Y0-BEC-958

General Information | 1

Tools and Techniques | 2

Troubleshooting | 3

Lubrication, Maintenance and Tune-up | 4

Engine Synchronization and Linkage Adjustments | 5

Fuel System | 6

Ignition and Electrical Systems | 7

Power Head | 8

Gearcase | 9

L-Drive Assembly and Exhaust System | 10

Manual Rewind Starters | 11

Power Trim and Tilt and Remote Control Systems | 12

Index | 13

Wiring Diagrams | 14

Contents

QUICK REFERENCE DATA IX

CHAPTER ONE
GENERAL INFORMATION 1

Manual organization 1
Notes, cautions and warnings 1
Torque specifications 2
Engine operation 2
Fasteners 2

Lubricants 8
Gasket sealant 10
Galvanic corrosion 11
Protection from galvanic corrosion 12
Propellers 14

CHAPTER TWO
TOOLS AND TECHNIQUES 21

Safety first 21
Basic hand tools 21
Test equipment 26

Service hints 28
Special tips 30
Mechanic's techniques 31

CHAPTER THREE
TROUBLESHOOTING 33

Operating requirements 33
Starting system 34
Choke solenoid or fuel primer valve circuits 43
Alternator charging system 46
Ignition system 50
Magneto ignition system 52
Battery breaker point ignition system 56
Prestolite magneto capacitor discharge ignition 58

Thunderbolt capacitor discharge ignition 81
Breakerless ignition module (BIM) system 89
Sem walbro capacitor discharge ignition 91
Capacitor discharge module (CDM) ignition 92
Ignition switch 100
Fuel system 101
Power head 102

CHAPTER FOUR
LUBRICATION, MAINTENANCE AND TUNE-UP 115

Lubrication.................................... 115
Storage...................................... 124
Complete submersion 127
Anticorrosion maintenance 128
Engine flushing 128
Tune-up 129
Compression check 129
Cylinder head bolt torque 130
Spark plugs 131

Gearcase and water pump check................. 134
Fuel system service 134
Breaker point ignition system service............ 135
Battery and starter motor check
  (electric start models) 138
Wiring harness check 138
Engine synchronization and adjustment 139
Performance test (on boat) 139

CHAPTER FIVE
ENGINE SYNCHRONIZATION AND LINKAGE ADJUSTMENTS 145

Engine timing and synchronization.............. 145
4, 5, 7.5, 9.9 and 15 hp models 146
25 hp 2-cylinder and 35 hp models............. 148

25 hp 3-cylinder models 150
40, 50 and 60 hp models 151
70-150 hp models (including L-Drive)........... 159

CHAPTER SIX
FUEL SYSTEM 168

Fuel pump 168
Carburetors 179
Carburetor removal/installation................. 179
Carburetor disassembly,
  reassembly and adjustment.................. 187
Carburetor cleaning and inspection.............. 213
Core plugs and lead shot 214

Reed valve assembly 215
Choke solenoid 222
Primer valve................................ 223
Integral fuel tank 223
Portable fuel tank........................... 223
Fuel hose and primer bulb..................... 224
Fuel recirculation system..................... 226

CHAPTER SEVEN
IGNITION AND ELECTRICAL SYSTEMS................................... 243

Battery 243
Alternator charging system 249
Electric starting system 253
Starter motor system 253
Ignition systems............................. 260
Breaker point magneto ignition................. 260
Battery breaker point ignition 263

Prestolite magneto CD ignition.................. 265
Thunderbolt capacitor discharge ignition 277
Breakerless ignition module (BIM) 282
Sem-walbro ignition system 284
Capacitor discharge module (CDM) ignition
  (40-120 hp models).......................... 285

CHAPTER EIGHT
POWER HEAD 294

Force model numbering system 295
Fasteners and torque specifications.............. 296
Power head removal/installation................. 300
Power head disassembly 320

Power head cleaning/inspection 352
Piston and connecting rod..................... 355
Connecting rod and crankshaft 361
Cylinder block and crankcase assembly 370

CHAPTER NINE
GEARCASE **391**

Service precautions 394
Propeller. 395
Gearcase. 399
Gearcase disassembly/reassembly. 408
Gearcase cleaning and inspection 461

Gearcase shimming 462
Gearcase pressure testing 472
Zinc anode. 473
Gear shift linkage adjustment 473
Water pump 476

CHAPTER TEN
L-DRIVE LOWER ASSEMBLY AND EXHAUST SYSTEM. **496**

Lower assembly removal/installation 496

Exhaust system 505

CHAPTER ELEVEN
MANUAL REWIND STARTERS **509**

Engine cover starter. 509
Spool starter. 512

Flywheel-mounted starter 517

CHAPTER TWELVE
POWER TRIM AND TILT AND REMOTE CONTROL SYSTEMS. **522**

Power trim and tilt. 522

Remote controls. 553

INDEX. **569**

WIRING DIAGRAMS **572**

QUICK REFERENCE DATA

RECOMMENDED SPARK PLUGS

Model	Champion Spark Plug Number (RFI*)	Gap in. (mm)
4 hp 1984-1987	L86C (RL86C)	.030 (0.76)
5 hp		
1988-1990B	L86C (RL86C)	.030 (0.76)
1991-1993	L87YC (RL87YC)	.030 (0.76)
1994-1996 (SEM-Walbro CD ignition)	L87YC (RL87YC)	.040 (1.02)
7.5 hp 1985	L86C (QL86C)	.030 (0.76)
9.9 hp		
1984-1991B	L86C (RL86C)	.030 (0.76)
1991C-1993	L87YC (RL87YC)	.030 (0.76)
1994-1996 (SEM-Walbro CD ignition)	L87YC (RL87YC)	.040 (1.02)
15 hp		
1984-1991B	L86C (RL86C)	.030 (0.76)
1991C-1992A	L87YC (RL87YC)	.030 (0.76)
1992B-1993	L82YC (RL82YC)	.030 (0.76)
1994-1996 (SEM-Walbro CD ignition)	L82YC (RL82YC)	.040 (1.02)
25 hp (1989 2 cylinder)	L82C (RL82C)	.030 (0.76)
25 hp (1996 3 cylinder)	L82C (RL82C)	.035 (0.89)
35 hp 1986-1991	L82C (RL82C)	.030 (0.76)
40 hp 1992-1996	L76V (QL76V)	NA
50 hp		
1984-1987B (battery-points ignition)	UL81C (RL81C)	.030 (0.76)
1987C-1989A	L82C (RL82C)	.030 (0.76)
1989B-1992A	UL18V (QL76V)	NA
1992C-1996	L76V (QL76V)	NA
60 hp 1985	L20V (QL76V)	NA
70 and 75 hp	L76V (QL76V)	NA
85 and 125 hp, including L-Drives	UL18V (QL76V)	NA
90 hp, not including L-Drives		
1990-1991C and 1991E (Prestolite CD)	UL18V (QL76V)	NA
1991D, 1991H-1996 (Thunderbolt/CDM)	L76V (QL76V)	NA
90 and 120 hp L-Drives		
1990-1991A (Prestolite CD ignition)	UL18V (QL76V)	NA
1991B-1992 (Thunderbolt ignition)	L76V (QL76V)	NA
120 hp, not including L-Drives		
1990-1991C (Prestolite CD ignition)	UL18V (QL76V)	NA
1991D-1996 (Thunderbolt/CDM)	L76V (QL76V)	NA
150 hp		
1989-1991A (Prestolite CD ignition)	UL18V (QL76V)	NA
1991B-1994 (Thunderbolt ignition)	L76V (QL76V)	NA

*Use resistor or suppression spark plugs where radio frequency interference (RFI) suppression is required.

GEARCASE GEAR RATIO AND APPROXIMATE LUBRICANT CAPACITY[1]

Outboard model	Gear Ratio (tooth count)	Lubricant Capacity
4 and 5 hp	2:1 (13:26)	4 oz. (118 ml)
7.5 hp	2:1 (13:26)	5 oz. (148 ml)
9.9 and 15 hp	1.57:1 (14:22)	5 oz. (148 ml)
25 hp (2 cylinder)	2:1 (13:26)	12 oz. (355 ml)
25 hp (3 cylinder)	2.25:1 (12:27)	7.6 oz. (225 ml)
35 hp	2:1 (13:26)	12 oz. (355 ml)
40-50 hp (through 1994)	1.62:1 (13:21)	12 oz. (355 ml)
40-50 hp (1995-on)	2:1 (13:26)	14.9 oz. (441 ml)
60 hp	not available	26 oz. (769 ml)
70 and 75 hp	1.64:1 (14:23)	12 oz. (355 ml)
85 hp (through 1989)	2:1 (15:30)	26 oz. (769 ml)
125 hp (through 1989)	1.73:1 (15:26)	26 oz. (769 ml)
90 and 120 hp (1990-1994)	1.93:1 (14:27)[2]	35 oz. (1035 ml)
90 hp (1995-on)	2.3:1 (13:30)	22.5 oz. (665 ml)
120 hp (1995-on)	2.07:1 (14:29)	22.5 oz. (665 ml)
150 hp (through 1991I)	1.93:1 (14:27)	26 oz. (769 ml)
150 hp (1991J-on)	1.93:1 (14:27)	35 oz. (1035 ml)
L-Drive models	1.93:1 (14:27)[2]	26 oz. (769 ml)

[1] Quicksilver Premium Blend Gearcase Lubricant or equivalent is recommended.
[2] A high altitude 2.2:1 (14:31) gear ratio is optional for these 90 and 120 hp models.

STANDARD TORQUE VALUES

Screw or Nut Size	in.-lb.	ft.-lb.	N•m
6-32	9	–	1.0
8-32	20	–	2.3
10-24	30	–	3.4
10-32	35	–	4.0
12-24	45	–	5.1
1/4-20	70	6	7.9
1/4-28	84	7	9.5
5/16-18	160	13	18.1
5/16-24	168	14	19.0
3/8-16	270	23	30.5
3/8-24	300	25	33.9
7/16-14	–	36	48.8
7/16-20	–	40	54.2
1/2-13	–	50	67.8
1/2-20	–	60	81.3

COMMON ENGINE SPECIFICATIONS

Fuel requirements	
Recommended	Regular unleaded from a major supplier, 87 pump posted octane minimum, with no alcohol
Minimum	Regular unleaded, 87 pump posted octane minimum, with no more than 10% ethanol[1]

(continued)

COMMON ENGINE SPECIFICATIONS (continued)

Fuel requirements (continued)	
Recommended fuel additives	Quicksilver Fuel System Treatment and Stabilizer part No. 92-78383A12
	Quicksilver Gasoline Stabilizer part No. 92-817529A12
	Quicksilver QuicKleen Fuel Treatment part No. 92-824074A12[2]
Oil	
Recommended	Force or Quicksilver NMMA approved TCW-3 outboard oil
Minimum	NMMA approved TCW-3 or TCW-II
Fuel to oil ratio	
After break-in	50:1
During break-in	25:1 for the first 12 gal. (45.4 L) of gasoline
Battery	Minimum of 630 CCA (490 MCA) and 100 minutes reserve capacity
Gear lubricant	Quicksilver Premium Blend Gear Lube or equivalent

[1] The use of methanol is not recommended. When using any alcohol extended (oxygenated) fuel, install a Quicksilver Water Separating Fuel Filter.

[2] QuicKleen is designed to remove existing combustion chamber deposits and prevent new deposits from forming.

RECOMMENDED LUBRICANTS, SEALANTS AND ADHESIVES

	Part No.
Lubricants	
Quicksilver Premium 2-Cycle TC-W3 outboard oil	(normal dealer stock item)
Quicksilver Special Lubricant 101	92-13872A-1
Quicksilver 2-4-C Multi-Lube	(normal dealer stock item in various sizes)
Quicksilver Anti-Corrosion Grease	92-78376A-6
Quicksilver Needle Bearing Grease	92-825265A-1
Quicksilver Power Trim and Steering Fluid	92-90100A12
Quicksilver Premium Blend Gearcase Lubricant	(normal dealer stock item)
Sealants	
Quicksilver Perfect Seal	92-34227-11
Loctite 5900 Ultra black RTV sealant	92-809826
Sealer (crankcase halves)	92-90113–2
Loctite Master Gasket Sealer	92-12564–2
Quicksilver Liquid Neoprene	92-25711–2
Loctite 567 PST pipe sealant	92-809822
Quicksilver Bellows Adhesive	92-86166–1
Adhesives	
Loquic Primer	92-809824
Loctite 271 threadlocking sealant (high strength)	92-809819
Loctite 242 threadlocking sealant (medium strength)	92-809821
Loctite RC680 high strength retaining compound	92-809833
Miscellaneous	
Quicksilver Power Tune Engine Cleaner	92-15104A12
Quicksilver Corrosion Guard	92-815869A12
Quicksilver Storage Seal Rust Inhibitor	92-86145A12

CLYMER®

FORCE

OUTBOARD SHOP MANUAL
4-150 HP (Includes -Drives) • 1984-1999

Introduction

This Clymer shop manual covers service and repair of all 1984-1999 Force 4-150 hp outboard motors including 85, 90, 120 and 125 hp L-Drives. Step-by-step instructions and hundreds of illustrations guide you through jobs ranging from simple maintenance to complete overhaul.

This manual can be used by anyone from a first time amateur to a professional mechanic. Easy to read type, detailed drawings and clear photographs give you all the information you need to do the work right.

Having a well-maintained engine will increase your enjoyment of your boat as well as assure your safety offshore. Keep this shop manual handy and use it often. It can save you hundreds of dollars in maintenance and repair bills and make yours a reliable, top-performing boat.

Engine model identification is covered in Chapter Eight.

Chapter One

General Information

This detailed, comprehensive manual contains complete information covering maintenance, repair and overhaul. Hundreds of photos and drawings guide you throughout every procedure.

Troubleshooting, tune-up, maintenance and repair are not difficult if you know what tools and equipment to use and what to do. Anyone not afraid to get their hands dirty, of average intelligence and with some mechanical ability can perform most of the procedures in this manual. See Chapter Two for more information on tools and techniques.

A shop manual is a reference. You want to be able to find information quickly. Clymer books are designed with you in mind. All chapters are thumb tabbed and important items are indexed at the end of the manual. All procedures, tables, photos and instructions in this manual assume the reader may be working on the machine or using the manual for the first time.

Keep the manual in a handy place in your toolbox or boat. It will help you to better understand how your boat runs, lower repair and maintenance costs and generally increase your enjoyment of your boat.

MANUAL ORGANIZATION

This chapter provides general information useful to boat owners and marine mechanics.

Chapter Two discusses the tools and techniques for preventative maintenance, troubleshooting and repair.

Chapter Three provides troubleshooting and testing procedures for all systems and individual components.

Following chapters describe specific systems, providing disassembly, inspection, assembly and adjustment procedures in simple step-by-step form. Specifications concerning a specific system are included at the end of the appropriate chapter.

NOTES, CAUTIONS AND WARNINGS

The terms NOTE, CAUTION and WARNING have specific meanings in this manual. A NOTE provides additional information to make a step or procedure easier or more clear. Disregarding a NOTE could cause inconvenience, but would not cause damage or personal injury.

A CAUTION emphasizes areas where equipment damage could cause permanent mechanical damage; however, personal injury is unlikely.

A WARNING emphasizes areas where personal injury or even death could result from negligence. Mechanical damage may also occur. WARNINGS *must* be taken seriously. In some cases, serious injury or death has resulted from disregarding similar warnings.

TORQUE SPECIFICATIONS

Torque specifications throughout this manual are given in foot-pounds (ft.-lb.), inch-pounds (in.-lb.) and newton meters (N•m.). Newton meters are being adopted in place of meter-kilograms (mkg) in accordance with the International Modernized Metric System. Existing torque wrenches calibrated in meter-kilograms can be used by performing a simple conversion: move the decimal point one place to the right. For example, 4.7 mkg = 47 N•m. This conversion is accurate enough for most mechanical operations even though the exact mathematical conversion is 3.5 mkg = 34.3 N•m.

ENGINE OPERATION

All marine engines, whether two or four-stroke, gasoline or diesel, operate on the Otto cycle of intake, compression, power and exhaust phases.

Two-Stroke Cycle

A two-stroke engine requires one crankshaft revolution (two strokes of the piston) to complete the Otto cycle. All engines covered in this manual are a two-stroke design. **Figure 1** shows gasoline two-stroke engine operation.

Four-Stroke Cycle

A four-stroke engine requires two crankshaft revolutions (four strokes of the piston) to complete the Otto cycle. **Figure 2** shows gasoline four-stroke engine operation.

FASTENERS

The material and design of the various fasteners used on marine equipment are carefully thought out and designed. Fastener design determines the type of tool required to work with the fastener. Fastener material is carefully selected to decrease the possibility of physical failure or corrosion. See *Galvanic Corrosion* in this chapter for information on marine materials.

Nuts, bolts and screws are manufactured in a wide range of thread patterns. To join a nut and bolt, the diameter of the bolt and the diameter of the hole in the nut must be the same. It is just as important that the threads are compatible.

The easiest way to determine if fastener threads are compatible is to turn the nut on the bolt, or bolt into its threaded opening, using fingers only. Be sure both pieces are clean. If much force is required, check the thread condition on each fastener. If the thread condition is good but the fasteners jam, the threads are not compatible.

Four important specifications describe the thread:
1. Diameter.
2. Threads per inch.
3. Thread pattern.

①

TWO-STROKE OPERATING PRINCIPLES

As the piston travels downward, it uncovers the exhaust port (A) allowing the exhaust gases to leave the cylinder. A fresh air-fuel charge, which has been compressed slightly in the crankcase, enters the cylinder through the transfer port (B). Since this charge enters under pressure, it also helps to push out the exhaust gases.

While the crankshaft continues to rotate, the piston moves upward, covering the transfer (B) and exhaust (A) ports. The piston compresses the new air-fuel mixture and creates a low-pressure area in the crancase at the same time. As the piston continues to travel, it uncovers the intake port (C). A fresh air-fuel charge from the carburetor (D) is drawn into the crankcase through the intake port.

As the piston almost reaches the top of the travel, the spark plug fires, igniting the compressed air-fuel mixture. The piston continues to top dead center (TDC) and is pushed downward by the expanding gases.

As the piston travels down, the exhaust gases leave the cylinder and the complete cycle starts all over again.

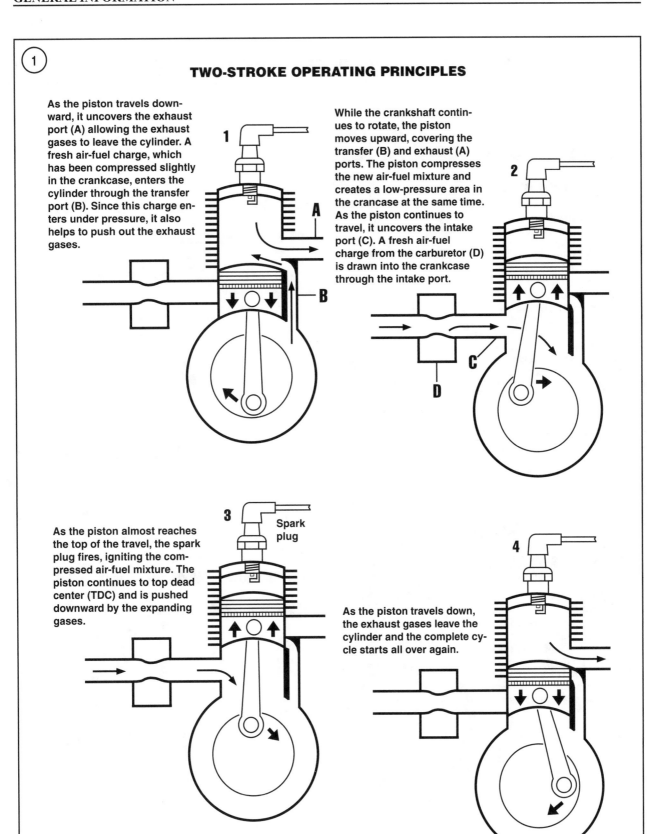

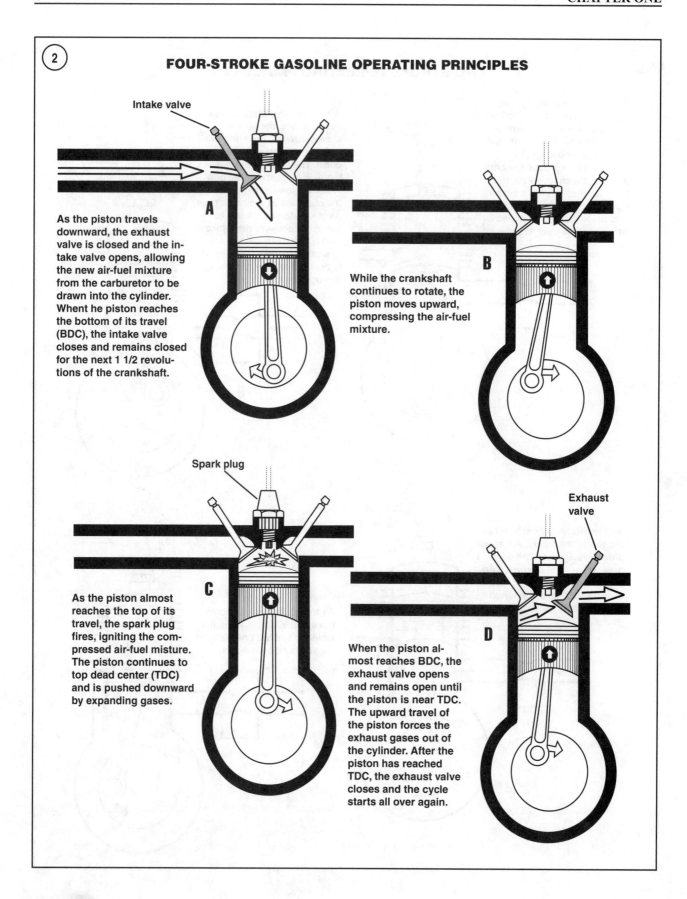

FOUR-STROKE GASOLINE OPERATING PRINCIPLES

Intake valve

A

As the piston travels downward, the exhaust valve is closed and the intake valve opens, allowing the new air-fuel mixture from the carburetor to be drawn into the cylinder. Whent he piston reaches the bottom of its travel (BDC), the intake valve closes and remains closed for the next 1 1/2 revolutions of the crankshaft.

B

While the crankshaft continues to rotate, the piston moves upward, compressing the air-fuel mixture.

Spark plug

C

As the piston almost reaches the top of its travel, the spark plug fires, igniting the compressed air-fuel misture. The piston continues to top dead center (TDC) and is pushed downward by expanding gases.

Exhaust valve

D

When the piston almost reaches BDC, the exhaust valve opens and remains open until the piston is near TDC. The upward travel of the piston forces the exhaust gases out of the cylinder. After the piston has reached TDC, the exhaust valve closes and the cycle starts all over again.

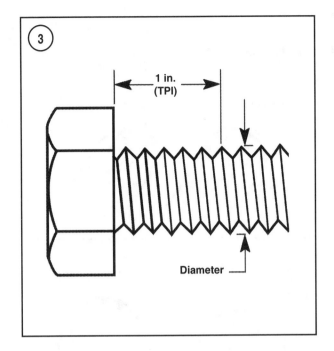

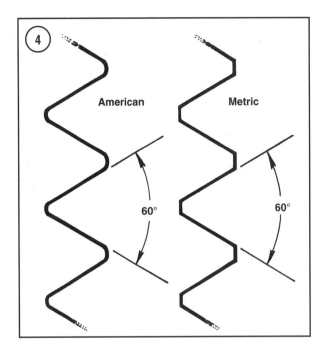

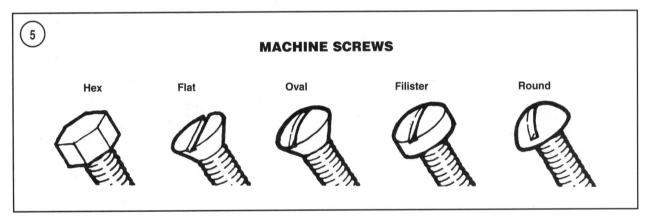

4. Thread direction

Figure 3 shows the first two specifications. Thread pattern is more subtle. Italian and British standards exist, but the most commonly used by marine equipment manufactures are American standard and metric standard. The root and top of the thread are cut differently as shown in **Figure 4**.

Most threads are cut so the fastener must be turned clockwise to tighten it. These are called right-hand threads. Some fasteners have left-hand threads; they must be turned counterclockwise to tighten. Left-hand threads are used in locations where normal rotation of the equipment would tend to loosen a right-hand threaded fastener. Assume all fasteners use right-hand threads unless the instructions specify otherwise.

Machine Screws

There are many different types of machine screws (**Figure 5**). Most are designed to protrude above the secured surface (rounded head) or be slightly recessed below the surface (flat head). In some applications the screw head is recessed well below the fastened sur-

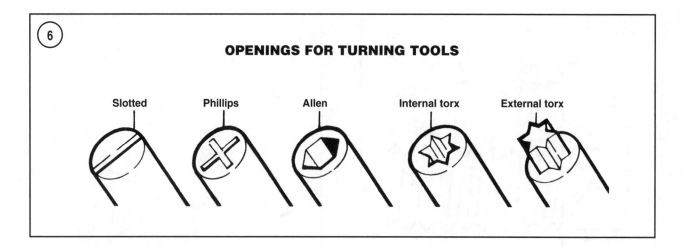

OPENINGS FOR TURNING TOOLS

Slotted   Phillips   Allen   Internal torx   External torx

face. **Figure 6** shows a number of screw heads requiring different types of turning tools.

Bolts

Commonly called bolts, the technical name for this fastener is cap screw. They are normally described by diameter, threads per inch and length. For example, 1/4-20 × 1 indicates a bolt 1/4 in. in diameter with 20 threads per inch, 1 in. long. The measurement across two flats of the bolt head indicates the proper wrench size required to turn the bolt.

Nuts

Nuts are manufactured in a variety of types and sizes. Most are hexagonal (six-sides) and fit on bolts, screws and studs with the same diameter and threads per inch.

Figure 7 shows several types of nuts. The common nut is usually used with some type of lockwasher. Self-locking nuts have a nylon insert that helps prevent the nut from loosening; no lockwasher is required. Wing nuts are designed for fast removal by hand. Wing nuts are used for convenience in non-critical locations.

To indicate the size of a nut, manufactures specify the diameter of the opening and the threads per inch. This is similar to a bolt specifi-

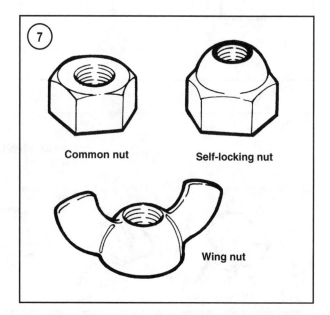

Common nut   Self-locking nut

Wing nut

cation, but without the length dimension. The measurement across two flats of the nut indicates the wrench size required to turn the nut.

Washers

There are two basic types of washers: flat washers and lockwashers. A flat washer is a simple disc with a hole that fits the screw or bolt. Lockwashers are designed to prevent a fastener from working loose due to vibration, expansion and contraction. **Figure 8** shows several types of lockwashers. Note that flat washers are often

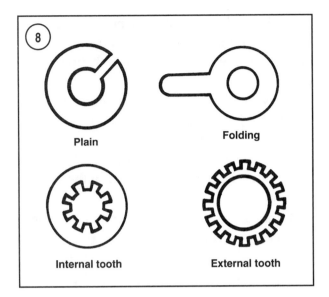

Plain

Folding

Internal tooth

External tooth

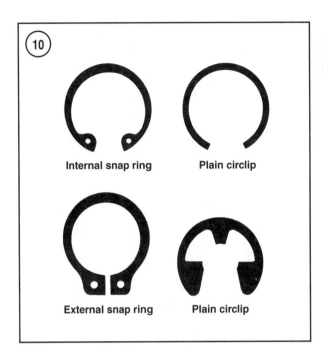

Internal snap ring

Plain circlip

External snap ring

Plain circlip

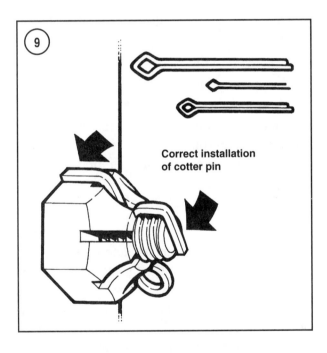

Correct installation
of cotter pin

plication. For this purpose, a cotter pin (**Figure 9**) and slotted or castellated nut is often used. To use a cotter pin, first make sure the pin fits snugly, but not too tight. Then, align a slot in the fastener with the hole in the bolt or axle. Insert the cotter pin through the nut and bolt or propeller shaft and bend the ends over to secure the cotter pin tightly. If the holes do not align, tighten the nut just enough to obtain the proper alignment. Unless specifically instructed to do so, never loosen the fastener to align the slot and hole. Because the cotter pin is weakened after installation and removal, never reuse a cotter pin. Cotter pins are available in several styles, lengths and diameters. Measure cotter pin length from the bottom of its head to the tip of its shortest prong.

Snap Rings

Snap rings (**Figure 10**) can be an internal or external design. They are used to retain components on shafts (external type) or inside openings (internal type). Snap rings can be reused if they are not distorted during removal. In some applications, snap rings of varying thickness

used between a lockwasher and a fastener to provide a smooth bearing surface. This allows the fastener to be turned easily with a tool.

Cotter Pins

In certain applications, a fastener must be secured so it cannot possibly loosen. The propeller nut on some marine drive systems is one such ap-

(selective fit) can be selected to position or control end play of parts assemblies.

LUBRICANTS

Periodic lubrication helps ensure long service life for any type of equipment. It is especially important with marine equipment because it is exposed to salt, brackish or polluted water and other harsh environments. The type of lubricant used is just as important as the lubrication service itself, although in an emergency, the wrong type of lubricant is better than none at all. The following paragraphs describe the types of lubricants most often used on marine equipment. Be sure to follow the equipment manufacture's recommendations for the lubricant types.

Generally, all liquid lubricants are called *oil*. They may be mineral-based (including petroleum bases), natural-based (vegetable and animal bases), synthetic-based or emulsions (mixtures). *Grease* is lubricating oil that has a thickening compound added. The resulting material then usually enhanced with anticorrosion, antioxidant and extreme pressure (EP) additives. Grease is often classified by the type of thickener added; lithium and calcium soap are the most commonly used.

Two-stroke Engine Oil

Lubrication for a two-stroke engine is provided by oil mixed with the incoming air/fuel mixture. Some of the oil mist settles out in the crankcase, lubricating the crankshaft, bearings and lower end of the connecting rod. The rest of the oil enters the combustion chamber to lubricate the piston, rings and the cylinder wall. This oil is then burned along with the air/fuel mixture during the combustion process.

Engine oil must have several special qualities to work well in a two-stroke engine. It must mix easily and stay in suspension in gasoline.

When burned, it cannot leave behind excessive deposits. It must also withstand the high operating temperature associated with two-stroke engines.

The National Marine Manufacturer's Association (NMMA) has set standards for oil used in two-stroke, water-cooled engines. This is the NMMA TC-W (two-cycle, water-cooled) grade. It indicates the oil's performance in the following areas:

1. Lubrication (preventing wear and scuffing).
2. Spark plug fouling.
3. Piston ring sticking.
4. Preignition.
5. Piston varnish.
6. General engine condition (including deposits).
7. Exhaust port blockage.
8. Rust prevention.
9. Mixing ability with gasoline.

In addition to oil grade, manufactures specify the ratio of gasoline and oil required during break-in and normal engine operation.

Gearcase Oil

Gearcase lubricants are assigned SAE viscosity numbers under the same system as four-stroke engine oil. Gearcase lubricant falls into the SAE 72-250 range. Some gearcase lubricants are multigrade. For example, SAE 80-90 is a common multigrade gear lubricant.

Three types of marine gearcase lubricants are generally available; SAE 90 hypoid gearcase lubricant is designed for older manual-shift units; type C gearcase lubricant contains additives designed for the electric shift mechanisms; high-viscosity gearcase lubricant is a heavier oil designed to withstand the shock loads of high performance engines or units subjected to severe duty use. Always use the gearcase lubricant specified by the manufacturer.

Grease

Greases are graded by the National Lubricating Grease Institute (NLGI). Greases are graded by number according to the consistency of the grease. These ratings range from No. 000 to No. 6, with No. 6 being the most solid. A typical multipurpose grease is NLGI No. 2. For specific applications, equipment manufactures may require grease with an additive such as molybdenum disulfide (MOS^2).

GASKET SEALANT

Gasket sealant is used instead of preformed gaskets on some applications, or as a gasket dressing on others. Three types of gasket sealant are commonly used: gasket sealing compound, room temperature vulcanizing (RTV) and anaerobic. Because these materials have different sealing properties, they cannot be used interchangeably.

Gasket Sealing Compound

This nonhardening liquid is used primarily as a gasket dressing. Gasket sealing compound is available in tubes or brush top containers. When exposed to air or heat it forms a rubber-like coating. The coating fills in small imperfections in gasket and sealing surfaces. Do not use gasket sealing compound that is old, has began to solidify or has darkened in color.

Applying Gasket Sealing Compound

Carefully scrape residual gasket material, corrosion deposits or paint from the mating surfaces. Use a blunt scraper and work carefully to avoid damaging the mating surfaces. Use quick drying solvent and a clean shop towel and wipe oil or other contaminants from the surfaces. Wipe or blow loose material or contaminants from the gasket. Brush a light coating on the mating surfaces and both sides of the gasket. Do not apply more compound than needed. Excess compound will be squeezed out as the surfaces mate and may contaminate other components. Do not allow compound into bolt or alignment pin holes

A hydraulic lock can occur as the bolt or pin compresses the compound, resulting in incorrect bolt torque.

RTV Sealant

This is a silicone gel supplied in tubes. Moisture in the air causes RTV to cure. Always place the cap on the tube as soon as possible if using RTV. RTV has a shelf life of approximately one year and will not cure properly after the shelf life expires. Check the expiration date on the tube and keep partially used tubes tightly sealed. RTV can generally fill gaps up to 1/4 in. (6.3 mm) and works well on slightly flexible surfaces.

Applying RTV Sealant

Carefully scrape all residual sealant and paint from the mating surfaces. Use a blunt scraper and work carefully to avoid damaging the mating surfaces. The mating surfaces must be absolutely free of gasket material, sealant, dirt, oil grease or other contamination. Lacquer thinner, acetone, isopropyl alcohol or similar solvents work well to clean the surfaces. Avoid using solvents with an oil, wax or petroleum base as they are not compatible with RTV compounds. Remove all sealant from bolt or alignment pin holes.

Apply RTV sealant in a continuous bead 0.08-0.12 in. (2-3 mm) thick. Circle all mounting bolt or alignment pin holes unless otherwise specified. Do not allow RTV sealant into bolt holes or other openings. A hydraulic lock can

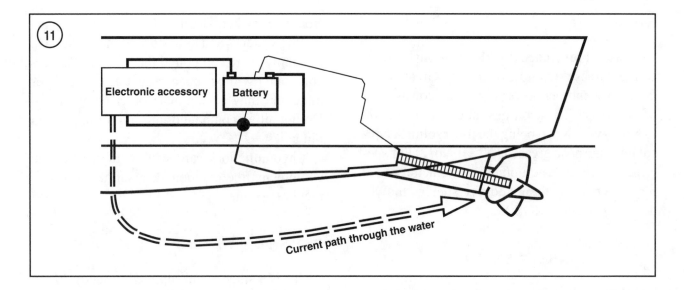

occur as the bolt or pin compresses the sealant, resulting in incorrect bolt torque. Tighten the mounting fasteners within 10 minutes after application.

Anaerobic Sealant

This is a gel supplied in tubes. It cures only in the absence of air, as when squeezed tightly between two machined mating surfaces. For this reason, it will not spoil if the cap is left off the tube. Do not use anaerobic sealant if one of the surfaces is flexible. Anaerobic sealant is able to fill gaps up to 0.030 in. (0.8 mm) and generally works best on rigid, machined flanges or surfaces.

Applying Anaerobic Sealant

Carefully scrape all residual sealant from the mating surfaces. Use a blunt scraper and work carefully to avoid damaging the mating surfaces. The mating surfaces must be absolutely free of gasket material, sealant, dirt, oil grease or other contamination. Lacquer thinner, acetone, isopropyl alcohol or similar solvents work well to clean the surfaces. Avoid using solvents

with an oil, wax or petroleum base as they are not compatible with anaerobic compounds. Clean a sealant from the bolt or alignment pin holes. Apply anaerobic sealant in a 0.04 in. (1 mm) thick continuous bead onto one of the surfaces. Circle all bolt and alignment pin openings. Do not apply sealant into bolt holes or other openings. A hydraulic lock can occur as the bolt or pin compresses the sealant, resulting in incorrect bolt torque. Tighten the mounting fasteners within 10 minutes after application.

GALVANIC CORROSION

A chemical reaction occurs whenever two different types of metal are joined by an electrical conductor and immersed in an electrolytic solution such as water. Electrons transfer from one metal to the other through the electrolyte and return through the conductor.

The hardware on a boat is made of many different types of metal. The boat hull acts as a conductor between the metals. Even if the hull is wooden or fiberglass, the slightest film of water (electrolyte) on the hull provides conductivity. This combination creates a good environment for electron flow (**Figure 11**). Unfortunately, this electron flow results in galvanic corrosion of the metal involved, causing one of the metals to be corroded or eroded away. The amount of electron flow, and therefore the amount of corrosion, depends on several factors:

1. The types of metal involved.
2. The efficiency of the conductor.
3. The strength of the electrolyte.

Metals

The chemical composition of the metal used in marine equipment has a significant effect on the amount and speed of galvanic corrosion. Certain metals are more resistant to corrosion than others. These electrically negative metals are commonly called *noble*; they act as the cathode in any reaction. Metals that are more subject to corrosion are electrically positive; they act as the anode in a reaction. The more *noble* metals include titanium, 18-8 stainless steel and nickel. Less *noble* metals include zinc, aluminum and magnesium. Galvanic corrosion becomes more severe as the difference in electrical potential between the two metals increases.

In some cases, galvanic corrosion can occur within a single piece of metal. For example, brass is a mixture of zinc and copper, and, when immersed in an electrolyte, the zinc portion of the mixture will corrode away as a galvanic reaction occurs between the zinc and copper particles.

Conductors

The hull of the boat often acts as the conductor between different types of metal. Marine equipment, such as the drive unit can act as the conductor. Large masses of metal, firmly connected together, are more efficient conductors than water. Rubber mountings and vinyl-based paint can act as insulators between pieces of metal.

Electrolyte

The water in which a boat operates acts as the electrolyte for the corrosion process. The more efficient a conductor is, the more severe and rapid the corrosion will be.

Cold, clean freshwater is the poorest electrolyte. Pollutants increase conductivity; therefore, brackish or saltwater is an efficient electrolyte. This is one of the reasons that most manufacturers recommend a freshwater flush after operating in polluted, brackish or saltwater.

Protection From Galvanic Corrosion

Because of the environment in which marine equipment must operate, it is practically impossible to totally prevent galvanic corrosion. However, there are several ways in which the process can be slowed. After taking these precautions, the next step is to *fool* the process into occurring only where you want it to occur. This is the role of sacrificial anodes and impressed current systems.

Slowing Corrosion

Some simple precautions can help reduce the amount of corrosion taking place outside the hull. These precautions are not substitutes for the corrosion protection methods discussed under *Sacrificial Anodes* and *Impressed Current Systems* in this chapter, but they can help these methods reduce corrosion.

Use fasteners made of metal more noble than the parts they secure. If corrosion occurs, the parts they secure may suffer but the fasteners are protected. The larger secured parts are more able to withstand the loss of material. Also major problems could arise if the fasteners corrode to the point of failure.

Keep all painted surfaces in good condition. If paint is scraped off and bare metal exposed, corrosion rapidly increases. Use a vinyl- or plastic-based paint, which acts as an electrical insulator.

Be careful when applying metal-based antifouling paint to the boat. Do not apply antifouling paint to metal parts of the boat or the drive unit. If applied to metal surfaces, this type of paint reacts with the metal and results in corrosion between the metal and the layer of paint. Maintain a minimum 1 in. (25 mm) border between the painted surface and any metal parts. Organic-based paints are available for use on metal surfaces.

Where a corrosion protection device is used, remember that it must be immersed in the electrolyte along with the boat to provide any protection. If you raise the gearcase out of the water with the boat docked, any anodes on the gearcase may be removed from the corrosion process rendering them ineffective. Never paint or apply any coating to anodes or other protection devices. Paint or other coatings insulate them from the corrosion process.

Any change in the boat's equipment, such as the installation of a new stainless steel propeller, changes the electrical potential and may cause increased corrosion. Always consider this when adding equipment or changing exposed materials. Install additional anodes or other protection equipment as required ensuring the corrosion protection system is up to the task. The expense to repair corrosion damage usually far exceeds that of additional corrosion protection.

Sacrificial Anodes

Sacrificial anodes are specially designed to do nothing but corrode. Properly fastening such pieces to the boat causes them to act as the anode in any galvanic reaction that occurs; any other metal in the reaction acts as the cathode and is not damaged.

Anodes are usually made or zinc, a far from a noble material. Some anodes are manufactured of an aluminum and indium alloy. This alloy is less noble than the aluminum alloy in drive system components, providing the desired sacrificial properties. The aluminum and indium alloy is more resistant to oxide coating than zinc anodes. Oxide coating occurs as the anode material reacts with oxygen in the water. An oxide coating will insulate the anode, dramatically reducing corrosion protection.

Anodes must be used properly to be effective. Simply fastening anodes to the boat in random locations will not do the job.

First determine how much anode surface is required to adequately protect the equipment's surface area. A good starting point is provided by the Military Specification MIL-A-818001, which states that one square inch of new anode protects either:

1. 800 square inches of freshly painted steel.
2. 250 square inches of bare steel or bare aluminum alloy.
3. 100 square inches of copper or copper alloy.

This rule is valid for a boat at rest. If underway, additional anode area is required to protect the same surface area.

The anode must be in good electrical contact with the metal that it protects. If possible, attach an anode to all metal surfaces requiring protection.

Good quality anodes have inserts around the fastener holes that are made of a more noble material. Otherwise, the anode could erode away around the fastener hole, allowing the anode to loosen or possibly fall off, thereby loosing needed protection.

Impressed Current System

An impressed current system can be added to any boat. The system generally consists of the anode, controller and reference electrode. The anode in this system is coated with a very noble

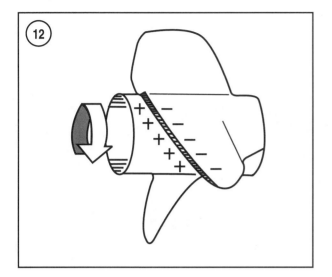

metal, such as platinum, so that it is almost corrosion-free and can last almost indefinitely. The reference electrode, under the boat's waterline, allows the control module to monitor the potential for corrosion. If the module senses that corrosion is occurring, it applies positive battery voltage to the anode. Current then flows from the anode to all other metal component, regardless of how noble or non-noble these components may be. Essentially, the electrical current from the battery counteracts the galvanic reaction to dramatically reduce corrosion damage.

Only a small amount of current is needed to counteract corrosion. Using input from the sensor, the control module provides only the amount of current needed to suppress galvanic corrosion. Most systems consume a maximum of 0.2 Ah at full demand. Under normal conditions, these systems can provide protection for 8-12 weeks without recharging the battery. Remember that this system must have constant connection to the battery. Often the battery supply to the system is connected to a battery switching device causing the operator to inadvertently shut off the system while docked.

An impressed current system is more expensive to install than sacrificial anodes but, considering its low maintenance requirements and the superior protection it provides, the long term cost may be lower.

PROPELLERS

The propeller is the final link between the boat's drive system and the water. A perfectly maintained engine and hull are useless if the propeller is the wrong type, is damaged or is deteriorated. Although propeller selection for a specific application is beyond the scope of this manual, the following provides the basic information needed to make an informed decision. The professional at a reputable marine dealership is the best source for a propeller recommendation.

How a Propeller Works

As the curved blades of a propeller rotate through the water, a high-pressure area forms on one side of the blade and a low-pressure area forms on the other side of the blade (**Figure 12**). The propeller moves toward the low-pressure area, carrying the boat with it.

Propeller Parts

Although a propeller is usually a one-piece unit, it is made of several different parts (**Figure 13**). Variations in the design of these parts make different propellers suitable for different applications.

The blade tip is the point of the blade furthest from the center of the propeller hub or propeller shaft bore. The blade tip separates the leading edge from the trailing edge.

The leading edge is the edge of the blade nearest the boat. During forward operation, this is the area of the blade that first cuts through the water.

The trailing edge is the surface of the blade furthest from the boat. During reverse operation,

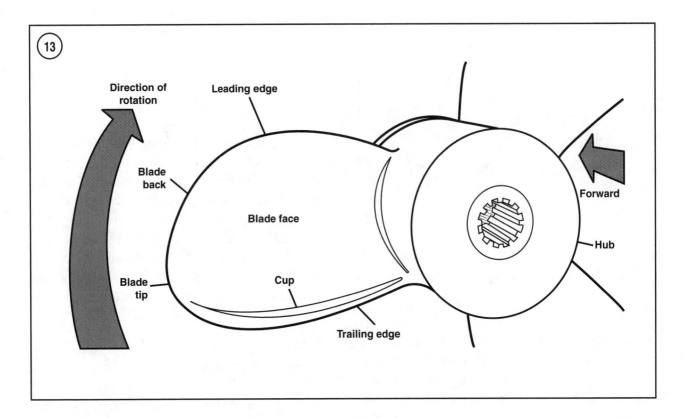

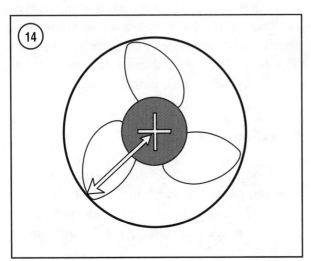

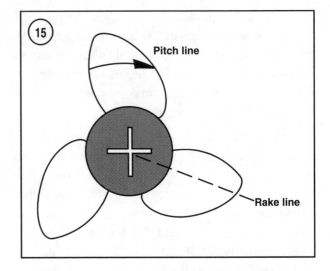

this is the area of the blade that first cuts through the water.

The blade face is the surface of the blade that faces away from the boat. During forward operation, high-pressure forms on this side of the blade.

The blade back is the surface of the blade that faces toward the boat. During forward gear operation, low-pressure forms on this side of the blade.

The cup is a small curve or lip on the trailing edge of the blade. Cupped propeller blades generally perform better than non-cupped propeller blades.

The hub is the center portion of the propeller. It connects the blades to the propeller shaft. On most drive systems, engine exhaust is routed through the hub; in this case, the hub is made up of an outer and inner portion, connected by ribs.

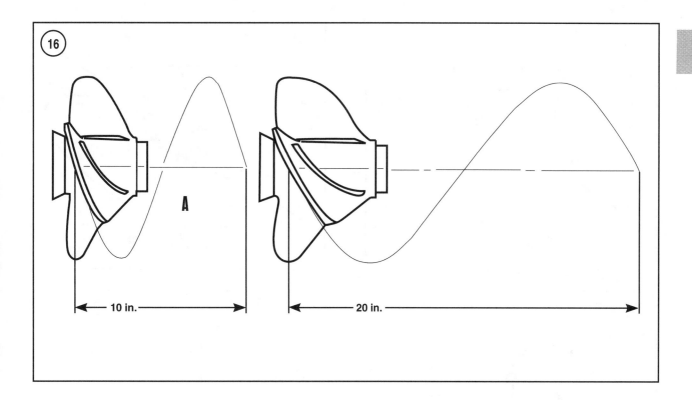

The diffuser ring is used on though- hub exhaust models to prevent exhaust gasses from entering the blade area.

Propeller Design

Changes in length, angle, thickness and material of propeller parts make different propellers suitable for different applications.

Diameter

Propeller diameter is the distance from the center of the hub to the blade tip, multiplied by two. Essentially it is the diameter of the circle formed by the blade tips during propeller rotation (**Figure 14**).

Pitch and rake

Propeller pitch and rake describe the placement of the blades in relation to the hub (**Figure 15**).

Pitch describes the theoretical distance the propeller would travel in one revolution. In A, **Figure 16**, the propeller would travel 10 inches in one revolution. In B, **Figure 16**, the propeller would travel 20 inches in one revolution. This distance is only theoretical; during operation, the propeller achieves only 75-85% of its pitch. Slip rate describes the difference in actual travel relative to the pitch. Lighter, faster boats typically achieve a lower slip rate than heavier, slower boats.

Propeller blades can be constructed with constant pitch (**Figure 17**) or progressive pitch (**Figure 18**). On a progressive propeller, the pitch starts low at the leading edge and increases toward the trailing edge. The propeller pitch specification is the average of the pitch across the entire blade. Propellers with progressive pitch usually provide better overall performance than constant pitch propellers.

Blade rake is specified in degrees and is measured along a line from the center of the hub to the blade tip. A blade that is perpendicular to the

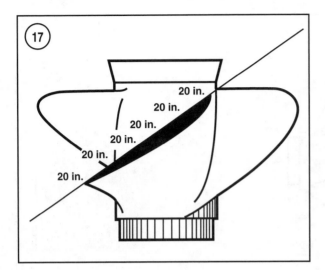

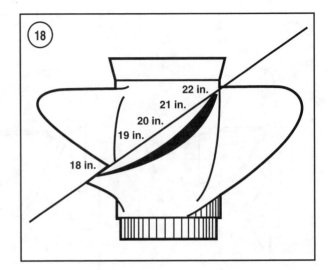

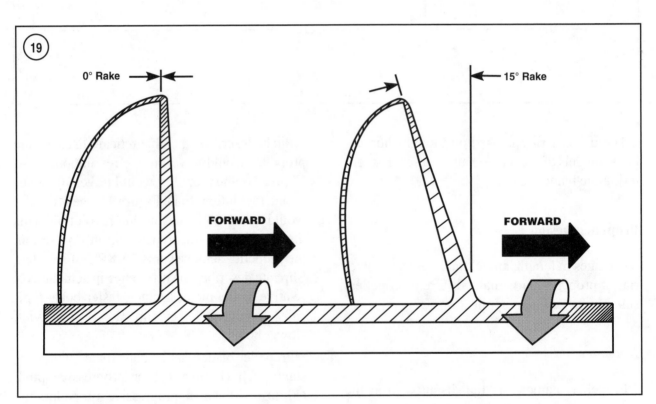

hub (**Figure 19**) has 0° rake. A blade that is angled from perpendicular (**Figure 19**) has a rake expressed by its difference from perpendicular. Most propellers have rakes ranging from 0-20°. Lighter faster boats generally perform better with propeller with a greater amount of rake. Heavier, slower boats generally perform better using a propeller with less rake.

Blade thickness

Blade thickness in not uniform at all points along the blade. For efficiency, blades are as thin a possible at all points while retaining enough strength to move the boat. Blades are thicker where they meet the hub and thinner at the blade tips (**Figure 20**). This is necessary to support the

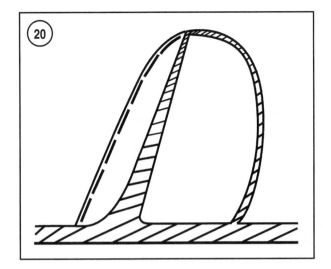

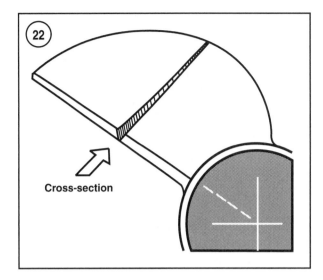

Cross-section

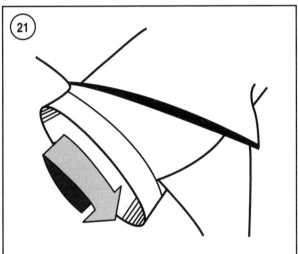

heavier loads at the hub section of the blade. Overall blade thickness is dependent on the strength of the material used.

When cut along a line from the leading edge to the trailing edge in the central portion of the blade (**Figure 21**), the propeller blade resembles and airplane wing. The blade face, where high-pressure exists during forward rotation, is almost flat. The blade back, where low-pressure exists during forward rotation, is curved, with the thinnest portions at the edges and the thickest portion at the center.

Propellers that run only partially submerged, as in racing applications, may have a wedge

shaped cross-section (**Figure 22**). The leading edge is very thin and the blade thickness increases toward the trailing edge, where it is thickest. If a propeller such as this is run totally submerged, it is very inefficient.

Number of blades

The number of blades used on a propeller is a compromise between efficiency and vibration. A one-bladed propeller would the most efficient, but it would create an unacceptable amount of vibration. As blades are added, efficiency decreases, but so does vibration. Most propellers have three or four blades, representing the most practical trade-off between efficiency and vibration.

Material

Propeller materials are chosen for strength, corrosion resistance and economy. Stainless steel, aluminum, plastic and bronze are the most commonly used materials. Bronze is quite strong but rather expensive. Stainless steel is more common than bronze because of its combination of strength and lower cost. Aluminum alloy and plastic materials are the least expensive

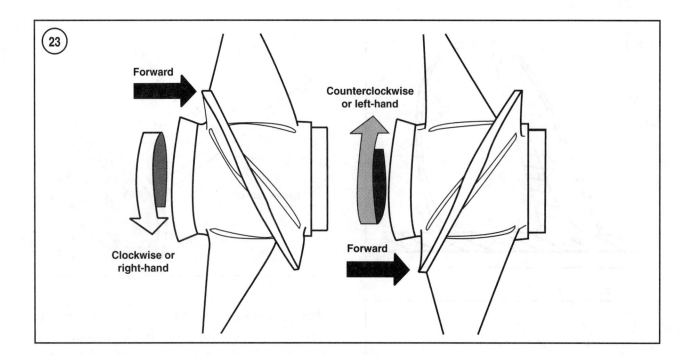

Direction of rotation

Propellers are made for both right-hand and left hand rotations although right-hand is the most commonly used. As viewed from the rear of the boat while in forward gear, a right-hand propeller turns clockwise and a left-hand propeller turns counterclockwise. Off the boat, the direction of rotation is determined by observing the angle of the blades (**Figure 23**). A right-hand propeller's blade slant from the upper left to the lower right; a left-hand propeller's blades are opposite.

Cavitation and Ventilation

Cavitation and ventilation are *not* interchangeable terms; they refer to two distinct problems encountered during propeller operation.

To help understand cavitation, consider the relationship between pressure and the boiling but usually lack the strength of stainless steel. Plastic propellers are more suited for lower horsepower applications.

point of water. At sea level, water boils at 212° F (100° C). As pressure increases, such as within an engine cooling system, the boiling point of the water increases—it boils at a temperature higher than 212° F (100° C). The opposite is also true. As pressure decreases, water boils at a temperature lower than 212° F (100° C). It the pressure drops low enough, water will boil at normal room temperature.

During normal propeller operation, low pressure forms on the blade back. Normally the pressure does not drop low enough for boiling to occur. However, poor propeller design, damaged blades or using the wrong propeller can cause unusually low pressure on the blade surface (**Figure 24**). If the pressure drops low enough, boiling occurs and bubbles form on the blade surfaces. As the boiling water moves to a higher pressure area of the blade, the boiling ceases and the bubbles collapse. The collapsing bubbles release energy that erodes the surface of the propeller blade.

Corroded surfaces, physical damage or even marine growth combined with high-speed operation can cause low pressure and cavitation on gearcase surfaces. In such cases, low pressure

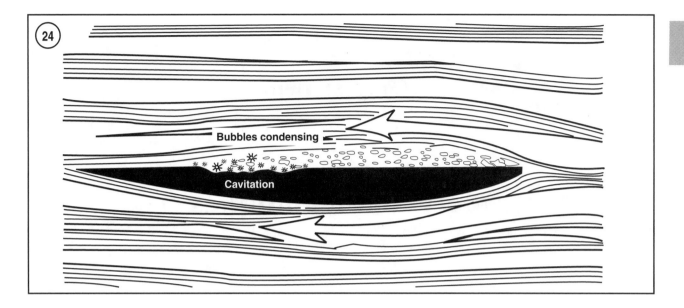

Bubbles condensing

Cavitation

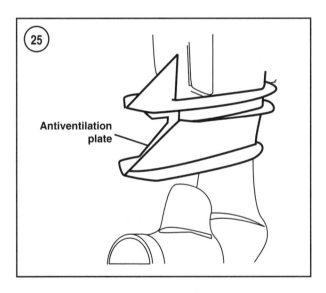

Antiventilation plate

forms as water flows over a protrusion or rough surface. The boiling water forms bubbles that collapse as they move to a higher pressure area toward the rear of the surface imperfection.

This entire process of pressure drop, boiling and bubble collapse is called *cavitation*. The ensuing damage is called *cavitation burn*. Cavitation is caused by a decrease in pressure, not an increase in temperature.

Ventilation is not as complex a process as cavitation. Ventilation refers to air entering the blade area, either from above the water surface or from a though-hub exhaust system. As the blades meet the air, the propeller momentarily looses it bite with the water and subsequently loses most of its thrust. An added complication is that the propeller and engine over-rev, causing very low pressure on the blade back and massive cavitation.

Most marine drive systems have a plate (**Figure 25**) above the propeller designed to prevent surface air from entering the blade area. This plate is correctly called an *anti-ventilation plate*, although it is often incorrectly called an *anticavitation plate*.

Most propellers have a flared section at the rear of the propeller called a diffuser ring. This feature forms a barrier, and extends the exhaust passage far enough aft to prevent the exhaust gases from ventilating the propeller.

A close fit of the propeller to the gearcase is necessary to keep exhaust gasses from exiting and ventilating the propeller. Using the wrong propeller attaching hardware can position the propeller too far aft, preventing a close fit. The wrong hardware can also allow the propeller to rub heavily against the gearcase, causing rapid wear to both components. Wear or damage to these surfaces will allow the propeller to ventilate.

Chapter Two

Tools and Techniques

This chapter describes the common tools required for marine engine repair and troubleshooting. Techniques that make the work easier and more effective are also described. Some of the procedures in this book require special skills or expertise; in some cases it is better to entrust the job to a specialist or qualified dealership.

SAFETY FIRST

Professional mechanics can work for years and never suffer a serious injury. Avoiding injury is as simple as following a few rules and using common sense. Ignoring the rules can and often does lead to physical injury and/or damaged equipment.

1. Never use gasoline as a cleaning solvent.

2. Never smoke or use a torch near flammable liquids, such as cleaning solvent. Dirty or solvent soaked shop towels are extremely flammable. If working in a garage, remember that most home gas appliances have pilot lights.

3. Never smoke or use a torch in an area where a battery is being charged. Highly explosive hydrogen gas is formed during the charging process.

4. Use the proper size wrench to avoid damaged fasteners and bodily injury.

5. If loosening a tight or stuck fastener, consider what could happen if the wrench slips. Protect yourself accordingly.

6. Keep the work area clean, uncluttered and well lighted.

7. Wear safety goggles while using any type of tool. This is especially important when drilling, grinding or using a cold chisel.

8. Never use worn or damaged tools.

9. Keep a Coast Guard approved fire extinguisher handy. Ensure it is rated for gasoline (Class B) and electrical (Class C) fires.

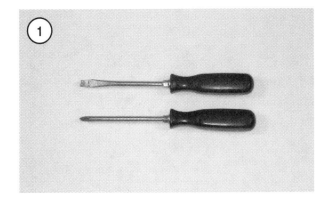

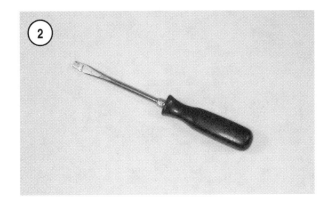

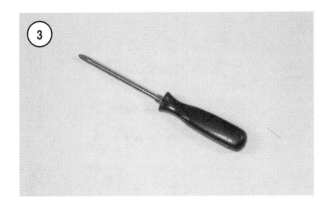

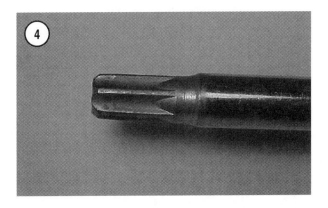

BASIC HAND TOOLS

A number of tools are required to maintain and repair a marine engine. Most of these tools are also used for home and automobile repair. Some tools are made especially for working on marine engines; these tools can be purchased from a marine dealership. Having the required tools always makes the job easier and more effective.

Keep the tools clean and in a suitable box. Keep them organized with related tools stored together. After using a tool, wipe it clean using a shop towel.

The following tools are required to perform virtually any repair job. Each tool is described and the recommended size given for starting a tool collection. Additional tools and some duplication may be added as you become more familiar with the equipment. You may need all U.S. standard tools, all metric size tools or a mixture of both.

Screwdrivers

A screwdriver (**Figure 1**) is a very basic tool, but if used improperly can do more damage than good. The slot on a screw has a definite dimension and shape. Always select a screwdriver that conforms to the shape of the screw. Use a small screwdriver for small screws and a large one for large screws or the screw head will be damaged.

Three types of screwdrivers are commonly required: a slotted (flat-blade) screwdriver (**Figure 2**), Phillips screwdriver (**Figure 3**) and Torx screwdriver (**Figure 4**).

Screwdrivers are available in sets, which often include an assortment of slotted Phillips and Torx blades. If you buy them individually, buy at least the following:

    a. Slotted screwdriver—5/16 × 6 in. blade.

    b. Slotted screwdriver—3/8 × 12 in. blade.

    c. Phillips screwdriver—No. 2 tip, 6 in. blade.

d. Phillips screwdriver—No. 3 tip, 6 in. blade.

e. Torx screwdriver—T15 tip, 6 in. blade.

f. Torx screwdriver—T20 tip, 6 in. blade.

g. Torx screwdriver—T25 tip, 6 in. blade.

Use screwdrivers only for driving screws. Never use a screwdriver for prying or chiseling. Do not attempt to remove a Phillips, Torx or Allen head screw with a slotted screwdriver; you can damage the screw head so that even the proper tool is unable to remove it.

Keep the tip of a slotted screwdriver in good condition. Carefully grind the tip to the proper size and taper if it is worn or damaged. The sides of the blade must be parallel and the blade tip must be flat. Replace a Phillips or Torx screwdriver if its tip is worn or damaged.

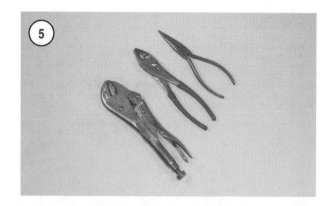

Pliers

Pliers come in a wide range of types and sizes. Pliers are useful for cutting, gripping, bending and crimping. Never use pliers to cut hardened objects or turn bolts or nuts. **Figure 5** shows several types of pliers.

Each type of pliers has a specialized function. General-purpose pliers are mainly used for gripping and bending. Locking pliers are used for gripping objects very tightly, like a vise. Use needlenose pliers to grip or bend small objects. Adjustable or slip-joint pliers (**Figure 6**) can be adjusted to grip various sized objects; the jaws remain parallel for gripping objects such as pipe or tubing. There are many more types of pliers. The ones described here are the most common.

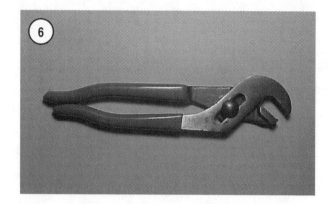

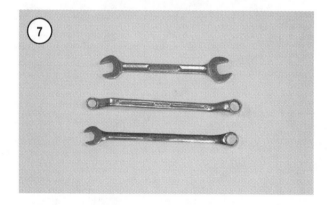

Box-end and Open-end Wrenches

Box-end and open-end wrenches (**Figure 7**) are available in sets in a variety of sizes. The number stamped near the end of the wrench refers to the distance between two parallel flats on the hex head bolt or nut.

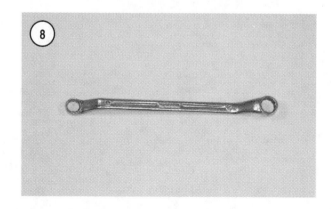

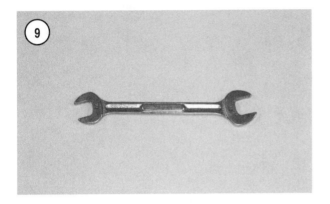

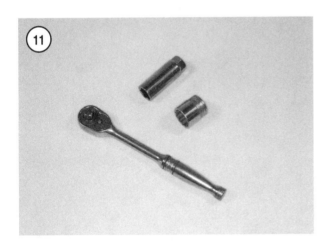

Box-end wrenches (**Figure 8**) provide a better grip on the nut and are stronger than open end wrenches. An open-end wrench (**Figure 9**) grips the nut on only two flats. Unless it fits well, it may slip and round off the points on the nut. A box-end wrench grips all six flats. Box-end wrenches are available with six-point or 12 point openings. The six-point opening provides

superior holding power; the 12-point allow a shorter swing if working in tight quarters.

Use an open-end wrench if a box-end wrench cannot be positioned over the nut or bolt. To prevent damage to the fastener, avoid using and open-end wrench if a large amount of tightening or loosening toque is required.

A combination wrench has both a box-end and open-end. Both ends are the same size.

Adjustable Wrenches

An adjustable wrench (**Figure 10**) can be adjusted to fit virtually any nut or bolt head. However, it can loosen and slip from the nut or bolt, causing damage to the nut and possible physical injury. Use an adjustable wrench only if a proper size open-end or box-end wrench in not available. Avoid using an adjustable wrench if a large amount of tightening or loosening torque is required.

Adjustable wrenches come in sized ranging from 4-18 in. overall length. A 6 or 8 in. size is recommended as an all-purpose wrench.

Socket Wrenches

A socket wrench (**Figure 11**) is generally faster, safer and more convenient to use than a common wrench. Sockets, which attach to a suitable handle, are available with six-point or 12-point openings and use 1/4, 3/8, and 1/2 in. drive sizes. The drive size corresponds to the square hole that mates with the ratchet or flex handle.

Torque Wrench

A torque wrench (**Figure 12**) is used with a socket to measure how tight a nut or bolt is installed. They come in a wide price range and in 1/4, 3/8, and 1/2 in. drive sizes. The drive size

2

corresponds to the square hole that mates with the socket.

A typical 1/4 in. drive torque wrench measures in in.-lb. increments, and has a range of 20-150 in.-lb. (2.2-17 N•m). A typical 3/8 or 1/2 in. torque measures in ft.-lb. increments, and has a range of 10-150 ft.-lb. (14-203 N•m).

Impact Driver

An impact driver (**Figure 13**) makes removal of tight fasteners easy and reduces damage to bolts and screws. Interchangeable bits allow use on a variety of fasteners.

Snap Ring Pliers

Snap ring pliers are required to remove snap rings. Snap ring pliers (**Figure 14**) usually come with different size tips; many designs can be switched to handle internal or external type snap rings.

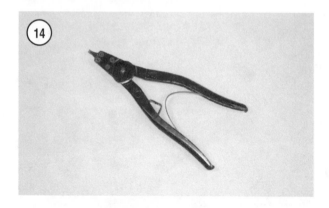

Hammers

Various types of hammers (**Figure 15**) are available to accommodate a number of applications. Use a ball-peen hammer to strike another tool, such as a punch or chisel. Use a soft-face hammer to strike a metal object without damaging it.

Never use a metal-faced hammer on engine and drive system components as severe damage will occur. You can always produce the same amount of force with a soft-faced hammer.

Always wear eye protection when using hammers. Make sure the hammer is in good condition and that the handle is not cracked. Select the correct hammer for the job and always strike the object squarely. Do not use the handle or the side of the hammer head to stroke an object.

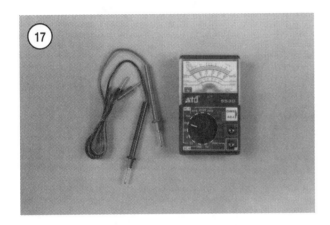

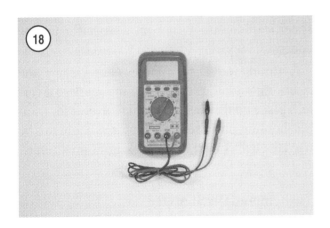

Feeler Gauges

This tool has either flat or wire measuring gauges (**Figure 16**). Use wire gauges to measure spark plug gap; use flat gauges for other measurements. A nonmagnetic (brass) gauge may be specified if working around magnetized components.

Other Special Tools

Many of the maintenance and repair procedures require special tools. Most of the necessary tools are available from a marine dealership or from tool suppliers. Instructions for their use and the manufacture's part number are included in the appropriate chapter.

Purchase the required tools from a local marine dealership or tool supplier. A qualified machinist, often at a lower price, can make some tools locally. Many marine dealerships and rental outlets will rent some of the required tools. Avoid using makeshift tools. Their use may result in damaged parts that cost far more than the recommended tool.

TEST EQUIPMENT

This section describes equipment used to perform testing, adjustments and measurements on marine engines. Most of these tools are available from a local marine dealership or automotive parts store.

Multimeter

This instrument is invaluable for electrical troubleshooting and service. It combines a voltmeter, ohmmeter and an ammeter in one unit. It is often called a VOM.

Two types of mutimeter are available, analog and digital. Analog meters (**Figure 17**) have a moving needle with marked bands on the meter face indicating the volt, ohm and amperage scales. An analog meter must be calibrated each time the scale is changed.

A digital meter (**Figure 18**) is ideally suited for electrical troubleshooting because it is easy to read and more accurate than an analog meter. Most models are auto-ranging, have automatic polarity compensation and internal overload protection circuits.

2

Either type of meter is suitable for most electrical testing described in this manual. An analog meter is better suited for testing pulsing voltage signals such as those produced by the ignition system. A digital meter is better suited for testing very low resistance or voltage reading (less than 1 volt or 1 ohm). The test procedure will indicate if a specific type of meter is required.

The ignition system produces electrical pulses that are too short in duration for accurate measurement with a using a conventional multimeter. Use a meter with peak-volt reading capability to test the ignition system. This type of meter captures the peak voltage reached during an electrical pulse.

Scale selection, meter specifications and test connections vary by the manufacturer and model of the meter. Thoroughly read the instructions supplied with the meter before performing any test. The meter and certain electrical components on the engine can be damaged if tested incorrectly. Have the test performed by a qualified professional if you are unfamiliar with the testing or general meter usage. The expense to replace damaged equipment can far exceed the cost of having the test performed by a professional.

Strobe Timing Light

This instrument is necessary for dynamic tuning (setting ignition timing while the engine is running). By flashing a light at the precise instant the spark plug fires, the position of the timing mark can be seen. The flashing light makes a moving mark appear to stand still next to a stationary mark.

Timing lights (**Figure 19**) range from inexpensive models with a neon bulb to expensive models with a xenon bulb, built in tachometer and timing advance compensator. A built in tachometer is very useful as most ignition timing

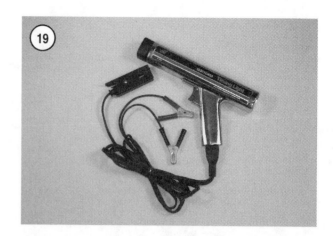

specifications are based on a specific engine speed.

A timing advance compensator delays the strobe enough to bring the timing mark to a certain place on the scale. Although useful for troubleshooting purposes, this feature should not be used to check or adjust the base ignition timing.

Tachometer/Dwell Meter

A portable tachometer (**Figure 20**) is needed to tune and test most marine engines. Ignition timing and carburetor adjustments must be performed at a specified engine speed. Tachometers are available with either an analog or digital display.

The fuel/air mixture must be adjusted with the engine running at idle speed. If using an analog

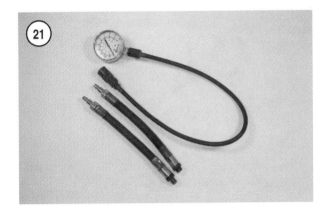

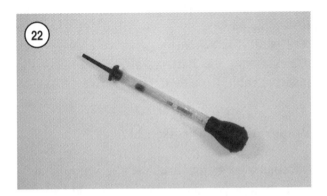

vide accurate measurement at all speeds without the need to change the range or scale. Many of these use an inductive pickup to receive the signal from the ignition system.

A dwell meter is often incorporated into the tachometer to allow testing and/or adjustments to engines with a breaker point ignition system.

Compression Gauge

This tool (**Figure 21**) measures the amount of pressure created in the combustion chamber during the compression stroke. Compression indicates the general engine condition making it one of the most useful troubleshooting tools.

The easiest type to use has screw-in adapters that fit the spark plug holes. Rubber tipped, press-in type gauges are also available. This type must be held firmly in the spark plug hole to prevent leakage and inaccurate test results..

Hydrometer

Use a hydrometer to measure specific gravity in the battery. Specific gravity is the density of the battery electrolyte as compared to pure water and indicates the battery's state of charge. Choose a hydrometer (**Figure 22**) with automatic temperature compensation; otherwise the electrolyte temperature must be measured during charging to determine the actual specific gravity.

Precision Measuring Tools

Various tools are required to make precision measurements. A dial indicator (**Figure 23**), for example, is used to determine piston position in the cylinder, runout and end play of shafts and assemblies. It is also used to measure free movement between the gear teeth (backlash) in the drive unit.

tachometer, choose one with a low range of 0-1000 rpm or 0-2000 rpm range and a high range of 0-6000 rpm. The high range setting is needed for testing purposes but lacks the accuracy needed at lower speeds. At lower speeds the meter must be capable of detecting changes of 25 rpm or less.

Digital tachometers are generally easier to use than most analog type tachometers. They pro-

Venier calipers (**Figure 24**), micrometers (**Figure 25**) and other precision tools are used to measure the size of parts, such as the piston.

Precision measuring equipment must be stored, handled and used carefully or it will not remain accurate.

SERVICE HINTS

Most of the service procedures in this manual are straightforward and can be performed by anyone reasonably handy with tools. It is suggested, however, that you consider your skills and available tools and equipment before attempting a repair involving major disassembly of the engine or drive unit.

Some operations, for example, require the use of a press. Other operations require precision measurement. Have the procedure or measurements performed by a professional if you do not have access to the correct equipment or are unfamiliar with its use.

Special Battery Precautions

Disconnecting or connecting the battery can create a spike or surge of current throughout the electrical system. This spike or surge can damage certain components of the charging system. Always verify the ignition switch is in the OFF position before connecting or disconnecting the battery or changing the selection on a battery switch.

Always disconnect both battery cables and remove the battery from the boat for charging. If the battery cables are connected, the charger may induce a damaging spike or surge of current into the electrical system. During charging, batteries produce explosive and corrosive gasses. These gases can cause corrosion in the battery compartment and creates an extremely hazardous condition.

Disconnect the cables from the battery prior to testing, adjusting or repairing many of the systems or components on the engine. This is nec-essary for safety, to prevent damage to test equipment and to ensure accurate testing or adjustment. Always disconnect the negative battery cable first, then the positive cable. When reconnecting the battery, always connect the positive cable first, then the negative cable.

Preparation for Disassembly

Repairs go much faster if the equipment is clean before you begin work. There are special cleaners such as Gunk or Bel-Ray Degreaser, for cleaning the engine and related components. Just spray or brush on the cleaning solution, let it stand, then rinse with a garden hose.

Use pressurized water to remove marine growth and corrosion or mineral deposits from external components such as the gearcase, drive shaft housing and clamp brackets. Avoid directing pressurized water directly as seals or gaskets; pressurized water can flow past seal and gasket surfaces and contaminate lubricating fluids.

> *WARNING*
> *Never use gasoline as a cleaning agent. It presents an extreme fire hazard. Always work in a well-ventilated area if using cleaning solvent. Keep a Coast Guard approved fire extinguisher, rated for gasoline fires, readily accessible in the work area.*

Much of the labor charged for a job performed at a dealership is usually for removal and disas-

sembly of other parts to access defective parts or assemblies. It is frequently possible to perform most of the disassembly then take the defective part or assembly to the dealership for repair.

If you decide to perform the job yourself, read the appropriate section in this manual, in its entirety. Study the illustrations and text until you fully understand what is involved to complete the job. Make arrangements to purchase or rent all required special tools and equipment before starting.

Disassembly Precautions

During disassembly, keep a few general precautions in mind. Force is rarely needed to get things apart. If parts fit tightly, such as a bearing on a shaft, there is usually a tool designed to separate them. Never use a screwdriver to separate parts with a machined mating surface, such as the cylinder head or manifold. The surfaces will be damaged and leak.

Make diagrams or take instant photographs wherever similar-appearing parts are found. Often, disassembled parts are left for several days or longer before resuming work. You may not remember where everything came from, or carefully arranged parts may become disturbed.

Cover all openings after removing parts to keep contamination or other parts from entering.

Tag all similar internal parts for location and mounting direction. Reinstall all internal components in the same location and mounting direction as removed. Record the thickness and

mounting location of any shims as they are removed. Place small bolts and parts in plastic sandwich bags. Seal and label the bags with masking tape.

Tag all wires, hoses and connections and make a sketch of the routing. Never rely on memory alone; it may be several days or longer before you resume work.

Protect all painted surfaces from physical damage. Never allow gasoline or cleaning solvent on these surfaces.

Assembly Precautions

No parts, except those assembled with a press fit, require unusual force during assembly. If a part is hard to remove or install, find out why before proceeding.

When assembling parts, start all fasteners, then tighten evenly in an alternating or crossing pattern unless a specific tightening sequence or procedure is given.

When assembling parts, be sure all shims, spacers and washers are installed in the same position and location as removed.

Whenever a rotating part butts against a stationary part, look for a shim or washer. Use new gaskets, seals and O-rings if there is any doubt about the conditions of the used ones. Unless otherwise specified, a thin coating of oil on gaskets may help them seal more effectively. Use heavy grease to hold small parts in place if they tend to fall out during assembly.

Use emery cloth and oil to remove high spots from piston surfaces. Use a dull screwdriver to remove carbon deposits from the cylinder head, ports and piston crown. *Do not* scratch or gouge these surfaces. Wipe the surfaces clean with a *clean* shop towel when finished.

If the carburetor must be repaired, completely disassemble it and soak all metal parts in a commercial carburetor cleaner. Never soak gaskets and rubber or plastic parts in these cleaners.

2

Clean rubber or plastic parts in warm soapy water. Never use a wire to clean jets and small passages because they are easily damaged. Use compressed air to blow debris from all passages in the carburetor body.

Take your time and do the job right. Break-in procedure for a newly rebuilt engine or drive is the same as for a new one. Use the recommended break-in oil and follow the instructions provided in the appropriate chapter.

SPECIAL TIPS

Because of the extreme demands placed on marine equipment, several points must be kept in mind when performing service and repair. The following are general suggestions that may improve the overall life of the machine and help avoid costly failure.

1. Unless otherwise specified, apply a threadlocking compound, such as Loctite Threadlocker, to all bolts and nuts, even if secured with a lockwasher. Use only the specified grade of threadlocking compound. A screw or bolt lost from an engine cover or bearing retainer could easily cause serious and expensive damage before the loss is noticed. When applying threadlocking compound, use only enough to lightly coat the threads. If too much is used, it can work its way down the threads and contaminate seals or bearings.

2. If self-locking fasteners are used, replace them with new ones. Do not install standard fasteners in place of self-locking ones.

3. Use caution when using air tools to remove stainless steel nuts or bolts. The heat generated during rapid spinning easily damages the threads of stainless steel fasteners. To prevent thread damage, apply penetrating oil as a cooling agent and loosen or tighten them slowly.

4. Use a wide chisel to straighten the tab of a fold-over type lockwasher. Such a tool provides a better contact surface than a screwdriver or pry bar, making straightening easier. During installa-

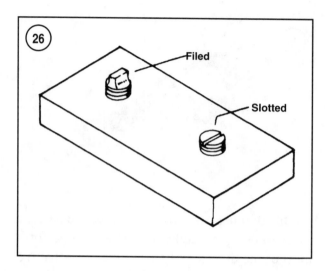

tion, use a new fold-over type lockwasher. If a new lockwasher is not available, fold over a tab on the washer that has not been previously used. Reusing the same tab may cause the washer to break, resulting in a loss of locking ability and a loose piece of metal adrift in the engine. When folding the tab into position, carefully pry it toward the flat on the bolt or nut. Use a pair or plies to bend the tab against the fastener. Do not use a punch and hammer to drive the tab into position. The resulting fold may be too sharp, weakening the washer and increasing its chance of failure.

5. Use only the specified replacement parts if replacing a missing or damaged bolt, screw or nut. Many fasteners are specially hardened for the application.

6. Install only the specified gaskets. Unless specified otherwise, install them without sealant. Many gaskets are made with a material that swells when it contacts oil. Gasket sealer prevents them from swelling as intended and can result in oil leakage. Most gaskets must be a specific thickness. Installing a gasket that is too thin or too thick in a critical area could cause expensive damage.

7. Make sure all shims and washers are reinstalled in the same location and position. Whenever a rotating part contacts a stationary part, look for a shim or washer.

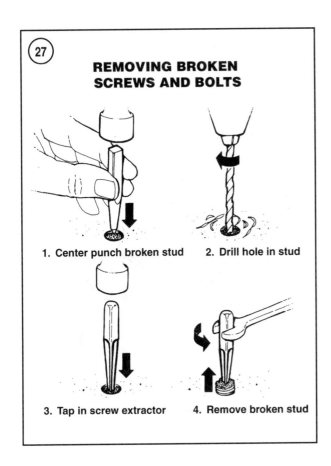

REMOVING BROKEN SCREWS AND BOLTS

1. Center punch broken stud

2. Drill hole in stud

3. Tap in screw extractor

4. Remove broken stud

MECHANICS TECHNIQUES

Marine engines are subjected to conditions very different from most engines. They are repeatedly subjected to a corrosive environment followed by periods of non-use for weeks or longer. Such use invites corrosion damage to fasteners, causing difficulty or breakage during removal. This section provides information that is useful for removing stuck or broken fasteners and repairing damaged threads.

Removing Stuck Fasteners

When a nut or bolt corrodes and cannot be removed, several methods may be used to loosen it. First, apply penetrating oil, such as Liquid Wrench or WD-40. Apply it liberally to the threads and allow it to penetrate for 10-15 minutes. Tap the fastener several times with a small

hammer; however, do not hit it hard enough to cause damage. Reapply the penetrating oil if necessary.

For stuck screws, apply penetrating oil as described, then insert a screwdriver in the slot. Tap the top of the screwdriver with a hammer. This looses the corrosion in the threads allowing it to turn. If the screw head is too damaged to use a screwdriver, grip the head with locking pliers and twist the screw from the assembly.

A Phillips, Allen or Torx screwdriver may start to slip in the screw during removal. If slippage occurs, stop immediately and apply a dab of course valve lapping compound onto the tip of the screwdriver. Valve lapping compound or a special screw removal compound is available from most hardware and automotive parts stores. Insert the driver into the screw and apply downward pressure while turning. The gritty material in the compound improves the grip on the screw, allowing more rotational force before slippage occurs. Keep the compound away from any other engine components. It is very abrasive and can cause rapid wear if applied onto moving or sliding surfaces.

Avoid applying heat unless specifically instructed because it may melt, warp or remove the temper from parts.

Removing Broken Bolts or Screws

The head of bolt or screw may unexpectedly twist off during removal. Several methods are available for removing the remaining portion of the bolt or screw.

If a large portion of the bolt or screw projects out, try gripping it with locking pliers. If the projecting portion is too small, file it to fit a wrench or cut a slot in it to fit a screwdriver (**Figure 26**). If the head breaks off flush or cannot be turned with a screwdriver or wrench, use a screw extractor (**Figure 27**). To do this, center punch the remaining portion of the screw or bolt. Select the proper size of extractor for the size of the fastener. Using the drill size specified on the extractor, drill a hole into the fastener. Do not drill deeper than the remaining fastener. Carefully tap the extractor into the hole and back the remnant out using a wrench on the extractor.

Remedying Stripped Threads

Occasionally, threads are stripped through carelessness or impact damage. Often the threads can be repaired by running a tap (for internal threads on nuts) or die (for external threads on bolts) through threads (**Figure 28**).

To clean or repair spark plug threads, use a spark plug tap. If an internal thread is damaged, it may be necessary to install a Helicoil or some other type of thread insert. Follow the manufacturer's instructions when installing their insert.

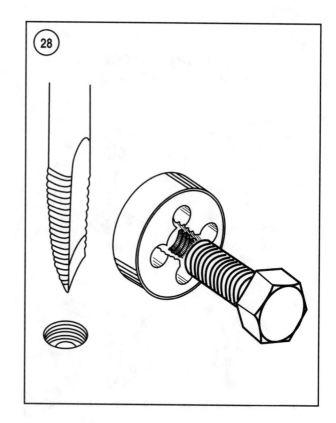

Chapter Three

Troubleshooting

Troubleshooting is a relatively simple matter when it is done logically. The first step in any troubleshooting procedure is to define the symptoms as closely as possible and then localize the problem. Subsequent steps involve testing and analyzing those areas which could cause the symptoms. A haphazard approach may eventually solve the problem, but it can be very costly in terms of wasted time and unnecessary parts replacement.

Proper lubrication, maintenance and periodic tune-ups as described in Chapter Four and Chapter Five will reduce the necessity for troubleshooting. Even with the best of care however, a marine engine is prone to problems which will require troubleshooting. This chapter contains brief descriptions of each operating system and troubleshooting procedures to be used. **Tables 1-3** present typical starting, ignition and fuel system problems with their probable causes and solutions. All tables are at the end of the chapter.

OPERATING REQUIREMENTS

All 2-stroke engines require 3 basic conditions to run properly. Crankcase and cylinder com-

pression, fuel and air mixed properly by the carburetor and spark delivered to the spark plug by the ignition system at the correct time. When troubleshooting it is helpful to remember: *compression, fuel and spark*. If any of these are lacking the motor will not run. Always verify the mechanical integrity of the engine by performing a compression test (Chapter Four). Once compression has been verified, test the ignition system with an air gap spark tester and then finally focus your attention on the fuel system. Troubleshooting in this order will provide the quickest results.

If a motor has been sitting for any length of time and refuses to start, check the condition of the battery first to make sure it has an adequate charge, then look to the fuel delivery system. This includes the gas tank, fuel pump, fuel lines and carburetor(s). Rust may have formed in the tank, obstructing fuel flow. Gasoline deposits may have gummed up carburetor jets and air passages. Gasoline tends to lose its potency after standing for long periods. Condensation may contaminate the fuel delivery system with water.

Connect a portable tank containing fresh fuel mix to help isolate the problem. Do not drain the old gasoline unless you are sure it is at fault. Always dispose of old gasoline in accordance with EPA regulations.

STARTING SYSTEM

Description

Two cylinder 25 hp and all 35 hp and larger outboard and L-Drive engines are equipped with an electric starter motor (**Figure 1**). The motor is mounted vertically on the engine. When battery current is supplied to the starter motor, its pinion gear is thrust upward to engage the teeth on the engine flywheel. Once the engine starts, the pinion gear disengages from the flywheel. This is similar to the method used in cranking an automotive engine.

The electric starting system requires a fully charged battery to provide the large amount of current required to operate the starter motor. Electric start motors are equipped with an alternator on the stator plate which charges the battery while the engine is running.

The electric starting system consists of the battery, ignition or starter switch, an interlock switch, starter motor and related wiring. A solenoid or starter relay carries the heavy electrical current to the starter motor. Depressing the starter switch or turning the ignition switch to the START position allows current to flow through the solenoid coil. The solenoid contacts close and allow current to flow from the battery through the solenoid to the starter motor.

A circuit breaker or fuse protects the switching circuits from damage due to excessive current flow.

An interlock switch, sometimes called a neutral safety switch, prevents the starter from engaging if the engine is in forward or reverse gear. This is called *start in gear protection*. The interlock switch is located in the control box or on the engine, but all electric start models must have start in gear protection.

Figure 2 is a simplified diagram of a typical starting system.

CAUTION
Do not operate an electric starter motor continuously for more than 15 seconds. Allow the motor to cool for at least 3 minutes between attempts to start the engine.

Troubleshooting Procedures

Refer to **Table 1** at the end of this chapter. Before troubleshooting the starting circuit, make sure that:

a. The battery is in acceptable condition and fully charged.
b. The shift mechanism is in NEUTRAL.
c. All electrical connections are clean and tight.
d. The wiring harness is in good condition, with no worn or frayed insulation.
e. Battery cables are the proper size and length. Replace cables that are undersize or relocate the battery to shorten the distance between battery and starter solenoid.
f. The fuel system is filled with an adequate supply of fresh gasoline that has been properly mixed with a recommended engine oil. See Chapter Four.

A 12-volt test lamp is a very simple and accurate device for troubleshooting the starting system when used with a wiring diagram for the engine being tested. One lead of the test lamp must be connected to a good ground at all times, unless otherwise specified. When the other lead is connected to a hot circuit, the test lamp will glow.

Before beginning any troubleshooting with a test lamp, connect the test lamp directly to the battery and observe the brightness of the bulb. You must reference the rest of your readings against this test. If the bulb does not glow as brightly as when it was hooked directly to the battery, a problem is indicated.

The troubleshooting procedures in this chapter are intended only to isolate a malfunction to a certain component. If further bench testing is then necessary, remove the suspected component for testing and inspection, or have it tested by an authorized service center. It is often less expensive to replace a faulty component than to have it tested and repaired. Refer to Chapter Seven for component removal and installation.

NOTE
*All 1984-1992 remote control models use terminal blocks for electrical connections. All 1993 and newer remote control models use Mercury style plug-in connections. Also, note that 1989 was a transition year for color code changes. Refer to **Table 17**.*

All Models With Mercury Style Plug In Connector, (1993 and Newer Models)

Refer to **Figure 3** for this procedure. Refer to Chapter Fourteen for individual model wiring diagrams.

1. Connect the test lamp lead to the *positive* terminal of the battery and touch the test lamp probe to metal anywhere on the engine block. The test lamp should light. If the lamp does not light or is dim, the battery ground cable connections are loose or corroded, or there is an open circuit in the battery ground cable. Check connections on both ends of the ground cable.

2. Place the shift lever into the NEUTRAL position and connect the test lamp lead to a good engine ground.

3. Connect the test lamp probe to the starter solenoid input terminal (1, **Figure 3**). The test lamp should light. If the lamp does not light or is very dim, the battery cable connections are loose or corroded, or there is an open in the cable between the battery and the solenoid. Clean and tighten connections or replace the battery cable as required.

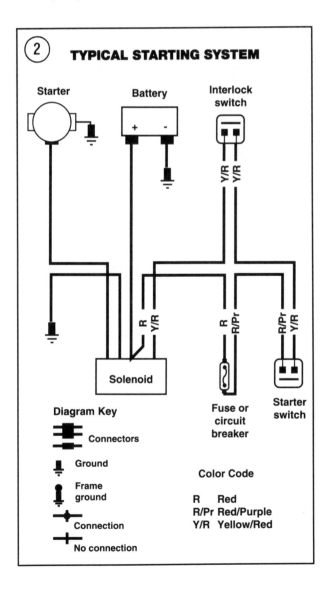

③

TYPICAL STARTING SYSTEM CIRCUIT
(1993 AND NEWER WITH MERCURY PLUG-IN)

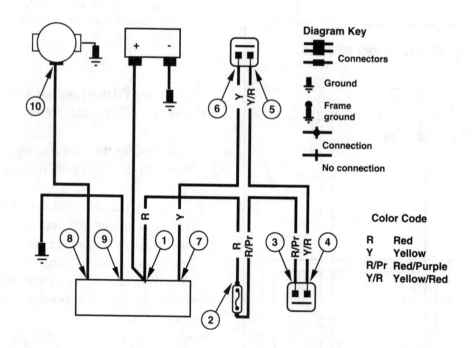

Diagram Key

Connectors

Ground

Frame ground

Connection

No connection

Color Code

R   Red
Y   Yellow
R/Pr Red/Purple
Y/R   Yellow/Red

4. Remove the 20 amp fuse and connect the test lamp probe to the input side of the fuse holder (2, **Figure 3**). If the lamp does not light, repair or replace the wire between the starter solenoid and the fuse holder.

5. Inspect the 20 amp fuse. Install a known good fuse into the fuse holder. Unplug the main 8-pin connector and connect the test light to pin No. 8 of the main engine harness connector. If the test lamp does not light, repair or replace the wire between the fuse holder and the main engine harness connector.

6. Reconnect the main harness connector and gain access to the ignition key on the dash or in the remote control box. Connect the test lamp to terminal B on the key switch (3, **Figure 3**). If the lamp does not light, repair or replace the wire between pin No. 8 of the main boat harness connector and the key switch terminal B.

7. Connect the test lamp to the key switch terminal S (4, **Figure 3**). With the key switch turned to the START position, observe the test lamp. If the test lamp does not light, replace the key switch.

8. Remove the cover from the remote control box and connect the test lamp to the ignition switch side of the interlock switch (5, **Figure 3**). With the key switch turned to the START position, observe the test lamp. If the test lamp does not light, repair or replace the wire between the interlock switch and the ignition switch.

9. Move the test lamp to the engine side of the interlock switch (6, **Figure 3**). With the key switch turned to the START position, observe the test lamp. If the test lamp does not light, make sure the remote control box is still in neutral and retest. Replace the interlock switch if the lamp does not light.

10. Connect the test lamp to the yellow/red wire terminal on the starter solenoid (7, **Figure 3**). With the key switch turned to the START position, observe the test lamp. If the test lamp does not light, repair or replace the wire between the interlock switch and the starter solenoid. This includes the main harness connector pin No. 7.

11. Connect the test lamp to the starter solenoid terminal leading to the starter motor (8, **Figure 3**). With the key switch turned to the START position observe the test lamp. If the test lamp does not light, connect the test lamp lead to the positive battery terminal and connect the test lamp to the ground terminal of the starter solenoid (9, **Figure 3**). If the test lamp does not light, repair or replace the ground wire between the starter solenoid and the engine block. If the test lamp lights, replace the starter solenoid.

12. Connect the test lamp to the starter motor terminal (10, **Figure 3**). With the key switch turned to the START position observe the test lamp. If the test lamp does not light, repair or replace the cable between the starter solenoid and the starter motor. If the test lamp lights, remove the starter and inspect for paint or corrosion on the mounting bolts and bosses. If paint or corrosion is found, clean the mounting bolts and bosses then reinstall the starter and test starter engagement. If the starter still will not engage, remove the starter for replacement or repair.

All Models (Except L-Drive) Equipped with Terminal Block Connections

Refer to **Figure 4** (typical, early models) or **Figure 5** (typical, later models) for this procedure. Refer to Chapter Thirteen for individual model wiring diagrams.

1. Place the engine in NEUTRAL and connect one test lamp lead to a good engine ground.

2. Connect the other lead to the starter relay input terminal (2, **Figure 4** or **Figure 5**). The test lamp should light. If the lamp does not light or is very dim, the battery cable terminal connections are loose or corroded, or there is an open in the cable between the battery and the starter relay. Clean and tighten terminal connections or replace the battery cable as required.

3

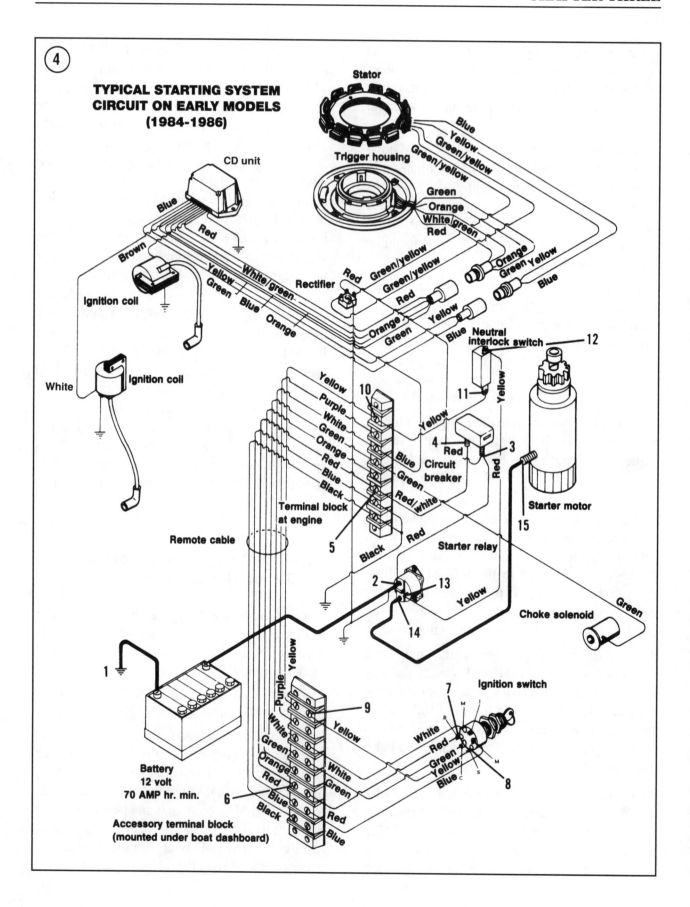

④

**TYPICAL STARTING SYSTEM
CIRCUIT ON EARLY MODELS
(1984-1986)**

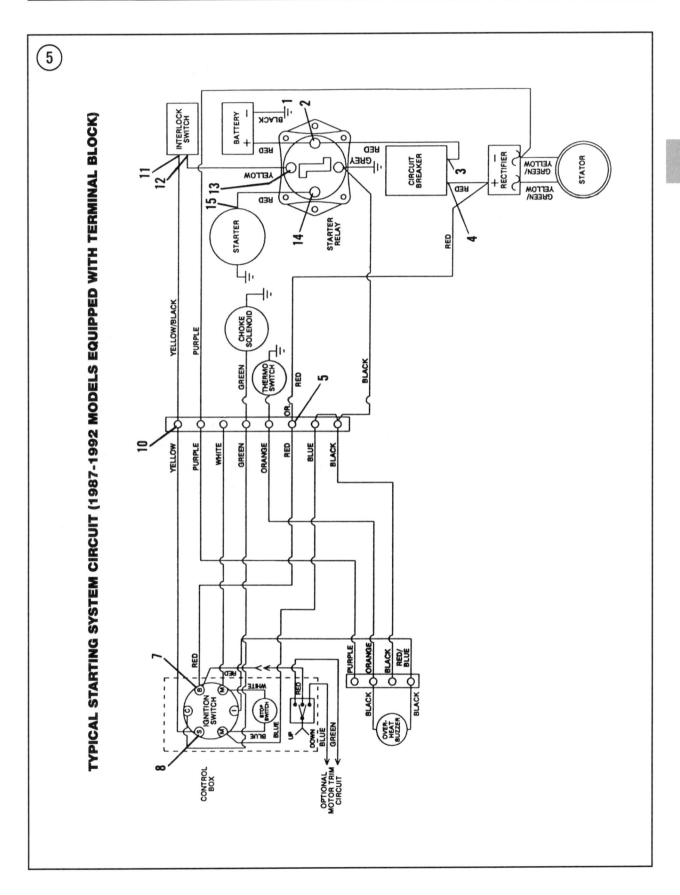

TYPICAL STARTING SYSTEM CIRCUIT (1987-1992 MODELS EQUIPPED WITH TERMINAL BLOCK)

3

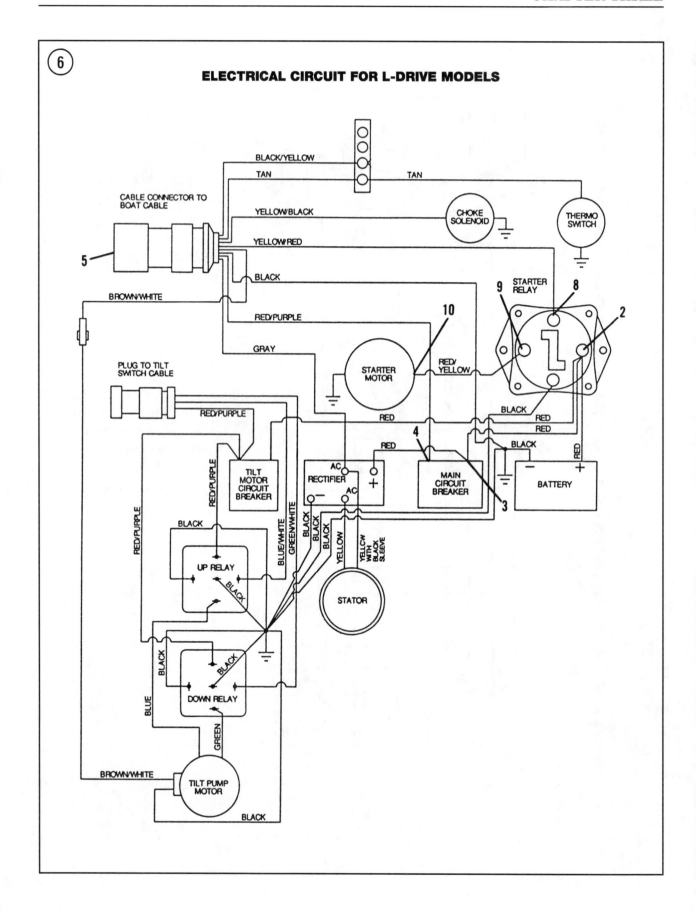

⑥ **ELECTRICAL CIRCUIT FOR L-DRIVE MODELS**

3. Connect the test lamp to the circuit breaker (or fuse) input terminal (3, **Figure 4** or **Figure 5**). If the lamp does not light, repair or replace the wire between the starter relay and circuit breaker (or fuse) as required.

NOTE
If the circuit breaker reset button pops out when depressed in Step 4, the circuit breaker is not necessarily defective. There is possibly a short circuit in the starting circuit that must be located and corrected.

4. Connect the test lamp to the circuit breaker (or fuse) output terminal (4, **Figure 4** or **Figure 5**). If the test lamp does not light, depress the reset button (or replace the fuse if so equipped). If the lamp still does not light, replace the circuit breaker.

5. Connect the test lamp to the red wire terminal on the terminal block (5, **Figure 4** or **Figure 5**). Note that the wire between the circuit breaker and terminal block or engine harness connector (5, **Figure 4** or **Figure 5**) may be red with a white tracer or red with a purple tracer. If the test lamp does not light, repair or replace the wire between the circuit breaker (or fuse) and terminal block or engine harness connector as required.

6. Connect the test lamp to the red wire terminal on the accessory block (6, **Figure 4**) on models so equipped. If not equipped with accessory block, proceed to Step 7. If the lamp does not light, repair or replace the red lead in the remote harness as required.

7. Connect the test lamp to the battery (B) terminal on the ignition switch (7, **Figure 4** or **Figure 5**). If the test lamp does not light, repair or replace the red (or red/purple) wire between the ignition switch and accessory block (if so equipped) or ignition switch and circuit breaker or fuse as required.

NOTE
The ignition switch must be held in the START position during Steps 8-15. Make

sure the shift lever is in the NEUTRAL position.

8. Connect the test lamp to the start (S) terminal on the ignition switch (8, **Figure 4**). If the lamp does not light, replace the ignition switch.

9. Connect the test lamp to the yellow (or yellow/red) wire terminal of the accessory block (9, **Figure 4**), on models so equipped. If not equipped with accessory block, proceed to Step 10. If the lamp does not light, repair or replace the yellow (or yellow/red) wire between the ignition switch and accessory block.

10. Connect the test lamp to the yellow or yellow/red wire terminal of the terminal block (10, **Figure 4** or **Figure 5**). If the lamp does not light, repair or replace the yellow (or yellow/red) wire in the remote harness as required.

11. Connect the test lamp to the interlock switch terminal (11, **Figure 4** or **Figure 5**). If the lamp does not light, repair or replace the wire between the interlock and ignition switches or between the terminal block and interlock switch.

12. Connect the test lamp to the interlock switch terminal (12, **Figure 4** or **Figure 5**). If the test lamp does not light, manually depress the interlock switch plunger. If the lamp still does not light, replace the switch.

13. Connect the test lamp to the starter relay yellow or yellow/red wire terminal. If the lamp does not light, repair or replace the wire between the starter relay and interlock switch as required.

14. Connect the test lamp to the starter relay-to-starter terminal (14, **Figure 4** or **Figure 5**). If the lamp does not light, replace the starter relay.

15. Connect the test lamp to the starter motor positive terminal (15, **Figure 4** or **Figure 5**). If the test lamp lights, the starter motor is defective and must be repaired or replaced.

L-Drive Models

Refer to **Figure 6** for this procedure.

3

1. Place the shift lever into the NEUTRAL position and connect test lamp lead to a good engine ground.

2. Connect test lamp to the starter relay input terminal (2, **Figure 6**). The test lamp should light. If the lamp does not light or is very dim, the battery cable terminal connections are loose or corroded, or there is an open in the cable between the battery and the starter relay. Clean and tighten terminal connections or replace the battery cable as required.

3. Remove the bracket containing the rectifier, main circuit breaker and 4-screw terminal block. Connect test lamp to the circuit breaker battery-input terminal (3, **Figure 6**). If the lamp does not light, repair or replace the wire between the starter relay and circuit breaker.

NOTE
If the circuit breaker reset button pops out when depressed in Step 4, the circuit breaker is not necessarily defective. There is possibly a short circuit in the starting system that must be located and corrected.

4. Connect the test lamp to the remaining circuit breaker (output) terminal (4, **Figure 6**). If the lamp does not light, depress the reset button. If the lamp still does not light, replace the circuit breaker. Reattach the bracket to the power head.

5. Disconnect the engine wiring harness connector (5, **Figure 6**) from the boat harness. Probe the No. 6 pin in engine harness connector (**Figure 7**) with the test lamp. If the test lamp does not light, repair or replace the red/purple wire between the circuit breaker and connector (5, **Figure 6**).

6. Reconnect the engine wiring harness connector to the boat harness connector. Remove the ignition switch from the boat instrument panel. Do not disconnect any wires from the ignition switch. Connect test lamp to terminal B (6, **Figure 8**) of ignition switch. If test lamp does not light, repair or replace wire between pin No.

6 of engine wiring harness connector (**Figure 7**) and terminal B (6, **Figure 8**) of ignition switch.

NOTE
The ignition switch must be held in the START position while performing Steps 7-12. Make sure the shift lever is in the NEUTRAL position.

7. Connect test lamp to the S terminal (7, **Figure 8**) of the ignition switch. Replace the ignition switch if the test lamp does not light.

8. Remove remote control box cover and connect test lamp to ignition switch side of interlock

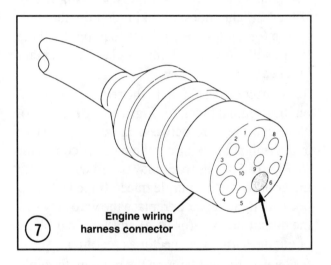

Engine wiring harness connector

⑦

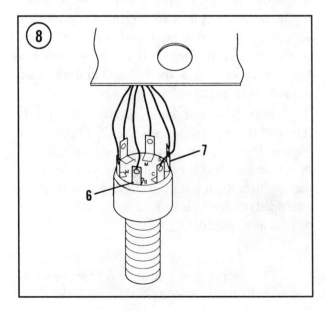

⑧

switch (**Figure 9**). If test lamp does not light, repair or replace wire between ignition switch S terminal and interlock switch.

9. Connect test lamp to the starter relay side of interlock switch (**Figure 9**). If test lamp does not light, replace interlock switch.

10. Connect test lamp to the yellow/red terminal (8, **Figure 6**) of starter relay. If test lamp does not light, repair or replace wire between interlock switch and relay yellow/red terminal (8, **Figure 6**).

11. Connect test lamp to the starter relay red/yellow terminal (9, **Figure 6**). If test lamp does not light, replace starter relay.

12. Connect test lamp to the red/yellow terminal at starter motor (10, **Figure 6**). If test lamp does not light, repair or replace the red/yellow wire

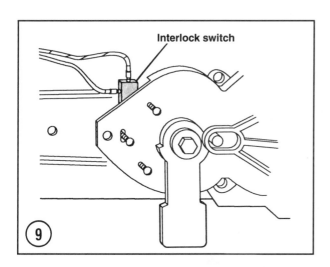

between starter relay and starter motor. If test lamp lights, remove starter motor for repair or replace starter motor as required.

Starter Current Draw Test (All Models)

A starter draw test may be performed to determine the overall condition of the starter motor by checking the current draw and voltage drop at the battery during cranking. A higher than specified current draw indicates the starter requires repair or replacement. The battery must be in good condition and fully charged for valid test results. Proceed as follows:

1. Disconnect the spark plug leads from the spark plugs. Securely ground the leads to the power head.

2. Place the shift lever in the NEUTRAL position.

3. Connect an ammeter in series (200 amp minimum) between positive battery terminal and positive battery cable, or connect a suitable inductive-type ammeter to positive battery cable.

4. Connect a suitable voltmeter to the battery.

5. Crank engine while noting ammeter and voltmeter.

6. Refer to **Table 6** for specifications. Minimum cranking voltage at the battery is 10.0 volts.

CHOKE SOLENOID OR FUEL PRIMER VALVE CIRCUITS

NOTE
*Choke models were last produced in 1994. All choke models can be identified by a mechanical linkage from the choke solenoid to the carburetor choke plates. Choke models enrich the air/fuel mixture by closing the choke plate at the front of the carburetor(s). Fuel primer models can be identified by the absence of choke plates on the carburetor(s) and the presence of fuel lines at the primer valve (**Figure 10**). Fuel primer models enrich*

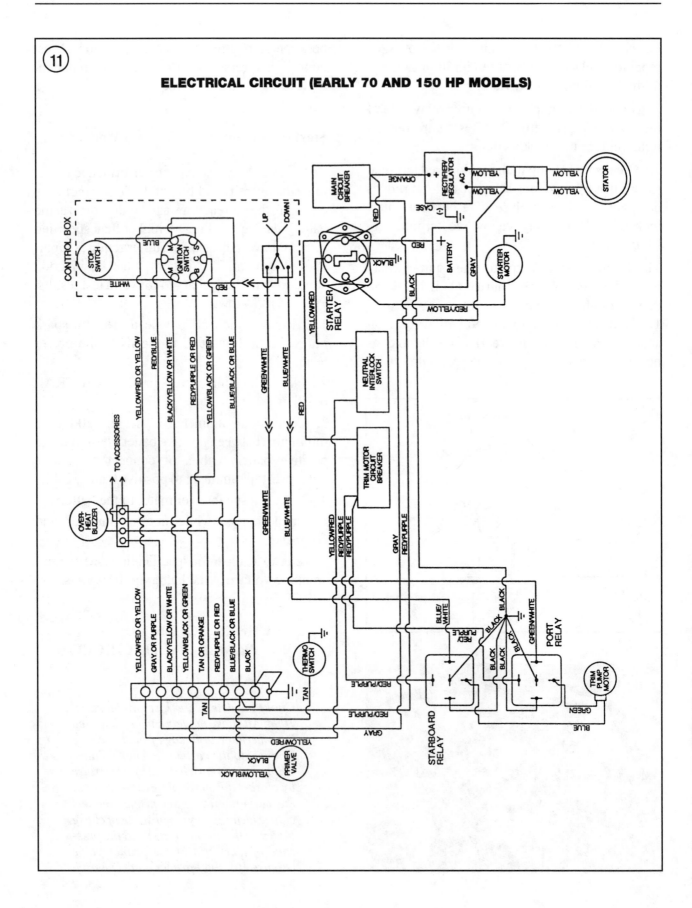

ELECTRICAL CIRCUIT (EARLY 70 AND 150 HP MODELS)

the air/fuel mixture by injecting fuel directly into the intake manifold.

Troubleshooting Choke Solenoid Models

NOTE
The key switch must be held in the CHOKE position for all of the following tests.

Refer to **Figures 4-6** for typical choke solenoid system wiring diagrams.

1. Check the choke linkage for binding or lack of lubrication. Correct any problems found.

2. Connect the test lamp lead to a good engine ground.

3. Gain access to the ignition switch terminal C (green or yellow/black wire). Connect the test lamp probe to this terminal. With the ignition switch in the CHOKE position, the test lamp should light. If it does not light, check terminal B of the key switch for power. If there is no power at terminal B, repair or replace the red or red/purple wire from terminal B of the ignition switch back through the main circuit breaker or 20 amp fuse to the starter solenoid.

4. Connect the test lamp probe to the green or yellow/black wire terminal at the choke solenoid. With the ignition switch in the CHOKE position the test lamp should light. If the test lamp does not light, repair or replace the green or yellow/black wire from the choke solenoid to the ignition switch.

5. Disconnect the green or yellow/black wire from the choke solenoid. Calibrate an ohmmeter set on the appropriate scale. Connect one lead of the ohmmeter to the electrical terminal of the choke solenoid and the other lead to the solenoid case. Replace the solenoid if the resistance is not 0.5-1.5 ohms on L-Drive models or 0.5-1.35 ohms on outboard models.

Troubleshooting Fuel Primer Valve Models

NOTE
The ignition switch must be held in the PRIME position for all of the following tests.

Refer to **Figure 11** for a typical fuel primer valve system wiring diagram.

1. Check the fuel lines going to and from the fuel primer valve for deterioration and obstructions. Correct any problems found.

2. Make sure the black wire coming out of the fuel primer valve is connected to a clean ground.

3. Connect the test lamp lead to a good engine ground.

4. Gain access to the ignition switch terminal C (yellow/black or green wire). Connect the test lamp probe to this terminal. With the ignition switch in the PRIME position the test lamp should light. If it does not light, check terminal B of the key switch for power. If there is no power at terminal B, repair or replace the red or red/purple wire from terminal B of the ignition switch back through the main 20 amp fuse to the starter solenoid.

5. Disconnect the yellow/black wire from the fuel primer valve. Connect the test lamp probe to the yellow/black or green wire on the engine harness side. With the ignition switch in the PRIME position the test lamp should light. If the test lamp does not light, repair or replace the yellow/black or green wire from the fuel primer valve to the ignition switch.

6. Disconnect the yellow/black and black wires from the fuel primer valve. Calibrate an ohmmeter on the appropriate scale to read 10-12 ohms. Connect one lead of the ohmmeter to the yellow/black wire of the fuel primer valve and the other lead to the black wire of the fuel primer valve. Replace the solenoid if the resistance is not within 10-12 ohms.

7. Disconnect the fuel hoses from the fuel primer valve and connect a short length of hose to the upper port of the valve. Blow into the hose while

depressing the manual valve button of top of the valve. Air should flow through the valve with the button depressed, but not when the button is released. Replace the valve if it does not perform as specified.

ALTERNATOR CHARGING SYSTEM

An alternator charging system is used on all electric start models. The job of the charging system is to keep the battery fully charged and supply current to run accessories. The charging system consists of the alternator stator coils, permanent magnets located within the flywheel, a rectifier or rectifier/regulator, a circuit breaker or 20 amp fuse, the battery and related wiring (**Figure 12**). Electricity is produced whenever a magnet is moved past a conductor. The rotating movement of the flywheel past the stator coils fulfills these requirements. The electricity produced from the stator is AC (alternating current) which cannot be used by the battery until it has been changed into DC (direct current). The rectifier changes AC to DC by utilizing a series of diodes, which are one-way electrical check valves. A rectifier/regulator (**Figure 13**) also changes AC to DC, but included in the rectifier/regulator is a circuit that controls the voltage going to the battery to prevent overcharging. Voltage regulators typically regulate battery voltage at approximately 14.5 volts. Refer to **Table 4** for alternator charging system specifications.

Another function of the alternator charging system is to provide the signal for the tachometer. The tachometer simply counts AC voltage pulses coming out of the stator before the AC voltage is rectified to DC. Tachometer failure is therefore, related to the charging system, not the ignition system.

Malfunctions in the charging system generally cause the battery to be undercharged and the tachometer to read erratically or totally fail. The following conditions will result in rectifier or rectifier/regulator failure.

a. Reversing the battery leads.
b. Disconnecting the battery leads while the engine is running.
c. Loose connections in the charging system circuits, including battery connections.

Preliminary Checks

Before troubleshooting the alternator charging system, visually check the following:
1. Make sure the red cable is connected to the positive battery terminal. If polarity is reversed, check for a damaged rectifier or rectifier/regulator.

NOTE
A damaged rectifier will generally be discolored or have a burned appearance.

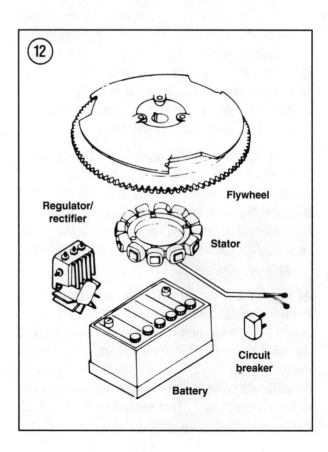

2. Check for corroded or loose connections. Clean and tighten connections, then insulate with liquid neoprene as required.

3. Check battery condition. Clean and recharge as required.

4. Check wiring harness between the stator and battery for damaged or deteriorated insulation and corroded, loose or disconnected connections. Repair, tighten or replace as required.

5. Perform the current draw test to make sure that the current demand placed on the charging system does not exceed its capacity.

> *NOTE*
> *If the load on the alternator charging system exceeds its rated capacity, the battery will always be discharging, not charging. Put simply, there may be nothing wrong with the charging system except that you are expecting more output than it is capable of producing.*

Current Draw Test
(All Models)

1. Disconnect the negative battery cable from the battery.

2. Disconnect the positive battery cable from the battery. Connect an ammeter (20 amp minimum) between positive battery post and cable as shown

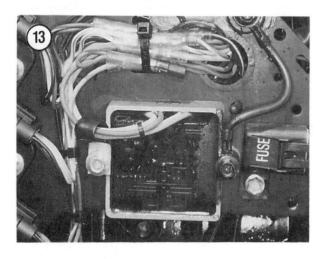

in **Figure 12**. Reconnect the negative battery cable.

3. Turn ignition switch to ON and turn on all accessories. Note the ammeter reading and compare to the maximum current draw provided in **Table 4**. If current draw exceeds the specified amperage, reduce the number of accessories used with the charging system.

Troubleshooting Nonregulated Models

Refer to **Table 4** for specifications and **Table 7** for ohmmeter guidelines

1. Disconnect the negative battery cable from the battery.

2. Connect an ammeter (of sufficient size to measure the maximum rated output of the charging system) in SERIES between the positive (+) output terminal of the rectifier and the wire that was hooked to the positive (+) output terminal of the rectifier. Hook the red lead of the ammeter to the rectifier terminal and the black lead of the ammeter to the rectifier engine harness lead. Make sure the connections are secure and insulated from any other wires or grounds.

3. Reconnect the negative battery cable

4. Install a shop tachometer according to its manufacturers instructions.

5. Start the engine and run it to the rpm specified in **Table 4** while observing the ammeter readings. If amperage output is less than specified, continue with Step 6. If amperage output is within specification, the charging system is functioning correctly.

6. To check the resistance of the stator, disconnect the negative battery cable. Disconnect the 2 stator wires connected to the AC terminals of the rectifier. Calibrate an ohmmeter on the appropriate scale to read the stator resistance specification (**Table 4**). Connect one lead of the ohmmeter to each of the stator wires. Note the reading.

Replace the stator if the measured resistance is out of the specification range.

7. To check the stator for shorts to ground, calibrate the ohmmeter on the high ohms scale. Connect one lead of the ohmmeter to a clean engine ground. Connect the other lead alternately to each of the 2 stator leads. The ohmmeter should read *infinity*. Any reading other than infinity means the stator is shorted to ground and must be replaced.

8. To check the diodes in the rectifier, disconnect the remaining rectifier leads. Calibrate the ohmmeter on the high ohms scale. Connect one ohmmeter lead to the rectifier negative (-) terminal and the other lead to one of the AC terminals (**Figure 14**). Note the ohmmeter reading. Reverse the ohmmeter leads and note the reading. The reading should be high in one polarity and low in the other. If the reading was high in both polarities or low in both polarities the rectifier must be replaced. Repeat the test for the other AC terminal.

9. Connect one lead of the ohmmeter, calibrated on the high ohms scale, to the rectifier positive (+) terminal and the other lead to one of the AC terminals (**Figure 14**). Note the ohmmeter reading. Reverse the ohmmeter leads and note the reading. The reading should be high in one polarity and low in the other. If the reading was high in both polarities or low in both polarities the rectifier must be replaced. Repeat the test for the other AC terminal.

10. To check the continuity of the rectifier positive (+) lead back to the battery, make sure the negative lead of the battery is disconnected. Make sure the rectifier positive (+) wire is disconnected from the rectifier. Calibrate the ohmmeter on the high ohms scale. Connect one lead of the ohmmeter to the battery positive terminal, connect the other lead of the ohmmeter to the rectifier end of the wire that connects to the rectifier positive (+) lead. Note the ohmmeter reading. A good circuit will have a zero or very low resistance reading. If the reading is not very

low, repair or replace the wire, connections, circuit breaker or fuse between the rectifier and the battery.

Troubleshooting Regulated Models

> *NOTE*
> *A regulated charging system only outputs the current necessary to maintain 14.5 volts at the battery. If the battery is fully charged the alternator will not produce its rated output unless enough accessory demand is present.*

Refer to **Table 4** for specifications and **Table 7** for ohmmeter guidelines

1. Disconnect the negative battery cable from the battery

2. Connect an ammeter of sufficient size to measure the maximum rated output of the charging system in SERIES between the positive (+) output lead of the rectifier/regulator and the wire that was hooked to the positive (+) output lead of the rectifier/regulator (**Figure 15**). Hook the red lead of the ammeter to the rectifier/regulator terminal and the black lead of the ammeter to the rectifier/regulator engine harness lead. Make sure the connections are secure and insulated from any other wires or grounds.

3. Reconnect the negative battery cable

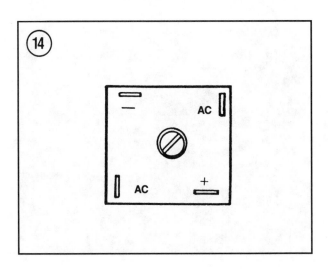

4. Install a shop tachometer according to its manufacturers instructions.

5. Connect a voltmeter to the battery terminals

6. Start the engine and run it to the speed specified in **Table 4** while noting both the ammeter and voltmeter readings. If the voltage exceeds 12.5 volts, turn on accessories or attach accessories to the battery to maintain battery voltage at 12.5 volts or less. If amperage output is less than specified, continue to Step 7. If amperage output is within specification, turn off or disconnect the accessories and run the engine at approximately 3000 rpm while observing the voltmeter. As the battery approaches full charge the voltage should rise to approximately 14.5 volts and stabilize. If the voltage stabilizes at approximately 14.5 volts, the voltage regulator is functioning correctly. If the voltage exceeds 14.5 volts, replace the rectifier/regulator.

7. To check the resistance of the stator, disconnect the negative battery cable. Disconnect the 2 stator wires connected to the AC terminals or

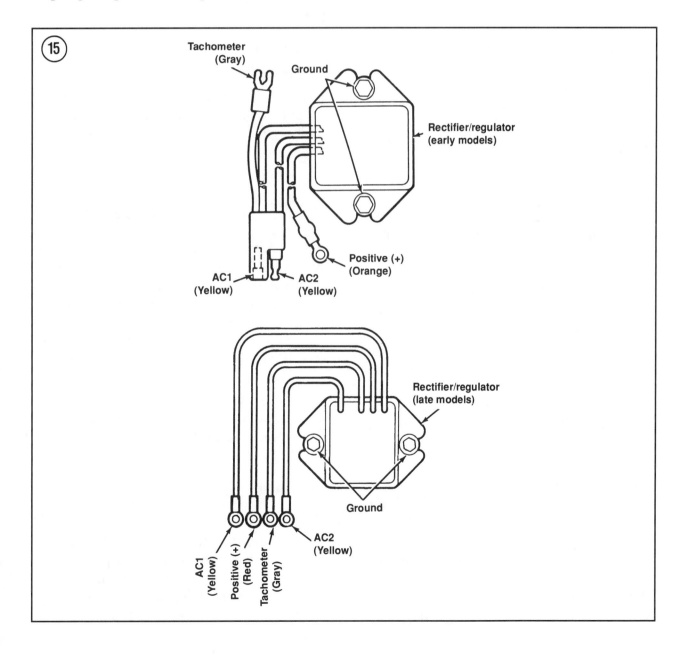

wires of the rectifier/regulator. Calibrate an ohmmeter on the appropriate scale (**Table 4**). Connect one lead of the ohmmeter to each of the stator wires. Note the reading. Replace the stator if its resistance is out of the specification range.

8. To check the stator for shorts to ground, calibrate the ohmmeter on the high ohms scale. Connect one lead of the ohmmeter to a clean engine ground. Connect the other lead alternately to each of the 2 stator leads. The ohmmeter should read *infinity*. Any reading other than infinity means the stator is shorted to ground and must be replaced.

9. To check the diodes in the rectifier/regulator, disconnect the remaining rectifier/regulator leads. Calibrate the ohmmeter on the high ohms scale. Connect one ohmmeter lead to the rectifier/regulator case and the other lead to one of the AC terminals or leads (**Figure 15**). Note the ohmmeter reading. Reverse the ohmmeter leads and note the reading. The reading should be relatively high in one polarity and relatively low in the other. If the reading was high in both polarities or low in both polarities the rectifier must be replaced. Repeat the test for the other AC terminal or lead.

10. Connect one lead of the ohmmeter, calibrated on the high ohms scale, to the rectifier positive (+) terminal or lead and the other lead to one of the AC terminals or leads (**Figure 15**). Note the ohmmeter reading. Reverse the ohmmeter leads and note the reading. The reading should be relatively high in one polarity and relatively low in the other. If the reading was high in both polarities or low in both polarities the rectifier must be replaced. Repeat the test for the other AC terminal or lead.

11. To check the continuity of the rectifier/regulator positive (+) lead back to the battery, make sure the negative lead of the battery is disconnected. Make sure the rectifier/regulator positive (+) wire is disconnected from the rectifier/regulator. Calibrate the ohmmeter on the high ohms scale. Connect one lead of the ohmmeter to the battery positive terminal, connect the other lead of the ohmmeter to the rectifier/regulator end of the wire that connects to the rectifier/regulator positive (+) lead. Note the ohmmeter reading. A good circuit will have a zero or very low resistance reading. If the reading is not very low, repair or replace the wire, connections, circuit breaker or fuse between the rectifier/regulator and the battery.

Circuit Breaker Test
(All Models)

1. Disconnect circuit breaker wires.

2. Depress the circuit breaker reset button.

3. Connect an ohmmeter or battery-powered test lamp between the circuit breaker terminals. Replace the circuit breaker if continuity is not present across the circuit breaker terminals.

IGNITION SYSTEM

The wiring harness used between the ignition switch and engine is adequate to handle the electrical needs of the outboard motor or L-Drive. It *will not* handle the electrical needs of accessories. Whenever an accessory is added, run new wiring between the battery and accessory, installing a separate fuse panel on the instrument panel.

If the ignition switch requires replacement, *never* install an automotive-type switch. A marine-type switch must always be used.

Description

Seven different ignition systems are used on models covered in this manual. A full description along with theory of operation is provided for each system in Chapter Seven. For the purposes of troubleshooting, the ignition systems can be divided into 7 basic types (see **Table 8**):

a. A magneto breaker-point ignition.

b. Battery breaker-point ignition.

c. Breakerless ignition module (BIM) system.

d. SEM-Walbro magneto capacitor discharge ignition system.

e. Prestolite magneto capacitor discharge ignition.

f. Thunderbolt capacitor discharge ignition (CDI).

g. Capacitor discharge module (CDM).

Two variations of the breakerless ignition module (BIM) ignition are used on 5-15 hp models. The 2 systems are similar, but the flywheels and ignition module/coil assemblies are different and can not be intermixed. For identification purposes, the flywheel magnets on BIM 1 systems are glued to the inner diameter of the flywheel and the ignition module/coil primary wires are blue and brown. On BIM 2, the flywheel magnets are machined and cast into the flywheel assembly and the ignition module/coil primary wires are black and gray.

In addition, 2 variations of the Prestolite ignition system are used on early 3- and 4-cylinder models. On early models, plug-in connectors are used to connect all components; later models make most electrical connections at terminal blocks. Test points differ according to system design.

Basic Troubleshooting Precautions

General troubleshooting procedures are provided in **Table 2**. The following precautions should be strictly observed to avoid damage to the ignition system:

1. Do not reverse the battery connections. This reverses polarity and can damage the rectifier or the CD module or switch box.

2. Do not "spark" the battery terminals with the battery cable connections to check polarity.

3. Do not disconnect the battery cables with the engine running unless specified in a test procedure.

4. Do not start the engine if the CDI module(s) is not properly grounded.

5. Do not touch or disconnect any ignition components when the engine is running, while the ignition switch is ON or while the battery cables are connected unless specified in a test procedure.

Troubleshooting Preparation

NOTE
To test the wiring harness for poor solder connections in Step 1, bend the molded rubber connector while checking each wire for continuity.

1. Check the wiring harness and all plug-in connections to make sure that all terminals are free of corrosion, all connectors are tight and the wiring insulation is in good condition.

2. Check all electrical components that are grounded to the engine for a good ground connection.

3. Make sure that all ground wires are properly connected and that the connections are clean and tight.

4. Check remainder of the wiring for disconnected wires and short or open circuits.

5. Make sure there is an adequate supply of fresh and properly mixed fuel available to the engine.

6. If the engine is to be operated during the test procedure, make sure that sufficient water is provided for proper cooling to avoid power head or gearcase overheating. Use a flush adapter, place the engine in a test tank or perform the procedure with the boat in the water.

7. Check the battery condition. Clean terminals and recharge the battery, if necessary.

8. Check spark plug cable routing. Make sure the cables are properly connected to their respective spark plugs.

3

9. Keep all spark plugs in the order of their removal. Check the condition of each plug. See Chapter Four.

MAGNETO IGNITION SYSTEM

A magneto ignition system generally contains 7 major components:

   a. Flywheel.

   b. Stator plate.

   c. Throttle cam.

   d. Breaker points.

   e. Condenser(s).

   f. Ignition coil(s).

   g. Spark plug(s).

A typical magneto ignition system is shown in **Figure 16**.

Coils and condensers can only be tested effectively with a suitable ignition analyzer. The manufacturer recommends using a Merc-O-Tronic analyzer. This test equipment is available through marine dealers or from Merc-O-Tronic Instruments Corporation, 215 Branch Street, Almont, MI 48003. The equipment comes complete with instructions and test specifications.

Troubleshooting

1. Install an air gap spark tester (**Figure 17**) between the plug wire and a good engine ground to check for spark at each cylinder. If a spark tester is not available, remove each spark plug and reconnect the proper plug cable to one plug. Lay the plug against the cylinder head so its base makes a good connection, then crank the engine. A bright blue spark should be noted at the spark plug.

2. Repeat Step 1 with each remaining plug if a spark tester is not used.

3. If a good spark is not produced at each cylinder in Steps 1-3, disconnect the wires from the ignition or stop switch and repeat Step 1. If a good spark is produced with the switch isolated, replace the switch.

4. If the spark is still not acceptable, remove the flywheel. See Chapter Eight. Check the breaker point condition and gap. Replace or adjust the points as required. See Chapter Four.

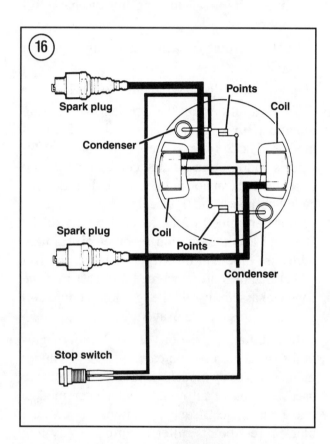

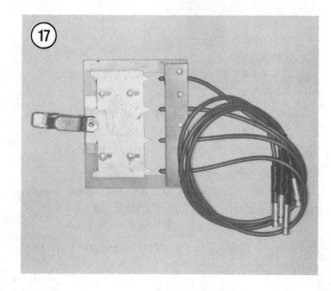

5. Remove the condenser(s) from the stator plate. Remove the coil(s) from the stator plate or power head. See Chapter Seven.

6. Test the condenser(s) and coil(s) as described in this chapter.

Condenser Capacity and Leakage Test

1. Plug the Merc-O-Tronic analyzer into an AC outlet and set the selector knob on position 4. Clip the analyzer test leads together, depress the red button and rotate the meter set knob to align the meter needle with the SET line on the meter scale. Release the red button and unclip the test leads.

2. Connect the small red test lead to the condenser lead and the small black test lead to the condenser body. See **Figure 18**.

3. Depress the red button and note the reading on the CONDENSER CAPACITY scale. If the reading is not within specifications (specifica-

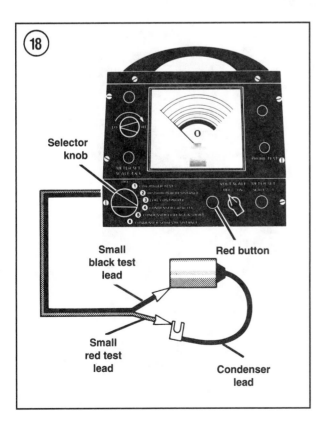

18

Selector knob

Small black test lead

Small red test lead

Red button

Condenser lead

tions provided with tester), replace the condenser. If the reading is within specifications, turn the selector knob OFF and continue testing.

4. With the test leads connected as shown in **Figure 18**, turn the selector knob to position 5. Depress the red button for 15 seconds and note the meter needle movement. It should move all the way to the right on the CONDENSER LEAKAGE AND SHORT scale, then return all the way to the left. Replace the condenser if the needle does not return. Turn the selector knob OFF, disconnect the test leads and continue testing.

5. Set the selector knob to position 6 and repeat Step 1 to align the meter needle with the SET line.

6. Repeat Step 2, then note the meter needle movement. Replace the condenser if the needle moves outside the green area at the right of the CONDENSER SERIES RESISTANCE scale.

7. Disconnect the test leads and unplug the analyzer.

Coil Test Sequence

WARNING
Perform this test on a wooden or insulated workbench to prevent leakage or shock hazards.

1. Plug the Merc-O-Tronic analyzer into an AC outlet. Connect the test leads as shown in **Figure 19** or **Figure 20**.

2. With the current control knob on LO, turn the selector knob to position 1.

3. Slowly rotate the current control knob clockwise until the meter needle reads 1.0 (external coil) or 1.5 (stator-mounted coil) on the COIL POWER TEST scale. If the spark gap is firing uniformly at this point, the coil can be considered acceptable. Rotate the current control knob back to LO and turn the selector knob OFF.

4. With the analyzer test leads connected as shown in **Figure 19** or **Figure 20**, turn the selector knob to position 1.

CAUTION
Complete Step 5 as quickly as possible to prevent tester or coil damage.

5. Rotate the current control knob clockwise until the meter needle reaches full scale. If the spark gap is firing uniformly at this point, the coil can be considered acceptable. Rotate the current control knob back to LO and turn the selector knob OFF.

6. Disconnect the large red test lead from the coil and plug the test probe into the analyzer jack.

7. Turn the selector knob to position 1 and rotate the current control knob clockwise until the meter needle reaches full scale. Quickly move the test probe over the insulated surfaces of the coil and spark plug lead. See **Figure 21**. A faint

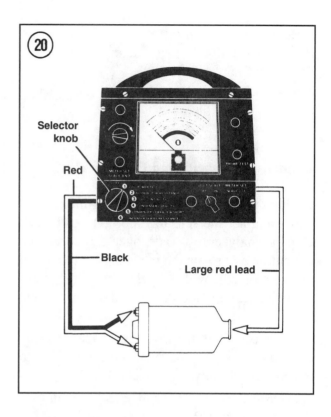

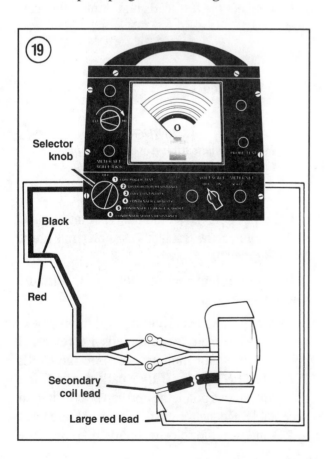

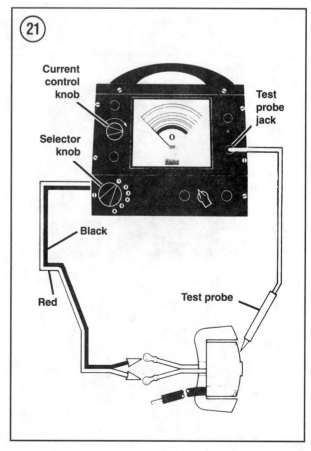

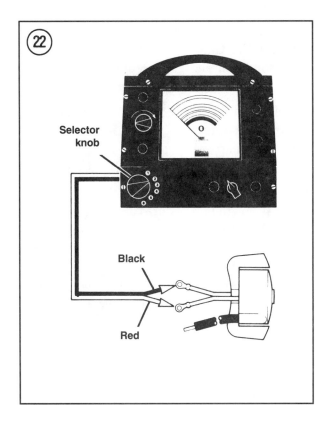

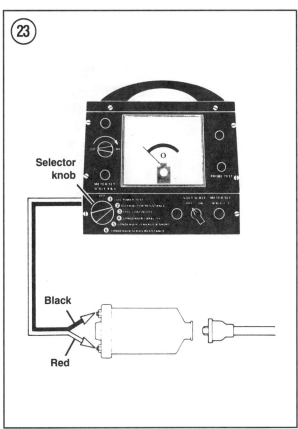

spark at the probe is acceptable; strong sparks indicate coil leakage. Rotate the current control knob back to LO and turn the selector knob OFF. Remove the test leads.

8. Turn the selector knob to position 2. Holding the test leads apart, rotate the meter set knob to align the needle with the SET line on the meter scale.

9. Connect the test leads as shown in **Figure 22** or **Figure 23**. Note the meter reading on the DISTRIBUTOR RESISTANCE scale and compare to the primary resistance specifications (**Table 5**). Replace the coil if the reading is not within specifications. Turn the selector knob OFF and disconnect the test leads.

10. Turn the selector knob to position 3. Clip the analyzer test leads together, rotate the meter set knob to align the meter needle with the SET line on the meter scale and unclip the test leads.

11. Connect the red test lead to the spark plug lead. Connect the black test lead to either primary terminal. See **Figure 24** or **Figure 25**. Note the meter reading on the COIL CONTINU-ITY scale and compare to the secondary

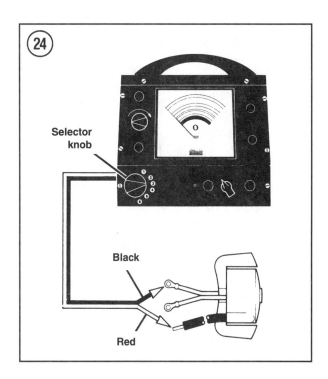

resistance specifications (**Table 5**). Replace the coil if the reading is not within specifications. Turn the selector knob OFF and disconnect the test leads.

BATTERY BREAKER POINT IGNITION SYSTEM

The battery ignition system uses a breaker plate and cam located under the flywheel. In addition, the system contains the following components:

a. Breaker points.
b. Condensers.
c. Ignition coils.
d. Spark plugs.

Coils and condensers can only be effectively tested using a suitable ignition analyzer. The manufacturer recommends using a Merc-O-Tronic analyzer. The test equipment is available through marine dealers or Merc-O-Tronic Instruments Corporation, 215 Branch Street, Almont, MI 48003. The equipment comes complete with instructions and test specifications.

Troubleshooting

Refer to the appropriate wiring diagram at the end of the manual.

1. Install a spark tester (**Figure 18**) between the plug wire and a good engine ground to check for spark at each cylinder. If a spark tester is not available, remove each spark plug and reconnect the proper plug cable to one plug. Lay the plug against the cylinder head so its base makes a good connection, then crank the engine. A bright blue spark should be noted at the spark plug.

2. If there is no spark or only a weak yellowish or red spark in Step 1, check for loose connections at the coil and battery and repair as required.

3. Repeat Step 1 with each remaining plug if a spark tester is not used. If the connections are good, continue testing.

4. If the spark is not acceptable, remove the flywheel. See Chapter Eight. Check the breaker point condition and gap. Replace or adjust the points as required. See Chapter Four.

5. Remove the condenser(s) from the stator plate. Remove the coil(s) from the stator plate or power head. See Chapter Seven.

6. Test the condenser(s) and coil(s) as described in this chapter.

The following procedures are performed with a 12-volt test lamp and require a fully charged battery with properly connected cables that are in good condition. It is assumed that all engine wiring and remote electric harness wiring is in good condition and properly connected.

Battery to Coil Test

The ignition switch must be in the ON position with the engine not running.

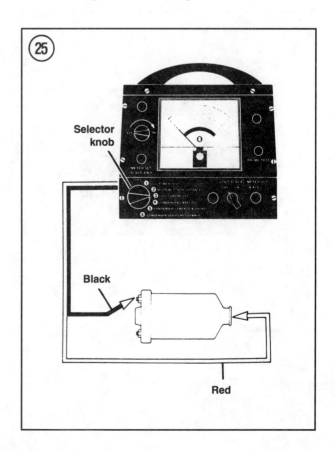

CAUTION
Avoid leaving the ignition switch in the
ON position for prolonged periods.

If the 12-volt test lamp does not light during one step, proceed to the following step. A dim light at any point in the procedure indicates a poor connection, high resistance or low voltage.

1. Connect one lead of the test lamp to a good engine ground. Probe the positive (+) terminal of each coil with the other test lead. If the test lamp lights at each coil positive terminal, the ignition circuit between the battery and coils is acceptable.

2. If the test lamp does not light at one or more coils in Step 1, move the test lead probe to the terminal block blue connector. If the lamp lights, repair or replace the blue wire between the terminal block and coils as required.

3. Move the test lead probe to the ignition switch I terminal. If the lamp lights, repair or replace the blue wire in the remote cable harness.

4. Move the test probe to the ignition switch B terminal. If the lamp lights, replace the ignition switch. If the lamp does not light, look for an open circuit in the wiring between the ignition switch and battery.

Coil and Condenser to Breaker Point Test

The ignition switch must be in the ON position with the engine not running.

CAUTION
Avoid leaving the ignition switch in the
ON position for prolonged periods.

If the 12-volt test lamp does not light during one step, proceed to the following step. A dim light at any point in the procedure indicates a poor connection, high resistance or low voltage.

1. Remove the spark plugs to prevent the engine from starting. See Chapter Four.

2. Connect one lead of the test light to a good engine ground. Probe the negative (−) terminal of the coil with the other test lead. If the breaker

points are closed, the test lamp will not light. If the breaker points are open, the lamp will light.

3. Rotate the flywheel 360° and watch the test lamp. It should come on for 90° and remain off for 270°.

4. If the test light remains on during the 360° rotation, an open circuit is present. Inspect the ignition system for:

   a. Breaker points insulated or not closing.

   b. A defective lead wire between the coil and breaker points.

5. If the test light remains off during the 360° rotation, a short circuit is indicated. Proceed as follows:

   a. Rotate the flywheel until one set of breaker points is open.

   b. Disconnect the breaker point lead at the negative (−) terminal of the coil. If the test lamp now shows voltage at the negative (−) terminal of the coil, either the lead wire or the breaker point set is shorted.

   c. If the test lamp does not light, disconnect the condenser lead wire. If the test lamp lights, the condenser is shorted.

6. Repeat Step 5 to test the other breaker point set and coil.

7. No. 1 cylinder only—Disconnect the tachometer lead wire (white) from the No. 1 coil negative (−) terminal. If the test lamp lights when the terminal is probed, there is a short in the tachometer or tachometer circuit.

8. Reinstall the spark plugs. See Chapter Four.

Ignition Circuit Test (Engine Running)

CAUTION
The engine must be provided with an adequate supply of water while performing this procedure. Install a flushing device, place the engine in a test tank or perform the procedure with the boat in the water.

This test is useful in locating a misfiring or dead cylinder.

1. Connect a tachometer according to its manufacturer's instructions.

2. Start the engine and run at 800-1,000 rpm in NEUTRAL.

3. Connect the test lamp lead to a good engine ground. Probe the negative (–) terminal of the ignition coil. The test lamp should flicker on and off as the breaker points open and close. If the test lamp remains on or off, stop the engine and perform the *Coil and Condenser to Breaker Point Test* in this chapter.

4. If the test lamp flickers in Step 3, and no loss of engine speed is noted, the primary ignition circuit is acceptable. Continue testing to locate the problem in the secondary circuit.

5. Stop the engine. Remove the spark plugs (Chapter Four), reconnect the plug wires to the plugs and ground the plugs to the cylinder head.

6. Turn the ignition switch ON and crank the engine. If the plugs do not fire with a crisp blue spark, check the spark plug wire and its connection to the coil and spark plug. If the wire and connections are good, test the coil as described in this chapter.

Condenser Capacity and Leakage Test

Test the condensers(s) as described for magneto ignition systems in this chapter.

Coil Test Sequence

Test the coils as described for magneto ignition systems in this chapter.

PRESTOLITE MAGNETO CAPACITOR DISCHARGE IGNITION

The Prestolite alternator-driven capacitor discharge (CD) ignition system consists of the following components (**Figure 26**):

  a. Flywheel.

  b. Stator assembly.

  c. Stator trigger assembly.

  d. CD module(s).

  e. Ignition coils.

  f. Spark plugs.

Two versions of the CD ignition are used on early 3- and 4-cylinder models. System A uses plug-in connectors on all components; system B makes most electrical connections through ter-

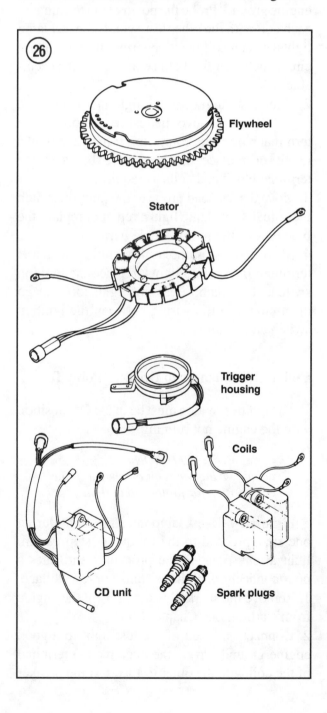

26

Flywheel

Stator

Trigger housing

Coils

CD unit

Spark plugs

minal blocks. All late models use terminal blocks for most electrical connections. Test points differ according to system design.

The circuit test consists of a preliminary and individual components tests. The test sequence requires the use of peak-reading voltmeter part No. 91-99750 (or equivalent) and spark tester FT-11295 (or equivalent). If a multimeter other than part No. 91-99750 is used, it must be capable of reading peak voltages; a conventional volt-ohm meter (VOM) will not work. A timing light is also required.

NOTE
The term Peak Volts is used interchangeably with DVA (Direct Voltage Adapter). The Mercury Marine multimeter (part No. 91-99750) has a DVA scale that should be used whenever the specification is in Peak Volts or listed as DVA. If the DVA or Peak Volts specification is listed as polarity sensitive, reverse your meter test leads and retest if the initial reading was unsatisfactory.

NOTE
Black CD modules are no longer available (NLA). Black modules are replaced with a blue module kit. This kit contains a blue module and 2 blue coils. Blue modules must use blue coils. If black coils are used with a blue module, ignition coil secondary voltage will be low and module life decreased. It is acceptable to have a blue module and a black module on the same engine as long as the ignition coil color matches the module color.

Preliminary Check (All Models)

This procedure determines if there is sufficient voltage in the secondary ignition system to fire the spark plugs.

NOTE
Slow engine cranking speed will affect the following test results. Make sure the starting system is operating properly.

1. Connect the spark tester to a good engine ground and adjust the spark gap to 7/16 in (11.1 mm).

2. Disconnect the spark plug leads and connect them to the corresponding leads on the spark tester.

3. Remove the spark plugs from the engine.

4. Crank the engine while observing the tester. If a good crisp spark is noted at each spark gap, the ignition system is functioning normally. Check spark plugs (Chapter Four) and check/adjust ignition timing (Chapter Five). If spark plugs are in acceptable condition and timing is properly adjusted, problem is not in the ignition system.

5. If one or more spark gaps are not firing properly, check all ground and wire connections in the system. Correct any defect found and repeat Step 4. If all spark gaps are now firing properly, further testing is not necessary.

6. If one or more spark gaps do not fire properly in Step 4, and no defects are noted during the inspection in Step 5, isolate the ignition system stop circuit from the boat wiring as follows:

   a. *7.5 hp*—Disconnect the stop button wires from both CD module/coil units (**Figure 27**).

   b. *50 hp 1987C-1988C*—Disconnect the stop circuit (brown) wires from both CD module/coil units at the main terminal strip on the engine. One will be connected to a white boat harness wire and the other will be connected to a blue boat harness wire.

   c. *All other remote control models*—The boat harness stop circuit wire is white on early models and black/yellow on later models. The CD module(s) stop circuit wire is blue, white or black/yellow. Disconnect the white, blue or black/yellow wire(s) from the CD module(s) side at the main terminal strip on the engine. The boat wiring harness lead can be left on the terminal strip. Refer to the end of the manual for wiring diagrams. Remember that the wire you are

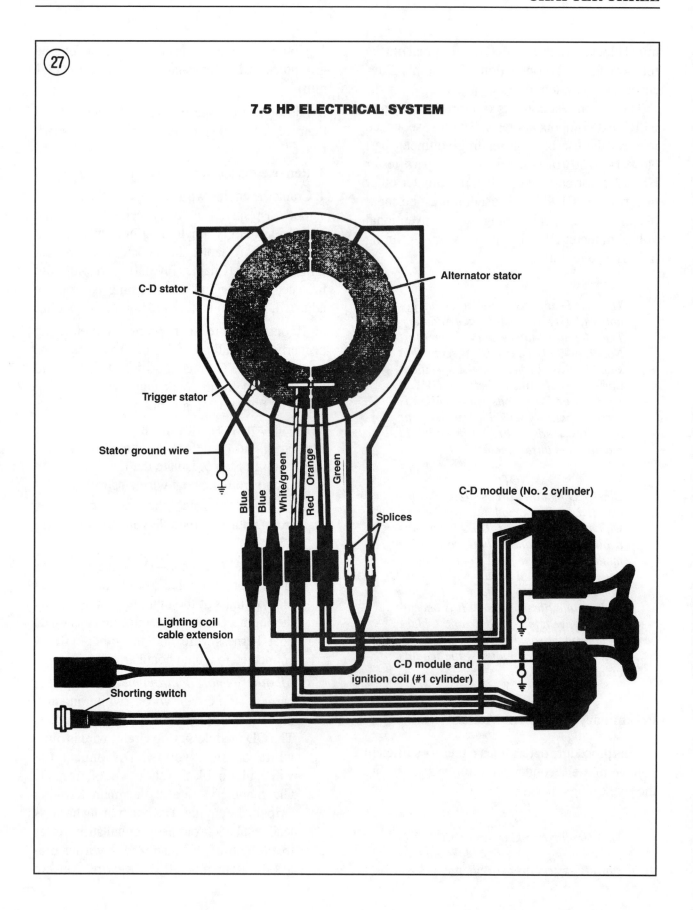

7.5 HP ELECTRICAL SYSTEM

looking for is hooked to the boat harness white or black/yellow terminal.

7. Make sure the disconnected leads are not grounded or touching, then crank the engine while observing the spark tester.

   a. If all spark gaps now fire normally, there is a problem in the boat wiring. Repair or replace the boat wiring or stop button as required.

   b. If one or more spark gaps still do not fire normally, proceed with the individual component tests.

NOTE
It is possible for a defective CD module to fire the 2 coils connected to it, while shorting out the stop circuits of the other CD modules on the engine. Separate and insulate the CD module stop circuit wires from each other and the main engine terminal strip and retest. If the engine now has good spark on the air gap tester, connect one pair of the CD module stop circuit wires together and retest. Continue in this manner until the failed CD module is isolated. Use only the air gap tester for this test, as the ignition switch and lanyard switch have been isolated.

Stator Test

25, 35 and 60 hp models

1. Disconnect the blue and yellow wire 2-pin connector between the stator assembly and CD module. See **Figure 28** and **Figure 29**.

2. Connect peak-reading voltmeter part No. 91-99750 or a suitable equivalent peak reading voltmeter (PRV) to the blue and yellow wire terminals in the stator end of the connector. Set the meter to the 400 DVA scale.

3. Crank the engine while observing the meter. Stator output should be 300 volts or more for 25 and 35 hp models and 210 volts or more for 60 hp model. If peak output is less than specification

or if the reading is intermittent, replace the stator assembly (Chapter Seven) and repeat this test.

7.5 and 50 hp models prior to 1988 D models

NOTE
The last letter in the model number indicates variations in individual models. Refer to the model number to determine which troubleshooting procedure to use.

1. Disconnect the blue stator wires at the terminal block or harness. See **Figure 27** or **Figure 30.**

2. Set meter to the 400 DVA scale and connect test leads to the blue stator wires.

3. Crank the engine while observing the meter. The meter should indicate 300 volts or more. If peak voltage is less than 300 volts or if reading is intermittent, replace the stator assembly (Chapter Seven) and repeat this test.

50 hp 1988 D and later models

NOTE
The last letter in the model number indicates variations in individual models. Refer to the model number to determine which troubleshooting procedure to use.

1. Disconnect the yellow and blue stator wires from the terminal block (**Figure 31**). The stator wires are numbered 1 through 4.

2. Set the meter to the 400 DVA scale and connect test leads to the Nos. 1 and 2 (yellow and blue) stator wires.

3. Crank engine while observing meter. Peak output voltage should be 210 volts or more.

4. Repeat Step 3 with meter connected to the Nos. 3 and 4 (yellow and blue) stator wires. Peak voltage should be 210 volts or more.

5. Replace the stator assembly (Chapter Seven) if reading is intermittent or if peak output voltage is less than 210 volts.

3

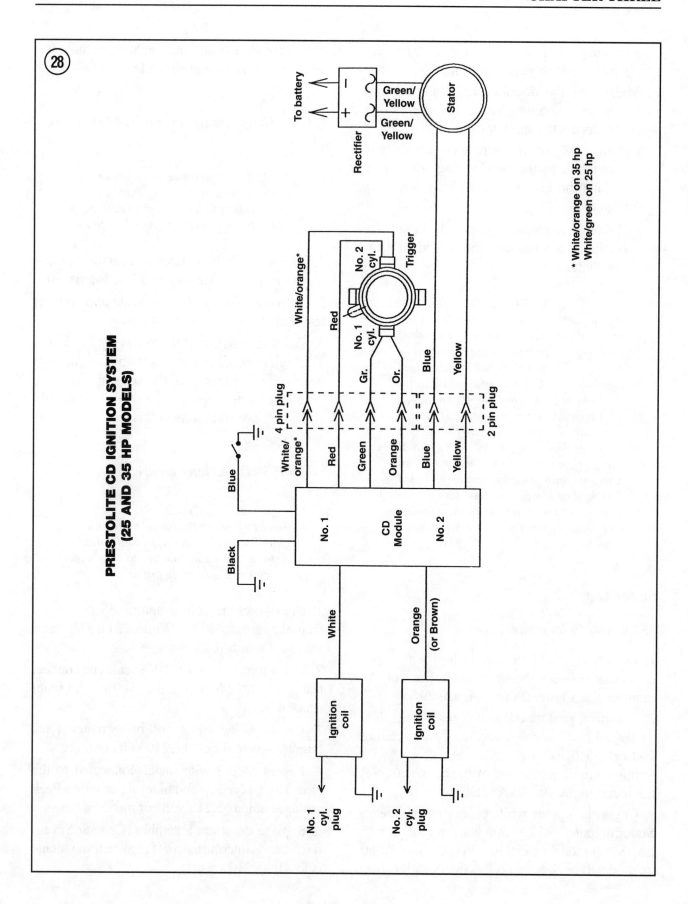

PRESTOLITE CD IGNITION SYSTEM
(25 AND 35 HP MODELS)

* White/orange on 35 hp
  White/green on 25 hp

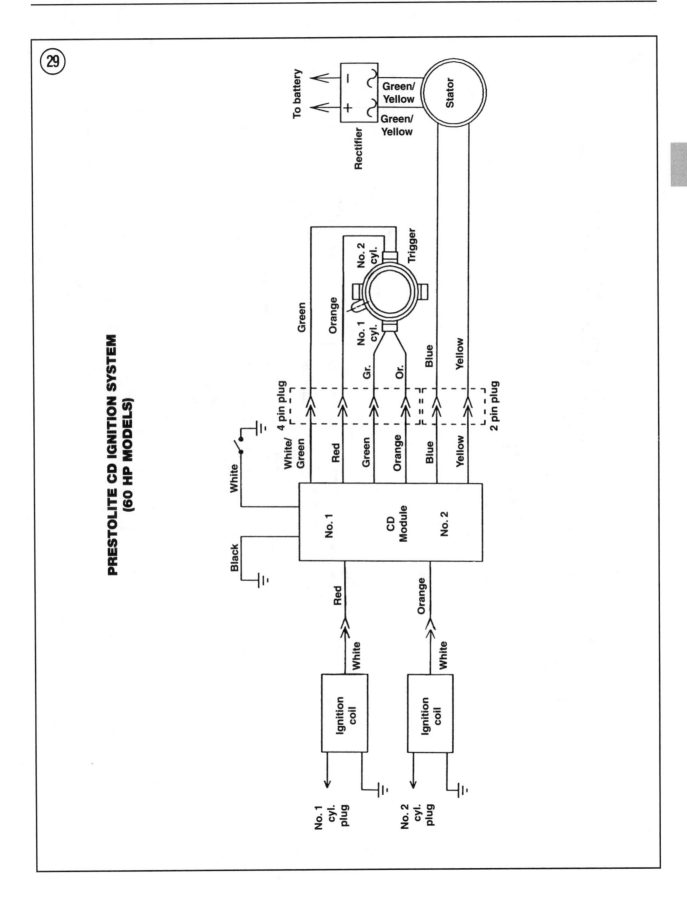

PRESTOLITE CD IGNITION SYSTEM (60 HP MODELS)

3

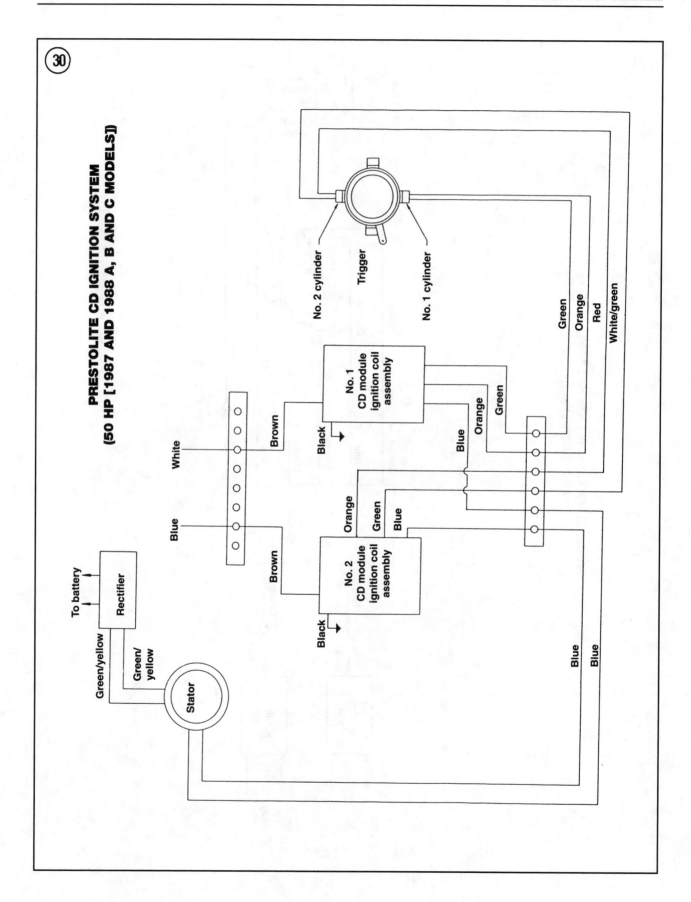

PRESTOLITE CD IGNITION SYSTEM
(50 HP [1987 AND 1988 A, B AND C MODELS])

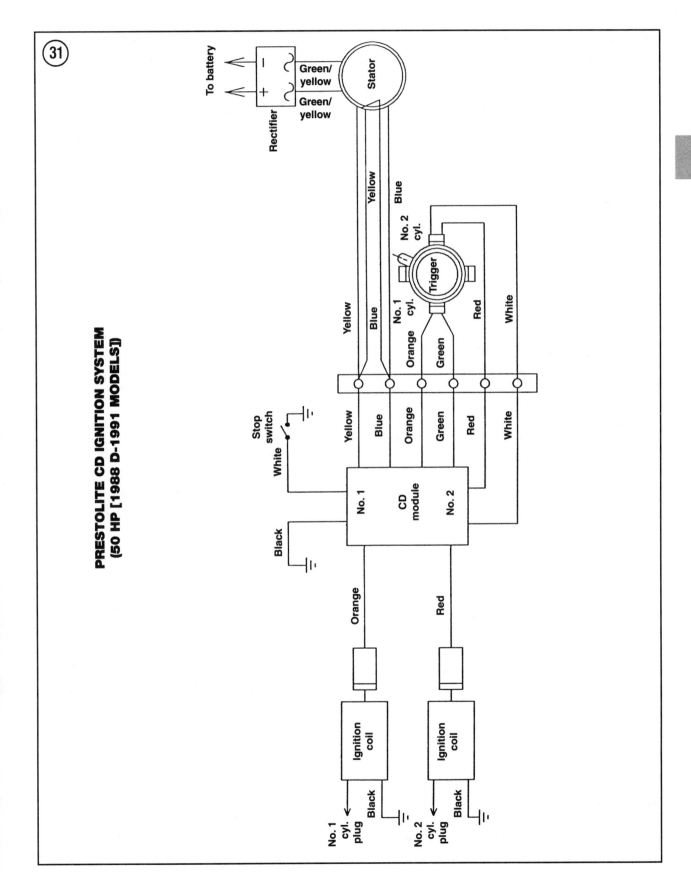

PRESTOLITE CD IGNITION SYSTEM (50 HP [1988 D-1991 MODELS])

Early 3- and 4-cylinder models (plug-in connectors)

NOTE
*Two variations of the CD ignition are used on early 85 (3-cylinder) and 125 (4-cylinder) hp models. System A (**Figures 32** and **33**) uses plug-in connectors to join all components. System B (**Figures 34** and **35**) makes most electrical connections using terminal blocks. Test points differ according to system design.*

1. Disconnect the blue and yellow wire connectors between the stator and CD modules.

2. With the meter set on the 400 DVA scale, connect its test leads between the yellow and blue wire terminals in the stator end of the plug. Crank the engine while observing the meter. Peak output voltage should be 210 volts or more. Replace stator if reading is intermittent or if peak voltage is less than 210 volts. See Chapter Seven.

3. Repeat Step 2 with meter connected to the remaining blue and yellow wire connector. Note that on 3-cylinder engines, both blue wires are contained in the same connector as one yellow wire. To perform this step, check the blue wire not checked in Step 2 and the single yellow wire connector. Peak output voltage should be 210 volts or more. Replace stator (Chapter Seven) if reading is intermittent or if peak voltage is less than 210 volts.

4. Set the meter on the ×100 scale and connect the test leads between one set of yellow and blue stator wires. The meter should indicate 675-800 ohms. If not, replace stator (Chapter Seven).

5. Repeat Step 4 to check the remaining set of blue and yellow wires. The meter should indicate 675-800 ohms. If not, replace stator (Chapter Seven).

6. Set the meter to the × 1 scale. Connect the negative test lead to a good engine ground. Alternately probe each yellow and blue wire while observing meter. Meter should show infinity at each wire. Continuity between any stator wire and engine ground indicates a shorted stator or stator wire. Repair shorted wire or replace stator assembly as required.

NOTE
If stator resistance is normal but the output voltage is consistently low, the flywheel magnets may be weak. Replace the flywheel and repeat the stator test.

Late 3- and 4-cylinder models including L-Drive (terminal block connectors)

Stator output voltage tests are provided for late 3- and 4-cylinder models equipped with terminal block connectors. **Figure 36** (3-cylinder) and **Figure 37** (4-cylinder) show ignition system components, wiring and terminal blocks.

1. Install spark tester FT-11295 or equivalent as outlined under *Preliminary Check* in this chapter.

2. Remove terminal block cover located below CD modules. The stator wires are located on the side of the terminal block closest to the ignition coils. See **Figure 38**.

3. Disconnect stator wires numbered 1 and 2 (brown/blue and brown/yellow on L-Drive, blue and yellow on all others) from the terminal block.

4. Set the meter on the 400 DVA scale and connect test leads to the two disconnected stator wires. Crank engine while observing meter. Peak voltage should be 210 volts or more. If peak voltage is less than 210 volts or if reading is intermittent, replace stator. See Chapter Seven.

5. Reconnect stator wires numbered 1 and 2. Disconnect stator wires numbered 3 and 4 (brown/black/blue and brown/black/yellow on L-Drive and blue and yellow on all others) from terminal block.

6. Repeat Step 4 to check stator output at the Nos. 3 and 4 wires. Note that on 3-cylinder engines, the No. 1 and the No. 3 stator wires are both connected to the same terminal. Peak voltage should be 210 volts or more. Replace stator

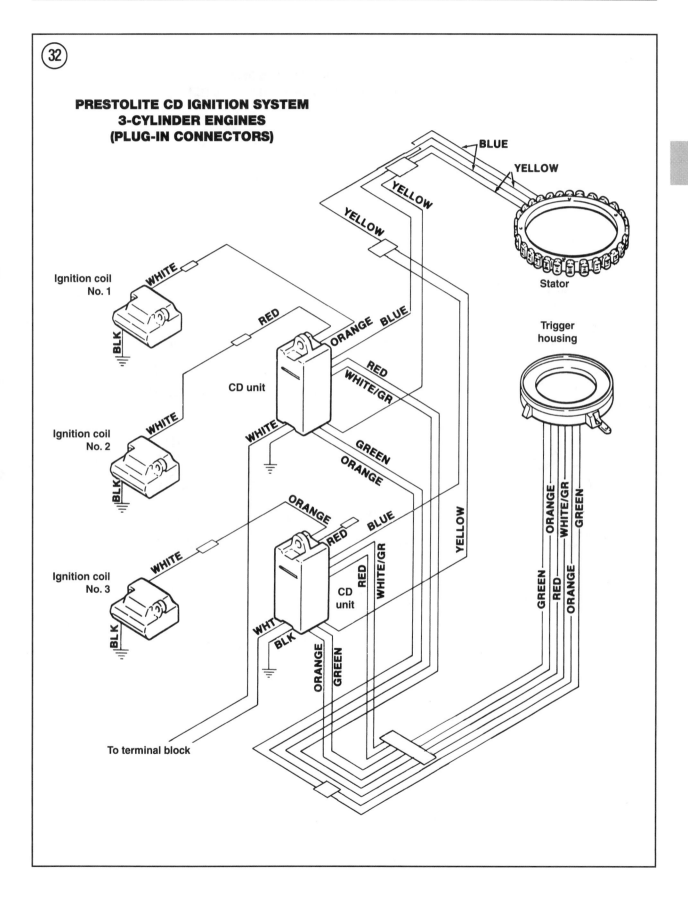

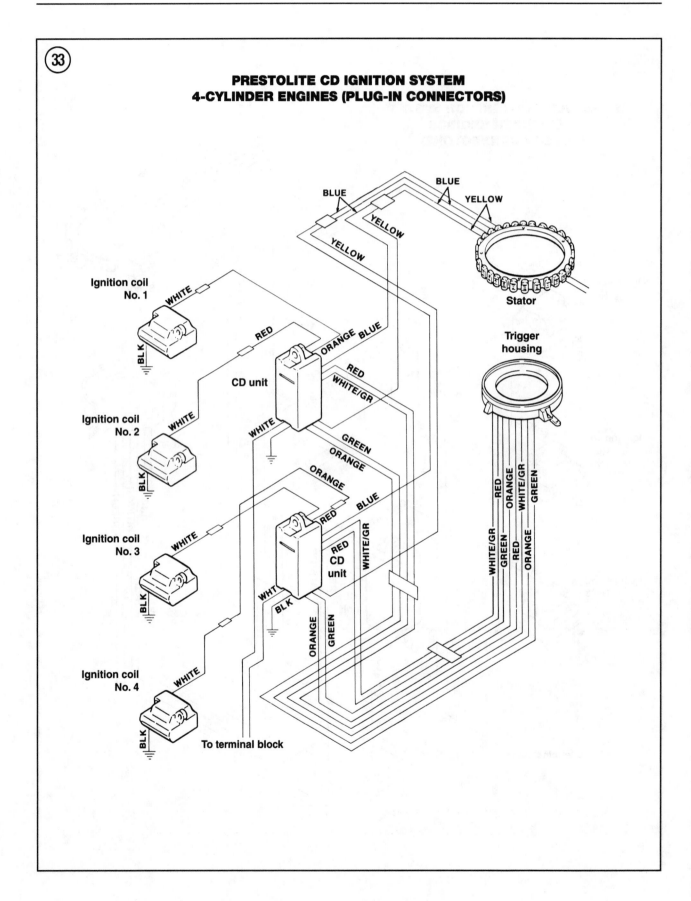

**PRESTOLITE CD IGNITION SYSTEM
4-CYLINDER ENGINES (PLUG-IN CONNECTORS)**

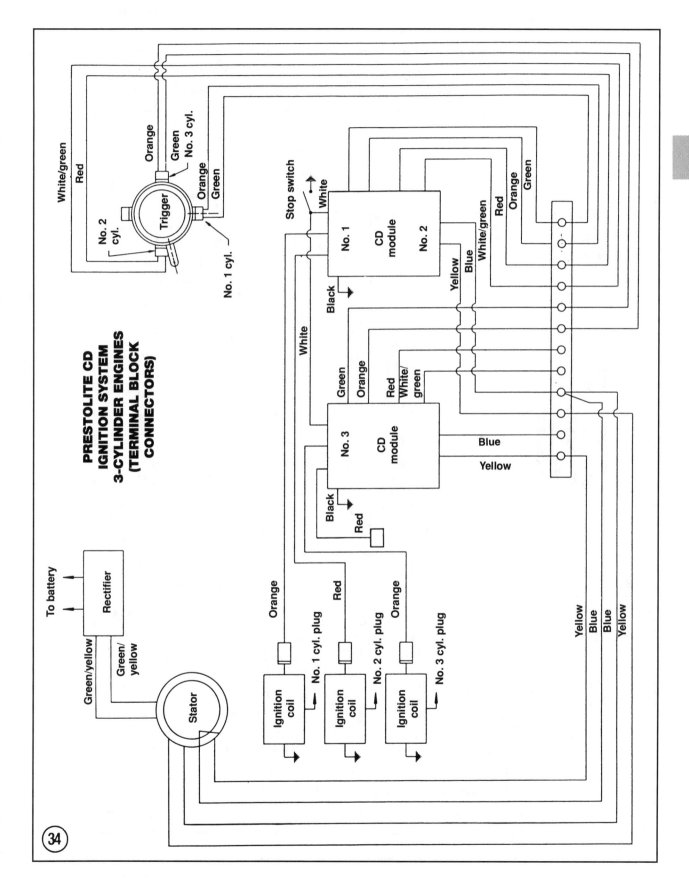

PRESTOLITE CD
IGNITION SYSTEM
3-CYLINDER ENGINES
(TERMINAL BLOCK
CONNECTORS)

34

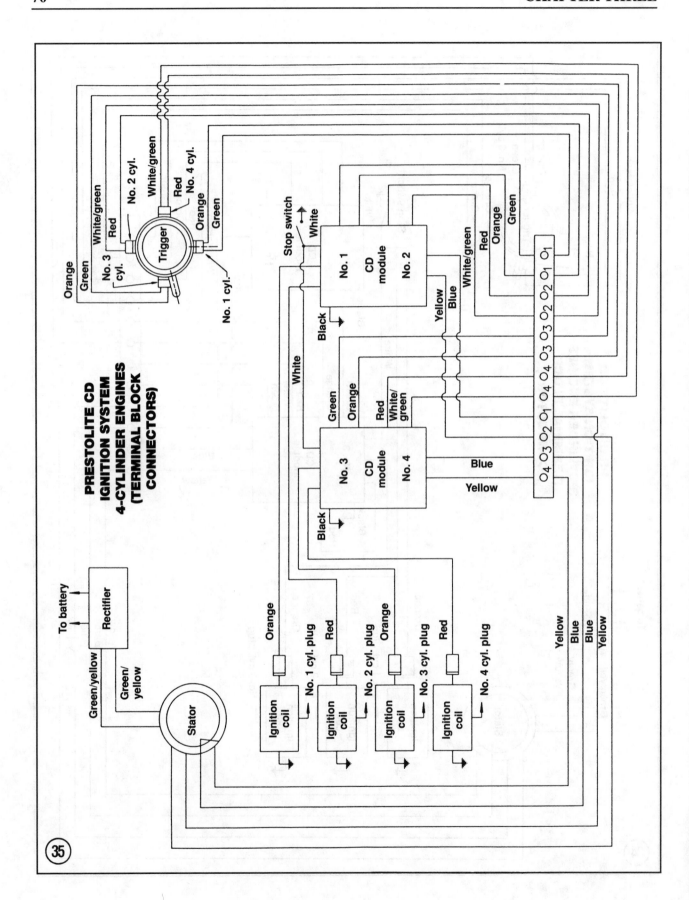

PRESTOLITE CD
IGNITION SYSTEM
4-CYLINDER ENGINES
(TERMINAL BLOCK
CONNECTORS)

35

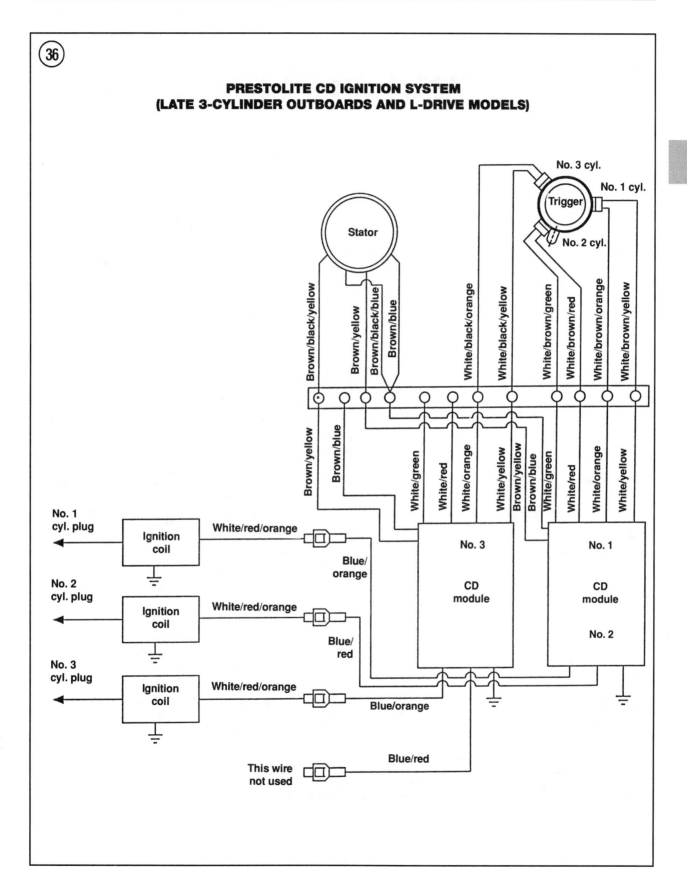

**PRESTOLITE CD IGNITION SYSTEM
(LATE 3-CYLINDER OUTBOARDS AND L-DRIVE MODELS)**

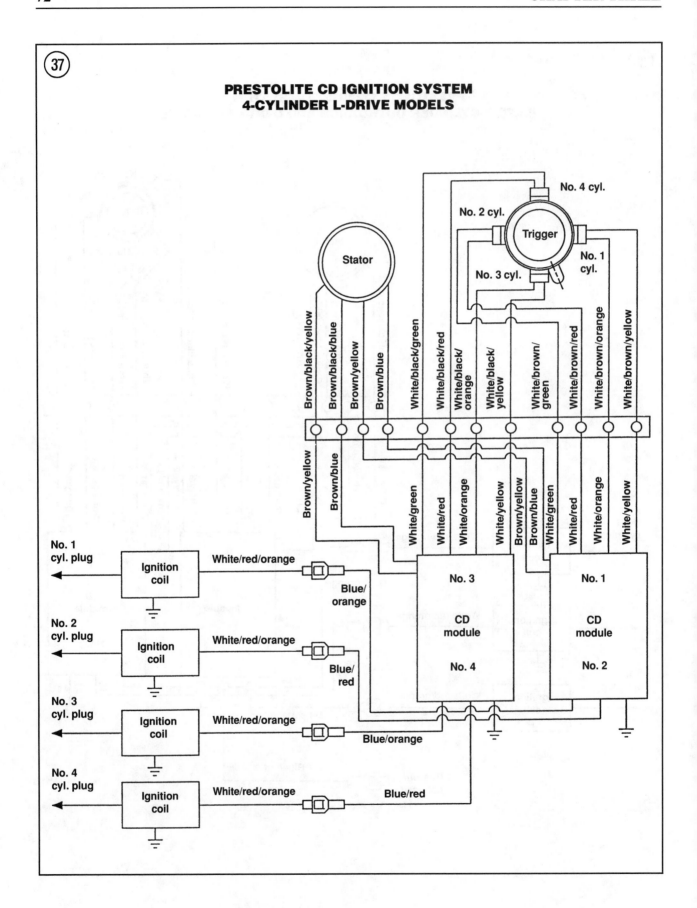

**PRESTOLITE CD IGNITION SYSTEM
4-CYLINDER L-DRIVE MODELS**

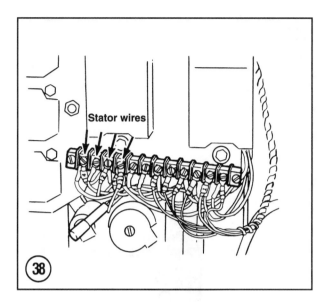

(Chapter Seven) if reading is intermittent or if peak reading is less than 210 volts.

7. If all test results are acceptable, proceed to the trigger tests.

150 hp models

Refer to **Figure 39** and **Figure 40** for this procedure. Stator wires are numbered for identification.

1. Remove terminal block cover from terminal block located between the two upper CD modules.

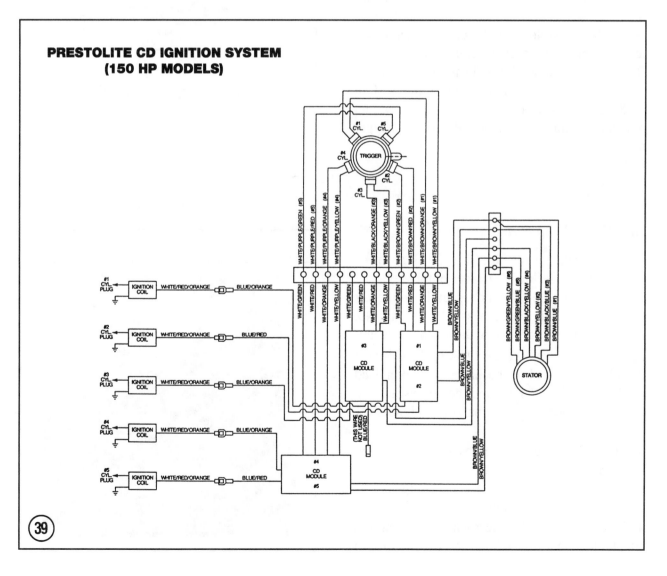

2. Disconnect stator wires numbered 1 (brown/blue) and 2 (brown/yellow).

3. Set the meter on the 400 DVA scale and connect the test leads to the No. 1 and No. 2 stator wires.

4. Crank the engine while observing the meter. Peak voltage should be 210 volts or more. Replace the stator assembly if reading is intermittent or if peak voltage is less than 210 volts.

5. Reconnect stator wires No. 1 and 2. Disconnect stator wires No. 3 (brown/black/blue) and No. 4 (brown/black/yellow), connect test leads to disconnected wires and repeat Step 4.

6. Reconnect stator wires No. 3 and 4. Disconnect wires No. 5 (brown/green/blue) and No. 6 (brown/green/yellow) and connect meter test leads to the disconnected wires. Repeat Step 4. Replace stator assembly if peak voltage is less than 210 volts or if reading is intermittent. If all readings are as specified, reconnect wires and reinstall terminal block cover. Proceed to trigger tests.

Trigger Test

7.5, 25 and 35 hp models

Harness adapter part No. FT-11201 is required to perform the following trigger output test.

1. Unplug the 4-pin trigger assembly connector (**Figure 41**). Connect harness adapter part No. T-11201 to the trigger end of the 4-pin connector.

2. Set the meter on the 2.0 DVA scale. Connect the black test lead to the harness adapter lead marked TRIGGER 1 (–) and the red test lead to the harness adapter lead marked TRIGGER 1 (+).

3. Crank the engine while observing the meter. Peak trigger output should be 1.4 volts or more. Replace trigger assembly if peak output is less than 1.4 volts or if reading is intermittent.

4. Connect meter black test lead to the harness adapter lead marked TRIGGER 2 (–) and the red

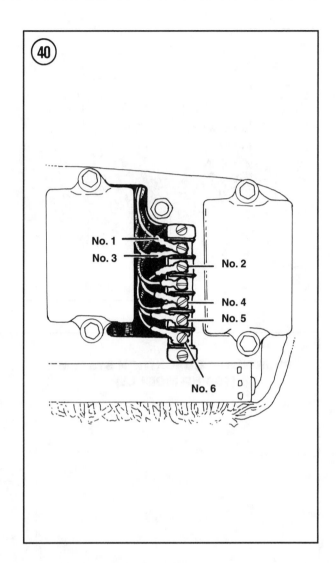

test lead to the lead marked TRIGGER 2 (+) and repeat Step 3. Replace trigger assembly if peak output is less than 1.4 volts or if reading is intermittent. If peak readings are as specified, reconnect the 4-pin connector and proceed to CD module test.

60 hp models

Harness adapter part No. FT11237 is required to perform the following trigger output test.

1. Unplug the 4-pin trigger assembly connector (**Figure 41**). Connect harness adapter part No. FT11237 to the trigger end of the 4 pin connector.

2. Set the meter on the 2.0 DVA scale. Connect the black test lead to the harness adapter lead marked TRIGGER 1 (-) and the red test lead to the harness adapter lead marked TRIGGER 1 (+).

3. Crank the engine while observing the meter. Peak trigger output should be 0.3 volts or more. Replace the trigger if peak output is less than 0.3 volts or if reading is intermittent.

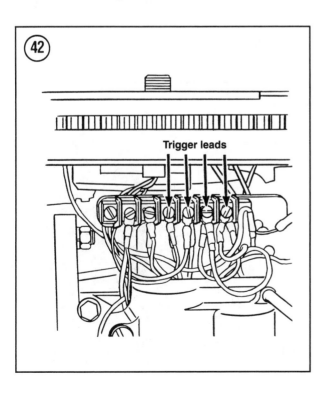

Trigger leads

4. Connect the black test lead to the harness adapter lead marked TRIGGER 2 (-) and the red test lead to the harness adapter lead marked TRIGGER 2 (+) and repeat Step 3. Replace trigger assembly if peak output is less than 0.3 volts or if reading is intermittent. If peak readings are as specified, reconnect the 4-pin connector and proceed to CD module test.

3

Early 50 hp models (prior to 1988 D models)

NOTE
The last letter in the model number indicates variations in individual models. Refer to the model number to determine which troubleshooting procedure to use.

1. Disconnect all 4 trigger wires from the terminal block (**Figure 42**).

2. Set the meter to the 2.0 DVA scale. Connect the black meter test lead to the red trigger wire and the red test lead to the white/green trigger wire.

3. Crank engine while observing the meter. Meter should indicate 0.5 volt or more peak output. If output is less than 0.5 volt or if reading is intermittent, replace the trigger assembly.

4. Reconnect the red and white/green trigger wires to the terminal block (**Figure 42**). Connect the meter black test lead to the green trigger wire and the red test lead to the orange trigger wire.

5. Repeat Step 3. If the meter indicates peak output of 0.5 volt or more, reconnect trigger wires and proceed to the CD module test. If peak output is less than 0.5 volt, or if reading is intermittent, replace the trigger assembly.

Late 50 hp (1988 D and later models)

NOTE
The last letter in the model number indicates variations in individual models. Refer to the model number to determine which troubleshooting procedure to use.

1. Disconnect the green and orange trigger wires from the terminal block (**Figure 43**).

2. Set the meter on the 2.0 DVA scale. Connect the black test lead to the green trigger wire and the red test lead to the orange trigger wire.

3. Crank the engine while observing the meter. If trigger output is 0.3 volt or more, proceed to Step 4. If peak reading is less than 0.3 volt or if reading is intermittent, replace the trigger assembly.

4. Reconnect the orange and green trigger wires and disconnect the white/green and red trigger wires. Connect the black test lead to the red trigger wire, the red test lead to the white/green trigger wire and repeat Step 3. If trigger output is 0.3 volt or more, reconnect wires to terminal block and proceed to CD module test. If output is less than 0.3 volt or if reading is intermittent, replace trigger assembly.

Early 3- and 4-cylinder models (plug-in connectors)

Voltage and resistance tests are provided to test the trigger assembly on early 3- and 4-cylinder models equipped with plug-in connectors. Refer to **Figure 32** (3-cylinder) and **Figure 33** (4-cylinder) for ignition components and wiring diagram.

1A. 3-Cylinder—Disconnect the 2-wire and 4-wire connectors between the trigger assembly and CD modules.

1B. 4-Cylinder—Disconnect both 4-wire connectors between the trigger assembly and CD modules.

2A. 3-Cylinder—Set the meter on the 2.0 volt scale. Connect the black test lead to the green wire terminal and the red test lead to the orange wire terminal in the trigger end of the 2-wire connector.

2B. 4-Cylinder—Set the meter on the 2.0 volt scale. Connect the black test lead to the green wire terminal and the red test lead to the orange

wire terminal in the trigger end of either 4-wire connector.

3. Crank the engine while observing the meter. Trigger output should be 0.3 volt or more.

4A. 3-Cylinder—Connect the black test lead to the green wire terminal and the red test lead to the orange wire terminal in the trigger end of the 4-wire connector.

4B. 4-Cylinder—Move the black test lead to the red wire terminal and the red test lead to the white/green wire terminal in the trigger end of the same 4-wire connector.

5. Crank the engine while observing the meter. It should indicate 0.3 volt or more.

6A. 3-Cylinder:

  a. Connect the black test lead to the red wire terminal and the red test lead to the white/green wire terminal in the trigger end of the 4-wire connector.

  b. Crank the engine while observing the meter. It should indicate 0.3 volt or more.

6B. 4-Cylinder—Repeat Steps 2B and 4B to check the remaining 4-wire connector. The meter reading should be 0.3 volt or more during each test.

7A. 3-Cylinder:

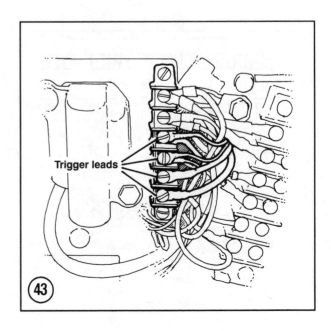

Trigger leads

43

a. Set the meter on the ×1 scale and connect the test leads between the green and orange wire terminals in the trigger end of the 2-wire connector. The meter should indicate 45-50 ohms.

b. Repeat Step 7a with the meter connected to the orange and green wire terminals in the 4-wire connector. The meter should indicate 45-50 ohms.

c. Connect the test leads between the white/green and red wire terminals in the 4-wire connector. The meter should indicate 45-50 ohms.

7B. 4-Cylinder:

a. With the meter set on the ×1 scale, connect the test leads to the orange and green wire terminals in either 4-wire connector. The meter should indicate 45-50 ohms.

b. Move the test leads to the white/green and red wire terminals in the same connector. The meter should indicate 45-50 ohms.

c. Repeat Steps 7a and 7b to check the remaining 4-wire connector. The meter should indicate 45-50 ohms during each test.

8. All Models—Connect the black test lead to a good engine ground. Alternately probe each

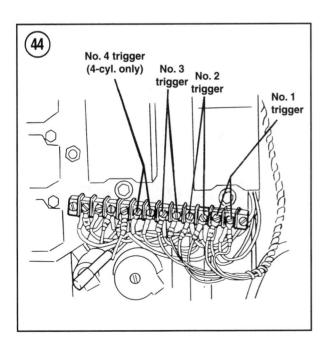

No. 4 trigger (4-cyl. only)
No. 3 trigger
No. 2 trigger
No. 1 trigger

trigger wire terminal with the red test lead. Infinity (no continuity) should be noted between ground and all trigger wires. Continuity between ground and any trigger wire indicates a shorted trigger or trigger wire. Repair trigger wire or replace trigger as required.

9. If test results are as specified, proceed to CD module test.

If any test results are not as specified, replace trigger assembly.

Late 3- and 4-cylinder including L-Drive models (terminal block connectors)

During the following trigger output tests, disconnect the trigger wires from the terminal block (**Figure 44**) one pair at a time, then reconnect them after performing the test. Trigger wires are numbered for identification. On L-Drive models, disconnect spark plug leads from the spark plugs and install spark tester T-11260-1 or equivalent as outlined in this chapter prior to performing tests. Refer to **Figure 34** (3-cylinder), **Figure 35** (4-cylinder), **Figure 36** (3-cylinder L-Drive) and **Figure 37** (4-cylinder L-Drive) for ignition components and wiring diagrams.

1. Place the remote control in the neutral position and disconnect the throttle cable from the carburetor tower shaft. This is necessary to enable manual throttle advance while cranking the engine.

2. Remove the cover from the terminal block below CD modules.

3. Disconnect the number 1 cylinder trigger wires from the terminal block (**Figure 44**).

4. Set the meter on the 2.0 DVA scale.

5A. L-Drive—Connect red test lead to the white/brown/orange trigger wire and the black test lead to the white/brown/yellow trigger wire.

5B. All others—Connect the red test lead to the orange trigger wire and the black test lead to the green trigger wire.

6. Crank the engine while observing the meter. While cranking, advance the throttle from idle to wide-open throttle, then back to idle. If trigger output is 0.3 volt or more, reconnect trigger wires and proceed to Step 7. If output is less than 0.3 volt or if reading is intermittent, replace trigger.

7A. L-Drive—Repeat Step 6 with meter connected as follows:

   a. No. 2 trigger—connect the red test lead to the white/brown/green wire and the black test lead to the white/brown/red wire.

   b. No. 3 trigger—connect the red test lead to the white/black/orange wire and the black test lead to the white/black/yellow wire.

   c. No. 4 trigger (4-cylinders only)—connect the red test lead to the white/black/green wire and the black test lead to the white/black/red wire.

7B. All others—Repeat Step 6 with the meter connected as follows:

   a. No. 2 trigger—connect the red test lead to the white/green wire and the black test lead to the red wire.

   b. No. 3 trigger—connect the red test lead to the orange wire and the black test lead to the green wire.

   c. No. 4 trigger (4-cylinders only)—connect the red test lead to the white/green wire and the black test lead to the red wire.

8. Trigger output should be 0.3 volt or more on all tests and models. If not, or if reading is intermittent, replace trigger assembly. If all trigger tests are as specified, proceed to CD module test.

150 hp

During the following trigger output tests, disconnect the trigger wires from the terminal block (**Figure 45**) one pair at a time, then reconnect them after performing the test. Trigger wires are numbered for identification. Refer to **Figure 39** for ignition components and wiring diagram.

1. Connect a jumper wire between the terminals of the neutral interlock switch.

2. Remove the cover from the terminal block located below the top CD modules.

3. Disconnect the No. 1 trigger wires (**Figure 45**) from the terminal block.

4. Set the meter to the 2.0 DVA scale. Connect the red test lead to the white/brown/orange trigger wire and the black test lead to the white/brown/yellow trigger lead.

5. Crank engine while observing the meter. While cranking, advance the throttle to wide-open throttle, then back to the idle position. If trigger output is 0.3 volt or more, reconnect the trigger wires and proceed to Step 6. If output is less than 0.3 volt or if reading is intermittent, replace the trigger assembly.

6. Disconnect the No. 2 trigger wires. Connect the red test lead to the white/brown/red wire and the white/brown/green wire. Repeat Step 5.

7. Disconnect the No. 3 trigger wires. Connect the red test lead to the white/black/orange wire and the black test lead to the white/black/yellow wire. Repeat Step 5.

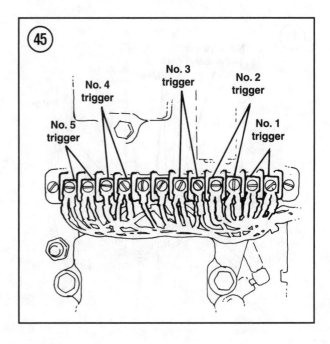

8. Disconnect the No. 4 trigger wires. Connect the red test lead to the white/purple/yellow wire and the black test lead to the white/purple/orange wire. Repeat Step 5.

9. Disconnect the No. 5 trigger wires. Connect the red test lead to the white/purple/red wire and the black test lead to the white/purple/green wire. Repeat Step 5.

10. If trigger output is as specified on all triggers, reconnect wires, reinstall the terminal block cover and remove the jumper wire from neutral interlock switch. Proceed to CD module test. Replace the trigger assembly if output is less than 0.3 volt or if the reading is intermittent on any trigger.

CD Module Test

25 and 35 hp models

Refer to **Figure 28** for ignition components and wiring diagram on 35 hp models.

1. Disconnect CD module output wire from either ignition coil. Note that CD output wire to the No. 1 coil is white and the output wire to the No. 2 coil is brown or orange.

2. Set the meter to the 200 DVA scale. Connect the red test lead to the disconnected CD module output wire and the black test lead to a good engine ground.

3. Crank the engine while observing the meter. If the CD module output is 175 volts or more, reconnect the module output wire to the ignition coil and proceed to Step 4. If the output is less than 175 volts or if reading is intermittent, replace the CD module.

4. Disconnect the CD module output wire to the remaining ignition coil. Connect the red test lead to the disconnected wire and the black test lead to a good engine ground. Repeat Step 3. Replace the CD module if output is less than 175 volts or if reading is intermittent.

7.5 hp and early 50 hp (prior to 1988 D models)

Refer to **Figure 27** and **Figure 30** for ignition components and wiring diagram on early 50 hp models.

No test for the CD module/ignition coil assemblies is provided. If one cylinder is misfiring, and the stator and trigger assemblies have tested to be in acceptable condition, replace the CD module/ignition coil assembly for the misfiring cylinder.

NOTE
Each CD module/ignition coil unit is equipped with a diode and a circuit for charging the capacitor in the opposite CD module/ignition coil. If the charging diode in one CD module/ignition coil fails, it will cause the opposite CD module/ignition coil to misfire. If a CD module/ignition coil unit is replaced, but the affected cylinder still misfires, replace the other CD module/ignition coil.

Late 50 hp (1988 D and later models) and 60 hp models

Refer to **Figure 31** for ignition components and wiring diagram on late 50 hp models. Refer to **Figure 29** for 60 hp models.

1. Remove the screws securing the CD module bracket to the power head and carefully pull the bracket out and away from the engine.

2. Disconnect the orange CD module output wire from the No. 1 ignition coil.

3. Set the meter on the 400 DVA scale. Connect the red test lead to a good engine ground and the black test lead to the orange output wire.

4. Crank the engine while observing the meter. If CD module output is 210 volts or more, reconnect the orange wire and proceed to Step 5. If output is less than 210 volts or if the reading is intermittent, replace the CD module.

5. Disconnect the module red output wire from the No. 2 ignition coil. Move the black test lead to the red wire and repeat Step 4. The module

3

output should be 210 volts or more. Replace the module if output is less than 210 volts or if reading is intermittent.

6. If CD module output is as specified at both coils, reconnect all wires and reinstall the module bracket to the power head.

3-, 4- and 5-cylinder models (including L-Drive)

The CD module output wire to ignition coil connections are located behind the bracket that secures the modules to the power head. Remove

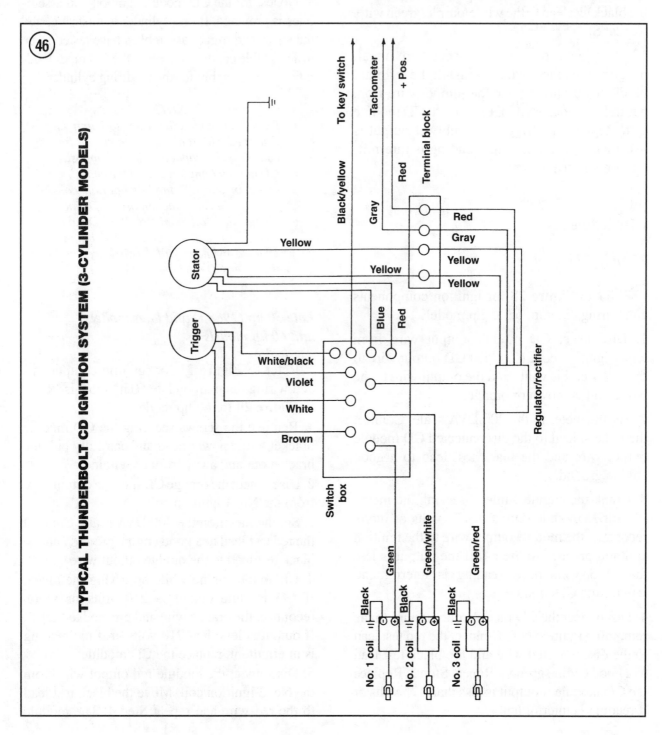

TYPICAL THUNDERBOLT CD IGNITION SYSTEM (3-CYLINDER MODELS)

the bracket and carefully pull it away from the power head to gain access to the connectors.

On L-Drive models, disconnect the spark plug leads from the spark plugs and install spark tester T-11260-1 or equivalent as described in this chapter.

Refer to **Figure 32** (early 3-cylinder), **Figure 33** (early 4-cylinder), **Figure 34** (late 3-cylinder), **Figure 35** (late 4-cylinder), **Figure 36** (3-cylinder L-Drive), **Figure 37** (4-cylinder L-Drive) and **Figure 39** (5-cylinder) for ignition components and wiring diagram.

NOTE
Each CD module contains 2 independent capacitor discharge circuits. The failure of one circuit does not necessarily indicate the remaining circuit is defective.

1. Remove the nuts or screws that secure the CD module bracket to the power head. Do not loose the spacers between the bracket and engine on models so equipped. Carefully pull the bracket away from the engine.

2. Disconnect the module output wire from the No. 1 ignition coil. Refer to the appropriate wiring diagram. Set the meter on the 400 DVA scale. Connect the black test lead to the No. 1 module output wire and the red test lead to a good engine ground.

3. Crank the engine while observing the meter. CD module output should be 220 volts or more on 1984-1986 3- and 4-cylinder models and 210 volts or more on 1987-on 3- and 4-cylinder, 5-cylinder and L-Drive models. Replace the module if the output is less than specified.

4. Refer to the appropriate wiring diagram and repeat Step 3 with the black test lead connected alternately to each CD module output wire and the red test lead connected to a good engine ground. Replace any module with output less than specified.

5. If the CD modules test to be acceptable, reconnect all wires and reinstall the CD module bracket to the power head.

Ignition Coil Test
(All Models)

A specific troubleshooting procedure is not provided on the ignition coil(s); however, if an ignition system malfunction is present, and the stator, trigger and CD modules test to be in acceptable condition, replace the ignition coil that is connected to the affected cylinder. The condition of the ignition coil can be verified by connecting the coil to the CD module of a known firing cylinder. Connect the coil spark plug lead to a spark tester and crank the engine. If no spark is noted at the spark gap, the coil has failed and must be replaced.

THUNDERBOLT CAPACITOR DISCHARGE IGNITION

WARNING
*High voltage is present in the ignition system. **Do not** touch or disconnect ignition components while engine is running.*

The Thunderbolt capacitor discharge (CD) ignition system consists of the following components:

   a. Flywheel.
   b. Stator assembly.
   c. Trigger assembly.
   d. Switch box (CD module).
   e. Converter box (150 hp).
   f. Ignition coils.
   g. Spark plugs.

See **Figure 46** for a wiring diagram typical of a 3-cylinder Thunderbolt ignition system. Refer to the appropriate wiring diagram at the end of the manual to assist troubleshooting. The circuit test consists of a preliminary and individual tests. The test sequence requires the use of peak-reading voltmeter (PRV) part No. 91-99750 (or equivalent and spark tester part No. FT-11295. If a meter other than peak-reading voltmeter (PRV) part No. 91-99750 is used, it must be capable of

3

reading peak voltage; a conventional voltmeter will not work.

The switch box and ignition coils cannot be tested without using a peak-reading voltmeter (PRV). However, all other ignition components can be tested using a conventional ohmmeter. Thus, the switch box and ignition coils can be tested by a process of elimination. For example, the condition of an ignition coil from a misfiring cylinder can be verified by connecting it to a known-firing cylinder. If the coil now operates correctly, and the charge coils and trigger assembly have tested good, the switch box is probably defective. If the coil still does not fire properly, the coil is probably defective.

Troubleshooting Thunderbolt CDI

2, 3, and 4 cylinder models

Perform the following tests in the order listed. Refer to **Tables 9-16** for specifications.
1. Preliminary check.
   a. Spark test.
   b. Stop circuit isolation.
2. Switch box stop circuit test.
3. Stator output tests.
4. Stator resistance tests.
5. Switch box bias test (70 and 90 hp only).
6. Trigger resistance tests.
7. Ignition coil primary input voltage tests.
8. Ignition coil ohmmeter tests.

5 cylinder models

Perform the following tests in the order listed. Refer to **Tables 9-16** for specifications.
1. Preliminary check.
   a. Spark test.
   b. Stop circuit isolation.
2. Converter box voltage tests.
3. Switch box stop circuit test.
4. Trigger resistance tests.
5. Ignition coil primary input voltage tests.

6. Ignition coil ohmmeter tests.

Preliminary Check

This procedure determines if there is sufficient voltage in the secondary ignition system to fire the spark plugs.

> *NOTE*
> *The engine must be capable of 600 rpm minimum cranking speed with the spark plugs removed for the following tests. Make sure the starting system is operating properly.*

1. Connect the spark tester to a good engine ground and adjust the spark gap to 7/16 in (0.44 mm).
2. Disconnect the spark plug leads and connect them to the corresponding leads on the spark tester.
3. Remove the spark plugs from the engine.
4. Make sure the lanyard cord is properly attached to the lanyard switch. Crank the engine

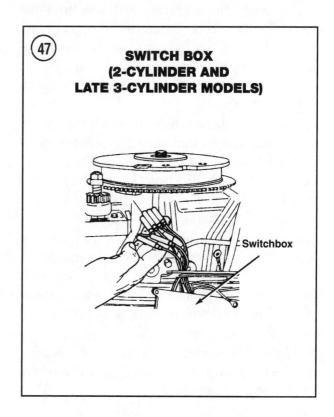

47 **SWITCH BOX (2-CYLINDER AND LATE 3-CYLINDER MODELS)**

Switchbox

while observing the tester. If a good crisp spark is noted at each spark gap, the ignition system is functioning normally. Check spark plugs (Chapter Four) and check/adjust ignition timing (Chapter Five). If spark plugs are in acceptable condition and timing is properly adjusted, problem is not in the ignition system.

5. If one or more spark gaps are not firing properly, check all ground and wire connections in the system. Correct any defect found and repeat Step 4. If all spark gaps are now firing properly, further testing is not necessary.

6. If one or more spark gaps do not fire properly in Step 4, and no defects are noted during the inspection in Step 5, isolate the ignition system from the stop circuit and boat wiring by disconnecting the black/yellow stop circuit wire from the switch box or its bullet connector located between the switch box and main terminal block or main harness plug-in connector. Be certain the wire is not contacting ground during Step 7.

7. Crank the engine while observing the spark tester. If all spark gaps now fire normally, check the ignition switch, stop switch, lanyard switch and related stop circuit and boat wiring for shorts to ground or other problems. Make the necessary repairs and repeat this test.

If one or more spark gaps still do not fire normally, continue with the next test in the troubleshooting procedure listed previously.

Switch Box Stop Circuit Test

Refer to **Figures 47-50** as necessary for this procedure.

1. Set the meter on the 400 DVA scale.

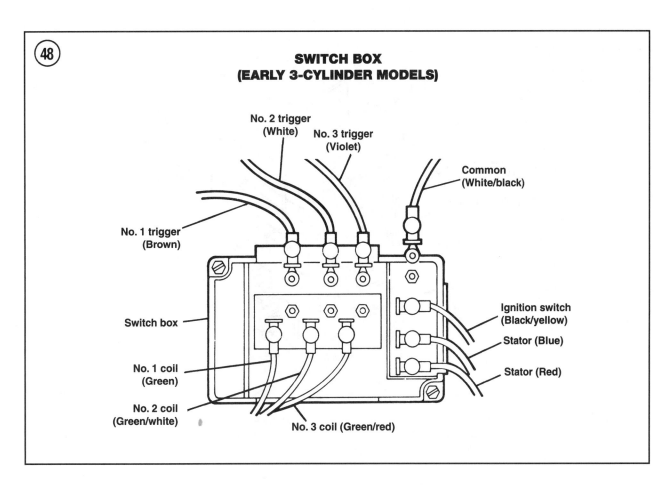

2. Connect the black PRV test lead to a good engine ground.

3. Connect the red PRV test lead to the black/yellow stop circuit wire terminal at the switch box or the black/yellow wire from the switch box.

4. Crank the motor while observing the meter. The switch box stop circuit voltage should be 200-360 volts.

   a. If 200-360 volts (or more) are noted, continue with the *Stator Output Test* in this chapter.

   b. If less than 200 volts are noted, continue at *Trigger Resistance* in this chapter. If trigger resistance is not within specifications, re-

place the trigger assembly. If trigger resistance is within specifications, replace the switch box.

Converter Box Output Test
5-Cylinder Models Only

Refer to **Figure 50** for this procedure.

1. Using a conventional voltmeter, check the voltage at the red wire terminal at the converter box. If battery voltage is not present at the terminal, check for an open circuit in the red wire between the converter box and starter relay. Repair or replace the wire as necessary.

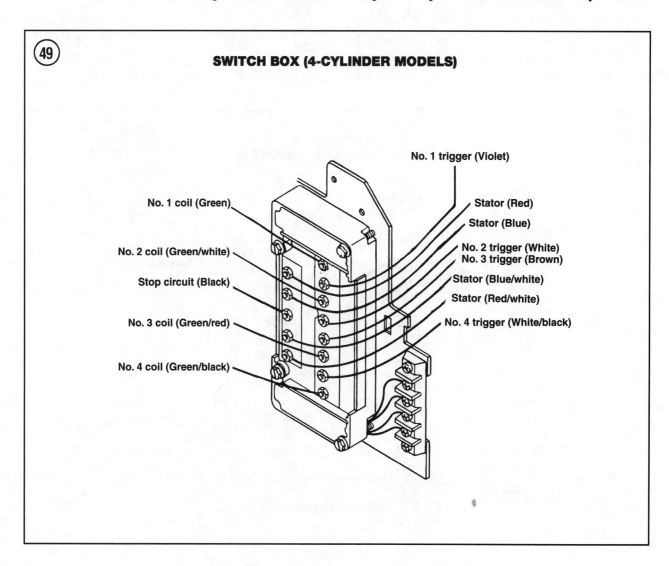

(49) **SWITCH BOX (4-CYLINDER MODELS)**

No. 1 coil (Green)
No. 2 coil (Green/white)
Stop circuit (Black)
No. 3 coil (Green/red)
No. 4 coil (Green/black)

No. 1 trigger (Violet)
Stator (Red)
Stator (Blue)
No. 2 trigger (White)
No. 3 trigger (Brown)
Stator (Blue/white)
Stator (Red/white)
No. 4 trigger (White/black)

2. Set the DVA meter selector switch to the 400 DVA position.

3. Connect the red test lead to the red wire terminal on the converter box and the black test lead to a good engine ground.

4. Crank the motor while observing the meter.

5. Converter box output should be 260-300 volts. If not, replace the converter box.

Ignition Coil Primary Input Voltage (All Models)

Refer to **Figures 47-50** as necessary for this procedure.

1. Set the meter on the 400 DVA scale.

2. Connect the red test lead to the No. 1 ignition coil positive (+) terminal and the black test lead to the No. 1 coil negative (–) terminal.

3

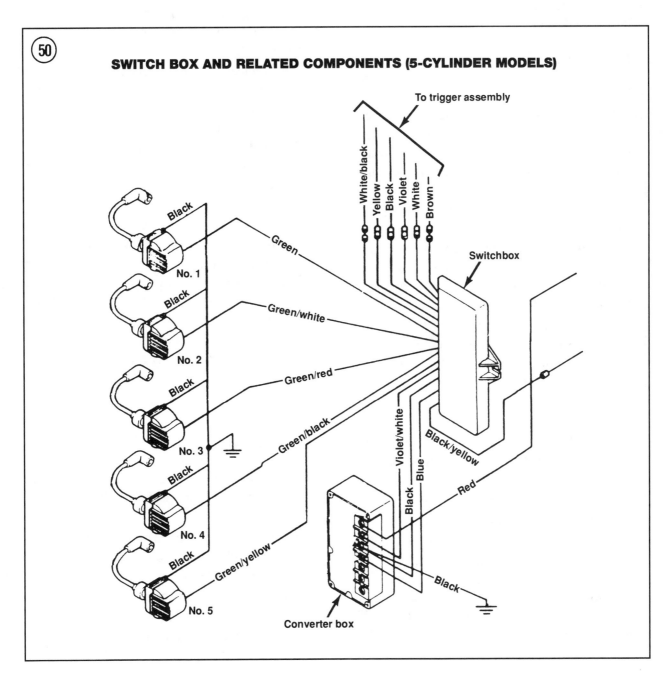

SWITCH BOX AND RELATED COMPONENTS (5-CYLINDER MODELS)

3. Crank the engine while observing the meter. If primary input voltage is within 150-250 volts, check ignition coil resistance as described in this chapter. If input voltage is less than 150 volts, replace the switch box.

4. Repeat Steps 2 and 3 on the remaining ignition coils.

Stator Output Test
(All Models Except 5-Cylinder)

The following procedure checks stator low-speed and high-speed charge coil output to the switch box. Both charge coils are contained within the stator assembly and are not serviced separately. Do not disconnect the stator wires from the switch box during the output tests. Refer to **Figures 47-49** as necessary for this procedure.

1. Set the meter selector switch to the 400 DVA scale.

2. To check low-speed charge coil output, connect the red test lead to the blue stator wire terminal at the switch box or bullet connector. Connect the black test lead to a good engine ground.

3. Crank the motor while observing the meter. Low-speed charge coil output should be 200 volts minimum on all models.

4. To check high-speed charge coil output, connect the red test lead to the red stator wire terminal at the switch box or bullet connector. Connect the black test lead to a good engine ground.

5. Crank the motor while observing the meter. High-speed output should be 20 volts minimum.

6. If either low-speed or high-speed charge coil output is less than specified, either the stator or switch box is defective. Check stator resistance as described in this chapter. If stator resistance is not within specification, replace the stator. If stator resistance is as specified, replace the switch box and repeat this test.

Stator Resistance Test
(All Models Except 5-Cylinder)

Refer to **Figures 47-49** as necessary for this procedure. Check low- and high-speed charge coil resistance using a suitable ohmmeter.

2-Cylinder models

1. To check low-speed charge coil resistance, first calibrate the ohmmeter on the R X 1,000 (1K) ohms scale.

2. Disconnect the red, red/white, blue and blue/white stator wires at their bullet connectors.

3. Connect the ohmmeter between the blue and blue/white stator wires and note the meter. Refer to **Tables 9-16** for specifications. If low-speed resistance is not as specified, replace the stator. See Chapter Seven.

4. To check high-speed charge coil resistance, calibrate the ohmmeter on the R X 1 scale.

5. Connect the ohmmeter between the red and red/white stator wires and note the meter. Refer to **Tables 9-16** for specifications. If high-speed resistance is not as specified, replace the stator. See Chapter Seven.

6. If both the low-speed and hi-speed stator resistance are within specifications, perform the trigger resistance tests as described in this chapter.

3- and 4-Cylinder Models

1. To check low-speed charge coil resistance, first calibrate the ohmmeter on the R × 1,000 (1K) ohms scale.

2. Then, disconnect the red and blue stator wires from the switch box or their bullet connectors.

3. Connect the ohmmeter between the red and blue wires and note the meter.

4. Refer to **Tables 9-16** for specifications.

   a. If resistance is not as specified, replace the stator assembly. See Chapter Seven.

b. If resistance is within specification, check high-speed charge coil resistance (Step 5).

5. To check high-speed charge coil resistance, calibrate the ohmmeter on the R × 1 scale.

6. Connect the ohmmeter between the red stator wire and a good engine ground and note the meter. If the stator is removed from the power head, connect the ohmmeter between the red and black (ground) stator wires. Refer to **Tables 9-16** for specifications. If resistance is out of specification, replace the stator assembly. See Chapter Seven. If resistance is within specification:

a. 3-cylinder models (70-90 hp)—Perform the switch box bias test as described in this chapter.

b. Except 3-cylinder models—Perform trigger resistance tests as described in this chapter.

Trigger Resistance Test

Test trigger resistance using a conventional ohmmeter. Calibrate the ohmmeter on the R × 100 ohms scale.

2-Cylinder Models

Refer to **Figure 47** for this procedure.

1. Disconnect the violet and white trigger wires from the switch box at the bullet connectors.

2. Connect the ohmmeter between the violet and white wires and note the meter.

3. If trigger resistance is within 700-1,000 ohms, check primary input voltage as described in this chapter. If resistance is not within 700-1,000 ohms, replace the trigger assembly. See Chapter Seven.

3-Cylinder models

Refer to **Figure 48** for this procedure.

1. Disconnect the following wires from the switch box:

a. Brown wire—No. 1 trigger.

b. White wire—No. 2 trigger.

c. Violet wire—No. 3 trigger.

d. White/black wire—common ground.

2. Connect the ohmmeter between the white/black common wire and the brown No. 1 trigger wire and note the meter reading.

3. Repeat Step 2 with the meter connected between the white/black common wire and the white No. 2 trigger wire, then the violet No. 3 trigger wire.

4. If trigger resistance is within 1,100-1,400 ohms at each wire, check primary input voltage as described in this chapter. If resistance is not as specified at any connection, replace the trigger assembly. See Chapter Seven.

4-Cylinder models

Refer to **Figure 49** for this procedure.

1. Disconnect the following wires from the switch box:

a. Violet wire—No. 1 trigger.

b. White wire—No. 2 trigger.

c. Brown wire—No. 3 trigger.

d. White/black wire—No. 4 trigger.

2. Connect the ohmmeter between the violet and white trigger wires and note the meter.

3. Next, connect the ohmmeter between the brown and white/black trigger wires and note the meter.

4. If trigger resistance is within 700-1,000 ohms, check primary input voltage as described in this chapter. If resistance is not within 700-1,000 ohms at either connection, replace the trigger assembly. See Chapter Seven.

5-Cylinder models

Refer to **Figure 50** for this procedure.

1. Disconnect the following trigger wires from the switch box at the bullet connectors:

a. Brown wire—No. 1 trigger.

b. White wire—No. 2 trigger.

c. Violet wire—No. 3 trigger.

d. Black wire—No. 4 trigger.

e. Yellow wire—No. 5 trigger.

f. White/black wire—common ground.

2. Connect the ohmmeter between the brown No. 1 trigger wire and the white/black common wire. Note the meter reading.

3. Repeat Step 2 with the ohmmeter connected between the white/black common wire and alternately to the white No. 2 trigger, violet No. 3 trigger, black No. 4 trigger and the yellow No. 5 trigger.

4. If the ohmmeter indicates 1,100-1,400 ohms at each trigger, check primary input voltage as described in this chapter. If resistance is not within 1,100-1,400 ohms at any trigger, replace the trigger assembly. See Chapter Seven.

Ignition Coil Resistance
(All Models)

Test ignition coil resistance using a conventional ohmmeter.

1. Calibrate the ohmmeter on the R × 1 scale.

2. Disconnect the positive (+) and negative (–) primary wires from the No. 1 ignition coil.

3. Connect the ohmmeter between the positive (+) and negative (–) ignition coil terminals and note the meter reading. Resistance should be 0.02-0.04 ohm.

4. Next, calibrate the ohmmeter on the R × 100 scale.

5. Connect the ohmmeter between the negative (–) coil terminal and the secondary coil terminal (spark plug lead removed). Resistance should be 800-1,100 ohms.

6. Repeat Steps 1-5 on each remaining ignition coil. Replace the coil if resistance is not as specified.

Switch Box Bias Test
(3-Cylinder Models Only)

Refer to **Figure 48** for this procedure.

1. Set the meter to the 20 DCV scale. *Do not* use the DVA scale during the switch box bias test.

2. Connect the red voltmeter lead to a good engine ground. Connect the black voltmeter lead to the white/black switch box terminal.

3. Crank the engine while observing the meter. If the meter indicates less than 2 volts DC, replace the switch box. If the meter indicates 2-10 volts DC, continue at *Trigger Resistance* in this chapter. If trigger resistance is not within specification, replace the trigger assembly. If trigger resistance is within specification, replace the switch box.

Running Output Tests

If an ignition system malfunction is intermittent, erratic or only occurs under load, it may be difficult to determine the defective component(s) with the cranking tests. Perform the running output tests to help locate intermittent problems.

To perform ignition system running output voltage tests, install a suitable test wheel and place the outboard motor in a test tank or place the boat in the water.

> *WARNING*
> *Do not attempt to perform running tests on a moving boat. Tie the boat to the dock to restrict movement.*

Connect the meter as outlined in the cranking tests and run the outboard at the engine speed the malfunction occurs. Refer to **Tables 9-16** for specifications.

Replace the stator if low-speed or high-speed output is less than specified, or if reading is intermittent. Replace the switch box if switch box stop circuit, switch box bias or ignition coil primary input voltage is not as specified, or if reading is intermittent.

BREAKERLESS IGNITION MODULE (BIM) SYSTEM

The breakerless ignition module (BIM) system operates similar to earlier breaker-point ignition, except it contains no mechanical breaker points. The BIM module(s) contains the trigger coil, silicon controlled rectifier (SCR) and the ignition coil. Refer to **Figure 51** (5 hp) or **Figure 52** (9.9 and 15 hp).

Two variations of the BIM system are used on 5-15 hp models, BIM 1 and BIM 2. The 2 systems are similar with operation and troubleshooting the same for both; however, the components from each system will not interchange. The systems can be identified by the flywheel and BIM module. On BIM 1, the flywheel magnets are glued to the inner diameter of the flywheel and the BIM module primary wires are blue and brown. On BIM 2, the magnets are cast into the flywheel and the BIM module primary wires are gray and black.

Proceed as follows to troubleshoot BIM ignition, should a malfunction occur:

NOTE
Make sure the lanyard cord is properly attached to the lanyard switch during all troubleshooting steps.

1. Disconnect the spark plug lead(s) from the spark plug(s). Connect spark tester part No. FT-11295 (or equivalent) and adjust the spark gap to 3/8 in.
2. Crank the engine while observing the spark tester.
3. If no spark (or weak spark) is noted, disconnect the brown wires (BIM 1) or red and black wires (BIM 2) from the lanyard switch.

3

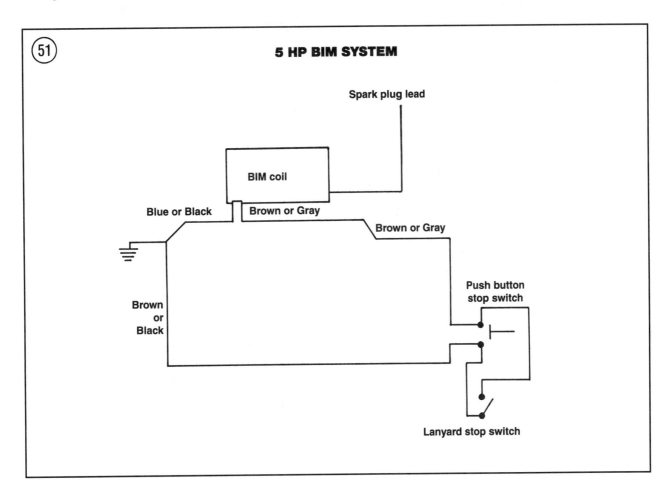

(51) **5 HP BIM SYSTEM**

Spark plug lead

BIM coil

Blue or Black   Brown or Gray

Brown or Gray

Push button stop switch

Brown or Black

Lanyard stop switch

4. Repeat Step 2. If good spark is now noted, replace the lanyard switch. If no spark is noted, continue at Step 5.

5. If no spark is noted in Step 4, disconnect the brown wires (BIM 1) or red and black wires (BIM 2) from the stop switch.

6. Repeat Step 2. If normal spark is now present, replace the stop switch. If no spark is noted, continue at Step 7.

7. Remove the flywheel. See Chapter Eight. Inspect all wires for clean, tight connections. Next, connect an ohmmeter between a good engine ground and the brown (BIM 1) or gray (BIM 2) wire terminal on the stator plate.

  a. If continuity is present between the terminal and ground, either the brown or gray wire, or the BIM module is shorted to ground.

Repair the shorted wire or replace the module as necessary.

  b. If no continuity is noted, continue at Step 8.

8. Connect an ohmmeter between a good engine ground and the blue (BIM 1) or black (BIM 2) module terminal.

  a. If no continuity is present, repair the open circuit in the blue or black wire.

  b. 5 hp—If continuity is noted and there is still no spark, replace the module.

  c. 9.9 and 15 hp—If continuity is noted and there is still no spark on one or more cylinders, continue at Step 9.

NOTE
The following step will test the isolation diode in each module. A module with a failed isolation diode will still produce

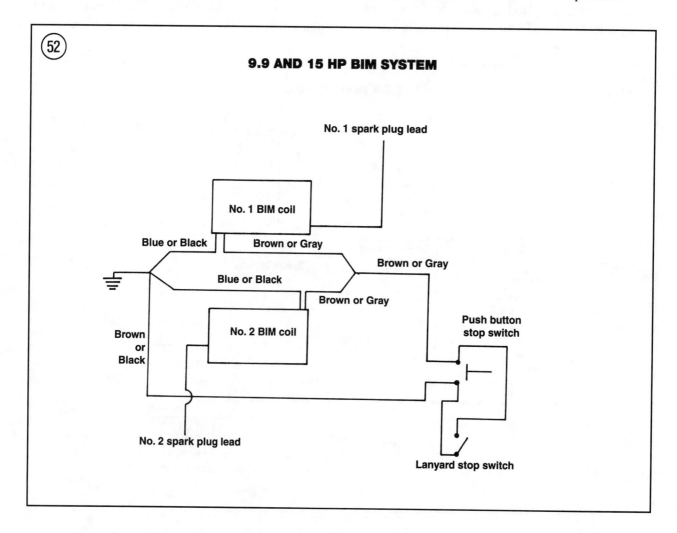

9.9 AND 15 HP BIM SYSTEM

spark, but will prevent the remaining module from sparking.

9. Disconnect the blue (BIM1) or gray (BIM2) module wires from the insulated screw on the stator plate. Calibrate an ohmmeter on the high ohms scale. Connect the red ohmmeter lead to the cylinder No.1 blue or gray module lead. Connect the black ohmmeter lead to the laminations of the module being tested. Observe the meter reading. Reverse the leads and retest. The meter should show a high reading in one polarity and a low reading in the other. Replace the module if the reading is high in both polarities or low in both polarities.

10. Repeat Step 9 for the cylinder No.2 module. If both modules pass the isolation diode test as

specified and spark is still not present, replace the suspect module.

SEM WALBRO CAPACITOR DISCHARGE IGNITION

The SEM capacitor discharge ignition is similar in design and operation to the earlier BIM ignition. The system consists of a flywheel, ignition module/coil assembly, spark plug(s), stop switch, lanyard switch and related wiring. The charge coil(s), trigger coil(s), SCR and related electronic circuitry is contained within the ignition module/coil assemblies. **Figure 53** shows a wiring diagram for 9.9 and 15 hp models; 5 hp models use only one ignition coil/module, while

3

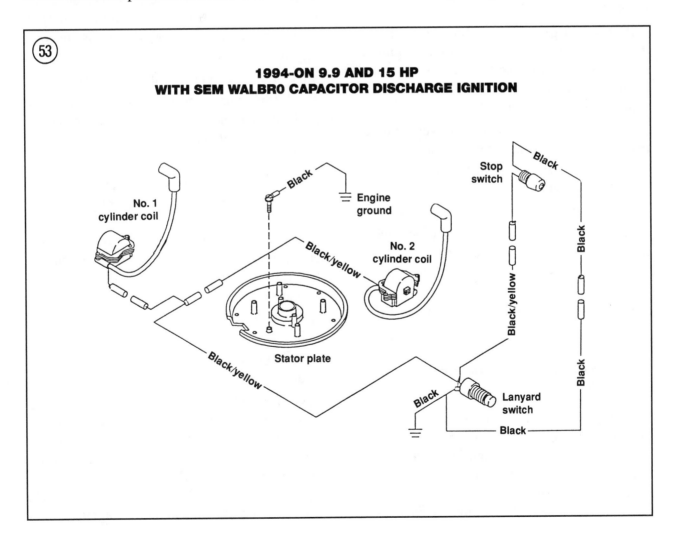

(53)

1994-ON 9.9 AND 15 HP WITH SEM WALBRO CAPACITOR DISCHARGE IGNITION

No. 1 cylinder coil

Black

Engine ground

Black/yellow

No. 2 cylinder coil

Stator plate

Black/yellow

Stop switch

Black

Black/yellow

Black

Black

Lanyard switch

Black

Black

25 hp models use three ignition coil/modules. All of the black/yellow wires are hooked together and routed to the stop switch and lanyard switch. The black/yellow leads must not touch ground or spark will not occur. Depressing the stop switch or pulling the lanyard connects the black/yellow leads to engine ground.

Should an ignition system malfunction occur, troubleshoot the system as follows:

1. Make sure the lanyard cord is properly attached to the lanyard switch.

2. Disconnect the spark plug lead(s) from the spark plug(s). Connect spark tester part No. FT-11295 (or equivalent) to the spark plug lead(s). Adjust the spark gap(s) to 3/8 in.

3. Crank the engine while observing the spark tester.

4. If a good crisp spark is noted at each spark gap, the problem is probably not in the ignition system. Inspect the fuel delivery system and carburetor for malfunctions. If weak or no spark is noted, continue at Step 5.

5. Disconnect the black and black/yellow wires from the lanyard switch. Repeat Step 3.
   a. If normal spark is now noted, replace the lanyard switch.
   b. If no spark is noted, continue at Step 6.

6. Disconnect the black and black/yellow wires from the stop switch. Repeat Step 3.
   a. If normal spark is now noted, replace the stop switch.
   b. If no spark is noted, continue at Step 7.

NOTE
An ohmmeter is required for the remaining tests.

7. Connect the black ohmmeter lead to a good ground on the power head and the red lead to the stator plate. Continuity should be noted. If no continuity is present between the engine and stator plate, repair the open circuit or poor connection in the black stator plate ground wire.

8. Next, move the black ohmmeter lead to the ignition module/coil lamination and note the meter. Continuity should be noted between the module/coil lamination and the power head. If not, make sure the module/coil is mounted to the stator plate securely. Check for corrosion between the module/coil and stator plate. Repeat this step on the remaining module/coil assembly(s) on 2 and 3-cylinder models.

9. Disconnect the black/yellow wire from the module/coil. Connect the red ohmmeter lead to the black/yellow module/coil wire and the black ohmmeter lead to the module/coil lamination. Note the meter reading, then reverse the ohmmeter leads. The meter should indicate continuity in one direction, but not the other. If no continuity, or continuity in both directions is noted, the isolation diode in the module/coil assembly is defective. Replace the module/coil assembly.

10. Repeat Step 9 on the remaining module/coil(s) on 2- and 3-cylinder models.

11. If the ohmmeter tests do not identify a problem, and there is still no spark, replace the suspect module/coil.

CAPACITOR DISCHARGE MODULE (CDM) IGNITION

The CDM ignition is an alternator driven, capacitor discharge, distributorless ignition system. The system consists of the following components (**Figure 54**).
   a. Flywheel.
   b. Stator.
   c. Trigger.
   d. CD module/ignition coil.
   e. Spark plugs.

The CDM module is unique in that it incorporates the ignition coil and CD module into one assembly. There will be one CDM module for each cylinder. All CDM modules are identical. Ignition test harness 84-825207A2 is required to test the CDM system without damaging the wiring harness and connectors. Multimeter 91-99750 or equivalent is required for voltage and resistance readings. The Mercury Marine (part No. 91-99750) multimeter has a DVA scale that should be used whenever the specification is in peak volts or listed as DVA. The term peak volts and DVA are used interchangeably. Normal AC voltage meters will give incorrect results.

WARNING
High voltage is present in the ignition system. Do not touch or disconnect igni-
tion components while the engine is running.

NOTE
All CDM modules must be connected when troubleshooting the system. Disconnecting the No. 1 CDM module will cause loss of spark on all cylinders, with the exception of the 4 cylinder models. Disconnecting either stator wire will always cause a loss of spark on all cylinders on all models.

On 2- and 3-cylinder models, the voltage return path for the No. 1 CDM module is *either* the

3

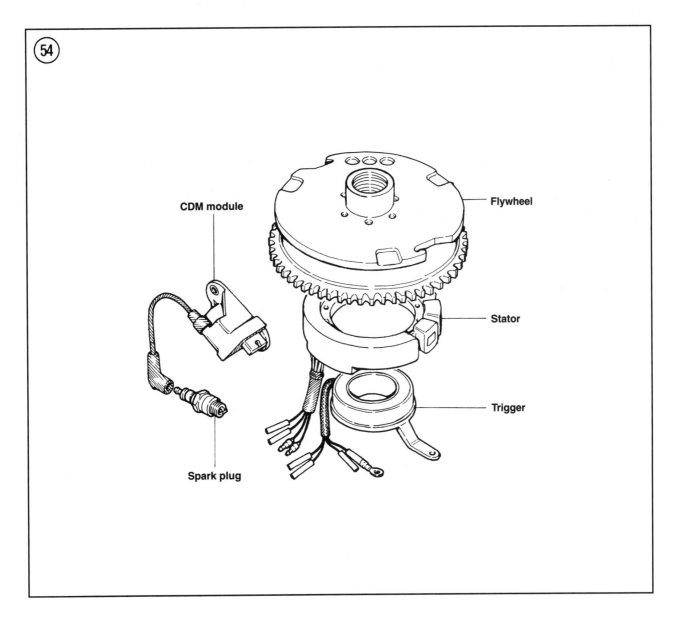

CDM module

Flywheel

Stator

Trigger

Spark plug

No. 2 or No. 3 CDM. The voltage return path for the No. 2 and No. 3 CDM is through the No. 1 CDM. See **Figure 55**.

On 4-cylinder models, the voltage return path for the No. 1 and No. 2 CDM is through *either* the No. 3 or No. 4 CDM. The voltage return path for the No. 3 and No. 4 CDM is through *either* the No. 1 or No. 2 CDM. See **Figure 56**.

On all models, the stator circuit must be complete from the stator to a CDM module and back to the stator through a different CDM module in order for the system to function.

CDM Troubleshooting Procedure

Perform the following tests in the order listed. Refer to **Tables 9-16** for specifications. Refer to **Figures 59-61** for wiring diagrams.

1. Preliminary checks.
   a. Spark test.
   b. Ground circuit verifications.

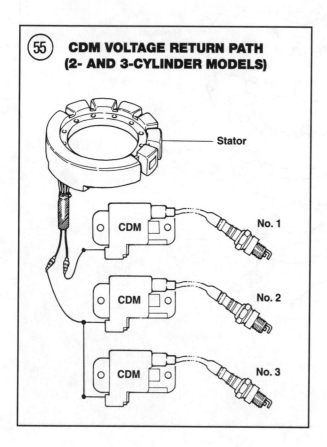

c. Stop circuit isolation.
2. Stator output.
3. Stator resistance.
4. Trigger output.
5. CDM module resistance test (optional).

> *CAUTION*
> *Do not reverse battery connections. Do not spark battery terminals to check polarity. Do not disconnect the battery cables while the engine is running.*

Preliminary Checks

Spark test

1. Check all plug-in connectors for corrosion, loose or damaged pins and mechanical damage.

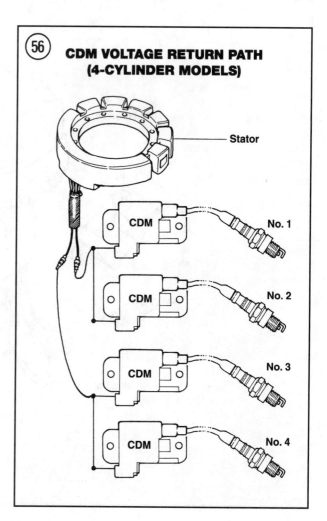

Check for disconnected wires and shorted or open circuits.

2. Check the battery cable connections at the battery and the engine for corrosion, loose connections and mechanical damage.

3. Remove the spark plugs. Connect the spark plug leads to the spark tester (part No. FT-11295 or equivalent) and set the air gap to 7/16 in. (0.44 mm).

4. Make sure the stop switch lanyard is connected to the stop switch.

5. Turn the ignition switch ON, crank the motor and observe the spark tester. If good spark is observed at each spark gap, the ignition system is functioning correctly. Check the spark plugs (Chapter Four) and replace as required. Go to Chapter Five to check ignition timing and linkage adjustments. If spark plugs are in

acceptable condition and timing is properly adjusted, the problem is not in the ignition system.

Ground circuit verification

NOTE
*Use the test harness adapter (part No. 84-825207A2) for all tests involving connection to the CDM module connectors (**Figure 57**). This will prevent damage to the connector pins.*

1. If one or more spark gaps are not firing correctly, disconnect all of the CDM module plugs and connect the test harness adapter to the ignition wiring harness connector for the No. 1 CDM module. Do not connect the tester to the CDM module. Calibrate an ohmmeter on the high ohms scale. Connect one lead of the ohmmeter to a clean engine ground. Connect the other ohmmeter lead to the black lead of the test harness. The ohmmeter must show continuity to ground. If high resistance or no continuity is shown, repair or replace the wire and connector as required.

2. Repeat Step 1 for each of the remaining cylinders. Continue to Step 3 once all CDM module grounds have been verified.

3. Verify the grounding of the ignition component mounting plate (3- and 4-cylinder models only) by connecting the one lead of the ohmmeter to a clean engine ground and the other

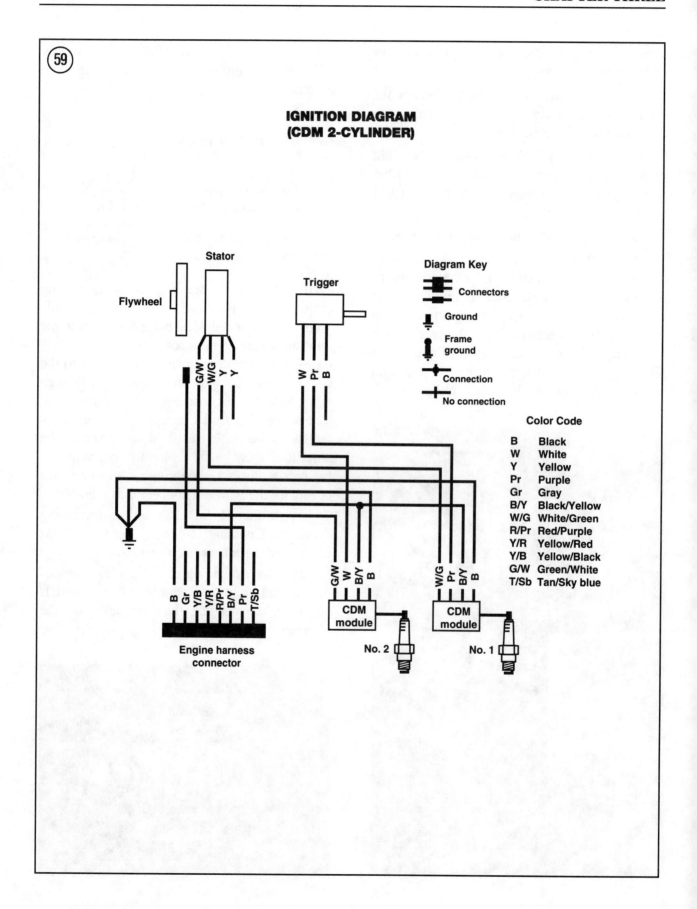

**IGNITION DIAGRAM
(CDM 2-CYLINDER)**

Flywheel

Stator

Trigger

Diagram Key

Connectors

Ground

Frame
ground

Connection

No connection

Color Code

B	Black
W	White
Y	Yellow
Pr	Purple
Gr	Gray
B/Y	Black/Yellow
W/G	White/Green
R/Pr	Red/Purple
Y/R	Yellow/Red
Y/B	Yellow/Black
G/W	Green/White
T/Sb	Tan/Sky blue

G/W
W/G
Y
Y

W
Pr
B

B
Gr
Y/B
Y/R
R/Pr
B/Y
Pr
T/Sb

G/W
W
B/Y
B

W/G
Pr
B/Y
B

CDM
module

CDM
module

Engine harness
connector

No. 2

No. 1

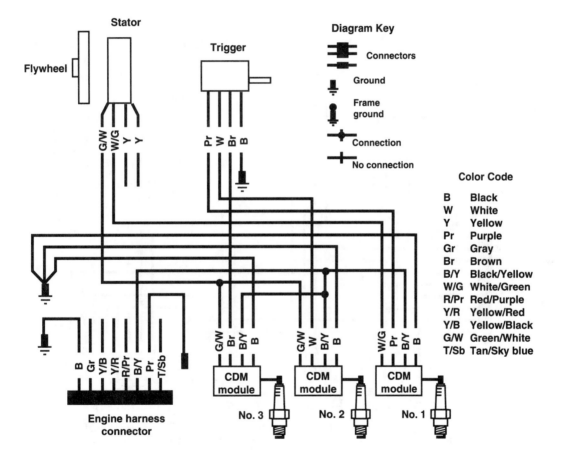

**IGNITION DIAGRAM
(CDM 3-CYLINDER)**

Flywheel

Stator

G/W W/G Y Y

Trigger

Pr W Br B

Diagram Key

Connectors

Ground

Frame
ground

Connection

No connection

Color Code

B   Black
W   White
Y   Yellow
Pr   Purple
Gr   Gray
Br   Brown
B/Y   Black/Yellow
W/G   White/Green
R/Pr Red/Purple
Y/R   Yellow/Red
Y/B   Yellow/Black
G/W   Green/White
T/Sb Tan/Sky blue

B Gr Y/B Y/R R/Pr B/Y Pr T/Sb

**Engine harness
connector**

G/W Br B/Y B

CDM
module

No. 3

G/W W B/Y B

CDM
module

No. 2

W/G Pr B/Y B

CDM
module

No. 1

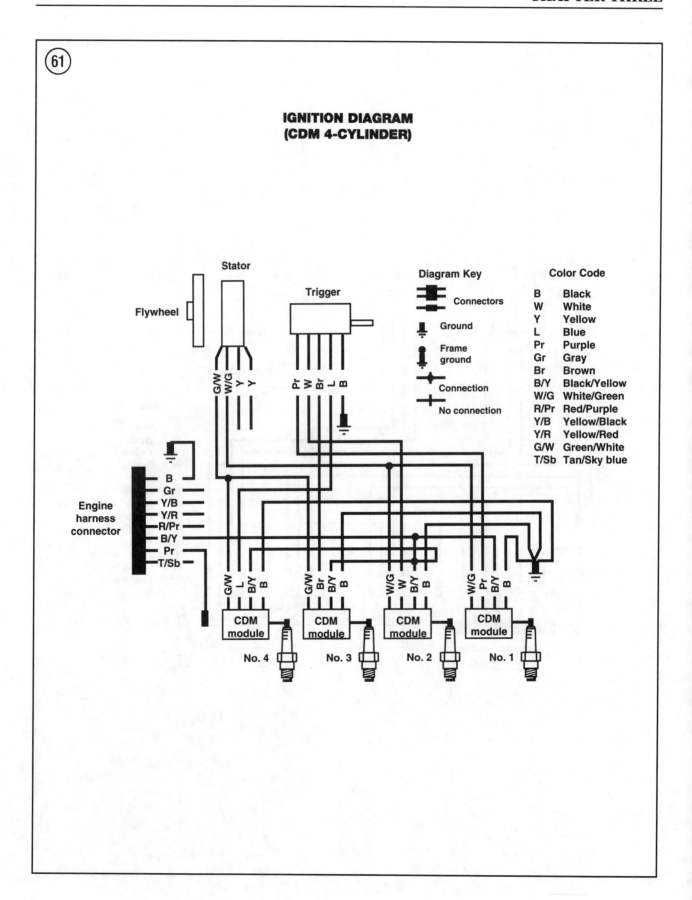

61

**IGNITION DIAGRAM
(CDM 4-CYLINDER)**

lead to the ground lead terminal (A, **Figure 58**) on the ignition component mounting plate. The ohmmeter must show continuity to ground. If high resistance or no continuity is shown, repair or replace the ground wires as required.

Stop circuit isolation

Isolate the stop circuit from the CDM ignition system by disconnecting the black/yellow bullet connector. This connector is in the tie-strapped bundle of wires near the voltage regulator (B, **Figure 58**). Make sure that that the black/yellow wire is not touching any other wire or ground. Turn the ignition switch ON, crank the motor and observe the spark tester. If good spark is now observed at each spark gap, the problem is in the stop circuit black/yellow lead. Check the black/yellow lead from the engine to the ignition switch for shorts to ground or other problems. Test the ignition switch and lanyard stop switch for malfunctions. The black/yellow lead must *not* have continuity to ground when the ignition switch and lanyard stop switches are in the ON position. The black/yellow lead must have continuity to ground when the ignition switch and lanyard stop switch are in the OFF positions. Repair or replace the circuit as required.

Stator Output

1. Install the test harness part No. 84-825207A2 between the No. 1 CDM and the ignition harness. Set the multimeter to the 400 DVA scale, connect the red lead of the meter to the test harness green lead and the black lead of the tester to the test harness black lead. Crank the engine and record the multimeter reading. Repeat the test for each CDM module. Each module should show at least 100 peak volts. If only one CDM is below specification, replace that CDM and retest. If all CDM stator voltage readings are below 100 volts, go to the stator resistance test.

NOTE
If all CDM stator voltages are below specification and stator resistance tests are within specification, replace each CDM module (one at a time) with a known good CDM module until the defective CDM module is located.

Stator Resistance

1. To check the resistance of the stator windings, disconnect the green/white and white/green stator lead bullet connectors. Calibrate an ohmmeter on the appropriate scale to read 500-600 ohms. Connect the red ohmmeter lead to the stator assembly white/green lead and the black ohmmeter lead to the stator assembly green/white lead. Resistance should be 500-600 ohms. If the resistance is out of specification or intermittent, replace the stator. If the resistance is within specification, continue to step 2.

2. To check for a grounded condition, connect the black ohmmeter lead to a clean engine ground. Connect the red ohmmeter lead to the green/white stator assembly wire. The ohmmeter should read *infinity*, which means that there is no continuity to ground. If the ohmmeter reads anything other than infinity, replace the stator. Repeat the test for the stator assembly white/green wire.

Trigger Output

NOTE
Pin C of the CDM module connector is the trigger lead. The trigger leads on the ignition harness are color coded for each cylinder. Cylinder No. 1 uses a purple trigger lead, cylinder No. 2 uses a white trigger lead, cylinder No. 3 uses a brown trigger lead and cylinder No. 4 uses a dark blue trigger lead. Connecting the wrong trigger lead to the wrong CDM module will cause the engine to fire out of time.

3

1. Install the test harness part No. 84-825207A2 between the No. 1 CDM and the ignition harness. Set the multimeter to the lowest DVA scale, connect the red lead of the meter to the test harness white lead and the black lead of the tester to the test harness black lead. Crank the engine and record the multimeter reading. Repeat the test for each CDM module. Each module should show 0.2-2.0 peak volts. If trigger voltage is below specification, replace the trigger and re-test. If trigger voltage is above specification, replace the CDM module.

NOTE
If a trigger voltage remains low after installing a new trigger, replace the CDM module.

CDM Module Resistance Test (Optional)

Refer to **Table 7** for ohmmeter guidelines.

1. Connect the test harness part No. 84-825207A2 to the No. 1 CDM, but *do not* connect the test harness to the ignition harness. This test is for the CDM module only. Calibrate the ohmmeter on an appropriate scale to read 1150-1350 ohms. Connect the red ohmmeter lead to the black test harness lead and the black ohmmeter lead to the white test harness lead. The ohmmeter should read 1150-1350 ohms. Replace the CDM module if the resistance is out of specification.

NOTE
On the following 3 steps the ohmmeter readings may be reversed depending on the polarity of the ohmmeter being used. As long as the first part of the test is opposite of the second part of the test, the test can be considered successful.

2. Calibrate the ohmmeter on the high ohms scale, connect the ohmmeter red lead to the green test harness lead and the black ohmmeter lead to the black test harness lead. The ohmmeter should show a low reading. Reverse the ohmmeter leads.

The ohmmeter should now show a high reading. Replace the CDM module if both tests show high or both tests show low.

3. Connect the ohmmeter red lead to the black/yellow test harness lead and the ohmmeter black lead to the green test harness lead. The ohmmeter should show a low reading. Reverse the ohmmeter leads. The ohmmeter should now show a high reading. Replace the CDM module if both tests show high or both tests show low.

4. Calibrate an ohmmeter on an appropriate scale to read 900-1200 ohms. Connect the red lead of the ohmmeter to the black lead of the test harness and connect the black lead of the ohmmeter to the spark plug terminal at the spark plug end of the spark plug wire. The ohmmeter should read 900-1200 ohms. Replace the CDM module if the resistance is out of specification.

IGNITION SWITCH

The ignition switch should be removed and all wires disconnected for testing.

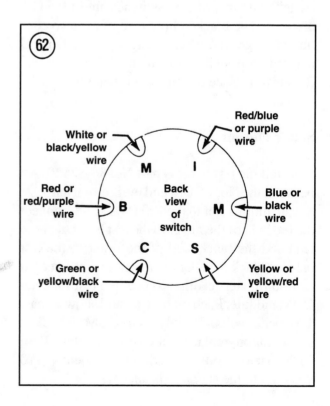

Continuity and Resistance Test

Refer to **Figure 62** for this procedure.

1. With the switch in the OFF position, connect a self-powered test lamp between terminals M and M. The lamp should light.

2. Turn the switch to the RUN position and connect the test lamp leads between terminals B and I. The lamp should light. Turn the key to the START position. The lamp should remain on.

3. Repeat Step 2 with the key depressed to engage the CHOKE position. The lamp should light and remain on as the switch is moved from the RUN to START position.

4. Turn the switch to the RUN position and connect the test lamp leads between terminals B and C. Depress key to engage CHOKE position. The lamp should light. Turn the key to the START position. The lamp should remain on.

5. With the switch in START, connect the test lamp between terminals B and S. The lamp should light. Hold switch in START and depress key to engage CHOKE position. The lamp should remain on.

NOTE
Reinstall ignition switch and reconnect all wires to perform the following steps.

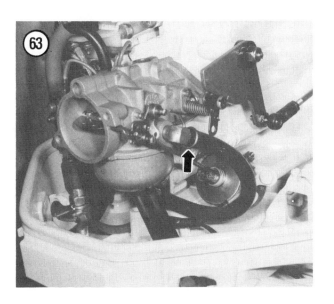

6. Disconnect the spark plug leads to prevent the engine from starting.

7. Connect a negative voltmeter lead to ground and the positive lead to switch terminal B. Turn switch to START to crank the engine. Note the voltmeter reading.

8. Move the positive voltmeter lead to terminal I and repeat Step 7. If voltage drops more than one volt, internal resistance is excessive. Replace the switch.

9. If the switch does not perform as specified, replace the switch.

FUEL SYSTEM

Many owners automatically assume that the carburetor is at fault when the engine does not run properly. While fuel system problems are not uncommon, carburetor adjustment is seldom the answer. In many cases, adjusting the carburetor only compounds the problem by making the engine run worse.

Fuel system troubleshooting should start at the fuel tank and work through the system, reserving the carburetor(s) as the final point. The majority of fuel system problems result from an empty fuel tank, sour fuel, a plugged fuel filter or a malfunctioning fuel pump. **Table 3** provides a series of symptoms and causes that can be useful in locating fuel system problems.

Troubleshooting

As a first step, check the fuel flow. Remove the fuel tank cap and look into the tank. If fuel is present, disconnect and ground the spark plug lead(s) as a safety precaution. Disconnect the fuel line from the carburetor (**Figure 63**, typical) and place it in a suitable container to catch discharged fuel. See if fuel flows freely from the fuel hose when the primer bulb is squeezed.

If no fuel flows from the hose, the fuel petcock may be shut off or blocked by rust or foreign matter, the fuel hose may be restricted or kinked or a primer bulb check valve may be defective. Make sure the vent on the fuel tank cap is open.

CAUTION
CD module damage may result if the engine is cranked with the spark plug lead(s) disconnected and in an open-circuit condition. When performing engine cranking tests with spark plug lead(s) disconnected, be sure to provide a spark gap by installing a suitable spark tester (part No. FT-11295) or securely grounding spark plug lead(s) to the engine.

If satisfactory fuel flow is noted, crank the engine several revolutions to check fuel pump operation. A properly operating pump will deliver a constant flow of fuel from the hose. If the fuel flow fluctuates from pulse to pulse, the fuel pump is probably failing.

The carburetor choke may also present problems. A choke that sticks open will result in hard starting; a choke that sticks closed will result in a flooding condition.

During a hot engine shut down, the fuel bowl temperature can rise above 200°, causing the fuel to boil inside the carburetor. While the carburetors are vented to prevent this condition, some fuel may percolate over the high-speed nozzle.

A leaking inlet needle and seat or a defective float will allow an excessive amount of fuel into the intake manifold. Pressure in the fuel hose after the engine is shut down forces fuel past the leaking inlet valve, raising the fuel bowl level, allowing fuel to overflow into the manifold.

Excessive fuel consumption may not necessarily indicate an engine or fuel system problem. Marine growth on the boat hull, a bent or otherwise damaged propeller or a fuel leak can cause an increase in fuel consumption. These areas should be checked *before* blaming the carburetor.

Spark plug wet fouling can occur on multicylinder engines if the fuel recirculating system is not functioning properly. If wet fouling proves a chronic problem, remove the recirculation hose from the carburetor adapter and try to blow through it. If you can, one or more of the check valves on the cylinder drain reed plate are not sealing properly.

POWER HEAD

Power head problems are generally symptoms of a malfunction in another system, such as ignition, fuel or starting system. If properly maintained and serviced, the power head should

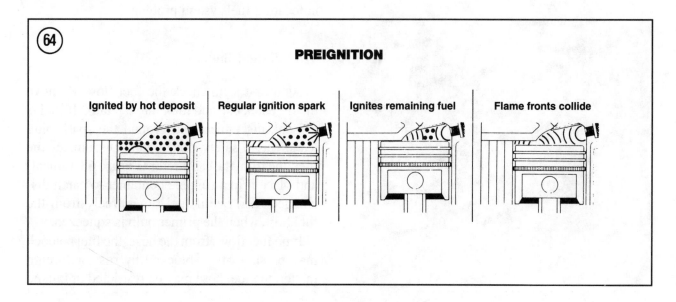

PREIGNITION

| Ignited by hot deposit | Regular ignition spark | Ignites remaining fuel | Flame fronts collide |

experience no problems other than those caused by age and wear.

However, mechanical problems in the power head cannot be overcome with adjustments to other systems, such as fuel and ignition. *Always* verify the mechanical condition of a power head by performing a compression test (Chapter Four).

Overheating and Lack of Lubrication

Overheating and lack of lubrication cause the majority of engine mechanical problems. Marine engines create a great deal of heat and are not designed to operate at a standstill for any length of time. Using a spark plug of the wrong heat range can burn a piston. Incorrect ignition timing, a propeller with too much pitch or diameter or an excessively lean fuel mixture can also cause the engine to overheat.

Preignition

Preignition is the premature ignition of the fuel charge before normal combustion occurs and is caused by hot spots in the combustion chamber (**Figure 64**). Glowing deposits in the combustion chamber, inadequate cooling or overheated spark plugs can all cause preignition. This is first noticed in the form of a power loss but will eventually result in extensive damage to the internal engine components because of excessive combustion chamber temperatures.

Detonation

Commonly called "spark knock," detonation is the violent explosion of fuel in the combustion chamber instead of the normal controlled burn that should take place (**Figure 65**). Severe engine damage can result. Use of low octane gasoline is a common cause of detonation.

Even when high octane gasoline is used, detonation can still occur if the ignition timing is over advanced. Other causes are lean fuel mixture at or near full throttle, inadequate engine cooling, cross-firing spark plugs, excessive accumulation of deposits on the piston and combustion chamber or the use of a propeller with too much pitch or diameter (overpropping).

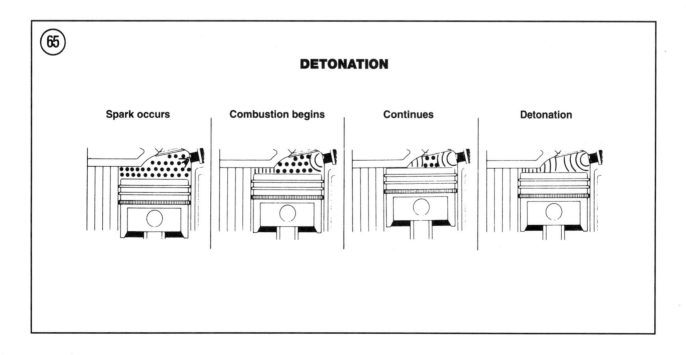

DETONATION

| Spark occurs | Combustion begins | Continues | Detonation |

Since outboard motors are relatively noisy, engine knock or detonation is likely to go unnoticed by the operator, especially at high engine speed when wind noise is also present. Such inaudible detonation is usually the cause when engine damage occurs for no apparent reason.

Poor Idle

Some common causes of poor idle are improper carburetor adjustment, crankcase or vacuum leakage, incorrect ignition timing or ignition system malfunction.

Misfiring

Common causes of misfiring are a weak spark, dirty, contaminated or fouled spark plug or excessively worn or defective spark plug. Check for chipped, cracked or broken reed valves. If misfiring only occurs under a heavy load, as when accelerating, it is usually caused by a defective spark plug or spark plug lead. Run the motor at night to check for spark leaks along the plug wire and under spark plug cap or use a spark tester.

WARNING
Never run engine in a dark garage to check for spark leak. There is considerable danger of carbon monoxide poisoning.

Water Leakage in Cylinder

The fastest and easiest method to check for water leakage into a cylinder is to check the spark plugs. Water inside the combustion chamber during combustion will turn to steam and thoroughly clean the spark plug and combustion chamber. If one spark plug on a multi-cylinder engine is very clean, and the other plugs show normal deposits, water ingestion is possibly taking place on the cylinder with the clean plug.

Water ingestion can be verified by installing used spark plugs with normal deposits into each cylinder. Run the engine in a test tank or on a boat in the water for 5-10 minutes. Stop the engine and allow it to cool. Remove and inspect the spark plugs. If one or more spark plugs are thoroughly clean, water leakage is probably occurring.

Flat Spots

If the engine seems to die momentarily when the throttle is opened and then recovers, check for a dirty or restricted main jet in the carburetor, water in the fuel or an excessively lean fuel mixture. Also check for vacuum leaks at the carburetor-to-intake manifold joint, intake manifold or crankcase mating surfaces.

Power Loss

Several factors can cause a lack of power and speed. Look for air leaks in the fuel line or fuel pump, restricted fuel filter, chipped cracked or broken reed valves or a choke/throttle valve that operates improperly. Check ignition timing adjustment.

A piston or cylinder that is galling, incorrect piston clearance or a worn/sticky piston ring may be responsible. Look for loose bolts, defective gaskets or leaking mating surfaces on the cylinder head, cylinder or crankcase. Also check the crankshaft seals; worn seals can result in pressure or vacuum leaks.

Piston Seizure

Piston seizure is commonly caused by incorrect piston-to-cylinder clearance, improper piston ring end gap, insufficient oil mixed with the gasoline, poor quality oil, spark plug with the wrong heat range or incorrect ignition timing. In addition, engine overheating may result in piston seizure.

Excessive Vibration

Excessive vibration may be caused by loose motor mounts, worn rubber bushings, worn bearings, bent or damaged propeller or a generally poor running motor.

Engine Noises

Experience is needed to diagnose accurately in this area. Noises are difficult to differentiate and even harder to describe. Deep knocking noises usually indicate main bearing failure. A slapping noise generally indicates excessive piston-to-cylinder clearance. A light knocking noise during acceleration may be a worn connecting rod bearing. Pinging should be corrected immediately or damage to the piston(s) will result. A compression leak at the cylinder head mating surface will sound like a rapid on-off squeal.

Table 1 STARTER MOTOR TROUBLESHOOTING*

Symptom	Probable Cause	Remedy
Low no-load speed with high current draw	Tight or dirty bushings. Shorted armature.	Clean and lubricate bushings. Test armature on growler.
Low no-load speed with low current draw	High resistance in the armature circuit.	Check brushes and springs. Test armature on growler. Clean and inspect commutator.
High current draw with no rotation	Stuck armature. Internal short to ground.	Clean and lubricate bushings, remove internal corrosion. Check brush leads for shorts.
No current draw with no rotation	Open armature circuit.	Check brushes and springs. Test armature on growler. Clean and inspect commutator.
Starter continues running after key is released	Solenoid stuck on. Key switch failure. Yellow or yellow/red wire circuit malfunction.	Replace solenoid. Test key switch. Remove yellow or yellow/red wire from solenoid. If starter now stops, repair or replace the yellow or yellow/red wire from the key switch to the starter solenoid.
Starter turns motor over too slowly	Solenoid has high internal resistance.	Measure voltage drop across the solenoid while starter is engaged. 0.2 volts maximum drop allowed. Connect red voltmeter lead to battery side of solenoid and black voltmeter lead to the starter side. Measure voltage with starter engaged.

(continued)

Table 1 STARTER MOTOR TROUBLESHOOTING* (continued)

Symptom	Probable Cause	Remedy
Starter turns motor over too slowly (continued)	Mechanical failure of power head or gearcase.	Turn flywheel by hand. If resistance is excessive, remove gearcase and recheck. Repair gearcase or power head.
	Battery cables too small or excessively long.	Do not use cables smaller than the manufacturer installed. If extending cable length, use larger diameter cables.
Starter spins but starter drive does not engage	Starter drive is corroded or needs lubrication.	Clean thoroughly and lubricate the splines under the starter drive.
	Starter is not producing necessary speed and torque to engage the drive.	Check the battery charge, battery cables and connections. Test the solenoid voltage drop (see Starter turns motor over too slowly). Disassemble the starter, then clean and lubricate bushings, clean and inspect commutator, check brushes and springs; and test armature on growler.

*The majority of Force starter motors use permanent magnets glued into main housing. Never strike a starter as this will damage the magnets. Inspect the magnets anytime the starter is disassembled. Replace the housing if the magnets are cracked, damaged or loose.

Table 2 IGNITION TROUBLESHOOTING

Symptom	Probable cause
Engine will not start, but fuel and spark are okay	Defective spark plugs. Spark plug gap set too wide. Improper spark timing.
Engine misfires at idle	Incorrect spark plug gap. Defective or loose spark plugs. Spark plugs of incorrect heat range. Leaking or broken high tension wires. Weak armature magnets. Defective coil or condenser. Defective ignition switch. Spark timing out of adjustment.
Engine misfires at high speed	See *Engine misfires at idle*. Coil breaks down. Coil shorts through insulation. Spark plug gap too wide. Wrong type spark plugs. Too much spark advance.
Engine backfires through exhaust	Cracked spark plug insulator. Improper timing. Crossed spark plug wires.

(continued)

Table 2 IGNITION TROUBLESHOOTING (continued)

Symptom	Probable cause
Engine backfires through carburetor	Improper ignition timing.
Engine preignition	Spark advanced too far. Incorrect type spark plug. Burned spark plug electrodes.
Engine noise (knocking at power head)	Spark advanced too far.
Ignition coil fails	Extremely high voltage. Moisture formation. Excessive heat from engine.
Spark plugs burn and foul	Incorrect type plug. Fuel mixture too rich. Inferior grade of gasoline. Overheated engine. Excessive carbon in combustion chambers.
Ignition causing high fuel consumption	Incorrect spark timing. Leaking high tension wires. Incorrect spark plug gap. Fouled spark plugs. Incorrect spark advance. Weak ignition coil. Preignition.

3

Table 3 FUEL SYSTEM TROUBLESHOOTING

Symptom	Probable cause
No fuel at carburetor	No fuel in tank. Air vent in fill cap not open. Air vent in fill cap clogged. Fuel tank sitting on fuel line. Fuel line fittings not properly connected to engine or fuel tank. Air leak at fuel connection. Fuel pickup clogged. Defective fuel pump.
Flooding at carburetor	Choke out of adjustment. High float level. Float stuck. Excessive fuel pump pressure. Float saturated beyond buoyancy.
Rough operation	Dirt or water in fuel. Reed valve open or broken. Incorrect fuel level in carburetor bowl. Carburetor loose at mounting flange.

(continued)

Table 3 FUEL SYSTEM TROUBLESHOOTING (continued)

Symptom	Probable cause
Rough operation (continued)	Throttle shutter valve not closing completely. Throttle shutter valve installed incorrectly.
Engine misfires at high speed	Dirty carburetor. Lean carburetor adjustment. Restriction in fuel system. Low fuel pump pressure.
Engine backfires	Poor quality fuel. Air/fuel mixture too rich or too lean.
Engine preignition	Excessive oil in fuel. Inferior grade of gasoline. Lean carburetor mixture.
Spark plugs burn and foul	Fuel mixture too rich. Inferior grade of gasoline.
High gas consumption **Flooding or leaking**	Cracked carburetor casting. Leaks at line connections. Defective carburetor bowl gasket. High float level. Plugged vent hole in cover. Loose needle and seat. Defective needle valve seat gasket. Worn needle valve and seat. Foreign matter clogging needle valve. Worn float pin or bracket. Float binding in bowl. High fuel pump pressure.
Overrich mixture	Choke lever stuck. High float level. High fuel pump pressure.
Abnormal speeds	Carburetor out of adjustment. Too much oil in fuel.

Table 4 CHARGING SYSTEM SPECIFICATIONS

Model	Minimum Output Amperage @ rpm	Stator Ohms	Maximum Output Amperage @ rpm	Regulated
7.5 hp*	1.0 @ 2000	NA	3.5 @ 4000	no
25-35 hp	0.5 @ 1800	1.0-2.0	2.0 @ 3500	no
40-50 hp				
1992C-1995	1.0 @ 1000	0.8-1.1	9.0 @ 3000	yes
1996-1999	8.0 @ 1200	0.15-0.20	14.0 @ 3000	yes
50 hp				
1984-1987	0.5 @ 1100	NA	6.0 @3500	no
1988-1992B	1.5 @ 1000	0.5-1.0	7.5 @ 3500	no
60 hp	0.5 @ 800	1.0	7.0 @ 3500	no

(continued)

Table 4 CHARGING SYSTEM SPECIFICATIONS (continued)

Model	Minimum Output Amperage @ rpm	Stator Ohms	Maximum Output Amperage @ rpm	Regulated
70 hp with original stator part No. 398-8778A10, A26 or A29	1.0 @ 1000	0.6-1.1	9.0 @ 5000	yes
70 hp with upgraded stator part No. 398-9873A24	8.0 @ 1200	0.1-0.5	14.0 @ 3000	yes
75 hp	8.0 @ 1200	0.22-0.24	14.0 @ 3000	yes
85 and 125 hp	1.0 @ 1000	0.5-1.0	7.0 @ 3500	no
90 hp				
Prestolite CD	1.0 @ 1000	0.5-1.0	7.0 @ 3500	no
Thunderbolt CDI with original stator part No. 398-8778A10, A16, A26 or A29	1.0 @ 1000	0.6-1.1	9.0 @ 5000	yes
Thunderbolt CDI with upgraded stator part No. 398-9873A24	8.0 @ 1200	0.1-0.5	14.0 @ 3000	yes
CDM	8.0 @ 1200	0.15-0.20	14.0 @ 3000	yes
120 hp				
Prestolite CD	1.0 @ 1000	0.5-1.0	7.0 @ 3500	no
Thunderbolt CDI	1.0 @ 1000	0.6-1.1	9.0 @ 3500	yes
CDM	8.0 @ 1200	0.15-0.20	14.0 @ 3000	yes
150 hp				
1989-1990C	1.0 @ 1000	2.0 or less	11.0 @ 3500	yes
1990D-1991A	1.0 @ 1000	2.0 or less	7.0 @ 3500	no
1991B-1994	9.0 @ 1000	0.17-0.19	16.0 @ 5000	yes
L-Drive				
1989-1991A	1.0 @ 1000	2.0 or less	7.0 @ 3500	no
1991B-1992	4.5 @ 1000	0.6-1.1	9.0 @ 3500	yes

* Specifications are for optional AC lighting kit or DC charging kit. Both are unregulated.

Table 5 IGNITION COIL SPECIFICATIONS (BREAKER-POINT IGNITION)

Model/Year	Operating amperage	Primary resistance (ohms)	Secondary resistance (ohms)
4 hp (1984-1986)			
Coil No. 12358	1.5	0.7-0.9	7,400
Coil No. 12369	1.5	0.7-0.9	13,500-16,500
5 hp (1987-on)		0.7-0.9	13,500-16,500
9.9/15 hp (1984-1986)			
Coil No. A12345	1.5	0.7-0.9	6,900-7,800
Coil No. 12370	1.5	0.7-0.9	13,500-16,500
9.9/15 hp (1987-on)		0.7-0.9	13,500-16,500
50 hp (1984-1986)	1.0	2.5-3.0	13,500-16,500

3

Table 6 STARTER SPECIFICATIONS

Model	Cranking Speed*	Current Draw
1984-1994 models including L-Drives		
25-35hp	550 rpm minimum	95-125 amps
40-50 hp	450 rpm minimum	80-125 amps
60-150 hp	300 rpm minimum	80-165 amps
1995-1999 models		
40-50 hp	300 rpm minimum	95 amps (20 amps no-load)
75-120 hp	300 rpm minimum	110-200 amps (80-165 amps no-load)

*Spark plugs should be installed. No-load test is a bench test.

Table 7 OHMMETER GUIDELINES*

A reading of:	0	The opposite reading is:	∞
Means:	Zero	The opposite reading is:	Infinity
Also means:	Continuity	The opposite reading is:	No continuity
Also called a:	Very low reading	The opposite reading is:	Very high reading
Visualized as:	A solid piece of wire (electricity can flow)	The opposite situation:	A wire broken in two (electricity cannot flow)

*When checking *short to ground* or testing *diodes*, calibrate on the highest scale available. If the ohmmeter is so equipped, never use the *low* scale to test a diode or short to ground. When checking for a specific ohm value, calibrate the ohmmeter on a scale that allows reading that specification as close to the middle of the meter movement as possible.

Table 8 IGNITION SYSTEM MODEL IDENTIFICATION

Model/Year	Ignition System
4 hp	Magneto breaker point
5 hp	
1988-1989A	Magneto breaker point
1989B-1993	BIM I or II (breakerless inductive module)
1994-1996	SEM-Walbro CD (capacitor discharge)
7.5 hp	Prestolite magneto CD* (capacitor discharge)
9.9 and 15 hp	
1984-1989A	Magneto breaker point
1989B-1993	BIM I or II (breakerless inductive module)
1994-1996	SEM-Walbro CD (capacitor discharge)
25 hp 2 cylinder	Prestolite magneto CD (capacitor discharge)
25 hp 3 cylinder	CDM (capacitor discharge module)
35 hp	Prestolite magneto CD (capacitor discharge)
40 and 50 hp	
1992C-1995	Thunderbolt CDI (capacitor discharge ignition)
1996	CDM (capacitor discharge module)
50 hp	
1984-1987B	Battery breaker-point
1987C-1988C	Prestolite magneto CD* (capacitor discharge)
1988D-1992B	Prestolite magneto CD (capacitor discharge)
60 hp	Prestolite magneto CD (capacitor discharge)
70 hp	Thunderbolt CDI (capacitor discharge ignition)

(continued)

Table 8 IGNITION SYSTEM MODEL IDENTIFICATION (continued)

Model/Year	Ignition System
75 hp	CDM (capacitor discharge module)
85 and 125 hp	Prestolite magneto CD (capacitor discharge)
90 and 120 hp	
1990-1991C and 90 hp 1991E	Prestolite magneto CD (capacitor discharge)
1991D-1995 except 90 hp 1991E	Thunderbolt CDI (capacitor discharge ignition)
1996-1999	CDM (capacitor discharge module)
150 hp	
1989-1991A	Prestolite magneto CD (capacitor discharge)
1991B and newer	Thunderbolt CDI (capacitor discharge ignition)
L-drives	
85 and 125 hp	Prestolite magneto CD (capacitor discharge)
90 and 120 hp 1990-1991A	Prestolite magneto CD (capacitor discharge)
90 and 120 hp 1991B-1992	Thunderbolt CDI (capacitor discharge ignition)

*CD modules and ignition coils are a single unit.

Table 9 BIM I AND II IGNITION SYSTEM SPECIFICATIONS

	BIM I	BIM II
Module wires that must always have continuity to ground	blue	black
Module wires that must not have continuity to ground	brown	gray

Table 10 SEM-WALBRO CD IGNITION SYSTEM SPECIFICATIONS

Ignition coil/module laminations must have continuity to engine ground at all times.
The black/yellow lead at an ignition coil/module should have continuity to its coil laminations in one polarity and have no continuity to its coil laminations in the opposite polarity.
Grounding the black/yellow lead shuts off the ignition.

Table 11 PRESTOLITE MAGNETO CD IGNITION SYSTEM SPECIFICATIONS

	Minimum voltages (peak/DVA)		
	Stator	Trigger*	CD module*
7.5 hp	300	1.4	NA
25-35 hp	300	1.4	175
50 hp 1987C-1988C	300	0.5	NA
50 hp 1988D-1992B	210	0.3	210
60-150 hp	210	0.3	210

Table 12 THUNDERBOLT CDI IGNITION SYSTEM
MINIMUM CRANKING PEAK/DVA VOLTAGE SPECIFICATIONS

Models	Stator low speed	Stator high speed	Switch box stop circuit	Ignition coil primary input	Switch box bias
2 cylinder	200	20	200	150	NA
3 cylinder with original stator part No. 398-8778A10, A26 or A29	200	20	200	150	2-10 VDC
3 cylinder with upgraded stator part No. 398-9873A24	215	10	215	145	2-10 VDC
4 cylinder	200	20	200	150	NA
5 cylinder	NA	NA	200	150	NA
Converter voltage on 5-cylinder models is: Input—12 VDC; Output—260-300.					

Table 13 THUNDERBOLT CDI IGNITION SYSTEM
PEAK/DVA VOLTAGE SPECIFICATIONS AT 1000-4000 RPM

Models	Stator low speed	Stator high speed	Switch box stop circuit	Ignition coil primary input	Switch box bias
2 cylinder	200-330	130-300	200-360	180-280	NA
3 cylinder with original stator part No. 398-8778A10, A26 or A29	200-330	130-300	200-360	180-280	10-30 VDC
3 cylinder with upgraded stator part No. 398-9873A24	260-340	205-255	260-340	200-250	10-30 VDC
4 cylinder	200-330	130-300	200-360	180-280	NA
5 cylinder	NA	NA	200-360	180-280	NA

Table 14 THUNDERBOLT CDI IGNITION SYSTEM RESISTANCE SPECIFICATIONS

Models	Stator low speed	Stator high speed	Trigger	Ignition coil primary	Ignition coil secondary
2 cylinder	6800-7600	90-140	700-1000	.02-.04	800-1100
3 cylinder with original stator part No. 398-8778A10, A26 or A29	3600-4200	90-140	1100-1400	.02-.04	800-1100
3 cylinder with upgraded stator part No. 398-9873A24	1100-1600	30-35	1100-1400	.02-.04	800-1100
4 cylinder	6800-7600	90-140	700-1000	.02-.04	800-1100
5 cylinder	NA	NA	1100-1400	.02-.04	800-1100

Table 15 CDM IGNITION SYSTEM OUTPUT TESTS

	Cranking	Running at Idle Speed
Stator output	100 DVA minimum	200 DVA minimum
Trigger output	0.2-2.0 DVA	2 DVA minimum
Stop circuit output	100 DVA minimum	200 DVA minimum

Table 16 CDM IGNITION SYSTEM RESISTANCE SPECIFICATIONS

Red Lead	Black lead	Specifications
Pin A	Pin C	1150-1350 ohms
Pin A	Pin D	High reading (low reading with leads reversed)
Pin B	Pin D	Low reading (high reading with leads reversed)
Pin A	Spark plug lead	900-1200 ohms
Stator resistance is 500-600 ohms.		

Table 17 WIRING HARNESS STANDARD COLOR CODE CHANGES

Circuit or system	Model year 1984-1989	Model year 1989-1992	Model year 1993 and newer
Starting	Yellow	Yellow/Red	Yellow/Red
Tachometer	Purple	Gray	Gray
Stop 1 (ignition side)	White	Black/Yellow	Black/Yellow
Stop 2 (ground side)	Blue	Blue/Black	Black
Choke or Primer	Green	Yellow/Black	Yellow/Black
Overheat Warning	Orange	Tan	Tan/Blue
Switched B+	Red/Blue	Red/Blue	Purple
Protected B+	Red	Red/Purple	Red/Purple
Grounds	Black	Black	Black

Table 18 IGNITION AND ELECTRICAL TEST EQUIPMENT AND TOOLS

Description	Part No.
Multimeter/DVA tester	91-99750
Spark tester (air gap)	FT-11295
Timing light	91-99379
Shop tachometer/dwell meter	91-59339
Digital shop tachometer	79-17391A-1
Interface module (spark plug wire)	825824A-2
(continued)	

Table 18 IGNITION AND ELECTRICAL
TEST EQUIPMENT AND TOOLS (continued)

Description	Part No.
CDM ignition test harness	84-825207A2
Prestolite magneto CD ignition test adapters	
Harness adapter (7.5, 25 and 35 hp)	FT-11201
Harness adapter (60 hp)	FT-11237

Chapter Four

Lubrication, Maintenance and Tune-up

The modern marine engine delivers more power and performance than ever before, with higher compression ratios, new and improved electrical systems and other design advances. Proper lubrication, maintenance and tune-ups have become increasingly important as ways in which you can maintain a high level of performance, extend engine life and extract the maximum economy of operation.

You can do your own lubrication, maintenance and tune-ups if you follow the correct procedures and use common sense. The following information is based on recommendations from the manufacturer that will help keep your outboard motor or L-Drive operating at its peak performance level.

Tables 1-7 are at the end of the chapter.

LUBRICATION

Proper Fuel Selection

Two-stroke engines are lubricated by mixing oil with the fuel. The various components of the engine are lubricated as the fuel-oil mixture passes through the crankcase and cylinders.

Since the fuel serves the dual function of producing combustion and distributing the lubrication, never use low octane marine white gasoline or any other fuel not intended for use in modern gasoline-powered engines. Among other problems, such gasoline has a tendency to cause piston ring sticking and port plugging.

The *recommended* fuel is regular unleaded gasoline from a major supplier with a minimum pump posted octane rating of 87 with no alcohol additives. The *minimum* fuel requirements are regular unleaded with a minimum pump posted octane rating of 87 with no more than 10% ethanol. The use of methanol in any quantity is not recommended. Recently *reformulated* fuels have been introduced in parts of the United States that have not achieved federally mandated reductions in emissions. Reformulated fuels are specifically blended to reduce emissions. Reformulated fuels normally contain oxygenates, such as ethanol, methanol or MTBE (methyl tertiary butyl ether). Reformulated fuels may be used as long as they do not contain methanol and normal precautions for alcohol (ethanol) extended fuels are taken. See *Alcohol Extended Gasoline*. If the engine is used for severe service, hard working conditions or if detonation is suspected to be caused by poor grade gasolines, use mid-grade gasoline of 89-91 pump posted octane from a major supplier with no alcohol. The installation of a Quicksilver Water Separating Fuel Filter is recommended as a preventative measure on all permanently installed fuel systems. The manufacturer specifically recommends the installation of the Quicksilver Water Separating Fuel Filter if any alcohol blended or alcohol extended gasoline is used.

Sour Fuel

Under ideal conditions, fuel should not be stored for more than 60 days (especially fuel with alcohol additives). Gasoline forms gum and varnish deposits as it ages. A good grade of gasoline stabilizer may be used to extend the storage life of gasoline, but it is usually better to drain the fuel tank when storage exceeding 30 days is anticipated. Always use fresh gasoline when mixing fuel for your outboard or L-Drive.

Alcohol Extended Gasoline

Although the manufacturer does not recommend the use of gasoline that contains alcohol, the minimum gasoline specifications allow for a maximum of 10% ethanol to be used. Methanol is not recommended since the detrimental effects of methanol are more extreme than ethanol. If alcohol extended gasoline is being used, the following must be considered.

1. Alcohol extended gasoline promotes leaner air/fuel ratios, which can:
   a. Raise combustion chamber temperatures, leading to preignition and/or detonation.
   b. Cause hesitation or stumbling on acceleration.
   c. Cause hard starting, hot and cold.
   d. Cause the engine to produce slightly less horsepower

2. Alcohol extended gasoline attracts moisture, which can:
   a. Cause a water buildup in the fuel system.
   b. Block fuel filters.
   b. Block fuel metering components.
   c. Cause corrosion of metallic components in the fuel system and power head.

3. Alcohol extended gasoline deteriorates non-metallic components, such as:
   a. Rubber fuel lines.
   b. Primer bulbs.
   c. Fuel pump internal components.
   d. Carburetor internal components.
   e. Fuel recirculation components.

4. Alcohol extended gasoline promotes vapor lock and hot soak problems.

> *NOTE*
> *When the moisture content of the fuel reaches 0.5%, the water separates from the fuel and settles to the low points of the fuel system. This includes the fuel tank, fuel filters and carburetor float chambers. Alcohol extended fuels aggravate this situation.*

If any or all of these symptoms are regularly occurring, consider testing the fuel for alcohol or simply changing to a different gasoline supplier. If the symptoms are no longer present after the change, continue using the gasoline from the new supplier.

If usage of alcohol extended fuels is unavoidable, perform regular maintenance and inspections more often than normal. Pay special attention to changing or cleaning the fuel filters, inspecting rubber fuel system components for deterioration, inspecting metallic fuel system components for corrosion and monitoring the power head for warning signs of preignition and/or detonation on a regular basis. It is sometimes necessary to enrichen the carburetor's metering circuits to compensate for the leaning effect of these gasolines.

Reformulated gasolines that contain MTBE (methyl tertiary butyl ether) in normal concentrations have no side effects other those listed under No.1. This does not apply to reformulated gasoline that contains ethanol or methanol.

The following is an accepted and widely used field procedure for detecting alcohol in gasoline. Note that the gasoline should be checked prior to mixing with the oil. Use any small transparent bottle or tube that can be capped and can be provided with graduations or a mark at approximately 1/3 full. A pencil mark on a piece of adhesive tape will be sufficient.

1. Fill the container with water to the 1/3 third full mark.

2. Add gasoline until the container is almost full. Leave a small air space at the top.

3. Shake the container vigorously, then allow it to set for 3-5 minutes. If the volume of water appears to have increased, alcohol is present. If the dividing line between the water and gasoline becomes cloudy, reference from the center of the cloudy band.

This procedure can not differentiate between types of alcohol (ethanol or methanol), nor is it considered to be absolutely accurate from a scientific standpoint, but it is accurate enough to determine if sufficient alcohol is present to cause the user to take precautions.

Recommended Fuel Mixture

The recommended oil is Quicksilver Premium Plus Blend 2-Cycle Outboard Oil or a suitable equivalent NMMA certified TCW-3 engine oil. If TCW-2 engine oil must be used, the manufacturer recommends adding Quicksilver QuicKleen Fuel Treatment (**Table 2**) to the fuel to prevent excessive combustion chamber deposits. Mix QuicKleen Fuel Treatment as indicated on the container.

CAUTION
Do not, under any circumstances, use multigrade automotive oil, or any other oil designed for use in 4-stroke engines. Such oil is harmful to 2-stroke engines

and will result in extensive internal engine damage.

On all models except 1992 120 hp L-Drives, mix the fuel and oil as follows:

a. During the break-in period of a new or rebuilt power head (first 12 gallons of fuel), thoroughly mix two 16-ounce containers of the recommended oil with each 6 gallons of gasoline (or 16 ounces with each 3 gallons) in the remote fuel tank. This mixture provides a 25:1 fuel-oil ratio.

b. After the engine break-in period, mix one 16-ounce container of the recommended oil with each 6 gallons of gasoline (or 8 ounces with each 3 gallons) in the remote tank. This mixture provides 50:1 a fuel-oil ratio.

On 1992 120 hp L-Drive models (with oil injection):

a. To provide the additional lubrication necessary during the break-in period (first 12 gallons of fuel), use a 50:1 fuel-oil mixture (16 ounces of oil per 6 gallons gasoline) in the remote tank in combination with the oil injection system. This provides the power head with a 25:1 fuel-oil ratio.

b. After the break-in period, confirm the the oil injection system is functioning properly, then switch to straight gasoline in the fuel tank.

Correct Fuel Mixing

Mix the fuel and oil outdoors or in a well-ventilated indoor location. Mix the fuel directly in the remote fuel tank.

WARNING
Gasoline is an extreme fire hazard. Never use gasoline near heat, sparks or flame. Never smoke while mixing fuel.

Measure the required amounts of gasoline and oil accurately. Pour a small amount of oil into the remote tank and add a small amount of gasoline. Mix thoroughly by shaking or stirring vigor-

4

ously, then add the balance of the gasoline and oil and mix again.

Using less than the specified amount of oil will result in insufficient lubrication and extensive engine damage. Using more oil than specified causes spark plug fouling, erratic carburetion, excessive smoking and rapid carbon accumulation.

Cleanliness is of prime importance. Even a very small particle of dirt can cause carburetor malfunction. Always use fresh gasoline. Gum and varnish deposits tend to form in gasoline stored in a tank for any length of time. Using sour fuel can result in carburetor problems and spark plug fouling.

Above 32°F (0°C)

Measure the required amount of gasoline and Quicksilver Premium Plus Blend 2-Cycle Outboard Oil accurately. Pour the oil into the remote tank and add the fuel. Install the tank fill cap and mix the fuel by tipping the tank from side-to-side several times. See **Figure 1**.

If a built-in tank is used, insert a large filter-type funnel into the tank fill neck. Carefully pour the specified oil and gasoline into the funnel at the same time. See **Figure 2**.

Below 32°F (0°C)

Measure the required amount of gasoline and Quicksilver Premium Plus Blend 2-Cycle Outboard Oil accurately. Pour approximately one gallon of gasoline into the tank and then add the required amount of oil. Install the tank fill cap and shake the tank vigorously to mix thoroughly the fuel and oil. Remove the cap, add the balance of the gasoline and shake the tank again.

If a built-in tank is used, insert a large filter-type funnel into the tank fill neck. Mix the required amount of oil with one gallon of gasoline in a separate container. Carefully pour the mixture into the funnel at the same time the tank is being filled with gasoline.

Consistent Fuel Mixtures

The carburetor idle circuit is sensitive to fuel mixture variations which result from the use of different oils and gasolines or from inaccurate measuring and mixing. This may require frequent readjustment of the idle speed and mixture. Consistently prepare each batch of fuel exactly as the previous mix to prevent having constantly to readjust the carburetor.

Gearcase Lubrication

Check the gearcase lubricant level after the first 30 hours of operation and replace the lubricant at 100 hour or 6 month intervals (once per season minimum). Check the gearcase lubricant at 50 hour intervals. The manufacturer recommends using Quicksilver Premium Blend Gear Lube. If the recommended lubricant is not available, use a high-quality SAE 90 EP outboard gear lubricant.

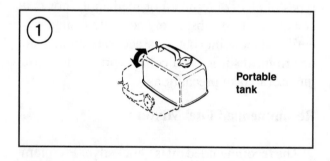

① Portable tank

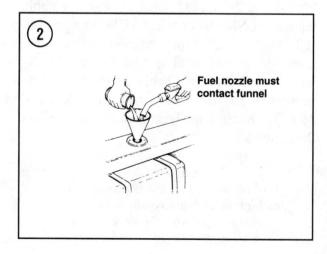

② Fuel nozzle must contact funnel

CAUTION
Do not use regular automotive grease in the gearcase. Its expansion and foam characteristics are not suitable for marine use.

Gearcase Lubricant Check

Before performing the gearcase lubricant check, identify the type of gearcase being seviced.

The lower gearcase on 4, 5, 9.9, 15, 25 (2-cylinder) and 35 hp models and 40 and 50 hp models prior to 1995 is identified by an exhaust exiting trim tab and the 2 plugs. See **Figure 3**. The top plug is a vent only. The bottom plug is fill and drain.

A Force 7.5 hp lower gearcase is dentified by an exhaust exiting trim tab and 3 plugs. The top plug's identification is cast into the gear housing. The top front plug is the fill, the top rear plug is the vent and the bottom plug is the drain. This gearcase is unique to the 7.5 hp model.

A Mercury small gearcase is used on 9.9 and 15 hp (1998) models. This gearcase utilizes a design that allows the exhaust to exit through the propeller. A single fill/drain plug and 1 vent plug is used on this type of gearcase.

A Force large engine lower gearcase (**Figure 4**) is identified by an exhaust exiting trim tab or

exhaust exiting trim tab and propeller. Both models have 3 plugs. The top plug's identification is cast into the gear housing. The top front plug is the fill, the top rear plug is the vent and the bottom plug is the drain. The drain plug on older models may be a pipe plug that is sealed with Loctite PST pipe sealant. This type of gearcase is used on 60, 85, 125, 150 hp and all L-Drive models. It is also used on 90 and 120 hp through 1994.

Mercury gearcases (**Figure 5**) are used on many of the newer models. The Mercury gearcases are identified by a anodic trim tab and exhaust exiting through the propeller. Some models use 2 vent plugs (**Figure 6**). The upper plugs are vents only and the lower plug is for draining and filling the gearcase. All vent plugs must be removed when draining and filling the gearcase lubricant.

A Mercury gearcase in used on all 25 hp 3-cylinder models. It utilizes a single drain/fill plug and 1 vent plug.

As with the 25 hp 3-cylinder models a Mercury gearcase is used on all 1995-1999 40 and 50 hp models. This gearcase uses a single drain/fill plug and 1 vent plug.

A similar gearcase (Mercury style) is used on all 1998 and prior 70 and 75 hp 3-cylinder models. It uses a single drain/fill plug and 2 vent plugs.

A Mercury large engine lower gearcase (**Figure 6**) is used on all 1995-1999 90-120 hp and

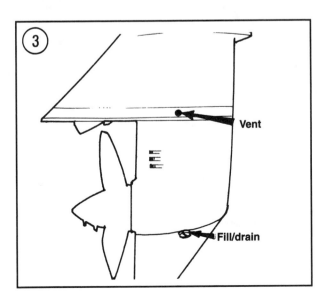

③ Vent

Fill/drain

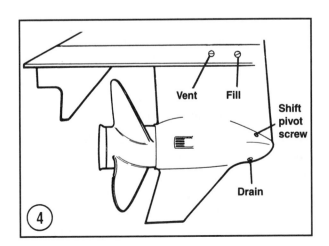

④ Vent Fill

Shift pivot screw

Drain

1999 75 hp models. This gearcase uses a single fill/drain plug and 2 vent plugs.

To ensure a correct gear lube check, the outboard motor must be in the upright position and not run for at least 2 hours prior to performing this procedure. Refer to **Figures 3-6** as required.

1. Remove the engine cover and disconnect the spark plug lead(s) as a safety precaution to prevent accidental starting of the engine.

2. Locate and loosen (but do not remove) the gearcase drain or fill/drain plug. Allow a small amount of lubricant to drain. If water is present inside the gearcase, it will drain before the lubricant. Retighten the drain plug securely.

3. If water is noted in Step 2, drain the lubricant completely and pressure test the gearcase to determine if a seal has failed or if the water is simply condensation in the gearcase. See Chapter Nine.

4. Remove the vent plug(s). Replace the accompanying sealing washer(s). The lubricant should be level with the bottom of the vent plug hole(s).

> *CAUTION*
> *The vent plug(s) are provided to vent displaced air while lubricant is added to the gearcase. Never attempt to fill or add lubricant without first removing the vent plug(s).*

5A. *Single vent models*—If the lubricant level is low, remove the fill or fill/drain plug. Replace the accompanying sealing washer. See **Figures 3-5**. Inject lubricant into the fill or fill/drain hole until lubricant flows from the vent plug.

   a. Install the vent plug. Install the fill or fill/drain plug. Tighten all plugs securely.
   b. Wipe any excess lubricant from the gearcase exterior.
   c. Recheck the lubricant level after 30 minutes.

5B. *Dual vent models*—If the lubricant level is low, remove the fill plug. Replace the accompanying sealing washer. See **Figure 6**. Inject lubricant into the fill hole until lubricant flows from a vent hole. Install the vent plug in the hole that is flowing oil. Continue to inject lubricant

until lubricant flows from the other vent hole. Install the last vent plug then install the fill plug. Tighten all plugs securely.

   a. Wipe any excess lubricant from the gearcase exterior.
   b. Recheck the lubricant level after 30 minutes.

Gearcase Lubricant Change

Refer to **Figures 3-6** for this procedure.

1. Remove the engine cover and disconnect the spark plug lead(s) to prevent accidental starting of the engine.

> *NOTE*
> *On models so equipped, do not mistake the shift pivot screw (**Figure 4** and **Figure 6**) for the drain plug. If the shift pivot screw is removed, complete disassembly of the gearcase will be required to reinstall the screw correctly.*

2. Place a clean container under the appropriate drain or fill/drain plug at the bottom of the gearcase and remove the plug. See **Figures 3-6**.

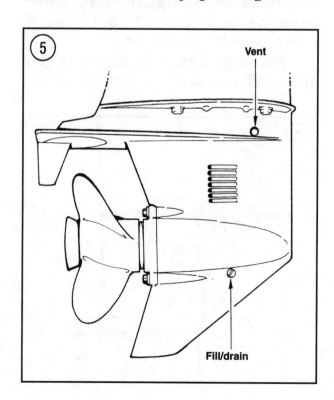

Remove the vent plug(s). Replace the sealing washers on all plugs. Allow the lubricant to drain fully from the gearcase.

3. Replace the drain plug on models that have a dedicated drain plug. Tighten the drain plug securely.

NOTE
If the lubricant has a milky color, water contamination is indicated. Pressure test

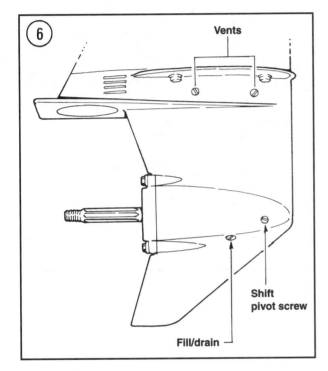

the gearcase (Chapter Nine) and correct any problems found. The presence of a small amount of metal filings and fine metal particles in the lubricant is normal, while an excessive amount of metal filings and larger chips indicates a problem. Remove and disassemble the gearcase to determine the source and cause of the metal filings and chips. Repair or replace any damaged parts. See Chapter Nine.

4. If no problems are indicated from the inspection of the used lubricant, refill the gearcase starting at Step 5 of *Gearcase Lubricant Check* in this chapter.

Propeller Shaft

The propeller shaft should be lubricated after every 100 hours of operation (50 hours of use in saltwater). Remove the propeller (Chapter Nine) and thoroughly clean any corrosion or dried grease, then coat the shaft spines with Quicksilver 2-4-C Marine Lubricant, Quicksilver Special Lube 101 or a suitable anticorrosion grease.

Other Lubrication Points

Refer to **Figures 7-21**, typical and **Table 1** for other lubrication points, frequency of lubrication and lubricant to be used. In addition to these lubrication points, some motors may also be equipped with grease fittings provided at critical locations where bearing surfaces are not externally exposed. These fittings should be lubricated at least once per season with an automotive type grease gun and Quicksilver 2-4-C Marine Lubricant or Quicksilver Special Lube 101.

CAUTION
When lubricating the steering cable on models so equipped, make sure its core is fully retracted into the cable housing. Lubricating the cable while extended may cause a hydraulic lock to occur.

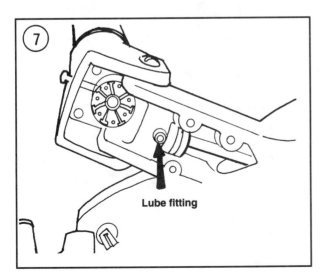

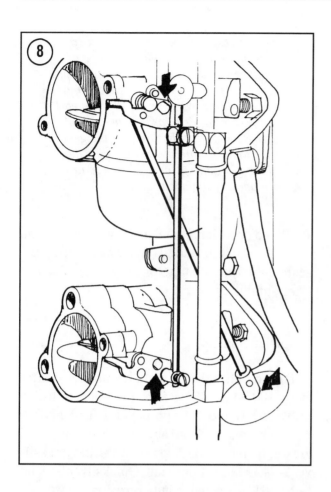

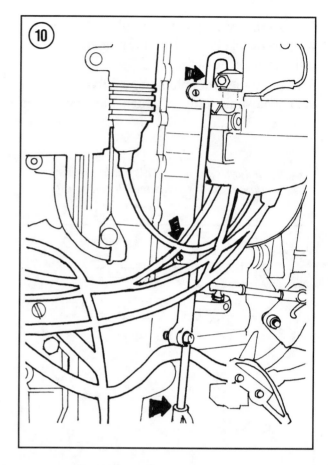

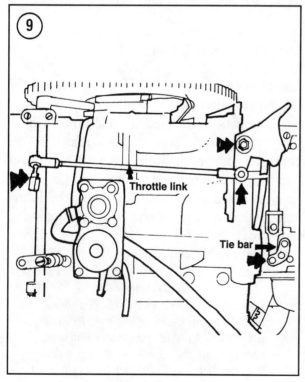

Throttle link

Tie bar

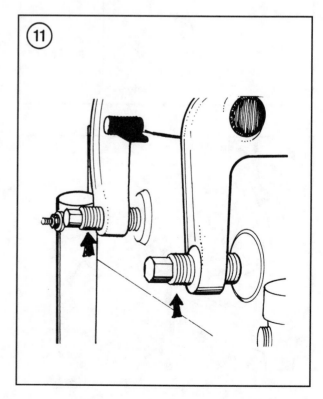

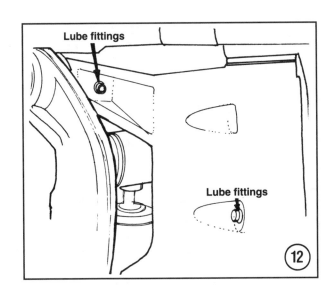

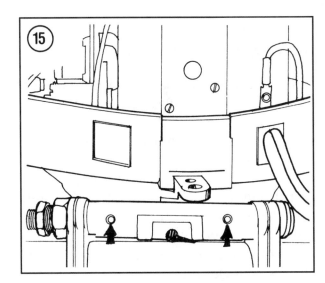

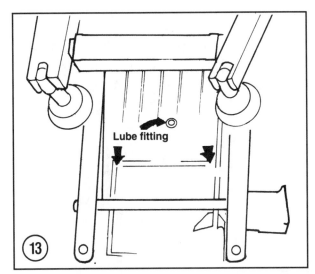

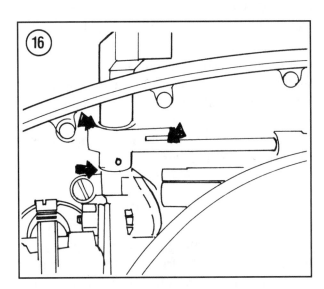

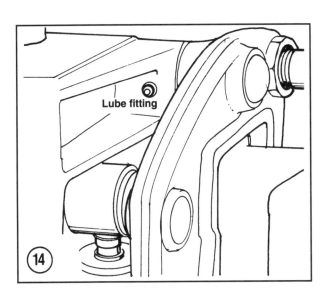

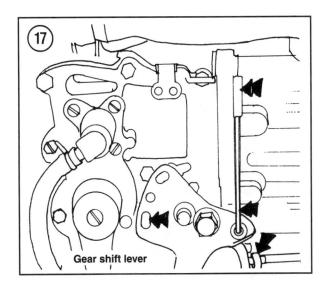

Saltwater Corrosion of
Gearcase Bearing Cage or Spool

Saltwater corrosion that is allowed to build up unchecked can eventually split the gearcase and destroy the lower unit. If the motor is used in saltwater, remove the propeller assembly, zinc anode or bearing cage cap and the bearing cage or spool (**Figure 22**, typical) at least once per year after the initial 30-hour inspection. Clean all corrosive deposits and dried lubricant from each end of the cage or spool.

Install new O-rings on cage or spool, wipe O-rings with Quicksilver 2-4-C Marine Lubricant or Quicksilver Special Lube 101 and install spool with new O-ring seals on spool bolts. If a zinc anode cover is used, apply a liberal amount of Loctite 242 to the anode screw threads. On models without the anode, coat the cap screw threads with a suitable antiseize compound. Coat propeller shaft splines with Quicksilver 2-4-C Marine Lubricant or a suitable antiseize grease, then install the propeller.

STORAGE

The major consideration when preparing an outboard motor or L-Drive for storage is to protect it from rust, corrosion, dirt or other contamination. The manufacturer recommends the following procedure:

1. Remove the engine cover.

2. Treat all fuel tanks with gasoline stabilizer. Mix according to manufacturers recommendations for *storage*. Gasoline stabilizer, when added to fresh gasoline:

   a. Prevents gum and varnish from forming in the fuel system.

   b. Controls moisture in the fuel system.

   c. Prevents modern fuels from reacting with brass and copper fuel system components.

   d. Stabilizes the fuel to prevent octane loss and prevents the fuel from going sour.

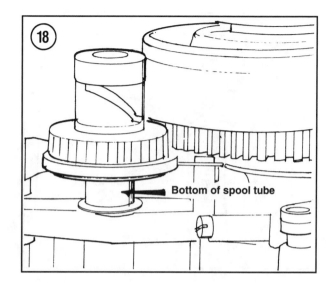

Bottom of spool tube

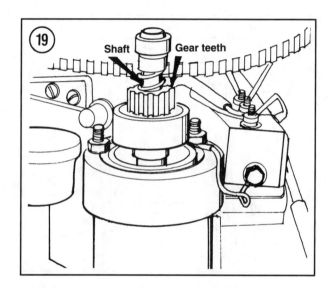

Shaft   Gear teeth

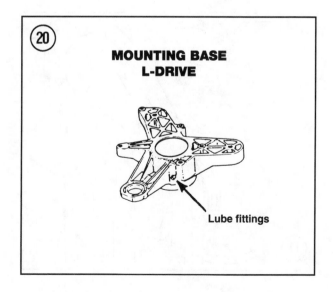

**MOUNTING BASE
L-DRIVE**

Lube fittings

3. Operate the engine in a test tank or on the boat in the water. Start the engine and run at fast idle until warmed up to operating temperature. This ensures that the gasoline stabilizer has had time to reach the carburetor(s).

4. With the engine running at fast idle, spray Quicksilver Storage Seal or equivalent (**Table 2**) into each carburetor throat, following the manufacturer's instructions. It is not necessary to disconnect the fuel supply line and run the engine out of fuel if gasoline stabilizer is used. Remove the motor from the water when the

application of Quicksilver Storage Seal is complete.

5. Remove spark plug(s) as described in this chapter. Pour approximately 1 ounce of Quicksilver Premium Plus Blend 2-Cycle Outboard Oil (or equivalent) into each spark plug hole. Manually rotate engine several revolutions to distribute the oil throughout the cylinder(s), then reinstall the spark plug(s).

NOTE
*Four types of engine mounted fuel filters are used. On newer engines, there is an in-line plastic fuel filter (**Figure 23**) between the fuel pump and the carburetor. On older 4 and 5 hp models with an integral gas tank, there is a filter mounted in the outlet fitting of the integral fuel tank. On older 5-15 hp models with portable fuel tanks, there is a filter*

UNIVERSAL JOINT HOUSING L-DRIVE

Lube fittings

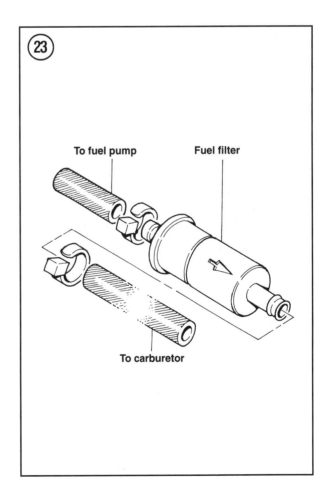

To fuel pump   Fuel filter

To carburetor

(*Figure 24*) in the inlet fitting of the fuel pump. On older 25-150 hp models, there is a filter (*Figure 25*) mounted in the fuel pump sediment bowl.

6. Service the in-line filter as follows:
   a. Cut the tie-straps from the fuel lines at each end of the filter. See **Figure 23**.
   b. Push the fuel lines off the filter with a flat-blade screwdriver. If the fuel lines are damaged or deteriorated, replace the lines.
   c. Install a new filter and secure with 2 new tie-straps or stainless steel worm clamps.
   d. Test the installation by squeezing the primer bulb and checking for fuel leaks.
7. Service the integral fuel tank filter as follows:
   a. Drain the fuel tank and remove the fuel tank outlet fitting.
   b. Clean the filter screen.
   c. Flush the fuel tank while the fitting is removed.
   d. Apply Loctite PST pipe sealant to the threads of the fitting. Reinstall the fitting.
   e. Replace the fuel line if it is damaged or deteriorated. Reconnect the fuel line and secure it with the original spring clamp, a tie-strap or a stainless steel worm clamp.
   f. Refill the fuel tank and check for fuel leaks.
8. Service the 5-15 hp models with the filter in the inlet fitting of the fuel pump as follows:
   a. Disconnect the fuel inlet hose from the lower fuel pump fitting. See **Figure 24**. Replace the fuel line if it is damaged or deteriorated.
   b. Remove the fuel pump inlet fitting and discard the filter.
   c. Install a new filter on the inlet fitting. Apply Loctite PST pipe sealant to the threads of the fitting
   d. Reinstall the fitting to the fuel pump.
   e. Reconnect the fuel line and secure it with the original spring clamp, a tie-strap or a stainless steel worm clamp.
   f. Test the installation by squeezing the primer bulb and checking for leaks.

9. Service the older 25-150 hp (including L-Drives) fuel pump filter as follows:
   a. Remove the fuel pump sediment bowl screw. See **Figure 25**.
   b. Remove the sediment bowl and filter from the fuel pump.
   c. Remove and clean or replace the filter screen.
   d. Install the screen into the sediment bowl with its turned edge facing the fuel pump.
   e. Install the sediment bowl and filter to the fuel pump with a new gasket. Tighten the bowl screw securely.
   f. Test the installation by squeezing the primer bulb and checking for fuel leaks.

10. Drain and refill gearcase as described in this chapter. Check condition of vent, fill or fill/drain plug gasket, and replace as required.

11. Refer to **Figures 7-21** and **Table 1** as appropriate and lubricate motor at all specified

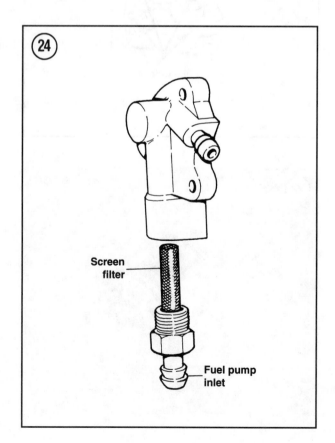

Screen filter

Fuel pump inlet

locations. See **Table 2** for recommended lubricants.

12. Clean the outboard motor or L-Drive, including all accessible power head parts. Coat with a good marine-type wax. Install the engine cover.

13. Remove the propeller and lubricate propeller shaft splines with Quicksilver 2-4-C Marine Lubricant, Special Lube 101 or a suitable anticorrosion grease, then reinstall the propeller.

14. Store the outboard motor in an upright position, in a dry and well-ventilated area.

15. Service the battery as follows:

a. Disconnect the negative, then the positive battery cables from the battery.

b. Remove all grease, corrosion and dirt from the battery surface.

c. Check the electrolyte level in each battery cell. If necessary, fill to the proper level with distilled water. Fluid level in each cell should not be higher than 3/16 in. above the battery plates.

d. Lubricate the terminal screws with a suitable anticorrosion grease or petroleum jelly.

CAUTION
A discharged battery can be damaged by freezing.

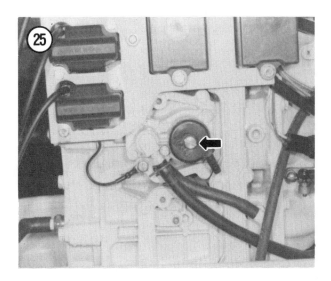

e. With the battery in a fully charged condition (specific gravity at 1.260-1.275), store in a dry area. If possible, store battery where ambient temperature will not drop to the freezing point.

f. Recharge the battery every 45 days or whenever the specific gravity drops below 1.230. Before charging, check electrolyte level and top up if necessary. The charging rate should not exceed 6 amps. Discontinue charging when the specific gravity reaches 1.260 at 80°F (27°C).

g. Before placing the battery back into service following storage, remove the excess grease from the terminals, leaving a small amount. Install battery in a fully charged condition.

COMPLETE SUBMERSION

An outboard motor which has been lost overboard should be recovered as quickly as possible. If the motor was running when submerged, disassemble and clean it immediately—any delay will result in rust and corrosion of internal components once it has been removed from the water. If the motor was not running and appears to be undamaged mechanically with no abrasive dirt or silt inside, take the following emergency steps *immediately*.

1. Wash the outside of the motor with clean water to remove weeds, mud and other debris.

2. Remove the engine cover.

3. If recovered from saltwater, flush motor completely with freshwater and spray entire power head with Quicksilver Corrosion Guard or a suitable equivalent rust preventive spray.

4. Remove the spark plug(s) as described in this chapter.

CAUTION
Do not force the motor if it does not turn over freely by hand in Step 5. This may be an indication of internal damage such

as a bent connecting rod or broken piston.

5. Drain as much water as possible from the power head by placing the motor in a horizontal position. Manually rotate the flywheel by hand with the spark plug hole(s) facing downward.

6. Dry and reinstall the spark plug(s).

7. Dry all ignition components and spray with Quicksilver Corrosion Guard or equivalent.

8. Drain the fuel lines and carburetor(s).

9. On models with an integral fuel tank, drain the tank and flush with fresh gasoline until all water is removed.

CAUTION
If there is a possibility that sand has entered the power head, do not try to start the motor or severe internal damage may occur.

10. Try starting the motor with a fresh fuel source. If the motor will start, allow it to run at least 1 hour to eliminate any water remaining inside the power head.

CAUTION
If it is not possible to disassemble and clean the motor immediately in Step 11, resubmerge the motor in water to prevent rust and corrosion. The motor should be retrieved from the water only when it can be properly serviced.

11. If the motor will not start in Step 10, attempt to determine if the cause is fuel, electrical or mechanical, then repair as necessary. If the motor cannot be started within 2 hours, the power head *must* be disassembled, cleaned and thoroughly oiled as soon as possible.

ANTICORROSION MAINTENANCE

1. Flush the cooling system with freshwater as described in this chapter after each time the

motor is used in saltwater. Wash exterior with freshwater.

2. Dry exterior of the motor and apply primer over any nicks and scratches. Use only Quicksilver Spray Paint of the appropriate color. Do not use paint containing mercury or copper. Do not paint sacrificial anodes.

3. Spray power head and all electrical connections with Quicksilver Corrosion Guard or a good quality corrosion/rust preventive.

4. Check sacrificial anodes. Replace any that are less than half their original size.

5. If the outboard motor or L-Drive is operated consistently in saltwater, reduce lubrication intervals in **Table 1** by one-half.

ENGINE FLUSHING

Periodic engine flushing will prevent salt or silt deposits from accumulating in the water passages. This procedure should also be performed whenever the outboard motor or L-Drive is operated in saltwater, brackish or polluted water.

Keep the motor in an upright position during and after flushing. This prevents water from passing into the power head through the drive shaft housing and exhaust ports during the flushing procedure. It also eliminates the possibility of residual water being trapped in the drive shaft housing or other passages.

1. Attach a flushing device according to the manufacturer's instructions.

2. Connect a garden hose between a water tap and the flushing device.

3. Open the water tap partially—do not use full pressure.

4. Shift into NEUTRAL, then start motor. Keep engine speed between 800-1,100 rpm.

5. Adjust water flow so that there is a slight loss of water around the rubber cups of the flushing device.

6. Check the motor to make sure that water is being discharged from the "tell-tale" nozzle. If

not, stop the motor *immediately* and determine the cause of the problem.

CAUTION
Flush the motor for at least 5 minutes if used in saltwater.

7. Flush the motor until discharged water is clean, then stop motor.

8. Close the water tap and remove the flushing device from the lower unit.

TUNE-UP

A tune-up consists of a series of inspections, adjustments and parts replacement to compensate for normal wear and deterioration of specific components. Regular tune-up is important for reliability, performance and economy. The manufacturer recommends that Force outboard motors and L-Drives be serviced every 6 months or after each 100 hours of operation, whichever occurs first. If subjected to limited use, the engine should be tuned at least once per year.

Since proper outboard motor and L-Drive operation depends upon a number of interrelated system functions, a tune-up should consist of a thorough and systematic procedure of analysis and correction. The best results are seldom obtained with a partial or limited tune-up.

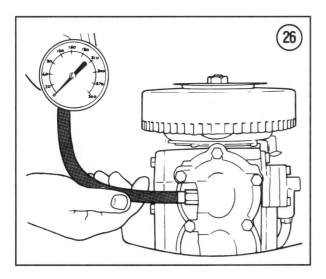

Prior to performing a tune-up, flush the motor as described in this chapter and check for satisfactory water pump operation.

The tune-up sequence recommended by the manufacturer includes the following:

 a. Compression check.
 b. Checking cylinder head torque.
 c. Spark plug service.
 d. Gearcase and water pump check.
 e. Fuel system service.
 f. Ignition system service.
 g. Battery, starter motor and solenoid check (if so equipped).
 h. Wiring harness check.
 i. Timing, synchronization and adjustment.
 j. Performance test (on boat).

Any time the fuel or ignition systems are adjusted, or if defective parts are replaced, the ignition timing, synchronization and adjustment *must* be checked and/or adjusted. These procedures are described in Chapter Five. Perform the timing, synchronization and adjustment procedure for your engine before running the performance test.

COMPRESSION CHECK

An accurate cylinder compression check gives a good idea of the condition of the basic working parts of the engine. It is also an important first step in any tune-up; a motor with low or unequal compression between cylinders *cannot* be satisfactorily tuned. Any compression problem discovered during this check must be corrected before continuing with the tune-up procedure.

1. With the engine warm, disconnect the spark plug wire(s) and remove the spark plug(s) as described in this chapter.

2. Ground the spark plug wire(s) to the engine to disable the ignition system.

3. Connect the compression tester to the top spark plug hole according to the tester manufacturer's instructions (**Figure 26**).

4. Make sure the throttle is set to the wide-open position and crank the engine through at least 4 compression strokes. Record the compression reading.

5. Repeat Step 3 and Step 4 on each cylinder of multicylinder models.

While minimum cylinder compression should not be less than shown in **Table 3**, the actual readings are *generally* not as important as the variation between cylinders when interpreting the results.

NOTE
*On some late model 3- and 4-cylinder models, the compression is staggered. On 3-cylinder models, the specification for cylinder No.1 is lower than the specifications for cylinders No.2 and No.3. On 4-cylinder models, the specifications for cylinders No.1 and No.4 are lower than the specifications for cylinders No.2 and No.3. Refer to **Table 4**.*

A variation of more than 15 psi (103 kPa) between 2 cylinders indicates a problem. Before disassembling and inspecting any part of the engine, treat the engine with Quicksilver Power Tune Engine Cleaner, following its manufacturer's instructions. Quicksilver Power Tune is designed to remove combustion chamber deposits and free stuck piston rings. Retest the compression after the treatment. If compression is restored, continue with the next step of the tune-up sequence.

If the compression is still unacceptable, remove the cylinder head and inspect the cylinder wall(s), piston(s) and head gasket condition. If the cylinder wall(s), piston(s) and head gasket show no evidence of damage or failure, the piston rings are worn and must be replaced.

NOTE
Using quality gasoline and 2-cycle oil will minimize combustion chamber deposits and piston ring sticking. If the use of poor quality gasoline and 2-cycle oil is unavoidable, use Quicksilver QuicKleen Fuel Treatment regularly. Perform

*Quicksilver Power Tune Engine Cleaner applications every 100 hours of operation or as required. See **Table 2**.*

Some high-hour outboard motors may be plagued by hard starting and generally poor running for which there seems to be no good cause. Carburetion and ignition check out satisfactorily and a compression test show that the piston(s), rings and cylinder(s) are in acceptable condition.

What a compression test does *not* show is lack of primary compression. In a 2-stroke engine, the crankcase must be alternately under high pressure and low pressure. After the piston closes the intake port, further downward movement of the piston causes the entrapped mixture to be pressurized so that it can rush quickly into the cylinder when the scavenging ports are opened. Upward piston movement creates a lower pressure in the crankcase, enabling the fuel-air mixture to be drawn into the crankcase from the carburetor.

When the crankshaft seals or crankcase gaskets leak, the crankcase cannot hold pressure and proper engine operation becomes impossible. Any other source of leakage, such as defective cylinder base gaskets or a porous or cracked crankcase casting, will result in the same condition.

If the power head shows evidence of overheating (discolored or scorched paint) but the compression test turns up nothing abnormal, check the cylinder(s) visually through the transfer ports for possible scoring. A cylinder can be slightly scored and still deliver a relatively good compression reading. In such cases, it is also a good idea to double-check the water pump operation as a possible cause for overheating.

CYLINDER HEAD BOLT TORQUE

Loosen each bolt and retighten to the specifications in **Table 5**. Refer to Chapter Nine for the proper tightening sequence according to engine.

SPARK PLUGS

Force outboard motors and L-Drives are equipped with Champion spark plugs selected for average use conditions. Under adverse or severe duty conditions, the recommended spark plug may foul or overheat. In such cases, check the ignition and carburetion systems to make sure they are operating correctly. If no defect is found, replace the spark plug with one of a hotter or colder heat range as required. **Table 7** lists the recommended spark plugs for all models covered in this manual.

Spark Plug Removal

CAUTION
Whenever the spark plugs are removed, dirt surrounding the base of the plugs can fall into the plug holes. This can result in expensive engine damage.

1. Clean the area around the base of the plug(s). Use clean air from an air compressor if available. If not, use a can of compressed inert gas, available from photo stores.
2. Disconnect the spark plug wire(s) by twisting the wire boot back and forth on the spark plug while pulling outward. Pulling on the wire instead of the boot may damage the wire.
3. Remove the plug(s) with an appropriate size spark plug socket or box-end wrench. On multicylinder engines, keep the plugs in the order they were removed.
4. Examine each spark plug. Compare its condition with **Figure 27** (conventional gap) or **Figure 28** (surface gap). Spark plug condition indicates engine condition and can warn of developing problems.
5. Check each plug for the correct make and heat range. All should be of the same make and number or heat range.
6. Discard the plugs. Although they could be cleaned and reused, if in good condition, the best tune-up results will be obtained by installing new spark plugs.

Spark Plug Gapping
(Conventional Gap Only)

New spark plugs should be carefully gapped to ensure a reliable, consistent spark. Use a special spark plug tool with a wire gauge. See **Figure 29** for a common type of plug gapping tool.

1. Remove the spark plugs and gaskets from the boxes and install the gaskets on the plugs.

NOTE
*Some spark plug brands may have small terminals that must be screwed onto the spark plug prior to installing. See **Figure 30**.*

2. Insert the appropriate wire gauge between the electrodes. If the gap is correct, there will be a slight drag as the wire is pulled through. If there is not drag or if the wire will not pull through, bend the side electrode with the gapping tool (**Figure 31**) to change the gap as necessary. Remeasure with the wire gauge. See **Table 7**.

CAUTION
Never attempt to close the electrode gap by tapping the spark plug on a solid surface. This can damage the plug internally. Always use the gapping tool to open or close the gap.

Spark Plug Installation

Improper installation is a common cause of poor spark plug performance in outboard motors and L-Drives. The spark plug seat in the cylinder

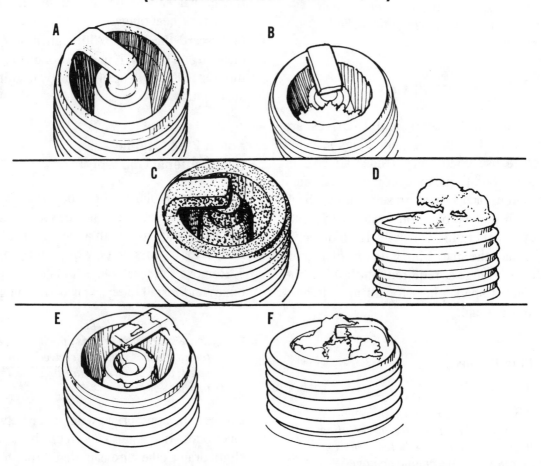

**SPARK PLUG ANALYSIS
(CONVENTIONAL GAP SPARK PLUGS)**

A. **NORMAL**—Light tan to gray color of insulator indicates correct heat range. Few deposits are present and the electrodes are not burned.

B. **CORE BRIDGING**—These defects are caused by excessive combustion chamber deposits striking and adhering to the firing end of the plug. In this case, they wedge or fuse between the electrode and core nose. They originate from the piston and cylinder head surfaces. Deposits are formed by one or more of the following:
1. Excessive carbon in cylinder.
2. Use of non-recommended oils.
3. Immediate high-speed operation after prolonged trolling.
4. Improper fuel-oil ratio.

C. **WET FOULING**—Damp or wet, black carbon coating over entire firing end of plug. Forms sludge in some engines. Caused by one or more of the following:
1. Spark plug heat range too cold.
2. Prolonged trolling.
3. Low-speed carburetor adjustment too rich.

4. Improper fuel-oil ratio.
5. Induction manifold bleed-off passage obstructed.
6. Worn or defective breaker points.

D. **GAP BRIDGING**—Similar to core bridging, except the combustion particles are wedged or fused between the electrodes. Causes are the same.

E. **OVERHEATING**—Badly worn electrodes and premature gap wear are indicative of this problem, along with a gray or white "blistered" appearance on the insulator. Caused by one or more of the following:
1. Spark plug heat range too hot.
2. Incorrect propeller usage, causing engine to lug.
3. Worn or defective water pump.
4. Restricted water intake or restriction somewhere in the cooling system.

F. **ASH DEPOSITS OR LEAD FOULING**—Ash deposits are light brown to white in color and result from use of fuel or oil additives. Lead fouling produces a yellowish brown discoloration and can be avoided by using unleaded fuels.

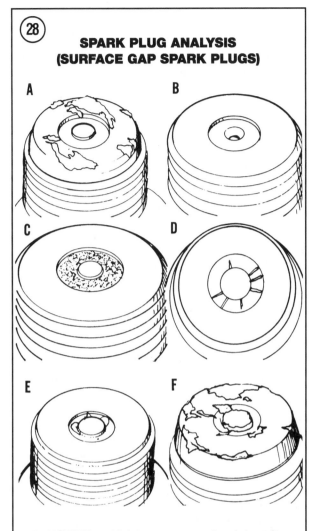

**SPARK PLUG ANALYSIS
(SURFACE GAP SPARK PLUGS)**

A. B.

C. D.

E. F.

A. **NORMAL** — Light tan or gray colored deposits
   indicate that the engine/ignition system condition
   is good. Electrode wear indicates normal spark
   rotation.
B. **WORN OUT** — Excessive electrode wear can
   cause hard starting or a misfire during acceleration.
C. **COLD FOULED** — Wet oil or fuel deposits are
   caused by "drowning" the plug with raw fuel mix
   during cranking, overrich carburetion or an improper fuel:oil ratio. Weak ignition will also con-
   tribute to this condition.
D. **CARBON TRACKING** — Electrically conductive
   deposits on the firing end provide a low-resis-
   tance path for the voltage.
E. **CONCENTRATED ARC** — Multi-colored appearance is normal. It is caused by electricity consistently following the same firing path. Arc path
   changes with deposit conductivity and gap erosion.
F. **EROSION THROW-OFF** — Caused by preignition.
   This is not a plug problem but the result of engine
   damage. Check engine to determine cause and
   extent of damage.

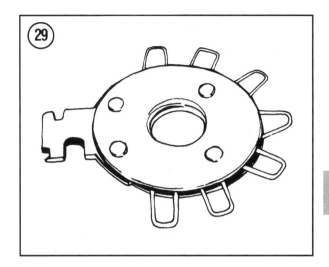

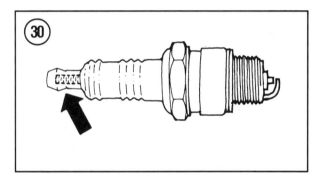

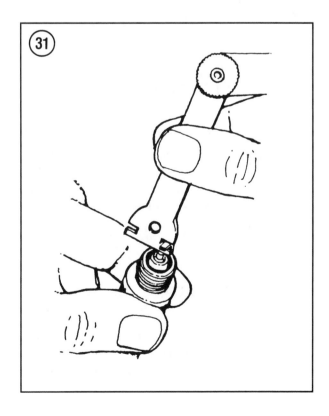

4

head must be clean and the spark plug gasket must be fully compressed against the seat for the required heat transfer to occur. This requires close attention to spark plug tightening during installation.

1. Inspect the spark plug hole threads. Clean threads with a thread chaser (**Figure 32**) if necessary. Wipe cylinder head seats clean before installing the plugs.

2. Screw each plug in by hand until it seats. Very little effort should be required. If force is necessary, the cause must be determined and corrected before installing plug.

3. Tighten the spark plugs to 10-15 ft.-lb. using a torque wrench, if available. If not, seat the plug finger-tight on the gasket, then tighten an additional 1/4 turn.

4. Inspect each spark plug wire before reconnecting to the spark plug. If insulation is damaged or deteriorated, install a new plug wire. Push wire boot onto plug terminal and make sure it seats fully.

GEARCASE AND WATER PUMP CHECK

A faulty water pump or one that performs below specifications may result in extensive engine damage. Thus, it is a good idea to replace the water pump impeller, seals and gaskets once per year or whenever the lower unit is removed for service. See Chapter Nine.

FUEL SYSTEM SERVICE

The clearance between the carburetor throat and choke valve should not be greater than 0.015 in. (0.38 mm) when the choke is closed or hard cold starting will result.

Fuel Hoses

1. Visually check all fuel hoses for kinks, leaks, deterioration or other damage.
2. Disconnect fuel hoses and blow out with compressed air to dislodge any contamination or foreign material.
3. Replace any damaged or deteriorated hoses. Use alcohol resistant replacement fuel hose.
4. Reconnect all hoses and secure with the original spring clamps, tie-straps or stainless steel worm clamps.
5. Test the installation by squeezing the primer bulb and checking for fuel leaks.

Engine Fuel Filter

NOTE
*Four types of engine mounted fuel filters are used. On newer engines, there is an in-line plastic fuel filter (**Figure 23**) between the fuel pump and the carburetor. On older 4 and 5 hp models with an integral gas tank, there is a filter mounted in the outlet fitting of the integral fuel tank. On older 5-15 hp models with portable fuel tanks, there is a filter (**Figure 24**) in the inlet fitting of the fuel pump. On older 25-150 hp models, there is a filter (**Figure 25**) mounted in the fuel pump sediment bowl.*

1. Service the in-line filter as follows:
   a. Cut the tie-straps from the fuel lines at each end of the filter. See **Figure 23**.
   b. Push the fuel lines off the filter with a flat blade screwdriver. If the fuel lines are damaged or deteriorated, replace the lines.
   c. Install a new filter and secure with 2 new tie-straps or stainless steel worm clamps.
   d. Test the installation by squeezing the primer bulb and checking for fuel leaks.
2. Service the integral fuel tank filter as follows:
   a. Drain the fuel tank and remove the fuel tank outlet fitting.
   b. Clean the filter screen.
   c. Flush the fuel tank while the fitting is removed.
   d. Apply Loctite PST pipe sealant to the threads of the fitting. Reinstall the fitting.
   e. Replace the fuel line if it is damaged or deteriorated. Reconnect the fuel line and secure it with the original spring clamp, a tie-strap or a stainless steel worm clamp.
   f. Refill the fuel tank and check for fuel leaks.
3. Service the 5-15 hp models with the filter in the inlet fitting of the fuel pump as follows:
   a. Disconnect the fuel inlet hose from the lower fuel pump fitting. See **Figure 24**. Replace the fuel line if it is damaged or deteriorated.
   b. Remove the fuel pump inlet fitting and discard the filter.
   c. Install a new filter on the inlet fitting. Apply Loctite PST pipe sealant to the threads of the fitting
   d. Reinstall the fitting to the fuel pump.
   e. Reconnect the fuel line and secure it with the original spring clamp, a tie-strap or a stainless steel worm clamp.
   f. Test the installation by squeezing the primer bulb and checking for leaks.
4. Service the older 25-150 hp (including L-Drives) fuel pump filter as follows:
   a. Remove the fuel pump sediment bowl screw. See **Figure 25**.

   b. Remove the sediment bowl and filter from the fuel pump.
   c. Remove and clean or replace the filter screen.
   d. Install the screen into the sediment bowl with its turned edge facing the fuel pump.
   e. Install the sediment bowl and filter to the fuel pump with a new gasket. Tighten the bowl screw securely.
   f. Test the installation by squeezing the primer bulb and checking for fuel leaks.

4

BREAKER POINT IGNITION SYSTEM SERVICE

The condition and gap of the breaker points will greatly affect engine operation. Burned or badly oxidized points will allow little or no current to pass through the contacts. A breaker point gap that is too narrow will cause the timing to be slow. Excessive breaker point gap will not allow the ignition coil to build up sufficient voltage resulting in a weak spark.

While slightly pitted points can be dressed with a point file, this should be considered temporary, as the points may arc excessively after filing. Oxidized, dirty or oily points can be cleaned with alcohol; however, new points are inexpensive and preferred when performing a tune-up.

The condenser absorbs the surge of primary current and prevents arcing across the contacts when the points open. Although condensers can be tested (Chapter Three), they are inexpensive and should be replaced as a matter of course when the breaker points are replaced.

NOTE
Breaker point gap must be adjusted correctly. An error of 0.015 in. (0.38 mm) will change ignition timing by as much as one degree. With multicylinder engines, variation in the gap between breaker point sets will affect timing by several degrees.

Breaker point gap on all models so equipped should be adjusted to 0.015 in. (0.38 mm)(50 hp) or 0.020 in. (0.51 mm)(all others). The following procedure involves adjusting breaker point gap with a flat feeler gauge. Some marine technicians prefer to use a test light to indicate precisely when the points open and close.

> *CAUTION*
> *Always rotate the crankshaft in a clockwise direction during the following procedure. If rotated counterclockwise, the water pump impeller may be damaged.*

Magneto Plate
Breaker Point Replacement
(1-Cylinder Models)

Refer to **Figure 33** for this procedure.

1. Disconnect the negative battery cable, if so equipped.
2. Remove the engine cover.
3. Remove the flywheel. See Chapter Eight.
4. Remove the 2 screws holding the breaker point set to the stator plate.
5. Disconnect the coil and condenser leads at the breaker point set. Remove the breaker point set.
6. Remove the screw holding the condenser to the stator plate and remove the condenser.
7. Install a new breaker point set on the stator plate. Install but do not tighten the breaker point screws.
8. Install a new condenser on the stator plate and tighten attaching screw securely, then connect the coil and condenser leads to the breaker point set.

> *CAUTION*
> *Do not over-lubricate the wick in Step 9. Excessive lubrication will result in premature breaker point failure.*

9. Squeeze the cam lube wick to determine if adequate lubrication is present in the wick. If dry, work a drop of motor oil into the wick with your fingers.

10. Adjust the breaker point gap as described in this chapter.

11. Reverse Steps 1-3 to complete installation.

Magneto Plate
Breaker Point Adjustment
(1-Cylinder Models)

1. Install the flywheel screw on the crankshaft and rotate the magneto stator to the full-throttle position.

2. Place a wrench on the flywheel screw and rotate the crankshaft clockwise until the cam index mark aligns with the breaker point cam follower. See **Figure 34**.

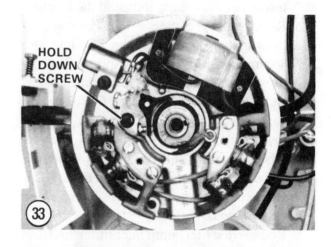

3. Turn the points adjusting screw to obtain a 0.020 in. gap when measured with a feeler gauge. The gap is correct when the feeler gauge offers a slight drag as it is slipped between the points. When the gap is correct, tighten the hold-down screw securely. Recheck the gap after tightening the screws.

4. Attach a spring tension gauge (part T-8974) and measure the breaker point spring tension (**Figure 35**) at right angles to the surface at the center of contact. Replace the breaker point set if the spring tension is not 16-32 oz.

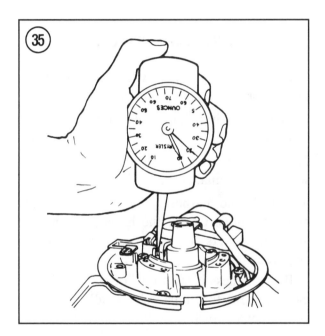

Magneto Plate
Breaker Point Replacement
(2-Cylinder Models)

1. Disconnect the negative battery cable.
2. Remove the engine cover.
3. Remove the flywheel. See Chapter Eight.
4. Remove the 2 screws securing the breaker points to the stator plate. See **Figure 36**.
5. Disconnect the coil and condenser leads at the breaker point set. Remove the breaker points.
6. Remove the screw securing the condenser to the stator plate and remove the condenser.
7. Repeat Steps 4-6 to remove the remaining breaker point set and condenser.
8. Install a new breaker point set on the stator plate. Install but do not tighten the hold-down screws.
9. Install a new condenser on the stator plate and tighten attaching screw securely, then connect the coil and condenser leads to the breaker points.
10. Repeat Step 8 and Step 9 to install the remaining point set and condenser.

> *CAUTION*
> *Do not over-lubricate the wick in Step 11. Excessive lubrication will result in premature breaker point failure.*

11. Squeeze the cam lube wick to determine if sufficient lubrication is present in the wick. If dry, work a drop of motor oil into the wick with your fingers.
12. Adjust the breaker point gaps as described in this chapter.
13. Reverse Steps 1-3 to complete installation.

Magneto Plate
Breaker Point Adjustment
(2-Cylinder Models)

> *CAUTION*
> *On 50 hp models check the ignition timing after breaker point replacement or adjustment. See Chapter Five.*

1. Move the magneto stator ring to the full-throttle position.

2. Install the flywheel nut onto the crankshaft so crankshaft can be rotated using a wrench. On 1984-1986 9.9/15 hp models, rotate the crankshaft clockwise until the breaker point rubbing block is approximately 10° beyond the top of the cam ramp (points will not open any wider). Place a mark on the cam for reference when adjusting the remaining breaker point set. On all other models, an index mark is provided on the cam. Rotate crankshaft clockwise to align index mark on cam with the breaker point rubbing block.

3. Turn the point set adjusting screw to obtain a 0.015 in. (0.38 mm) gap on 50 hp models and 0.020 in. (0.51 mm) on all other models. The gap is correct when the feeler gauge offers a slight drag as it is slipped between the points. When the gap is correct, tighten the hold-down screw securely, then recheck gap.

4. Rotate the crankshaft clockwise 2 full revolutions and recheck the point gap.

5. Rotate the crankshaft clockwise until the index mark is aligned with the rubbing block on the remaining breaker point set.

6. Repeat Step 3 and Step 4 to adjust the second breaker point set.

7. Attach a spring tension gauge (part No. T-8974) and measure the breaker point spring tension (**Figure 35**) at right angles to the surface at the center of contact. Replace breaker points if the spring tension is not within 24-32 oz. on 50 hp models or 16-32 oz. on all other models.

BATTERY AND STARTER MOTOR CHECK (ELECTRIC START MODELS)

1. Check the battery state of charge. See Chapter Seven.

2. Connect a voltmeter between the starter motor positive terminal (**Figure 37**) and ground.

3. Turn the ignition to the START position and note the voltmeter reading while the engine is cranking.

    a. If the voltage is 9.5 volts or higher and the cranking speed is normal, the starting system is functioning normally and the battery is of sufficient capacity for the engine.

    b. If the voltage is below 9.5 volts and/or the cranking speed is below normal, the starting system is malfunctioning. Refer to Chapter Three.

WIRING HARNESS CHECK

Figure 38 shows typical wiring harness installations for terminal block models.

1. Check the wiring harness for frayed or chafed insulation.

2. Check for loose connections between the wires and terminal ends.

3. Check the harness connectors for bent electrical pins. Check the harness connector and pin sockets for corrosion, and clean as required.

4. If the harness is suspected of contributing to electrical malfunctions, check all wires for continuity and resistance between harness con-

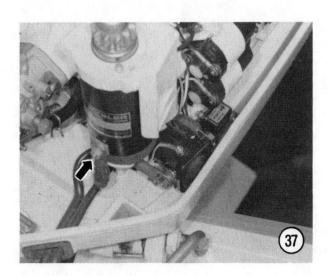

nectors and terminal ends. Repair or replace as required.

ENGINE SYNCHRONIZATION AND ADJUSTMENT

See Chapter Five.

PERFORMANCE TEST (ON BOAT)

Before performance testing the engine, make sure that the boat bottom is cleaned of all marine growth. Inspect the boat bottom for excessive hook or rocker (**Figure 39**). Any of these condi-

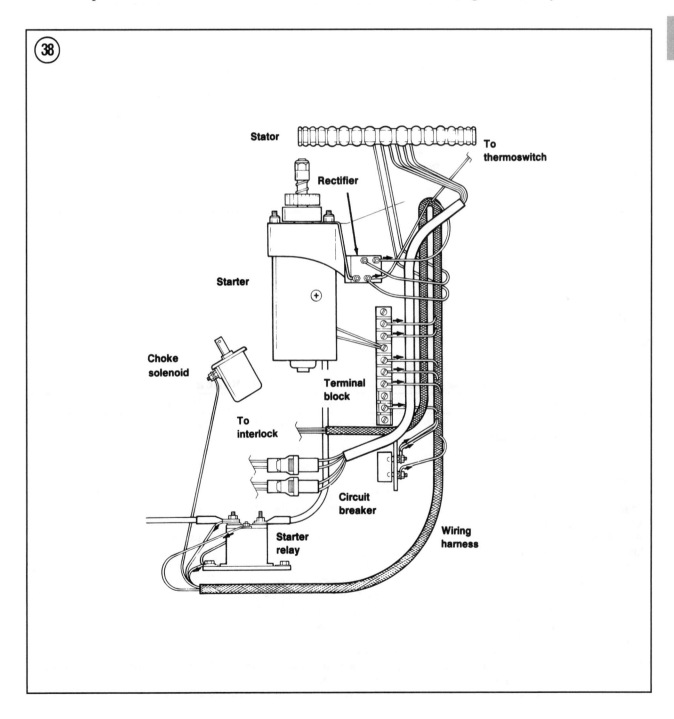

38

Stator

To thermoswitch

Rectifier

Starter

Choke solenoid

Terminal block

To interlock

Circuit breaker

Starter relay

Wiring harness

tions will reduce performance considerably. The boat should be performance tested with an average load and with the motor tilted or trimmed at the optimum running angle.

Check engine rpm at full throttle. If not within the recommended operating range as specified in Chapter Five, check the propeller pitch. A higher pitch propeller will reduce engine speed while a lower pitch propeller will increase speed.

Readjust the idle mixture and speed under actual operating conditions as required to obtain the optimum low-speed engine performance.

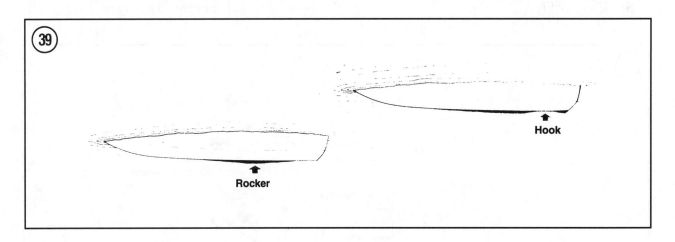

Hook

Rocker

Table 1 LUBRICATION AND MAINTENANCE

Lubrication points	Quicksilver Lubricant	Figure
Steering arm	2-4-C or Special Lube 101	5
Carburetor and choke linkage	2-4-C	6
Throttle linkage	Special Lube 101	7
Tower shaft	Special Lube 101	8
Clamp screws	2-4-C or Special Lube 101	9
Swivel bracket and tilt lock	Special Lube 101	10, 11
Stern bracket	2-4-C or Special Lube 101	12
Steering support tube	2-4-C	13
Shift linkage	Special Lube 101	14, 15
Manual starter pinion gear	2-4-C	16
Electric starter pinion gear	2-4-C	17
Propeller shaft splines	Anticorrosion grease, 2-4-C or Special Lube 101	
Drive shaft splines	2-4-C or Special Lube 101	
Steering mount (L-Drive)	2-4-C or Special Lube 101	18
Universal joint housing (L-Drive)	2-4-C	19

Perform lubrication service at 100 hours or once per season when operated in fresh water. Lubrication intervals are every 50 hours of operation when operated in saltwater.

Table 2 RECOMMENDED LUBRICANTS, SEALANTS AND ADHESIVES

	Part No.
Lubricants	
Quicksilver Premium 2-Cycle TC-W3 outboard oil	(normal dealer stock item)
Quicksilver Special Lubricant 101	92-13872A-1
Quicksilver 2-4-C Multi-Lube	(normal dealer stock item in various sizes)
Quicksilver Anti-Corrosion Grease	92-78376A-6
Quicksilver Needle Bearing Grease	92-825265A-1
Quicksilver Power Trim and Steering Fluid	92-90100A12
Quicksilver Premium Blend Gearcase Lubricant	(normal dealer stock item)
Sealants	
Quicksilver Perfect Seal	92-34227-11
Loctite 5900 Ultra black RTV sealant	92-809826
Sealer (crankcase halves)	92-90113–2
Loctite Master Gasket Sealer	92-12564–2
Quicksilver Liquid Neoprene	92-25711–2
Loctite 567 PST pipe sealant	92-809822
Quicksilver Bellows Adhesive	92-86166–1
Adhesives	
Loquic Primer	92-809824
Loctite 271 threadlocking sealant (high strength)	92-809819
Loctite 242 threadlocking sealant (medium strength)	92-809821
Loctite RC680 high strength retaining compound	92-809833
Miscellaneous	
Quicksilver Power Tune Engine Cleaner	92-15104A12
Quicksilver Corrosion Guard	92-815869A12
Quicksilver Storage Seal Rust Inhibitor	92-86145A12

4

Table 3 GEARCASE LUBRICANT APPROXIMATE CAPACITIES*

	Lubricant Capacity
Outboard model	
4 and 5 hp	4 oz. (118 ml)
7.5, 9.9 and 15 hp	5 oz. (148 ml)
25 hp (2 cylinder)	12 oz. (355 ml)
25 hp (3 cylinder)	7.6 oz. (225 ml)
35-50 hp (through 1994)	12 oz. (355 ml)
40-50 hp (1995-on)	14.9 oz. (441 ml)
60 hp	26 oz. (769 ml)
70 and 75 hp	12 oz. (355 ml)
85 and 125 hp	26 oz. (769 ml)
90 and 120 hp (1990-1994)	35 oz. (1035 ml)
90 and 120 hp (1995-on)	22.5 oz. (665 ml)
150 hp (through 1991I)	26 oz. (769 ml)
150 hp (1991J-on)	35 oz. (1035 ml)
L-Drive models	26 oz. (769 ml)

*Quicksilver Premium Blend Gearcase Lubricant or equivalent is recommended.

Table 4 POWER HEAD COMPRESSION SPECIFICATIONS

	Compression specification
Outboard model	
4 and 5 hp	110-125 psi (758-862 kPa)
7.5 hp	115-130psi (793-896 kPa)
9.9 hp 1984-1987	115-125 psi (793-862 kPa)
15 hp and 9.9 hp 1988 and newer	125-135 psi (862-931 kPa)
25 hp (2 cylinder)	95-105 psi (655-724 kPa)
25 hp (3 cylinder)	Maximum 15 psi (103 kPa) variation.
35 hp 1986-1989	120-130 psi (827-896 kPa)
35 hp 1990-1991	130-150 psi (896-1034 kPa)
50 hp 1984-1987	125-150 psi (862-1034 kPa)
50 hp 1988-1989	135-150 psi (931-1034 kPa)
50 hp 1990-1994	140-160 psi (965-1103 kPa)
40 hp 1992-1994	140-160 psi (965-1103 kPa)
40 and 50 hp 1995-1996	Maximum 15 psi (103 kPa) variation
60 hp	150-165 psi (1034-1138 kPa)
70 and 75 hp	Maximum 15 psi (103 kPa) variation
85 and 125 hp 1984-1988	145-165 psi (1000-1138 kPa)
85 hp 1989	135-155 psi (931-1069 kPa)
125 hp 1989	140-160 psi (965-1103 kPa)
90 hp 1990A	135-155 psi (931-1069 kPa)
90 hp 1990B-1996*	
Cylinder No.1	135-150 psi (931-1034 kPa)
Cylinders No. 2 and No. 3	145-160 psi (1000-1103 kPa)
120 hp 1990A	140-160 psi (965-1103 kPa)
120 hp 1990B-serial No.OE093938	145-165 psi (1000-1138 kPa)
120 hp serial No.OE093939 and up*	
Cylinders No. 1 and No. 4	135-150 psi (931-1034 kPa)
Cylinders No. 2 and No. 3	145-160 psi (1000-1103 kPa)
150 hp	145-165 psi (1000-1138 kPa)
L-Drive model	
85 and 125 hp	125-145 psi (862-1000 kPa)
90 and 120 hp 1990A models	125-145 psi (862-1000 kPa)
90 hp 1990B-1991A	
Cylinder No. 1	135-155 psi (931-1069 kPa)
Cylinders No. 2 and No. 3	145-160 psi (1000-1103 kPa)
120 hp 1990B-1991A	145-165 psi (1000-1138 kPa)
90 and 120 hp 1991B-1992	Maximum 15 psi (103 kPa) variation

*These engines have staggered compression. No.1 (and No.4 on the 120 hp) cylinder will normally be 5-10 psi (34.5-69 kPa) lower than No. 2 and No. 3.

Table 5 CYLINDER HEAD BOLT TORQUE SPECIFICATIONS

	Torque specification
Outboard model	
4-15 hp	130 in.-lbs. (14.7 N•m)
25 hp (2 cylinder) and 35 hp	190 in.-lbs. (21.5 N•m)
25 hp (3 cylinder)	250 in.-lbs. (28.2 N•m)
50 hp 1984-1989B (3/8 in. bolts)	270 in.-lbs. (30.5 N•m)
50 hp 1989C-1996 (5/16 in. bolts)	225 in.-lbs. (25.4 N•m)
40, 60, 70, 85, 125 and 150 hp	225 in.-lbs. (25.4 N•m)

(continued)

Table 5 CYLINDER HEAD BOLT TORQUE SPECIFICATIONS (continued)

	Torque specification
Outboard model (continued)	
75 hp	Torque and turn*
90 and 120 hp up to serial No.OE138599	225 in.-lbs. (25.4 N•m)
90 and 120 hp serial No. OE138600 and on	Torque and turn*
L-Drive models	225 in.-lbs. (25.4 N•m)

*On 1996-1999 (serial No. OE138600-on) 75, 90 and 120 hp models use a new torque procedure for the cylinder head bolts. Lightly oil the threads and the underside of the head of the bolts. Torque in sequence to 120 in.-lbs. (13.5 N•m). Then turn each head bolt, in sequence, an additional 90°.

Table 6 COMMON ENGINE SPECIFICATIONS

Fuel requirements	
Recommended	Regular unleaded from a major supplier, 87 pump posted octane minimum, with no alcohol
Minimum	Regular unleaded, 87 pump posted octane minimum, with no more than 10% ethanol[1]
Recommended fuel additives	Quicksilver Fuel System Treatment and Stabilizer part No. 92-78383A12
	Quicksilver Gasoline Stabilizer part No. 92-817529A12
	Quicksilver QuicKleen Fuel Treatment part No. 92-824074A12[2]
Oil	
Recommended	Force or Quicksilver NMMA approved TCW-3 outboard oil
Minimum	NMMA approved TCW-3 or TCW-II
Fuel to oil ratio	
After break-in	50:1
During break-in	25:1 for the first 12 gal. (45.4 L) of gasoline
Battery	Minimum of 630 CCA (490 MCA) and 100 minutes reserve capacity
Gear lubricant	Quicksilver Premium Blend Gear Lube or equivalent

[1]The use of methanol is not recommended. When using any alcohol extended (oxygenated) fuel, install a Quicksilver Water Separating Fuel Filter.

[2]QuicKleen is designed to remove existing combustion chamber deposits and prevent new deposits from forming.

Table 7 RECOMMENDED SPARK PLUGS

Model	Champion Spark Plug Number (RFI*)	Gap in. (mm)
4 hp 1984-1987	L86C (RL86C)	.030 (0.76)
5 hp		
1988-1990B	L86C (RL86C)	.030 (0.76)
1991-1993	L87YC (RL87YC)	.030 (0.76)
1994-1996 (SEM-Walbro CD ignition)	L87YC (RL87YC)	.040 (1.02)
7.5 hp 1985	L86C (QL86C)	.030 (0.76)
9.9 hp		
1984-1991B	L86C (RL86C)	.030 (0.76)
1991C-1993	L87YC (RL87YC)	.030 (0.76)
1994-1997 (SEM-Walbro CD ignition)	L87YC (RL87YC)	.040 (1.02)
	(continued)	

Table 7 RECOMMENDED SPARK PLUGS (continued)

Model	Champion Spark Plug Number (RFI*)	Gap in. (mm)
15 hp		
1984-1991B	L86C (RL86C)	.030 (0.76)
1991C-1992A	L87YC (RL87YC)	.030 (0.76)
1992B-1993	L82YC (RL82YC)	.030 (0.76)
1994-1996 (SEM-Walbro CD ignition)	L82YC (RL82YC)	.040 (1.02)
25 hp (1989 2 cylinder)	L82C (RL82C)	.030 (0.76)
25 hp (1996 3 cylinder)	L82C (RL82C)	.035 (0.89)
35 hp 1986-1991	L82C (RL82C)	.030 (0.76)
40 hp 1992-1996	L76V (QL76V)	NA
50 hp		
1984-1987B (battery-points ignition)	UL81C (RL81C)	.030 (0.76)
1987C-1989A	L82C (RL82C)	.030 (0.76)
1989B-1992A	UL18V (QL76V)	NA
1992C-1996	L76V (QL76V)	NA
60 hp 1985	L20V (QL76V)	NA
70 and 75 hp	L76V (QL76V)	NA
85 and 125 hp, including L-Drives	UL18V (QL76V)	NA
90 hp, not including L-Drives		
1990-1991C and 1991E (Prestolite CD)	UL18V (QL76V)	NA
1991D, 1991H-1996 (Thunderbolt/CDM)	L76V (QL76V)	NA
90 and 120 hp L-Drives		
1990-1991A (Prestolite CD ignition)	UL18V (QL76V)	NA
1991B-1992 (Thunderbolt ignition)	L76V (QL76V)	NA
120 hp, except L-Drives		
1990-1991C (Prestolite CD ignition)	UL18V (QL76V)	NA
1991D-1999 (Thunderbolt/CDM)	L76V (QL76V)	NA
150 hp		
1989-1991A (Prestolite CD ignition)	UL18V (QL76V)	NA
1991B-1994 (Thunderbolt ignition)	L76V (QL76V)	NA

*Use resistor or suppression spark plugs where radio frequency interference (RFI) suppression is required

Chapter Five

Engine Synchronization and Linkage Adjustments

For an outboard motor or L-Drive to deliver optimum performance, the ignition must be timed and the carburetor operation synchronized with the ignition. This procedure normally is the final step of a tune-up. It must also be performed whenever the fuel or ignition systems are serviced or adjusted.

Procedures for engine synchronization and linkage adjustment on Force outboards and L-Drives differ according to model and ignition system. This chapter is divided into self-contained sections dealing with particular models/ignition systems for fast and easy reference.

Each section specifies the appropriate procedure and sequence to be followed and provides the necessary tune-up data. Read the general information at the beginning of the chapter and then select the section pertaining to your outboard motor or L-Drive.

Table 1 lists recommended test equipment. **Tables 2-9** list engine specifications called out for in this chapter. All tables are at the end of the chapter.

ENGINE TIMING AND SYNCHRONIZATION

Ignition timing advance and throttle opening must be synchronized to occur at the proper time for the engine to perform properly. Synchronizing is the process of timing the carburetor operation to the ignition spark advance.

Required Equipment

The manufacturer recommends that static timing of engines equipped with breaker-point ignition be accomplished by setting the breaker point gap with a feeler gauge. A test lamp or ohmmeter can also be used to determine precisely when the points open and close.

A stroboscopic timing light must be used to check timing mark alignment on specified models. As the engine is cranked or run, the timing light flashes each time the spark plug fires. When the light is pointed at the moving flywheel, the mark on the flywheel appears to stand still. The flywheel mark should align with the stationary timing pointer on the power head.

An accurate shop tachometer (not the boat tachometer) should be used to determine engine speed during idle and high-speed adjustments.

> *CAUTION*
> *Never operate the engine without water circulating through the gearcase to the power head. Running the outboard motor without water will damage the water pump and may cause the gearcase and power head to overheat.*

Some form of water supply is required whenever the engine is operated during the adjustment procedure. Using a test tank is the most convenient method, although the procedures may be performed using a flushing device or with the boat in the water.

> *WARNING*
> *Never attempt to make adjustments on a moving boat. Boat movement should be restrained by securely fastening the boat to a dock when working around a running power head.*

4, 5, 7.5, 9.9 AND 15 HP MODELS

Throttle Pick-up Point Adjustment

1. Remove the engine cover.
2A. 4 and 5 hp (prior to 1989 B) and early (1984-1986) 9.9 and 15 hp:
   a. Advance the throttle control until the throttle cam just contacts the throttle shaft fol-

lower. If adjustment is correct, the index mark on the throttle cam will be aligned with the center of the throttle shaft follower. See **Figure 1**.
   b. If adjustment is required, loosen the screw holding the throttle cam to the stator plate.
   c. Pivot the throttle cam in or out as required to align the index mark with the center of the follower. Retighten the throttle cam screw securely.
   d. Recheck adjustment by repeating sub-step a, and readjust as necessary.
2B. 4 and 5 hp (1989 B-on) and 9.9 and 15 hp (1987-on):
   a. Loosen throttle cam follower adjustment screw (A, **Figure 2**) on models so equipped using an appropriate Allen wrench. On late 4 and 5 hp (1989 B-on) and 1990-on 15 hp models, throttle pick-up adjustment screw is located at B, **Figure 2**.
   b. Advance the throttle control until the throttle cam just contacts the follower roller (**Figure 2**). The carburetor throttle valves must be completely closed at this point. If not, back out idle speed screw (**Figure 3**) as necessary.
   c. The carburetor throttle valve must be fully closed during this step. On models prior to early 1990, align the index mark with the

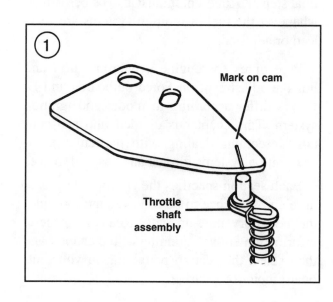

center of the roller, then retighten the adjustment screw (A, **Figure 2**) securely. On late 1990-on models, adjust the screw (B, **Figure 2**) as necessary to align the index mark with the center of the follower roller.

d. To check adjustment, advance throttle control until the throttle cam just contacts the

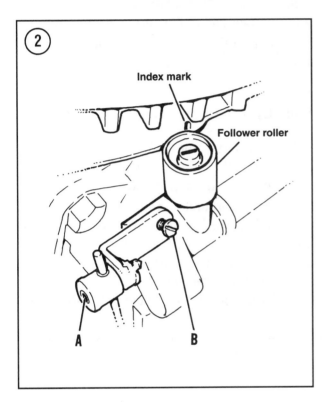

Index mark

Follower roller

A   B

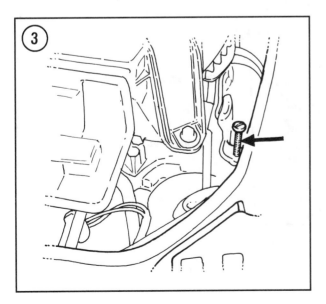

follower roller. If the index mark is not aligned with the center of the roller, repeat the adjustment procedure.

2C. 7.5 hp models:

a. Advance the throttle control until the edge of the throttle follower arm is aligned with the stamped mark on the throttle cam (located on the stator plate). The throttle should just begin to move as this mark aligns with the throttle follower arm.

b. Adjust the screw on the throttle follower arm as required to achieve proper operation.

Carburetor Adjustment

1. Turn the idle mixture adjustment screw clockwise until it is lightly seated. Do not turn the screw tightly into the carburetor or the tip will be damaged.

2. Back out the mixture screw to specification.

3. Start the motor and warm to normal operating temperature.

4. Shift the outboard into FORWARD gear.

5. Set the throttle lever control to the idle position. If necessary adjust the idle speed screw temporarily to obtain the recommend idle speed.

NOTE
Idle mixture cannot be properly set unless the carburetor is operating on the idle circuit. Setting the idle mixture at higher speeds will give inaccurate results. It may be necessary to switch back and forth between idle mixture adjustments and idle speed adjustments several times to achieve proper adjustment. Always adjust the idle speed last.

6. Slowly turn the idle mixture screw counterclockwise until the engine speed decreases and idle becomes rough due to overrich mixture. Note the position of the mixture screw slot.

7. Slowly turn the mixture screw clockwise. Engine idle will gradually become smooth and speed will increase. Continue turning screw clockwise until the engine speed slows again

5

and/or misfires due to a too-lean condition. Note the position of the mixture screw slot.

8. Turn the mixture screw to a midpoint between the settings noted in Step 6 and Step 7.

9. Adjust the idle stop screw on the tiller handle, the starboard side of the support plate or as shown in **Figure 3** to bring the idle speed to specification.

25 HP 2-CYLINDER AND 35 HP MODELS

Throttle Pick-up Point Adjustment

1. Remove the engine cover.

NOTE
Do not disconnect the throttle cam rod at the throttle cam. The effort required to do so can distort the cam.

2. Disconnect the throttle cam rod from the throttle arm. See **Figure 4**.

3. Loosen the locknut on the eccentric screw (S, **Figure 5**) that secures the nylon roller to the throttle arm.

4. Turn eccentric screw (S, **Figure 5**) to the furthest point from the throttle cam, then turn the screw counterclockwise to align the index mark with the center of the roller. See **Figure 5**.

5. Secure the position of the eccentric screw with a screwdriver and tighten the screw locknut.

6. Reconnect the throttle cam rod to the throttle arm.

Wide-Open Throttle Stop Adjustment

1. Advance the throttle to the wide-open position. Make sure the throttle arm is against the wide-open throttle stop (**Figure 4**).

2. Check the carburetor throttle valve position. If the throttle valve is not in the fully open position, disconnect the throttle cam rod from the throttle arm. Loosen the jam nut(s) and rotate the rod to lengthen or shorten rod as required. Reconnect the rod and recheck the carburetor throttle valve.

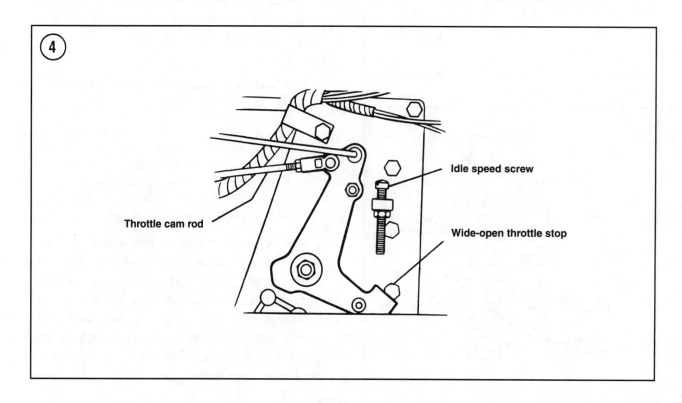

(4)

Throttle cam rod

Idle speed screw

Wide-open throttle stop

Repeat this step until the throttle valve is completely open (exactly horizontal).

3. Retighten the jam nut(s) securely.

Carburetor Adjustment

This procedure should be performed with the boat in the water or the outboard motor in a test tank with the correct test wheel installed in place of the propeller.

> *WARNING*
> *Never attempt to make adjustments to the outboard motor on a moving boat. Boat movement should be restrained by securely fastening the boat to a dock when working around a running power head.*

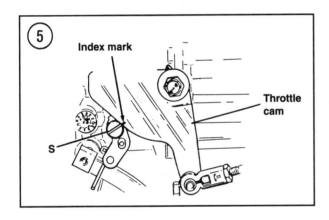

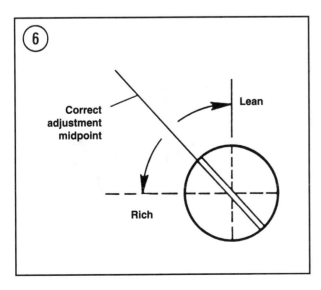

1. Connect an accurate shop tachometer according to the manufacturer's instructions.

2. Turn the idle mixture adjustment screw clockwise until lightly seated. Do not force the screw tightly into the carburetor or the tip will be damaged.

3. Back out the mixture screw to specification.

4. Start the engine and run at 2,000 rpm until warmed to normal operating temperature. Once operating temperature is reached, allow the motor to idle 1-2 minutes to stabilize the motor and allow the fuel recirculation system to begin functioning.

5. Move the throttle arm to the idle position. If necessary, adjust the idle speed screw temporarily to obtain the recommend idle speed.

> *NOTE*
> *Idle mixture cannot be properly set unless the carburetor is operating on the idle circuit. Setting the idle mixture at higher speeds will give inaccurate results. It may be necessary to switch back and forth between idle mixture adjustments and idle speed adjustments several times to achieve proper adjustment. Always adjust the idle speed last.*

6. Slowly turn the idle mixture screw counterclockwise in 1/8 turn increments, pausing at least 10 seconds between turns. Continue this step until the idle speed decreases and idle becomes rough due to an overly rich mixture. Note the position of the mixture screw slot.

7. Slowly turn the idle mixture screw clockwise in 1/8 turn increments, pausing at least 10 seconds between turns. The idle speed will gradually become smooth and speed will increase. Continue this step until the engine speed begins to slow again and/or misfire due to the excessively lean mixture. Note the position of the mixture screw slot.

8. Position the mixture screw at a midpoint between the settings noted in Step 6 and Step 7. See **Figure 6**.

9. Quickly, snap the throttle open. The engine will accelerate cleanly without hesitation if the mixture is adjusted correctly.

10. Adjust the idle speed (**Figure 4**) to specification.

25 HP 3-CYLINDER MODELS

Adjusting Throttle Plate Position

1. Disconnect the spark plug leads to prevent accidental starting.

2. Shift the motor into FORWARD gear. Rotate the propeller to make sure the gearcase is fully engaged into gear.

3. Advance the throttle to the wide-open position.

NOTE
The throttle must be in the wide-open position to adjust the throttle valve plate.

4. Check the position of the throttle valve plate in the carburetor bore. The throttle plate must be horizontal.

5. Turn the throttle plate adjustment screw (**Figure 7**) until the throttle plate is exactly horizontal.

6. Return the throttle back to the idle position and shift the motor into NEUTRAL.

7. Reconnect the spark plug leads.

Carburetor Adjustment

1. Connect an accurate shop tachometer according to its manufacturer's instructions.

2. Turn the idle mixture screw (**Figure 7**) clockwise until it is lightly seated. Do not force the screw tightly into the carburetor or the tip and the carburetor will be damaged.

3. Back out the mixture screw to specification.

4. Start the engine and run at 2000 rpm until warmed up to normal operating temperature. Once operating temperature is reached, allow the motor to idle 1-2 minutes to stabilize the motor

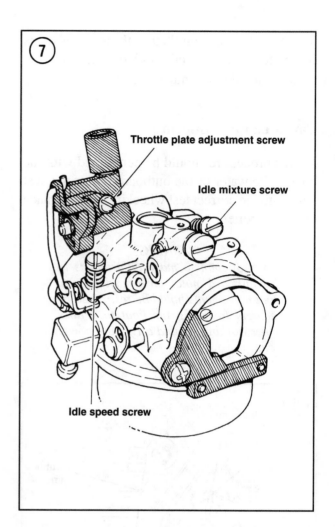

Throttle plate adjustment screw
Idle mixture screw
Idle speed screw

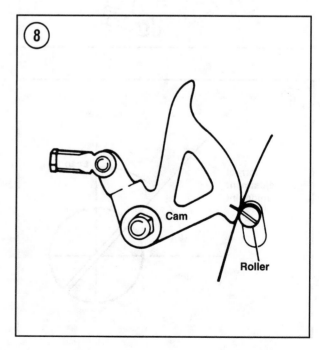

Cam
Roller

and allow the fuel recirculation system to begin functioning.

5. Set the throttle control to the idle position. If necessary adjust the idle speed screw (**Figure 7**) temporarily to obtain the recommend idle speed.

NOTE
Idle mixture cannot be properly set unless the carburetor is operating on the idle circuit. Setting the idle mixture at higher speeds will give inaccurate results. It may be necessary to switch back and forth between idle mixture adjustments and idle speed adjustments several times to achieve proper adjustment. Always adjust the idle speed last.

6. Slowly turn the idle mixture screw (**Figure 7**) counterclockwise in 1/8 turn increments, pausing at least 10 seconds between turns. Continue this step until the idle speed decreases and idle becomes rough due to an overly rich mixture. Note the position of the mixture screw slot.

7. Slowly turn the idle mixture screw clockwise in 1/8 turn increments, pausing at least 10 seconds between turns. The idle speed will gradually become smooth and speed will increase. Continue this step until the engine speed begins to slow again and/or misfires due to the excessively lean mixture. Note the position of the mixture screw slot.

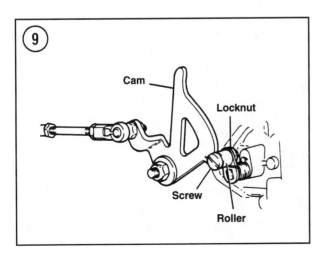

8. Position the mixture screw at a midpoint between the settings of Step 6 and Step 7. See **Figure 6**.

9. Quickly accelerate the engine to wide open throttle and back to idle. The engine will accelerate cleanly and without hesitation if the mixture is adjusted correctly. Readjust as necessary.

10. Adjust the idle speed (**Figure 7**) to specifications.

40, 50 AND 60 HP MODELS

Throttle Pick-up Point Adjustment

The throttle cam pick-up point must be properly adjusted or the low-speed timing will not be correct and the outboard motor will not idle and/or accelerate properly.

CAUTION
Do not disconnect the throttle cam rod at the throttle cam. The pressure required to do so can distort the throttle cam.

1. Disconnect the throttle rod from the tower shaft.

2. Rotate the throttle cam until it *just* contacts the roller. At this point, the mark on the throttle cam should be aligned with the center of the roller. See **Figure 8**.

3. If adjustment is necessary, loosen the locknut on the eccentric screw holding the nylon roller to the throttle shaft arm. See **Figure 9**.

4. Turn the eccentric screw until the mark on the cam intersects the center of the roller (**Figure 8**).

5. While holding the eccentric screw from turning, tighten the locknut. Repeat Step 2.

6. Reconnect the throttle cam rod to the tower shaft on 40 and 50 hp models.

Throttle Plate Synchronization (60 hp)

> *NOTE*
> *The 60 hp has 2 carburetors. The throttle linkage on a motor with multiple carburetors must be adjusted so that all carburetors open and close at exactly the same time. If the throttle valves are not synchronized, the motor will idle and accelerate poorly.*

1. Verify that the throttle cam rod is disconnected from the tower shaft.

2. Loosen the throttle tie bar adjustment screw (**Figure 10**), open both throttle valves and allow them to snap closed.

3. Verify that both throttle valves are fully closed.

4. Support the tie bar and tighten the tie bar adjustment screw securely.

5. Open and close the top carburetor using the throttle roller arm. Verify that both throttle valves open and close at the same time. Readjust the tie bar as necessary.

6. Reconnect the throttle cam rod to the tower shaft.

Wide-open Throttle Linkage Adjustment

The wide-open throttle linkage should be adjusted to ensure the carburetor throttle valve(s) opens to its full-throttle position.

1. Place the throttle linkage in the wide-open throttle position.

> *NOTE*
> *Do not adjust the throttle valve(s) past the horizontal position in Step 2. Adjusting the valve(s) past horizontal has the same effect as the throttle not opening fully.*

2. Check the carburetor throttle valve position(s). If the valve(s) are not completely open (horizontal), disconnect the throttle cam rod from the tower shaft. Loosen the jam nuts and rotate the rod to lengthen or shorten it is required. See

Figure 11. After adjustment, the rod should be centered between the rod end connectors.

3. Check adjustment by repeating Steps 1 and 2. Repeat the adjustment until the throttle valve(s) is fully open with the rod installed, then retighten the jam nuts.

Neutral Warm-up Speed Adjustment (Models So Equipped)

Perform this adjustment with the boat in the water, the outboard in a test tank or connected to a flushing device.

1. Connect a shop tachometer to the outboard motor according to its manufacturer's instructions.

2. Start the outboard motor and allow to idle in NEUTRAL.

3. Depress the neutral warm-up button on the remote control assembly.

4. Advance the throttle lever to the full-throttle position and note the engine speed. Fast idle warm-up speed should be 1,500-1,800 rpm.

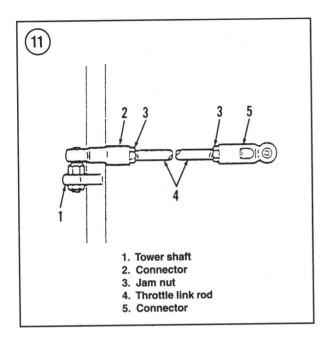

1. Tower shaft
2. Connector
3. Jam nut
4. Throttle link rod
5. Connector

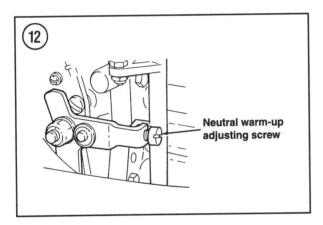

Neutral warm-up
adjusting screw

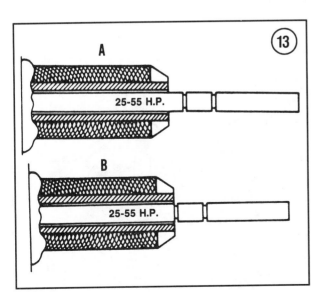

A

25-55 H.P.

B

25-55 H.P.

5. If adjustment is necessary, turn the neutral warm-up screw (**Figure 12**) as required to obtain the specified engine speed.

Ignition Timing
(Early 50 hp with Battery Breaker-Point Ignition)

1. Disconnect the negative (–) battery cable from the battery.

2. Remove the spark plugs. See Chapter Four.

3. Remove the flywheel. See Chapter Eight.

4. Check and adjust the breaker points as necessary. An error in the breaker point gap of only 0.0015 in. will change ignition timing up to 1°.

5. Thread the barrel of timing tool part No. T-2937-1 into the No. 1 (top) spark plug hole.

6. Insert the timing tool rod into the barrel. Make sure the 2 marks (grooves) on the rod are facing the outside. Note that the distance between the marks represents 32°.

7. While holding the rod lightly against the piston, rotate the crankshaft clockwise until the rod is at its maximum outward travel. At this point, the piston is at top dead center (TDC). See A, **Figure 13**.

8. Screw the barrel of the timing tool in or out as necessary to align the inner mark on the rod with the edge of the barrel. See B, **Figure 13**.

NOTE
If the crankshaft is rotated too far in Step 9 (outer line past the edge of the barrel), continue turning the crankshaft clockwise and repeat the step. Do not rotate the crankshaft counterclockwise to position the rod or the water pump may be damaged.

9. Apply light finger pressure on the end of the rod to prevent it from shooting out during the piston compression stroke. Rotate the crankshaft clockwise nearly 1 full turn, until the outer mark on the rod is aligned with the edge of the barrel.

See **Figure 14**. At this point, the piston is positioned at 32° before top dead center (BTDC).

10. Disconnect the throttle link at the tower shaft. Place the tower shaft in the wide-open throttle position by rotating it until the nylon stop rests against the cylinder crankcase cover.

11. Disconnect the lead wires from the slide terminal of the No. 1 breaker point set.

12. Connect a self-powered test lamp between the No. 1 cylinder breaker point lead wire and a good engine ground.

13. Loosen the locknut on the spark control link (**Figure 15**).

    a. If the test lamp is on, rotate the spark control link counterclockwise until the lamp just goes out.

    b. If the lamp is off, rotate the spark control link clockwise until the lamp just comes on.

14. Check the adjustment by lightly pushing against the crankshaft. The lamp should flicker on and off with each push.

15. Hold the spark control link from turning and tighten the locknut.

16. Remove the timing tool from the No. 1 spark plug hole and install it in the No. 2 spark plug hole. It is necessary to remove the rear engine cover bracket to install the tool into the hole.

17. Repeat Steps 6-9 to locate the 32° BTDC position for the No. 2 cylinder.

18. Disconnect the No. 2 cylinder breaker point lead wires at the slide terminal.

NOTE
Do not adjust the spark control link to adjust the No. 2 cylinder timing or the No. 1 cylinder timing will be affected. Make adjustment by adjusting the No. 2 cylinder breaker point gap.

19. Connect a self-powered test lamp between the No. 2 cylinder breaker point lead wire and a good engine ground.

    a. If the test light is off, adjust (close) the No. 2 cylinder breaker point gap until the lamp just goes off.

    b. If the test lamp is on, adjust (open) the No. 2 cylinder breaker point gap until the lamp just goes off.

    c. Check the adjustment by lightly pushing against the crankshaft. The light should flicker on and off with each push.

20. Remove the timing tool from the No. 2 spark plug hole. Reinstall both spark plugs, reconnect the breaker point leads, install the flywheel (Chapter Eight) and reconnect the negative battery cable to the battery.

21. Connect a spark tester (part No. FT-11295) to the spark plug wires as described in Chapter Four. Adjust the tester spark gap to 3/8 in. (9.5 mm).

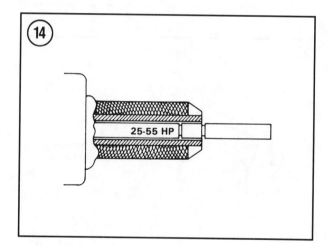

14

25-55 HP

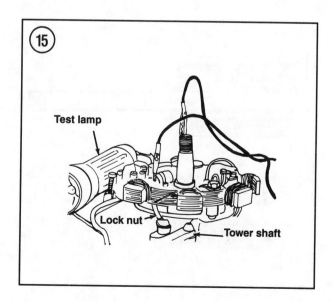

15

Test lamp

Lock nut

Tower shaft

22. Connect a timing light to the No. 1 spark plug lead according the manufacturer's instructions.

23. Move the tower shaft to the wide-open position (timing fully advanced).

NOTE
Force 50 hp outboard motors may be adjusted to 30° or 32° BTDC at the factory. The manufacturer recommends adjusting all 50 hp models to 30° BTDC. Figure 16 shows the differences between the 2 decals for factory timed engines.

24. Crank the engine while noting the timing marks with the timing light.

25. Connect the timing light to the No. 2 spark plug lead.

26. Repeat Step 24 and note the timing with the timing light. The firing positions of the 2 cylinders should be the same. If not, adjust the No. 2 cylinder breaker point gap until the No. 2 cylinder fires at the same position as No. 1 cylinder.

27. If the cylinders are firing exactly 180° apart, (same position on the timing tab), reconnect the timing light to the No. 1 spark plug lead. Determine if the No. 1 cylinder is firing at 30° BTDC. If it is not, readjust the spark control link until it does. When the cylinders are properly

synchronized, both cylinders will fire at 30° BTDC.

28. Remove the timing light and spark tester.

**Ignition Timing
(40, 50 and 60 hp with Electronic Ignition)**

Before adjusting ignition timing, first locate TDC for the No. 1 piston so the correct timing mark alignment can be verified. Two different tools can be used to accomplish this, timing tool part No. FTA-2937-1 or dial indicator part No. 91-58222A1 (or equivalent).

1. Disconnect the spark plug leads and remove the spark plugs.

2. If using timing tool part No. FTA-2937-1, thread the barrel of the tool approximately 3/4 into the No. 1 spark plug hole.

   a. Insert the timing tool rod into the tool barrel.

   b. While lightly holding the rod against the piston, rotate the crankshaft clockwise until the rod reaches its maximum outward travel. At this point, the piston is at TDC.

3. If using dial indicator part No. 91-58222A1 (or equivalent), install the indicator into the No. 1 spark plug hole. While observing the dial indicator, rotate the flywheel clockwise until the piston is at TDC.

4. With the No. 1 piston at TDC, make sure the TDC mark on the flywheel is aligned with the timing pointer. If the pointer and TDC mark are aligned, continue at Step 5. If not, remove the flywheel (Chapter Eight) and check for a sheared flywheel key or damaged key slot in the flywheel or crankshaft. Repair as necessary.

5. Remove the timing tool or dial indicator from the No. 1 spark plug hole. Connect spark tester part No. FT-11295 (or equivalent) to the spark plug leads.

WARNING
The outboard motor must be shifted into FORWARD gear to be able to advance the throttle to the wide-open position

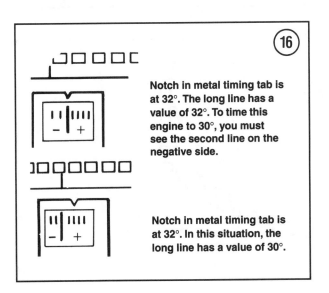

⑯

Notch in metal timing tab is at 32°. The long line has a value of 32°. To time this engine to 30°, you must see the second line on the negative side.

Notch in metal timing tab is at 32°. In this situation, the long line has a value of 30°.

5

(maximum spark advance). To prevent personal injury, remove the propeller prior to performing this procedure.

6. On models with the interlock switch on the engine, connect a jumper lead across the interlock switch to allow the engine to crank while in gear. See **Figure 17**. On newer models with the interlock switch in the remote control box, connect a push button remote starter switch across the starter solenoid yellow or yellow/red terminal and the battery positive (+) terminal. Either of these methods will allow starter activation while in gear.

7. Connect a timing light to the No.1 (top) spark plug lead.

8. Move the tower shaft to the wide-open throttle position. Crank the engine while observing the timing marks with the timing light. **Figure 18** shows a typical Prestolite magneto CD flywheel and timing marks. **Figure 19** shows a typical Thunderbolt CDI or CDM flywheel and timing grid.

> *NOTE*
> *Due to the electronic characteristics of the different CD ignition systems, timing at cranking speed must be set 2 degrees **retarded** on engines with Prestolite magneto CD ignition systems and 2 degrees **advanced** on engines with Thunderbolt CDI or CDM ignition systems. It is rec-*

ommended to verify timing at wide-open throttle with a test wheel, if available. The Tables give both cranking and wide-open throttle specifications. It is more important that the timing is correct at wide-open throttle than at cranking speed.

9. If adjustment is necessary, loosen the jam nut and turn the timing rod (**Figure 20**) as necessary. Retighten the jam nut and recheck the timing.

10. Disconnect and remove the spark tester, reinstall the spark plugs and remove the jumper lead from the neutral interlock switch.

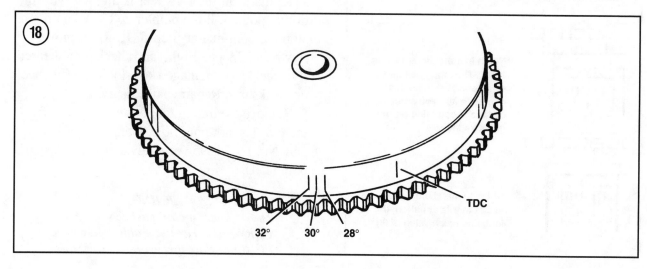

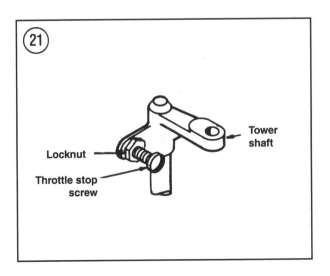

Locknut

Throttle stop
screw

Tower
shaft

Carburetor Adjustment

Idle mixture should be performed with the boat in the water or the outboard motor in a test tank. Do not attempt to adjust the carburetor with the outboard connected to a flushing device. If using a test tank, remove the propeller and install the correct test wheel.

WARNING
Never attempt to make adjustments on a moving boat. Restrain movement by securely fastening the boat to a dock when working on a running power head.

1. Connect an accurate shop tachometer according to its manufacturer's instructions.

NOTE
The 60 hp model has 2 carburetors. The idle mixture has to be properly set on both carburetors. Adjust the top carburetor first, then the bottom. It may be necessary to switch back and forth between the carburetors several times to get the mixture correct. If necessary, reset the mixture screws to the initial settings and try again.

2. Turn the idle mixture screw(s) clockwise until lightly seated. Do not force the screw(s) tightly into the carburetor or the tip(s) and the carburetor(s) will be damaged.

3. Back out the mixture screw(s) to specification.

4. Start the engine and run at 2000 rpm until warmed up to normal operating temperature. Once operating temperature is reached, allow the motor to idle 1-2 minutes to stabilize the motor and allow the fuel recirculation system to begin functioning.

5. Set the throttle lever control to the idle position. If necessary adjust the throttle stop screw (**Figure 21**) temporarily to obtain the recommended idle speed.

NOTE
Idle mixture cannot be properly set unless the carburetor(s) are operating on

5

*the idle circuit(s). Setting the idle mix-
ture at higher speeds will give inaccurate results. It may be necessary to
switch back and forth between idle mixture adjustments and idle speed adjustments several times to achieve proper
adjustment. Always adjust the idle speed
last.*

6. Slowly turn the idle mixture screw counterclockwise in 1/8 turn increments, pausing at least
10 seconds between turns. Continue this step
until the idle speed decreases and idle becomes
rough due to an overly rich mixture. Note the
position of the mixture screw slot.

7. Slowly turn the idle mixture screw clockwise
in 1/8 turn increments, pausing at least 10
seconds between turns. The idle speed will
gradually become smooth and speed will increase. Continue this step until the engine speed
begins to slow again and/or misfires due to the
excessively lean mixture. Note the position of the
mixture screw slot.

8. Position the mixture screw at a midpoint
between the settings of Step 6 and Step 7. See
Figure 22. Repeat Step 6 and Step 7 for the
bottom carburetor on 60 hp models.

9. Quickly accelerate the engine to wide-open
throttle. The engine will accelerate cleanly and
without hesitation if the mixture is adjusted
correctly. Readjust as necessary.

10. Adjust the idle speed (**Figure 21**) to
specifications.

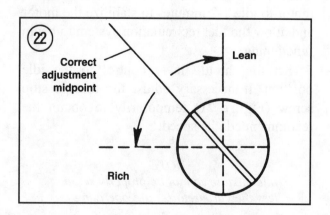

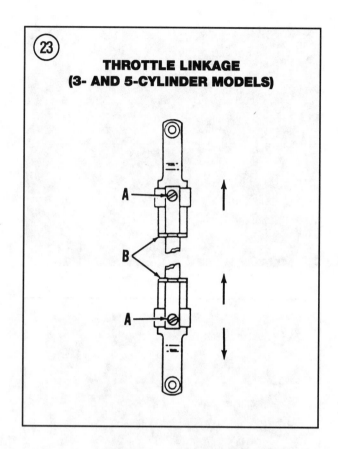

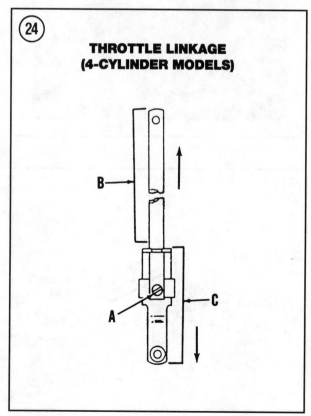

70-150 HP MODELS
(INCLUDING L-DRIVE)

Carburetor Linkage Adjustment
(Except 70 and 75 hp)

The throttle linkage on multi-carburetor motors, must be adjusted so the carburetor throttle valves open and close at exactly the same time. If the throttle valves are not synchronized, the outboard motor will idle and accelerate poorly.

1. Disconnect the throttle link connector from the tower shaft. Rotate the throttle cam away from the cam follower roller.

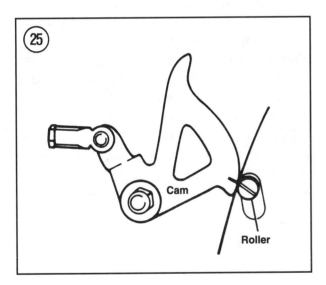

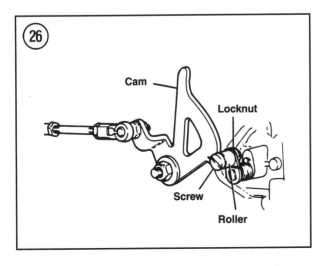

2. Loosen the carburetor linkage tie bar screws (A, **Figure 23** or **Figure 24**).

3A. *3- and 5-cylinder models*—Remove any play in the tie bar by applying light pressure to the tie bar ends (B, **Figure 23**) in the direction of the arrows. Make sure all throttle valves are fully closed, then tighten the tie bar screws (A, **Figure 23**).

3B. *4-cylinder models*—Remove any play in the tie bar by applying light pressure to the upper tie bar (B, **Figure 24**) in the direction of the arrow while holding downward on the lower link (C). While applying pressure, make sure all throttle valves are fully closed, then tighten the tie bar screw (A, **Figure 24**).

4. Slowly operate the throttle cam roller while observing the throttle valves. All throttle valves should open and close simultaneously. If not, repeat this procedure.

Throttle Cam Pick-up Point

The throttle cam pick-up point must be properly adjusted or the low-speed timing will not be correct and the outboard motor will not idle and/or accelerate properly.

1. If necessary, disconnect the throttle link connector from the tower shaft.

2. Loosen the locknut and back out the throttle stop screw (**Figure 21**) until the throttle valve(s) is fully closed.

NOTE
If the throttle cam has 2 marks, the roller should be centered between the marks in Step 3.

3. Rotate the throttle cam until the cam *just* contacts the cam follower roller. At this point, the mark on the throttle cam should be aligned with the center of the roller. See **Figure 25**.

4. If adjustment is necessary, loosen the locknut on the eccentric screw holding the nylon roller to the throttle shaft arm. See **Figure 26**.

5. Turn the eccentric screw until the mark on the cam intersects the center of the roller (**Figure 25**).

6. While holding the eccentric screw from turning, tighten the locknut. Repeat Step 2.

7. Reconnect the throttle link to the tower shaft.

Wide-open Throttle Linkage Adjustment

The wide-open throttle linkage should be adjusted to ensure the carburetor throttle valve(s) opens to its full-throttle position.

1. Place the throttle linkage in the wide-open throttle position.

NOTE
Do not adjust the throttle valve past the horizontal position in Step 2. Adjusting the valve past horizontal has the same effect as the throttle not opening fully.

2. Check the carburetor throttle valve position. If the valve is not completely open (horizontal), disconnect the throttle link rod from the tower shaft. Loosen the jam nuts and rotate the rod to lengthen or shorten it is required. See **Figure 27**. After adjustment, the rod should be centered between the rod end connectors.

3. Check adjustment by repeating Steps 1 and 2. Repeat the adjustment until the throttle valve is fully open with the rod installed, then retighten the jam nuts.

Ignition Timing (Cranking)

Before checking and adjusting ignition timing, first locate TDC for the No.1 piston so the correct timing mark alignment can be verified. Two different tools can be used to accomplish this, timing tool part No. FT2937-1 or dial indicator part No.91-85222A1 (or equivalent).

1. Disconnect the spark plug leads and remove the spark plugs.

2. If using timing tool part No. FT2937-1, thread the barrel of the tool approximately 3/4 into the No. 1 spark plug hole. See **Figure 28**.

   a. Insert the timing tool rod into the tool barrel.

   b. While lightly holding the rod against the piston, rotate the crankshaft clockwise until the rod reaches its maximum outward travel. At this point, the piston is at TDC.

3. If using dial indicator part No. 91-58222A1 (or equivalent), install the indicator into the No. 1 spark plug hole. While observing the dial indicator, rotate the flywheel clockwise until the piston is at TDC.

4. With the No. 1 piston at TDC, make sure the TDC mark on the flywheel is aligned with the timing pointer. If the pointer and TDC mark are aligned, continue at Step 5. If not, remove the flywheel (Chapter Eight) and check for a sheared flywheel key or damaged key slot in the flywheel or crankshaft. Repair as necessary.

5. Remove the timing tool or dial indicator from the No. 1 spark plug hole. Connect spark tester

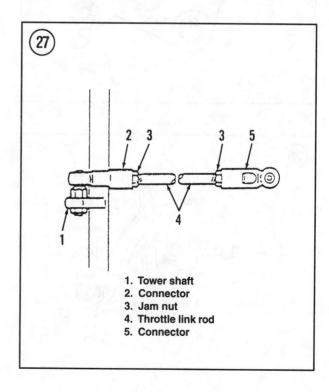

1. Tower shaft
2. Connector
3. Jam nut
4. Throttle link rod
5. Connector

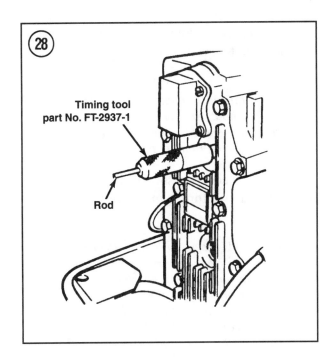

Timing tool
part No. FT-2937-1

Rod

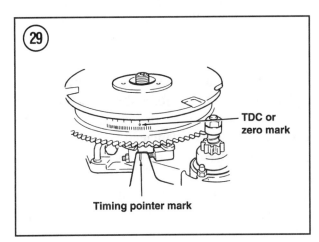

TDC or
zero mark

Timing pointer mark

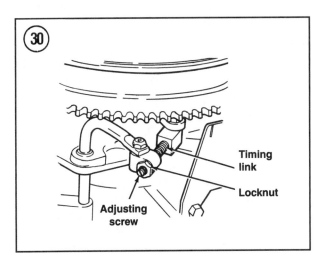

Timing
link

Locknut

Adjusting
screw

part No. FT-11295 (or equivalent) to the spark plug leads.

WARNING
The outboard motor must be shifted into FORWARD gear to be able to advance the throttle to the wide-open position (maximum spark advance). To prevent personal injury, remove the propeller prior to performing this procedure.

6. On models with the interlock switch on the engine, connect a jumper lead across the interlock switch to allow the engine to crank while in gear. See **Figure 17**, typical. On newer models with the interlock switch in the remote control box, connect a push button remote starter switch across the starter solenoid yellow or yellow/red terminal and the battery positive (+) terminal. Either of these methods will allow starter activation while in gear.

7. Connect a timing light to the No.1 (top) spark plug lead.

8. Move the tower shaft to the wide-open throttle position. Crank the engine while observing the timing marks with the timing light. See **Figure 29**.

NOTE
*Due to the electronic characteristics of the different CD ignition systems, timing at cranking speed must be set 2 degrees **retarded** on engines with Prestolite magneto CD ignition systems and 2 degrees **advanced** on engines with Thunderbolt CDI or CDM ignition systems. It is recommended to verify timing at wide-open throttle (dynamically) with a test wheel, if available. The engine specification Tables give both cranking and wide-open throttle specifications. It is more important that the timing is correct at wide-open throttle than at cranking speed.*

9. If adjustment is necessary, loosen the timing link locknut and turn the adjusting screw as required. See **Figure 30**. Tighten the locknut and recheck the timing to verify adjustment.

10. After adjustment, remove the interlock jumper wire or remote starter switch. Remove the spark tester, reinstall the spark plugs and connect the spark plug leads.

**Ignition Timing
(Dynamic)**

Dynamic ignition timing must be checked with the outboard motor running at wide-open throttle. Therefore, this procedure must be performed with the boat in the water or the outboard mounted in a test tank.

1. Remove the propeller (Chapter Nine) and install a suitable test wheel.

*WARNING
Never attempt to make adjustments to the engine on a moving boat. Boat movement should be restrained by securely fastening the boat to a dock.*

2. Connect a timing light to the No. 1 (top) spark plug lead according to its manufacturer's instructions.

3. Connect a shop tachometer according to its manufacturer's instructions.

4. Start the outboard and warm to normal operating temperature. Shift into forward gear.

5. Advance the throttle to the wide-open throttle position. If the specified mark on the flywheel does not align with the timing pointer mark, throttle back to idle and stop the motor.

6. Loosen the timing link locknut (**Figure 30**) and turn the adjusting screw as required.

7. Tighten the locknut and repeat Steps 5 and 6 as necessary.

Idle Mixture Adjustment

Idle mixture should be performed with the boat in the water or the outboard motor in a test tank. Do not attempt to adjust the carburetor with the outboard connected to a flushing device. If using a test tank, remove the propeller and install the specified test wheel.

*WARNING
Never attempt to make adjustments on a moving boat. Restrain movement by securely fastening the boat to a dock when working on a running power head.*

1. Connect an accurate shop tachometer according to its manufacturer's instructions.

*NOTE
All models except the 70 and 75 hp models have 2 or more carburetors. The idle mixture has to be properly set on all carburetors. Adjust the top carburetor first, middle next (if applicable) and the bottom carburetor last. It may be necessary to switch back and forth between the carburetors several times to get the mixture correct. If necessary, reset the mixture screws to the initial settings and try again.*

2. Turn the idle mixture screw(s) clockwise until lightly seated. Do not force the screw(s) tightly into the carburetor(s) or the tip(s) and the carburetor(s) will be damaged.

3. Back out the mixture screw(s) to specifications.

4. Start the engine and run at 2000 rpm until warmed up to normal operating temperature. Once operating temperature is reached, allow the motor to idle 1-2 minutes to stabilize the motor and allow the fuel recirculation system to begin functioning.

5. Set the throttle lever control to the idle position. If necessary adjust the throttle stop screw (**Figure 21**) temporarily to obtain the recommended idle speed.

*NOTE
Idle mixture cannot be properly set unless the carburetor(s) are operating on the idle circuit(s). Setting the idle mixture at higher speeds will give inaccurate results. It may be necessary to switch back and forth between idle mix-*

ture adjustments and idle speed adjustments several times to achieve proper adjustment. Always adjust the idle speed last.

6. Slowly turn the idle mixture screw counterclockwise in 1/8 turn increments, pausing at least 10 seconds between turns. Continue this step until the idle speed decreases and idle becomes rough due to an overly rich mixture. Note the position of the mixture screw slot.

7. Slowly turn the idle mixture screw clockwise in 1/8 turn increments, pausing at least 10 seconds between turns. The idle speed will gradually become smooth and speed will increase. Continue this step until the engine speed begins to slow again and/or misfires due to the excessively lean mixture. Note the position of the mixture screw slot.

8. Position the mixture screw at a midpoint between the settings of Step 6 and Step 7. See **Figure 22**. On 60 hp models, repeat Step 6 and Step 7 for the bottom carburetor.

9. Quickly accelerate the engine to wide-open throttle and back to idle. The engine will accelerate cleanly and without hesitation if the mixture is adjusted correctly. Readjust as necessary.

10. Adjust the idle speed screw (**Figure 21**) to specifications.

11. *1992 120 hp L-Drive models*—Synchronize the oil injection pump to the throttle opening as described in Chapter Six.

Choke Valve Synchronization (On models so equipped)

1. Loosen the screw on each choke swivel to free the choke link.

2. Adjust the top end of the link approximately 1/16 to 1/8 in. (1.6-3.2 mm) beyond the top of the choke swivel and tighten the screw to hold the link in that position.

3. Close the top carburetor choke valve completely and hold in that position. Close the bottom carburetor choke completely then tighten the bottom choke swivel screw.

4. Loosen the 2 solenoid attaching screws just enough to permit the solenoid to be moved.

5. Slip a small piece of writing paper about 1/2 inch wide into each carburetor air horn. The paper will provide sufficient clearance to prevent the choke valve from sticking in the closed position.

6. Depress the solenoid plunger (not the rod) to close the choke valves. Slide the solenoid against the plunger and tighten the solenoid attaching screws.

7. Pull the papers from the air horns. There should be a slight drag as the papers are removed. If drag is excessive, repeat Step 5 and Step 6.

8. Release the solenoid plunger. If the choke valves are not horizontal, bend the choke valve stop groove pin in the carburetor air horn(s) as required to bring the valves into a horizontal position.

Tables 1-9 are on the following pages.

Table 1 IGNITION AND ELECTRICAL TEST EQUIPMENT AND TOOLS

Description	Part No.
Multimeter / DVA tester	91-99750
Timing light	91-99379
Shop tachometer / dwell meter	91-59339
Digital shop tachometer	79-17391A-1
Interface module (spark plug wire)	825824A-2
Timing tool (older 25-55 hp)	FT-2937-1
Dial Indicator Timing Tool	91-58222A–1
Spark Tester (air gap)	FT-11295
Push Button Remote Starter Switch	Locally available

Table 2 GENERAL ENGINE SPECIFICATIONS (4, 5 AND 7.5 HP)

Recommended full throttle operating range	
4 hp and 5 hp 1988-1989	4750-5250 rpm
5 hp 1990 and newer	5500-6500 rpm
7.5 hp	4250-5250 rpm
Idle speed in forward gear	
4 hp and 5 hp 1988-1994	800-1000 rpm
5 hp 1995 and newer	700-800 rpm
7.5 hp	600-750 rpm
Initial idle mixture screw adjustment	1 turn out from lightly seated position
Ignition timing	not adjustable
Test wheel part No.	
4 and 5 hp	use standard propeller
7.5 hp	not available

Table 3 GENERAL ENGINE SPECIFICATIONS (9.9 AND 15 HP)

Recommended full throttle operating range	
9.9 hp 1984-1987	4250-5250 rpm
9.9 hp 1988-1989	4600-5600 rpm
9.9 hp 1990-1992	4500-5500 rpm
9.9 hp 1993 and newer	4000-5000 rpm
15 hp 1984-1987	4600-5600 rpm
15 hp 1988-1989	4750-5250 rpm
15 hp 1990 and newer	5500-6500 rpm
Idle speed in forward gear	
All models 1984-1987	750 rpm maximum
All models 1988-1992	600-700 rpm
All models 1993 and newer	700-800 rpm
Initial idle mixture screw adjustment	1 turn out from lightly seated position
Ignition timing	not adjustable
Test wheel part No.	not available

Table 4 GENERAL ENGINE SPECIFICATIONS (25 HP)

Recommended full throttle operating range	
2-cylinder	4250-5250 rpm
3-cylinder	5000-6000 rpm

(continued)

Table 4 GENERAL ENGINE SPECIFICATIONS (25 HP) (continued)

Idle speed in forward gear	700-800 rpm
Initial idle mixture screw adjustment	
2-cylinder	1-1/4 turns from lightly seated position
3-cylinder	1-1/2 turns from lightly seated position
Ignition timing	not adjustable
Test wheel part No. (minimum test rpm)	
2-cylinder	FT8968A (4800 rpm)
3-cylinder	not available

Table 5 GENERAL ENGINE SPECIFICATIONS (35, 40 AND 50 HP)

Recommended full throttle operating range	
35 hp 1986-1987	4500-5500 rpm
35 hp 1988-1989	4250-5250 rpm
35 hp 1990-1991	5000-5250 rpm
50 hp 1984-1989	4500-5500 rpm
50 hp 1990-1991	5000-5500 rpm
40 and 50 hp 1992-1999	4750-5250 rpm
Idle speed in forward gear	
All models 1984-1987	750 rpm maximum
All models 1988-1999	700-800 rpm
Initial idle mixture screw adjustment	1 turn out from lightly seated position
Ignition timing at wide-open throttle	
with a test wheel (at cranking speed)	
35 hp 1986-1991	Not adjustable
50 hp 1984-1987B (Battery breaker point)	30° BTDC[1]
50 hp 1987C-1989A	30° BTDC (28° BTDC)[2]
50 hp 1989B-1992B	32° BTDC (30° BTDC)[2]
40 and 50 hp 1992C-1995	30° BTDC (32° BTDC)[3]
40 and 50 hp 1996-1999	32° BTDC (34° BTDC)[4]
Test wheel part No. (minimum test rpm)	
35 hp	T2955A (4800 rpm)
50 hp 1984-1994	T2955A (5000 rpm)
40 hp 1992-1994	T2955A (not available)
40 and 50 hp 1995-1999	not available

[1] Checked only at cranking rpm. Timing must be checked on both cylinders.
[2] Prestolite magneto CD (capacitor discharge) ignition.
[3] Thunderbolt CDI (capacitor discharge ignition).
[4] CDM (capacitor discharge module) ignition.

Table 6 GENERAL ENGINE SPECIFICATIONS (60, 70 AND 75 HP)

Recommended full throttle operating range	4750-5250 rpm
Idle speed in forward gear	750 rpm maximum
Initial idle mixture screw adjustment	1 turn out from lightly seated position
Ignition timing at wide open throttle	
with a test wheel (cranking rpm)	
60 hp	32° BTDC (30° BTDC)[1]
70 and 75 hp	30° BTDC (32° BTDC)[2]
	(continued)

Table 6 GENERAL ENGINE SPECIFICATIONS (60, 70 AND 75 HP) (continued)

Test wheel part No. (minimum test rpm)	
60 hp	FT11200 (5000)
70 and 75 hp	Modified 48-816704A40 (5000 rpm)
Standard 13 in. aluminum propeller	
modified to 9 in. diameter by a propeller shop.	

[1]Prestolite magneto CD (capacitor discharge) ignition.
[2]70 hp—Thunderbolt CDI (capacitor discharge ignition).
[2]75 hp—CDM (capacitor discharge module) ignition.

Table 7 GENERAL ENGINE SPECIFICATIONS (85, 90, 120 AND 125 HP OUTBOARDS)

Recommended full throttle operating range	
85 hp	4500-5500 rpm
90 and 120 hp 1990A	4500-5500 rpm
90 and 120 hp 1990B-1994	5000-5500 rpm
90 and 120 hp 1995-1999	4750-5250 rpm
125 hp 1984-1988B	4250-5250 rpm
125 hp 1988C-1989	4500-5500 rpm
Idle speed in forward gear	700-800 rpm
Initial idle mixture screw adjustment	
85 hp 1984-1988	1-1/4 turns out from lightly seated position
85 hp 1989	3/4 turn out from lightly seated position
90 hp 1990-1994	3/4 turn out from lightly seated position
90 hp 1995-1999	1 turn out from a lightly seated position
120 hp 1990-1999	1 turn out from a lightly seated position
125 hp 1984-1988C	1-1/4 turns out from lightly seated position
125 hp 1988C-1989	1 turn out from a lightly seated position
Ignition timing at wide-open throttle with a test wheel (cranking rpm)	
85 and 125 hp	30° BTDC (28° BTDC)[1]
90 and 120 hp 1990-1991C and 90 hp 1991E	30° BTDC (28° BTDC)[1]
90 and 120 hp 1991D-1995, except 90 hp 1991E	30° BTDC (32° BTDC)[2]
90 and 120 hp 1996-1999	30° BTDC (32° BTDC)[3]
Test wheel part No. (minimum test rpm)	
All single port exhaust lower units	TA8999 (5000 rpm with plugs installed)
Dual port exhaust lower units*	
90 hp 1990-1991	Modified 48-FP685-3 (5000-5150 rpm)
120 hp 1990-1991	Modified 48-FP685-3 (5200 rpm)
90 and 120 hp 1992-1994	Modified 48-77340A40 (5000 rpm)
90 hp and 120 hp 1995-1999	not available

*Check 1991 and older engines with dual port exhaust (exhaust exits propeller hub and trim tab) with a 17 in. pitch aluminum propeller (part No. 48-FP685-3) turned down by a propeller shop to a diameter of 9 in. for the 90 hp and 9-7/8 in. for the 120 hp. Check 1992-1994 engines with dual port exhaust with a 13 in. pitch aluminum propeller (part No. 48-77340A40) turned down by a propeller shop to a diameter of 9 in. for the 90 hp and 10 in. for the 120 hp.

[1]Prestolite magneto CD (capacitor discharge) ignition.
[2]Thunderbolt CDI (capacitor discharge ignition).
[3]CDM (capacitor discharge module) ignition.

Table 8 GENERAL ENGINE SPECIFICATIONS (150 HP)

Recommended full throttle operating range	5000-5500 rpm
Idle speed in forward gear	700-800 rpm
Initial idle mixture screw adjustment	1 turn out from lightly seated position
Ignition timing at wide open throttle	
with at test wheel (cranking rpm)	
1989-1991A	32° BTDC (30° BTDC)[1]
1991B-1994	32° BTDC (34° BTDC)[2]
Test wheel part No. (minimum test rpm)	
Single port exhaust lower unit	TA8999 (5000 rpm with plugs removed)
Dual port exhaust lower unit*	
1989-1991	Modified 48-FP685-3 (5150-5200)
1992-1994	Modified 48-77340A40 (5000)

*Check 1989-1991 engines with dual port exhaust, (exhaust exits the propeller hub and the trim tab) with a 17 in. pitch aluminum propeller (part No. 48-FP685-3) turned down by a propeller shop to a diameter of 11 in. Check 1992-1994 engines with dual port exhaust with a 13 in. pitch aluminum propeller (part No. 48-77340A40) turned down by a propeller shop to a diameter of 9-1/2 in.

[1]Prestolite magneto CD (capacitor discharge) ignition.
[2]Thunderbolt CDI (capacitor discharge ignition).

Table 9 GENERAL ENGINE SPECIFICATIONS (85, 90, 120 AND 125 HP L-DRIVES)

Recommended full throttle operating range	
85 and 125 hp 1989	4500-5500 rpm
90 and 120 hp 1990A	4500-5500 rpm
90 and 120 hp 1990B-1992	5000-5500 rpm
Idle speed in forward gear	700-800 rpm
Initial idle mixture screw adjustment	
85 and 90 hp	3/4 turn out from lightly seated position
120 and 125 hp	1 turn out from a lightly seated position
Ignition timing at wide-open throttle	
with a test wheel (at cranking rpm)	
85 and 125 hp	30° BTDC (28° BTDC)[1]
90 and 120 hp 1990A models	30° BTDC (28° BTDC)[1]
90 and 120 hp 1990B-1991A	32° BTDC (30° BTDC)[1]
90 and 120 hp 1991B-1992	30° BTDC (32° BTDC)[2]
Test wheel part No. (minimum test rpm)	
All single port exhaust lower units	TA8999 (5000 rpm with plugs installed)
Dual port exhaust lower units*	
90 hp 1990-1991	Modified 48-FP685-3 (5000-5150 rpm)
120 hp 1990-1991	Modified 48-FP685-3 (5200 rpm)
120 hp 1992	Modified 48-77340A40 (5000 rpm)

*Check 1991 and older L-Drive engines with dual port exhaust (exhaust exits propeller hub and trim tab) with a 17 in. pitch aluminum propeller (part No. 48-FP685-3) turned down by a propeller shop to a diameter of 9 in. for the 90 hp and 9-7/8 in. for the 120 hp. Check 1992 120 hp dual port exhaust L-Drive engines with a 13 in. pitch aluminum propeller (part No. 48-77340A40) turned down by a propeller shop to a diameter of 10 in. for the 120 hp.

[1]Prestolite magneto CD (capacitor discharge) electronic.
[2]Thunderbolt CDI (capacitor discharge ignition) electronic.

5

Chapter Six

Fuel System

This chapter contains removal, overhaul, installation and adjustment procedures for fuel pumps, carburetors, reed valves, fuel tanks and connecting lines used with all engines covered in this manual. **Tables 1-3** list general torque specifications, reed valve specifications and fuel pump pressure specifications. **Tables 4-7** list carburetor specifications. All tables are at the end of the chapter.

FUEL PUMP

All outboard motors equipped with an integral fuel tank use a gravity flow fuel delivery system and require no fuel pump or primer bulb. The diaphragm-type fuel pump used on models with a remote fuel tank is operated by crankcase pressure/vacuum pulsations. Since this type of fuel pump cannot create sufficient suction to draw fuel from the tank during cranking, fuel is trans-

ferred to the carburetor(s) for starting by operating the primer bulb installed in the fuel hose.

> *WARNING*
> *L-Drive models cannot use a conventional primer bulb. If a priming type device is to be used on an L-Drive, it must pass Coast Guard regulations for permanently installed inboard-style fuel systems.*

A single-stage diaphragm displacement pump is used on 5-15 hp models. Pressure pulsations created by movement of the piston(s) reach the fuel pump through a passage between the crankcase and the pump. Changes in the crankcase pressure of the No. 1 cylinder cause the pump diaphragm to flex back and forth, transmitting the pressure to an inlet and outlet reed (check valve) mounted on a plate inside the pump.

Upward piston motion creates a low pressure on the pump diaphragm. This low pressure opens the inlet check valve in the pump, drawing fuel from the line into the pump. At the same time, the low pressure draws the air/fuel mixture from the carburetor into the crankcase.

Downward piston motion creates a high pressure on the pump diaphragm. This pressure closes the inlet check valve and opens the outlet check valve, forcing the fuel into the carburetor and drawing the air-fuel mixture from the crankcase into the cylinder for combustion. **Figure 1** shows the operational sequence of a typical single stage diaphragm fuel pump.

Either a 2-stage diaphragm pump or a square-type diaphragm pump is used on all other models. Pump operation is essentially the same as a

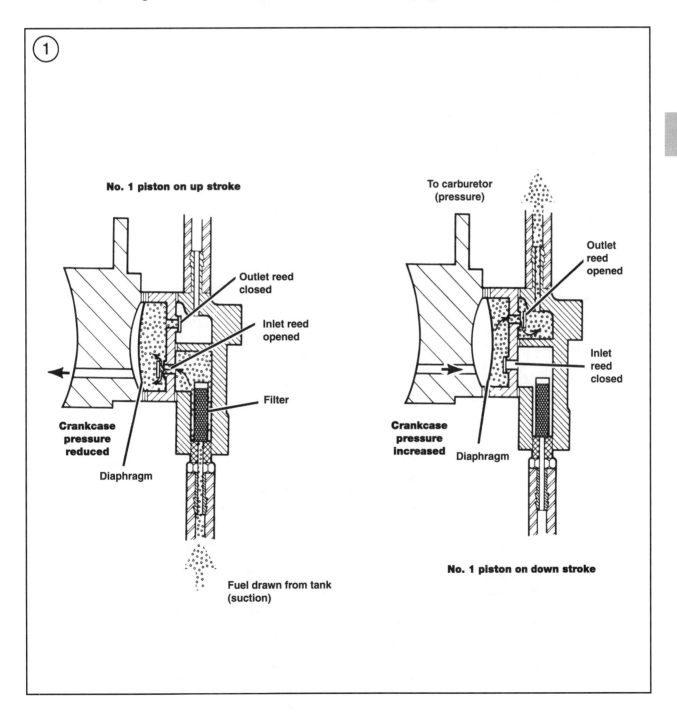

6

single-stage diaphragm pump. **Figure 2** shows the operational sequence of a typical 2-stage pump used on a 3-cylinder motor. **Figure 3** shows a typical square-type pump used on late models. On 5-cylinder models equipped with 2 fuel pumps, the lower pump is operated by the No. 4 and No. 5 cylinders. It delivers fuel to the upper pump (operated by the No. 3 and No. 4 cylinders) where it is delivered to the carburetors.

The fuel pumps used on all models are self-contained units mounted on the power head. Pump design is extremely simple and reliable in operation. Diaphragm failures are the most common problem, although the use of dirty or improper fuel-oil mixtures can cause check valve malfunction.

Fuel Pump Output Test

NOTE
If the cylinder(s) that supplies crankcase pressure and vacuum to a fuel pump mechanically fails, all of the cylinders will starve for fuel. Check the compression of the engine before condemning the fuel pump. See Chapter Four.

The fuel pump output test must be performed with the motor in a test tank with the correct test wheel installed or with the motor mounted on a boat in the water. Do not run the motor at wide-open throttle while connected to a flushing device.

1. Disconnect the fuel pump output hose that leads to the carburetor(s).
2. Connect a fuel pressure gauge between the fuel pump and the carburetor line using a T-fitting and appropriate fuel line and clamps. Squeeze the primer bulb and check for leaks.
3. Disconnect the fuel inlet hose from the fuel pump.
4. Install a short piece of clear vinyl hose between the fuel inlet hose and the fuel pump using the appropriate fittings and clamps.
5. *Permanent fuel tank*—Check that the fuel vent fitting and vent line are not obstructed.
6. *Portable fuel tank*—Open the fuel tank vent to relieve any pressure that may be present and verify that the tank is no more than 24 in. (61 cm) below the level of the fuel pump.
7. Start the motor and allow it to reach operating temperature. Refer to **Table 3** for fuel pump specifications. Run the engine in FORWARD gear to the speed listed in **Table 3**. Observe the fuel pressure gauge and the clear hose at each engine speed.
8. If air bubbles are visible in the clear hose at any test speed, check the fuel supply line back to

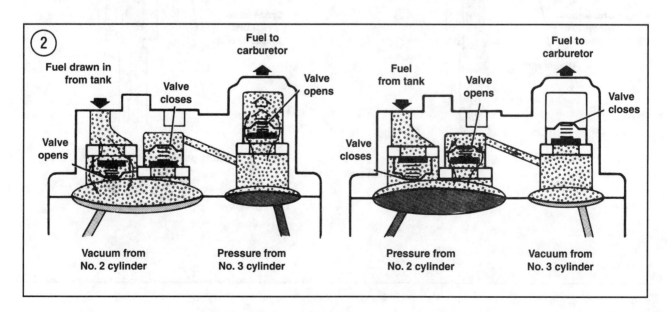

the pickup tube in the gas tank for loose fittings, clamps, a defective primer bulb, damaged filter or any problems that would allow air to leak into the fuel line. The fuel pump cannot develop the specified pressure if air is present. Correct any problems and retest.

9. If no air bubbles are visible in the clear hose and the fuel pressure is below specification, repair or replace the fuel pump(s)as necessary.

10. If no air bubbles are visible in the clear hose and fuel pressure is within specification, the fuel pump and fuel supply system are not the problem.

Removal/Installation (Single-stage Pump)

1. Disconnect the fuel hose from the support plate quick-disconnect fitting.

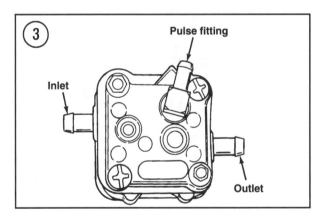

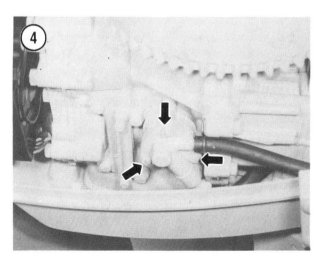

2. *15 hp*—Remove the manual rewind starter assembly. Refer to Chapter Eleven.

3. Remove the 3 screws securing the pump cover to the power head or transfer port cover (**Figure 4**).

4. Label fuel hoses for reference during reassembly. Compress the fuel hose clamp with hose clamp pliers and slide the clamp away from the fitting. Repeat this step to disconnect the remaining fuel hose from the pump cover.

5. Separate the reed plate and pump diaphragm from the power head.

6. Unscrew the lower fitting from the pump cover and remove the filter from the pump cover.

7. Clean all gasket residue from the power head mounting pad. Work carefully to prevent gouging, scratching or damaging the mounting surface.

8. Installation is the reverse of removal. Sandwich the diaphragm between the new gaskets. Make sure the diaphragm is completely flat and extends beyond the gasket on all sides.

Removal/Installation (2-Stage Pump)

1. Disconnect the fuel hose from the support plate quick-disconnect fitting.

2. Unscrew sediment bowl screw and remove sediment bowl (**Figure 5**) and remove filter screen (**Figure 6**).

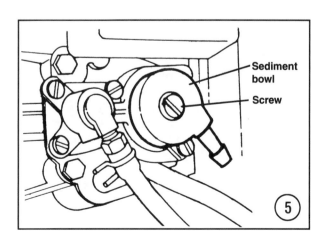

3. Label fuel hoses for reference during reassembly. Compress the fuel hose fitting clamp with hose clamp pliers and slide the clamp off the fitting. Repeat this step to disconnect the remaining fuel hose from the pump cover.

4. Remove the 6 fuel pump body screws and lockwashers. See **Figure 7**, typical. Remove the pump body.

5. Remove the fuel hose and pulse hose fitting from the fuel pump cover.

6. Remove the 4 fuel pump cover screws. See **Figure 8**, typical. Remove the cover and gasket.

7. Repeat Steps 2-6 to remove the second fuel pump on models so equipped.

8. Clean all gasket residue from the engine mounting pad. Work carefully to avoid gouging, scratching or damaging the mounting surface.

9. Installation is the reverse of removal. Always use new gaskets. Apply a suitable sealant to the impulse hose and fuel line fittings and tighten securely. Install filter screen in the sediment bowl with the turned edges facing the engine (**Figure 6**). Install new pump body gasket with slot over the pump body key (**Figure 7**). Install sediment bowl with hose fitting positioned as shown in **Figure 9**.

Removal/Installation (Square-Type Fuel Pump)

1. Label the hoses at the pump for correct reinstallation. Disconnect the hoses from the pump.

> *NOTE*
> *The fuel pump is secured to the power head by 2 Phillips or slotted screws. The fuel pump components are held together by 2 hex-head screws. See **Figure 10**. During fuel pump removal, do not remove the hex-head screws unless pump disassembly is necessary.*

2. Remove the 2 Phillips or slotted screws securing the pump to the power head. See **Figure 10**. Lift the pump off the power head.

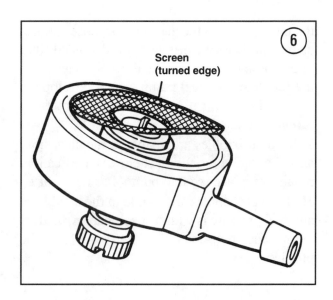

Screen (turned edge)

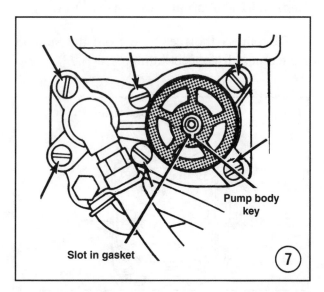

Pump body key

Slot in gasket

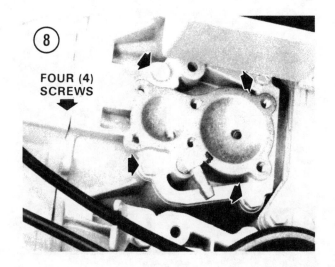

FOUR (4) SCREWS

3. Carefully clean the fuel pump-to-power head gasket or O-ring from the power head or fuel pump.

4. Install a new gasket or O-ring between the pump and power head.

5. Install the pump on the power head and secure with the 2 mounting screws. Tighten the screws evenly, to 55 in.-lb.

6. Reconnect the hoses to their respective fittings on the pump assembly. Securely clamp the hoses.

Disassembly/Assembly (Single-Stage Pump)

The single-stage fuel pump is completely disassembled during removal. Proceed to *Cleaning and Inspection (Single-stage Pump)* in this chapter.

Disassembly/Assembly (2-Stage Pump)

Figure 11 shows an exploded view of a typical 2-stage fuel pump.

1. Remove the 2 screws securing the middle check valve to the pump body. See **Figure 12**.

Remove the valve and gasket from the pump body.

NOTE
To make a hooked tool for use in Step 2, use a length of 16 gage wire and a pair of needlenose pliers.

2. If replacement is necessary, pry out the pressed-in second stage valve (**Figure 13**) using a suitable hooked tool. Note that the valve will be destroyed during removal.

3. Remove the pressed-in first stage valve (**Figure 13**) by inserting a pin punch into the hole in the pump body behind the valve, then tapping it lightly with a hammer.

4. Install a new center valve gasket in the pump body. Install the center valve with the spring side facing the pump body (**Figure 13**). Install and securely tighten the 2 retaining screws.

5. Press the first and second stage valves into the pump body until they bottom out. Make sure the valves are positioned as shown in **Figure 12**.

NOTE
*5-cylinder models with 2-stage pumps use a boost spring and retainer on each pump. The boost spring is installed wide side down into the pump body and valve assembly (10, **Figure 11**). The boost spring retainer is installed smooth side*

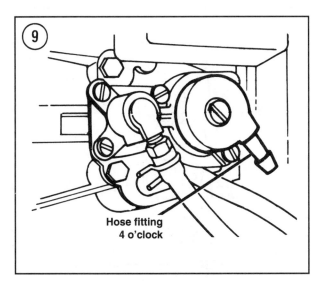

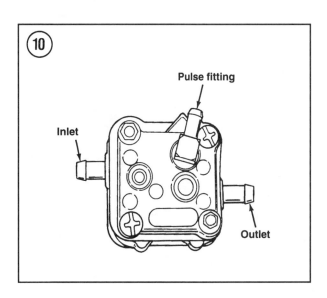

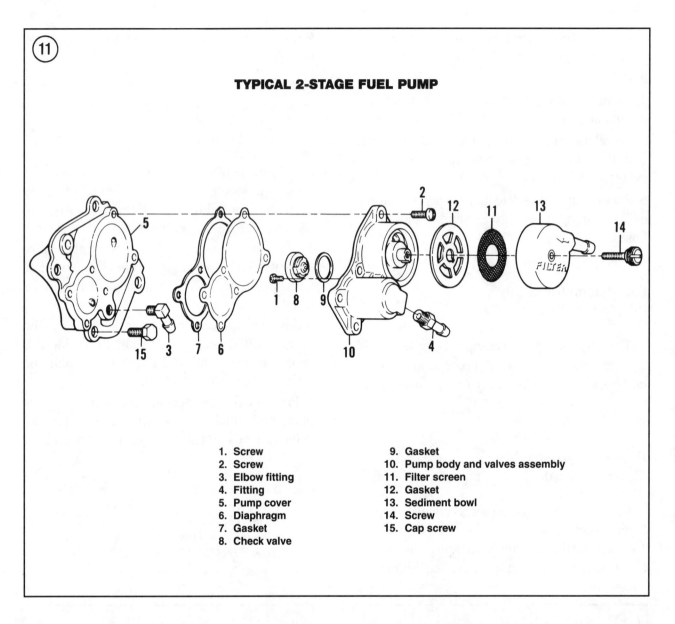

TYPICAL 2-STAGE FUEL PUMP

1. Screw
2. Screw
3. Elbow fitting
4. Fitting
5. Pump cover
6. Diaphragm
7. Gasket
8. Check valve
9. Gasket
10. Pump body and valves assembly
11. Filter screen
12. Gasket
13. Sediment bowl
14. Screw
15. Cap screw

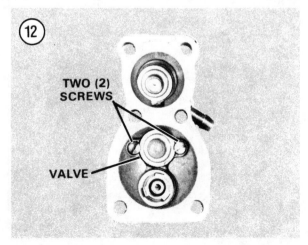

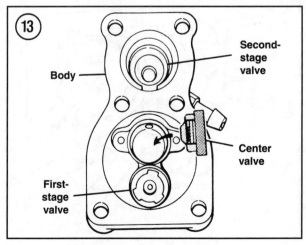

*up and will push against the diaphragm (6, **Figure 11**). Compress the boost spring by pushing the diaphragm down with a clean, smooth putty knife or similar tool. Assemble the pump cover to the pump body and carefully slide the putty knife out.*

Disassembly/Reassembly (Square-Type Fuel Pump)

Refer to **Figure 14** or **Figure 15** for an exploded view of the pump assembly.

NOTE
The pump diaphragms and gaskets should be replaced any time the pump is disassembled.

1. Remove the pump assembly as outlined in this chapter.

2. Remove the hex-head screws holding the pump together.

3. Separate the pump cover, gaskets and diaphragms from the pump body and base. Discard the gaskets and diaphragms.

4. *40 hp and larger*—Using needle nose pliers remove the check valve retainers from the pump body. Remove the plastic discs and check valves from the retainers.

5. *40 hp and larger*—Remove the cap and spring from the pump cover. Remove the cap and boost spring from the pump body.

6. *25 hp*—Using needle nose pliers remove the check valves from the pump body. Make sure the

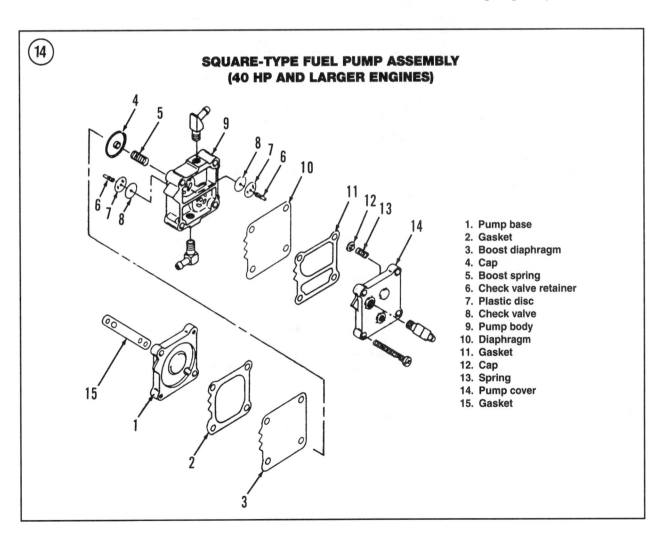

**SQUARE-TYPE FUEL PUMP ASSEMBLY
(40 HP AND LARGER ENGINES)**

1. Pump base
2. Gasket
3. Boost diaphragm
4. Cap
5. Boost spring
6. Check valve retainer
7. Plastic disc
8. Check valve
9. Pump body
10. Diaphragm
11. Gasket
12. Cap
13. Spring
14. Pump cover
15. Gasket

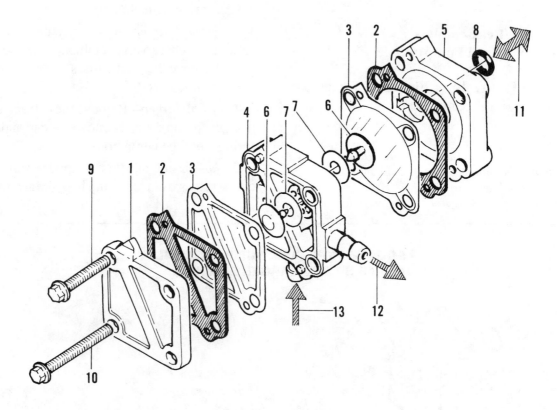

**SQUARE-TYPE FUEL PUMP
25 HP (3-CYLINDER) MODELS**

1. Pump cover
2. Gasket
3. Diaphragm
4. Pump body
5. Pump base
6. Check valve
7. Washer
   (not serviced separately)
8. O-ring
9. Cover screw
10. Mounting screw
11. Crankcase pressure/vacuum
    pulses
12. Fuel outlet
13. Fuel inlet

washers under the check valves are not damaged in this process. Discard the check valves.

Check valve installation

1. *25 hp*—Lubricate the new check valve with motor oil and install a washer onto the valve.

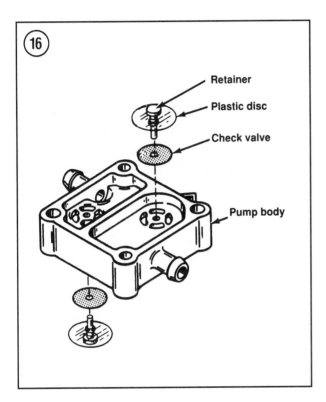

Gently press the valve and washer into the pump body. Do not use any tools or sharp objects. Do not pull the check valve through from the other side. Repeat the step for the other check valve.

2. *40 hp and larger*—Insert the check valve retainer into the plastic disc, then into the check valve. See **Figure 16**. Repeat the step for the other check valve.

3. *40 hp and larger*—Lubricate the check valve retainers with motor oil. Insert the check valve and retainer assemblies into the pump body. See **Figure 16**.

4. *40 hp and larger*—Bend the check valve retainer stem from side to side, until the stem breaks off flush with the retainer cap. See **Figure 17**. Repeat the step for the other retainer.

5. *40 hp and larger*—Insert the broken retainer stem into the retainer as shown in **Figure 18**. Using a small hammer and punch, tap the stem into the retainer until flush with the retainer cap.

> *NOTE*
> *Fuel pump components have one or more V tabs on one side for directional reference during assembly. Be certain the V tabs on all components are aligned. To ensure the correct alignment of pump components, use 1/4 in. bolts or dowels*

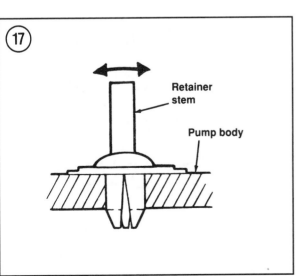

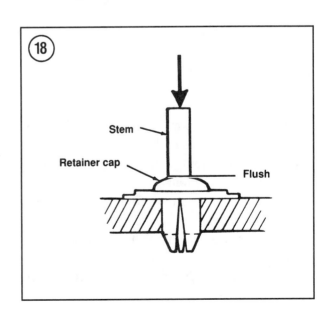

as guides. Insert the guides through the pump mounting screw holes.

6. Reassemble the pump by reversing the order of disassembly. Do not use gasket sealer on the pump gaskets or diaphragms. Be sure that all pump components are properly aligned.

7. Install the hex-head screws and tighten securely. Install the pump on the power head as outlined in this chapter.

Cleaning and Inspection (Single-Stage Pump)

1. Clean all metal parts in solvent and dry with compressed air.

2. Check filter screen for damage and replace as required.

3. Hold the diaphragm up to a strong light and check for pin holes, breaks or excessive stretching. Diaphragm should be replaced if in questionable condition.

4. Check fuel pump reeds. If warpage, tension or curling of the reed tips (**Figure 19**) is noted, replace the reeds.

Cleaning and Inspection (2-Stage Pump)

1. Clean all metals parts in solvent. Dry pump housing and body using compressed air. Allow check valves to air dry.

2. Check the filter screen for damage and replace as required.

3. Hold the diaphragm up to a strong light and check for pin holes, breaks or excessive stretching. The diaphragm should be replaced if in questionable condition.

4. Inspect the check valves for spring tension by depressing the check valve discs using a screwdriver or other suitable tool. Make sure the valves seat firmly when released. Replace any valve that is slightly warped, has weak spring tension or broken springs.

5. Check pump body and housing condition. Make sure the valve seats provide a flat contact area for the valve disc. Replace the body or housing if cracks or rough gasket mating surfaces are noted.

Cleaning/Inspection (Square-Type Fuel Pump)

1. Clean the pump components using a suitable solvent (except check valves) and dry with compressed air.

2. Inspect check valves and plastic discs for cracks, holes or other damage. Replace as necessary.

3. Inspect the fuel fittings on the pump cover or base for looseness, leakage or other damage. Tighten or replace the fittings as necessary.

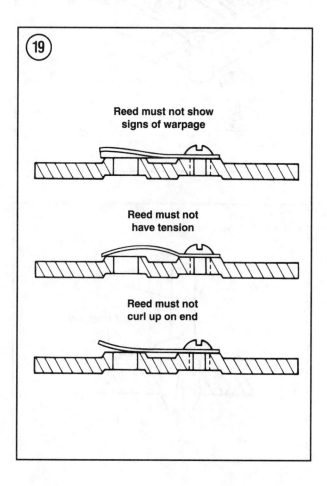

(19)

Reed must not show
signs of warpage

Reed must not
have tension

Reed must not
curl up on end

CARBURETORS

Force outboard motors and L-Drives use a variety of Tillotson and Walbro carburetors. All operate essentially the same, but housing shape and design vary slightly according to engine size. Some Tillotson carburetors do not use an idle tube.

When installing a carburetor, make sure that the mounting nuts (**Figure 20**) are securely tightened. A loose carburetor will allow air to enter around the mating surface resulting in a lean-running condition, which could cause engine damage.

Prior to removing and disassembling any carburetor, be sure the correct overhaul kit, the proper tools and a sufficient quantity of fresh

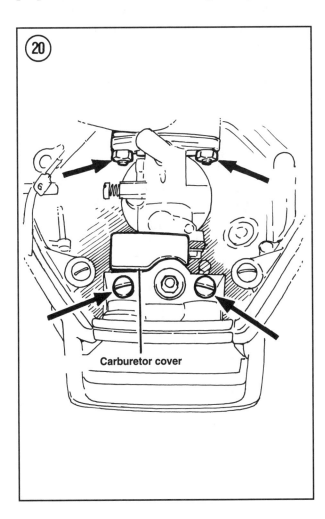

Carburetor cover

cleaning solvent is available. Force dealers offer a gasket kit and a repair kit for each carburetor.

CARBURETOR REMOVAL/INSTALLATION

4 and 5 hp Models (Prior to 1989 B)

1. Remove the engine cover.
2A. *Prior to 1988 B models*:
   a. Drain and remove the fuel tank as described in this chapter.
   b. Slide the fuel hose clamp from the fuel fitting with hose clamp pliers and disconnect the fuel hose from the shut-off valve.
   c. Pull the fuel shut-off knob from the fuel shut-off valve. Remove the fuel shut-off valve using an open-end wrench.
   d. Disconnect the stop switch wires. Remove the nut securing the stop switch to the front support plate cover and remove stop switch.
2B. *1988 B-1989 A*:
   a. Slide the fuel hose clamps from the fittings using hose clamp pliers.
   b. Disconnect the fuel hoses from the fuel fittings.
   c. Remove the nut securing the fuel fitting to the front support plate cover and remove the fuel fitting.
3. *All models*—Remove the retaining clip (if so equipped) securing the choke link to the carburetor choke shaft. Remove the screw securing the choke knob to the choke link. Pull the choke knob out of the front support plate cover and remove the choke link.
4. Remove 2 front support plate cover screws (**Figure 20**). Remove the front support plate cover.
5. Remove the carburetor cover (**Figure 20**).
6. Remove the 2 nuts securing the carburetor to the adapter plate (**Figure 20**). Remove the carburetor and gasket.
7. Installation is the reverse of removal. Always use a new gasket between carburetor and adapter

plate. Be certain that all fuel hose connections are securely clamped to prevent leakage. Perform synchronization and linkage adjustment as outlined in Chapter Five.

5 hp Models (1989 B-on)

1. Remove the rewind starter as described in Chapter Eleven.

2. Disconnect the choke link (A, **Figure 21**) from the carburetor.

3. Disconnect the fuel delivery hose (B, **Figure 21**) from the fitting in the front cover.

4. Remove the 2 front cover attaching screws (C, **Figure 21**). Remove the front cover.

5. Disconnect the primer hose (**Figure 22**) from the carburetor.

6. Remove the E-ring and washer that secures the throttle cam follower shaft to the carburetor. See **Figure 22**. Slide the follower shaft out of the carburetor and disconnect the throttle link from the throttle lever.

7. Remove the 2 carburetor mounting nuts and slide the carburetor away from the power head. Disconnect the fuel delivery hose and remove the carburetor.

8. To install the carburetor, place a new gasket (without sealant) on the carburetor mounting studs.

9. Place the carburetor into position. Attach the fuel delivery hose to the carburetor and securely clamp using a new tie strap. Attach the throttle link to the throttle lever.

10. Install the carburetor and 2 mounting nuts. Tighten the nuts evenly and securely.

11. Install the throttle cam follower shaft and secure it with the washer and E-ring (**Figure 22**).

12. Complete the remaining installation by reversing the removal procedure. Perform synchronization and linkage adjustment as described in Chapter Five.

7.5, 9.9 and 15 hp Models (1984-1987)

1. Remove engine cover.

2. Remove the choke rod retaining clip from the choke rod and disconnect the choke rod from the carburetor.

3. Remove 2 nuts securing the carburetor to the adapter plate. Pull carburetor back away from mounting studs. On 7.5 hp models, unhook the throttle link.

4. Slide the fuel hose clamp away from the fitting using hose clamp pliers. Disconnect the fuel hose and remove carburetor.

5. Using a new gasket, install carburetor by reversing removal procedure. Be certain that all fuel hose connections are securely clamped to prevent leakage. Adjust carburetor as outlined in Chapter Five.

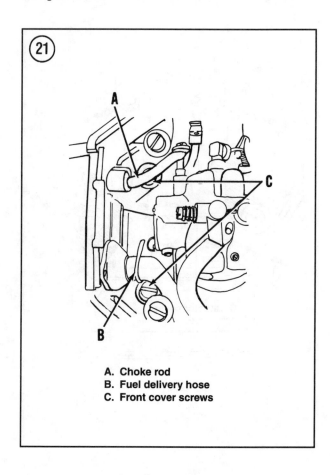

A. Choke rod
B. Fuel delivery hose
C. Front cover screws

9.9 and 15 hp and 25 hp (3-cylinder) Models (1988-on)

1. Remove engine cover.

2. Remove the rewind starter assembly as outlined in Chapter Eleven.

3. Remove the retainer clip securing the choke rod to the carburetor and disconnect the choke rod.

4. Disconnect the fuel primer hose from the carburetor (**Figure 22**).

5. Remove the E-ring and washer that secures the throttle cam follower shaft to the carburetor. Slide the follower shaft out of the carburetor. See **Figure 22**.

6. Remove the 2 nuts securing the carburetor to the intake manifold, then lift the carburetor off the power head.

7. Using a new gasket, install the carburetor by reversing the removal procedure. Be certain that all fuel hose connections are securely clamped to prevent leakage. Perform synchronization and linkage/adjustments as outlined in Chapter Five.

25 hp (2-cylinder), 35 and 50 hp Models (Prior to 1992)

1. Remove the engine cover.

2. Loosen the swivel screw that secures choke solenoid rod to the choke lever, then slide the rod out of the swivel.

3. Slide the fuel hose clamp away from the carburetor and disconnect the fuel hose.

4. If necessary, remove the throttle cam from the power head.

5. Remove the 2 nuts securing the carburetor to the intake manifold, then remove the carburetor and gasket.

6. Using a new gasket, install the carburetor by reversing the removal procedure. Be certain that all fuel hose connections are securely clamped to prevent leakage. Perform synchronization and linkage/adjustments as outlined in Chapter Five.

40 and 50 hp Models (1992-on)

1. If equipped with a choke, loosen the choke linkage swivel screw and disconnect the choke linkage.

2. Disconnect the fuel delivery hose from the carburetor.

3. Remove the nut (**Figure 23**) securing the throttle cam to the stud on the power head, then remove the throttle cam.

6

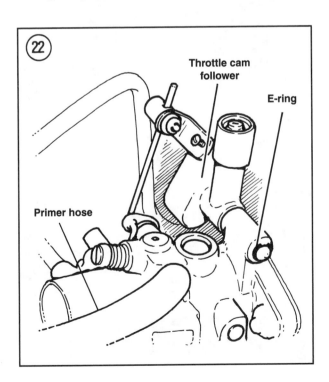

② Throttle cam follower

E-ring

Primer hose

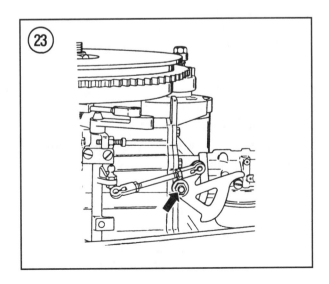

㉓

4. Remove the 2 carburetor mounting studs. Remove the carburetor from its mounting flange. Remove and discard the carburetor gasket.

5. To install the carburetor, place a new gasket (without sealant) on the mounting studs.

6A. If equipped with a choke—Place the carburetor into position while guiding the choke linkage into the swivel.

6B. If equipped with a primer—Place the carburetor into position while connecting the primer hoses to the carburetor.

7. Place the carburetor on the mounting studs. Install and tighten the mounting nuts evenly and securely.

8. Reconnect the fuel delivery hose to the carburetor. Install the throttle cam on its stud. Install and tighten the throttle cam attaching nut.

9. Complete the remaining installation by reversing the removal procedure. Perform synchronization and linkage/carburetor adjustments as described in Chapter Five.

60 hp Models

1. Remove the engine cover.

2. Disconnect the fuel hose from the fuel pump at the bottom carburetor.

3. Remove four screws from the front of the air silencer. Remove the air silencer.

4. Disconnect the throttle link from the tower shaft. If necessary, remove the nut securing the throttle cam to the stud on the power head, then remove the throttle cam. See **Figure 23**, similar.

5. Remove the throttle tie bar from both carburetors by removing the retaining rings from the throttle arms. See **Figure 24**.

6. Disconnect the choke linkage by removing the cotter pin, washers, O-rings and pin from each choke arm.

NOTE
To remove one carburetor only, disconnect the fuel line that connects the top and bottom carburetors together.

7. Install new gaskets on the carburetors' mounting studs. Install the carburetor(s) by reversing the removal procedure. Be certain that all fuel hose connections are securely clamped and checked for leaks. Perform synchronization and linkage adjustments as outlined in Chapter Five.

70 and 75 hp Models (1984-1998)

1. Remove the engine cover.

2. Disconnect the throttle link from the tower shaft. Rotate the throttle cam away from the carburetor.

3. Label fuel inlet and primer hoses for reference during reassembly. Using hose clamp pliers, slide the fuel inlet hose clamp away from the carburetor, then disconnect the inlet hose and primer hoses from the carburetor.

4. Remove 2 nuts securing the carburetor to the intake manifold, then remove the carburetor and gasket.

5. Install a new gasket on the carburetor mounting studs. Install the carburetor by reversing the removal procedure. Be certain that all fuel hose connections are securely clamped to prevent leakage. Perform synchronization and linkage/carburetor adjustments as outlined in Chapter Five.

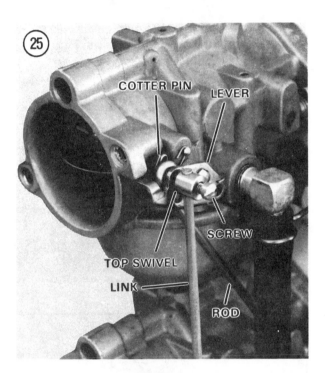

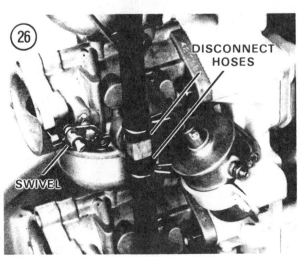

85 hp Models (1984-1987)

Top carburetor

1. Remove the carburetor intake cover and gaskets.

2. Remove the retaining rings holding the throttle tie bar to the top and middle carburetor throttle levers. Disconnect the tie bar. See **Figure 24**.

3. Loosen all 3 choke lever swivel screws. Allow the choke link to slide down.

4. Remove and discard the cotter pin holding the choke rod and swivel to the top lever. See **Figure 25**.

5. Remove washer, choke rod and 2 O-rings from swivel, then remove the swivel.

6. Slide the fuel hose clamp from the carburetor fuel fitting with hose clamp pliers, then disconnect fuel hose from the carburetor.

7. Remove the 2 nuts securing the carburetor to the adapter flange. Remove the carburetor and gasket.

8. Installation is the reverse of removal. Use a new gasket and cotter pin. If the fuel hose fitting was removed from the carburetor, coat threads of fitting with a suitable sealant and reinstall with barb facing straight down. Be certain that all fuel hose connections are securely clamped to prevent leakage. Perform synchronization and linkage/carburetor adjustments as outlined in Chapter Five.

Center carburetor

1. Remove the carburetor intake cover and gasket.

2. Remove the retaining rings holding throttle tie bar to the top and center carburetor throttle levers. Disconnect the tie bar. See **Figure 24**.

3. Loosen all 3 choke arm swivel screws, then remove choke link.

4. Remove and discard the cotter pin holding the choke rod and swivel to the center lever. See **Figure 26**.

5. Remove washer, 2 O-rings and swivel from the center carburetor.

6. Slide the fuel hose clamp from each barb on the fuel inlet fitting (**Figure 26**) and disconnect the hoses.

7. Remove the 2 nuts securing the carburetor to the adapter flange. Remove the carburetor and gasket.

8. Installation is the reverse of removal. Use new gaskets and cotter pin. Be certain fuel hose connections are securely clamped to prevent leakage. Perform synchronization and linkage/carburetor adjustments as outlined in Chapter Five.

Bottom carburetor

1. Remove the carburetor intake cover and gaskets.

2. Disconnect the throttle link at the tower shaft ball joint.

3. Remove the retaining rings holding the throttle tie bar to the center and bottom carburetor throttle levers. Disconnect the tie bar. See **Figure 27**.

4. Loosen all 3 choke arm swivel screws. Pull choke link up and out of the way.

5. Remove and discard the cotter pin holding the choke rod and swivel to the bottom choke lever.

6. Remove washer, 2 O-rings and swivel from the bottom lever.

7. Slide the fuel hose clamp from the carburetor fuel inlet fitting and disconnect the hose.

8. Remove the 2 nuts securing the carburetor to the adapter flange. Remove the carburetor and gasket.

9. Installation is the reverse of removal. Use new gaskets and cotter pin. Be certain fuel hose connections are securely clamped to prevent leakage. Perform synchronization and linkage/carburetor adjustments as outlined in Chapter Five.

85 and 90 hp Models (Including L-Drive) (1988-on)

NOTE
The carburetors may be removed individually, but due to the design of the support plate and intake cover, it is usu-

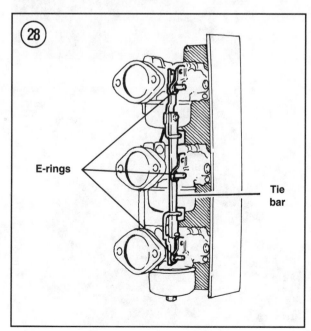

ally easier to remove the carburetors and intake cover as an assembly

1. Remove the engine cover.

2. Remove the nut securing the throttle cam to the power head. Slide the cam off its mounting stud and lay it aside. If necessary, disconnect the throttle link from the tower shaft.

3. Remove the clamp and disconnect the fuel delivery hose from the bottom carburetor.

4. Remove the 6 nuts securing the carburetors to the intake manifold.

NOTE
On models so equipped, leave choke solenoid plunger and rod connected to the top carburetor during carburetor removal. The plunger will slide out of the solenoid as the carburetors are pulled away from the power head.

5. Carefully pull carburetors away from power head and off the mounting studs. Disconnect the primer hoses on models so equipped. Push down in the choke link to gain clearance for the choke solenoid plunger on models so equipped.

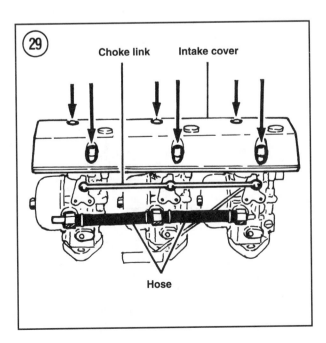

6. Disconnect the drain hose from the bottom of the intake cover and lift out the carburetors/intake cover assembly.

7. Remove 3 E-rings (**Figure 28**) attaching the tie bar to the carburetors and disconnect tie bar. Disconnect the carburetor vent hoses from the carburetors on L-Drive models.

8. Using hose clamp pliers, slide hose clamps off carburetor fittings, then disconnect the fuel hoses (**Figure 29**).

9. Remove and discard the 3 cotter pins attaching the choke link swivels to the choke levers, if so equipped. See **Figure 29**. Remove the choke link with swivels attached. Be sure to retrieve the flat washers and O-rings at each lever.

10. Remove 6 screws attaching the intake cover to the carburetors and remove cover.

11. Reinstall the carburetors by reversing the removal procedure, while noting the following: Install new gaskets and cotter pins during installation. Be sure that carburetors are installed in their original location; the top carburetor has an elbow fuel fitting and bottom carburetor is equipped with the throttle cam follower and roller. Reconnect the intake cover drain hose before installing carburetors/intake cover assembly onto mounting studs. Carefully guide the choke solenoid plunger (if so equipped) into solenoid when installing carburetors. Be certain fuel hose connections are securely clamped to prevent leakage. Perform synchronization and linkage/carburetor adjustments as outlined in Chapter Five.

**120 and 125 hp Models
(Including L-Drive)**

1. Remove the engine cover. Remove the carburetor covers and gaskets.

2A. *L-Drive models*—Disconnect the throttle rod from the tower shaft. Rotate the throttle cam away from the carburetors.

2B. *All others*—Remove the nut securing the throttle cam to the power head. Slide the cam off the stud and lay it aside.

3. Disconnect the fuel delivery hose from the bottom carburetor. Disconnect the fuel hose between the carburetors. On L-Drive models, disconnect the carburetor vent hoses.

4. Remove the retaining ring holding each throttle lever to the tie bar. See **Figure 30**.

5. If equipped with a choke, disconnect the choke link at both carburetor choke levers. The choke solenoid plunger and rod can remain attached to the bottom carburetor.

6. Remove the 2 nuts securing each carburetor to the adapter flange.

7A. *If equipped with a choke*—Remove the carburetors while guiding the choke solenoid plunger out of the solenoid.

7B. *If equipped with a primer*—Disconnect the primer hoses, then remove the carburetors.

8. Remove and discard the carburetor mounting gaskets.

9. Installation is the reverse of removal. Use new carburetor mounting gaskets and cotter pins. On models equipped with a choke, slide the choke solenoid plunger into the solenoid as the carburetors are installed. Be certain all fuel hose connections are securely clamped to prevent leakage. Perform synchronization and linkage/carburetor adjustments as described in Chapter Five.

150 hp Models

1. Remove the engine cover.

2. Disconnect the throttle link from the tower shaft. Rotate the throttle cam away from the carburetors.

3. Remove the retaining rings securing the tie bar to the carburetor throttle levers. Remove the washers and the tie bar. See **Figure 31**.

4. Disconnect the fuel delivery and fuel primer hoses from the carburetors.

5. Remove the nuts securing the carburetors to the adapter flange. Remove the carburetors and gaskets.

6. Reinstall the carburetors by reversing the removal procedure. Use new gaskets. Be certain

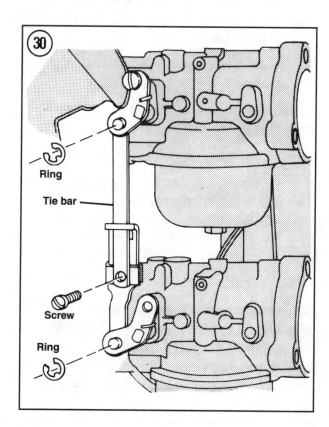

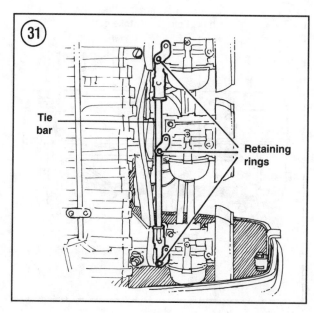

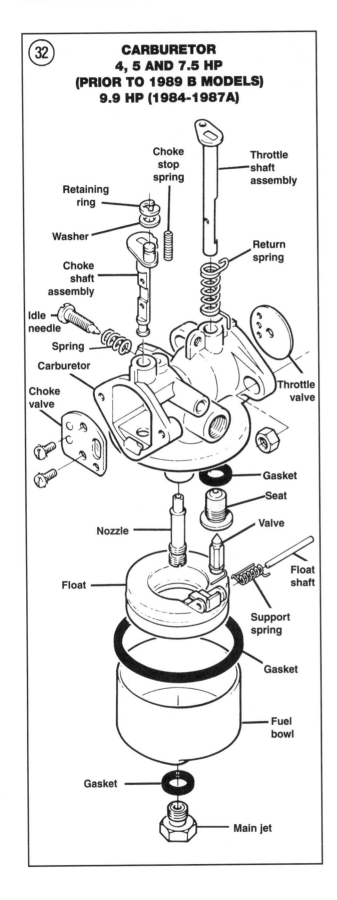

**CARBURETOR
4, 5 AND 7.5 HP
(PRIOR TO 1989 B MODELS)
9.9 HP (1984-1987A)**

(Labels in figure: Choke stop spring, Throttle shaft assembly, Retaining ring, Washer, Choke shaft assembly, Return spring, Idle needle, Spring, Carburetor, Choke valve, Throttle valve, Gasket, Seat, Valve, Nozzle, Float shaft, Float, Support spring, Gasket, Fuel bowl, Gasket, Main jet)

that all hose connections are securely clamped to prevent fuel leakage. Perform synchronization and linkage/carburetor adjustments as outlined in Chapter Five.

CARBURETOR DISASSEMBLY, REASSEMBLY AND ADJUSTMENT

Work slowly and carefully, follow the disassembly procedures and refer to the appropriate exploded drawing during carburetor disassembly. Note that some carburetors may not use all of the components shown in the exploded drawing.

It should not be necessary to use excessive force at any time during disassembly or reassembly. It is generally not necessary to disassemble the carburetor linkage or remove other external components. Remove the throttle and choke valves and shafts only if excessive wear, binding or other damage is noted.

The fuel jets on multiple carburetor models are often different sizes. Keep the carburetor parts separate if disassembling all carburetors. Make sure the carburetors are reinstalled in their original locations on the power head. Refer to **Tables 4-7** for specifications.

**Disassembly/Reassembly
(4, 5 and 7.5 hp
[Prior to 1989 B] Models)**

Cold-start fuel enrichment on these models is provided by a manually operated choke valve. Idle-speed fuel mixture is controlled by an adjustable needle valve. High-speed fuel mixture is controlled by a fixed main jet.

Refer to **Figure 32** for this procedure.

1. Remove the idle mixture screw and spring.

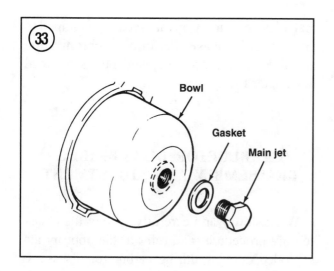

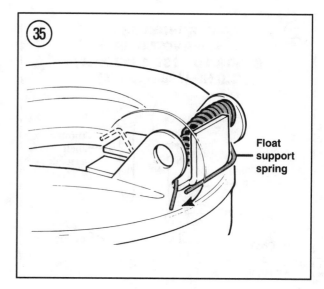

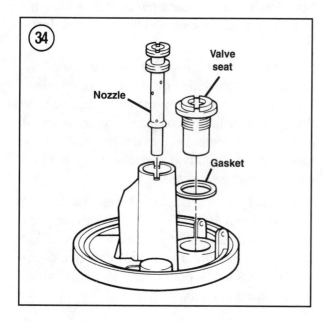

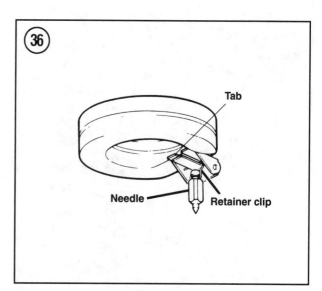

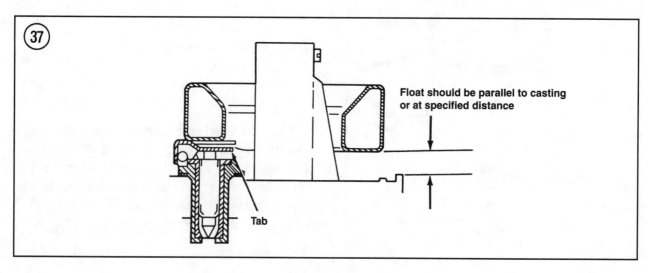

2. Unscrew the main jet from the fuel bowl. Remove the main jet and gasket. Remove the float bowl and gasket. See **Figure 33**.

3. Push the float shaft from the carburetor body using a small punch or similar tool. Remove the float along with the float support spring and inlet needle.

4. Using a wide-blade screwdriver, remove the nozzle and inlet valve seat. See **Figure 34**. Remove and discard the inlet seat gasket.

NOTE
Do not remove the throttle and choke valves and shafts unless replacement is necessary.

5. If necessary, remove the screws securing the choke and throttle valves to their respective shafts. After removing the valves, the throttle and choke shafts can be removed from the carburetor body.

6. Thoroughly clean and inspect all components as described under *Cleaning and Inspection* in this chapter.

7. If removed, slide the throttle shaft return spring on the throttle shaft, then insert the shaft into the carburetor body. Rotate the shaft so the flat side is facing out.

8. Apply a Loctite 271 thread locking compound to the throttle valve attaching screws, then install the valve and screws. Tighten the screws snugly. Open and close the throttle to ensure the throttle valve is properly centered, then tighten the valve attaching screws securely.

9. If removed, insert the choke shaft into the carburetor body. Rotate the shaft so the flat side is facing out.

10. Apply Loctite 271 thread locking compound to the choke valve attaching screws. Install the choke valve and screws. Tighten the screws snugly. Open and close the choke to properly center the valve, then tighten the attaching screws securely.

11. Install the nozzle and tighten securely. Install the inlet valve seat using a new gasket. Tighten securely. See **Figure 34**.

12. Install the support spring on the float as shown in **Figure 35**.

13. Secure the inlet valve needle to the float using the retainer clip. See **Figure 36**.

14. Install the float into position on the carburetor body. Make sure the inlet needle properly enters the inlet valve seat, then install the float shaft to secure the float assembly.

15. Next, adjust the float level as follows:
   a. Invert the carburetor (float facing up) and allow the weight of the float to close the inlet valve. Refer to **Figure 37** and **Table 4** for specifications.
   b. If adjustment is required, bend the tab (**Figure 36**) as necessary.

16. Adjust the float drop as follows:
   a. Hold the carburetor in the upright position.
   b. Measure the distance between the carburetor body and the end of the float (opposite inlet valve) as shown in **Figure 38**. Refer to **Table 4** for specifications.
   c. If adjustment is required, bend the tab (**Figure 38**) as necessary.

NOTE
If the float chamber has a flattened portion, position the flattened portion over the inlet valve needle. This will allow unrestricted float movement.

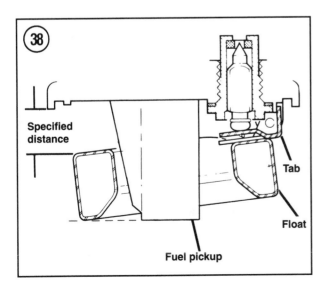

38

Specified
distance

Tab

Float

Fuel pickup

6

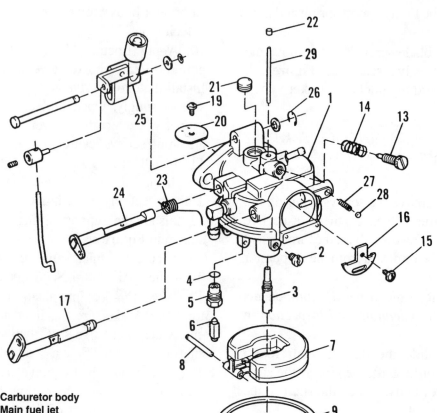

CARBURETOR
5 HP (1989 B-ON) AND 9.9 (1988A-ON) AND 15 HP (1988A-1990A)

1. Carburetor body
2. Main fuel jet
3. Main nozzle
4. Gasket
5. Inlet valve seat
6. Inlet valve needle
7. Float
8. Float pin
9. Gasket
10. Gasket
11. Float bowl
12. Float bowl retaining screw
13. Idle mixture screw
14. Spring
15. Screw
16. Choke valve
17. Choke shaft
19. Screw
20. Throttle valve
21. Plug
22. Plug
23. Throttle shaft return spring
24. Throttle shaft
25. Throttle cam follower assembly
26. E-ring
27. Spring
28. Choke shaft friction ball
29. Idle tube

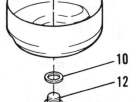

17. Install a new fuel bowl gasket into its groove in the carburetor body. Install a new gasket on the main jet, then install the fuel bowl and jet. Tighten the jet securely. See **Figure 32**.

18. Install the idle mixture screw and spring. Turn the screw clockwise until *lightly* seated, then back out 1 full turn.

19. Install carburetor as described in this chapter.

Disassembly/Reassembly (5 hp [1989B-on], 9.9 and 15 [1988A-on] and 25 hp [3-cylinder])

Refer to **Figure 39** for 5 hp, 9.9 hp and 15 hp (1988A-1990A) models. Refer to **Figure 40** for 15 hp (1990B-on) models. Refer to **Figure 41** for the 25 hp 3-cylinder model.

6

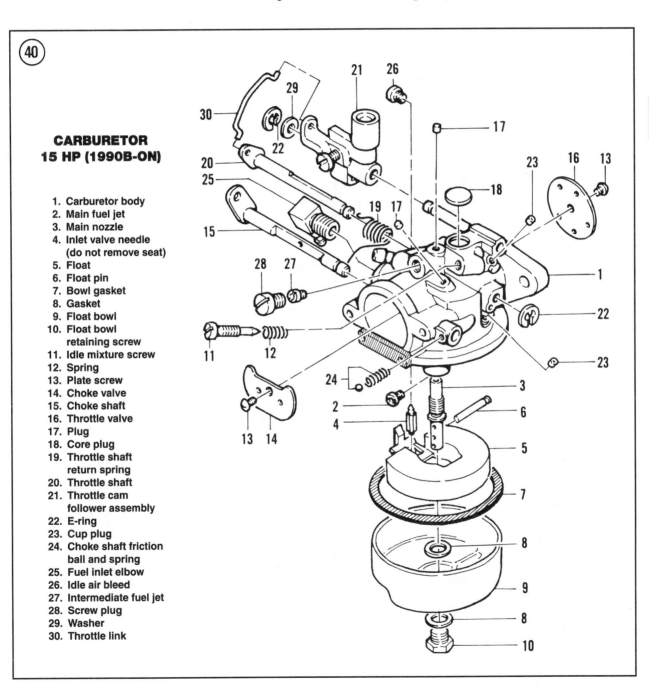

40

CARBURETOR 15 HP (1990B-ON)

1. Carburetor body
2. Main fuel jet
3. Main nozzle
4. Inlet valve needle (do not remove seat)
5. Float
6. Float pin
7. Bowl gasket
8. Gasket
9. Float bowl
10. Float bowl retaining screw
11. Idle mixture screw
12. Spring
13. Plate screw
14. Choke valve
15. Choke shaft
16. Throttle valve
17. Plug
18. Core plug
19. Throttle shaft return spring
20. Throttle shaft
21. Throttle cam follower assembly
22. E-ring
23. Cup plug
24. Choke shaft friction ball and spring
25. Fuel inlet elbow
26. Idle air bleed
27. Intermediate fuel jet
28. Screw plug
29. Washer
30. Throttle link

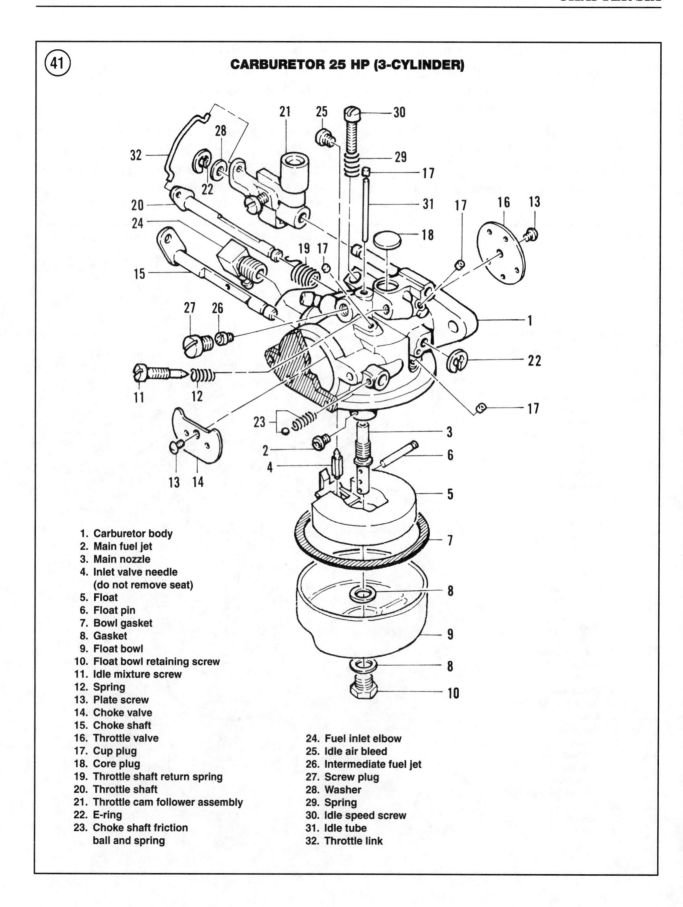

41

CARBURETOR 25 HP (3-CYLINDER)

1. Carburetor body
2. Main fuel jet
3. Main nozzle
4. Inlet valve needle
   (do not remove seat)
5. Float
6. Float pin
7. Bowl gasket
8. Gasket
9. Float bowl
10. Float bowl retaining screw
11. Idle mixture screw
12. Spring
13. Plate screw
14. Choke valve
15. Choke shaft
16. Throttle valve
17. Cup plug
18. Core plug
19. Throttle shaft return spring
20. Throttle shaft
21. Throttle cam follower assembly
22. E-ring
23. Choke shaft friction
    ball and spring
24. Fuel inlet elbow
25. Idle air bleed
26. Intermediate fuel jet
27. Screw plug
28. Washer
29. Spring
30. Idle speed screw
31. Idle tube
32. Throttle link

1. Remove the idle mixture screw and spring.

2. *Late 15hp and 25 hp 3-cylinder*—Remove the idle air bleed. Refer to **Figure 40** or **Figure 41**.

3. Remove the float bowl. Remove and discard the bowl gasket and the 2 bowl retaining screw gaskets. Refer to **Figure 42**.

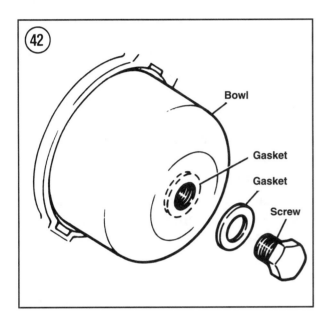

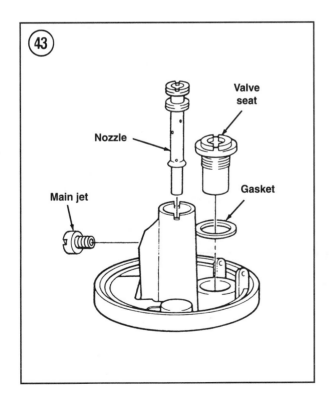

NOTE
The float pin is knurled on one end. When removing the pin, be sure to push on the end that is not knurled.

4. Invert the carburetor and remove the float pin by pushing it out with a small pin punch.

5. Remove the float and inlet valve needle.

6. *5, 9.9 and early 15 hp*—Remove the main jet, main nozzle and the inlet valve seat and gasket. See **Figure 43**.

7. *Late 15 hp and 25 hp 3-cylinder*—Remove the main jet and main nozzle. Do not attempt to remove the inlet valve seat. It is not serviced separately.

8. *Late 15 hp and 25 hp 3-cylinder*—Remove the screw plug and intermediate jet. See **Figure 44**.

NOTE
*Further disassembly of the carburetor is not necessary for routine cleaning. Refer to **Core Plug and Lead Shot Service** in this chapter if leakage is noted or if internal passages are plugged. Make sure replacement parts are available before attempting service on these components.*

9. Inspect the choke valve shaft for wear, binding or damage. If necessary, remove the choke valve attaching screw, then remove the valve and shaft. Be careful not to lose the choke shaft friction ball and spring as the shaft is removed from the carburetor body. See **Figures 39-41**.

10. Inspect the throttle valve shaft for wear, binding or damage. If necessary, remove the

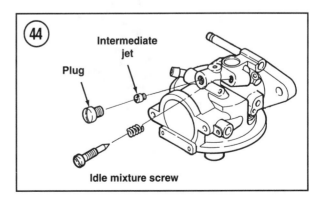

6

throttle valve attaching screw, then remove the valve. Remove the e-ring from the end of the shaft. Be careful to note the position of the throttle shaft return spring, then slide the shaft from the carburetor body. See **Figures 39-41**.

11. Thoroughly clean and inspect all components as described under *Cleaning and Inspection* in this chapter.

12. If removed, install the throttle shaft and return spring into the carburetor body. Install the e-ring on the end of the shaft. Turn the shaft clockwise so the flat side is facing out.

13. Install the throttle valve and apply Loctite 271 threadlocking adhesive to the attaching screw. Tighten the screw *finger-tight*.

14. Open and close the throttle to ensure the valve is properly centered. Adjust the valve position as necessary, then tighten the attaching screw securely.

15. If removed, install the choke shaft friction spring and ball into the carburetor body. Depress the ball and spring with a small punch and install the choke shaft into the carburetor body. Turn the shaft so the flat side is facing out.

16. Install the choke valve and apply Loctite 271 threadlocking adhesive to the attaching screw. Tighten the screw *finger-tight*.

17. Open and close the choke to ensure the valve is properly centered. Adjust the valve position as necessary, then tighten the attaching screw securely.

18. *5, 9.9 and early 15 hp*—Install the inlet valve seat using a new gasket. Securely tighten the seat using a wide-blade screwdriver or suitable tool. Do not damage the seat.

19. Install the main nozzle and main jet. Securely tighten the nozzle and jet with a wide-blade screwdriver or suitable tool. Do not damage the nozzle or jet.

20. *Late 15 hp and 25 hp 3-cylinder*—Install the intermediate jet and screw plug and the idle air bleed. Refer to **Figure 40** or **Figure 41** and **Figure 44**. Tighten the components securely with an appropriate screwdriver. Do not damage the idle air bleed or intermediate jet.

21. Install a new float bowl gasket into its groove in the carburetor body.

22. Place the inlet valve needle into the inlet seat.

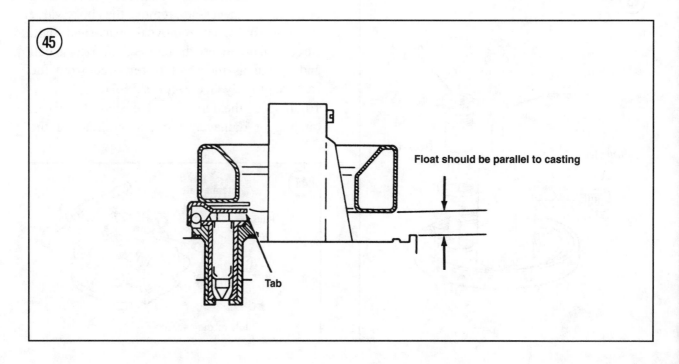

(45)

Float should be parallel to casting

Tab

23. Install the float and float pin. Insert the non-knurled end of the pin first. Lightly tap the float pin into position with a small hammer.

24. Adjust the float level as follows:

   a. Invert the carburetor and allow the weight of the float to close the inlet valve assembly.

   b. Refer to **Table 4** for specifications. Bend the tab as necessary to adjust the float level. See **Figure 45**.

25. Adjust the float drop as follows:

   a. Place the carburetor upright and allow the float to hang by its own weight.

   b. Measure the distance between the float bowl mating surface and the top edge of the float as show in **Figure 46**. Refer to **Table 4** for specifications.

   c. Bend the tab as necessary to adjust float drop. See **Figure 46**.

NOTE
If the float chamber has a flattened portion, position the flattened portion over the inlet valve needle. This will allow unrestricted float movement.

26. Install a new gasket on the float bowl retaining screw. Insert the screw and gasket through the float chamber. Install another gasket onto the screw inside the float chamber. See **Figure 42**. Install the float chamber assembly to

the carburetor body and tighten the retaining screw securely.

27. Install the idle mixture screw and spring. Turn the screw clockwise until *lightly* seated. Back the screw out the specified number of turns. See **Table 4**.

28. Install the carburetor as described in this chapter.

Disassembly/Reassembly (35 hp [1986-1989B] and 50 hp [1984-1989C])

Refer to **Figure 47** for this procedure.

1. Remove the idle mixture screw and spring.

2. Remove the air bleed from the side of the carburetor body. Refer to 23, **Figure 47**.

3. Remove the float bowl. Do not lose the main nozzle spring. Remove and discard the bowl gasket and the 2 bowl retaining screw gaskets. Refer to **Figure 42**.

NOTE
Most float pins are knurled on one end. When removing the pin, be sure to push on the end that is not knurled.

4. Invert the carburetor and remove the float pin by pushing it out with a small pin punch.

5. Remove the float, float support spring and inlet valve needle.

6. Remove the main jet with a suitable screwdriver.

7. Remove the main nozzle from the carburetor body by pushing on the nozzle from inside the carburetor bore. Replace the nozzle if it is damaged during removal.

CAUTION
The inlet valve seat is destroyed during removal in Step 8. Be sure to check the availability of a new seat prior to removing the old one.

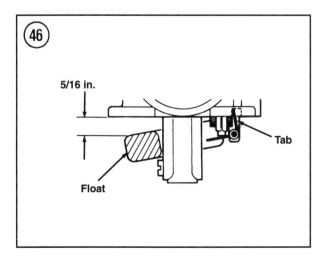

5/16 in.

Tab

Float

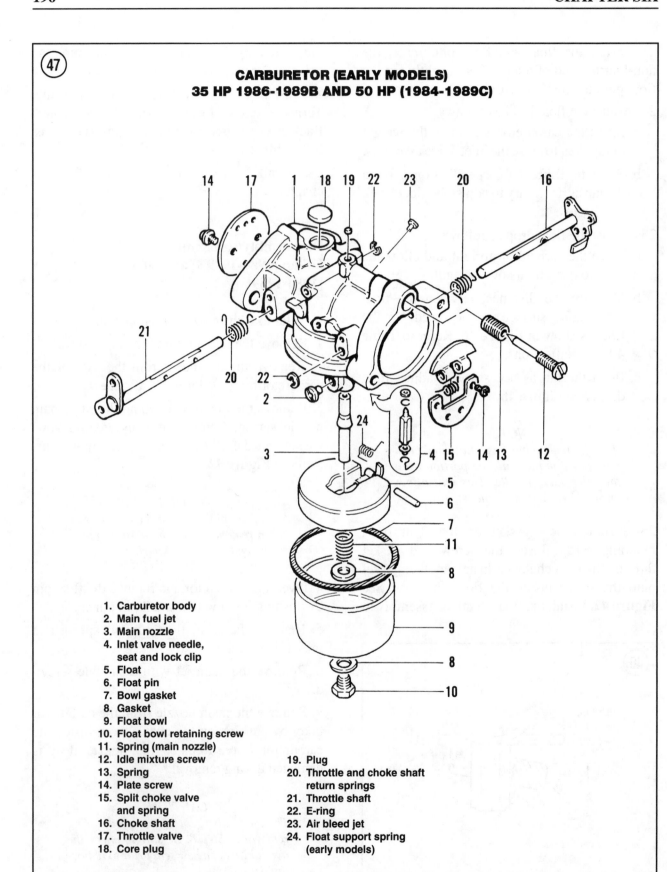

CARBURETOR (EARLY MODELS)
35 HP 1986-1989B AND 50 HP (1984-1989C)

1. Carburetor body
2. Main fuel jet
3. Main nozzle
4. Inlet valve needle,
   seat and lock clip
5. Float
6. Float pin
7. Bowl gasket
8. Gasket
9. Float bowl
10. Float bowl retaining screw
11. Spring (main nozzle)
12. Idle mixture screw
13. Spring
14. Plate screw
15. Split choke valve
    and spring
16. Choke shaft
17. Throttle valve
18. Core plug

19. Plug
20. Throttle and choke shaft
    return springs
21. Throttle shaft
22. E-ring
23. Air bleed jet
24. Float support spring
    (early models)

8. Remove the inlet valve seat retaining ring and valve seat with a small hooked tool. See **Figure 43**.

NOTE
*Further disassembly of the carburetor is not necessary for routine cleaning. Refer to **Core Plug and Lead Shot Service** in this chapter if leakage is noted or if internal passages are plugged. Make sure replacement parts are available before attempting service on these components.*

9. Inspect the choke valve shaft for wear, binding or damage. If necessary, remove the lower choke valve attaching screws and the valve. Remove the e-ring on the end of the shaft. Note the position of the choke shaft return spring, then slide the shaft out of the carburetor body. Be careful not to lose the upper choke plate and spring as the shaft is removed from the carburetor body. See **Figure 47**.

10. Inspect the throttle valve shaft for wear, binding or damage. If necessary, remove the throttle valve attaching screws and the valve. Remove the e-ring on the end of the shaft. Note the position of the throttle shaft return spring, then slide the shaft from the carburetor body. See **Figure 47**.

11. Thoroughly clean and inspect all components as described under *Cleaning and Inspection* in this chapter.

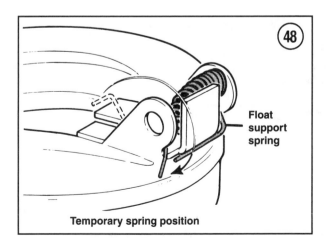

Temporary spring position

Float support spring

12. If removed, install the throttle shaft and return spring into the carburetor body. Install the e-ring on the end of the shaft. Turn the shaft clockwise so the flat side is facing out.

13. Install the throttle valve and apply Loctite 271 threadlocking adhesive to the attaching screws. Tighten the screws *finger-tight*.

14. Open and close the throttle to ensure the valve is properly centered. Adjust the valve position as necessary, then tighten the attaching screws securely.

15. If removed, position the upper portion of the split choke plate and the spring into the carburetor bore. Install the choke shaft and return spring into the carburetor body making sure the shaft passes through the upper choke plate and spring. Install the e-ring on the end of the shaft. Turn the shaft clockwise so the flat side is facing out.

16. Install the lower portion of the choke valve and apply Loctite 271 threadlocking adhesive to the attaching screws. Tighten the screws *finger-tight*.

17. Open and close the choke to ensure the lower valve is properly centered. Adjust the valve position as necessary, then tighten the attaching screws securely.

18. Manually hold the choke shaft in the choke position. Push the upper split choke plate open and ensure that it springs shut when released.

19. Install the inlet valve seat by pressing it gently into the carburetor body. Install the retaining clip. Do not damage the inlet valve seat.

20. Install the main jet. Securely tighten the jet with a wide-blade screwdriver or suitable tool. Do not damage the jet.

21. Install the air bleed on the side of the carburetor body. Refer to **Figure 47**. Tighten the air bleed securely with an appropriate screwdriver. Do not damage the air bleed.

22. Install a new float bowl gasket into its groove in the carburetor body.

23. Install the float support spring to the float. See **Figure 48**. Install the inlet valve needle to the float with the retainer clip. See **Figure 49**.

6

24. Install the float and float pin. Insert the non-knurled end of the pin first. Make sure the pin goes through the center of the float support spring. Lightly tap the float pin into position with a small hammer.

25. Adjust the float level as follows:
    a. Invert the carburetor and allow the weight of the float to close the inlet valve assembly.
    b. Refer to **Table 5** for specifications. Bend the tab as necessary to adjust the float level. See **Figure 50**.

26. Adjust the float drop as follows:
    a. Place the carburetor upright and allow the float to hang by its own weight.
    b. The float should stop just short of touching the carburetor casting. See **Figure 51**.
    c. Bend the tab as necessary to adjust float drop. See **Figure 51**.

27. Push the main nozzle into the carburetor body. Position the spring over the nozzle. See **Figure 47**.

28. Install a new gasket on the float bowl retaining screw. Insert the screw and gasket through the float chamber. Install another gasket onto the screw inside the float chamber. See **Figure 42**. Install the float chamber assembly to the carburetor body and tighten the retaining screw securely.

29. Install the idle mixture screw and spring. Turn the screw clockwise until *lightly* seated. Back the screw out the specified number of turns. See **Table 5**.

30. Install the carburetor as described in this chapter.

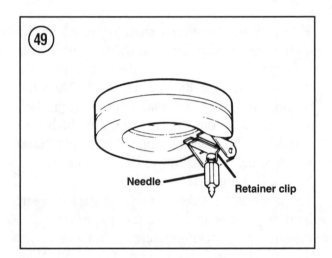

(49)

Needle   Retainer clip

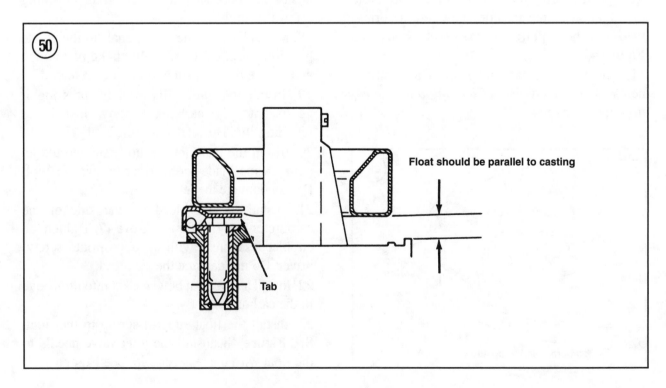

(50)

Float should be parallel to casting

Tab

**Disassembly/Reassembly
(25 hp 2-cylinder and 60 hp)**

Refer to **Figure 52** for this procedure. The 60 hp uses 2 carburetors, do not intermix components. Install each carburetor in its original location.

1. Remove the idle mixture screw and spring.

2. Remove the float bowl. Do not lose the main nozzle spring. Remove and discard the bowl gasket and the bowl retaining screw gasket. Refer to **Figure 52**.

NOTE
Most float pins are knurled on one end. When removing the pin, be sure to push on the end that is not knurled.

3. Invert the carburetor and remove the float pin by pushing it out with a small pin punch.

4. Remove the float, float support spring and inlet valve needle.

5. Remove the main jet with a suitable screwdriver.

6. Remove the main nozzle from the carburetor body by pushing on the nozzle in the carburetor bore. Replace the nozzle if it is damaged during removal. Do not damage or distort the idle tube. See **Figure 52**.

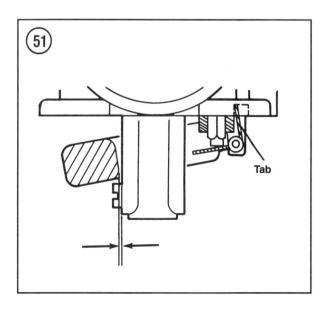

CAUTION
The inlet valve seat is destroyed during removal in Step 8. Be sure to check the availability of a new seat prior to removing the old one.

7. Remove the inlet valve seat retaining ring and valve seat with a small hooked tool. See **Figure 53**.

NOTE
*Further disassembly of the carburetor is not necessary for routine cleaning. Refer to **Core Plug and Lead Shot Service** in this chapter if leakage is noted or if internal passages are plugged. Make sure replacement parts are available before attempting service on these components.*

8. Inspect the choke valve shaft for wear, binding or damage. If necessary, remove the choke valve attaching screws and the valve. Remove the e-ring on the end of the shaft. Note the position of the choke shaft return spring, then slide the shaft out of the carburetor body. See **Figure 52**.

9. Inspect the throttle valve shaft for wear, binding or damage. If necessary, remove the throttle valve attaching screws and the valve. Note the position of the throttle shaft return spring, then slide the shaft from the carburetor body. See **Figure 52**.

10. If idle tube removal is necessary, measure and note the depth of the idle tube in the carburetor body. Also note the orientation of the idle tube in relation to the main nozzle. Invert the carburetor and using a small punch and hammer, tap the idle tube and plug out of the body. See **Figure 54**.

11. Thoroughly clean and inspect all components as described under *Cleaning and Inspection* in this chapter.

12. If removed, install the throttle shaft and return spring into the carburetor body. Turn the shaft clockwise so the flat side is facing out.

6

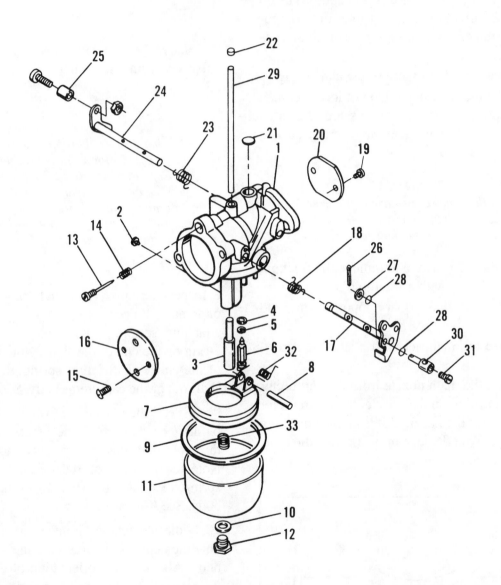

**CARBURETOR
(25 HP 2-CYLINDER AND 60 HP MODELS)**

1. Carburetor body
2. Main fuel jet
3. Main nozzle
4. Inlet valve seat
5. Valve seat retainer
6. Inlet valve needle
7. Float
8. Float pin
9. Gasket
10. Gasket
11. Float bowl
12. Float bowl retaining screw
13. Idle mixture screw
14. Spring
15. Screw
16. Choke valve
17. Choke shaft
18. Choke shaft return spring
19. Screw
20. Throttle valve
21. Plug
22. Plug
23. Throttle shaft return spring
24. Throttle shaft
25. Throttle cam follower roller
26. Cotter pin
27. Washer
28. O-ring
29. Idle tube
30. Swivel
31. Screw
32. Spring
33. Spring

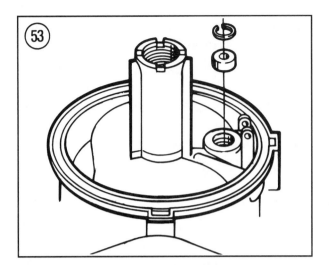

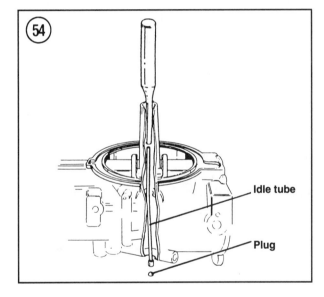

Idle tube

Plug

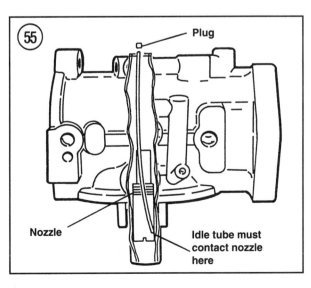

Plug

Nozzle

Idle tube must contact nozzle here

13. Install the throttle valve and apply Loctite 271 threadlocking adhesive to the attaching screws. Tighten the screws *finger-tight*.

14. Open and close the throttle to ensure the valve is properly centered. Adjust the valve position as necessary, then tighten the attaching screws securely.

15. If removed, install the choke shaft and return spring into the carburetor body. Install the e-ring on the end of the shaft. Turn the shaft clockwise so the flat side is facing out.

16. Install the choke valve and apply Loctite 271 threadlocking adhesive to the attaching screws. Tighten the screws *finger-tight*.

17. Open and close the choke to ensure the valve is properly centered. Adjust the valve position as necessary, then tighten the attaching screws securely.

18. Reinstall the idle tube to the depth and orientation noted in Step 10. Install a new plug into its bore above the idle tube. Seal the plug with nail polish. See **Figure 55**.

19. Install the inlet valve seat by pressing it gently into the carburetor body. Install the retaining clip. Do not damage the inlet valve seat. See **Figure 53**.

20. Install the main jet. Securely tighten the jet with a wide-blade screwdriver or suitable tool. Do not damage the jet.

21. Install a new float bowl gasket into its groove in the carburetor body.

22. Install the float support spring to the float. See **Figure 48**. Install the inlet valve needle to the float with the retainer clip. See **Figure 49**.

23. Install the float and float pin. Insert the non-knurled end of the pin first. Make sure the pin goes through the center of the float support spring. Lightly tap the float pin into position with a small hammer.

24. Adjust the float level as follows:

    a. Invert the carburetor and allow the weight of the float to close the inlet valve assembly.

6

b. Refer to **Table 4** or **Table 5** for specifications. Bend the tab as necessary to adjust the float level. See **Figure 56**.

25. Adjust the float drop as follows:

a. Place the carburetor upright and allow the float to hang by its own weight.

b. *25 hp 2-cylinder*—Measure from the bottom of the carburetor bowl mounting flange to the bottom edge of the float. Refer to **Table 4** for specifications. See **Figure 57**.

b. *60 hp*—The float should stop just short of touching the carburetor casting. See **Figure 59**.

c. Bend the tab as necessary to adjust float drop. See **Figure 57**.

26. Push the main nozzle into the carburetor body. Position the spring over the nozzle. See **Figure 52**.

27. Install a new gasket on the float bowl retaining screw. Insert the screw and gasket through the float chamber. Install the float chamber assembly to the carburetor body and tighten the retaining screw securely.

28. Install the idle mixture screw and spring. Turn the screw clockwise until *lightly* seated.

Back the screw out the specified number of turns. See **Table 4** or **Table 5**.

29. Install the carburetor as described in this chapter.

Disassembly/Reassembly
(85 and 90 hp Outboard and L-Drives)

Refer to **Figures 58-60** for these procedures.

The 85 and 90 hp carburetors have gone through many mid-year changes. The main differences are the inlet valve seats and main nozzle design. Some 85 and 90 hp carburetors may have an idle tube, but the majority will not. Consult the manufacturer's parts catalog for information on parts availability before disassembly. Carburetors may incorporate features from more than one of the typical carburetors shown in **Figures 58-60**. Choke plates are not used after serial No.OE009500.

On multiple-carburetor motors, do not intermix components between carburetors. In addition, be certain that each carburetor is reinstalled in its original location from which it was re-

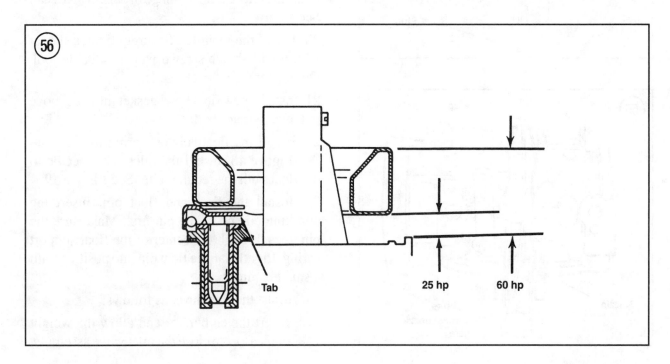

(56)

Tab   25 hp   60 hp

moved. Refer to **Table 6** or **Table 7** for specifications.

1. Remove the idle mixture screw and spring.

2. Remove the idle air bleed if so equipped. See **Figure 60**.

3. Remove the float bowl. Remove and discard the bowl gasket and the 2 bowl retaining screw gaskets. Do not lose the main nozzle spring (**Figure 58**), if so equipped. Refer to the appropriate **Figures 58-60**.

NOTE
The float pin is knurled on one end. When removing the pin, be sure to push on the end that is not knurled.

4. Invert the carburetor and remove the float pin by pushing it out with a small pin punch.

5. Remove the float and inlet valve needle. Remove the float support spring if so equipped.

6. Remove the main jet.

7. Remove the main nozzle by one of the following procedures:

   a. **Figure 58**—Push on the nozzle from inside the carburetor bore. Do not damage or distort the idle tube, if so equipped.

   b. **Figures 59-60**—Unscrewing the nozzle with a wide-bladed screwdriver or appropriate tool.

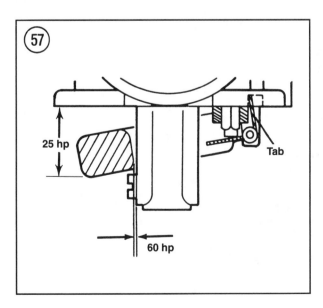

NOTE
The inlet valve seat is destroyed during removal in Step 8. Many carburetors have non-serviceable inlet valve seats. Attempts at removal will destroy the carburetor body. Only remove the inlet valve seat when the manufacturers parts catalog shows an inlet valve seat replacement part No. and that part No. is currently available.

8. If the carburetor has an inlet valve seat that is serviceable, follow the appropriate procedure listed below. If the inlet valve seat is not serviceable, under no circumstances attempt to remove it.

   a. *Figure 61*—Remove the inlet valve seat retaining ring and valve seat with a small hooked tool. Discard the seat.

   b. *Figure 62*—Remove the inlet valve seat by threading an appropriate size screw into the inlet valve seat. Remove the seat by pulling or prying on the screw head. Do not damage the carburetor body.

NOTE
Further disassembly of the carburetor is not necessary for routine cleaning. Refer to **Core Plug and Lead Shot Service** *in this chapter if leakage is noted or if internal passages are plugged. Make sure replacement parts are available before attempting service on these components.*

9. Inspect the choke valve shaft for wear, binding or damage. If necessary, remove the choke valve attaching screws and the valve. Remove the e-ring on the end of the shaft. Note the position of the choke shaft return spring, then slide the shaft out of the carburetor body. See **Figures 58-60**.

10. Inspect the throttle valve shaft for wear, binding or damage. If necessary, remove the throttle valve attaching screws and the valve. Note the position of the throttle shaft return spring, then slide the shaft from the carburetor body. See **Figures 58-60**.

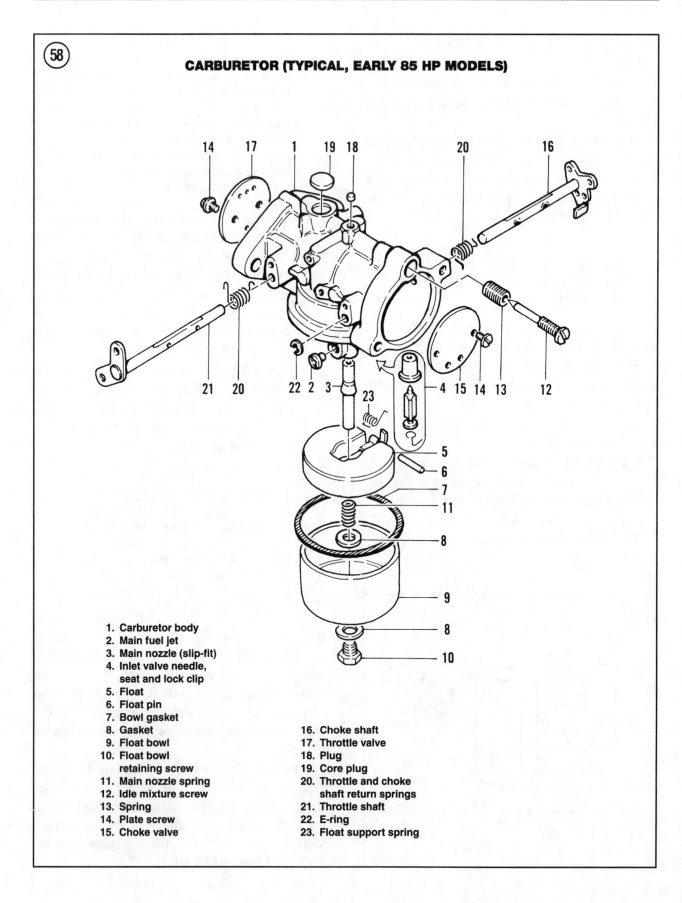

CARBURETOR (TYPICAL, EARLY 85 HP MODELS)

1. Carburetor body
2. Main fuel jet
3. Main nozzle (slip-fit)
4. Inlet valve needle,
   seat and lock clip
5. Float
6. Float pin
7. Bowl gasket
8. Gasket
9. Float bowl
10. Float bowl
    retaining screw
11. Main nozzle spring
12. Idle mixture screw
13. Spring
14. Plate screw
15. Choke valve
16. Choke shaft
17. Throttle valve
18. Plug
19. Core plug
20. Throttle and choke
    shaft return springs
21. Throttle shaft
22. E-ring
23. Float support spring

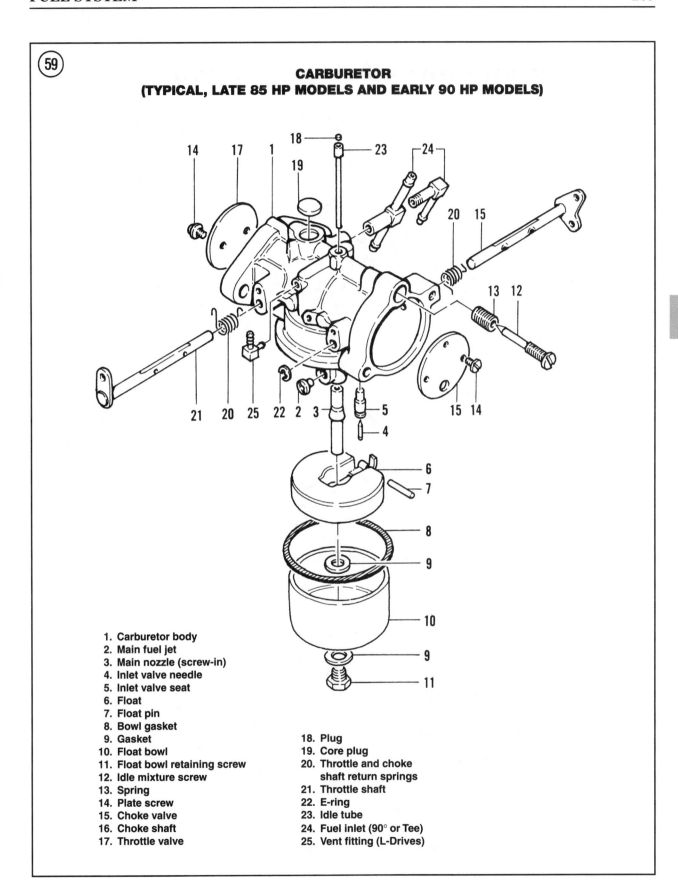

**CARBURETOR
(TYPICAL, LATE 85 HP MODELS AND EARLY 90 HP MODELS)**

1. Carburetor body
2. Main fuel jet
3. Main nozzle (screw-in)
4. Inlet valve needle
5. Inlet valve seat
6. Float
7. Float pin
8. Bowl gasket
9. Gasket
10. Float bowl
11. Float bowl retaining screw
12. Idle mixture screw
13. Spring
14. Plate screw
15. Choke valve
16. Choke shaft
17. Throttle valve
18. Plug
19. Core plug
20. Throttle and choke
    shaft return springs
21. Throttle shaft
22. E-ring
23. Idle tube
24. Fuel inlet (90° or Tee)
25. Vent fitting (L-Drives)

6

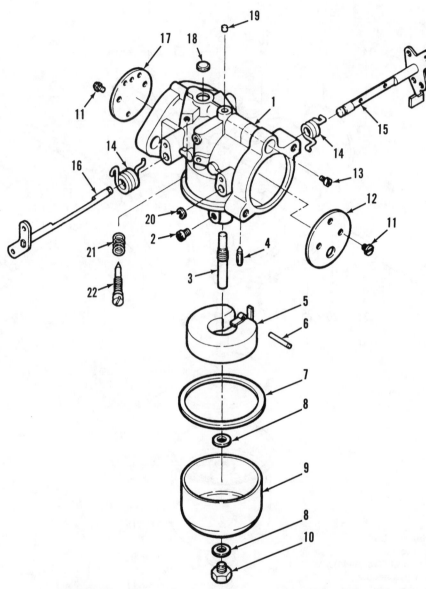

CARBURETOR (1999 75 HP AND LATE 90 HP MODELS, TYPICAL)

1. Carburetor body
2. Main jet
3. Main nozzle
4. Inlet valve needle
5. Float
6. Float pin
7. Gasket
8. Gasket
9. Float bowl
10. Bowl retaining screw
11. Screw
12. Choke valve*
13. Intermediate air jet
14. Return spring
15. Choke shaft*
16. Throttle shaft
17. Throttle valve
18. Plug
19. Plug
20. E-ring
21. Spring
22. Idle mixture screw

* Not used on fuel primer valve models

11. If so equipped and removal of the idle tube is necessary, measure and note the depth of the idle tube in the carburetor body. Also note the orientation of the idle tube in relation to the main nozzle. Invert the carburetor and using a small punch and hammer, tap the idle tube and plug out of the body. See **Figure 63**.

12. Thoroughly clean and inspect all components as described under *Cleaning and Inspection* in this chapter.

13. If removed, install the throttle shaft and return spring into the carburetor body. Turn the shaft clockwise so the flat side is facing out.

14. Install the throttle valve and apply Loctite 271 threadlocking adhesive to the attaching screws. Tighten the screws *finger-tight*.

15. Open and close the throttle to ensure the valve is properly centered. Adjust the valve position as necessary, then tighten the attaching screws securely.

16. If removed, install the choke shaft and return spring into the carburetor body. Turn the shaft clockwise so the flat side is facing out.

17. Install the choke valve and apply Loctite 271 threadlocking adhesive to the attaching screws. Tighten the screws *finger-tight*.

18. Open and close the choke to ensure the valve is properly centered. Adjust the valve position as necessary, then tighten the attaching screws securely.

19. Install the main nozzle by one of the following procedures:

   a. Press the nozzle into its bore until it is seated. See **Figure 58**. Do not damage or distort the idle tube, if so equipped.

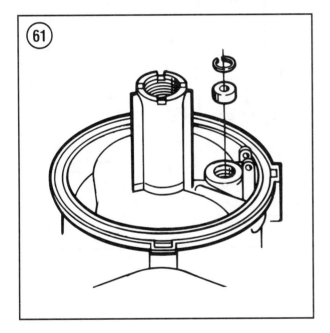

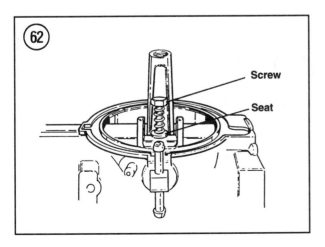

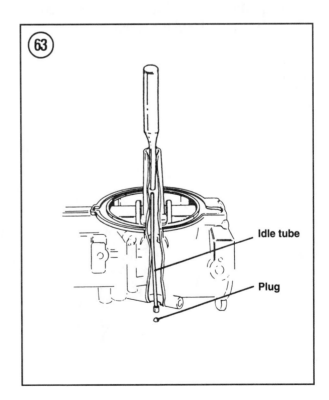

b. Screw the nozzle in and tighten securely with a wide-bladed screwdriver or appropriate tool. See **Figures 59** or **Figure 60**.

NOTE
The idle tube must contact the front of the main nozzle as shown in **Figure 64** *or the carburetor will operate excessively lean.*

20. If removed, reinstall the idle tube to the depth and orientation noted in Step 11. Install a new plug into its bore above the idle tube. Seat the plug with a punch and hammer. Seal the plug with nail polish. See **Figure 64**.

21. If the carburetor inlet valve seat was removed, follow the appropriate procedure listed below to install a new seat.

a. Install the inlet valve seat (**Figure 61**) by pressing it gently into the carburetor body. Install the retaining clip. Do not damage the inlet valve seat.

b. Install the inlet valve seat (**Figure 62**) by pressing it firmly into the carburetor body. If necessary, use a wooden dowel and hammer. Make sure the inlet valve seat is completely seated into the carburetor body.

22. Install the main jet. Securely tighten the jet with a wide-blade screwdriver or suitable tool. Do not damage the main jet.

23. Install the idle air bleed if so equipped. Refer to **Figure 60**. Tighten the air bleed securely with an appropriate screwdriver. Do not damage the idle air bleed.

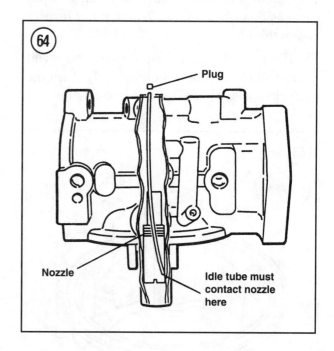

Plug

Nozzle

Idle tube must contact nozzle here

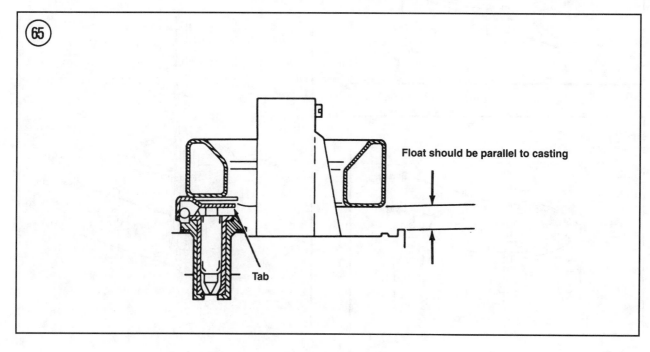

Float should be parallel to casting

Tab

24. Install a new float bowl gasket into its groove in the carburetor body.

25A. *Models with float springs*:

    a. Install the float support spring to the float. See **Figure 48**. Install the inlet valve needle to the float with the retainer clip. See **Figure 49**.

    b. Install the float, inlet valve needle and float pin. Insert the non-knurled end of the pin first. Make sure the pin goes through the center of the float support spring. Lightly tap the float pin into position with a small hammer.

25B. *Models without float springs*:

    a. Place the inlet valve needle into the inlet seat.

    b. Install the float and float pin. Insert the non-knurled end of the pin first. Lightly tap the float pin into position with a small hammer.

26. Adjust the float level as follows:

    a. Invert the carburetor and allow the weight of the float to close the inlet valve assembly.

    b. Refer to **Table 6** or **Table 7** for specifications. Bend the tab as necessary to adjust the float level. See **Figure 65**.

27. Adjust the float drop as follows:

    a. Place the carburetor upright and allow the float to hang by its own weight.

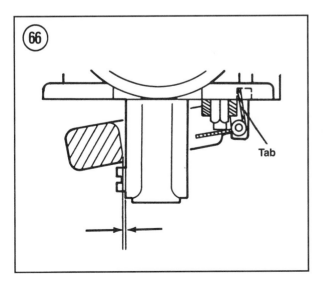

b. The float should stop just short of touching the carburetor casting. See **Figure 66**.

c. Bend the tab as necessary to adjust float drop. See **Figure 66**.

28. On models so equipped, position the main nozzle spring over the main nozzle. See **Figure 58**.

29. Install a new gasket on the float bowl retaining screw. Insert the screw and gasket through the float chamber. Install another gasket onto the screw inside the float chamber. Install the float chamber assembly to the carburetor body and tighten the retaining screw securely.

30. Install the idle mixture screw and spring. Turn the screw clockwise until *lightly* seated. Back the screw out the specified number of turns. See **Table 6** or **Table 7**.

31. Install the carburetor as described in this chapter.

Disassembly/Reassembly
(35 hp [1989C-on], 50 hp [1989D-on], 40, 70, 75 and 120-150 hp Outboards and L-Drives)

Refer to **Figure 67** for these procedures.

There are only minor differences in these carburetors; mainly the style of inlet valve seats and whether or not idle tubes are used. Inlet valve seats are either a replaceable insert or not serviceable. Idle tubes are present on all but a few models. Consult the manufacturer's parts catalog for information on parts availability before disassembly. Choke plates are not used after serial No. OE009500. Refer to **Table 5**, **Table 6** or **Table 7** for specifications.

On multiple-carburetor motors, do not intermix components between carburetors. In addition, be certain that each carburetor is reinstalled in its original location from which it was removed.

1. Remove the idle mixture screw and spring.

2. Remove the screw plug and intermediate jet. See 31 and 32, **Figure 67**.

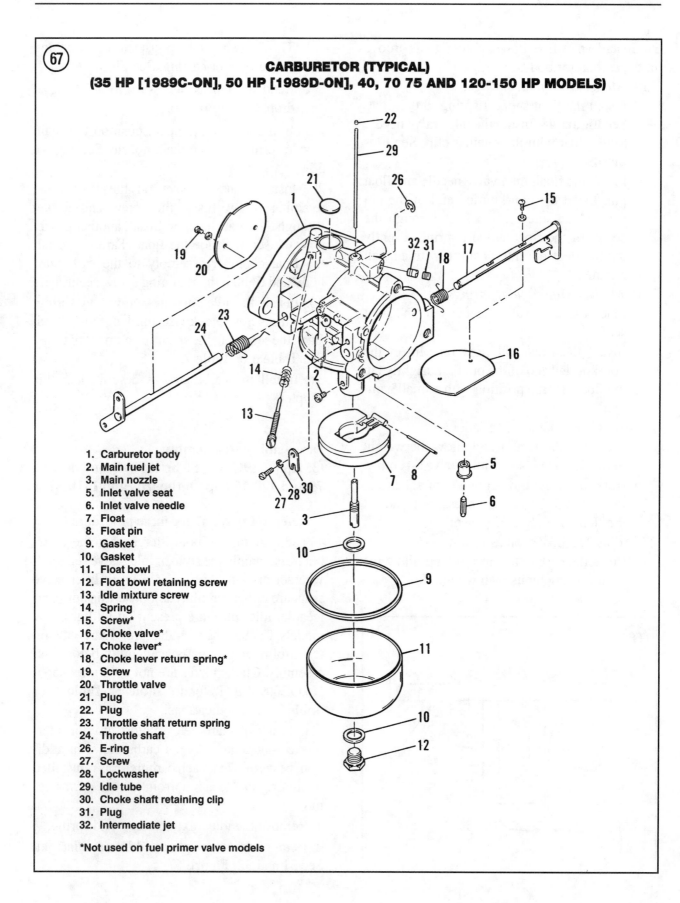

CARBURETOR (TYPICAL)
(35 HP [1989C-ON], 50 HP [1989D-ON], 40, 70 75 AND 120-150 HP MODELS)

1. Carburetor body
2. Main fuel jet
3. Main nozzle
5. Inlet valve seat
6. Inlet valve needle
7. Float
8. Float pin
9. Gasket
10. Gasket
11. Float bowl
12. Float bowl retaining screw
13. Idle mixture screw
14. Spring
15. Screw*
16. Choke valve*
17. Choke lever*
18. Choke lever return spring*
19. Screw
20. Throttle valve
21. Plug
22. Plug
23. Throttle shaft return spring
24. Throttle shaft
26. E-ring
27. Screw
28. Lockwasher
29. Idle tube
30. Choke shaft retaining clip
31. Plug
32. Intermediate jet

*Not used on fuel primer valve models

3. Remove the float bowl. Remove and discard the bowl gasket and the 2 bowl retaining screw gaskets.

NOTE
The float pin is knurled on one end. When removing the pin, be sure to push on the end that is not knurled.

4. Invert the carburetor and remove the float pin by pushing it out with a small pin punch.

5. Remove the float and inlet valve needle.

6. Remove the main jet and main nozzle with a wide-bladed screwdriver or appropriate tool.

NOTE
The inlet valve seat is destroyed during removal in Step 7. Many carburetors have a non-serviceable inlet valve seat. Attempts at removal will destroy the carburetor body. Only remove the inlet valve seat if the manufacturers parts catalog shows an inlet valve seat replacement part No. and that part No. is currently available.

7. If the inlet valve seat is not serviceable, under no circumstances attempt to remove it. If the carburetor has an inlet valve seat that is serviceable, thread an appropriate size screw into the inlet valve seat (**Figure 68**). Remove the seat

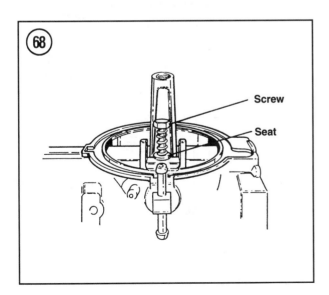

by pulling or prying on the screw head. Do not damage the carburetor body.

NOTE
*Further disassembly of the carburetor is not necessary for routine cleaning. Refer to **Core Plug and Lead Shot Service** in this chapter if leakage is noted or if internal passages are plugged. Make sure replacement parts are available before attempting service on these components.*

8. If so equipped, inspect the choke valve shaft for wear, binding or damage. If necessary, remove the choke valve attaching screws and the valve. Remove the screw and retainer from the end of the shaft. Note the position of the choke shaft return spring, then slide the shaft out of the carburetor body. See **Figure 67**.

9. Inspect the throttle valve shaft for wear, binding or damage. If necessary, remove the throttle valve attaching screws and the valve. Note the position of the throttle shaft return spring, then slide the shaft from the carburetor body. See **Figure 67**.

10. If so equipped and removal of the idle tube is necessary, measure and note the depth of the idle tube in the carburetor body. Also note the orientation of the idle tube in relation to the main nozzle. Invert the carburetor and using a small punch and hammer, tap the idle tube and plug out of the body. See **Figure 69**.

11. Thoroughly clean and inspect all components as described under *Cleaning and Inspection* in this chapter.

12. If removed, install the throttle shaft and return spring into the carburetor body. Turn the shaft clockwise so the flat side is facing out.

13. Install the throttle valve and apply Loctite 271 threadlocking adhesive to the attaching screws. Tighten the screws *finger-tight*.

14. Open and close the throttle to ensure the valve is properly centered. Adjust the valve position as necessary, then tighten the attaching screws securely.

15. If removed, install the choke shaft and return spring into the carburetor body. Turn the shaft clockwise so the flat side is facing out.

16. Install the choke valve and apply Loctite 271 threadlocking adhesive to the attaching screws. Tighten the screws *finger-tight*.

17. Open and close the choke to ensure the valve is properly centered. Adjust the valve position as necessary, then tighten the attaching screws securely.

18. Install the choke shaft retainer and screw on the end of choke shaft.

19. Install the main nozzle and tighten it securely with a wide-bladed screwdriver or appropriate tool.

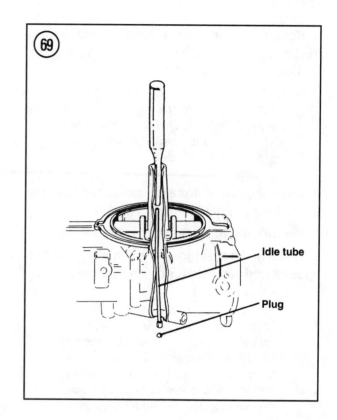

NOTE
*The idle tube must contact the front of the main nozzle as shown in **Figure 70** or the carburetor will operate excessively lean.*

20. If removed, reinstall the idle tube to the depth and orientation noted in Step 10. Install a new plug into its bore above the idle tube. Seat the plug with a punch and hammer. Seal the plug with nail polish. See **Figure 70**.

21. If the carburetor inlet valve seat was removed, install a new inlet valve seat by pressing it firmly into the carburetor body. If necessary, use a wooden dowel and hammer. Make sure the inlet valve seat is completely seated into the carburetor body.

22. Install the main jet. Securely tighten the jet with a wide-blade screwdriver or suitable tool. Do not damage the main jet.

23. Install the intermediate jet and screw plug. Refer to 31 and 32, **Figure 67**. Tighten the intermediate jet and screw plug securely with an appropriate screwdriver. Do not damage the intermediate jet.

24. Install a new float bowl gasket into its groove in the carburetor body.

25. Place the inlet valve needle into the inlet seat.

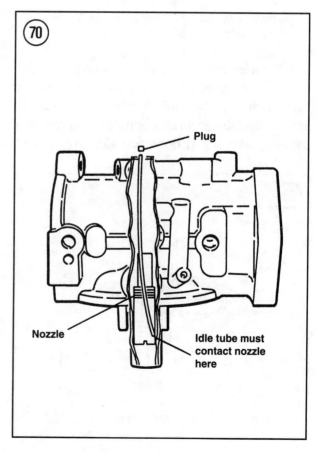

26. Install the float and float pin. Insert the non-knurled end of the pin first. Lightly tap the float pin into position with a small hammer.

27. Adjust the float level as follows:

    a. Invert the carburetor and allow the weight of the float to close the inlet valve assembly.

    b. Refer to **Table 5**, **Table 6** or **Table 7** for specifications. Bend the tab as necessary to adjust the float level. See **Figure 71**.

28. Adjust the float drop as follows:

    a. Place the carburetor upright and allow the float to hang by its own weight.

    b. The float should stop just short of touching the carburetor casting. See **Figure 72**.

    c. Bend the tab as necessary to adjust float drop. See **Figure 72**.

29. Install a new gasket on the float bowl retaining screw. Insert the screw and gasket through the float chamber. Install another gasket onto the screw inside the float chamber. Install the float chamber assembly to the carburetor body and tighten the retaining screw securely.

30. Install the idle mixture screw and spring. Turn the screw clockwise until *lightly* seated.

Back the screw out the specified number of turns. See **Table 5**, **Table 6** or **Table 7**.

31. Install the carburetor as described in this chapter.

CARBURETOR CLEANING AND INSPECTION

Clean carburetor components with an aerosol-type solvent and a brush. Spray the solvent on the casting and other components and clean any gum or varnish using a small brush. Spray the solvent through the casting metering passages. Never clean passages with a wire or drill bit as you may enlarge the passage and alter the carburetor calibration. Dry castings and other components with compressed air. Thoroughly clean all gasket material from mating surfaces. Do not nick, scratch or damage mating surfaces.

Check the float for fuel absorption. Check the float arm for wear in the hinge pin and needle valve contacts areas. Replace the float as necessary.

6

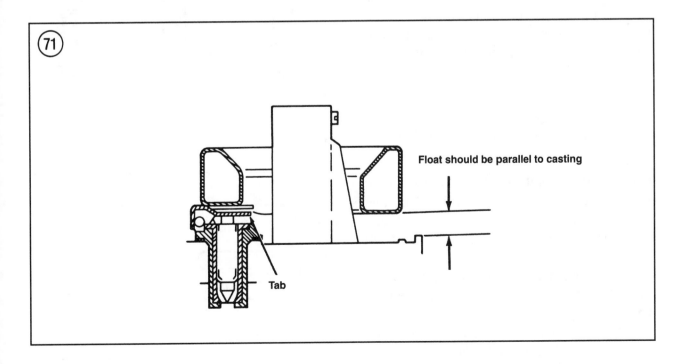

(71)

Float should be parallel to casting

Tab

Check the idle mixture screw tip for grooving, nicks or scratches. **Figure 73** shows an acceptable tip (1), a tip damaged from excessive pressure when seating (2) and one with wear on one side caused by excessive vibration such as could result from operation with a damaged propeller.

Check the inlet valve needle tip for grooving, nicks or scratches. See **Figure 74**.

Check throttle and choke shafts for excessive wear or play. The throttle and choke valves must move freely without binding.

CORE PLUGS AND LEAD SHOT

Certain passages in the carburetor casting are covered with a core plug or a lead shot. These usually require service only if the plug is leaking or if the carburetor passages are plugged. **Figure 75** shows a carburetor with the core plug over the low-speed orifices (A) removed and a typical lead shot installed (B).

Core Plug Service

1. If core plug leakage is noted, secure the carburetor in a vise with protective jaws.

2. Hold a flat punch in the center of the core plug and tap carefully to spread the plug. Seal the plug with fingernail polish.

> *CAUTION*
> *Do not drill more than 1/16 in. below the core plug in Step 3 or the casting will be damaged.*

3. If leakage is still noted, or the carburetor passages are plugged, carefully drill a 1/8 in. hole through the center of the core plug. Pry the plug from the carburetor casting using a small screwdriver or similar tool.

4. Clean all residue from the core plug hole in the casting. If the hole is out of round, replace the carburetor casting.

5. If the low-speed passages are plugged, clean with a brush and carburetor cleaner.

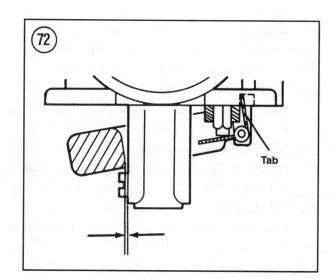

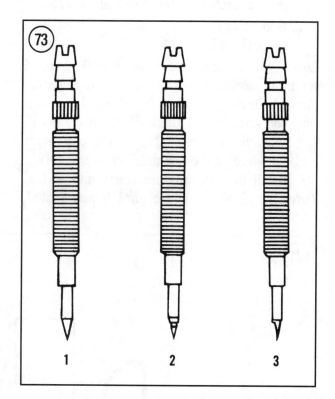

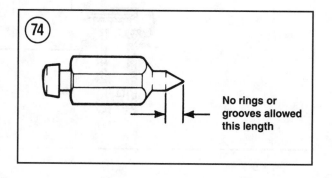

6. Place a new core plug in the casting with the convex side facing out.

7. Using a flat punch, carefully tap the center of the plug to spread it out.

8. Seal the core plug with fingernail polish.

Lead Shot Service

1. If leakage is noted, secure the carburetor in a vise with protective jaws.

2. Tap the center of the lead shot with a small hammer and appropriate size punch.

3. If leakage remains, carefully pry the lead shot from the casting using an awl or other suitable tool.

4. Clean any residue from the casting.

5. Install a new shot in the opening and flatten out with a hammer and appropriate size punch.

6. If necessary, seal the area with fingernail polish.

REED VALVE ASSEMBLY

The reed valve assembly is mounted on the rear of the carburetor adapter plate or intake manifold. Reed valves control the passage of air-fuel mixture into the crankcase by opening and closing as crankcase pressure changes. When crankcase pressure is high, the reeds maintain contact with the reed plate to which they are attached. As crankcase pressure drops on the compression stroke, the reeds move away from the plate and allow the air-fuel mixture to enter the crankcase. Reed travel is limited by the reed stop. As crankcase pressure increases, the reeds return to the seated position against the reed plate.

Figures 76-82 show typical reed plate and intake manifold configurations. Late 1-cylinder

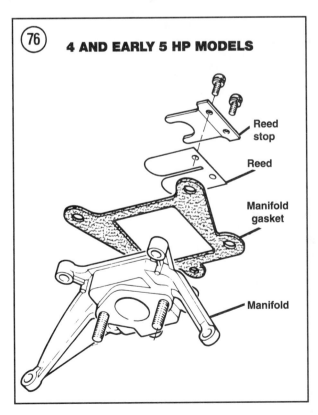

4 AND EARLY 5 HP MODELS

Reed stop

Reed

Manifold gasket

Manifold

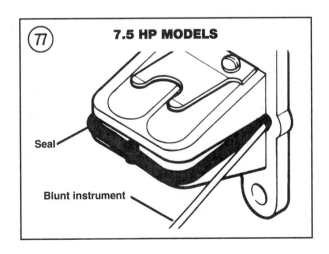

7.5 HP MODELS

Seal

Blunt instrument

**25 HP 3-CYLINDER MODELS
(9.9 AND 15 HP SIMILAR DESIGN)**

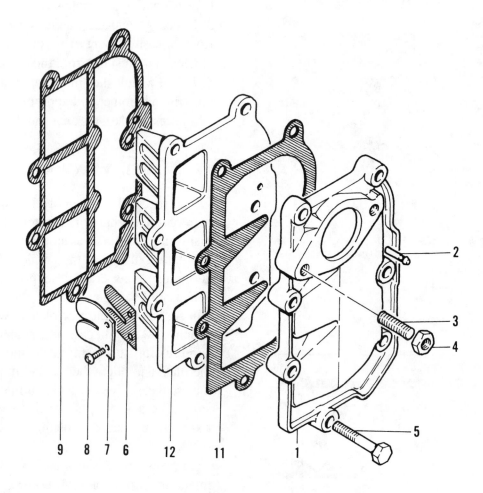

1. Intake manifold
2. Recirculation check valve
3. Carburetor mounting stud
4. Hex nut
5. Intake manifold
   mounting screws
6. Reed
7. Reed stop
8. Machine screw
9. Gasket
10. Reed plate
11. Gasket

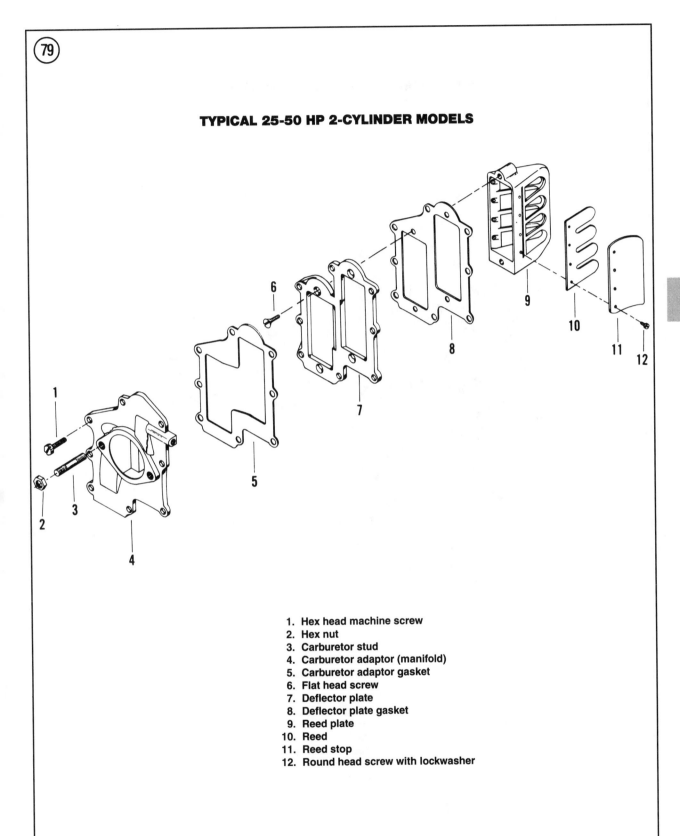

TYPICAL 25-50 HP 2-CYLINDER MODELS

1. Hex head machine screw
2. Hex nut
3. Carburetor stud
4. Carburetor adaptor (manifold)
5. Carburetor adaptor gasket
6. Flat head screw
7. Deflector plate
8. Deflector plate gasket
9. Reed plate
10. Reed
11. Reed stop
12. Round head screw with lockwasher

6

⑧⓪

3-CYLINDER 75 HP MODELS (1984-1998)

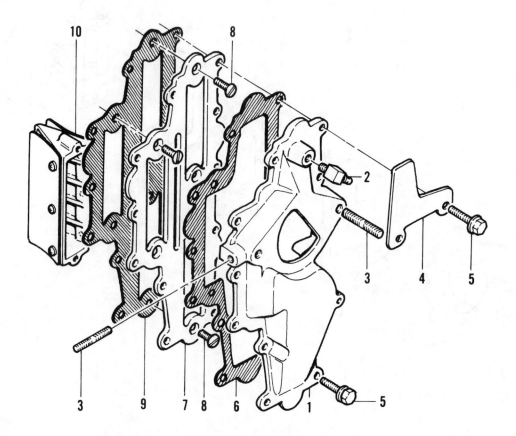

1. Intake manifold
2. Elbow
3. Carburetor mounting stud
4. Timing pointer
5. Intake manifold mounting screws
6. Gasket
7. Reed plate adapter
8. Machine screw
9. Gasket
10. Reed Assembly

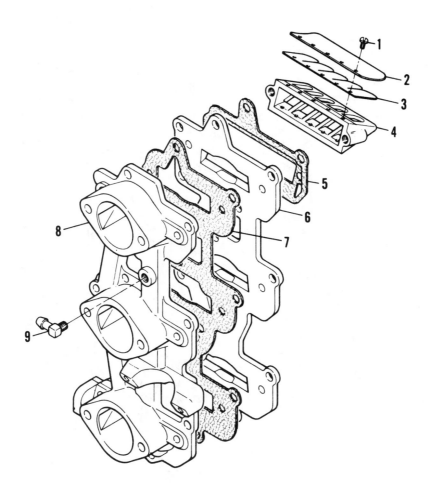

81

3-CYLINDER 75 HP MODELS (1999)
AND ALL 85 AND 90 HP MODELS

6

1. Screw and lockwasher
2. Reed stop
3. Reed
4. Reed plate
5. Reed plate adapter gasket
6. Reed plate adapter
7. Intake manifold gasket
8. Intake manifold
9. Elbow

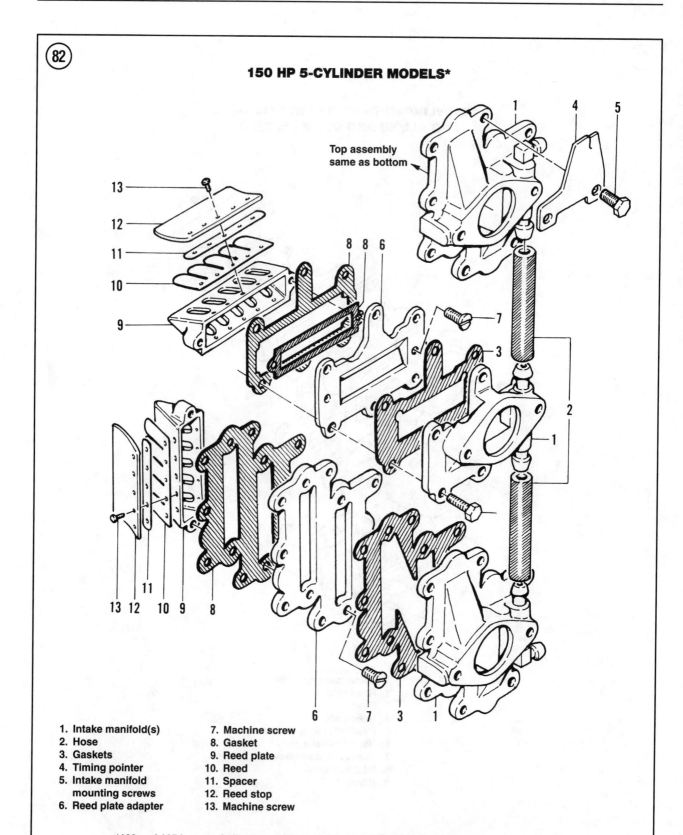

150 HP 5-CYLINDER MODELS*

Top assembly
same as bottom

1. Intake manifold(s)
2. Hose
3. Gaskets
4. Timing pointer
5. Intake manifold
   mounting screws
6. Reed plate adapter
7. Machine screw
8. Gasket
9. Reed plate
10. Reed
11. Spacer
12. Reed stop
13. Machine screw

*120 and 125 hp use similar top and bottom intake manifold assemblies (no middle assembly)

models are equipped with a V-type reed block assembly. Note that larger engines have a deflector plate or reed plate adapter between the intake manifold/carburetor adapter and the reed valve assemblies.

Removal/Installation

1. Remove the carburetor(s) as described in this chapter.

NOTE
On 1990 B-on 5 hp models, the V-type reed block assembly is located between

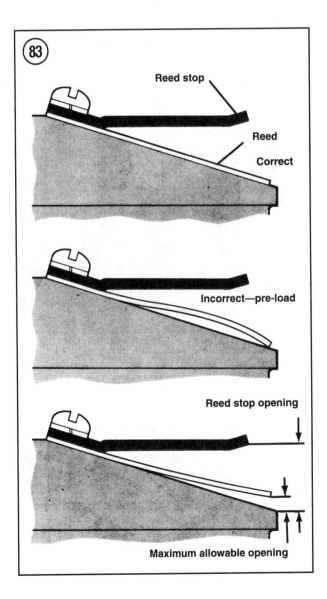

(83)

Reed stop

Reed

Correct

Incorrect—pre-load

Reed stop opening

Maximum allowable opening

the carburetor and manifold. Therefore, it is not necessary to remove the manifold to service the reed valves. The reed block assembly can be removed from the manifold after removing the carburetor

2. Disconnect any hoses connected to the intake manifold or carburetor adapter.

3. On 3-, 4- and 5-cylinder models, it may be necessary to remove the throttle cam from the intake manifold. Remove the primer valve or choke solenoid as required.

4. Remove the screws holding the intake manifold or carburetor adapter to the crankcase cover.

5. Remove the intake manifold or carburetor adapter and gasket. Discard the gasket.

6. If a deflector or adapter plate is used, separate it from the intake manifold/carburetor adapter and remove the screws holding the reed valve assemblies.

7. Thoroughly clean all gasket surfaces. Use care not to scratch, nick or damage mating surfaces.

8. Installation is the reverse of removal, plus the following:

   a. Apply a thin bead of RTV sealant around the reed plate opening on the power head.

   b. *7.5 hp*—Remove and discard the oil seal. Lubricate reed plate groove with engine oil and install a new seal, pushing its ends through the reed plate hole with a blunt tool. See **Figure 77**. Seal ends should extend no more than 0.06 in. abovethe outside face of the plate after installation.

   c. Use new gaskets.

   d. Tighten intake manifold/carburetor adapter screws to specifications. See **Table 1**.

Disassembly, Inspection and Reassembly

Refer to **Figure 83** for this procedure.

1. Check reeds for cracking or other damage. Replace reeds if any defects are noted.

2. Reeds should lie flat on the reed plate with no preload. To check flatness, gently push each reed

6

petal out. Constant resistance should be felt with no noise.

3. If reeds do not lie perfectly flat on the reed plate, measure the amount they are open and compare to maximum allowable reed opening specifications (**Table 2**).

4. Measure the distance between the tip of the reed stop and the reed plate. Compare to specifications (**Table 2**).

5. Replace any reeds that do not meet the specifications in Step 3. Replace the reed stop if the measurement (Step 4) is not within specifications.

Reed Replacement

> *NOTE*
> *Some models do not have replaceable reed petals. The reed block and reed petals must be replaced as an assembly.* **Table 2** *identifies these models. Also 85-150 hp models use spacers between the reed stop and the reed petals.*

1. Remove the screws, spacers (if used) and lockwashers securing the reed stop and reeds to the reed plate.

2. Remove the reed stop and reeds.

3. Place a new reed on the reed plate and check for flatness.

4. Locate reed over reed plate openings. There should be a minimum overlap of 0.030 in. (4-15 hp) or 0.040 in. (all others) over the reed plate opening. See **Figure 84** (4-25 hp 3 cylinder) or **Figure 85** (25 hp [2-cylinder] and 35-150 hp).

5. Install reed stop with screws, spacers (if used) and lockwashers. Apply Loctite 271 threadlocking adhesive to the screws.

6. Check reed stop opening as described in this chapter.

CHOKE SOLENOID

A choke solenoid is used on 25 hp (2-cylinder) 35-125 hp (except 70 hp) models prior to serial No. OE009500. Test procedure is described in Chapter Three.

Removal/Installation

1. Disconnect the solenoid terminal wire. Note the position of the terminal for reference during reinstallation.

2. Loosen the fastener(s) securing the solenoid clamp.

3. Remove solenoid from clamp and disconnect it from the plunger.

4. Remove the strap securing the wire to the solenoid body.

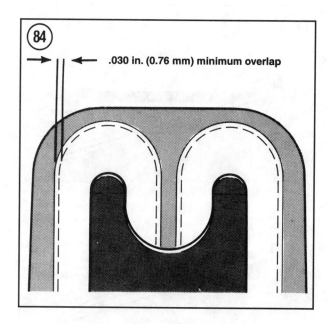

84 .030 in. (0.76 mm) minimum overlap

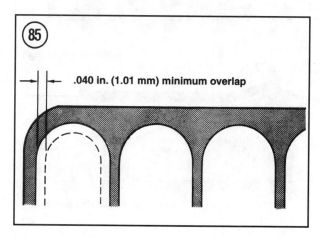

85 .040 in. (1.01 mm) minimum overlap

5. Installation is the reverse of removal. Install solenoid with the terminal located in the same position noted in Step 1.

PRIMER VALVE

All models 70 and 150 hp and 40-120 hp serial No. OE009500-on are equipped with a fuel primer valve. Test procedures are provided in Chapter Three.

Removal/Installation

1. Disconnect the battery negative (−) terminal from the battery.
2. Disconnect primer valve black and yellow/black wires from the engine terminal block.
3. Label fuel hoses for reference during reinstallation, then disconnect fuel hoses from primer valve.
4. Remove the bolt securing the valve to the power head, then remove valve.
5. Installation is the reverse of removal. Make sure all fuel hose connections are tight and securely clamped.

INTEGRAL FUEL TANK

All 1-cylinder models prior to 1988 B are equipped with an integral fuel tank.

Removal/Installation

1. Remove the engine cover as follows:
    a. Loosen the thumb screws securing the rear of the engine cover to the lower cover.
    b. Remove the fuel tank cap. Compress the fuel tank cap anchor and remove it from the tank.
    c. Pry the rope retainer from the starter handle. Untie the knot and remove the handle. Do not allow starter rope to wind into the starter housing.
    d. Lift the engine cover and allow the starter rope to slide through rope guide. Remove the engine cover, then tie a knot in the starter rope to prevent the rope from winding into the starter housing.
2. Using hose clamp pliers, slide the hose clamp from the fuel tank fitting. Disconnect the fuel hose from the tank and drain the fuel into an approved container.
3. Remove the 4 screws securing the rewind starter to the fuel tank, then lift off the starter.
4. Remove the 2 front and 2 rear fuel tank mounting screws and washers. Remove the tank mounting screws on each side of the tank.
5. Position the throttle lever to the SHIFT position to gain clearance between the tank mounting bracket and throttle cam.
6. Lift the tank up and forward to remove.
7. Install the tank by reversing the removal procedure. When installing the rewind starter, be sure the starter friction shoes (or pawl on late models) properly engage the starter cup.

PORTABLE FUEL TANK

Figure 86 shows the components of the metal portable fuel tank, including the fuel cap gauge sender and primer bulb assembly. Later models are equipped with the plastic portable fuel tank shown in **Figure 87**.

On metal tanks, the fuel tank adapter threads into the top of the tank and serves as the fuel pickup. A screen clamped to the end of the adapter prevents fuel sediment from reaching the fuel pump.

On plastic tanks, the fuel pickup is attached to the gauge assembly. A screen is attached to the pickup to prevent sediment from entering the fuel hoses.

When some oils are mixed with gasoline and stored in a warm area, a bacterial substance will form. This clear substance covers the fuel pickup, restricting fuel flow. Bacterial formation can be prevented by using a good-quality fuel

6

conditioner on a regular basis. If present, it can be removed with a good marine engine cleaner.

To remove any dirt or water and to prevent the build up of gum and varnish, clean the inside of the tank once per season by flushing with clean gasoline or kerosene.

Check metal tanks for rust, leakage or corrosion. Replace the tank as required. Do not attempt to patch the tank using automotive fuel tank repair materials.

To check the fuel tank adapter screen for possible restrictions, remove the adapter or gauge assembly. Inspect the hose and screen for damage. Remove the screen and clean with solvent, then dry with compressed air.

FUEL HOSE AND PRIMER BULB

WARNING
L-Drive models cannot use a conventional primer bulb. If a priming type device is to be used on an L-Drive, it must pass Coast Guard regulations for permanently installed inboard-style fuel systems.

When priming the engine, the primer bulb should gradually become firm. If it does not become firm or if it stays firm even when disconnected, the check valve inside the primer bulb is malfunctioning and the bulb should be replaced.

The fuel hose should be checked periodically for cracks, breaks, restrictions and chafing. The bulb should be checked periodically for proper

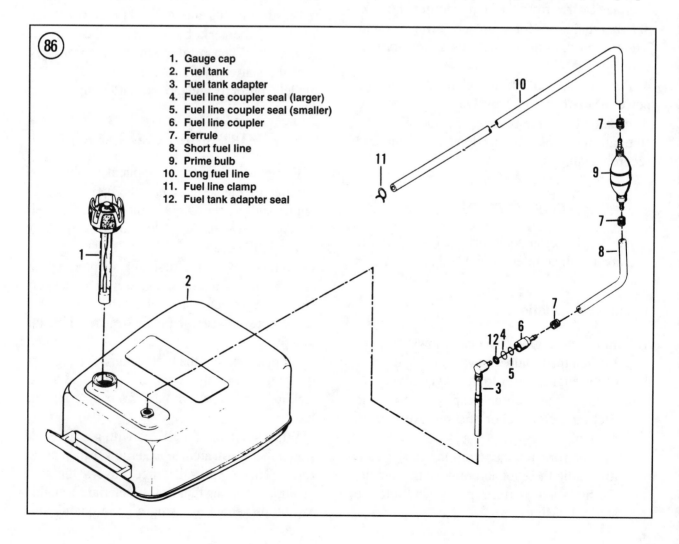

86

1. Gauge cap
2. Fuel tank
3. Fuel tank adapter
4. Fuel line coupler seal (larger)
5. Fuel line coupler seal (smaller)
6. Fuel line coupler
7. Ferrule
8. Short fuel line
9. Prime bulb
10. Long fuel line
11. Fuel line clamp
12. Fuel tank adapter seal

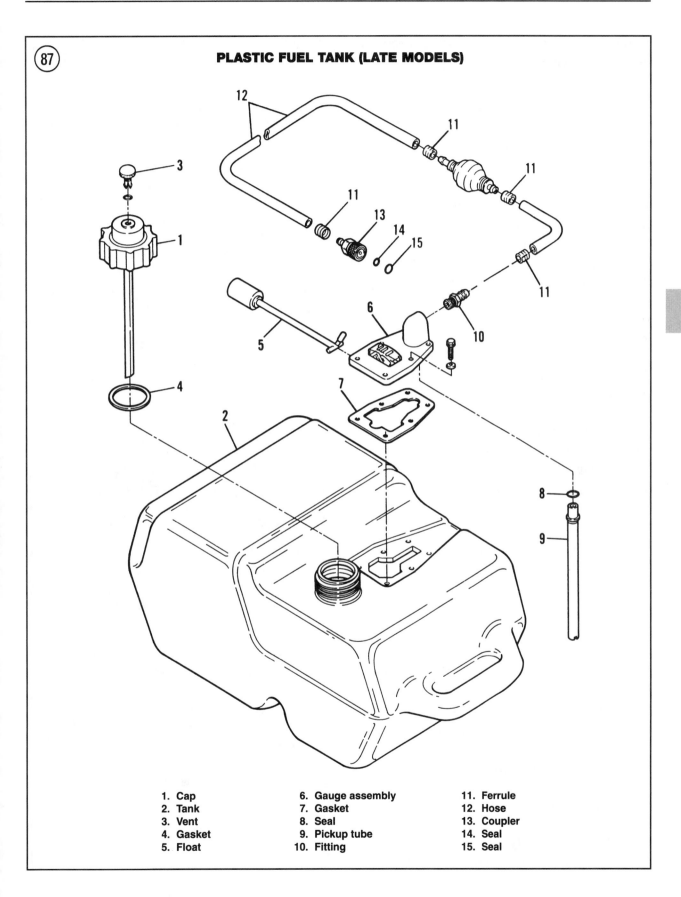

PLASTIC FUEL TANK (LATE MODELS)

6

1. Cap
2. Tank
3. Vent
4. Gasket
5. Float
6. Gauge assembly
7. Gasket
8. Seal
9. Pickup tube
10. Fitting
11. Ferrule
12. Hose
13. Coupler
14. Seal
15. Seal

operation. Make sure all fuel hose connections are tight and securely clamped.

FUEL RECIRCULATION SYSTEM

Multiple cylinder motors are equipped with a fuel recirculation system designed to collect unburned fuel and oil from the low spots of the individual crankcase areas. Since the intake system used by 2-stroke engines does not completely transfer all of the fuel sent through the crankcase to the combustion chamber (especially during low-speed operation), the recirculation system provides a method of collecting the fuel and oil pooled in the low spots of the crankcase and transferring it to the intake ports or intake manifold where it can be burned.

Correct recirculation system operation is vitally important to efficient engine operation. If the system fails, excessive amounts of fuel and oil will puddle in the crankcase and not reach the combustion chamber during low-speed operation, causing a lean mixture. When the engine is accelerated, the puddles of fuel and oil are quickly drawn into the engine causing a temporary, excessively rich mixture. This will result in the following symptoms:

1. Poor low-speed performance.

2. Poor acceleration.

3. Spark plug fouling.

4. Stalling or spitting at idle.

5. Excessive smoke on acceleration.

Two distinct systems are used. Early models use a cylinder drain cover that contains reed or check valves. The drain cover collects the fuel and transfers it to a hose which is connected to the intake manifold or transfer port cover.

Newer models do not use special drain covers to mount the valves. The valves are contained in special fittings screwed into the transfer port covers, intake manifolds or directly to the crankcase. There is normally 1 check-valve for each cylinder. A check-valve should allow flow out

from the crankcase puddle area but not back into the crankcase.

Recirculation System Service
(Early Models with Cylinder Drain Covers)

Refer to the appropriate **Figure 88-97** for this procedure.

NOTE
On 25 and 35 hp 2-cylinder models, the check valves are pressed into the transfer

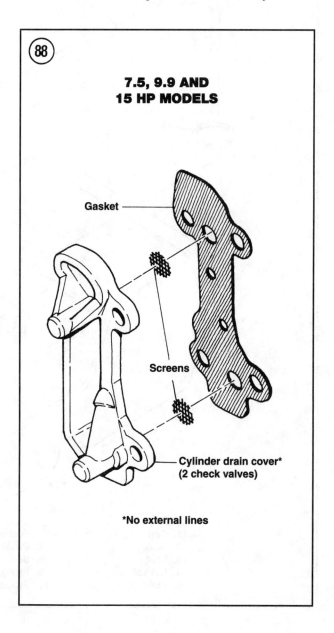

(88)

7.5, 9.9 AND 15 HP MODELS

Gasket

Screens

Cylinder drain cover*
(2 check valves)

*No external lines

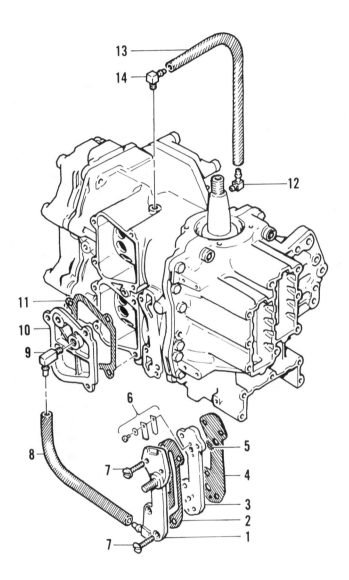

**FUEL RECIRCULATION SYSTEM
(EARLY 40 AND 50 HP MODELS)**

6

1. Cylinder drain cover
2. Gasket
3. Cylinder drain plate
4. Gasket
5. Screen
6. Reed petal, reed stop,
   screw and lockwasher
7. Cover screw
8. Recirculation hose
9. Fitting
10. Cylinder No. 2
    transfer port cover
11. Gasket
12. Check valve
13. Recirculation hose
14. Fitting

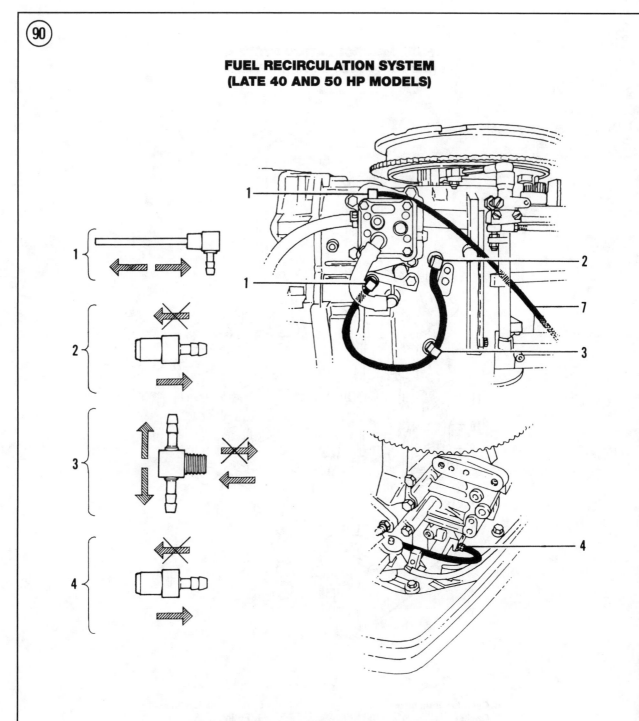

⑨⓪

**FUEL RECIRCULATION SYSTEM
(LATE 40 AND 50 HP MODELS)**

1. Extended fittings, cylinder No. 1 and No. 2 transfer port covers
2. Check valve, cylinder No. 1 crankcase passage
3. Tee check valve, cylinder No. 2 crankcase passage
4. Check valve, lower main bearing
5. Hose, No. 1 crankcase check valve to No. 2 crankcase tee check valve
6. Hose, No. 2 crankcase tee check valve to No. 2 transfer port cover fitting
7. Hose, lower main bearing check valve to No. 1 transfer port cover fitting

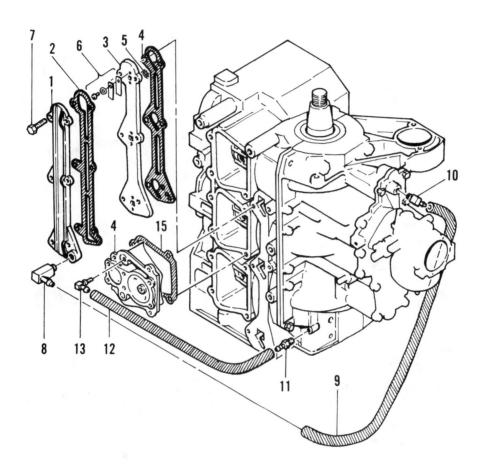

**FUEL RECIRCULATION SYSTEM
(EARLY 70, 85 AND 90 HP MODELS)**

1. Cylinder drain cover
2. Gasket
3. Cylinder drain plate
4. Gasket
5. Screen
6. Reed petal, reed stop,
   screw and lockwasher
7. Cover screw
8. Fitting
9. Recirculation hose
10. Fitting, intake manifold
11. Check valve (70 hp models only)
12. Recirculation hose
    (70 hp models only)
13. Fitting (70 hp models only)
14. Cylinder No. 2 transfer
    port cover (70 hp models only)
15. Gasket (70 hp models only)

6

FUEL RECIRCULATION SYSTEM
(LATE 70 AND 75 HP MODELS)

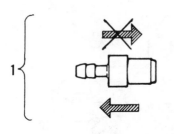

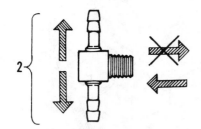

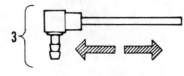

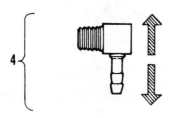

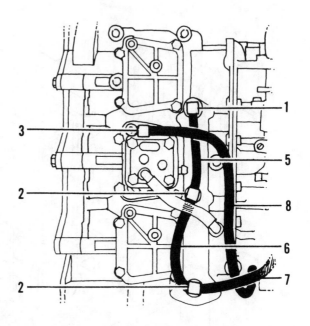

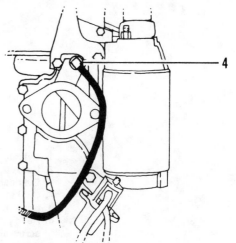

1. Check valves, cylinder No. 1 crankcase passage and lower main bearing (lower main bearing check valve not shown)
2. Tee check valves, cylinder No. 2 and No. 3 crankcase passages
3. Extended fitting, cylinder No. 2 transfer port cover
4. Fitting, intake manifold
5. Hose, No. 1 crankcase check valve to No. 2 crankcase tee check valve
6. Hose, No. 2 crankcase tee check valve to No. 3 crankcase tee check valve
7. Hose, No. 3 crankcase tee check valve to intake manifold fitting
8. Hose, Lower main bearing check valve to No. 2 transfer port cover fitting

FUEL RECIRCULATION SYSTEM
(1999 75 HP AND LATE 90 HP MODELS)

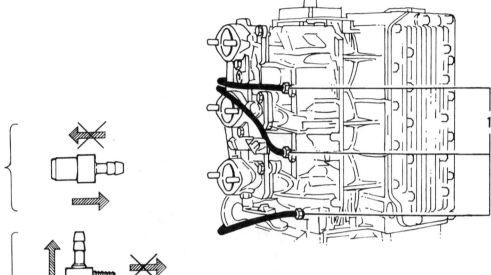

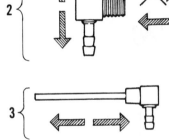

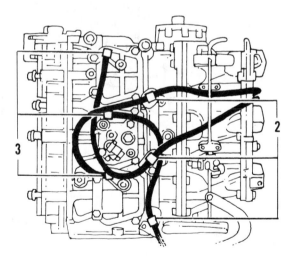

6

1. Check valves
2. Tee check valves
3. Extended fittings

**FUEL RECIRCULATION SYSTEM
(EARLY 120 AND 125 HP MODELS)**

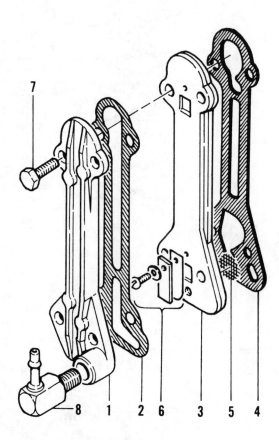

1. Cylinder drain cover
2. Gasket
3. Cylinder drain plate
4. Gasket
5. Screen
6. Reed petal, reed stop,
   screw and lockwasher
7. Cover screw
8. Hose fitting

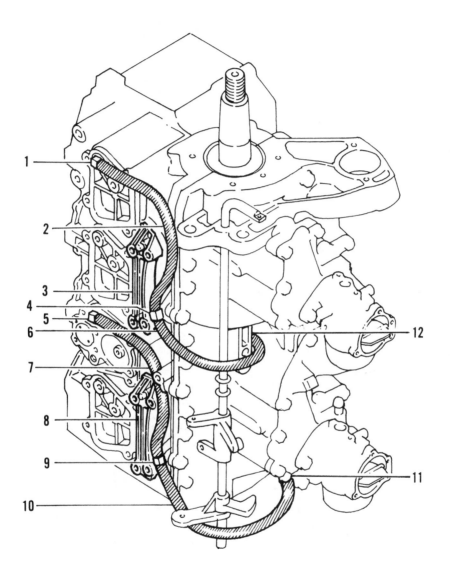

**FUEL RECIRCULATION SYSTEM
(120 HP 1990A-SERIAL NO. OE065371)**

1. Cylinder No. 1 extended fitting
2. Hose, upper assembly to
   No. 1 transfer port cover fitting
3. Upper cylinder drain cover assembly
4. Tee fitting
5. Cylinder No. 3 extended fitting
6. Hose, upper assembly to upper check valve
7. Hose, lower assembly to
   No. 3 transfer port cover fitting
8. Lower cylinder drain cover assembly
9. Tee fitting
10. Hose, lower assembly to lower check valve
11. Upper check valve, cylinders No. 1 and No. 2
12. Lower check valve, cylinders No. 3 and No. 4

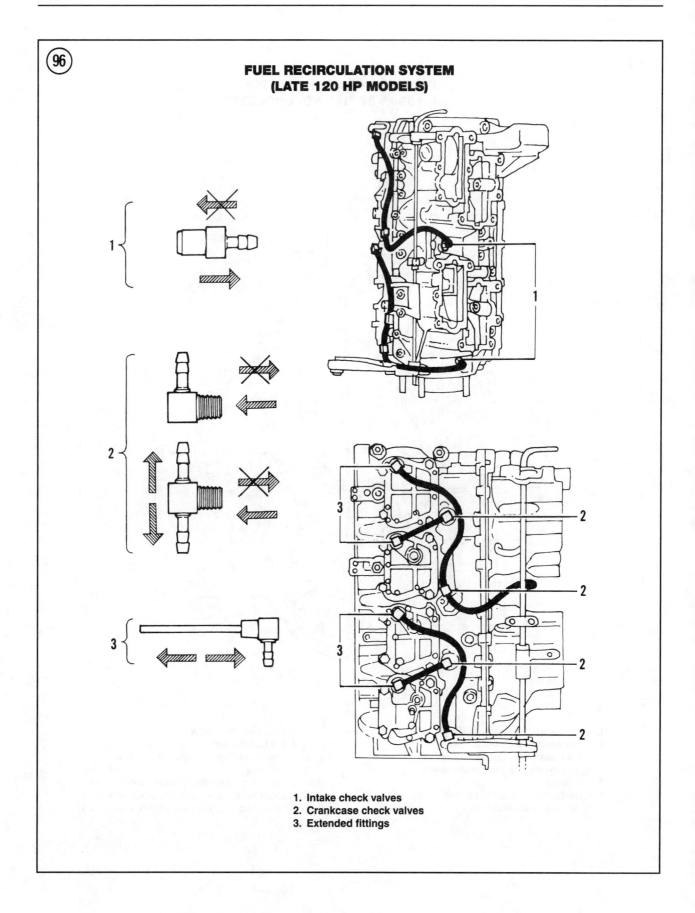

**FUEL RECIRCULATION SYSTEM
(LATE 120 HP MODELS)**

1. Intake check valves
2. Crankcase check valves
3. Extended fittings

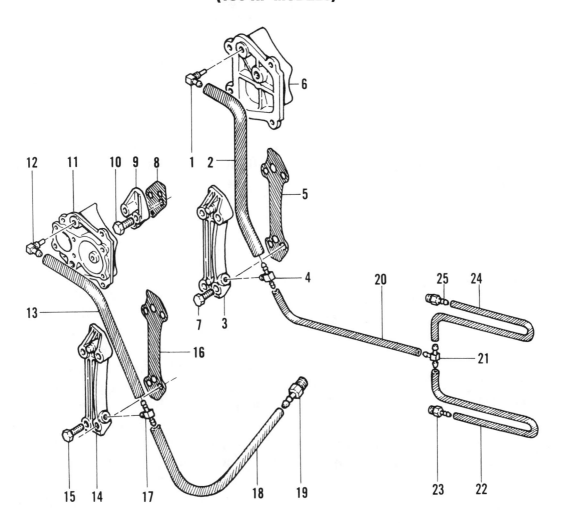

**FUEL RECIRCULATION SYSTEM
(150 HP MODELS)**

6

1. Cylinder No. 1 extended fitting
2. Hose, upper assembly to
   No. 1 transfer port cover fitting
3. Upper cylinder drain cover assembly
4. Tee fitting (90° elbow on early models)
5. Gasket
6. Cylinder No. 1 transfer port cover
7. Mounting screw
8. Gasket
9. Middle cylinder drain cover assembly
10. Mounting screw
11. Cylinder No. 4 transfer port cover
12. Cylinder No. 4 extended fitting
13. Hose, lower assembly to
    No. 4 transfer port cover fitting.
14. Lower cylinder drain cover assembly

15. Mounting screw
16. Gasket
17. Tee fitting (90° elbow on early models)
18. Hose, lower assembly to
    lower check valve (late models only)
19. Upper check valve, cylinders
    No. 1 and No. 2 (late models only)
20. Hose, Upper assembly to
    intake cover tee (late models only)
21. Tee (late models only)
22. Hose, intake tee to middle intake
    cover check valve (late models only)
23. Middle intake check valve (late models only)
24. Hose, intake tee to upper intake cover
    check valve (late models only)
25. Upper intake check valve (late models only)

port cover. Remove the transfer port cover to inspect and test the recirculation system on these models. Thread a sheet metal screw into the check valves and pry or pull the screw to remove the check valves. Sixty hp models use a puddle drain valve with a metering cap on the front crankcase half, directly in front of the lower main bearing. This is connected to another puddle drain valve with a metering cap located on the lower port side of the No.1 cylinder intake manifold runner. Make sure the drain valves are not blocked and the connecting hose is not damaged or deteriorated.

1. Disconnect and remove the necessary electrical components positioned in front of the cylinder drain cover(s).

2. Remove the cover, plate (reed valve models only) and gasket assembly. Repeat this step as necessary for 4 and 5 cylinder models. Do not damage the cover and plate when removing the gaskets.

3. *Reed valve models*—Carefully separate the cover from the plate and discard the gasket.

4. *Reed valve models*—Remove the reed valves and reed stops. Inspect the reeds for flatness and replace if cracked, chipped, damaged or distorted.

5. *Check valve models*—Test the check valves with a short piece of 5/32 in. rubber hose. Trim one end of the hose square. Press the trimmed end of the hose firmly down over a check valve to provide an airtight seal. Inhale and exhale into the open end of the hose. Air should flow when exhaling but not when inhaling. Test each check valve in the cylinder drain cover. Replace the cylinder drain cover if any of the valves do not function correctly.

6. *Check valve models*—Repeat Step 5 for each cylinder drain cover on the motor.

7. Remove the screens using a small hooked tool and clean in solvent. Replace the screens if they are damaged or impossible to clean.

8. Inspect the condition of all hoses connected to the recirculation system. Replace any damaged or deteriorated hoses.

9. Clean all components in solvent and dry with compressed air.

10. Reverse removal procedure to reinstall. Use new gaskets for installation. Apply Loctite PST sealant to all fittings.

Recirculation System Service (Late Models without Cylinder Drain Covers)

Refer to the appropriate **Figure 88-97** for this procedure.

On late models without cylinder drain covers, the check valves are mounted directly to the crankcase or intake manifold. The fittings are mounted to the transfer port cover(s) or intake manifold(s). A check valve should flow in the direction of the arrow on the appropriate diagram, but not flow in the opposite direction. Use a small syringe and a piece of recirculation line to quickly test the system.

All check valves should only flow in the direction of the arrow on the appropriate diagram. Fittings should flow in both directions. Replace or clean any fitting that will not flow in both directions. Replace any check valve that flows in both directions or will not flow in either direction. Push on the syringe plunger to check flow into a fitting or check valve. Pull on the syringe plunger to check flow out of a fitting or check valve.

When replacing fittings or check valves, coat the threads with Loctite PST pipe sealant. Also, inspect and replace any recirculation lines that are damaged or deteriorated.

NOTE
The 25 hp 3-cylinder has 2 check valves in the intake manifold and 1 check valve in the front crankcase half, directly in line with the lower main bearing. There are 3 fittings on the transfer port cover,

1 for each check valve (cylinder). Make sure each check valve flows out from the intake manifold or crankcase half, but not back into the valve. Make sure each fitting on the transfer port cover flows both directions. Replace the valves or fittings as necessary.

OIL INJECTION
(1992 120 HP L-DRIVE)

Two-stroke engines are lubricated by mixing oil with the gasoline. The various internal engine components are lubricated as the fuel and oil mixture passes through the crankcase and cylinders. The optimum fuel-oil ratio required by an outboard motor depends on engine speed and load condition. Without oil injection, the oil and gasoline must be mixed at a predetermined ratio to ensure sufficient lubrication is provided at all engine speeds and load conditions. While this predetermined ratio is adequate for high-speed operation, it may contain more oil than necessary during idle and slow-speed operation. This can result in excessive smoking and fouled spark plugs when operated at slow speed.

Oil injection eliminates the need to hand mix oil and gasoline together in the fuel tank. On models equipped with oil injection, the amount of oil delivered to the engine can be varied instantly and accurately to supply the optimum fuel-oil ratio for all engine speeds and load conditions.

Operation

The injection system delivers oil to the power head relative to engine speed and throttle position. A linkage rod (5, **Figure 98**) connects the oil pump control lever to the throttle linkage and varies the oil pump stroke according to throttle opening. The fuel/oil ratio is varied from approximately 100:1 at idle to approximately 50:1 at wide-open throttle.

An engine-mounted oil reservoir feeds oil to the oil pump. Oil reservoir capacity is 1-1/2 gal.

(5.7 L) The oil reservoir is equipped with a low-oil sensor that activates a warning horn should the oil level drop to a predetermined level.

A crankshaft-driven oil injection pump injects oil into a mixing valve (12, **Figure 98**) where the oil and gasoline is mixed for delivery to the power head.

Throttle and Oil Pump Synchronization

The oil injection pump should be synchronized to the throttle opening after adjusting carburetor idle speed.

1. Make sure the idle speed is correctly adjusted. See Chapter Five.
2. With the throttle lever in the IDLE position, the match marks on the pump control lever and pump housing should be aligned. See **Figure 99**.
3. To adjust, disconnect the control rod from the control lever. Loosen the locknut and turn the connector end as necessary to align the match marks.
4. Reconnect the control rod and securely tighten the locknut.

Oil Injection Pump Removal/Installation

Refer to **Figure 98** for this procedure.
1. Carefully cut the tie strap clamps securing oil hoses to the pump. Disconnect the hoses.
2. Disconnect the pump control rod from the pump control lever.
3. Remove the screws securing the pump assembly to the power head. Remove the pump and O-ring. If the pump drive shaft comes out with the pump, reinstall it into the power head, making sure it properly engages the pump drive gear.
4. To install the pump, install a new O-ring (3, **Figure 98**) on the pump base.
5. Install the pump on the power head. Make sure the drive shaft properly engages the pump.
6. Install the pump attaching screws and tighten them securely.

6

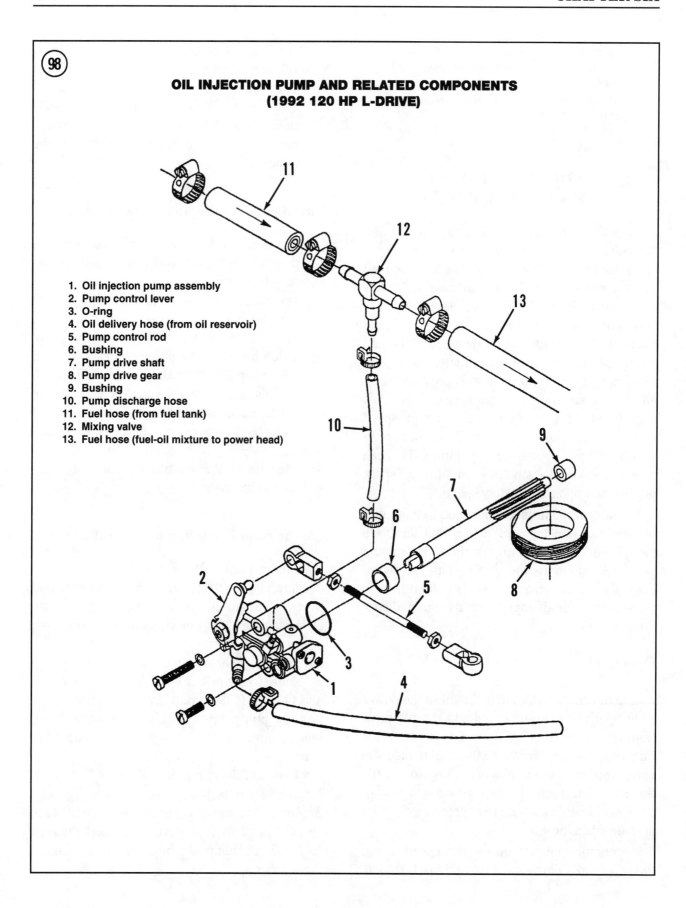

98

OIL INJECTION PUMP AND RELATED COMPONENTS
(1992 120 HP L-DRIVE)

1. Oil injection pump assembly
2. Pump control lever
3. O-ring
4. Oil delivery hose (from oil reservoir)
5. Pump control rod
6. Bushing
7. Pump drive shaft
8. Pump drive gear
9. Bushing
10. Pump discharge hose
11. Fuel hose (from fuel tank)
12. Mixing valve
13. Fuel hose (fuel-oil mixture to power head)

7. Connect the oil hoses to the pump. Securely clamp the hoses using new tie straps.

8. Connect the pump control rod. Synchronize the pump and throttle and bleed the injection system as described in this chapter.

Bleeding Injection System

If air enters the oil injection system, or if any injection system components are replaced, the air must be purged (bled) from the pump and hoses before operating the motor. To bleed the injection system, proceed as follows:

1. Place a shop towel under the oil pump to absorb spilled oil.

2. Connect a remote fuel tank containing a 50:1 fuel-oil mixture to the motor.

3. Open the pump bleed screw (**Figure 99**) 2-3 turns.

4. Start the motor and run at idle speed. Continue idling the motor until the oil discharged from the bleed screw is free of air bubbles.

5. Tighten the bleed screw. Disconnect the remote fuel supply and reconnect the boat's fuel tank.

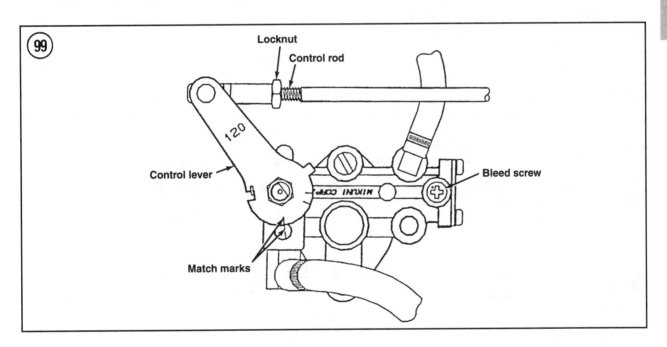

Locknut
Control rod
Control lever
Match marks
Bleed screw

Table 1 STANDARD TORQUE VALUES

Screw or Nut Size	in.-lbs.	ft.-lbs.	N•m
6-32	9	–	1.0
8-32	20	–	2.3
10-24	30	–	3.4
10-32	35	–	4.0
12-24	45	–	5.1
1/4-20	70	6	7.9
1/4-28	84	7	9.5
5/16-18	160	13	18.1
5/16-24	168	14	19.0
(continued)			

Table 1 STANDARD TORQUE VALUES (continued)

Screw or Nut Size	in.-lbs.	ft.-lbs.	N•m
3/8-16	270	23	30.5
3/8-24	300	25	33.9
7/16-14	–	36	48.8
7/16-20	–	40	54.2
1/2-13	–	50	67.8
1/2-20	–	60	81.3

Table 2 REED VALVE SPECIFICATIONS

Model	Maximum Stand Open	Minimum Overlap	Reed Stop Opening
4, 5, 9.9 and 15 hp	.006 in. (0.15 mm)	.030 in. (0.76 mm)	.240-.260 in. (6.1-6.6 mm)
7.5 hp	.012 in. (0.30 mm)	.030 in. (0.76 mm)	.200-.220 in. (5.1-5.6 mm)
25 hp (2 cylinder)	.010 in. (0.25 mm)	.040 in. (1.02 mm)	.270-.290 in. (6.9-7.4 mm)
25 hp (3 cylinder)	.003 in. (0.08 mm)	N/A	N/A
35-60, 85 and 90[1] hp, 1999 75 hp	.010 in. (0.25 mm)	.040 in. (1.02 mm)	.270-.290 in. (6.9-7.4 mm)
70 and 75 hp[2], 1984-1998	.010 in. (0.25 mm)	N/A	N/A
120[3],125 and 150 hp	.010 in. (0.25 mm)	.040 in. (1.02 mm)	.300-.320 in. (7.6-8.1 mm)

[1]The 1991A and newer 90 hp models do not have serviceable reeds. Check only the maximum stand open. Replace the reed block assembly if any defects are noted.
[2]All 70 and 75 hp models do not have serviceable reeds. Replace the reed block assembly if any defects are noted.
[3]The 1995-1999 120 hp models do not have serviceable reeds. Check only the maximum stand open. Replace the reed block assembly if any defects are noted.

Table 3 FUEL PUMP SPECIFICATIONS

Model (includes L-Drives)	Minimum psi (kPa)
5-15 hp	
at 600 rpm	1 (6.9)
at 2500-3000 rpm	1.5 (10.3)
at 4500 rpm	2.5 (17.2)
25 hp (2-cylinder)	
at 600 rpm	1 (6.9)
at 2500-3000 rpm	1.5 (10.3)
at 4500 rpm	2.5 (17.2)
25 hp (3-cylinder)	
at 4500 rpm	2.5 (17.2)
35-70 hp (two stage pump)	
at 600 rpm	1 (6.9)
at 2500-3000 rpm	1.5 (10.3)
at 4500 rpm	2.5 (17.2)
40-120 hp (square pump)	
at 750 rpm	3-4 (20.7-27.6)
at 5000 rpm	5-7 (34.5-48.3)
85-150 hp (two stage pump)	
at 5000 rpm	4 (27.6)

Table 4 CARBURETOR SPECIFICATIONS (4-25 HP MODELS)

4, 5, 9.9 and 15 hp	
Float level	Parallel to body flange
Float drop (top edge of float to carburetor body)	5/16 in. (7.93 mm)
Initial idle mixture screw adjustment (except 1998 9.9 and 15 hp)	1 turn out from a lightly seated position
9.9 and 15 hp	1-1 1/2 turns out from a lightly seated position
Standard main jet (carburetor number)	
4 and 5 hp	.039 in.
9.9 hp 1984-1987	.049 in.
9.9 hp 1988A (HO2C)	.059 in.
9.9 hp 1988 B-1990A (HO1C)	.063 in.
9.9 hp 1991A and newer (HO5A)	.057 in.
15 hp 1984-1987	.0625 in.
15 hp 1988A-1990A (HO1C)	.063 in.
15 hp 1990C and newer (FO-1B)	.070 in.
7.5 hp	
Float level (top edge of float to carburetor body)	1/8 in. (3.18 mm)
Float drop (top edge of float to carburetor body)	5/16 in. (7.93 mm)
Standard main jet	.041 in.
Initial idle mixture screw adjustment	1 turn out from lightly seated position
25 hp 2-cylinder	
Float level (top edge of float to carburetor body)	.150-.190 in. (3.81-4.83 mm)
Float drop (lowest edge of float to carburetor body)	1.00-1.08 in. (25.4-27.43 mm)
Main jet (standard)	.066 in.
Initial idle mixture screw adjustment	1-1/4 turns out from lightly seated position
25 hp 3-cylinder	
Float level	Parallel to body flange
Float drop (top edge of float to carburetor body)	5/16 in. (7.93 mm)
Main jet (standard)	.058 in.
Initial idle mixture screw adjustment	1-1/2 turns out from lightly seated position

6

Table 5 CARBURETOR SPECIFICATIONS: 35-60 HP

Float level 35-50 hp	Parallel to body flange
Float level 60 hp	25/64-27/64 in. (9.9-10.7 mm)[1]
Float drop[2]	
Initial idle mixture screw adjustment	1 turn out from lightly seated position
Standard main jet (carburetor numbers)	
35 hp 1986-1990B (WE-15,16,16A,16B,103A)	.074 in.
35 hp 1990C-1991 (WB-106A)	.088 in.
40 hp 1992C-serial No. OE065371 (WB-107A,110A)	.076 in.
40 hp serial No. OE093700-138599 (WB-117A,127A)	.060 in.
40 hp serial No. OE138600 and up (TC-131A)	.062 in.
50 hp 1984-1985 (WE-8)	.086 in.
50 hp 1986-1989A (WE-13,17,17A)	.084 in.
50 hp 1989B-1990B (WE-27C, WB-102A)	.088 in.
50 hp 1990C-1992C (TC-102A,102B,121A)	.098 in.
50 hp serial No. OE063572-OE093699 (WB-118A)	.082 in.

(continued)

Table 5 CARBURETOR SPECIFICATIONS (35-60 HP) (continued)

Standard main jet (carburetor numbers) (continued)	
50 hp serial No. OE093700-OE138599 (TC-130A)	.094 in.
50 hp serial No. OE138600 and up (TC-134A)	.096 in.
60 hp	.074 in.

[1]Measured from the lowest edge of float to the carburetor body.
[2]Float should hang just short of touching the carburetor casting.

Table 6 CARBURETOR SPECIFICATIONS (70-150 HP OUTBOARD MODELS)

Float level	Parallel to body flange
Float drop*	
Initial idle mixture screw adjustment	
70, 75, 120 and 150 hp	1 turn out from lightly seated position
75 hp (1999) and 90 hp 1995-1999	1 turn out from a lightly seated position
85 hp 1984-1988	1-1/4 turns out from lightly seated position
85 hp 1989	3/4 turn out from lightly seated position
90 hp 1990-1994	3/4 turn out from lightly seated position
125 hp 1984-1988C	1-1/4 turns out from lightly seated position
125 hp 1988C-1989	1 turn out from a lightly seated position
Standard main jet (carburetor numbers)	
70 hp	
1991-serial No. OE065371 (TC-111A)	.096 in.
1991-serial No. OE065371 (TC-125A)	.090 in.
Serial No. OE065372-OE138599 (TC-111B)	.094 in.
75 hp 1996 (TC-111B)	.094 in.
85 hp	.074 in.
90 hp 1990	Top .074 in., center .072 in., bottom .072 in.
90 hp 1991A-1999	Top .076 in., center .074 in., bottom .074 in.
120 hp 1990-1996	.094 in.
125 hp 1984-1985	.094 in.
125 hp 1986-1989C	Top .101 in., bottom .094 in.
125 hp 1989D and 1989E	Top .098 in., bottom .096 in.
150 hp	Top .094 in., center .078 in., bottom .094 in.

*Float should hang just short of touching the carburetor casting.

Table 7 CARBURETOR SPECIFICATIONS (L-DRIVE MODELS)

Float level	Parallel to body flange
Float drop*	
Initial idle mixture screw adjustment	
85 and 90 hp	3/4 turn out from lightly seated position
120 and 125 hp	1 turn out from a lightly seated position
Standard main jet	
85 hp 1989	.074 in.
90 hp 1990	Top .074 in., center .072 in., bottom .072 in.
90 hp 1991A-1996	Top .076 in., center .074 in., bottom .074 in.
120 hp 1990-1992	.094 in.
125 hp 1989C	Top .101 in., bottom .094 in.
125 hp 1989D and 1989E	Top .098 in., bottom .096 in.

*Float should hang just short of touching the carburetor casting.

Chapter Seven

Ignition and Electrical Systems

This chapter provides service procedures for the battery, charging system, starter motor (electric start models) and ignition system on all models covered by this manual. Wiring diagrams are located at the end of the book. Tables covering battery information, ignition system identification, wire color coding and general torque specifications are located at the end of the chapter.

BATTERY

Batteries used in marine applications endure far more rigorous treatment than those used in automotive applications. Marine batteries have a thicker exterior case to cushion the plates during tight turns and rough water operation. Thicker plates are also used, with each one individually fastened within the case to prevent premature failure. Spill-proof caps on the battery cells prevent electrolyte from spilling into the bilges.

Automotive batteries should be used in a boat *only* during an emergency situation when a suitable marine battery is not available.

Battery Rating Methods

The battery industry has developed specifications and performance standards to evaluate batteries and their energy potential. Several rating methods are available to provide meaningful information on battery selection. Force recommends a battery with a *minimum rating* of 630 cold cranking amps (CCA) or 490 marine cranking amps (MCA) and 100 minutes reserve capacity.

Cold cranking amps (CCA)

This figure represents in amps the current flow the battery can deliver for 30 seconds at 0° F (-17.6° C) without dropping below 1.2 volts per cell (7.2 volts on a standard 12 volt battery). The higher the number, the more amps it can deliver to crank the engine. CCA × 1.3 = MCA.

Marine cranking amps (MCA)

This figure is similar to the CCA test figure except that the test is run at 32 F° (0° C) instead of 0° F (-17.6° C). This is more in line with actual boat operating environments. MCA × 0.77 = CCA.

Reserve capacity

This figure represents the time (in minutes) that a fully charged battery at 80° F (26.7° C) can deliver 25 amps, without dropping below 1.75 volts per cell (10.5 volts on a standard 12 volt battery). The reserve capacity rating defines the length of time that a typical vehicle can be operated after the charging system fails. The 25 amp figure takes into account the power required by the ignition, lighting and other accessories. The higher the reserve capacity rating, the longer the vehicle could be operated after a charging system failure.

Amp-hour rating

The ampere hour rating method is also called the 20 hour rating method. This rating represents the steady current flow that the battery will deliver for 20 hours while at 80° F (26.7° C) without dropping below 1.75 volts per cell (10.5 volts on a standard 12 volt battery). The rating is actually the steady current flow times the 20 hours. Example: A 60 amp-hour battery will deliver 3 amps continuously for 20 hours. This method has been largely discontinued by the battery industry. Cold cranking amps (or MCA) and reserve capacity ratings are now the most common battery rating methods.

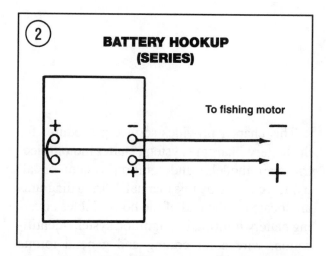

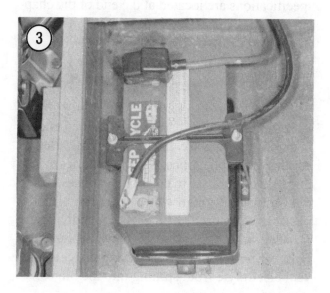

CAUTION
*Sealed or maintenance-free batteries are **not** recommended for use with the unregulated charging systems used on some Force outboard motors and L-Drives. Excessive charging during continued high-speed operation will cause the electrolyte to boil, resulting in its loss. Since water cannot be added to sealed batteries, unregulated overcharging will destroy the battery.*

Separate batteries may be used to provide power for any accessories such as lighting, fish finders and depth finders. To determine the required capacity of such batteries, calculate the accessory current (amperage) draw rate and refer to **Table 1**.

Two batteries may be connected in parallel to double the ampere-hour capacity while maintaining the required 12 volts. See **Figure 1**. For accessories which require 24 volts, batteries may be wired in series (**Figure 2**), but only accessories specifically requiring 24 volts should be connected to the system. If charging becomes necessary, batteries connected in a parallel or series circuit should be disconnected and charged individually.

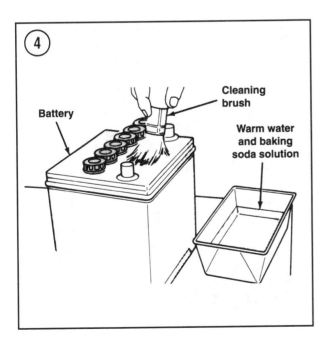

Battery Installation in Aluminum Boats

If the battery is not properly secured and grounded when installed in an aluminum boat, it may contact the hull and short to ground. This will burn out remote control cables, tiller handle cables or wiring harnesses.

The following preventive steps should be observed when installing a battery in any boat, and especially a metal boat.

1. Choose a location as far as practical from the fuel tank while providing access for maintenance.
2. Install the battery in a plastic battery box with cover and tie-down strap.
3. If a covered battery box is not used, cover the positive battery terminal with a nonconductive shield or boot (**Figure 3**).
4. Make sure the battery is secured inside the battery box and that the box is fastened in position with a suitable tie-down strap.

Care and Inspection

1. Remove the battery box cover or the battery hold-down fixture (**Figure 3**).
2. Disconnect the negative battery cable, then disconnect the positive cable.
3. Remove battery from the battery tray or box.
4. Inspect the entire battery case for cracks or other damage.
5. Inspect the battery tray or box for corrosion and clean if necessary with a solution of baking soda and water.

CAUTION
Do not allow the baking soda and water cleaning solution to enter the battery cells in Step 6 or the electrolyte will be severely weakened.

6. Clean the top of the battery with a stiff brush using the baking soda and water solution (**Figure 4**). Rinse the battery case with clear water and wipe dry with a clean cloth or paper towel.

7. Position the battery in the battery tray or box.

8. Clean the battery cable terminal ends (**Figure 5**) and the battery terminals (**Figure 6**) with a suitable battery cable/terminal cleaning tool or a stiff wire brush.

> *CAUTION*
> *Be sure the battery cables are connected to the proper terminals. Reversing the battery polarity will result in rectifier and ignition system damage.*

9. Securely tighten the battery connections. Coat the connections with petroleum jelly or a light grease to minimize corrosion.

> *NOTE*
> *Do not overfill the battery cells in Step 10. The electrolyte expands due to heat from charging and will overflow if the level is more than 3/16 in. above the battery plates.*

10. Remove the filler caps and check the electrolyte level. Add distilled water, if necessary, to bring the level up to 3/16 in. above the battery plates (**Figure 7**).

Testing

Hydrometer testing is the best method to check the battery's state of charge (specific gravity). Use a hydrometer with numbered graduations from 1.100-1.300 points rather than one with color-coded bands. To use the hydrometer, squeeze the rubber bulb, insert the tip into a cell, then release bulb to fill the hydrometer (**Figure 8**).

> *NOTE*
> *Do not test specific gravity immediately after adding water to the battery cells, as the water will dilute the electrolyte (lower specific gravity). To obtain accurate hydrometer readings, the battery must be charged after adding water.*

Draw sufficient electrolyte to raise the float inside the hydrometer. When using a temperature-compensated hydrometer, discharge the electrolyte back into the battery cell and repeat the process several times to adjust the temperature of the hydrometer to that of the electrolyte.

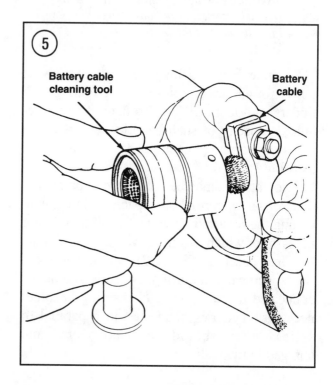

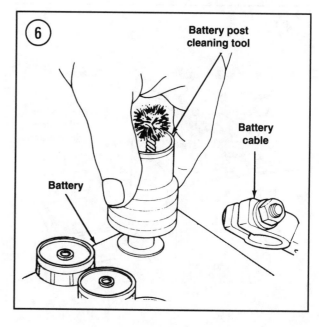

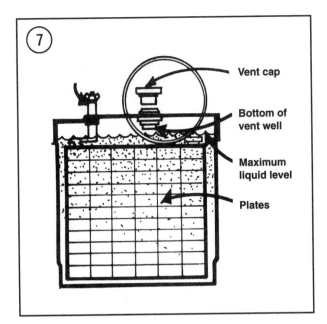

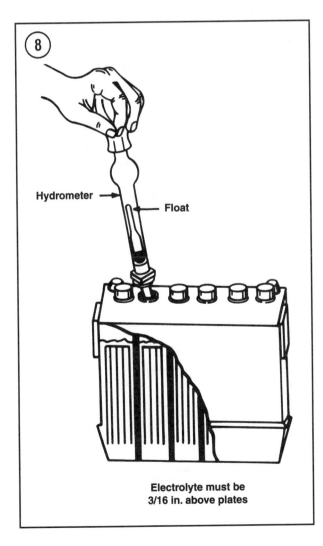

Electrolyte must be
3/16 in. above plates

Hold the hydrometer upright and note the number on the float that is even with the surface of the electrolyte (**Figure 9**). This number is the specific gravity for the cell. Discharge the electrolyte into the cell from which it came.

The specific gravity of a cell is the indicator of the cell's state of charge. A fully charged cell

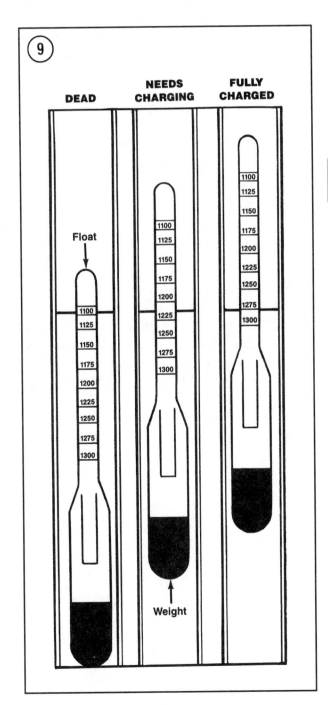

7

will read 1.260 or more at 80°F (26.7°C). A cell that is 75% charged will read from 1.220-1.230 while a cell with a 50% charge will read from 1.170-1.180. Any cell reading 1.120 or less should be considered discharged. All cells should be within 30 points specific gravity of each other. If over 30 points variation is noted, the battery condition is questionable. Charge the battery and recheck the specific gravity. If 30 points or more variation remains between cells after charging, the battery has failed and should be replaced.

NOTE
If a temperature-compensated hydrometer is not used, add 4 points specific gravity to the actual reading for every 10° above 80°F (26.7°C). Subtract 4 points specific gravity for every 10° below 80°F (26.7°C).

Battery Storage

Wet cell batteries slowly discharge when stored. They discharge faster when warm then when cold. See **Table 2**. Before storing a battery, clean the case with a solution of baking soda and water. Rinse with clear water and wipe dry. The battery should be fully charged (no change in specific gravity when 3 readings are taken 1 hour apart) and then stored in a cool, dry location. Check electrolyte level and state of charge frequently during storage. If specific gravity falls to 40 points or more below full charge (1.260), recharge battery.

Charging

A good state of charge should be maintained in batteries used for starting. Check the battery with a voltmeter as shown in **Figure 10**. Any battery that cannot deliver at least 9.6 volts under starting load should be recharged. Replace battery if it cannot deliver at least 9.6 volts under cranking load after proper recharging.

The battery does not have to be removed from the boat for charging, but it is a recommended safety procedure, since a charging battery releases highly explosive hydrogen gas. In many boats, the area around the battery is not well ventilated and the gas may remain in the area for hours after the charging process has been completed. Sparks or flames occurring near the battery can cause it to explode, spraying battery acid over a wide area.

For this reason, it is important to observe the following precautions:

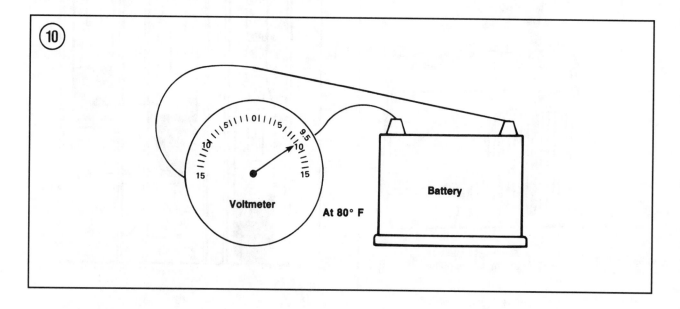

a. Never smoke around batteries that are charging, or have been recently charged.

b. Do not disconnect a live circuit at the battery creating a spark that can ignite any hydrogen gas that may be present.

Disconnect the negative battery cable first, then the positive cable. Make sure the electrolyte is at the proper level.

Connect the charger to the battery, negative charger lead to negative battery terminal, positive charger lead to positive battery terminal. If the charger output is variable, select a 4 ampere setting. Set the voltage switch to 12 volts and switch the charger on.

WARNING
Be extremely careful not to create any sparks around the battery when connecting the battery charger.

If the battery is severely discharged, allow it to charge for at least 8 hours. **Table 3** provides approximate state of charge percentages for batteries used primarily for engine starting. Check the charging process with a hydrometer. The battery should be considered fully charged when the specific gravity of all cells does not increase when checked at 3 intervals of 1 hour, and all cells are gassing freely.

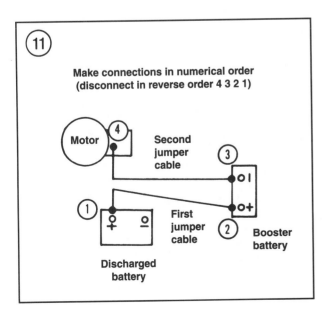

Make connections in numerical order
(disconnect in reverse order 4 3 2 1)

Motor — Second jumper cable — First jumper cable — Discharged battery — Booster battery

Jump Starting

If the battery becomes severely discharged, it is possible to "jump start" the engine from another battery. If the proper procedure is not followed, however, jump starting can be dangerous. Check the electrolyte level of the discharged battery before attempting the jump start. If the electrolyte is not visible or if it appears to be frozen, do not jump start the discharged battery.

WARNING
*Use extreme caution when connecting a booster battery to one that is discharged to avoid personal injury or damage to the system. **Be certain** the jumper cables are connected in the correct polarity.*

1. Connect the jumper cables in the order and sequence shown in **Figure 11**.

WARNING
An electrical arc may occur when the final connection is made. This could cause an explosion if it occurs near the battery. For this reason, the final connection should be made to a good engine ground, away from the battery and to the battery itself.

2. Check that all jumper cables are clear of moving engine components.

3. Start the engine. Once started, run at a fast idle speed.

CAUTION
Running the engine at full throttle with a discharged battery may damage the charging system.

4. Remove the jumper cables in the exact reverse order shown in **Figure 11**. Remove the cables at point 4, then 3, 2 and 1.

ALTERNATOR CHARGING SYSTEM

An alternator charging system is standard on all electric start models and optional on 4-15 hp models equipped with an AC lighting system.

7

Figure 12 shows the typical charging system components.

The alternator charging system consists of the alternator stator, permanent magnets located along the inner periphery of the flywheel (**Figure 13**), a rectifier or rectifier/regulator, circuit breaker or fuse, battery and connecting wiring.

Rotation of the flywheel magnets around the stator induces alternating current into the alternator stator (**Figure 14**). The induced current is sent to the rectifier (**Figure 15** or **Figure 16**, typical) where it is converted to direct current (DC) to charge the battery or power the accessories.

A malfunction in the battery charging system will normally result in an undercharged battery. Perform the following visual inspection prior to testing the alternator stator and rectifier or rectifier/regulator as described in Chapter Three.

1. Make sure that the battery cables are properly connected. The red cable must be connected to the positive (+) battery terminal. Reversed battery polarity will damage the rectifier or rectifier/regulator.

2. Make sure the battery terminal connections are clean and tight. Clean and tighten as required.

3. Inspect the physical condition of the battery. Look for bulges or cracks in the case, leaking electrolyte or corrosion.

4. Carefully check the wiring between the stator coils, rectifier and battery for chafing, deterioration or other damage.

5. Check the circuit wiring for corroded, loose or disconnected wires. Clean, tighten or repair as required.

6. Determine if the accessory load on the battery exceeds the charging system or battery capacity. See Chapter Three.

Stator Removal/Installation

Remove the negative battery cable from the battery anytime the electrical system is serviced. Remove the engine cover, disconnect the spark

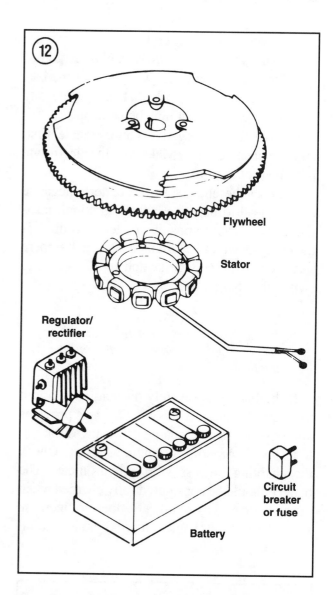

Flywheel

Stator

Regulator/ rectifier

Circuit breaker or fuse

Battery

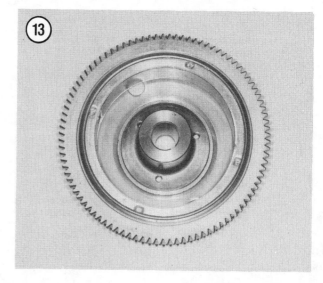

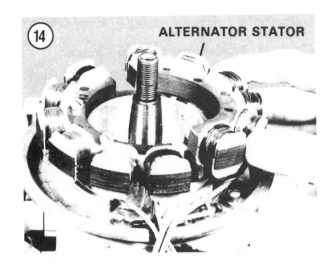

ALTERNATOR STATOR

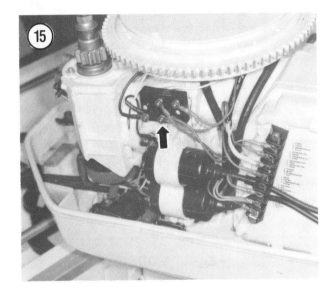

plug leads and ground the plug leads to the power head.

The alternator and ignition windings of the stator are integrated into one assembly on all models except the 50 hp with battery breaker point ignition and manual start models converted to battery charging system. Stator removal and installation procedures for all other models are covered under *Ignition Systems* in this chapter. Refer to Table Seven for ignition system model identification.

50 hp (battery breaker-point ignition)

1. Remove the flywheel. See Chapter Eight.

2. Pull the breaker point leads off the stator spade terminals. Remove the terminal mounting screws and terminals from the stator assembly. See **Figure 17**.

3. Remove 3 screws securing stator to the bearing cage, then lift stator assembly off bearing cage.

4. Reinstall by reversing removal procedure. Make sure all wires are routed to prevent contact or interference with any moving components.

7

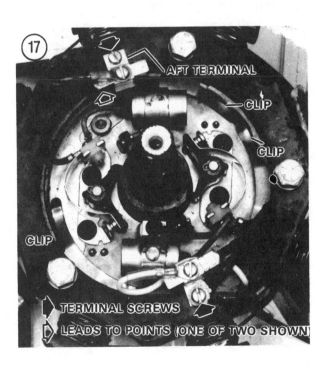

AFT TERMINAL

CLIP

CLIP

CLIP

TERMINAL SCREWS

LEADS TO POINTS (ONE OF TWO SHOWN)

Stator Removal/Installation
(Manual Start Models Converted
to Battery Charging System)

1. Disconnect the negative battery cable.

2. Remove the engine cover.

3. Remove the flywheel. See Chapter Eight.

4. Remove the screws securing the alternator stator to the trigger stator.

5. Cut any straps holding stator wires to other wiring.

6. Unwrap the lighting coil cable splices. Cut stator wires from splices. Remove stator from the power head.

7. Installation is the reverse of removal. Make sure stator wires are routed to prevent contact or interference with any moving components.

Rectifier or Rectifier/Regulator
Removal/Installation

Refer to **Figure 18**, **Figure 19** and **Figure 20**, typical for this procedure.

1. Disconnect the negative battery cable.

2. Remove the engine cover.

3. Label all wires for reference during reassembly. Disconnect the wires at the rectifier or rectifier/regulator.

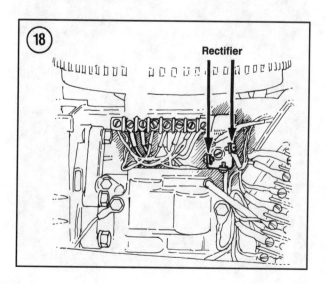

4. Remove the screw(s) securing the rectifier or rectifier/regulator to the power head or mounting bracket.

5. Remove the rectifier or rectifier/regulator.

6. Reverse removal to reinstall.

Circuit Breaker Replacement

The circuit breaker is generally located on or near the terminal block. See **Figure 21** for typical location.

1. Disconnect the negative battery cable.

2. Remove the engine cover.

NOTE
Depending upon the circuit breaker location and positioning, it may be easier to reverse Step 3 and Step 4 on some models.

3. Remove the 2 screws and washers holding the circuit breaker to the terminal board bracket or crankcase cover. See **Figure 22**, typical.

4. Remove the nuts and disconnect the wires from the circuit breaker terminals (**Figure 22**, typical).

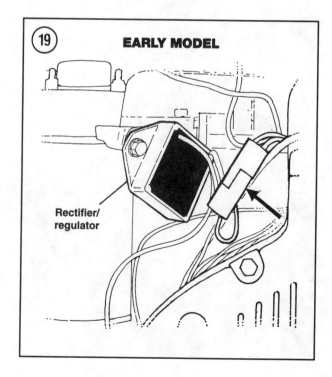

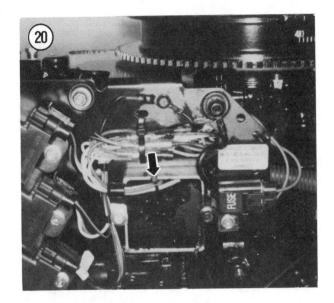

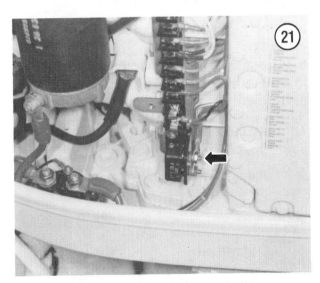

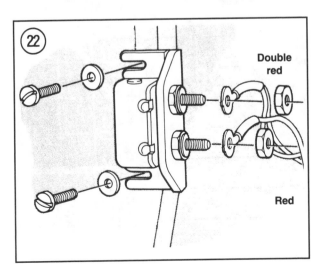

Double red

Red

5. Installation is the reverse of removal.

Fuse Replacement

The fuse is generally located near the rectifier/regulator. See **Figure 20**, typical.

1. Carefully lift the lock clip and slide the fuse holder out of the protective cover.

2. Pull the defective fuse out of the fuse holder.

3. Push a new fuse into the fuse holder.

4. Push the fuse holder into the protective cover until the lock clip snaps into place.

ELECTRIC STARTING SYSTEM

The models covered in this manual may use a rope-operated rewind starter or an electric starting system. The electric starting system consists of the battery, an ignition or starter switch, a neutral interlock switch, the starter motor and connecting wiring. All models use a starter solenoid or relay in the circuit.

Starting system operation and troubleshooting are described in Chapter Three.

STARTER MOTOR SYSTEM

Marine starter motors are very similar in design and operation to those found on automotive engines. They use an inertia-type drive in which external spiral splines on the armature shaft engage internal spiral splines on the drive assembly.

The starter motor is capable of producing a very high torque, but only for a brief time, due to rapid heat buildup. To prevent overheating, never operate the starter motor continuously for more that 15 seconds. Allow the motor to cool for at least 3 minutes before further operation.

If the starter motor does not crank the engine, check the battery and all connecting wiring for loose or corroded connections, shorted or open circuits, or other defects. If this inspection does

7

not determine the problem, refer to Chapter Three for troubleshooting procedures.

Starter Motor Removal/Installation (1984-1987 35 hp and 25 hp 2-cylinder)

Refer to **Figure 23** for this procedure.
1. Disconnect negative battery cable from the battery.
2. Remove the engine cover.
3. Remove the nuts and disconnect the positive battery cable and starter cable from the starter solenoid.
4. Disconnect the 2 small wires from the solenoid.
5. Remove the screws securing the solenoid to the starter bracket and remove solenoid.
6. Remove the screws securing the circuit breaker to the starter bracket and position circuit breaker aside.
7. Remove the screw securing the top of the terminal block to the starter bracket.
8. Remove the screws securing the starter bracket to the power head. Lift starter to gain access to the lower terminal block screw, then remove the lower terminal block screw.
9. Remove the starter motor and bracket assembly from the power head.
10. Remove the bracket from the starter motor.
11. Installation is the reverse of removal.

Starter Motor Removal/Installation (1988-on 35 hp)

1. Disconnect the negative battery cable.
2. Remove the engine cover.
3. Remove the screw securing the clamp around the center of the starter motor to the power head.
4. Remove the starter bracket mounting screws (**Figure 24**).
5. Lift starter and bracket assembly sufficiently to remove the starter cable.
6. Lift starter motor and bracket assembly from power head.

7. Remove the nuts securing the bracket to the motor and separate the bracket from the motor.

8. Installation is the reverse of removal.

Starter Motor Removal/Installation (1984-1992A 50 hp)

1. Disconnect the negative battery cable.

2. Remove the engine cover.

3. Remove the choke solenoid.

4. Remove 2 screws securing the bottom of the starter bracket to the power head (behind carburetor).

5. Remove 3 nuts securing starter bracket to the power head.

6. Lift starter and bracket assembly sufficiently to remove the starter cable from the bottom of the motor.

7. Lift starter and bracket assembly from the power head. Separate the bracket from the motor.

8. Installation is the reverse of removal.

STARTER

(▶ REMOVE)
(PLUS ONE SCREW NOT SHOWN)

Starter Motor Removal/Installation (1992C-1995 40 and 50 hp)

1. Disconnect the negative battery cable from the battery.

2. Remove the screws (A, **Figure 25**) holding the upper starter bracket to the crankcase cover.

3. Then, remove the screw (B, **Figure 25**) holding the main engine wiring harness connector to the power head.

4. Remove the 2 switch box mounting bracket screws (C, **Figure 25**). Move the bracket aside as necessary to expose the starter lower mounting fastener(s). Remove the lower fastener(s).

5. Pull the starter motor away from the power head, then remove the starter cable from the motor. Remove the motor.

6. To install, attach the starter cable to its terminal. Install the terminal nut and tighten securely.

7. Install the starter motor on the power head and install the lower mounting bracket fastener(s), then the upper mounting fasteners.

8. Install the switch box mounting bracket screws. Install the main engine wiring harness connector clamp screw. Reconnect the negative battery cable.

Starter Motor Removal/Installation (60 hp)

1. Disconnect the negative battery cable.
2. Remove the engine cover.
3. Remove the starter cable from the starter motor.
4. Remove the three screws holding the starter to the engine.
5. Installation is the reverse of removal.

Starter Motor Removal/Installation (70-150 hp [Including L-Drive] and 1996 40-50 hp)

1. Disconnect the negative battery cable.
2. Remove the engine cover.

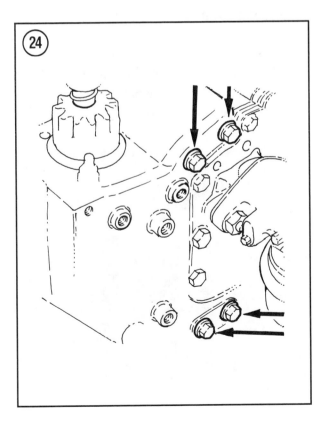

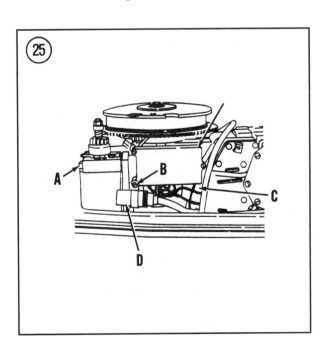

7

3. Remove the 2 nuts securing the starter to the upper starter bracket (A, **Figure 26**).

4. Remove the screw holding the lower starter bracket to the crankcase cover (B, **Figure 26**).

5. Disconnect the starter-to-relay lead at the starter terminal (C, **Figure 26**).

6. Lower the starter and remove from the power head.

7. Installation is the reverse of removal.

Brush Replacement

Refer to **Figure 27** for an exploded view of the starter motor typical of most models equipped with electric start.

Fabricate a brush retainer tool from a putty knife with a 1 × 1/2 in. opening as shown in **Figure 28**. This tool is necessary to position the brushes properly and prevent damaging them when reassembling the starter end cap to the housing.

1. Remove the starter motor as described in this chapter.

2. Remove the 2 through-bolts and commutator end cap from the starter. Do not lose the brush springs from end cap.

3. Inspect the brushes in the end cap. Replace the brushes if any are pitted, cracked, oil-soaked or worn to 1/4 in. or less.

4. If replacement is necessary, remove the screws holding the ground brushes. Remove the hex nut and washers from the positive terminal. Remove the positive terminal and insulated brushes from the end cap. See **Figure 29**.

5. Install new insulated brush and terminal assembly in end cap, positioning the long brush lead in the cap slot. See **Figure 30**.

6. Install new ground brushes to holder. Tighten retaining screws securely.

7. Fit springs and brushes into the holder. Retain the brushes with the brush holder tool and lower the starter housing into place, aligning the starter housing rib with the cap notch. See **Figure 31**.

8. Remove the brush holder tool and install the through-bolts. Tighten the through-bolts *securely*.

Starter Drive Replacement

1. Remove the starter as described in this chapter.

2. Rotate the drive assembly to the end of the armature shaft. Clamp the hex nut affixed to the back side of the starter drive assembly into a vise with protective jaws.

3. Remove the armature shaft stop nut.

4. Remove starter from the vise and slide the spring seat, spring and drive assembly off armature shaft.

5. Inspect drive gear for chipped or broken teeth or other damage.

6. Reassemble starter by reversing disassembly. Lightly lubricate armature shaft spiral splines with SAE 10 motor oil.

Starter Solenoid (Relay) Replacement

Two designs of solenoids (relays) are used. See **Figure 32** and **Figure 33**, typical.

1. Disconnect the negative battery cable.
2. Remove the engine cover.

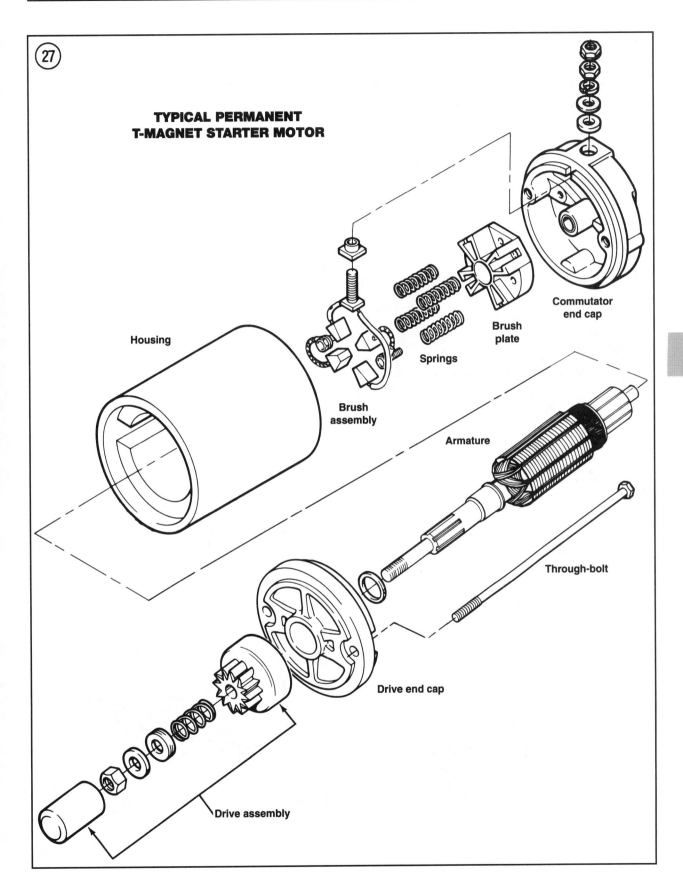

㉗

**TYPICAL PERMANENT
T-MAGNET STARTER MOTOR**

Housing

Brush
assembly

Springs

Brush
plate

Commutator
end cap

Armature

Through-bolt

Drive end cap

Drive assembly

7

3. Note the wire colors connected to each terminal for reference during reinstallation.

4. Remove the nut from each terminal and disconnect the wire(s) from the terminals.

5. Remove the 2 screws holding the solenoid to the support plate. Note that a ground wire is attached to the forward screw. Remove the solenoid.

6. Installation is the reverse of removal. Be sure to reattach the correct wire(s) to each terminal as

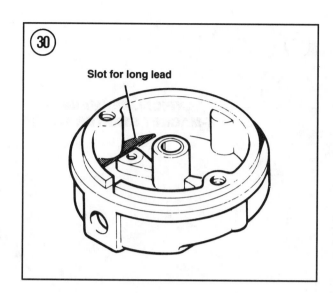

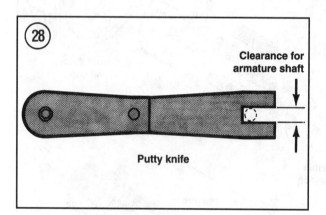

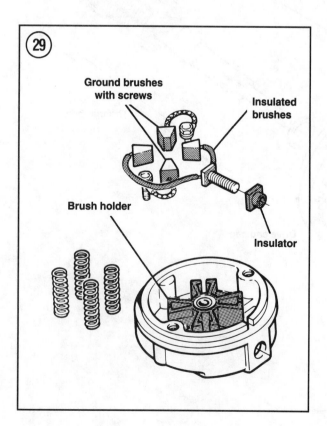

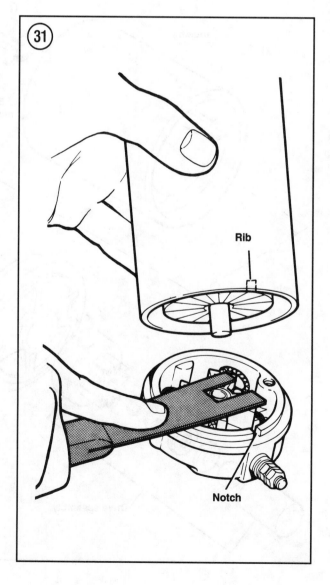

noted in Step 3. Refer to wiring diagrams at the end of this manual.

Neutral Interlock Switch Replacement (Electric Start Except L-Drive)

The neutral start interlock switch is designed to prevent starter motor operation unless the gearcase is in NEUTRAL. On 1993-on models equipped with a Commander 2000 remote control assembly, the neutral start interlock switch is located inside the remote control box. On all other models, the switch is generally located in the area of the throttle cam. See **Figure 34**. Only replacement of the engine-mounted switch is covered in this chapter.

1. Disconnect the negative battery cable. Remove the engine cover.
2. Disconnect the lead wires at each end of the interlock switch.
3. Remove the switch mounting screws and washers, then remove switch.
4. Installation is the reverse of removal. Test installation by shifting into gear (forward or reverse) and attempting to crank engine. Starter should be operational *only* with shift lever in the neutral position.

Neutral Interlock Switch Replacement (L-Drive Models)

1. Remove the engine cover.
2. Disconnect the negative battery cable.
3. Remove the remote control cover.

7

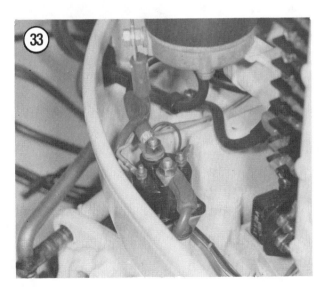

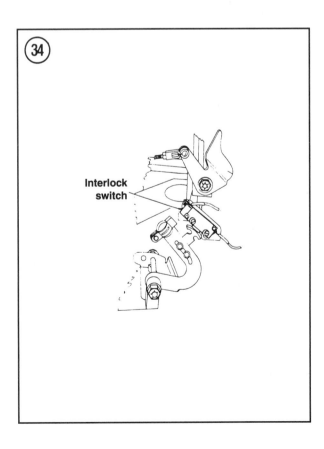

4. Disconnect interlock switch wires (A, **Figure 35**).

5. Remove screws (B, **Figure 35**) and remove switch.

6. Installation is the reverse of removal. Test installation by shifting remote control into forward or reverse gear and attempt to crank engine. Starter should be operational *only* with remote control in the neutral position.

Terminal Block Replacement

Refer to **Figure 36**, typical for this procedure.

1. Remove the engine cover.

2. Disconnect the negative battery cable.

3. Disconnect each lead wire from the terminal block. If the wire connection decal on the power head is damaged, be sure to record the color and location of each wire before to disconnecting it.

4. Remove the 2 mounting screws and remove the terminal block.

5. Install by reversing removal procedure.

IGNITION SYSTEMS

The models covered in this manual use one of the following ignition systems:

    a. Magneto breaker-point ignition.

    b. Battery breaker-point ignition.

    c. Breakerless ignition module (BIM) ignition.

    d. SEM-Walbro magneto capacitor discharge (CD) ignition.

    e. Prestolite magneto capacitor discharge (CD) ignition.

    f. Thunderbolt capacitor discharge ignition (CDI).

    g. Capacitor discharge module (CDM) ignition.

Refer to **Table 5** for ignition system model identification.

BREAKER POINT MAGNETO IGNITION

Manual start models prior to 1989B use a magneto ignition with a combined primary/secondary ignition coil, condenser and one set of breaker points for each cylinder. The breaker points are mounted on a stator plate. The primary section of the coil connects to the stationary breaker point and is grounded to the stator plate.

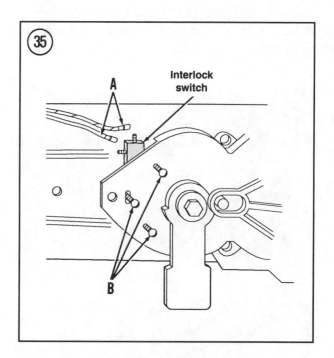

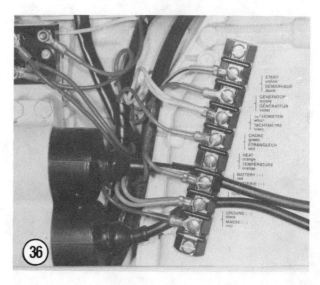

The secondary section of the coil connects to the spark plug and is also grounded to the stator plate.

Refer to Chapter Three for a schematic of a magneto ignition showing the location and relationship of the components. Troubleshooting and test procedures are also provided in Chapter Three.

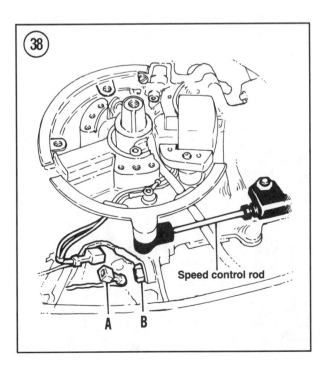

Speed control rod

Operation

As the flywheel rotates, magnets around its inner diameter induce a current that flows through the closed breaker points into the ignition coil primary windings. The induced current builds a magnetic field in the primary coil windings. When the breaker cam opens the breaker points, the magnetic field collapses, inducing a high voltage in the ignition coil secondary windings, which flows through the high tension lead to the spark plug. While the points are open, the condenser absorbs any residual current remaining in the primary circuit preventing arcing across the open breaker point contacts. The breaker points close and the flywheel continues to rotate, duplicating the sequence. Activating the stop switch grounds the primary circuit thus stopping ignition.

7

Stator Plate Removal/Installation (1-Cylinder Breaker Point Magneto)

1. Remove the engine cover.
2. Disconnect the spark plug lead from the spark plug.
3. Remove the flywheel. See Chapter Eight.
4. Loosen the stator plate friction screw (A, **Figure 37**).
5A. *Prior to 1988 B:*
    a. Remove screw (B, **Figure 37**) and disconnect stator plate ground wire.
    b. Disconnect breaker point ground wire from stop switch.
5B. *1988 B and later:*
    a. Disconnect wire (A, **Figure 38**).
    b. Remove screw and disconnect ground wire (B, **Figure 38**).
    c. Remove the screw securing speed control rod (**Figure 38**) to the stator plate.
6. Lift stator plate assembly off the power head.
7. To reinstall, carefully place stator plate on power head.

8. On models prior to 1988 B, reconnect stator plate ground wire to crankcase (B, **Figure 37**) and reconnect the breaker point ground wire to the stop switch. On 1988 B and later models, reconnect speed control rod, ground wire (B, **Figure 38**) and lanyard switch wire (A, **Figure 38**).

9. Adjust stator friction screw (A, **Figure 37**), by turning friction screw clockwise until a definite drag is noted when rotating stator plate. Stator plate should not "creep" when motor is operated at wide-open throttle.

10. Adjust breaker point gap (Chapter Four) and synchronize the speed control linkage (Chapter Five).

Stator Plate Removal/Installation (2-Cylinder Breaker Point Magneto)

1. Disconnect the negative battery cable.

2. Remove the engine cover.

3. Remove the flywheel. See Chapter Eight.

4. Disconnect the spark plug leads from the spark plugs. Remove plug leads from exhaust port cover clip, if so equipped.

NOTE
On some engines, the ground lead is attached under one of the stator mounting screws.

5. Disconnect the stator ground wire at the fuel pump or stator.

6. Disconnect the stop switch wires. Disconnect the lanyard switch wires, if so equipped.

7. Remove 4 screws securing stator plate assembly to the stator ring. See **Figure 39**, typical.

8. Lift stator plate and unhook the throttle cam link from the magneto control lever.

9. Invert stator plate and remove throttle cam screws.

10. Installation is the reverse of removal. Adjust the breaker points (Chapter Four). Adjust the

throttle pickup point and ignition timing as required (Chapter Five).

Breaker Point and Condenser Replacement

Refer to *Tune-up*, Chapter Four.

Ignition Coil Removal/Installation (1- and 2-Cylinder Models)

1. Disconnect the negative battery cable.

2. Remove the engine cover.

3. Disconnect the spark plug leads from the spark plugs.

4. Remove the flywheel as described in Chapter Eight.

5. Disconnect the coil lead wires from the breaker points and ground. See **Figure 40**.

6. Using pliers, straighten the coil lamination which holds the coil. See **Figure 41**.

7. Pry the lip of the coil wedge spring from the coil laminations with a screwdriver, then pull coil free of the laminations. Be sure to note how the spark plug lead is routed.

8. Remove the spark plug terminal boot and terminal spring from spark plug lead.

9. Pull the spark plug lead through the stator plate grommet and remove the coil.

10. If necessary, repeat Steps 5-9 to remove the remaining coil on 2-cylinder models.

11. To reinstall the coil, position coil at the stator plate lamination with spark plug lead routed as noted in Step 7.

12. Fit coil wedge spring in the coil with small lip facing downward.

13. Insert the coil halfway into lamination, making sure that the spark plug lead remains properly routed. Insert end of the spark plug lead through the grommet in the stator plate.

14. Push down on coil until the wedge spring snaps into place at the rear of the laminations.

The large lip on the spring must be positioned over the front surface of the coil.

15. Pull any excess spark plug lead through the stator plate, then bend the bottom lamination up with pliers to retain the coil in place.

16. Connect the coil lead wires to the breaker points and ground.

17. Reinstall the spark plug terminal spring and boot.

18. Reverse Steps 1-4 to complete reinstallation.

BATTERY BREAKER POINT IGNITION

Early 50 hp models are equipped with a battery ignition with a condenser and one set of breaker points for each cylinder mounted on a breaker plate. Two externally mounted ignition coils are used. The primary section of the coil connects to the stationary breaker point and the battery. The secondary section of the coil connects to the spark plug and is also grounded to the breaker plate.

Troubleshooting and testing procedures are provided in Chapter Three.

Operation

When the ignition switch is in the RUN position, current from the battery flows through the closed breaker points to the ignition coil primary windings, creating a magnetic field in the primary windings. When the breaker cam opens the No. 1 breaker points, the magnetic field collapses, inducing a high voltage in the coil secondary windings, which flows through the high tension lead to the No. 1 spark plug. The condenser absorbs residual current to prevent arcing across the breaker contacts while the points are open. This sequence is repeated at the No. 2 points, ignition coil and spark plug.

7

Breaker Plate Removal/Installation

Refer to **Figure 42** for this procedure.

1. Remove the engine cover.
2. Disconnect the battery negative cable.
3. Disconnect the spark plug leads from the spark plugs.
4. Remove the flywheel. See Chapter Eight.
5. Pull the breaker point leads from the spade terminals.
6. Remove the 2 screws holding the spade terminals in place. Remove the terminals.
7. Remove the 3 screws securing the breaker plate to the bearing cage.
8. Lift the breaker plate up and over the crankshaft end. Carefully place the breaker plate aside.
9. Remove the 3 clips, disconnect the spark control link and remove the breaker plate.
10. Installation is the reverse of removal. Position clips so their long tabs curl upward. The hole in each tab should align with the breaker plate mounting screw holes. Adjust ignition timing (Chapter Five).

Breaker Points and Condenser Replacement

See *Tune-up*, Chapter Four.

Ignition Coil Removal/Installation

1. Disconnect the negative battery cable.
2. Remove the engine cover.
3. Disconnect the spark plug leads from each ignition coil.
4. Disconnect the blue and white wires from the top coil. Disconnect the blue and brown (or gray/white) wires from the bottom coil.

> *NOTE*
> *A crowsfoot wrench or a thin open-end wrench may be required to remove the lower coil clamp screws in Step 5.*

5. Remove the 2 upper and 2 lower coil clamp mounting screws. See **Figure 43**.

6. Remove the ignition coils.

7. To reinstall, connect a blue wire to the positive (+) terminal of each coil.

8. Connect the white wire to the negative (–) terminal of the top coil and the brown (or gray/white) wire to the negative (–) terminal of the bottom coil.

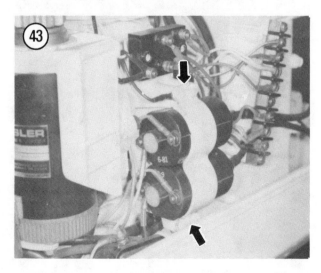

9. Fit the coils in place and install the coil clamp. Be sure to reinstall the rectifier ground wire under the upper left-hand bracket screw.

10. Connect the spark plugs leads to their respective coils.

PRESTOLITE MAGNETO CD IGNITION

This is an alternator-driven CD ignition system. The major components include the fly-wheel, alternator stator, trigger stator, stator ring or throttle cam, CD module(s), ignition coils, spark plugs and connecting wiring. See **Figure 44** and **Figure 45** for typical views of ignition components. Refer to the wiring diagrams located in Chapter Three or Chapter 14.

Operation

A series of permanent magnets are contained along the outer rim of the flywheel. As the fly-

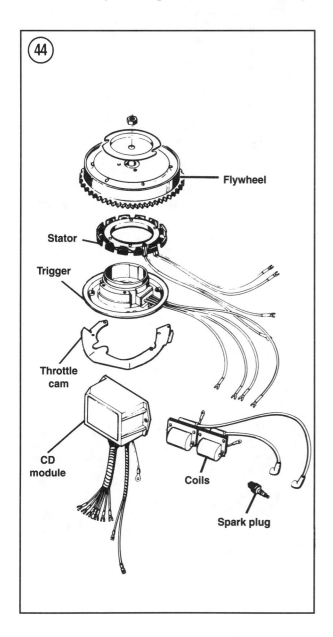

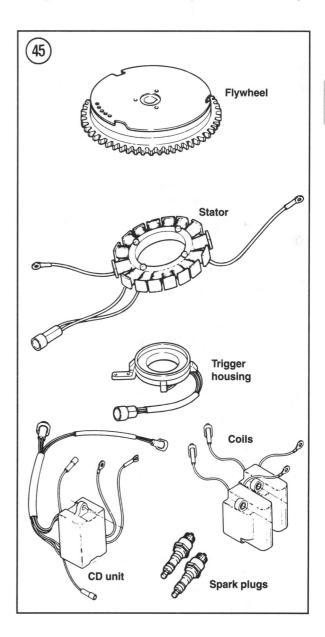

7

wheel rotates around the stator, alternating current (AC) is induced into the stator charge coil windings. The AC current flows to the CD module where it is converted into direct current (DC) by a full-wave rectifier, then stored in the capacitor.

Timing magnets in the flywheel hub rotate inside the trigger stator and induce a low voltage signal into the No. 1 trigger coil. This voltage pulse causes an electronic switch in the CD module to close, allowing the stored voltage in the capacitor to discharge into the ignition coil. The coil increases the voltage to approximately 24,000-32,000 volts. The voltage then flows through the high tension lead to the spark plug. This sequence of events is duplicated for each cylinder of the engine, and is repeated upon each revolution of the flywheel. Activating the stop switch, turning off the ignition switch or disengaging the lanyard cord shorts the CD module output to ground, stopping the ignition.

Spark timing is advanced or retarded by rotating the trigger assembly, changing the trigger coil position in relation to the permanent magnets in the flywheel hub.

Stator Removal/Installation (7.5 hp)

1. Remove the engine cover.
2. Remove the flywheel. See Chapter Eight.
3. Disconnect the 2 blue stator wires from the engine harness.
4. Note the routing and orientation of the stator wires leading to the wiring harness. Loosen any clamps holding the stator wires in position.
5. Remove the 2 stator mounting screws and lift the stator off the trigger assembly.

CAUTION
Make sure the new stator and stator wires are installed in same position and orientation on the trigger assembly to prevent contact or interference with the flywheel.

6. Install the new stator onto the trigger assembly. Route the wires to the engine harness. Reinstall any clamps holding the wires in position.

7. Apply Loctite 242 threadlocking sealant to the 2 stator mounting screws. Install and securely tighten the screws.

8. Connect the stator wires to the engine harness.

9. Install the flywheel. See Chapter Eight.

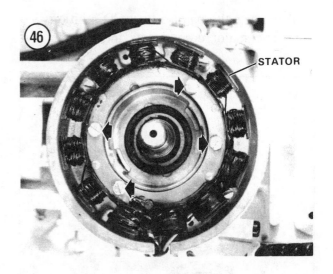

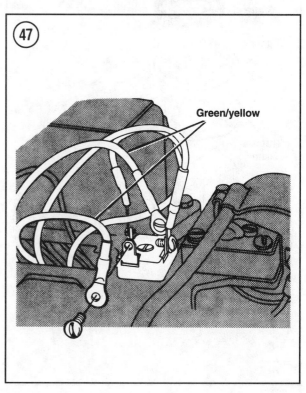

Stator Removal/Installation
(25 hp 2-Cylinder, 35 hp and 60 hp)

1. Disconnect the negative battery cable.
2. Remove the engine cover.
3. Remove the flywheel. See Chapter Eight.
4. Remove the screws holding the stator to the trigger. See **Figure 46**.
5. Disconnect the 2 green/yellow wires from the rectifier (**Figure 47**).
6. Unwrap the wiring harness cover to separate the stator and trigger leads.
7. Disconnect the 2-pin stator lead connector (**Figure 48**).
8. Remove the stator.
9. Installation is the reverse of removal. Make sure all wires are routed to prevent contact or interference with moving components.

Stator Removal/Installation
(50, 85-125 and 150 hp [Including L-Drives])

1. Disconnect the negative battery cable.
2. Remove the engine cover.
3. Remove the flywheel. See Chapter Eight.

4. Disconnect the 2 green/yellow (early models) or 2 yellow wires (late models) from the rectifier or rectifier/regulator. Refer to **Figure 47** and **Figure 49**, typical.

NOTE
The 50-125 hp (except 1987C-1988C 50 hp) models use stators with 4 ignition wires. The 50 hp models use only 2 terminals to connect these 4 stator wires to the terminal block. 85 and 90 hp models use 3 terminals and the 120 and 125 hp use 4 terminals. Due to mid-year changes, it is very important to label the wires to ensure they are reinstalled in the correct location. Helpful wiring diagrams are located in Chapter Three and at the end of the manual.

5. Disconnect and label the following stator wires from the terminal block. Do not disconnect the wires from the engine side of the terminal block.

  a. *50 hp (1987C-1988C [combined CD module/ignition coil])*—Disconnect the 2 blue wires from the terminal block. See **Figure 50**.

7

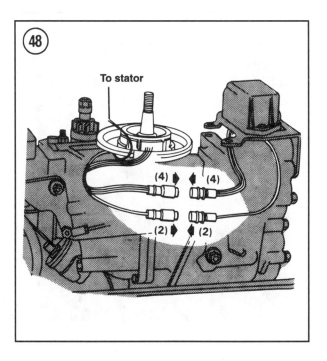

To stator

(4) (4)

(2) (2)

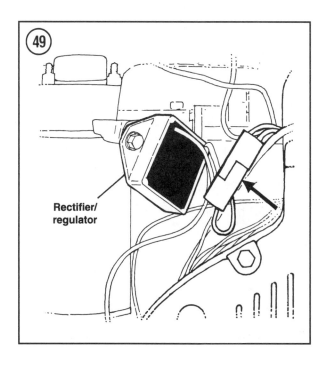

Rectifier/
regulator

b. *50-125 hp (early models)*—Disconnect the 2 yellow and 2 blue wires from the terminal block. On 50 hp models, refer to **Figure 50**. On 85-125 hp models, refer to **Figure 51**.

c. *50-125 hp (late models)*—Disconnect the 4 brown based wires from the terminal block: (brown/black/blue, brown/black/yellow, brown/blue and brown/yellow). On 50 hp models, refer to **Figure 50**. On 85-125 hp models, refer to **Figure 51**.

d. *150 hp*—Disconnect the 6 brown based wires from the terminal block: (brown/blue, brown/black/blue, brown/yellow, brown/black/yellow, brown/green/blue, brown/green/yellow). See **Figure 52**.

6. Note the routing and orientation of the stator wires leading to the terminal block. Loosen any clamps holding the wires in position.

7. Remove the 4 stator mounting screws and lift the stator off the bearing cage.

CAUTION
Make sure the new stator and stator wires are installed in same position and orientation on the bearing cage to prevent contact or interference with the flywheel.

8. Install the new stator on the bearing cage. Route the wires to the terminal block. Reinstall any clamps holding the wires in position.

9. Apply Loctite 242 threadlocking sealant to the 4 stator mounting screws. Install and securely tighten the screws.

10. Install the stator wires to the terminal block in the same position that they were removed. Tighten the terminal block screws securely. Refer to Chapter Three or Chapter Fourteen for wiring diagrams.

11. Install the flywheel. See Chapter Eight.

12. Reconnect the negative battery cable.

Trigger Assembly Removal/Installation (7.5 hp)

1. Remove the stator assembly as described in this chapter.

2. Disconnect the two, 2-pin trigger connectors (red and white/green and green and orange) from the CD modules.

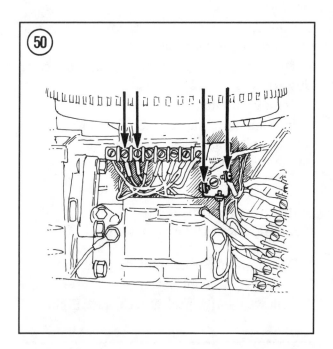

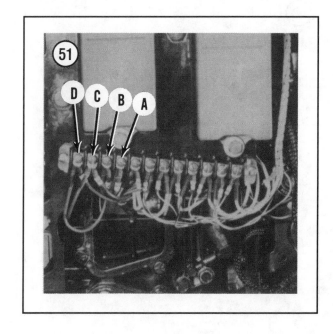

3. Remove the 4 trigger assembly mounting screws. See Figure 53.

4. Disconnect the stator link connector from the ball joint stud.

5. Lift the trigger assembly off of the engine.

6. Installation is reverse of removal. Be sure all wires are routed to prevent contact with the flywheel.

Trigger Assembly Removal/Installation (25 hp 2-cylinder, 35 and 60 hp)

1. Remove the stator assembly as described in this chapter.

2. *25 and 35 hp*—Remove the 4 trigger assembly mounting screws. See **Figure 53**.

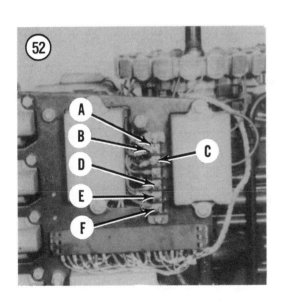

150 HP:
A. No. 1 (brown/blue)
B. No. 3 (brown/black/blue)
C. No. 2 (brown/yellow)
D. No. 4 (brown/black/yellow)
E. No. 5 (brown/green/blue)
F. No. 6 (brown/green/yellow)

3. Lift the trigger assembly sufficiently to remove the wiring harness from the stator ring hook.

4. Remove the clamp securing the wiring harness.

5. Disconnect the 4-pin connector between the trigger and the CD module. See **Figure 48**.

6. Remove trigger assembly from the power head.

7. Installation is the reverse of removal. Make sure all of the wires are routed to prevent contact or interference with any moving components.

Trigger Assembly Removal/Installation (1987-1991 50 hp)

1. Remove the stator assembly as described in this chapter.

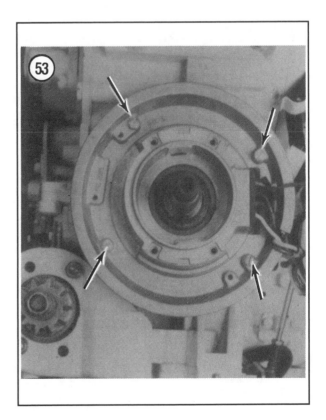

2A. *Prior to 1988 D*—Disconnect the wires from the terminal block above the CD module/ignition coil units. See **Figure 54**.

2B. *1988 D and later*—Disconnect the trigger wires from the terminal block (**Figure 55**).

3. Detach the spark control rod (**Figure 56**) from the trigger assembly.

4. Remove the trigger assembly from the bearing cage.

5. Installation is the reverse of removal. Refer to **Figure 54** (prior to 1988 D) or **Figure 55** (1988 D and later) when connecting trigger wires to terminal blocks.

Trigger Assembly Removal/Installation (85-125 hp [Including L-Drive])

1. Remove the stator assembly as described in this chapter.

2. Remove the cover from the terminal block on the starboard side of the motor. Disconnect the

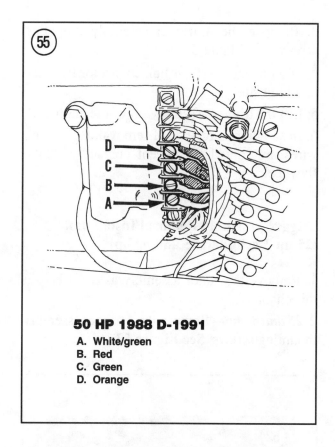

50 HP 1988 D-1991
A. White/green
B. Red
C. Green
D. Orange

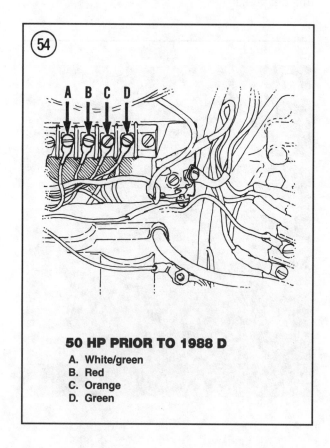

50 HP PRIOR TO 1988 D
A. White/green
B. Red
C. Orange
D. Green

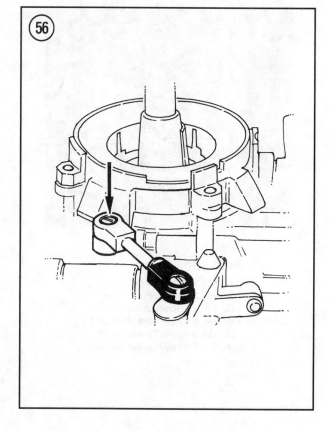

trigger wires from the terminal block (**Figure 57**).

NOTE
*Trigger wires (G and H, **Figure 57**) are used on 4-cylinder models only.*

3. Disconnect spark control rod from the tower shaft (**Figure 58**, typical).

4. Lift the trigger assembly off the bearing cage. If trigger assembly is being replaced, remove the spark control rod and transfer to the new trigger.

5. Installation is the reverse of removal. Refer to **Figure 57** when connecting trigger wires. Adjust ignition timing and pickup point as described in Chapter Five.

Trigger Assembly Removal/Installation (150 hp)

1. Remove the stator assembly as described in this chapter.

2. Remove the cover from the terminal block between upper and lower CD modules.

3. Disconnect the trigger wires from the terminal block (**Figure 59**).

4. Disconnect the spark control rod from the tower shaft (**Figure 58**, typical).

5. Lift trigger assembly off bearing cage.

6. Installation is the reverse of removal. Lubricate outer lip of trigger with a suitable water-resistant grease. Locate trigger wires between the CD module mounting bracket and the power head. Connect trigger wires to terminal block as shown in **Figure 59**.

Ignition Coils Removal/Installation (25 hp 2-cylinder, 35 hp and 60 hp)

1. Disconnect the negative battery cable.

2. Remove the engine cover.

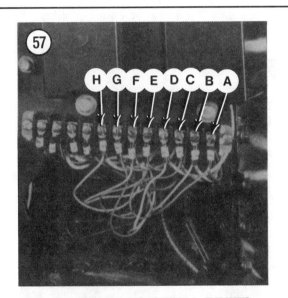

85-125 HP (EXCEPT L-DRIVE)
A. Green
B. Orange
C. Red
D. White/green
E. Green
F. Orange
G. Red (4-cylinder only)
H. White/green (4-cylinder only)

85-125 HP L-DRIVE
A. White/brown/yellow
B. White/brown/orange
C. White/brown/red
D. White/brown/green
E. White/black/yellow
F. White/black/orange
G. White/black/red (4-cylinder only)
H. White/black/green (4-cylinder only)

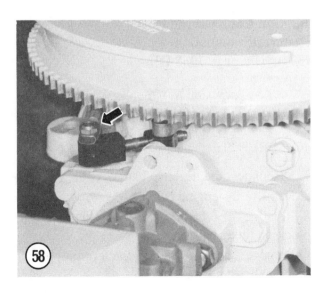

3. Disconnect the coil high tension leads at the spark plugs.

4. Note and record the color code of the coil primary wires, then disconnect the primary wires.

5. Remove the coil mounting screws and remove coils.

6. Installation is the reverse of removal.

Ignition Coils/CD Modules Removal/Installation (7.5 hp)

NOTE
On 7.5 hp models the ignition coils and CD modules are unit assemblies.

1. Remove the engine cover.

2. Disconnect the module trigger and stator wires at the engine harness connectors.

3. Disconnect the module stop switch wire at the stop switch.

4. Disconnect the spark plug lead.

5. Remove the 2 module mounting screws, remove the module.

6. Installation is the reverse of removal. Make sure the ground wire is connected to a mounting screw.

Ignition Coils/CD Modules Removal/Installation (50 hp [Prior to 1988 D])

NOTE
On 50 hp models prior to 1988 D, the ignition coils and CD modules are unit assemblies.

1. Disconnect the negative battery cable.

2. Remove the engine cover.

3. Remove the 2 brown wires from the terminal block on the exhaust cover.

4. Remove 2 screws securing the terminal block to the exhaust cover.

5. Remove the coil/module mounting screws. Note the location of the ground wires.

6. Disconnect the coil/module assembly wires from the terminal block (**Figure 60**), then remove the coil/module assemblies from the mounting bracket.

7. Installation is the reverse of removal. Connect the coil/module wires as shown in **Figure 60**. Make sure the ground wires are installed under the coil/module mounting screws.

Ignition Coil Removal/Installation (50 hp [1988 D-1992A])

1. Disconnect the negative battery cable.

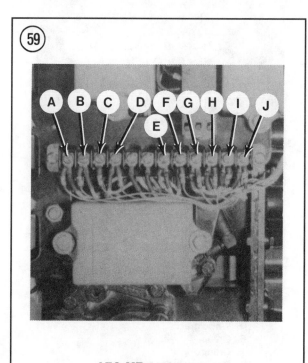

150 HP

A. White/purple/green
B. White/purple/red
C. White/purple/orange
D. White/purple/yellow
E. White/black/orange
F. White/black/yellow
G. White/brown/green
H. White/brown/red
I. White/brown/orange
J. White/brown/yellow

2. Remove the engine cover.

3. Disconnect the high tension leads from the spark plugs.

4. Remove 2 screws securing the terminal block to the ignition coils mounting bracket.

5. Remove the screws securing the coil bracket to the power head. Pull the bracket away from the power head sufficiently to gain access to rear of the bracket.

6. Unplug the 2 CD module output-to-coil connectors located on back side of coil mounting bracket.

7. Remove the coil mounting screws and remove coils from bracket.

8. Installation is the reverse of removal. Connect the No. 1 coil to the orange CD module output

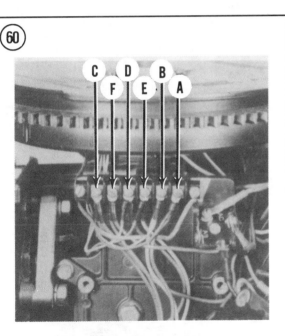

50 HP (PRIOR TO 1988 D)
Top module/coil assembly:
A. Green
B. Orange
C. Blue

Lower module/coil assembly:
D. Green
E. Orange
F. Blue

wire and the No. 2 coil to the red CD module output wire.

Ignition Coil Removal/Installation (85-150 hp [Including L-Drive])

1. Disconnect the negative battery cable.
2. Remove the engine cover.
3. Disconnect the high tension leads from the spark plugs.
4. On L-Drive models, remove the flywheel cover.
5. Remove nuts or screws securing CD module bracket to the power head or shock mounts. Pull bracket away from power head to gain access to rear of bracket.
6. Disconnect the coil input wire at plug between CD module and coil.
7. Remove nuts and screws securing coil(s) to the CD module mounting bracket and remove coil(s).
8. Installation is the reverse of removal plus the following:
   a. Reinstall the ground wire under the top mounting screw of each coil.
   b. On early 3- and 4-cylinder models, connect the No. 1 (top) coil to the front CD module orange wire; the No. 2 coil to front CD module red wire; the No. 3 coil to the rear CD module orange wire; the No. 4 coil (4-cylinders only) to the rear CD module red wire.
   c. On 3- and 4-cylinder models, connect the No. 1 (top) coil to the port CD module blue/orange wire; the No. 2 coil to the port CD module blue/red wire; the No. 3 coil to the starboard CD module blue/orange wire; the No. 4 coil (4-cylinders) to the starboard blue/red wire.
   d. On 5-cylinder models, connect the No. 1 (top) coil to the front CD module blue/orange wire; the No. 2 coil to the front CD module blue/red wire; the No. 3 coil to the rear CD module blue/orange wire; the No.

7

4 coil to the rear CD module blue/orange wire and the No. 5 coil to the bottom CD module blue/red wire. Note that the blue/red wire on the rear CD module is not used on 150 hp models.

CD Module Removal/Installation (25 hp 2-cylinder and 35 hp)

1. Disconnect the negative battery cable.
2. Remove the engine cover.
3. Disconnect the high tension leads from the spark plugs.
4. Remove 3 head bolts securing the CD module mounting bracket to the cylinder head. Remove 2 screws securing the bracket to the power head.
5. Remove 2 screws securing the CD module to the bracket.
6. Disconnect the trigger and stator plugs (**Figure 61**).
7. Installation is the reverse of removal. Make sure the CD module ground wire is positioned under the CD module mounting screw. Tighten the 3 cylinder head screws to 190 in.-lbs (21.5 N•m).

CD Module Removal/Installation (50 hp Prior to 1988D and 7.5 hp)

CD modules and ignition coils are unit assemblies on 50 hp models prior to 1988 D and 7.5 hp models. Refer to *Ignition Coil Removal/Installation*.

CD Module Removal/Installation (50 hp 1988 D-1992A)

1. Disconnect the negative battery cable.
2. Remove the engine cover.
3. Disconnect CD module wires from terminal block (**Figure 62**).
4. Remove the screws securing module mounting bracket to the power head. Pull bracket away

from power head sufficiently to gain access to rear of bracket.

5. Unplug CD module output wires (C and D, **Figure 63**).

6. Remove nut (B, **Figure 63**) to remove module ground wire.

7. Remove nuts (A, **Figure 63**) and remove module.

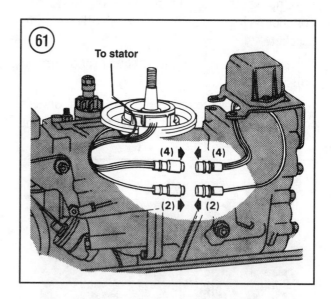

(61) To stator

(4) (4)

(2) (2)

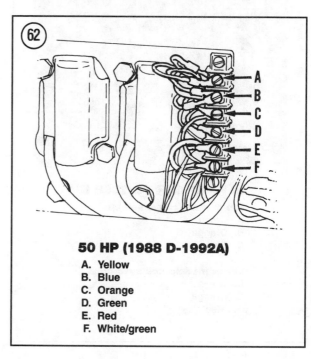

(62)

50 HP (1988 D-1992A)
A. Yellow
B. Blue
C. Orange
D. Green
E. Red
F. White/green

8. Installation is the reverse of removal while noting the following:

   a. Be sure to install module ground wire under nut (B, **Figure 63**).

   b. Connect red module output wire (C, **Figure 63**) to the No. 2 ignition coil. Connect the orange module output wire (D, **Figure 63**) to the No. 1 ignition coil.

   c. Connect CD module wires to terminal block as shown in **Figure 62**.

CD Module Removal/Installation (60 hp)

1. Disconnect the negative battery cable.

2. Remove the engine cover.

3. Disconnect the trigger and stator plugs. See **Figure 61**.

4. Disconnect the module white wire at the terminal strip.

5. Disconnect the module ground screw at top center of cylinder head.

6. Remove the 2 module mounting nuts, 4 washers and 2 bushings, remove the module.

7. Installation is the reverse of removal. Torque the cylinder head ground bolt to 225 in.-lb (25.4 N•m).

CD Modules Removal/Installation (85-125 hp [Including L-Drive])

NOTE
The following procedure outlines the removal of all CD modules; however, if replacement is required, only the defective module(s) requires removal.

1. Disconnect the negative battery cable.

2. Remove the engine cover.

3. Disconnect the spark plug high tension leads from the spark plugs.

4. On L-Drive models, remove the flywheel cover.

5. Remove the terminal block cover from starboard side terminal block.

6. Note and record the location and color code of CD module wires. Disconnect CD module wires from the starboard terminal block (**Figure 64**).

NOTE
Do not remove the numbered wires from the terminal block.

7. Disconnect the white (black/yellow on late models) module stop circuit wires from the

7

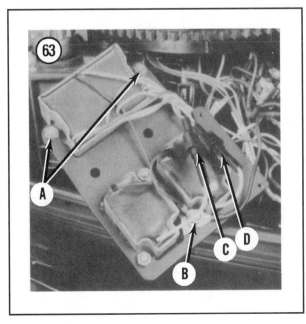

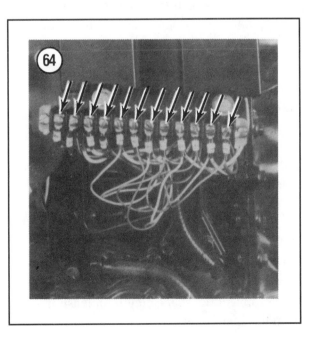

terminal block on port side of the engine (**Figure 65**).

8. Remove the screws securing CD module mounting bracket to the power head. Pull the bracket away from the power head sufficiently to gain access to the rear of the bracket.

9. Remove CD module ground wires from under the appropriate ignition coil mounting screw.

10. Remove the module mounting nuts and screws. Remove CD modules.

11. Disconnect module output leads from the ignition coils. See *Ignition Coil Removal/Installation* in this chapter.

12. Installation is the reverse of removal while noting the following:

    a. Make sure both CD module ground wires are properly installed.

    b. Connect the CD module output wires to the ignition coils as described in *Ignition Coil Removal/Installation* in this chapter.

    c. The white (or black/yellow on late models) stop circuit wires should be routed over power head and connected to the port side terminal block (**Figure 65**).

    d. Tighten CD module mounting bracket screws to 160 in.-lbs.

    e. Refer to the appropriate wiring diagrams in Chapter Fourteen when connecting CD module wires at the terminal blocks.

CD Modules Removal/Installation (150 hp)

The front CD module control cylinders No. 1 and 2, the rear CD module controls cylinder No. 3 and the lower CD module controls cylinders No. 4 and 5. The following procedure outlines the removal of all modules; however, only the defective module requires removal.

1. Disconnect the negative battery cable.

2. Remove the engine cover.

3. Disconnect the spark plug high tension leads from the spark plugs.

4. Remove the covers from terminal blocks (**Figure 66**).

NOTE
Do not remove the numbered wires from terminal blocks.

5. Note location and color code of CD module wires. Disconnect wires A-F, **Figure 66**, for the front CD module (cylinders 1 and 2), wires G-L, **Figure 66**, for the rear CD module (cylinder 3) and wires M-R, **Figure 66**, for the lower CD module (cylinders 4 and 5).

6. Remove the ground wire attached to the bottom ignition coil mounting screw.

7. Remove the nuts securing the CD module mounting bracket to the power head. Pull bracket away from the power head sufficiently to gain access to the rear of the bracket.

8. Disconnect the black/yellow wires from the terminal block on rear of bracket.

9. Remove the CD module ground wires from the No. 3 cylinder ignition coil mounting screw.

10. Disconnect the CD module output wires from the ignition coils.

11. Remove the nuts and screws securing CD modules to the bracket. Remove the modules.

12. Installation is the reverse of removal while noting the following:

    a. Make sure all module ground wires are properly connected to the No. 3 cylinder ignition coil mounting screw.

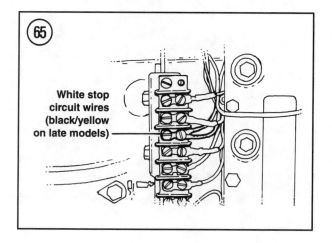

White stop circuit wires (black/yellow on late models)

b. Connect module output wires to the ignition coils as described in *Ignition Coil Removal/Installation* in this chapter.

c. Refer to **Figure 66** when connecting module wires to terminal blocks.

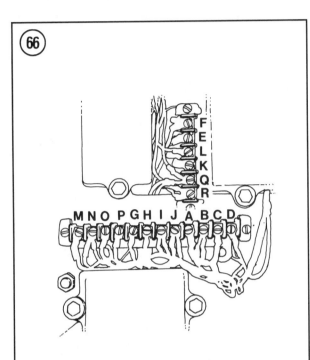

150 HP

Front module:
A. White/green
B. White/red
C. White/orange
D. White/yellow
E. Brown/yellow
F. Brown/blue

Rear module:
G. White/green
H. White/red
I. White/orange
J. White/yellow
K. Brown/blue
L. Brown/yellow

Lower module:
M. White/green
N. White/red
O. White/orange
P. White/yellow
Q. Brown/blue
R. Brown/yellow

THUNDERBOLT CAPACITOR DISCHARGE IGNITION

Thunderbolt ignition on all models except 150 hp, is an alternator-driven capacitor discharge ignition (CDI) system. The major components include the flywheel, stator (charge coils), trigger assembly, switch box, ignition coils and spark plugs.

The stator assembly is located under the flywheel. On 2- and 3-cylinder models, the stator contains 2 charge coils: 1 low-speed coil and 1 high-speed coil. On 4-cylinder models, the stator contains 4 charge coils: 2 low-speed coils and 2 high-speed coils. The low-speed charge coil(s) provides capacitor charging current at engine speeds under 2,500 rpm. The high-speed charge coil(s) provides capacitor charging current at engine speeds above 2,000 rpm.

The trigger assembly (located under the flywheel), contains 1 trigger coil on 2-cylinder models, 3 trigger coils on 3-cylinder models and 2 trigger coils on 4-cylinder models.

Thunderbolt ignition used on 150 hp models, is a battery-driven capacitor discharge ignition (CDI) system. The major components include the battery, flywheel, converter box, trigger assembly, switch box, ignition coils and spark plugs.

The converter box contains the electronic circuitry necessary to allow battery current to charge the capacitors inside the switch box. The trigger assembly contains a trigger coil for each cylinder.

Operation (Except 150 hp)

A series of permanent magnets are contained along the outer rim of the flywheel. As the flywheel rotates, alternating current (AC) is induced into the stator charge coil windings. The AC current flows to the switch box where it is converted (rectified) into direct current (DC) and

7

stored in the capacitor contained within the switch box.

Another series of permanent magnets are mounted to the flywheel hub. These magnets rotate inside the trigger assembly and induce a low voltage current into the trigger coil(s). This voltage signal causes an electronic switch (SCR) in the switch box to close, allowing the stored voltage in the capacitor to discharge into the ignition coil at the correct time and in the correct firing order. The ignition coil greatly amplifies the voltage and discharges it into the high tension lead to the spark plug. This sequence of events is duplicated for each cylinder of the engine, and is repeated upon each revolution of the flywheel. Ignition timing is advanced or retarded by rotating the position of the trigger assembly in relation to the magnets mounted on the flywheel inner hub. See Chapter Three for troubleshooting procedures.

Operation (150 hp)

A series of permanent magnets are mounted to the flywheel inner hub. As these magnets rotate inside the trigger assembly, a small voltage is generated and conducted to the switch box. Inside the switch box, this trigger voltage will follow 2 separate circuit paths.

On 1 circuit, the trigger signal closes an electronic switch (SCR) inside the converter box. This allows the converter box to convert the 12-volt DC battery voltage into AC voltage. A transformer then amplifies this AC voltage (DC voltage cannot be transformed) up to approximately 280 volts. The AC voltage is then converted back to DC (AC voltage cannot be stored) and stored in a capacitor inside the switch box.

The trigger signal that follows the second circuit activates a SCR located inside the switch box which triggers the stored DC voltage in the capacitor to discharge into the ignition coil primary windings. The ignition coil greatly amplifies the voltage and conducts it into the high

tension lead to the spark plug. This sequence of events is duplicated for each cylinder of the engine, and is repeated upon each revolution of the flywheel. Ignition timing is advanced or retarded by rotating the position of the trigger assembly in relation to the magnets mounted on the flywheel inner hub. See Chapter Three for troubleshooting procedures.

Component Wiring

Modern outboard motor electrical systems are quite complex, especially on the higher output engines. For this reason, electrical wiring is color-coded, and the terminals on the components to which each wire connects are sometimes embossed with the correct wire color. When used in conjunction with the correct electrical diagram, incorrect wire connections should be held to a minimum.

In addition, wire routing is very important to prevent possible electrical interference and/or damage to the wiring harnesses from moving engine parts or vibration. Modern outboards are shipped from the factory with all wiring har-

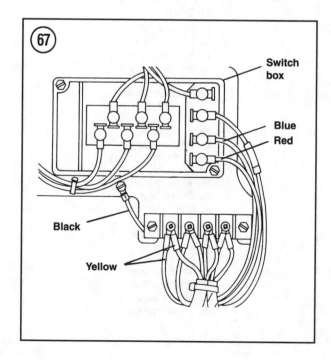

nesses and leads properly positioned and secured with clamps and plastic tie straps.

Should component replacement become necessary, it is highly recommended that you take the time to either carefully draw a sketch of the area to be serviced, noting the positioning of all wire harnesses involved, or use an instant camera to take several photographs at close range of the harness routing and location. Either method can be invaluable when it comes time to reroute the wiring for reassembly. Be sure to install all clamps and new tie straps where necessary to maintain the correct wire routing.

Stator Removal/Installation

1. Disconnect the negative battery cable from the battery. Disconnect the spark plug leads from the spark plugs to prevent accidental starting.

2. Remove the flywheel as described in Chapter Eight.

3A. *40 and 50 hp*—Disconnect the yellow stator wires from the rectifier/regulator. Disconnect the red, blue, blue/white and red/white stator wires from the switch box.

3B. *70 and 90 hp*—Disconnect the red and blue wires from the switch box. See **Figure 67**. Disconnect the 2 yellow stator wires from the terminal block below the switch box (**Figure 67**). Disconnect the black stator ground wire (**Figure 67**).

3C. *120 hp*—Disconnect the yellow stator wires from the terminal block adjacent to the switch box. Disconnect the red, blue, red/white and blue/white stator wires from the switch box. See **Figure 68**.

3D. *150 hp*—Disconnect the yellow stator wires from the terminal block (or unplug the 2-pin

7

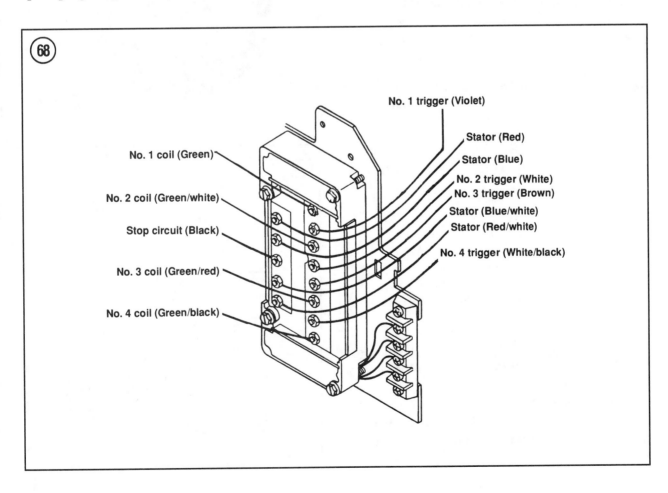

connector) between the stator and rectifier/regulator.

4. Remove the stator mounting fasteners. See **Figure 69**, typical. Lift the stator off the bearing cage.

5. To install, place the stator on the bearing cage so the wiring harness is positioned on the port side of the power head on 40 and 50 hp models or the starboard side on all other models. Make sure all stator wires are routed to prevent contact or interference with moving components.

6. Install the stator mounting fasteners and tighten securely. Install the flywheel as described in Chapter Eight.

Trigger Assembly Removal/Installation

1. Disconnect the negative battery cable from the battery. Disconnect the spark plug leads from the spark plugs to prevent accidental starting.

2. Remove the stator as described in this chapter.

> *NOTE*
> *Late models may have molded or bullet connectors that join the various ignition components*

3A. *40 and 50 hp*—Disconnect the white and violet trigger wires from the switch box wires at the bullet connectors.

> *NOTE*
> *Early 70 hp models use ring terminals and nuts to secure leads to the switch box studs. Later 70 hp models use bullet connectors on the switch box and harness leads. All color codes are the same.*

3B. *70-120 hp*—Disconnect the brown, white, violet and white/black trigger wires from the switch box. See **Figure 70** (3, cylinder) or **Figure 68** (4-cylinder).

3C. *150 hp*—Disconnect the brown, white, violet, black, yellow and white/black trigger wires from the switch box wires, at the bullet connectors.

4. Remove the nut securing the spark control rod to the tower shaft. See **Figure 71**, typical. Separate the rod from the tower shaft.

5. Lift the trigger assembly off the bearing cage. If the trigger is being replaced, remove the spark control rod from the old trigger assembly and install it on the new trigger.

6. Install the trigger assembly on the bearing cage and connect the spark control rod to the tower shaft.

STATOR

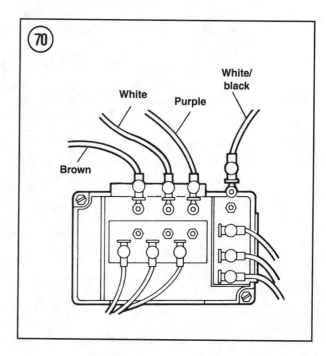

7. Lubricate the outer lip of the trigger assembly with a suitable water-resistant grease.

8. Route the trigger wires between the power head and switch box bracket. Reconnect the trigger wires to the switch box.

9. Complete the remaining installation by reversing the removal procedure. Perform linkage synchronization and adjustment as described in Chapter Five.

Converter Box Removal/Installation (150 hp)

1. Disconnect the negative battery cable.

2. Remove the engine cover.

3. Note the position of the converter box leads.

4. Disconnect the 4 converter box terminal leads. See A, **Figure 72**.

5. Remove the 4 screws holding the converter box to the ignition bracket (B, **Figure 72**).

6. Install the new converter box and tighten the 4 mounting screws securely.

7. Attach the leads to the 4 terminals as noted on removal. Only the ground leads (black) will not

have a protective cap over the terminal. See **Figure 72**.

8. Reconnect the negative battery cable.

Ignition Coil Removal/Installation

1. Disconnect the negative battery cable from the battery. Disconnect the spark plug leads from the spark plugs to prevent accidental starting.

2A. *40 and 50 hp*—Remove the 3 screws holding the coil mounting bracket to the exhaust cover, then remove the coils and mounting bracket from the exhaust cover.

2B. *70-150 hp*—Remove the screws securing the coil cover to the power head. Remove the coils and cover assembly.

3. Disconnect the ignition primary wires from the coil(s) to be removed. Slide the coil(s) out of the coil cover.

4. Installation is the reverse of removal. Connect the ignition primary wires as follows:

    a. *40 and 50 hp*—Connect the green wire to the No. 1 coil and the green/white wire to the No. 2 coil.

7

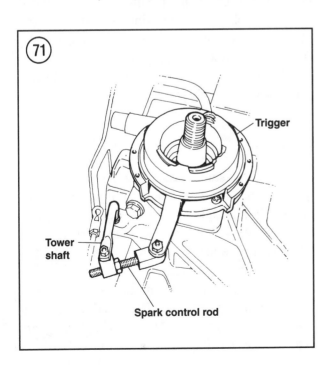

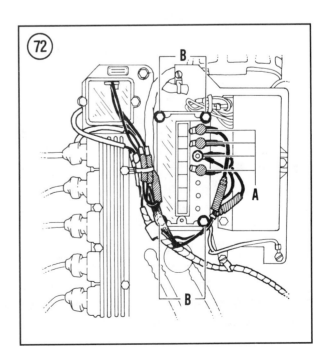

b. *70 and 90 hp*—Connect the green wire to the No. 1 coil, green/white wire to the No. 2 coil and the green/red wire to the No. 3 coil.

c. *120 hp*—Connect the green wire to the No. 1 coil, the green/white wire to the No. 2 coil, the green/red wire to the No. 3 coil and the green/black wire to the No. 4 coil.

d. *150 hp*—Connect the green wire to the No. 1 coil, the green/white wire to the No. 2 coil, the green/red wire to the No. 3 coil, the green/black wire to the No. 4 coil and the green/yellow wire to the No. 5 coil.

Switch Box (CD Module) Removal/Installation

1. Disconnect the negative battery cable from the battery. Disconnect the spark plug leads from the spark plugs.

2A. *40 and 50 hp*—Remove three screws and clamp securing the switch box to its mounting bracket. Disconnect the switch box wires at the bullet connectors and remove the switch box.

> *NOTE*
> *Early 70 hp models use ring terminals and nuts to secure leads to the switch box studs. Later 70 hp models use bullet connectors on the switch box and harness leads. All color codes are the same.*

2B. *70 and 90 hp*—Remove the nuts and disconnect the switch box wires from their terminals. Remove the 2 screws securing the switch box to its mounting bracket, then remove the switch box. Be sure to retrieve 2 spacers at each switch box mounting screw.

2C. *120 hp*—Remove the nuts and disconnect the wires from their terminals. Remove the 4 screws securing the switch box to its mounting bracket, then remove the switch box. Be sure to retrieve the spacers located behind the switch box at each mounting screw.

2D. *150 hp*—Disconnect the violet/white, black and blue switch box wires from the converter box. Remove the switch box mounting screws, disconnect the remaining switch box wires at their bullet connectors and remove the switch box.

3. Installation is the reverse of removal. Make sure all wires are connected to the correct switch box terminal or bullet connector. Be sure all connections are clean and tight.

BREAKERLESS IGNITION MODULE (BIM)

The BIM system consists of the flywheel, BIM module(s), spark plug(s), lanyard switch, stop switch and connecting wiring. See **Figure 73** for an exploded view of the BIM system used on 1-cylinder models (2-cylinder models are similar).

Two variations of the BIM system are used on 5-15 hp models. The 2 systems are similar, but the flywheels and ignition module/coil assemblies are different and can not be intermixed. For identification purposes, the flywheel magnets on BIM 1 systems are glued to the inner diameter of the flywheel and the ignition module/coil primary wires are blue and brown. On BIM 2, the flywheel magnets are machined and cast into the flywheel assembly and the ignition module/coil primary wires are black and gray.

Operation

The BIM system operates similar to a conventional breaker point magneto ignition except breaker points and condensers are not used. The trigger system, primary and secondary ignition coil windings and related circuitry are contained in the 1-piece BIM module.

The flywheel magnets induce a voltage into the ignition coil primary windings the same as a breaker-point system. The flywheel magnets also induce a voltage into a trigger coil which

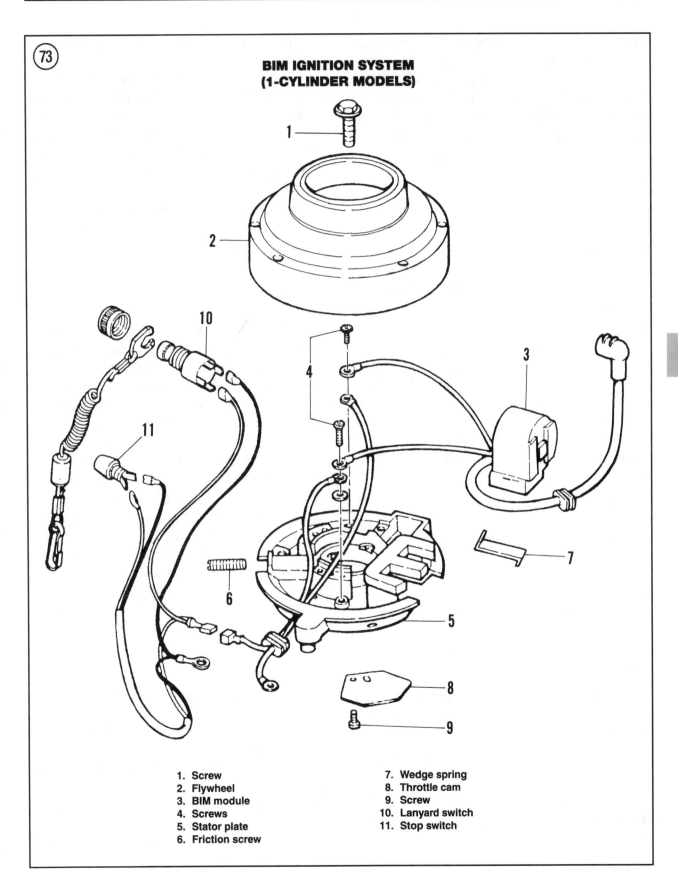

73

**BIM IGNITION SYSTEM
(1-CYLINDER MODELS)**

7

1. Screw
2. Flywheel
3. BIM module
4. Screws
5. Stator plate
6. Friction screw
7. Wedge spring
8. Throttle cam
9. Screw
10. Lanyard switch
11. Stop switch

opens an electronic switch (SCR). When the SCR opens, the magnetic field in the coil primary windings collapses, inducing a high voltage in the coil secondary windings. The high secondary voltage is conducted into the high tension lead to the spark plug.

See Chapter Three for troubleshooting procedures.

BIM Module
Removal/Installation

1. Disconnect the spark plug lead(s) from the spark plug(s).

2. Remove the flywheel. See Chapter Eight.

3. Remove the spark plug lead terminal and boot.

4. Push the spark plug lead grommet through the stator plate.

5. Remove the screws securing the BIM module ground and stop circuit wires to the stator plate.

6. Remove the BIM module mounting screws and lift the module off the stator plate.

7. Repeat Steps 3-6 to remove the remaining module (2-cylinder models) if necessary.

8. Installation is the reverse of removal.

Stator Plate
Removal/Installation

1. Disconnect the spark plug lead(s) from the spark plug(s).

2. Remove the flywheel. See Chapter Eight.

3. Remove the BIM module as described in this chapter.

4. Disconnect the stator plate ground wire and the BIM module stop circuit wire.

5. Loosen the stator plate friction screw (6, **Figure 73**) and lift the stator plate off the bearing cage.

6. Installation is the reverse of removal.

SEM-WALBRO IGNITION SYSTEM

SEM ignition is a capacitor discharge ignition (CDI) system. The system consists of the flywheel, ignition module(s), stator plate, stop switch, lanyard switch, spark plug(s) and related circuitry. See **Figure 74** for a diagram of the SEM ignition system used on 1-cylinder models (2 and 3-cylinders are similar).

The charge coil, trigger coil, ignition coil, capacitor and related electronic circuitry is contained in the 1-piece ignition module(s).

Operation

As the flywheel rotates, the permanent magnets contained in its outer rim create a magnetic field that induces an AC voltage into the charge coil located inside the module. The AC voltage is converted (rectified) to DC voltage by an internal diode, then stored in the capacitor. As the flywheel continues to rotate, a voltage signal is induced into the trigger coil. The trigger coil voltage signal closes an electronic switch which allows the voltage in the capacitor to be conducted into the ignition coil primary windings. The sudden flow of voltage in the primary windings creates a voltage rise in the coil secondary windings (up to 30,000 volts) which is conducted to the high tension (spark plug) lead. This series of events is repeated with each revolution of the flywheel.

Ignition Module
Removal/Installation

1. Disconnect the spark plug lead(s) from the spark plug(s).

2. Remove the flywheel as described in Chapter Eight.

3. Disconnect the black/yellow module primary wire at its bullet connector.

4. Remove the module mounting screws and lift the module off the stator plate.

5. Repeat Step 2 and Step 3 to remove the remaining modules on 2 and 3-cylinder models (if necessary).

6. Installation is the reverse of removal. Make sure all connections are clean and tight. Tighten the module mounting screws securely. Use Coil Setting Tool part No. 91-830230T to locate the coils on the 25 hp model.

Stator Plate
Removal/Installation

1. Disconnect the spark plug lead(s) from the spark plug(s).

2. Remove the flywheel as described in Chapter Eight.

3. Remove the ignition module(s) as described in this chapter.

4. Remove the screw and disconnect the stator plate ground wire.

5. Remove the stator plate mounting fasteners and lift the stator plate off the bearing cage.

6. Installation is the reverse of removal. Make sure all connections are clean and tight.

CAPACITOR DISCHARGE MODULE (CDM) IGNITION (40-120 HP MODELS)

The CDM ignition is an alternator driven, capacitor discharge, distributorless ignition sys-

7

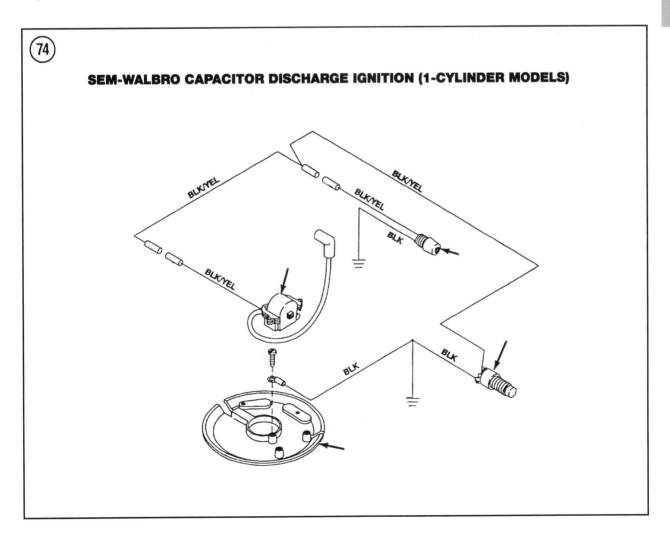

(74)

SEM-WALBRO CAPACITOR DISCHARGE IGNITION (1-CYLINDER MODELS)

tem. The system consists of the following components (**Figure 75**).

a. Flywheel.
b. Stator assembly.
c. Trigger assembly.
d. CD module/ignition coil.
e. Spark plugs

The CDM module is unique in that it incorporates the ignition coil and CD module into one assembly. There is one CDM module for each cylinder. All CDM modules are identical. CDM modules are mounted on the exhaust cover (40-50 hp models) or on an ignition plate (75-120 hp models) located on the starboard side of the engine (**Figure 76**). Models with an ignition

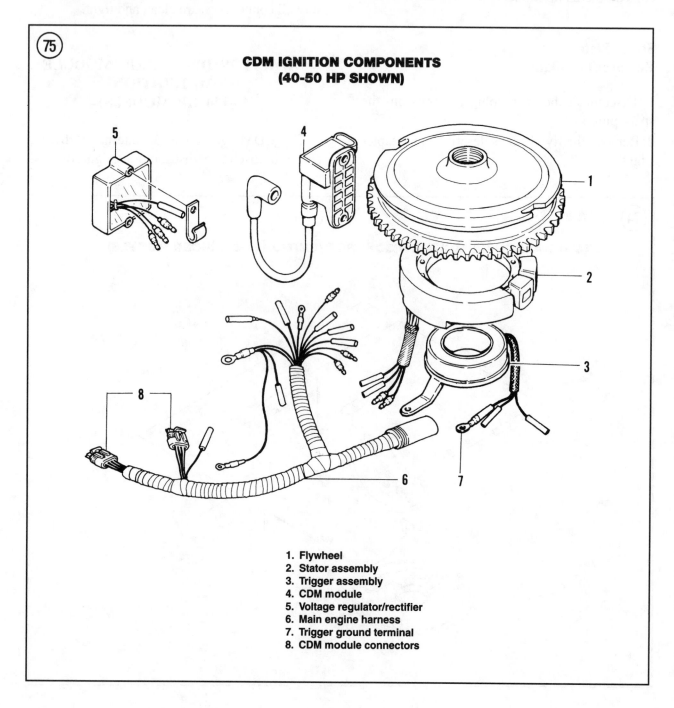

**CDM IGNITION COMPONENTS
(40-50 HP SHOWN)**

1. Flywheel
2. Stator assembly
3. Trigger assembly
4. CDM module
5. Voltage regulator/rectifier
6. Main engine harness
7. Trigger ground terminal
8. CDM module connectors

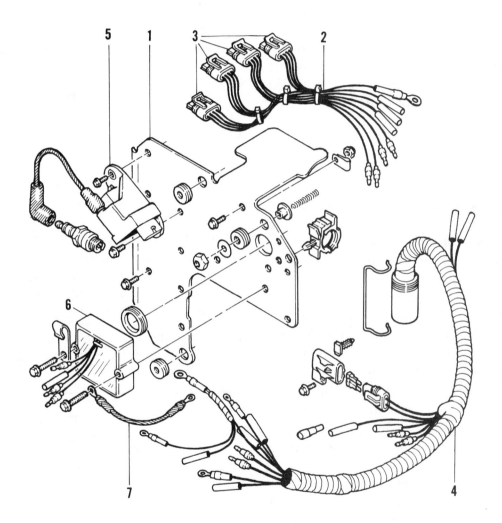

CDM IGNITION PLATE:
(75-120 HP MODELS [120 HP SHOWN])

7

1. Ignition plate
2. CDM harness
3. CDM module connectors
4. Main engine harness
5. CDM module
6. Voltage regulator/rectifier
7. Voltage regulator/rectifier
   ground lead

plate use a separate harness (CDM harness) to connect the CDM modules to the main engine harness.

Component Wiring

A special test harness has been developed to prevent damage to the waterproof connectors used on this system. Ignition test harness part No.84-825207A2 is used for all troubleshooting procedures involving connections to the CDM modules and wiring harness. Refer to Chapter Three for troubleshooting procedures.

Operation

The stator assembly is located under the flywheel. All models use a stator that contains one charge coil winding. The flywheel has permanent magnets mounted to the outer rim. As the flywheel rotates it carries the magnets past the charge coil windings and induces an AC voltage in the charge coil which is sent to all of the CDM modules. Each CDM module has a rectifier and a capacitor. The rectifier changes the charge coil AC voltage into DC voltage which can be stored in the capacitor. The capacitor holds this charge until the SCR (silicon controlled rectifier), which is simply an electronic switch, sends the voltage to the ignition coil windings, also mounted in the CDM. The SCR is triggered by a small voltage signal from the trigger assembly. The trigger assembly has one coil for each cylinder. A second set of magnets, mounted on the flywheel inner hub rotates past the trigger assembly and induces voltage (relatively low) which triggers the SCR. The ignition coil windings transform the capacitor voltage into a voltage high enough to jump the gap at the spark plug. Spark timing is advanced and retarded by rotating the trigger assembly which changes the mechanical relationship between the magnets in the flywheel hub and the trigger coil. A spark cycle occurs once per crankshaft revolution for each cylinder.

Connecting the black/yellow lead to ground shorts out the CDM module and spark ceases.

Stator Removal/Installation

1. Disconnect the negative battery cable.

2. Remove the engine cover.

3. Remove the flywheel. See Chapter Eight.

4. Note the orientation of the stator assembly and stator wires before proceeding.

> *NOTE*
> *It may be necessary to remove the ignition plate (75-120 hp models) to gain access to all of the stator bullet connections. See* ***Figure 76***.

5. Cut the tie-strap on the wire bundle above the rectifier/regulator. Disconnect 2 stator bullet connectors (green/white and white/green) from the engine harness (40-50 hp models) or CDM harness (75-120 hp models).

6. Disconnect 2 stator yellow wire bullet connectors from the voltage regulator/rectifier.

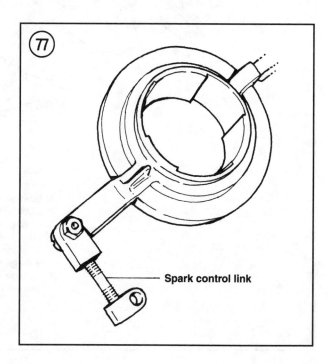

⑦

Spark control link

7. Remove the 6 stator mounting screws. Loosen any clamps holding the stator wires and remove the stator.

8. Set the new stator onto the bearing cage with the wire harness to the port side for 40-50 hp models or to the starboard side for 75-120 hp models. Route the stator wires to the CDM harness or engine harness and reinstall any clamps.

9. Install and torque the 6 stator screws to 50 in.-lbs.(5.6 N•m).

10. Connect the 2 stator yellow wire bullet connectors to the voltage regulator/rectifier.

11. Connect the stator white/green and green/white wire bullet connectors to the engine harness (40-50 hp models) or CDM harness (75-120 hp models). Secure all wires to the wire bundle with a ty-strap.

12. Reinstall the flywheel. See Chapter Eight.

13. Reconnect the negative battery cable.

Trigger Assembly Removal/Installation

1. Disconnect the negative battery cable.

2. Remove the engine cover.

3. Remove the flywheel. See Chapter Eight.

4. Remove the stator as outlined in this section.

NOTE
The trigger has a common black ground wire and 1 signal wire for each cylinder. Make sure the ground wire is securely attached to a clean engine ground when

reinstalling the trigger. Trigger colors denote the cylinder number. Purple is No. 1, white is No. 2, brown is No. 3 and dark blue is No. 4.

5. Disconnect the trigger signal leads from the engine harness (40-50 hp models) or CDM harness (75-120 hp models).

   a. *40 and 50 hp*—The 2 trigger signal wires are purple and white.

   b. *75 and 90 hp*—The 3 trigger signal wires are purple, white and brown.

   c. *120 hp*—The 4 trigger signal wires are purple, white, brown and dark blue.

6. Remove the black trigger ground screw and wire from the ignition plate or power head.

7. Disconnect the spark control link from the tower shaft. See **Figure 71**.

8. Lift the trigger assembly off of the bearing cage.

9. Install the spark control link to the new trigger. See **Figure 77**.

10. Lubricate the bearing surface of the new trigger with 2-4-C Multi-Lube grease or equivalent.

11. Place the trigger assembly onto the bearing cage with the wire harness to the port side for 40-50 hp models or the starboard side for 75-120 hp models.

12. Secure the spark link to the tower shaft. See **Figure 71**.

13. Reinstall the flywheel. See Chapter Eight.

14. Reconnect the negative battery cable.

15. Perform synchronization and linkage adjustments as described in Chapter Five.

CDM Module Removal/Installation

1. Disconnect the negative battery cable.

2. Remove the engine cover.

3. Unplug the CDM wire harness plug.

4. Remove the 2 screws mounting the CDM module to the ignition plate (75-120 hp models) or exhaust cover (40-50 hp models) and remove the module. See **Figure 78** or **Figure 79**.

7

5. Install the new module and secure it with the 2 mounting screws. Tighten the screws securely.

6. Reconnect the CDM wire harness plug.

7. Reconnect the negative battery cable.

8. Perform synchronization and linkage adjustments as described in Chapter Five.

Ignition Switch Removal/Installation

1. Disconnect the negative battery cable.

2. Gain access to the ignition switch in the dash or remote control box. See Chapter Twelve for remote control box service.

3. Remove the switch by unscrewing the nut holding it in place.

4. Label all leads for reassembly. Disconnect all leads. See **Table 6** for color code changes.

5. Connect all leads to the new switch. Refer to **Figure 80** and **Figure 81** for typical switch wiring. Refer to Chapter Fourteen for specific wiring diagrams.

6. Install the switch to the dash or control box and hand-tighten the nut.

7. Reconnect the negative battery cable.

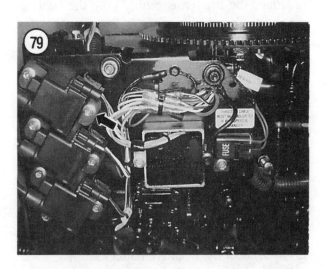

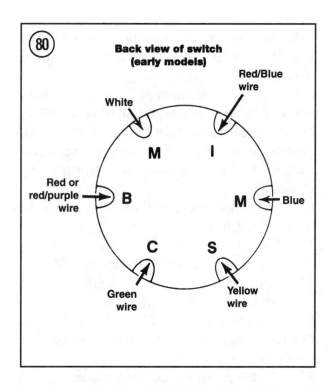

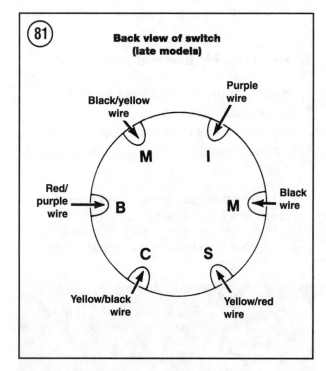

Table 1 BATTERY CAPACITY (HOURS)

Accessory draw	Provides continuous power for:	Approximate recharge time
80 amp-hour battery		
5 amps	13.5 hours	16 hours
15 amps	3.5 hours	13 hours
25 amps	1.8 hours	12 hours
105 amp-hour battery		
5 amps	15.8 hours	16 hours
15 amps	4.2 hours	13 hours
25 amps	2.4 hours	12 hours

Table 2 SELF-DISCHARGE RATE

Temperature	Approximate allowable self-discharge per day for first 10 days (specific gravity)
100°F (37.8°C)	0.0025 points
80°F (26.7°C)	0.0010 points
50°F (10.0°C)	0.0003 points

7

TABLE 3 BATTERY CHARGE PERCENTAGE

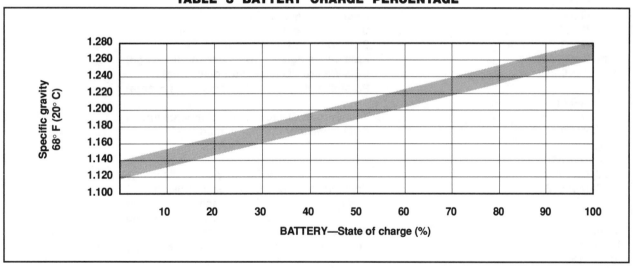

Table 4 STANDARD TORQUE VALUES

Screw or nut size	in.-lbs.	ft.-lbs.	N•m
6-32	9	–	1.0
8-32	20	–	2.3
10-24	30	–	3.4
10-32	35	–	4.0
12-24	45	–	5.1
		(continued)	

Table 4 STANDARD TORQUE VALUES (continued)

Screw or nut size	in.-lbs.	ft.-lbs.	N•m
1/4-20	70	6	7.9
1/4-28	84	7	9.5
5/16-18	160	13	18.1
5/16-24	168	14	19.0
3/8-16	270	23	30.5
3/8-24	300	25	33.9
7/16-14	–	36	48.8
7/16-20	–	40	54.2
1/2-13	–	50	67.8
1/2-20	–	60	81.3

Table 5 IGNITION SYSTEM MODEL IDENTIFICATION

Model/Year	Ignition System
4 hp	Magneto breaker-point
5 hp	
1988-1989A	Magneto breaker-point
1989B-1993	BIM I or II (breakerless inductive module)
1994-1998	SEM-Walbro CD (capacitor discharge)
7.5 hp	Prestolite magneto CD* (capacitor discharge)
9.9 and 15 hp	
1984-1989A	Magneto breaker-point
1989B-1993	BIM I or II (breakerless inductive module)
1994-1999	SEM-Walbro CD (capacitor discharge)
25 hp 2 cylinder	Prestolite magneto CD (capacitor discharge)
25 hp 3 cylinder	SEM-Walbro CD (capacitor discharge)
35 hp	Prestolite magneto CD (capacitor discharge)
40 and 50 hp	
1992C-1995	Thunderbolt CDI (capacitor discharge ignition)
1996-1999	CDM (capacitor discharge module)
50 hp	
1984-1987B	Battery breaker-point
1987C-1988C	Prestolite magneto CD* (capacitor discharge)
1988D-1992B	Prestolite magneto CD (capacitor discharge)
60 hp	Prestolite magneto CD (capacitor discharge)
70 hp	Thunderbolt CDI (capacitor discharge ignition)
75 hp	CDM (capacitor discharge module)
85 and 125 hp	Prestolite magneto CD (capacitor discharge)
90 and 120 hp	
1990-1991C and 90 hp 1991E	Prestolite magneto CD (capacitor discharge)
1991D-1995 except 90 hp 1991E	Thunderbolt CDI (capacitor discharge ignition)
1996-1999	CDM (capacitor discharge module)
150 hp	
1989-1991A	Prestolite magneto CD (capacitor discharge)
1991B and newer	Thunderbolt CDI (capacitor discharge ignition)
L-drives	
85 and 125 hp	Prestolite magneto CD (capacitor discharge)
90 and 120 hp 1990-1991A	Prestolite magneto CD (capacitor discharge)
90 and 120 hp 1991B-1992	Thunderbolt CDI (capacitor discharge ignition)

*CD modules and ignition coils are a single unit.

Table 6 WIRING HARNESS STANDARD COLOR CODE CHANGES

Circuit or System	Model Year 1984-1989	Model Year 1989-1992	Model Year 1993 and Newer
Starting	Yellow	Yellow/Red	Yellow/Red
Tachometer	Purple	Gray	Gray
Stop 1 (ignition side)	White	Black/Yellow	Black/Yellow
Stop 2 (ground side)	Blue	Blue/Black	Black
Choke or Primer	Green	Yellow/Black	Yellow/Black
Overheat Warning	Orange	Tan	Tan/Blue
Switched B+	Red/Blue	Red/Blue	Purple
Protected B+	Red	Red/Purple	Red/Purple
Grounds	Black	Black	Black

7

Chapter Eight

Power Head

This chapter covers the basic repair of Force power heads 4-150 hp.

The procedures involved are similar from model to model, with some minor differences. Some procedures require the use of special tools, which can be purchased from a dealer. Certain tools may also be fabricated by a machinist, often at substantial savings. Power head stands are available from specialty shops such as Bob Kerr's Marine Tool Company (P.O. Box 1135, Winter Garden, FL 32787).

Work on the power head requires considerable mechanical ability. Carefully consider your own capabilities before attempting any operation involving major disassembly of the engine.

Much of the labor charge for dealer repairs involves the removal and disassembly of other parts to reach the defective component. Even if you decide not to perform the entire power head overhaul after studying the text and illustrations in this chapter, it can be less expensive to perform the preliminary operations yourself and then take the power head to your dealer. Since many ma-

rine dealers have lengthy waiting lists for service (especially during the spring and summer seasons), this practice can reduce the time your unit is in the shop. If you have done much of the preliminary work, your repairs can be scheduled and performed much quicker.

Repairs go much faster and easier if your motor is clean before you begin work. There are special cleaners for washing the motor and related parts. Just spray or brush on the cleaning solution, let stand, then rinse it away with a garden hose. Clean all oily or greasy parts with fresh solvent upon removal.

WARNING
Never use gasoline as a cleaning agent. It presents an extreme fire hazard. Be sure to work in a well-ventilated area when using cleaning solvents. Keep a fire extinguisher rated for gasoline and oil fires nearby in case of emergency.

If you decide to do the repair yourself, read this chapter thoroughly until you have a good idea of what is involved in completing the overhaul satisfactorily. Make arrangements to obtain any special tools and all replacement parts necessary before starting on the repair.

Before beginning the repair, read Chapter Two of this manual. You will do a better job with this information fresh in mind.

Remember that new engine break-in procedures should be followed after an engine is overhauled. Refer to your owner's manual for specific instructions.

Since this chapter covers a large range of models over a lengthy time period, the procedures are somewhat generalized to accommodate all models. Where individual differences occur, they are specifically pointed out. The

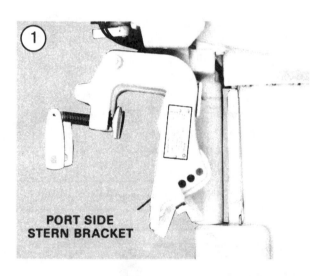

PORT SIDE
STERN BRACKET

power heads shown in the accompanying pictures are current designs. While it is possible that the components shown in the pictures may not be identical with those being serviced, the step-by-step procedures may be used with all models covered in this manual.

Tables covering torque specifications (**Tables 1-5**), engine specifications (**Tables 6-7**), sealants, lubricants and adhesives (**Table 8**) and special tools (**Tables 9-10**) are located at the end of the chapter.

FORCE MODEL NUMBERING SYSTEM

Force engines are identified *primarily* by the model number *or* the serial number. A model and serial number plate is located on the midsection of an outboard motor (**Figure 1**, typical) or on the mount plate of an L-Drive (**Figure 2**).

Prior to the 1993 model year, product identification was based primarily on the model number. The model number identified the product's horsepower, features, original boat manufacturer (purchaser), model year and model year revision. This was the U.S. Marine system. See **Figure 3**.

The U.S. Marine model number has 1 to 3 digits designating the horsepower, 1 digit or 2 letters designating the features, 1 letter designating the boat manufacturer, 1 or 2 digits designating the model year and 1 digit designating the model revision. Horsepower ranges from 4 to 150.

Model year revisions change any time a major change is made to the product. It is imperative that all parts are ordered from a parts catalog that matches the engine's model year revision code. Model year revision codes follow the alphabet upwards as changes occur.

Late 1992 and all 1993 and newer models use the serial number for primary identification. There is still a model number, but it cannot be used as stand alone identification. The serial

8

number should begin with the OE prefix. This is the Mercury System. See **Figure 4**.

FASTENERS AND TORQUE SPECIFICATIONS

Always replace a worn or damaged fastener with one of equal size, type and torque requirement.

Power head tightening torques are given in **Tables 1-5**. Where a specification is not provided for a given fastener, use the standard bolt and nut torque according to fastener size.

> *CAUTION*
> *Metric and American fasteners are used on newer model outboards. Always match a replacement fastener to the original. Do not run a tap or thread chaser into a hole (or over a bolt) without first verifying thread size and pitch. Newer model parts catalogs list every standard fastener by diameter, length and pitch. Always have engine model and serial numbers when ordering a parts catalog from a dealer.*

> *CAUTION*
> *1995 and newer 40-120 hp models use a new torque process for the connecting rod bolts. The 1996 and newer 75-120 hp models also employ the same new process for torquing the cylinder head bolts. This procedure is called "torque and turn." Be sure to follow the new procedure as outlined in this chapter to prevent damaging components.*

When installing the cylinder head after it has been removed, the fasteners should be torqued in sequence and in the recommended increments to prevent warpage. Torque sequences are listed in the *assembly* section of this chapter.

The recommended procedure for all models not covered by torque and turn is:

1. *4-15 hp models*—Torque initially to 50 in.-lb. (5.6 N•m) in sequence and continue in 25 in.-lb. (2.8 N•m) increments (sequentially) to the specified torque.

2. *25-150 hp models*—Torque initially to 75 in.-lb. (8.5 N•m) in sequence and continue in 50 in.-lb. (5.6 N•m) increments (sequentially) to the specified torque. See **Table 2**.

Tighten other power head fasteners in 2 steps. Tighten to one half of the final value in the first step, then to the specified final torque in the second step.

Retighten cylinder head bolts after the engine has been run until it reaches operating tempera-

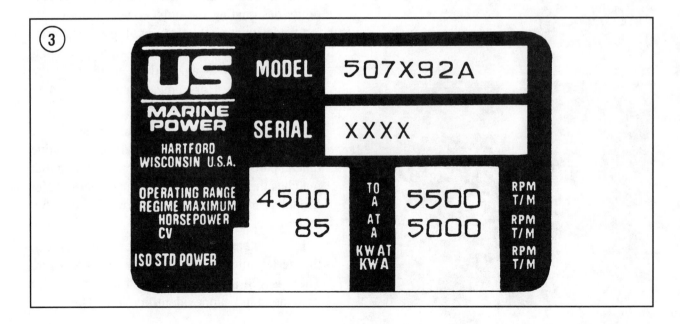

③

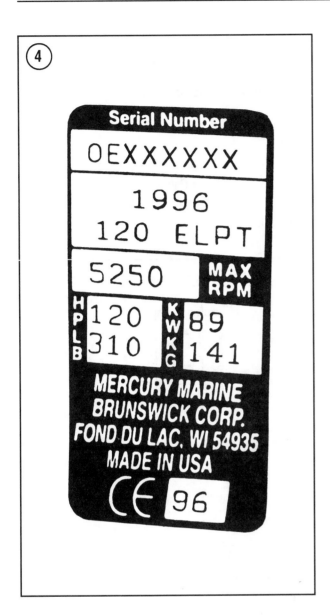

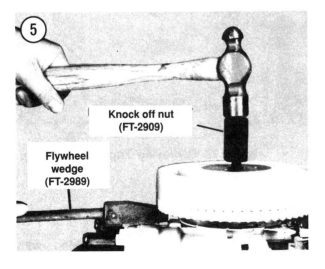

Knock off nut
(FT-2909)

Flywheel
wedge
(FT-2989)

ture and then allowed to cool. It is recommended to retighten the head bolts again after 10 hours of operation.

To retighten the power head mounting fasteners properly, back fasteners out 1 turn, then retighten to the specified torque.

When spark plugs are installed after an overhaul, tighten plugs to to specified torque. Warm the engine to normal operating temperature, allow power head to cool, then retighten to specified value.

Removal/Installation (4-35 hp)

WARNING
Disconnect and ground the spark plug lead(s) to the power head to prevent accidental starting.

1A. *Integral fuel tank models*—Remove the fuel tank as outlined in Chapter 6.

1B. *Remote fuel tank models*—Remove the rewind starter, if necessary. See Chapter Eleven.

2. Remove the bolt or nut holding the flywheel to the crankshaft. Use a strap wrench or flywheel wrench part No.91-52344 to hold the flywheel stationary.

3. Thread the flywheel knock-off tool (**Table 9**) completely onto the crankshaft, then unthread the tool 2 full turns.

4. Insert the flywheel removal wedge tool (**Table 9**) between the flywheel and power head. Rotate the flywheel clockwise until the flywheel key is aligned with the wedge tool.

CAUTION
Use caution not to pry against the stator windings on models so equipped. Do not strike the knock-off tool with excessive force or the crankshaft and/or bearings may be damaged.

5. Pry upward on the flywheel with the wedge tool and strike the knock-off tool with a 16 oz. hammer. See **Figure 5**.

6. When the flywheel breaks loose, remove the pry tool and unscrew the knock-off tool, then remove the flywheel from the crankshaft.

7. Remove the flywheel key.

8. Inspect the flywheel and key carefully as described in this chapter.

9. Clean and inspect the crankshaft and flywheel tapers. Both tapers must be completely clean, dry and free of oil before reassembly.

10. Install the flywheel key. Outer edge of the key must be parallel to the crankshaft center line. See **Figure 6**.

11. Install the flywheel onto the crankshaft. Align the key and keyway.

12. Install the bolt or nut and tighten to specifications (**Table 3**). Use a strap wrench or flywheel wrench part No.91-52344 to hold the flywheel stationary.

13A. *Integral fuel tank models*—Install the fuel tank (Chapter Six) and reconnect the spark plug lead.

13B. *Remote fuel tank models*—Install the rewind starter if removed. Reconnect the spark plug lead(s).

Removal/Installation (1984-1995 40-150 hp [Including L-Drive])

1. Remove the engine cover.

2. Disconnect the spark plug leads and ground to the power head to prevent accidental starting.

3. *L-Drive*—Remove 2 screws and 1 nut, then lift flywheel cover off power head.

4. Remove the flywheel nut. Use flywheel wrench part No. 91-52344 to hold the flywheel stationary.

5. Install flywheel puller (part No. FT-8948-1) on the flywheel as shown in **Figure 7**. Screw puller bolts into the flywheel in equal amounts.

6. Tighten puller screw until tight against crankshaft.

CAUTION
Do not strike puller screw with excessive force in Step 7 or crankshaft and/or bearing damage may result.

7. Strike top of puller screw with a suitable hammer.

8. When flywheel breaks loose from crankshaft taper, lift puller and flywheel off crankshaft and remove flywheel key. Remove puller from flywheel.

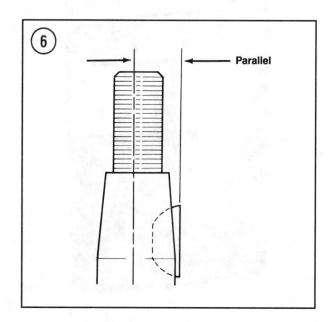

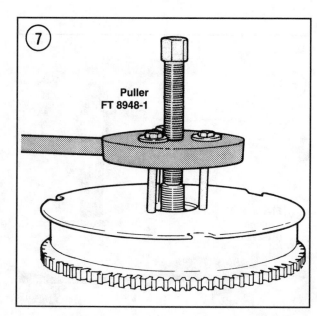

9. Inspect flywheel and key carefully as described in this chapter.

10. Crankshaft and flywheel tapers must be clean, dry and free of oil or other contamination. Clean tapered surfaces with solvent and dry with compressed air.

11. Install flywheel key with outer edge parallel to crankshaft centerline. See **Figure 6**.

12. Install flywheel on the crankshaft.

13. Install flywheel nut and tighten to specification (**Table 3**).

Removal/Installation
(1996-1999 40-120 hp Models)

WARNING
Disconnect and ground the spark plug leads to the power head to prevent accidental starting.

1. Remove the plastic thread protecting plug from the flywheel. Remove the nut and washer holding the flywheel to the crankshaft. Use flywheel wrench part No. 91-52344 to hold the flywheel stationary.

2. Place the protector cap part No. 91-24161 from flywheel puller kit part No. 91-73687A1 onto the end of the crankshaft. See **Figure 8**.

3. Thread the flywheel puller tool completely into the flywheel.

4. Hold the tool with a wrench and tighten the center bolt until the flywheel comes free. See **Figure 9**.

5. Remove the tool from the flywheel and lift the flywheel off of the crankshaft.

6. Remove the flywheel key.

7. Inspect the flywheel and key carefully as described in this chapter.

8. Clean and inspect the crankshaft and flywheel tapers. Both tapers must be completely clean, dry and free of oil before reassembly.

9. Install the flywheel key. Outer edge of the key must be parallel to the crankshaft center line. See **Figure 6**.

10. Install the flywheel onto the crankshaft. Align the key and keyway.

11. Install the washer and nut and tighten to specifications (**Table 3**). Use flywheel wrench part No.91-52344 to hold the flywheel stationary.

12. Replace the plastic thread protecting plug. Reconnect the spark plug leads.

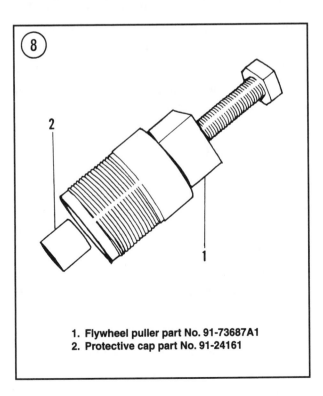

1. Flywheel puller part No. 91-73687A1
2. Protective cap part No. 91-24161

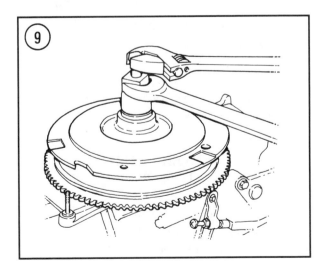

8

Flywheel Inspection

1. Check the flywheel carefully for cracks or breaks.

WARNING
A cracked or chipped flywheel must be replaced. A damaged flywheel may fly apart at high rpm, throwing fragments over a large area. Do not attempt to repair a damaged flywheel.

2. Inspect flywheel and crankshaft tapers for wear or other damage. Flywheel and crankshaft tapers may be lapped if wear in tapered areas is minimal.

CAUTION
When lapping, use fine (240 grit or higher) water based compound. Oscillate the flywheel back and forth several times through no more than 90° total rotation. Lift and turn the flywheel 1/4 turn and repeat the oscillations. Do not attempt to achieve 100% contact; 80% contact is satisfactory. Make sure all lapping compound is removed before reinstalling the flywheel.

3. Inspect crankshaft and flywheel key slot for wear or damage.
4. Carefully inspect flywheel key. Replace key if in questionable condition.
5. Inspect flywheel for loose or damaged magnets. Flywheel must be replaced if magnets are loose or damaged.

NOTE
Arc burns on the flywheel timing magnets are a normal condition.

POWER HEAD REMOVAL/INSTALLATION

When removing the power head, it is a good idea to make a sketch or take an instant photograph of the location, routing and positioning of electrical wiring, brackets and clamps for reference during reassembly. Take notes as you remove wires, washers and engine grounds so they may be reinstalled in the correct position. Unless specified otherwise, always install lockwashers on the engine side of ground wires to ensure a good connection.

4 hp (1984-1987)

1. Remove the engine cover.

2. Disconnect and ground the spark plug lead to the power head. Remove the spark plug.

3. Remove the fuel tank. See Chapter Six.

4. Pull fuel shut-off valve knob off the valve shaft.

5. Remove the fuel shut-off valve.

6. Remove E-ring securing choke lever to carburetor.

7. Remove the carburetor.

8. Disconnect the stop switch wires from the switch.

9. Remove the screws and nuts securing the support plate and remove the support plate.

10. Remove the flywheel as described in this chapter.

11. Remove the ignition components and stator plate. See Chapter Seven.

12. Remove the screws holding the power head to the motor leg (**Figure 10**). Lift power head off motor leg.

13. Installation is the reverse of removal plus the following:

  a. Install a new gasket between motor leg and power head.

  b. Align motor leg drive shaft splines with power head crankshaft splines when installing power head.

  c. Apply RTV sealant to threads of motor leg screws and tighten to specification (**Table 4**).

d. Perform linkage adjustments and synchronization. See Chapter Five.

5 hp (1988-on)

1. Remove the engine cover.

2. Disconnect and ground the spark plug lead to the power head. Remove the spark plug.

3. *1988A models*—Remove fuel tank. See Chapter Six.

4. Remove the flywheel as described in this chapter. Remove the flywheel key.

5. Remove the stator plate. See Chapter Seven. Remove breaker point cam on models so equipped.

6. Remove carburetor and carburetor adapter. See Chapter Six.

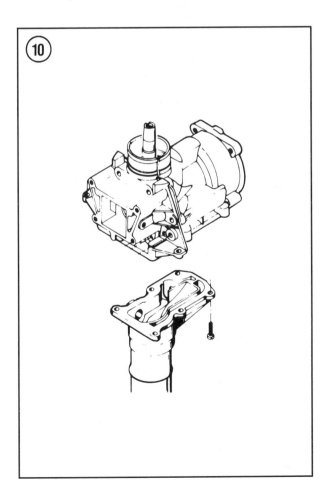

7. Remove the spark plug. On 1988B-on models, remove the fuel pump.

8. Remove the 6 screws securing the lower engine cover and then remove the cover. Disconnect the lanyard switch on later models so equipped.

9. Remove the 2 screws securing the support plate to the power head. Remove support plate.

10. Remove the screws (3 on each side) securing the power head to the motor leg. Lift power head off the motor leg.

11. Installation is the reverse of removal plus the following:

   a. Install a new gasket between the power head and motor leg.

   b. Lubricate the drive shaft splines with a suitable anticorrosion grease.

   c. When lowering the power head onto the motor leg, shift the gearcase into gear and rotate the propeller to align the drive shaft and crankshaft splines.

   d. Apply a suitable RTV sealant to the threads of the power head-to-motor leg screws. Tighten the screws to specification (**Table 4**).

   e. Adjust breaker point gap (prior to 1990) and perform linkage adjustment and synchronization. See Chapter Five.

7.5 hp

1. Remove the engine cover.

2. Disconnect and ground the spark plug leads to the power head. Remove the spark plugs.

3. Remove the flywheel and ignition components (stator, trigger and CD module assemblies). See Chapter Seven.

4. Remove the carburetor, intake manifold and fuel pump. See Chapter Six.

5. Remove the manual rewind starter. See Chapter Eleven.

8

6. Remove the tower shaft assembly. See **Figure 11**.

7. Disconnect the shift interlock link from the lever on the crankcase cover. See **Figure 12**.

8. Remove the 8 screws (4 on each side) securing the power head to the motor leg. Lift the power head off of the motor leg.

9. Installation is the reverse of removal plus the following:

    a. Install a new gasket between the power head and motor leg.

    b. Lubricate the drive shaft splines with a 2-4-C Multi-Lube grease (**Table 8**).

    c. Align drive shaft splines with the power head splines when installing power head.

    d. Apply RTV sealant to threads of the 8 motor leg screws and tighten to specifications (**Table 4**).

    e. Perform synchronization and linkage adjustments. See Chapter Five.

9.9-15 hp

1. Remove the engine cover.

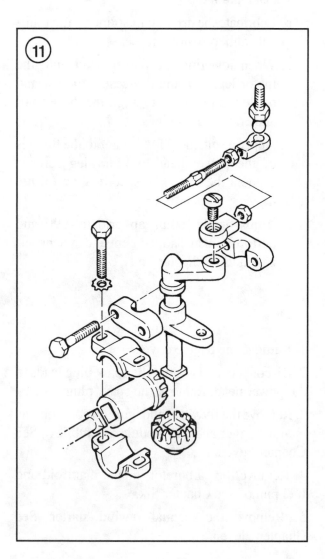

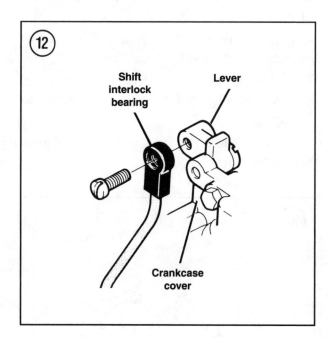

2. Disconnect and ground the spark plug leads to the power head. Remove the spark plugs.

3A. *1984-1987*—Remove the rewind starter handle. Tie a suitable knot into starter rope to prevent rope from winding onto starter spool.

3B. *1988-on*—Remove the rewind starter. See Chapter Eleven.

4. Disconnect the choke link from the carburetor and remove carburetor. See Chapter Six.

5. Disconnect the fuel delivery hose at the support plate.

6. Remove the fuel pump. See Chapter Six.

7. Disconnect the stop switch wires from the stop switch.

8. Remove the flywheel as described in this chapter.

9. Remove the stator plate. See Chapter Seven.

10. Disconnect interlock rod from the lever. See **Figure 12** (1984-1987) or **Figure 13** (1988-on).

11. Remove the 6 screws (**Figure 14**) securing power head to the motor leg.

12. Lift power head sufficiently to disconnect the magneto shaft link from the magneto control rod, then lift power head off motor leg. Remove and discard the power head-to-motor leg gasket.

13. Installation is the reverse of removal plus the following:

   a. Install a new gasket between the power head and motor leg.

   b. Apply antiseize lubricant to the drive shaft splines.

   c. Rotate crankshaft or propeller (gearcase in gear) to align crankshaft and drive shaft splines when installing power head.

   d. Apply a suitable RTV sealant to threads of power head-to-motor leg screws. Tighten screws to specification (**Table 4**).

   e. Adjust breaker point gap (prior to 1990) and perform linkage adjustment and synchronization. See Chapter Five.

25 hp (3-cylinder)

1. Remove the engine cover.

2. Disconnect and ground the spark plug leads to the power head. Remove the spark plugs.

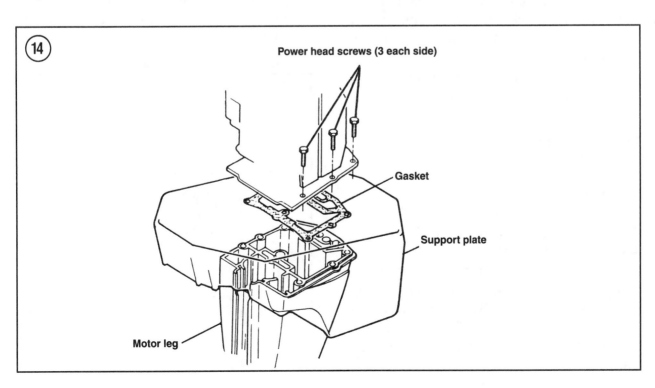

(14) Power head screws (3 each side)

Gasket

Support plate

Motor leg

3. Remove the manual rewind starter. See Chapter Eleven.

4. Remove the flywheel and the stator plate assembly. See Chapter Seven.

5. Remove the carburetor and fuel pump. See Chapter Six.

6. Disconnect the shift interlock link from the lever on the crankcase cover. See **Figure 13**.

7. Remove the 6 screws (3 on each side) securing the power head to the motor leg. Lift the power head off of the motor leg. See **Figure 14**.

8. Lay the power head on a work bench and remove the 3 screws, lock washers and flat washers holding the exhaust tube to the power head. Remove the exhaust tube.

9. Installation is the reverse of removal plus the following:

    a. Apply Loctite 271 threadlocking adhesive to the exhaust tube screws.

    b. Install a new gasket between the power head and motor leg.

    c. Lubricate the drive shaft splines with 2-4-C Multi-Lube grease.

    d. Align drive shaft splines with the power head splines when installing power head.

    e. Apply RTV sealant to threads of the 6 motor leg screws and tighten to specifications (**Table 4**).

    f. Perform synchronization and linkage adjustments. See Chapter Five.

25 hp (2-cylinder)

1. Disconnect the negative battery cable.

2. Remove the engine cover.

3. Disconnect and ground the spark plug leads to the power head. Remove the spark plugs.

4. Disconnect the throttle and shift cables.

5. Disconnect the wires from the interlock switch

6. Remove the electric starter bracket (including terminal strip) assembly. See Chapter Seven.

7. Remove the flywheel. See Chapter Eight.

8. Remove the stator and trigger assemblies. See Chapter Seven.

9. Remove the 3 head bolts holding the ignition bracket (CD module and ignition coils) to the power head. Disconnect any remaining leads and remove the bracket.

10. Remove the carburetor and fuel pump. See Chapter Six.

11. Remove the 5 upper screws (3 on starboard and 2 on port) securing the power head (spacer plate) to the motor leg.

12. Remove the 2 lower screws holding the power head to the lower leg. See B, **Figure 15**.

13. Remove the 2 screws from the upper shock mount cover. See **Figure 16**.

> *WARNING*
> *At this point, there should be no hoses, wires or linkages connecting the power head to the motor leg. Be sure that nothing will interfere with power head removal.*

14. Install a lift eye (**Table 9**). Use a suitable hoist and lift the power head off of the motor leg.

15. Lay the power head on a workbench and remove the 6 screws holding the spacer plate to the power head. Remove the spacer plate.

16. Installation is the reverse of removal plus the following:

a. Replace all gaskets and seals.

b. Lubricate the drive shaft splines with 2-4-C Multi-Lube grease.

c. Align drive shaft splines with the power head splines when installing power head.

d. Apply RTV sealant to threads of the power head, spacer plate and motor leg screws and tighten to specifications (**Table 4**).

e. Perform synchronization and linkage adjustments. See Chapter Five.

35 hp (1986-1987)

1. Disconnect the negative battery cable.

2. Remove the engine cover.

3. Disconnect and ground the spark plug leads to the power head. Remove the spark plugs.

4. Disconnect the throttle and shift cables.

5. Disconnect the wires from the interlock switch.

6. Remove the electric starter bracket (including terminal strip) assembly. See Chapter Seven.

7. Remove the flywheel. See Chapter Eight.

8. Remove the stator and trigger assemblies. See Chapter Seven.

9. Remove the 3 head bolts holding the ignition bracket (CD module and ignition coils) to the

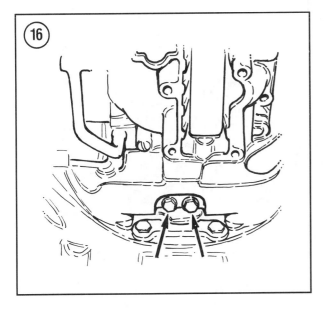

power head. Disconnect any remaining leads and remove the bracket.

10. Remove the carburetor and fuel pump. See Chapter Six.

11. Remove the 6 screws holding the rear motor leg cover to the front cover. Remove the rear motor leg cover.

12. Remove the 2 upper side shock mount nuts (1 on each side).

13. Remove the lower shock mount side covers, then remove the side mounts and front mount from the lower motor leg.

14. Engage the reverse lock, pull motor leg back enough to slip the front motor leg cover down, sideways and off.

15. Remove the 6 screws (3 on each side) securing the power head to the motor leg.

NOTE
At this point, there should be no hoses, wires or linkages connecting the power head to the motor leg. Be sure that nothing will interfere with power head removal.

16. Install a lift eye (**Table 9**). Use a suitable hoist and lift the power head off of the motor leg.

17. Installation is the reverse of removal plus the following:

a. Install a new gasket between the power head and motor leg.

b. Lubricate the drive shaft splines with 2-4-C Multi-Lube grease.

c. Align drive shaft splines with the power head splines when installing power head.

d. Apply RTV sealant to threads of the 6 motor leg screws and tighten to specifications (**Table 4**).

e. Perform synchronization and linkage adjustments. See Chapter Five.

60 hp

1. Disconnect both battery cable connections at the battery.

8

2. Remove the engine cover.

3. Disconnect and ground the spark plug leads to the power head. Remove the spark plugs.

4. Disconnect the throttle and shift cables.

5. Disconnect and plug the fuel inlet line from the fuel pump, then pull it out of the lower support half.

6. Note the position or label the wires on the boat harness side of the terminal strip. Remove the boat wiring harness from the terminal block and pull it out of the lower support half.

NOTE
Power head removal is simplified by removal of the split lower support plates from each side of the power head. Steps 7-11 detail this procedure.

7. Remove the rear support plate cover by removing the 3 inside and 2 outside screws.

8. Remove 1 screw from either side of each of the 2 brackets that hold the rear of the lower support halves together.

9. Remove 1 screw from either side of the front support cover (located in front of the lower carburetor).

10. Remove 1 screw on the outside of the lower support cover, located just above the steering arm base (port side).

11. Remove the 4 screws (2 on each side) that hold the lower support halves to the shock mounts on the power head. Remove both lower support cover halves.

12. Disconnect the yellow wires from the interlock switch.

13. Disconnect the green wire from the choke solenoid.

14. Disconnect the wire from the temperature switch on the cylinder head.

15. Remove the electric starter motor. See Chapter Seven.

16. Remove the positive battery cable from the starter solenoid. Remove the 2 starter solenoid mounting screws. Pull the solenoid away from the power head and remove the battery ground cable from the power head. Remove the battery cable assembly.

17. Remove the flywheel as described previously in this chapter.

18. Remove the stator and trigger assemblies. See Chapter Seven.

19. Remove the ignition coils and CD module. See Chapter Seven.

20. Remove the 2 mounting screws from each of the following: terminal strip, circuit breaker and rectifier. Remove the terminal strip, circuit breaker, rectifier and wiring harness as a unit.

21. Remove the carburetors and fuel pump. See Chapter Six.

22. Remove the 4 screws securing the tower shaft assembly. Disconnect the throttle link at the tower shaft and remove the tower shaft assembly.

23. Remove the cotter pin, washer and pin securing the gear shift bellcrank to the shift rod clevis (located at the base of the steering arm).

24. Remove the 9 lock nuts holding the power head to the motor leg.

WARNING
At this point, there should be no hoses, wires or linkages connecting the power

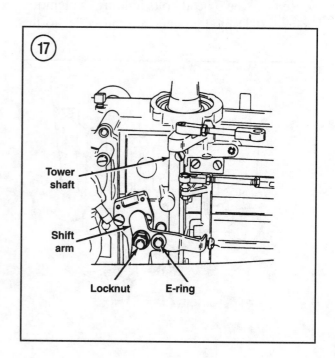

head to the motor leg. Be sure that nothing will interfere with power head removal. Do not attempt to lift the power head without a hoist. Portable hoists are available from rental centers.

25. Install lift eye (**Table 9**). Use a suitable hoist and lift the power head off of the motor leg.

26. Installation is the reverse of removal plus the following:

    a. Install a new gasket between the power head and motor leg.

    b. Lubricate the drive shaft splines with 2-4-C Multi-Lube grease.

    c. Align drive shaft splines with the power head splines when installing power head.

    d. Tighten the 9 lock nuts to specifications (**Table 4**).

    e. Perform synchronization and linkage adjustments. See Chapter Five.

50 hp (1984-1987B)

1. Disconnect the negative battery cable.

2. Remove the engine cover.

3. Disconnect and remove the spark plugs.

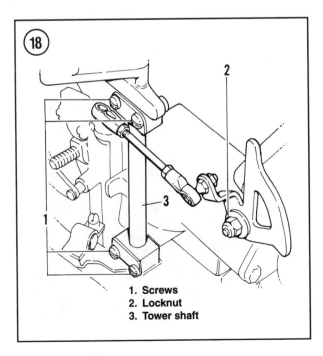

1. Screws
2. Locknut
3. Tower shaft

4. Remove the flywheel as described earlier in this chapter.

5. Remove the interlock switch mounting screws and cable clamp.

6. Remove the stator and breaker point plate. See Chapter Seven.

7. Remove the rectifier from the mounting bracket. Do not remove the wires.

8. Remove the boat wiring harness from the terminal strip and loosen any clamps holding the harness to the power head. Do not remove the engine harness from the terminal strip. Remove the 2 terminal strip mounting screws.

9. Remove the ignition coil clamp screws. Do not remove the wires from the coils.

10. Remove the circuit breaker mounting screws. Do not remove the wires from the circuit breaker.

11. Remove the carburetor and fuel pump. See Chapter Six.

12. Disconnect the green wire from the choke solenoid and remove the choke solenoid.

13. Remove the electric starter motor and bracket as an assembly. See Chapter Seven. Remove the starter solenoid mounting screws.

14. Remove the engine wiring harness and remaining electrical components as an assembly.

15. Remove the locknut and washer (**Figure 17**) holding the shift arm to the cylinder drain cover. Leave the e-ring attached to the shift arm. Remove the 4 screws (1, **Figure 18**) and the locknut and washer (2, **Figure 18**) and remove the tower shaft and throttle arm assembly.

16. Remove the intake manifold and reed block assembly. See Chapter Six.

17. Remove the screws holding the motor lower leg cover halves to each other. Remove the lower motor leg cover halves from the lower leg.

18. Remove the 2 screws holding the exhaust cover to the rear of the lower leg.

19. Remove the 9 screws holding the motor to the lower leg (4 on each side and 1 at the rear).

20. Remove the intake baffle in the lower support cover. Remove the 2 screws that support the

8

upper shock mount to the upper shock mount cover. See **Figure 16**.

> *WARNING*
> *At this point, there should be no hoses, wires or linkages connecting the power head to the motor leg. Be sure that nothing will interfere with power head removal. Do not attempt to lift the power head without a hoist. Portable hoists are available at rental centers.*

21. Thread the lift eye (**Table 9**) fully onto the crankshaft and lift the power head off of the lower leg with a suitable hoist.

22. Installation is the reverse of removal plus the following:

    a. Replace all gaskets and seals.

    b. Lubricate the drive shaft splines with 2-4-C Multi-Lube grease.

    c. Align drive shaft splines with the power head splines when installing power head.

    d. Apply RTV sealant to threads of the 9 motor leg screws and tighten to specifications (**Table 4**).

    e. Perform synchronization and linkage adjustments. See Chapter Five.

35 hp (1989-1991), 40 hp (1992C-1994) and 50 hp (1987C-1994)

1. Disconnect the negative battery cable.

2. Remove the engine cover.

3. Disconnect and remove the spark plugs.

4A. *1992 and earlier*—Remove the boat wiring harness from the terminal block and loosen any clamps holding it to the power head. Remove the 2 terminal block mounting screws.

4B. *1993 and later*—Disconnect the boat harness at the main plug-in connector.

5. Disconnect the throttle and shift cables.

6. Remove the flywheel as described earlier in this chapter.

7. Remove the stator and trigger assemblies. See Chapter Seven.

8A. *35 hp*—Remove the 3 head bolts holding the ignition bracket (CD module and ignition coils) to the power head. Disconnect any remaining leads and remove the bracket.

8B. *40 and 50 hp*—Remove the CD module or switch box, ignition coils and the ignition bracket. See Chapter Seven.

9. Remove the carburetor and fuel pump. See Chapter Six.

10. Remove the electric starter motor. See Chapter Seven.

11. Remove the starter solenoid and circuit breaker mounting screws. Remove the negative battery cable from the lower support plate.

12. *1992 and earlier*—Remove the interlock switch and its cable clamp mounting screws.

13. Disconnect the wire(s) from the choke solenoid or fuel primer valve.

14. Disconnect the temperature switch lead from the terminal strip or bullet connector.

15. Remove the engine wiring harness and remaining electrical components.

16. Remove the intake manifold and reed valve assembly. See Chapter Six.

17A. *35 hp*—Remove the locknut, washer and e-clip from the gear shift arm. Remove the detent

spring and ball from behind the gear shift arm. See **Figure 17**.

17B. *40 and 50 hp*—Remove the lock nut, washer and e-ring from the gear shift lever. Remove the gear shift lever. See **Figure 17**.

17C. *40 and 50 hp*—Remove the throttle cam locknut and washer (2, **Figure 18**) and the 4 screws (1, **Figure 18**) holding the tower shaft to the power head. Remove the tower shaft and throttle cam as an assembly.

18. Disconnect the lower shift rod from the upper shift rod. See **Figure 19**.

19. Remove the 6 top screws holding the power head to the lower leg. See **Figure 14**.

20. Remove the nuts and washers from the upper side shock mounts. See A, **Figure 15**.

21. Remove the 2 lower screws holding the power head to the lower leg. See B, **Figure 15**.

22. Remove the 2 screws from the upper shock mount cover. See **Figure 16**.

> *WARNING*
> *At this point, there should be no hoses, wires or linkages connecting the power head to the motor leg. Be sure that nothing will interfere with power head removal. Do not attempt to lift the power head without a hoist. Portable hoists are available at rental centers.*

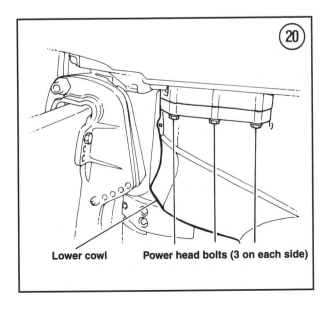

Lower cowl   **Power head bolts (3 on each side)**

23. Thread the lift eye (**Table 9**) fully onto the crankshaft and lift the power head off of the lower leg with a suitable hoist.

24. Lay the power head on a workbench and remove the spacer plate screws (6 screws on the 35 hp, 7 screws on the 40 and 50 hp). Remove the spacer plate from the power head.

25. Installation is the reverse of removal plus the following:

   a. Replace all gaskets and seals.

   b. Lubricate the drive shaft splines with 2-4-C Multi-Lube grease.

   c. Align drive shaft splines with the power head splines when installing power head.

   d. Apply RTV sealant to threads of all motor leg and spacer plate screws and tighten to specifications (**Table 4**).

   e. Perform synchronization and linkage adjustments. See Chapter Five.

40 and 50 hp (1995-1999)

1. Disconnect the negative battery cable.

2. Remove the engine cover.

3. Disconnect and remove the spark plugs.

4. Disconnect the boat harness at the main plug-in connector.

5. Disconnect the throttle and shift cables.

6. Remove the carburetor, fuel primer valve and fuel pump. See Chapter Six.

7. Remove the electric starter motor. See Chapter Seven.

8. Remove the positive battery cable from the starter solenoid and the negative battery cable from the cylinder block.

9. Remove the trim relay ground leads from the cylinder block near the fuel pump mounting boss.

10. Remove the lower cowl bolt, nut and washer. Slide the lower cowl down the motor leg to gain access to the power head mounting bolts. See **Figure 20**.

8

11. Remove the 6 (3 on each side) power head mounting bolts. See **Figure 20**.

> *WARNING*
> *At this point, there should be no hoses, wires or linkages connecting the power head to the motor leg. Be sure that nothing will interfere with power head removal. Do not attempt to lift the power head without a hoist. Portable hoists are available at rental centers.*

12A. *1995 models*—Remove the flywheel nut and install the lift eye (**Table 9**). Lift the power head from the lower leg with a suitable hoist.

12B. *1996-1999 models*—Remove the flywheel thread protecting cap and thread the lift eye (**Table 9**) fully into the flywheel. Lift the power head from the lower leg with a suitable hoist.

13. Lay the power head on a work bench and remove the spacer plate screws. Remove the spacer plate.

14. Remove the flywheel as outlined previously in this chapter.

15. Remove the stator and trigger assemblies. See Chapter Seven.

16A. *1995 models*—Remove the switch box, ignition coils, voltage regulator and fuse from the ignition plate assembly. Remove the ignition plate from the cylinder block. Remove the main wiring harness and any remaining electrical components from the power head. See Chapter Seven.

16B. *1996-1999 models*—Remove the CDM modules from the cylinder head. Remove the voltage regulator, fuse holder and starter solenoid from the port side of the power head. Remove the main wiring harness and any remaining electrical components from the power head. See Chapter Seven.

17. Remove the intake manifold and reed block assembly from the power head. See Chapter Six.

18. Remove the tower shaft from the starboard side of the power head. See **Figure 18**, typical.

19. Installation is the reverse of removal plus the following:

   a. Replace all gaskets and seals.

   b. Lubricate the drive shaft splines with 2-4-C Multi-Lube grease.

   c. Align the drive shaft splines with the power head splines when installing the power head.

   d. Apply RTV sealant to threads of all motor leg and spacer plate screws and tighten to specifications (**Table 4**).

   e. Perform synchronization and linkage adjustments. See Chapter Five.

70 and 75 hp (1998 and Prior)

1. Disconnect the negative battery cable.

2. Remove the engine cover.

3. Disconnect and remove the spark plugs.

4A. *1992 and earlier*—Remove the boat wiring harness from the terminal block and loosen any clamps holding it to the power head. Remove the 2 terminal block mounting screws.

4B. *1993 and later*—Disconnect the boat harness at the main plug-in connector.

5. Disconnect the throttle and shift cables.

6. Remove the carburetor, fuel primer valve and fuel pump. See Chapter Six.

7. Remove the electric starter motor. See Chapter Seven.

8. Remove the starter solenoid mounting screws from the lower support plate or the port side of the power head.

9. Remove the negative battery cable from the lower support plate or the power head.

10. *1992 and earlier*—Remove the interlock switch and its cable clamp mounting screws.

11. Disconnect the temperature switch lead from the terminal strip or bullet connector.

12. Remove the intake manifold and reed valve assembly. See Chapter Six.

13. Remove the tell-tale water discharge hose from the lower support plate if so equipped.

14. *75 hp*—Remove the 2 trim relay mounting screws from the port side of the power head.

15. Disconnect the lower shift rod from the upper shift rod. See **Figure 19**.

16. Remove the 5 top screws holding the power head to the lower leg. Remove the throttle cable anchor bracket to gain access to the starboard middle screw.

17. Remove the nuts and washers from the upper side shock mounts. See A, **Figure 15**.

18. Remove the 2 lower screws holding the power head to the lower leg. See B, **Figure 15**.

19. Remove the 2 screws from the upper shock mount cover. See **Figure 16**.

> *WARNING*
> *At this point, there should be no hoses, wires or linkages connecting the power head to the motor leg. Be sure that nothing will interfere with power head removal. Do not attempt to lift the power head without a hoist. Portable hoists are available at rental centers.*

20A. *70 hp*—Remove the flywheel nut. Thread the lift eye (**Table 10**) fully onto the crankshaft and lift the power head off of the lower leg with a suitable hoist.

20B. *75 hp (1994-1998)*—Thread the lift eye (**Table 10**) fully into the flywheel and lift the power head off of the lower leg with a suitable hoist.

21. Lay the power head on a workbench and remove the 6 spacer plate screws. Remove the spacer plate from the power head.

22. Remove the flywheel as outlined previously in this chapter.

23. Remove the stator and trigger assemblies. See Chapter Seven.

24A. *70 hp*—Remove the switch box, ignition coils, voltage regulator and fuse from the ignition plate assembly. Remove the ignition plate from the cylinder block. Remove the main wiring harness and any remaining electrical components from the power head. See Chapter Seven.

24B. *75 hp (1998 and prior)*—Remove the ignition plate assembly from the starboard side of the power head along with the main wiring harness and any remaining electrical components from the power head. See Chapter Seven.

25. Remove the tower shaft and shift linkage from the starboard side of the power head.

26. Installation is the reverse of removal plus the following:

  a. Replace all gaskets and seals.

  b. Lubricate the drive shaft splines with 2-4-C Multi-Lube grease.

  c. Align drive shaft splines with the power head splines when installing the power head.

  d. Apply RTV sealant to threads of all motor leg and spacer plate screws and tighten to specifications (**Table 4**).

  e. Perform synchronization and linkage adjustments. See Chapter Five.

85-150 hp (1984-1994 [except L-Drive])

1. Disconnect the negative battery cable.

2. Remove the engine cover.

3. Disconnect and remove the spark plugs.

4A. *1992 and earlier*—Remove the boat wiring harness from the terminal block and loosen any clamps holding it to the power head. Remove the 2 terminal block mounting screws.

4B. *1993 and later*—Disconnect the boat harness at the main plug-in connector.

5. Disconnect the throttle and shift cables.

6. Remove the flywheel as outlined previously in this chapter.

7. Remove the stator and trigger assemblies. See Chapter Seven.

8. *1992 and earlier*—Remove the interlock switch mounting screws.

8

9. Disconnect the temperature switch lead from the terminal strip or bullet connector. See **Figure 21** (150 hp shown).

10. Remove the choke solenoid or fuel primer valve. See Chapter Six.

11. Remove the negative battery cable from the power head.

12. If equipped with power trim, perform the following:

  a. Disconnect the relay ground lead from the power head.

  b. Disconnect the plugs from the power trim relays. See **Figure 22**.

  c. Insert a small screwdriver or similar tool into the receiving end of the connector plugs to unlock the blue and green leads from the appropriate connector. See **Figure 23**.

  d. Remove the power trim circuit breaker mounting screws. See **Figure 24**, typical.

13. Remove the electric starter motor. See Chapter Seven.

14. Remove the starter solenoid mounting screws from the lower support plate.

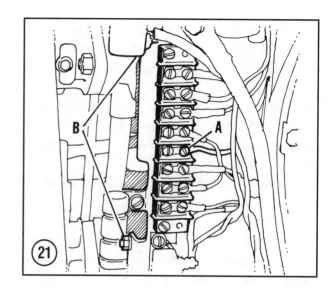

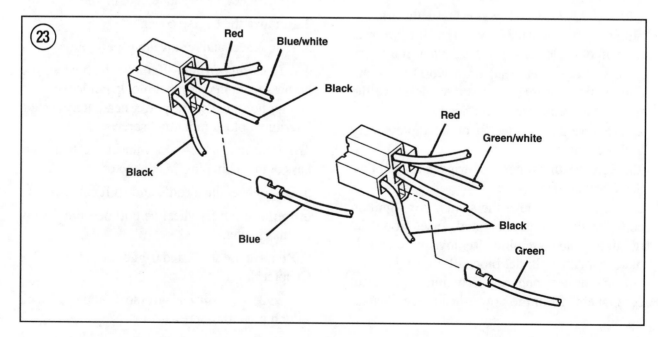

15. If the rectifier or rectifier/regulator is not mounted on the ignition components bracket, remove the rectifier or rectifier/regulator mounting screw(s). Early model rectifiers use a separate ground wire. Disconnect the rectifier ground wire if so equipped.

16. Remove the 3 nuts holding the ignition components bracket to the power head. If so equipped, remove the bracket ground wire from the power head. Remove the main wiring harness and any remaining electrical components from the power head. See Chapter Seven.

17. Remove the 3 ignition bracket shock mounts from the power head.

18. Remove the carburetor(s) and fuel pump(s). See Chapter Six.

19. Remove the intake manifold(s) and reed valve assembly(s). See Chapter Six.

20. Disconnect the shift rod nut from the interlock assembly. See **Figure 25**, typical.

21. Remove the 6 screws holding the rear motor leg cover to the front motor leg cover. Remove the 6 screws holding the rear motor leg cover to the support cover. Remove the rear motor leg cover. See **Figure 26**.

22. *85-125 hp*—Remove the 7 screws holding the lower support plate to the front motor leg

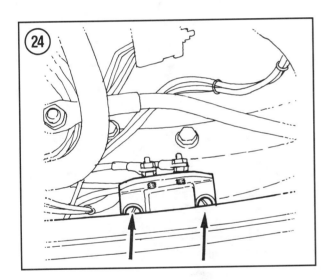

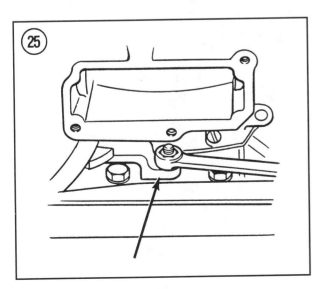

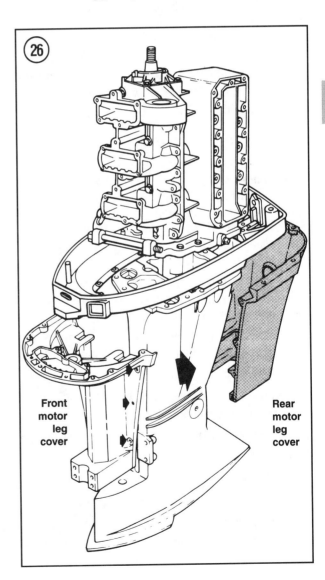

8

Front
motor
leg
cover

Rear
motor
leg
cover

cover. Remove the support plate from the engine. See **Figure 27**.

23. Remove the 6 top screws (5 on the 150 hp) holding the power head to the lower leg.

24. Remove the 6 lower lock nuts holding the power head to the lower leg.

> *WARNING*
> *At this point, there should be no hoses, wires or linkages connecting the power head to the motor leg. Be sure that nothing will interfere with power head removal. Do not attempt to lift the power head off without a hoist. Portable hoists are available at rental centers. Lift the power head slowly and guide the exhaust tube flange carefully past the water tube mount or damage will result.*

25. Thread the lift eye (**Table 10**) fully onto the crankshaft and lift the power head off of the lower leg with a suitable hoist.

> *NOTE*
> *A gasket (or seal) is used between the spacer plate and the power head. RTV sealant is used in place of a gasket between the spacer plate and motor leg. A rubber gasket seals the exhaust tube to the motor leg.*

26. Lay the power head on a workbench and remove the 4 spacer plate lock nuts. Remove the spacer plate from the power head. Inspect the exhaust tube and spacer plate. Remove the exhaust tube from the spacer plate only if replacement is required.

27. Remove the tower shaft from the starboard side of the power head.

28. Installation is the reverse of removal plus the following:

a. Replace all gaskets and seals.

b. Position the rubber gasket on the lower edge of the exhaust tube flange. A small amount of contact adhesive may be used to hold it in place.

c. Apply RTV sealant (**Table 8**) to the sealant surface (machined surface) of the motor leg.

d. Lubricate the drive shaft splines with 2-4-C Multi-Lube grease.

e. When lowering the power head onto the motor leg, guide the exhaust tube flange carefully past the water tube mount and align drive shaft splines with the power head splines.

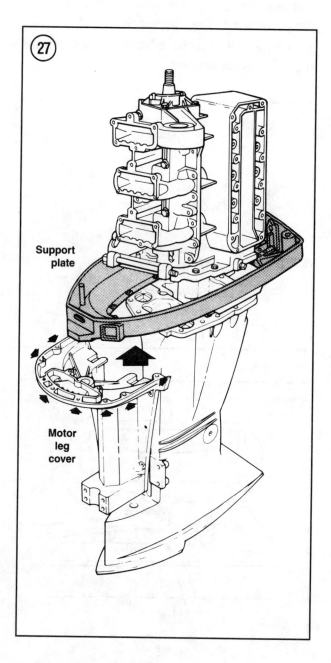

Support plate

Motor leg cover

g. Apply RTV sealant to threads of all motor leg and spacer plate screws and tighten to specifications (**Table 4**).

h. Adjust the gear shift and interlock assembly. See Chapter Nine.

i. Perform synchronization and linkage adjustments. See Chapter Five.

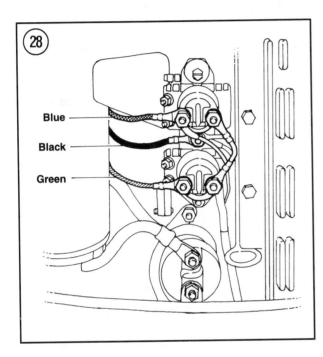

Blue

Black

Green

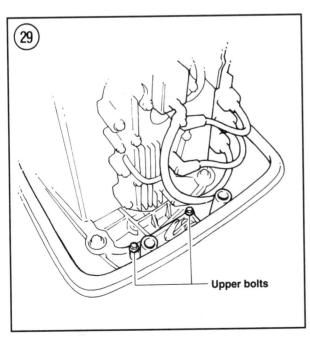

Upper bolts

75 hp (1999),
90 and 120 hp (1995-1999)

1. Disconnect the negative battery cable.

2. Remove the engine cover.

3. Disconnect and remove the spark plugs.

4. Disconnect the boat harness from the main plug-in connector.

5. Disconnect the throttle and shift cables.

6. Remove the carburetor, fuel primer valve and fuel pump. See Chapter Six.

7. Remove the tell-tale water discharge hose from the lower cover.

8. Remove the electric starter motor. See Chapter Seven.

9. Remove the positive battery cable from the starter solenoid and the negative battery cable from the cylinder block.

10. Remove the 3 power trim motor leads from the trim solenoids. See **Figure 28**.

11. Remove the 2 upper and 2 lower trim cover screws. Remove the trim cover. See **Figure 29** and **Figure 30.**

8

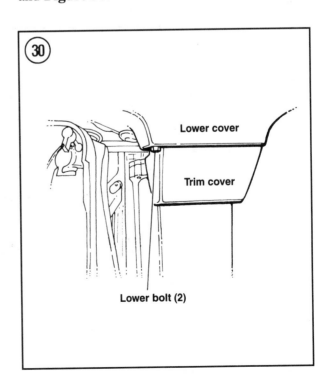

Lower cover

Trim cover

Lower bolt (2)

12. Remove the 4 screws holding the adapter plate to the lower cover. See **Figure 31**.

13. Remove the 8 locknuts and washers securing the power head to the motor leg.

> *WARNING*
> *At this point, there should be no hoses, wires or linkages connecting the power head to the motor leg. Be sure that nothing will interfere with power head removal. Do not attempt to lift the power head without a hoist. Portable hoists are available at rental centers.*

14A. *1995 models*—Remove the flywheel nut and install the lift eye (**Table 10**). Lift the power head from the lower leg with a suitable hoist.

14B. *1996-1999 models*—Remove the flywheel thread protecting cap and thread the lift eye (**Table 10**) fully into the flywheel. Lift the power head from the lower leg with a suitable hoist.

15. Lay the power head on a work bench and remove the 10 spacer plate screws. Remove the spacer plate.

16. Remove the flywheel as outlined previously in this chapter.

17. Remove the stator and trigger assemblies. See Chapter Seven.

18A. *1995 models*—Remove the 3 nuts holding the ignition components bracket to the power head. Remove the bracket ground wire from the power head. Remove the bracket, the main wiring harness and any remaining electrical components from the power head. See Chapter Seven.

18B. *1996-1999 models*—Remove the ignition plate assembly from the starboard side of the power head along with the main wiring harness and any remaining electrical components from the power head. See Chapter Seven.

19. Remove the tower shaft from the starboard side of the power head.

20. Installation is the reverse of removal plus the following:

    a. Replace all gaskets and seals.

    b. Lubricate the drive shaft splines with 2-4-C Multi-Lube grease.

    c. Align drive shaft splines with the power head splines when installing power head.

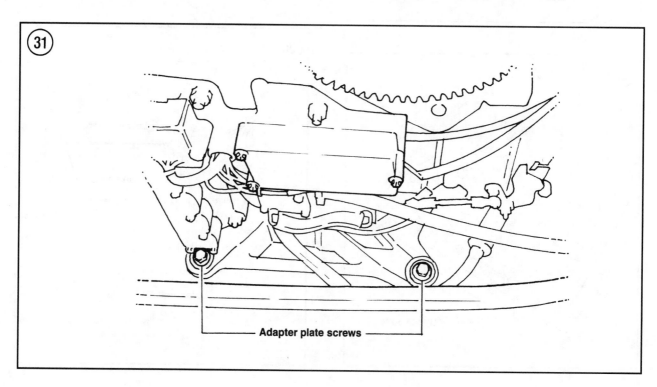

(31)

Adapter plate screws

d. Apply RTV sealant to threads of all motor leg and spacer plate screws and tighten to specifications (**Table 4**).

e. Perform synchronization and linkage adjustments. See Chapter Five.

L-Drive

1. Lift the port-side seat back up to gain access to the battery. Disconnect the negative battery cable.

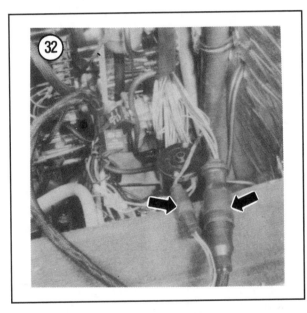

2. Remove the center seat cover.

3. Remove the seat center panel and center cushion.

4. Disconnect the wiring harness plugs (**Figure 32**).

5. Remove the clamp, then disconnect and plug the fuel delivery hose (E, **Figure 33**).

6. Disconnect the throttle cable from the stud (A, **Figure 33**). Remove screw and clamp (B, **Figure 33**).

7. Remove nuts (C, **Figure 33**) securing steering cable. Remove spring and washers (D, **Figure 33**) and lift off steering cable.

8. Unplug the power trim/tilt relays (**Figure 34**).

9. Using a small screwdriver or similar tool, remove the blue/white and green/white wires from the connectors. Push down on the tab holding wires in the connectors and pull wires out.

10. Remove 2 screws securing the power trim/tilt pump assembly to the mounting bracket.

11. Remove the trim components bracket (**Figure 34**) from the transom plate without disconnecting electrical leads. Using a length of wire, fasten the bracket to the power head.

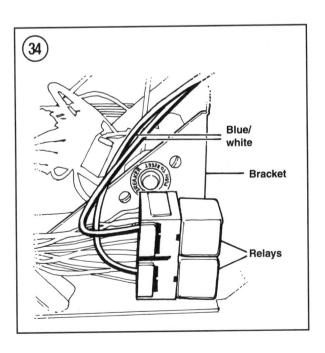

8

12. Remove clamp and disconnect the water inlet hose located between the transom plate and spacer plate (lower rear side of motor). Late models are equipped with an additional hose between spacer plate and exhaust flange that must be disconnected.

13. Loosen clamps (A, **Figure 35**) and disconnect the 2 water hoses (B) from the top of the exhaust manifold. Exhaust manifold on late models is internally cooled and not equipped with water hoses (B, **Figure 35**).

14. Loosen the clamps (C, **Figure 35**) securing the exhaust hose (D) to the manifold. The exhaust hose will slide off the manifold when the engine is raised.

NOTE
At this point, there should be no hoses, wires or linkages connecting the power head to the motor leg. Make sure nothing will interfere with power head removal.

15. Remove the 5 screws securing the spacer plate to the transom plate (**Figure 36**).

WARNING
Do not attempt to lift the power head without a hoist. Portable hoists are available at rental centers.

16. Remove the flywheel nut. Thread the lift eye (**Table 10**) fully onto the crankshaft and lift the power head off of the transom plate with a suitable hoist.

17. Set the power head on a workbench or mount it in a suitable holding fixture.

18. Remove the flywheel as outlined previously in this chapter.

19. Remove the stator and trigger assemblies. See Chapter Seven.

20. Remove the electric starter motor. See Chapter Seven.

21. Remove the wire from the choke solenoid terminal stud.

22. Remove the 3 nuts holding the ignition components bracket to the power head. If so equipped, remove the bracket ground wire from

the power head. Remove the main wiring harness and any remaining electrical components from the power head. See Chapter Seven.

23. Remove the 3 ignition bracket shock mounts from the power head.

24. Remove the carburetor(s) and fuel pump. See Chapter Six.

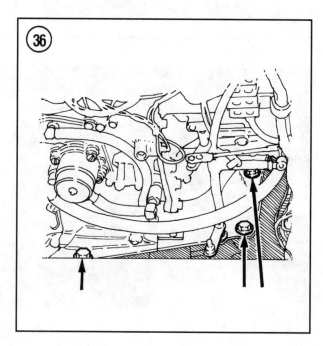

25. Remove the intake manifold(s) and reed valve assembly(s). See Chapter Six.

26. Lay the power head on its side and remove the 10 spacer plate screws. Remove the spacer plate from the power head.

27. Remove the tower shaft assembly from the starboard side of the power head.

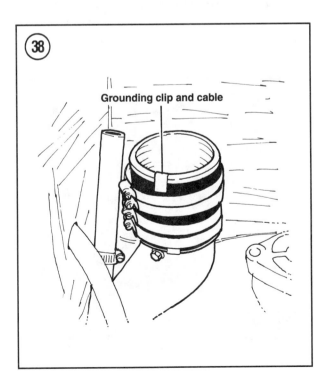

Grounding clip and cable

NOTE
All 4-cylinder and certain 3-cylinder L-Drive models did not originally use a gasket between the power head and spacer plate. Currently, replacement gasket part No.27-819381 is recommended for use between the power head and spacer plate on all L-Drive models.

28. Installation is the reverse of removal plus the following:

  a. Replace all seals and gaskets.

  b. Apply a suitable water-resistant grease (Quicksilver Special Lube 101) to the drive shaft splines (**Figure 37**).

  c. Apply bellows adhesive (**Table 8**) to the inner diameter of the exhaust hose (**Figure 38**). Make sure the grounding clip and cable (**Figure 38**) are properly installed on the exhaust hose.

  d. While lowering power head onto transom plate, guide exhaust manifold outlet into exhaust hose (**Figure 38**). When tightening exhaust hose clamps, be sure grounding clips are not directly under clamp screws. Rotate crankshaft or propeller shaft as necessary to align crankshaft and drive shaft splines.

  e. Tighten all fasteners to specifications (**Table 4**).

  f. Perform engine synchronization and linkage adjustments. Adjust engine timing. See Chapter Five.

29. Adjust steering linkage as follows:

  a. Place lower unit gearcase in the straight-ahead position.

  b. Rotate steering wheel completely to port while counting steering wheel revolutions. Place gearcase in the straight-ahead position.

  c. Rotate steering wheel completely to starboard while counting steering wheel revolutions.

  d. The number of turns required for full starboard and full port turns should be equal. If

8

not, loosen jam nuts (A, **Figure 39**) on steering cable and turn guide tube (B, **Figure 39**) as required. Tighten jam nuts to specification (**Table 4**). Recheck adjustment to ensure equal turns are required for full port and starboard turns.

POWER HEAD DISASSEMBLY

Power head overhaul gasket sets are available for most Force engines. It is often more economical and simpler to order the overhaul gasket set instead of each component individually. It is a good mechanical practice to replace every gasket, seal and o-ring during a power head reassembly. The piston rings should also be replaced if the pistons are taken out of the cylinder bore. All power head components should be cleaned and inspected before any reassembly occurs. If the power head has had a catastrophic failure, it may be more economical (in time and money) to replace the short block as an assembly.

Special tools recommended for the following procedures can be found in **Table 9** for the 4-60 hp and **Table 10** for the 70-150 hp. Remember that parts damaged by not using the correct tool can often be more expensive than the original cost of the tool. Recommended sealants, lubricants and adhesives are listed in **Table 8**.

4 and 5 hp

> *NOTE*
> *Mark all internal components that are to be reused for original location and direction for reference during reassembly.*

Refer to **Figure 40** for this procedure.

1. Remove the 4 cylinder head screws. Remove the cylinder head and gasket. Discard the gasket.

2. With crankcase and cylinder block on a solid surface, drive out the 2 locating pins with a pin punch. See **Figure 41**.

3. Remove the 6 screws holding the crankcase cover to the cylinder.

4. Carefully separate the crankcase cover from the cylinder by prying at the pry points provided with a putty knife or similar tool.

5. Remove the connecting rod cap screws using special tool part No. FT-8929 or equivalent. See **Figure 42**.

6A. *Prior to 1988 B*—Remove the connecting rod cap, roller bearings and bearing cages from the connecting rod and cap. Place the bearings and cages in a clean container.

6B. *1988 B-on*—Remove the connecting rod cap and 56 loose bearing rollers (not caged). If any bearing rollers fall into the crankcase during removal, remove them using a swab covered with grease. *Do not* use a magnet to retrieve loose rollers. Place the bearing rollers in a clean container.

7. Remove the crankshaft assembly from the cylinder block. Remove the upper crankshaft bearing and lower crankshaft seal. Remove the O-ring from the crankshaft lower splined bore.

8. Reinstall connecting rod cap on the connecting rod. Push the piston toward the cylinder head end of the crankcase until the piston rings can be seen.

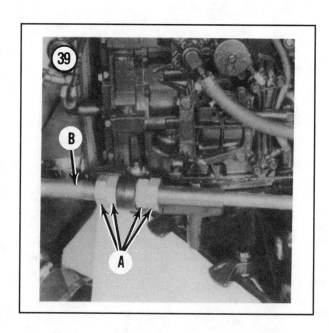

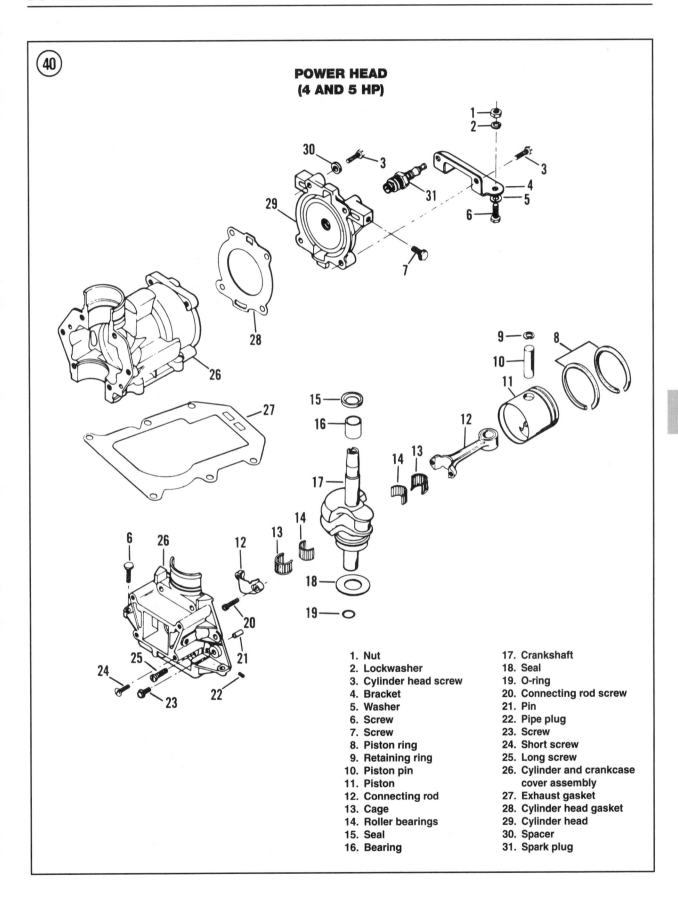

**POWER HEAD
(4 AND 5 HP)**

8

1. Nut
2. Lockwasher
3. Cylinder head screw
4. Bracket
5. Washer
6. Screw
7. Screw
8. Piston ring
9. Retaining ring
10. Piston pin
11. Piston
12. Connecting rod
13. Cage
14. Roller bearings
15. Seal
16. Bearing
17. Crankshaft
18. Seal
19. O-ring
20. Connecting rod screw
21. Pin
22. Pipe plug
23. Screw
24. Short screw
25. Long screw
26. Cylinder and crankcase cover assembly
27. Exhaust gasket
28. Cylinder head gasket
29. Cylinder head
30. Spacer
31. Spark plug

9. Remove and discard the piston rings using ring expander tool part No. FT-8926 or equivalent. See **Figure 43**.

10. Remove the piston and connecting rod from the crankcase.

11. If the piston is to be removed from the connecting rod, remove the piston pin retaining rings with snap rings pliers.

12. Place piston in pillow block (part No. FT-2990) and remove the piston pin with special tool part No. FT-8919. See **Figure 44**.

7.5, 9.9 and 15 hp

> *NOTE*
> *All internal components that are to be reused should be marked for original location and direction for reference during reassembly.*

Refer to **Figure 45** or **Figure 46** for this procedure.

1. Remove the screws holding the exhaust tube to the power head, if so equipped.

2. Remove the cylinder head bolts and washers. Remove the cylinder head and gasket. Discard the gasket.

3. Remove the cylinder drain cover screws. Remove the cover and gasket. Discard the gasket.

4. Remove the transfer port cover screws. Remove the cover and gasket. Discard the gasket.

5. Remove the 4 upper bearing cage screws. Remove the upper bearing cage from the power head. Remove and discard the gasket. Press the seal out of the bearing cage with a suitable mandrel. Discard the seal. Remove the stator ring from the power head.

6. With crankcase and cylinder block assembly on a solid surface, drive out the 2 locating pins with a suitable pin punch.

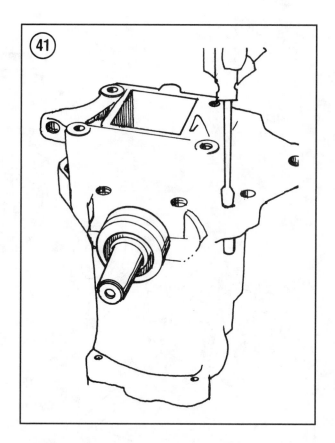

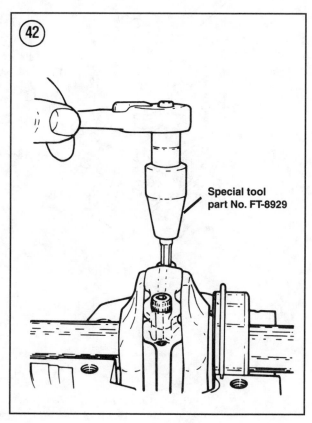

Special tool part No. FT-8929

7. Remove the crankcase cover-to-cylinder block screws.

NOTE
If the top half of the main bearing liner comes off when the cover is removed in Step 8, retrieve any loose bearing rollers from the cylinder with a swab covered with grease. **Do not** *use a magnet to retrieve loose rollers.*

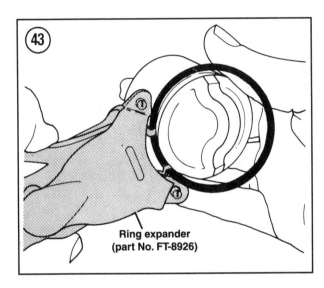

Ring expander
(part No. FT-8926)

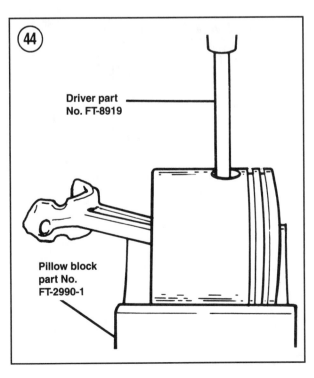

Driver part
No. FT-8919

Pillow block
part No.
FT-2990-1

8. Carefully pry the crankcase cover and cylinder block apart using a suitable pry tool at the pry points provided. Remove the cover from the block.

9. Remove the main bearing liner and roller bearings. Place in a clean container.

10. Lift the crankshaft slightly at the lower main journal. Slide seal and lower main bearing off the crankshaft. Remove the o-ring from the crankshaft lower splined bore.

11. Mark the cylinder number on each connecting rod and cap. Also mark the rods and caps for directional reference during reassembly. Be sure to keep the components from each cylinder separate.

NOTE
When servicing the connecting rod and big end bearing, observe the following: 7.5 hp models use steel rods with 16 rollers held by 2 bearing cages. Early 9.9 and 15 hp use aluminum rods with 2 steel bearing liner inserts and 52 loose needles. Late model 9.9 and 15 hp use steel rods with 56 loose needles.

12. Remove each connecting rod cap. Remove all loose bearing rollers that can be reached.

13. Remove the crankshaft from the cylinder block.

14. Remove the remaining connecting rod and main bearings and place into separate containers.

15. Reinstall the rod cap to its respective connecting rod. Remove each piston and connecting rod assembly from its cylinder. Mark the cylinder number on the top of the piston with a felt-tipped pen.

16. Remove and discard the piston rings with ring expander tool (part No. FT-8926) or equivalent. See **Figure 43**.

17. If the piston is to be removed from the connecting rod, remove the piston pin retaining rings with snap ring pliers (part No. FT-1749) or equivalent.

8

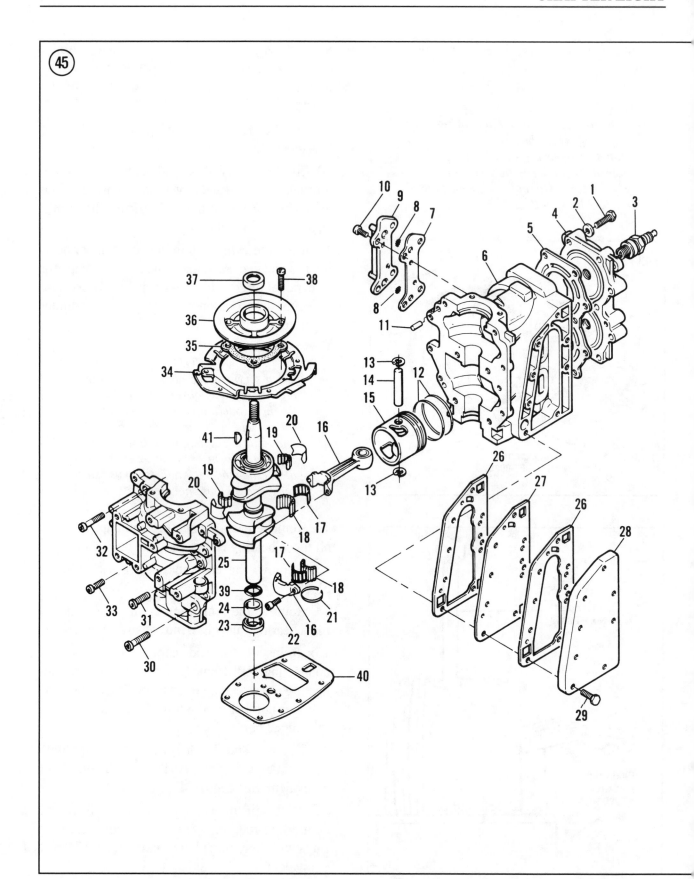

POWER HEAD
(7.5 HP)

1. Cylinder head screw
2. Plain washer
3. Spark plug
4. Cylinder head
5. Head gasket
6. Cylinder and crankcase
   cover assembly
7. Drain cover gasket
8. Drain screen
9. Drain cover
10. Screw
11. Locating pin
12. Piston rings
13. Piston pin retainer
14. Piston pin
15. Piston
16. Connecting rod
17. Bearing cage
18. Roller bearings
19. Center main roller bearings
20. Center main bearing liner
21. Crankshaft seal
22. Connecting rod screw
23. Lower crankshaft seal
24. Lower main bearing
25. Crankshaft and upper main
    bearing assembly
26. Exhaust plate gasket
27. Exhaust plate
28. Exhaust cover
29. Screw
30. Screw
31. Screw
32. Screw
33. Screw
34. Stator ring
35. Bearing cage gasket
36. Bearing cage
37. Upper crankshaft seal
38. Screw
39. Crankshaft spline seal
40. Cylinder mounting gasket
41. Woodruff key

8

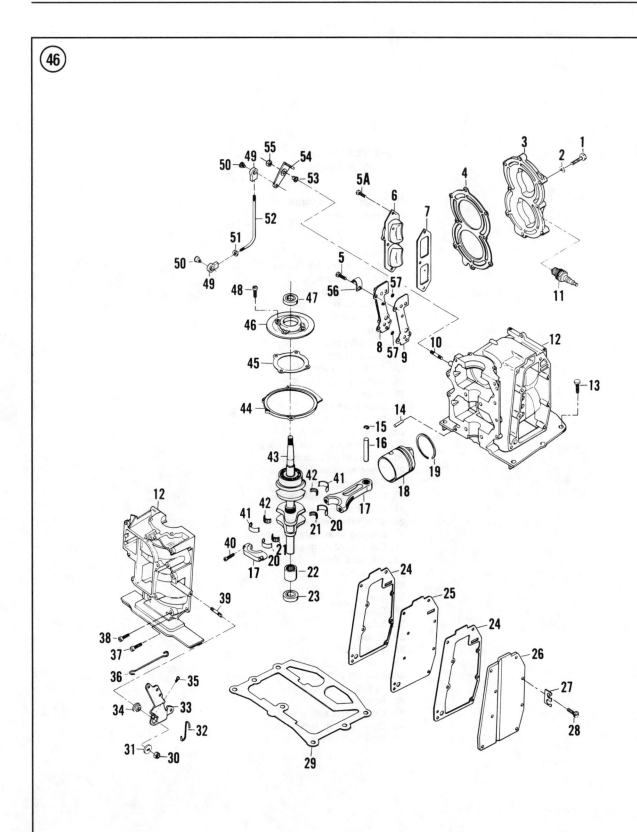

8

POWER HEAD (9.9 AND 15 HP)

1. Cylinder head screw
2. Plain washer
3. Cylinder head
4. Head gasket
5. Screw
6. Transfer port cover
7. Transfer port gasket
8. Drain cover
9. Drain cover gasket
10. Interlock lever stud
11. Spark plug
12. Cylinder and crankcase
    cover assembly
13. Cap screw
14. Locating pin
15. Piston pin retaining ring
16. Piston pin
17. Connecting rod
    (aluminum rod shown)
18. Piston
19. Piston rings
20. Connecting rod liner set
    (aluminum rod only)
21. Roller bearings
22. Lower main crankshaft bearing
23. Crankshaft lower seal
24. Exhaust cover gasket
25. Exhaust plate
26. Exhaust cover
27. Lead wire clip
28. Screw
29. Power head mounting gasket
30. Stop nut
31. Washer
32. Magneto control rod link
33. Magneto control lever
34. Control lever bearing
35. Screw
36. Throttle cam link
37. Screw
38. Screw
39. Magneto lever stud
40. Connecting rod screw
41. Main bearing liner set
42. Roller bearings
43. Crankshaft and upper
    main bearing assembly
44. Magneto stator ring
45. Bearing cage gasket
46. Bearing cage
47. Crankshaft upper seal
48. Screw
49. Interlock lever bearing
50. Interlock rod bearing swivel
51. Hex nut
52. Interlock rod
53. Interlock lever bearing
54. Interlock lever
55. Stop nut
56. Hose clamp
57. Screen

18. Place piston in pillow block (part No. FT-2990) and remove the piston pin with driver part No. FT-8919. See **Figure 44**.

25 hp (3-cylinder)

NOTE
All internal components should be marked (if possible) or stored in separate containers for reference during reassembly.

Refer to **Figure 47** and **Figure 48** for this procedure.

1. Remove the 4 upper bearing cage screws. Remove the upper bearing cage from the power head. Remove and discard the gasket. Press the seal out of the bearing cage with a suitable mandrel. Discard the seal.

2. Remove the 7 intake manifold screws. Carefully pry the intake manifold and reed block assembly from the crankcase cover. Carefully separate the intake manifold from the reed block. Remove and discard the gaskets.

3. Remove the 8 transfer port cover screws. Carefully pry the transfer port cover loose from the cylinder block. Remove and discard the gasket.

4. Remove the 14 exhaust cover screws. Carefully remove the exhaust cover and inner exhaust plate from the cylinder block and each other. Remove and discard the gaskets.

5. Remove the 10 cylinder head screws. Carefully remove the cylinder head from the cylinder block. Carefully remove the cylinder head cover and thermostat components from the cylinder head. Remove and discard all gaskets and seals.

6. Remove the 11 crankcase cover outer screws and the 6 main bearing screws from the power head. Carefully pry the crankcase cover from the cylinder block. Do not scratch the sealing surfaces.

7. Remove any loose center main bearing rollers and the 2 center main bearing liners from the crankcase cover. Retrieve as many loose rollers as possible from cylinder block with a swab covered with needle bearing assembly grease (**Table 8**). Do not use a magnet to pick up the loose rollers. Place all bearing components in separate containers.

8. Mark the pistons, rod caps and connecting rods with a permanent felt tip marker as to the cylinder and direction that they were removed from.

9. Remove the rod cap screws, rod caps and rod bearing cage sets. Place each rod assembly's parts in separate containers.

10. Remove the crankshaft. Slide the lower seal and bearing from the crankshaft. Remove any remaining center main bearing loose rollers and the 2 center main liners from cylinder block. Place all rollers and each liner with the appropriate liner and rollers from the crankcase cover. There are a total of 32 loose rollers and 2 liners for each center main bearing assembly.

NOTE
Do not remove the upper bearing unless it is going to be replaced. If replacement is necessary, thread the flywheel nut onto the crankshaft to protect the threads. Use a bearing separator plate and press the bearing off of the crankshaft. Use a suitable mandrel to press the bearing back onto the crankshaft. Support the crankshaft under the top counterweight when pressing the bearing on.

11. Reinstall the connecting rod caps and screws. Tighten the screws finger tight. Remove the piston and rod assemblies from the cylinder block.

12. Remove and discard the piston rings with the ring expander tool (part No. FT-8926) or equivalent. See **Figure 43**.

13. If the pistons are to be removed from the connecting rods, remove both lock clips from each piston with a needle nose pliers. Discard the lock clips.

14. Place the piston in pillow block (part No. FT-2990) and press the pin from the piston with

POWER HEAD (25 HP 3-CYLINDER)

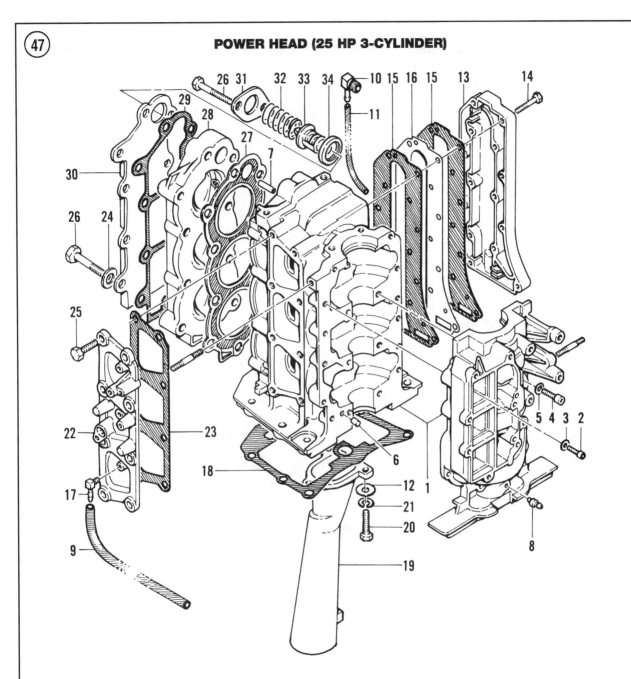

8

1. **Cylinder block and crankcase cover assembly**	11. **Tube (tell-tale water discharge)**	23. **Gasket**
2. **Crankcase cover outer screws**	12. **Flat washer**	24. **Washer**
3. **Washer**	13. **Exhaust cover**	25. **Screw**
4. **Main bearing screws**	14. **Screw**	26. **Screw**
5. **Washer**	15. **Gasket**	27. **Gasket**
6. **Dowel pin**	16. **Inner exhaust plate**	28. **Cylinder head**
7. **Water deflector**	17. **Elbow, recirculation**	29. **Gasket**
8. **Check valve (recirculation)**	18. **Gasket**	30. **Cylinder head cover**
9. **Hose (recirculation)**	19. **Exhaust Tube**	31. **Thermostat cover**
10. **Elbow (tell-tale water discharge)**	20. **Screw**	32. **Thermostat spring**
	21. **Lockwasher**	33. **Thermostat**
	22. **Transfer port cover**	34. **Grommet**

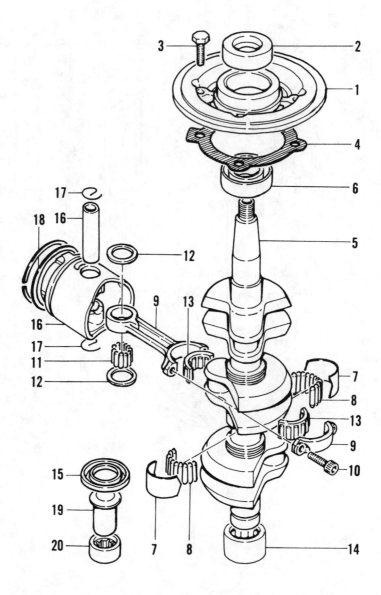

48

CRANKSHAFT ASSEMBLY (25 HP 3-CYLINDER)

1. Upper bearing cage
2. Seal
3. Screw
4. Gasket
5. Crankshaft
6. Upper main ball bearing
7. Center main bearing liner
8. Main bearing roller set
9. Connecting rod and
   cap assembly
10. Screw

11. Bearing roller set
12. Thrust bearing
13. Bearing halves
14. Lower main bearing
15. Seal
16. Piston and pin assembly
17. Lock ring
18. Piston rings
19. Drive shaft spline seal
20. Seal retainer

driver (part No. 91-13663). Collect the 2 thrust bearings and 24 loose needles. Keep all piston and rod assembly parts separate from the other rod assemblies. Repeat this step for the remaining pistons.

25 hp 2-cylinder and 35 hp

NOTE
All internal components that are to be reused should be marked for original location and direction for reference during reassembly.

Refer to **Figure 49** and **Figure 50** for this procedure.

1. Remove the exhaust port covers screws. Remove the cover, plate and 2 gaskets. Discard the gaskets.

2. Remove the transfer port cover screws. Remove the cover and gasket. Discard the gasket.

3. Remove the thermostat cover screws. Remove the cover and gasket. Discard the gasket.

4. Remove the cylinder head screws. Remove the cylinder head and gasket. Discard the gasket.

5. Remove the 4 upper bearing cage screws. Remove the upper bearing cage from the power head. Remove and discard the gasket. Press the seal out of the bearing cage with seal remover (part No. FT-3012) or equivalent. Discard the seal. Remove the stator ring from the power head.

6. Remove the crankcase cover screws. Note that 2 crankcase screws are located inside the reed plate opening. See **Figure 51**.

7. With crankcase and cylinder block assembly on a solid surface, drive out the 2 locating pins with a suitable punch.

8. Carefully pry the cover and block apart using a suitable pry tool at the pry points provided. See **Figure 52**. Separate the cover and block.

9. Remove the main bearing race half and bearing rollers. Place into a clean container.

10. Mark the connecting rods and caps for reference during reassembly. Remove each connecting rod cap, bearings and bearing cage.

Note that each connecting rod bearing contains 16 bearing rollers. Place bearings and cage from each rod into separate containers.

11. Remove the crankshaft from the cylinder block. Remove the o-ring from the crankshaft lower splined bore.

12. Remove the remaining connecting rod and main bearing rollers and place into separate containers.

13. Reinstall each rod cap on its respective connecting rod. Remove each piston and connecting rod assembly from its cylinder. Mark the cylinder number on the top of the piston with a felt-tipped pen.

14. Remove the crankshaft upper main bearing, lower main bearing collar seal and crankcase seal ring. See **Figure 53**.

NOTE
Do not remove the lower crankshaft bearing unless it is going to be replaced. If replacement is necessary, use a bearing separator plate and press the bearing off of the crankshaft. Use a suitable mandrel to press the bearing back onto the crankshaft. Support the crankshaft under the bottom counterweight when pressing the bearing on.

15. Remove and discard the piston rings with ring expander part No. FT-8926 or equivalent. See **Figure 43**.

16. If the piston requires removal from the connecting rod, remove the piston pin retaining rings with snap ring pliers.

17. Place piston in pillow block part No. FT-2990 and remove the piston pin with a suitable driver. See **Figure 54**. Remove the piston, spacers and 26 bearing rollers. Repeat procedure for remaining piston if necessary.

40 and 50 hp

NOTE
The 1996-1999 40 and 50 hp models use a top-guided power head design. This

8

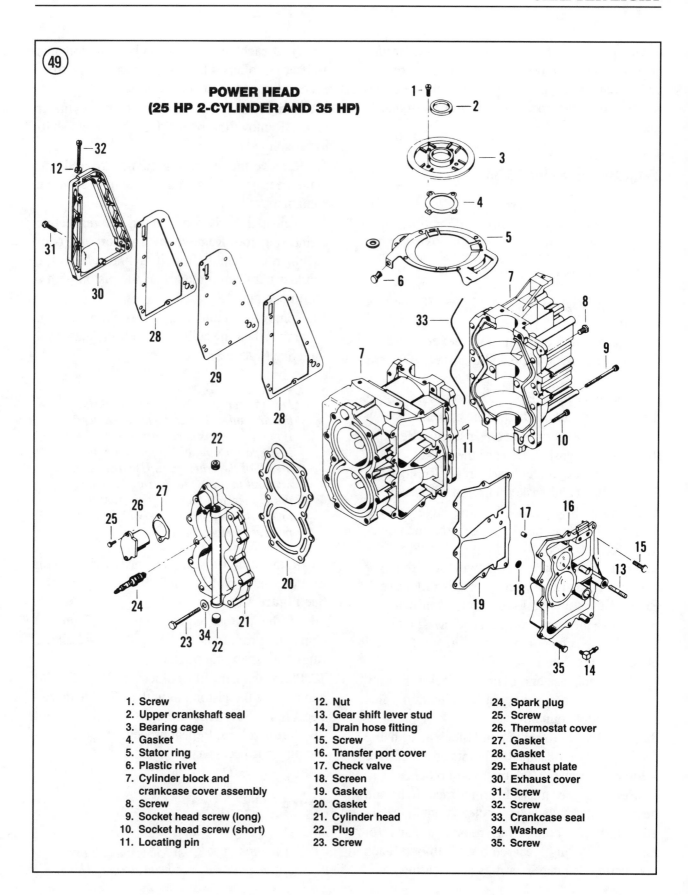

**POWER HEAD
(25 HP 2-CYLINDER AND 35 HP)**

1. Screw
2. Upper crankshaft seal
3. Bearing cage
4. Gasket
5. Stator ring
6. Plastic rivet
7. Cylinder block and
   crankcase cover assembly
8. Screw
9. Socket head screw (long)
10. Socket head screw (short)
11. Locating pin
12. Nut
13. Gear shift lever stud
14. Drain hose fitting
15. Screw
16. Transfer port cover
17. Check valve
18. Screen
19. Gasket
20. Gasket
21. Cylinder head
22. Plug
23. Screw
24. Spark plug
25. Screw
26. Thermostat cover
27. Gasket
28. Gasket
29. Exhaust plate
30. Exhaust cover
31. Screw
32. Screw
33. Crankcase seal
34. Washer
35. Screw

⑤⓪

CRANKSHAFT AND PISTONS
(25 HP 2-CYLINDER AND 35 HP)

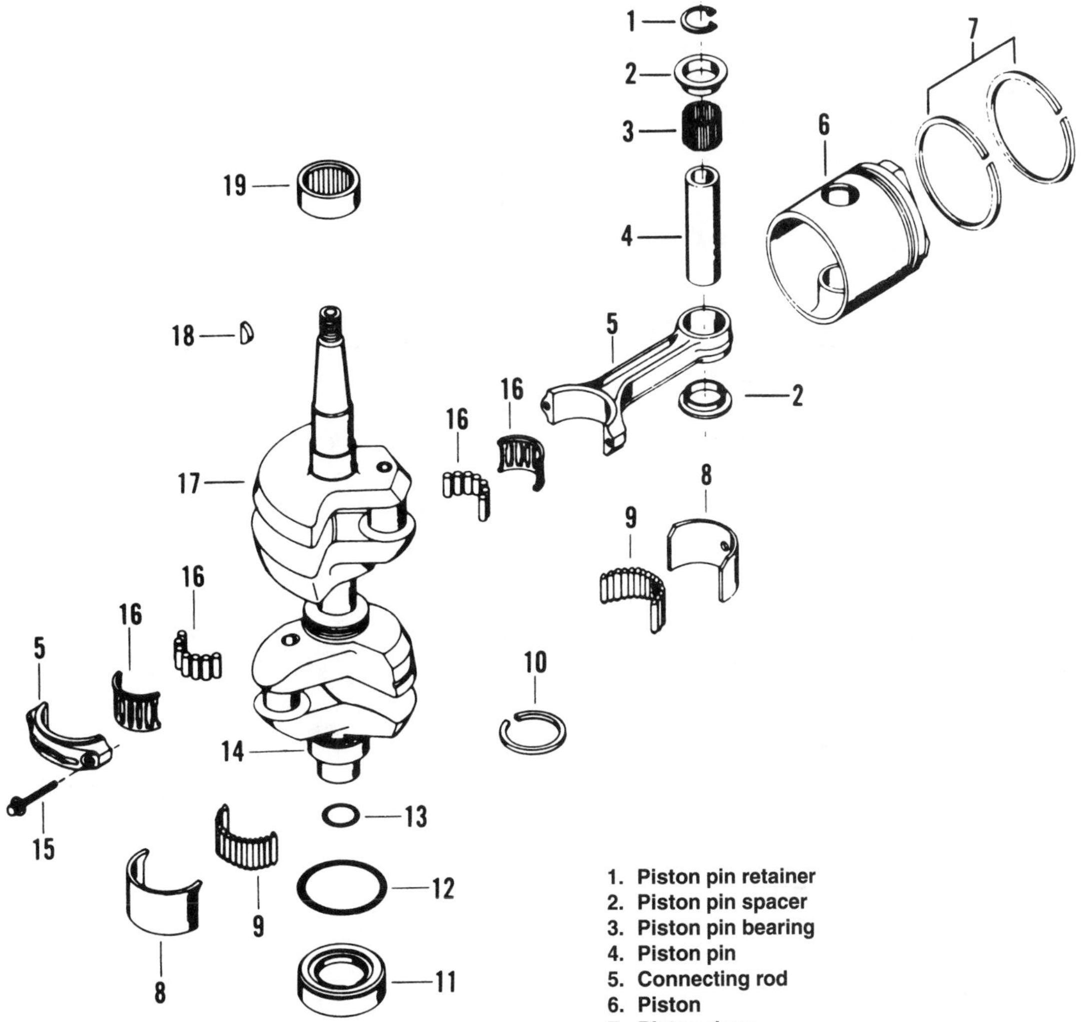

1. Piston pin retainer
2. Piston pin spacer
3. Piston pin bearing
4. Piston pin
5. Connecting rod
6. Piston
7. Piston rings
8. Center main bearing liner
9. Center main bearings
10. Crankcase seal
11. Crankshaft lower seal and collar
12. Crankshaft collar seal
13. Crankshaft spline seal
14. Crankshaft lower main bearing
15. Connecting rod screw
16. Bearing cage and roller bearing assembly
17. Crankshaft
18. Flywheel key
19. Crankshaft upper main bearing

8

*means that the connecting rods are cen-
tered vertically by the piston, not the
crankshaft. While service procedures are
similar between the new top guided
power head and the older bottom guided
power head, very few parts are interchangeable.*

NOTE
*Mark all internal components (if possi-
ble) or store in separate containers for
reference during reassembly.*

Refer to **Figure 55**, **Figure 56** and **Figure 57**
for this procedure.

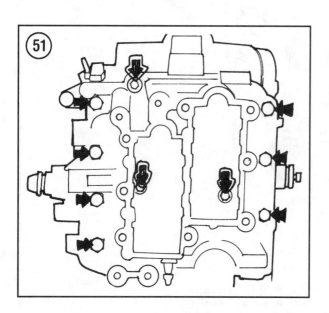

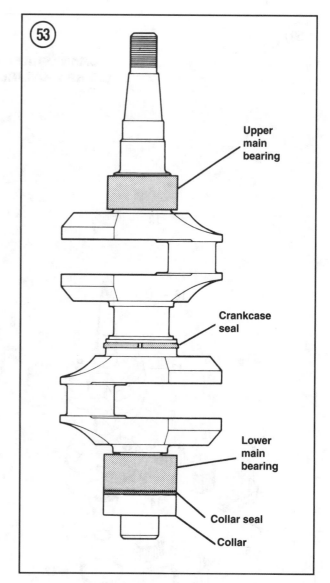

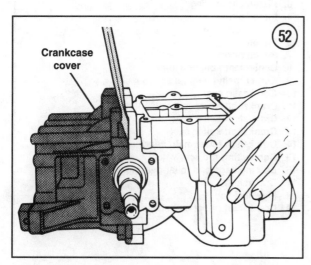

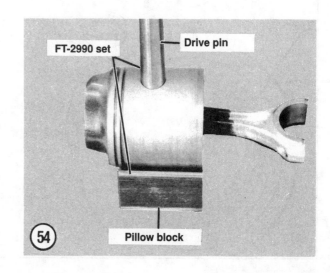

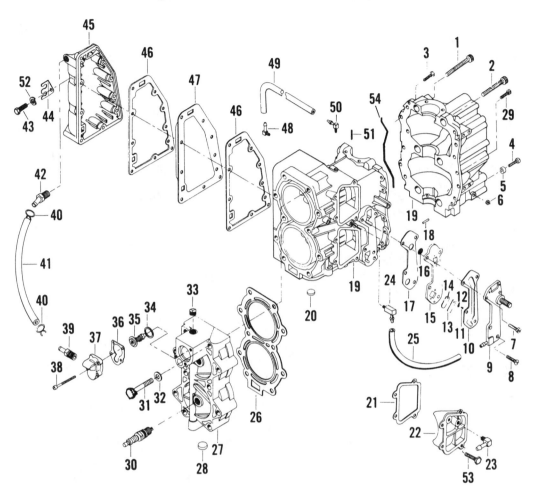

**POWER HEAD
(EARLY 40 AND 50 HP MODELS)**

1. Socket head cap screw (long)
2. Socket head cap screw (short)
3. Slot head screw
4. Screw
5. Bumper
6. Stop nut
7. Pan head screw
8. Screw
9. Drain cover
10. Drain cover gasket
11. Screw
12. Plain washer
13. Drain reed stop
14. Drain reed
15. Drain reed plate
16. Drain reed plate screen
17. Drain reed plate gasket
18. Locating pin
19. Cylinder and crankcase
    cover assembly
20. Welch plug
21. Transfer port cover gasket
22. Transfer port cover
23. Fuel line elbow
24. Elbow
25. Hose
26. Cylinder head gasket
27. Cylinder head
28. Welch plug
29. Screw (short)
30. Spark plug
31. Screw (long)
32. Plain washer
33. Pipe plug
34. Thermostat grommet
35. Thermostat
36. Thermostat cover gasket
37. Thermostat cover
38. Screw
39. Thermostat fitting
40. Clamp
41. Thermostat water tube
42. Thermostat fitting
43. Screw
44. Lead wire clip
45. Exhaust port cover
46. Exhaust port plate gasket
47. Exhaust port plate
48. Fitting
49. Elbow
50. Elbow with metering cup
51. Roll pin
52. Spring lockwasher
53. Screw
54. Spaghetti seal

8

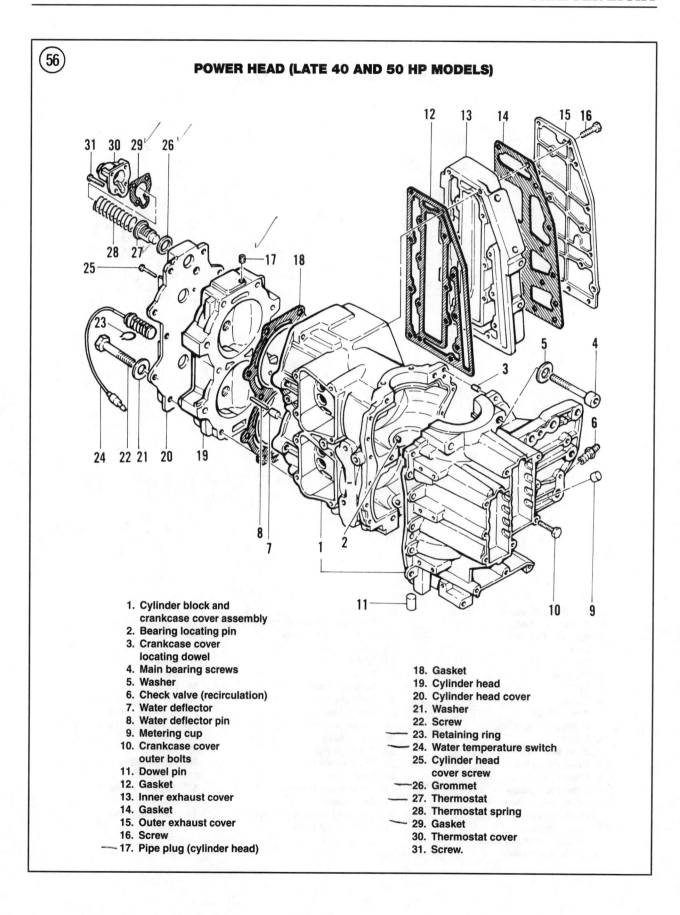

POWER HEAD (LATE 40 AND 50 HP MODELS)

1. Cylinder block and
   crankcase cover assembly
2. Bearing locating pin
3. Crankcase cover
   locating dowel
4. Main bearing screws
5. Washer
6. Check valve (recirculation)
7. Water deflector
8. Water deflector pin
9. Metering cup
10. Crankcase cover
    outer bolts
11. Dowel pin
12. Gasket
13. Inner exhaust cover
14. Gasket
15. Outer exhaust cover
16. Screw
17. Pipe plug (cylinder head)
18. Gasket
19. Cylinder head
20. Cylinder head cover
21. Washer
22. Screw
23. Retaining ring
24. Water temperature switch
25. Cylinder head
    cover screw
26. Grommet
27. Thermostat
28. Thermostat spring
29. Gasket
30. Thermostat cover
31. Screw.

⑤⑦

CRANKSHAFT AND PISTONS
(40 AND 50 HP [TYPICAL])

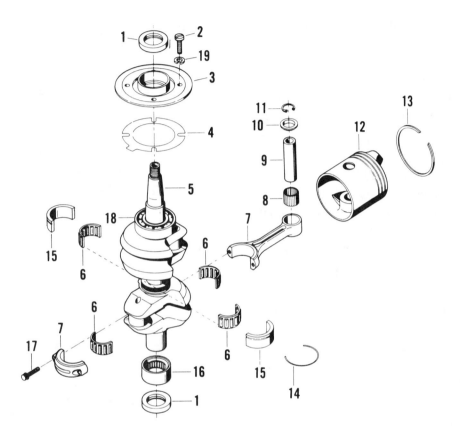

1. Seal
2. Screw
3. Bearing cage
4. Gasket
5. Crankshaft
6. Bearing half
7. Connecting rod and cap
8. Bearing
9. Piston pin
10. Spacer
11. Retainer ring
12. Piston
13. Piston ring
14. Retaining ring
15. Center main bearing race
16. Lower main bearing
17. Screw
18. Upper main bearing
19. Lockwasher

8

1. Remove the 4 upper bearing cage screws. Remove the upper bearing cage from the power head. Remove and discard the gasket. Press the seal out of the bearing cage with a suitable mandrel. Discard the seal.

2. *Early models*—Remove the clamps and disconnect the thermostat water tube. See **Figure 58**.

3. Remove the screws holding the thermostat cover to the cylinder head. Remove the cover, spring (late models), thermostat, grommet and gasket. Discard the gasket. See **Figure 59** (early models).

4. Remove the cylinder head bolts. Remove the cylinder head and gasket. Discard the gasket.

5. Remove the water temperature switch from the cylinder head.

6. *Late models*—Remove the 2 cylinder head cover screws. Carefully remove the cylinder head cover and gasket. Discard the gasket.

7. Remove the exhaust cover screws. Carefully pry the outer and inner exhaust covers from the cylinder block and each other. Discard the gaskets.

8. Remove the screws from both transfer port covers. Carefully pry the transfer port covers loose from the cylinder block. Remove and discard the gaskets.

9. *Early models*—Remove the cylinder drain cover screws. Carefully pry the cylinder cover loose from the cylinder block. Remove and discard the gasket. See **Figure 60**.

10. *Early models*—Remove the 5 screws securing the shock mount cover to the cylinder block. See **Figure 61**.

11. Remove the crankcase cover outer screws and the main bearing screws from the power head. See **Figure 62** for main bearing screw location.

12. With the crankcase and cylinder block assembly on a solid surface, drive out the 2 locating pins using a suitable punch.

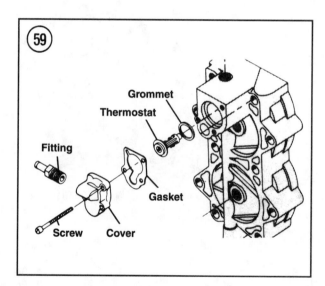

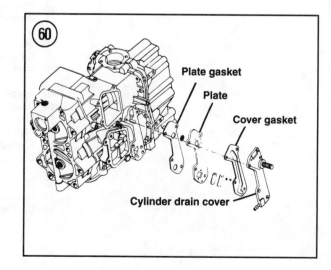

SHOCK MOUNT COVER

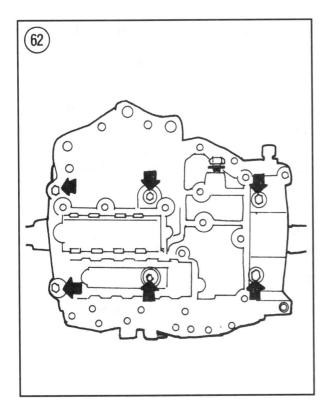

SEAL

13. Carefully pry the crankcase cover from the cylinder block. Do not scratch the sealing surfaces. Remove the crankcase seal from each side of the crankcase if so equipped. See **Figure 63**.

14. Mark the pistons, rod caps and connecting rods with a permanent felt tip marker as to the cylinder and direction they were removed from.

NOTE
A 1984-1995 connecting rod crankpin bearing consists of 2 bearing cages and 16 loose rollers. A 1996 top guided connecting rod crankpin bearing consists of 2 bearing cage and roller assemblies. If the rollers fall out of a 1996 bearing cage, the bearing cage and roller assembly must be replaced.

15. Remove the rod cap screws, rod caps and rod bearing cage sets or bearing cages and rollers. Place each rod assembly's parts in separate containers.

16. Remove the crankshaft. Slide the lower seal and bearing from the crankshaft. Discard the seal. Carefully pry the retaining ring from the center main bearing race. Expand the ring just enough to remove it.

17A. *1984-1995 models*—Remove the bearing race halves and 2 roller cages. The rollers and cages are serviced as an assembly.

17B. *1996-1999 models*—Top guided power heads use 14 loose rollers in the center main bearing. The bearing race, rollers and retaining ring are serviced as an assembly. Do not remove the center seal ring unless the center main bearing is being replaced. The seal ring comes only as an assembly with the center main bearing, it is not serviced separately.

NOTE
Do not remove the upper bearing unless it is going to be replaced. If replacement is necessary, thread the flywheel nut onto the crankshaft to protect the threads. Use a bearing separator plate and press the bearing off of the crankshaft. Use a suitable mandrel to press the bearing back

8

onto the crankshaft. Support the crank-shaft under the top counterweight when pressing the bearing on. Most early models use a thrust washer on top of the upper bearing. Check the manufac-turer's parts catalog if necessary. See **Figure 64**.

18. Reinstall the connecting rod caps and screws. Tighten the screws finger tight. Remove the piston and rod assemblies from the cylinder block.

19. Remove and discard the piston rings with the ring expander (part No. FT-8926) or equivalent. See **Figure 65**.

20A. *1984-1987 models*—If the pistons are to be removed from the connecting rods, remove both snap rings from each piston with a snap ring pliers (part No. FT-1749). Discard the snap-rings.

20B. *1988-1989A models*—The piston pins are retained by an interference fit between the piston pin bore and the piston pin.

20C. *1989B-1999 models*—If the pistons are to be removed from the connecting rods, remove both lock rings from each piston by carefully prying them out with lock ring tool part No. 91-77109A-2 or equivalent. Discard the lock rings.

21A. *1988-1989A models*—Place the piston in pillow block (part No. FT-2990) and insert the end of the shim bar (from FT-2990 kit) marked 295 between the spacer and needles. Press the pin from the piston with the stepped end of the driver (from FT-2990 kit). Collect the 2 spacers and 26 loose needles. Keep all rod assembly parts separate from the other rod assemblies. Repeat this step for the remaining pistons. See **Figure 66**.

21B. *1984-1987 and 1989B-1995 models*—Place the piston in pillow block (FT-2990) and press the pin from the piston with a suitable driver. Collect the 2 spacers and 26 loose needles. Keep all rod assembly parts separate from the other rod assemblies. Repeat this step for the remaining pistons. See **Figure 54**.

21C. *1996 models*—Place the piston in pillow block (part No. FT-2990) and press the pin from the piston with driver (part No. 91-74607A-3). Collect the 2 spacers and 29 loose needles. Keep all rod assembly parts separate from the other rod assemblies. Repeat this step for the remaining pistons. See **Figure 54**.

60 hp

NOTE
All internal components should be marked (if possible) or stored in sepa-rate containers for reference during re-assembly.

Refer to **Figure 67** and **Figure 68** for this procedure.

1. Remove the 6 upper bearing cage screws. Remove the upper bearing cage from the power

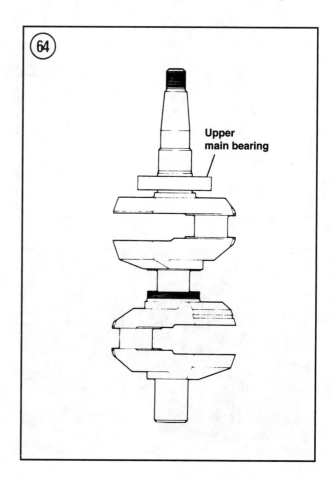

(64)

Upper
main bearing

head. Remove and discard the gasket. Press the seal out of the bearing cage with a suitable mandrel. Discard the seal.

2. Remove the 2 screws holding the bypass valve to the cylinder head. Remove the bypass valve and gasket. Discard the gasket.

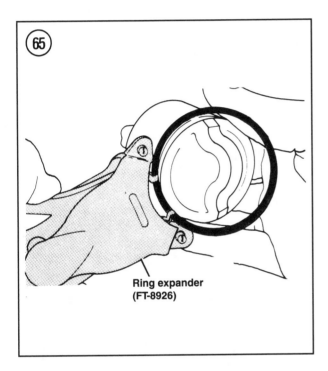

Ring expander (FT-8926)

3. Remove the 3 screws holding the thermostat cover to the cylinder head. Remove the cover, thermostat, grommet and gasket. Discard the gasket. See **Figure 67**.

4. Remove the water temperature switch from the cylinder head.

5. Remove the cylinder head bolts. Remove the cylinder head and gasket. Discard the gasket.

6. Remove the 2 cylinder head cover screws. Carefully remove the cylinder head cover and gasket. Discard the gasket.

7. Remove the exhaust cover screws. Carefully pry the outer and inner exhaust covers from the cylinder block and each other. Discard the gaskets.

8. Remove the 4 screws holding the forward stabilizer to the cylinder head. Remove the stabilizer. See **Figure 69**.

9. Remove the 4 screws holding the lower bearing cage to the power head. Remove the lower bearing cage.

10. Remove the 4 screws holding the gear shift and lever to the power head. Remove the gear shift and lever. See **Figure 70**.

8

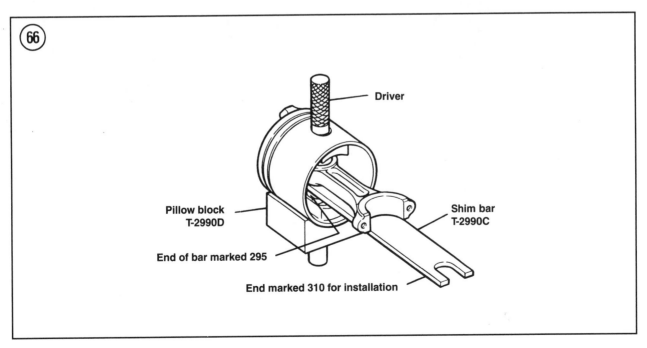

Driver

Pillow block
T-2990D

Shim bar
T-2990C

End of bar marked 295

End marked 310 for installation

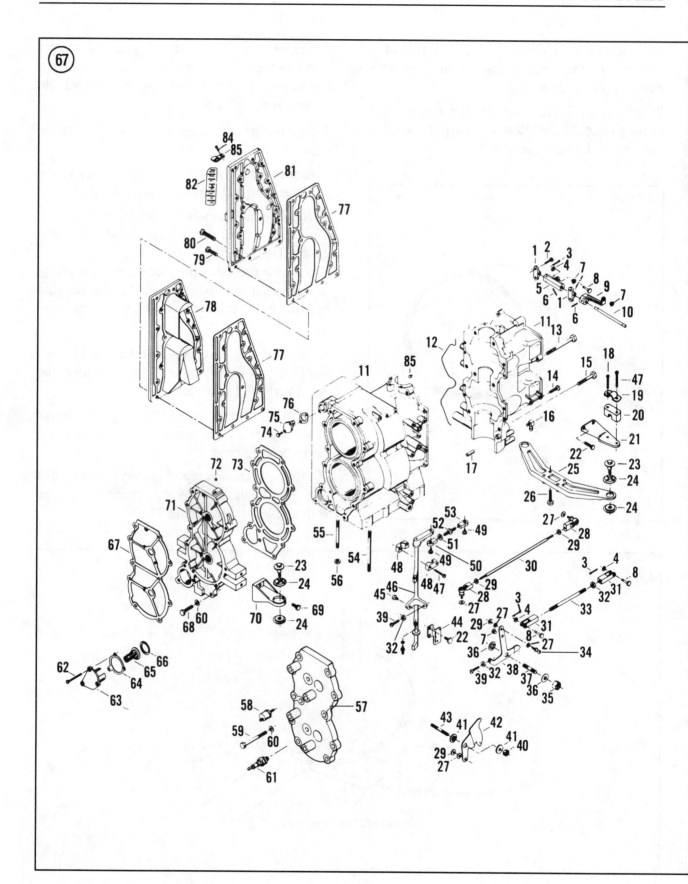

POWER HEAD (60 HP MODELS)

1. Bearing
2. Screw
3. Cotter pin
4. Plain washer
5. Gear shift pivot
6. Roll pin
7. Shift coupler
8. Gear shift pin
9. Gear shift lever
10. Gear shift shaft
11. Cylinder and crankcase cover assembly
12. Spaghetti seal
13. Cap screw
14. Hex head screw
15. Hex head cap screw
16. Drain fitting
17. Locating pin
18. Slotted screw
19. Cable clamp
20. Control cable spacer
21. Remote cable bracket
22. Cap screw
23. Support plate mount fastener
24. Mount
25. Front stabilizer
26. Hex cap screw
27. Internal tooth lockwasher
28. Ball-joint and bearing
29. Hex nut
30. Throttle link
31. Coupler
32. Hex nut
33. Gear shift link
34. Connecter stud rod end
35. Stop nut
36. Shift arm bearing
37. Shift arm stud
38. Shift arm
39. Screw
40. Stop nut
41. Throttle cam bearing
42. Throttle cam
43. Throttle cam stud
44. Interlock switch bracket
45. Plastic rivet
46. Tower shaft
47. Screw
48. Tower shaft bearing
49. Spark control swivel
50. Spark control bearing
51. Hex nut
52. Spark control link
53. Control link bearing
54. Cylinder stud
55. Cylinder stud
56. Locknut
57. Cylinder head cover
58. Thermoswitch
59. Hex cap screw
60. Plain washer
61. Spark plug
62. Hex cap screw
63. Thermostat cover
64. Thermostat cover gasket
65. Thermostat
66. Thermostat grommet
67. Cylinder head cover gasket
68. Hex cap screw
69. Hex cap screw
70. Rear stabilizer
71. Cylinder head
72. Cylinder head plug
73. Cylinder head gasket
74. Hex cap screw
75. Bypass valve cover
76. Bypass valve cover gasket
77. Exhaust port plate gasket
78. Exhaust port plate
79. Hex cap screw
80. Hex cap screw
81. Exhaust port cover
82. Wiring decal
83. Clamp
84. Screw and lockwasher
85. Locating pin

8

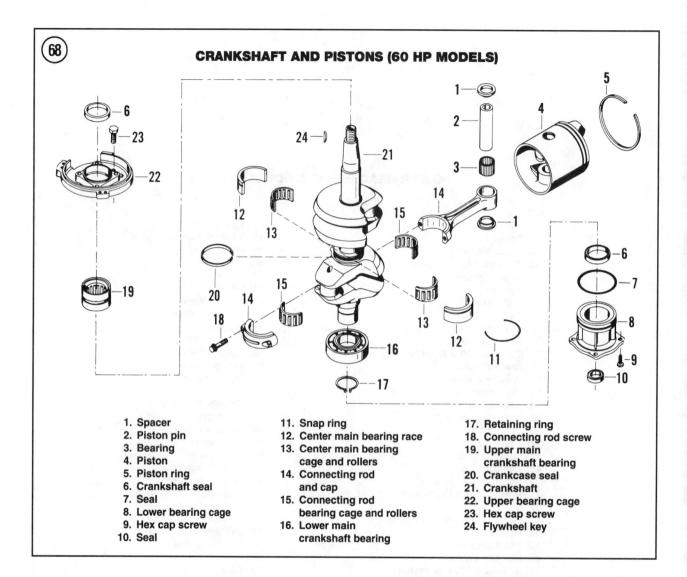

CRANKSHAFT AND PISTONS (60 HP MODELS)

1. Spacer
2. Piston pin
3. Bearing
4. Piston
5. Piston ring
6. Crankshaft seal
7. Seal
8. Lower bearing cage
9. Hex cap screw
10. Seal
11. Snap ring
12. Center main bearing race
13. Center main bearing
   cage and rollers
14. Connecting rod
   and cap
15. Connecting rod
   bearing cage and rollers
16. Lower main
   crankshaft bearing
17. Retaining ring
18. Connecting rod screw
19. Upper main
   crankshaft bearing
20. Crankcase seal
21. Crankshaft
22. Upper bearing cage
23. Hex cap screw
24. Flywheel key

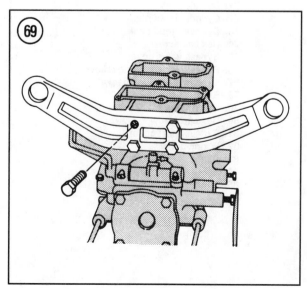

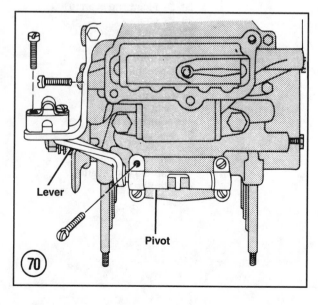

Lever

Pivot

11. Remove the 8 crankcase cover outer screws and the 6 main bearing bolts from the power head.

12. With the crankcase and cylinder block assembly on a solid surface, drive out the 2 locating pins using a suitable punch.

13. Carefully pry the crankcase cover from the cylinder block. Do not scratch the sealing surfaces. Remove the crankcase seal from each side of the crankcase. See **Figure 63**.

14. Mark the pistons, rod caps and connecting rods with a permanent felt tip marker as to the cylinder and direction they were removed from.

15. Remove the rod cap screws, rod caps and rod bearing cage sets. Place each rod assembly's parts in separate containers. There are 16 rollers on each connecting rod bearing.

16. Remove the crankshaft. Slide the upper bearing from the crankshaft. Carefully pry the retaining ring from the center main bearing race. Expand the ring just enough to remove it. Remove the bearing race halves and 2 roller cages. The rollers and cages are serviced as an assembly. Remove and discard the center seal ring.

NOTE
Do not remove the lower bearing unless it is going to be replaced. If replacement is necessary, remove the snap ring. Use a bearing separator plate and press the bearing off of the crankshaft. Use a suitable mandrel to press the bearing back onto the crankshaft. Support the crankshaft under the bottom counterweight when pressing the bearing on.

17. Reinstall the connecting rod caps and screws. Tighten the screws finger tight. Remove the piston and rod assemblies from the cylinder block.

18. Remove and discard the piston rings with the ring expander (part No. FT-8926) or equivalent. See **Figure 65**.

19. Further disassembly is not warranted as the piston and connecting rod are serviced as an assembly.

70-150 hp (Including L-Drives)

NOTE
*The 1996-1999 75, 90 and 120 hp models use a top-guided power head design. This means that the connecting rods are centered vertically by the piston, not the crankshaft. While service procedures are similar between the new top guided power head and the older bottom guided power heads, very few parts are interchangeable. See **Figure 71**.*

NOTE
Mark all internal components (if possible) and/or store in separate containers for reference during reassembly. Due to the large volume of fasteners on larger power heads, use a container (such as a cupcake tin) or zipper strip sandwich bags to keep the fasteners organized.

Figure 72 and **Figure 73** show typical early model 3 and 4-cylinder power heads. The 5-cylinder power head is simply a 4-cylinder with another cylinder added in the middle. The main visual difference between the 70/75 hp and 85/90 hp 3-cylinder models is the intake manifold mounting pad, internal power head components are quite similar. L-Drives use unique pistons, so do not interchange with outboard models. All L-Drive pistons use snap rings to retain the piston pins. The 1984-1994 outboard models use an interference fit to retain the piston pin, while 1995 and newer outboard models use snap rings or lock clips to retain the piston pin. Late outboard models use check valves and elbows for the recirculation system instead of cylinder drain covers. Refer to Chapter Six for recirculation system diagrams.

1. Remove the upper bearing cage screws. Remove the upper bearing cage from the power

8

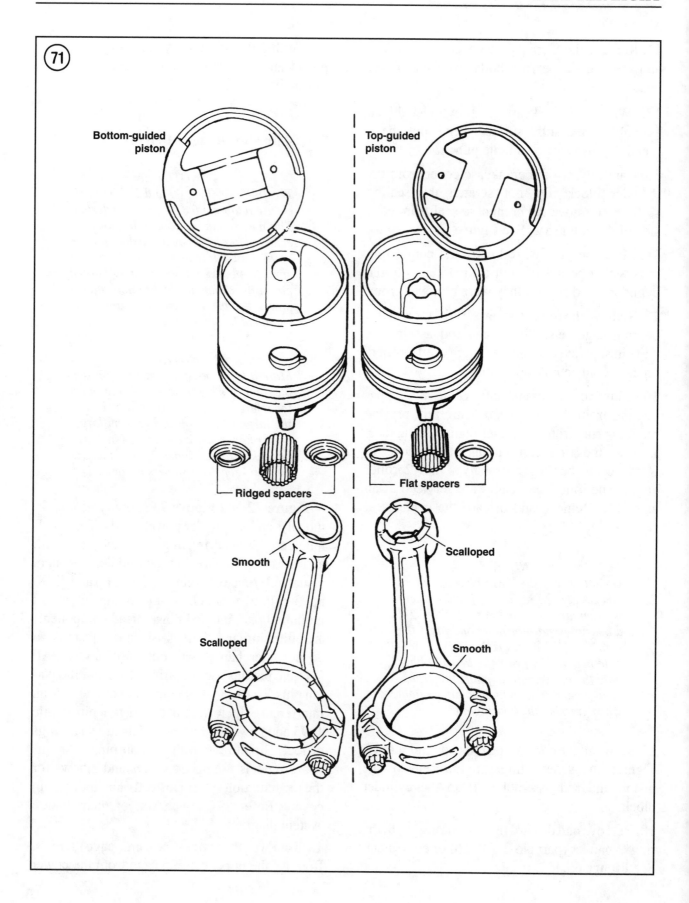

71

Bottom-guided
piston

Top-guided
piston

Ridged spacers

Flat spacers

Smooth

Scalloped

Scalloped

Smooth

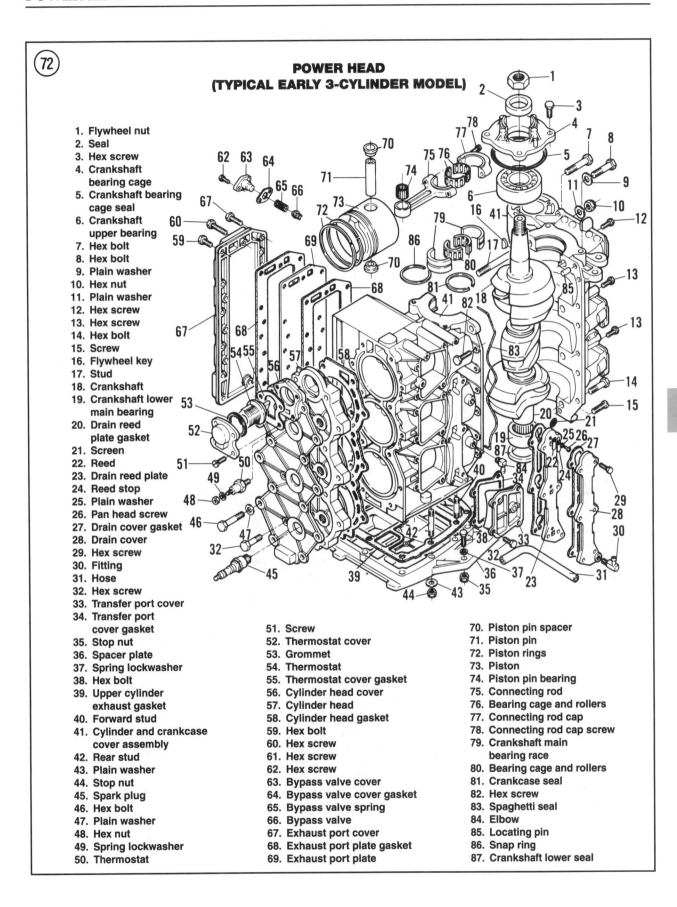

**POWER HEAD
(TYPICAL EARLY 3-CYLINDER MODEL)**

1. Flywheel nut
2. Seal
3. Hex screw
4. Crankshaft bearing cage
5. Crankshaft bearing cage seal
6. Crankshaft upper bearing
7. Hex bolt
8. Hex bolt
9. Plain washer
10. Hex nut
11. Plain washer
12. Hex screw
13. Hex screw
14. Hex bolt
15. Screw
16. Flywheel key
17. Stud
18. Crankshaft
19. Crankshaft lower main bearing
20. Drain reed plate gasket
21. Screen
22. Reed
23. Drain reed plate
24. Reed stop
25. Plain washer
26. Pan head screw
27. Drain cover gasket
28. Drain cover
29. Hex screw
30. Fitting
31. Hose
32. Hex screw
33. Transfer port cover
34. Transfer port cover gasket
35. Stop nut
36. Spacer plate
37. Spring lockwasher
38. Hex bolt
39. Upper cylinder exhaust gasket
40. Forward stud
41. Cylinder and crankcase cover assembly
42. Rear stud
43. Plain washer
44. Stop nut
45. Spark plug
46. Hex bolt
47. Plain washer
48. Hex nut
49. Spring lockwasher
50. Thermostat

51. Screw
52. Thermostat cover
53. Grommet
54. Thermostat
55. Thermostat cover gasket
56. Cylinder head cover
57. Cylinder head
58. Cylinder head gasket
59. Hex bolt
60. Hex screw
61. Hex screw
62. Hex screw
63. Bypass valve cover
64. Bypass valve cover gasket
65. Bypass valve spring
66. Bypass valve
67. Exhaust port cover
68. Exhaust port plate gasket
69. Exhaust port plate

70. Piston pin spacer
71. Piston pin
72. Piston rings
73. Piston
74. Piston pin bearing
75. Connecting rod
76. Bearing cage and rollers
77. Connecting rod cap
78. Connecting rod cap screw
79. Crankshaft main bearing race
80. Bearing cage and rollers
81. Crankcase seal
82. Hex screw
83. Spaghetti seal
84. Elbow
85. Locating pin
86. Snap ring
87. Crankshaft lower seal

8

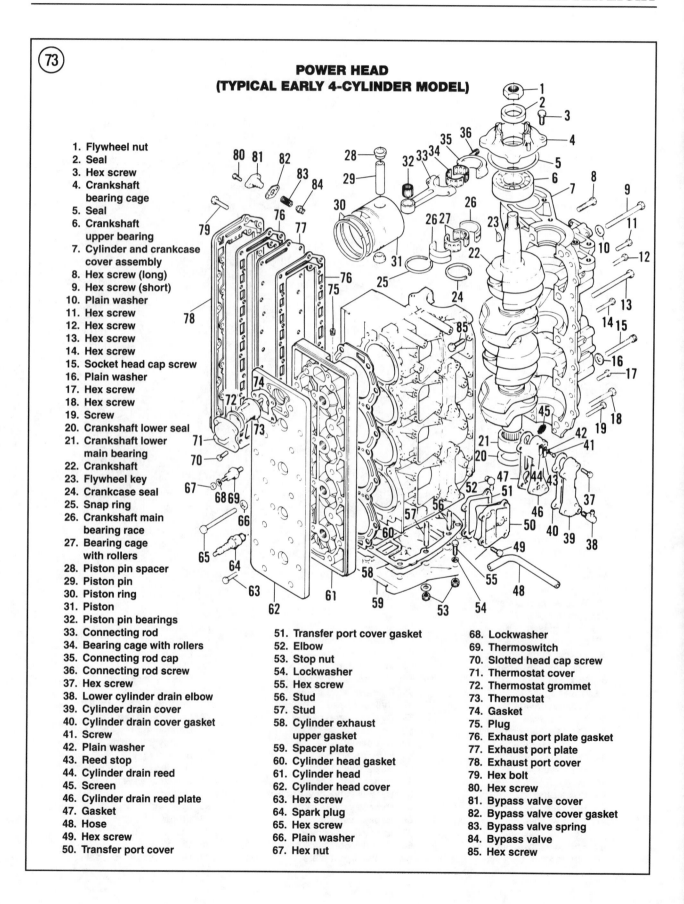

**POWER HEAD
(TYPICAL EARLY 4-CYLINDER MODEL)**

1. Flywheel nut
2. Seal
3. Hex screw
4. Crankshaft
   bearing cage
5. Seal
6. Crankshaft
   upper bearing
7. Cylinder and crankcase
   cover assembly
8. Hex screw (long)
9. Hex screw (short)
10. Plain washer
11. Hex screw
12. Hex screw
13. Hex screw
14. Hex screw
15. Socket head cap screw
16. Plain washer
17. Hex screw
18. Hex screw
19. Screw
20. Crankshaft lower seal
21. Crankshaft lower
    main bearing
22. Crankshaft
23. Flywheel key
24. Crankcase seal
25. Snap ring
26. Crankshaft main
    bearing race
27. Bearing cage
    with rollers
28. Piston pin spacer
29. Piston pin
30. Piston ring
31. Piston
32. Piston pin bearings
33. Connecting rod
34. Bearing cage with rollers
35. Connecting rod cap
36. Connecting rod screw
37. Hex screw
38. Lower cylinder drain elbow
39. Cylinder drain cover
40. Cylinder drain cover gasket
41. Screw
42. Plain washer
43. Reed stop
44. Cylinder drain reed
45. Screen
46. Cylinder drain reed plate
47. Gasket
48. Hose
49. Hex screw
50. Transfer port cover

51. Transfer port cover gasket
52. Elbow
53. Stop nut
54. Lockwasher
55. Hex screw
56. Stud
57. Stud
58. Cylinder exhaust
    upper gasket
59. Spacer plate
60. Cylinder head gasket
61. Cylinder head
62. Cylinder head cover
63. Hex screw
64. Spark plug
65. Hex screw
66. Plain washer
67. Hex nut

68. Lockwasher
69. Thermoswitch
70. Slotted head cap screw
71. Thermostat cover
72. Thermostat grommet
73. Thermostat
74. Gasket
75. Plug
76. Exhaust port plate gasket
77. Exhaust port plate
78. Exhaust port cover
79. Hex bolt
80. Hex screw
81. Bypass valve cover
82. Bypass valve cover gasket
83. Bypass valve spring
84. Bypass valve
85. Hex screw

head. Press the seal out of the bearing cage with a suitable mandrel. Discard the seal.

2. *Early 85 and 125 hp models*—Remove the 2 bolts securing the bypass valve to the power head (located in the front lower exhaust cover area). Remove the bypass valve assembly and gasket. Discard the gasket.

3. Remove the 4 screws holding the thermostat cover to the cylinder head. Remove the cover, by-pass spring (late models), thermostat, grommet and gasket. Discard the gasket. See **Figure 74**, late models.

4. Remove the cylinder head bolts. Remove the cylinder head and gasket. Discard the gasket.

5. Remove any remaining cylinder head cover screws and the water temperature switch. Carefully remove the cylinder head cover and gasket. Discard the gasket.

NOTE
Updated L-Drive models use a new 1 piece gasket to take the place of the inner exhaust plate and gaskets. 3-cylinder L-Drive gasket update kit is part No. 819477A-1. 4-cylinder gasket kit is part No. 819729A-1. These kits were introduced to suppress water entry into the cylinders. An updated 4-cylinder exhaust manifold kit part No. FK698866

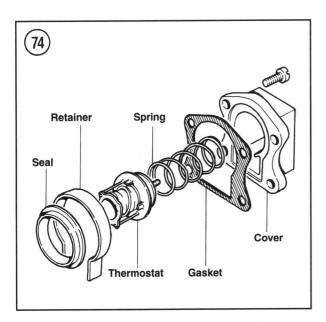

(exhaust manifold, water pump, water hose and gasket and fastener kit) is also available. Follow the instructions included with the kit.

6A. *Outboards*—Remove the exhaust cover screws. Carefully pry the outer exhaust cover and inner exhaust plate from the cylinder block and each other. Discard the gaskets.

6B. *L-Drives*—Remove the exhaust manifold screws. Remove the exhaust manifold and gasket(s). Discard the gasket(s). See **Figure 75**.

7. Remove the screws from all transfer port covers. Disconnect any recirculation hoses. Carefully pry the transfer port covers loose from the cylinder block. Remove and discard the gaskets.

8. *Early models*—Remove the cylinder drain cover(s) screws. Carefully pry the cylinder cover(s) loose from the cylinder block. Separate the plate from the cylinder drain cover(s) if so equipped. Remove and discard all gasket(s). See Chapter Six.

9. Remove the crankcase cover outer screws and the main bearing screws from the power head. There are 2 crankcase cover outer screws on the cylinder head side of the power head.

NOTE
On 3-cylinder L-Drive engines, the lower locating pin cannot be driven completely out in Step 10.

10. With the crankcase and cylinder block assembly on a solid surface, drive out the 2 locating pins using a suitable punch. See **Figure 76**.

NOTE
Pry points are located on the same corners as the locating pins on 3-cylinder models. On 4 and 5-cylinder models, the pry points are located at the opposite corners of the locating pins.

11. Carefully pry the crankcase cover from the cylinder block. Do not scratch the sealing

8

surfaces. Remove the crankcase seal from each side of the crankcase if so equipped.

12. Mark the pistons, rod caps and connecting rods with a permanent felt tip marker as to the cylinder and direction they were removed from.

13. Using special tool part No. FT-2953 or equivalent 12 point socket, remove the rod cap screws, rod caps and rod bearing cage sets. Place each rod assembly's parts in separate containers.

CAUTION
*Retrieve any dropped bearing rollers using a swab covered with needle bearing assembly grease (**Table 8**). Do not use a magnet on rollers or other internal components.*

14. Remove the crankshaft. Slide the lower seal and bearing down just far enough to insert a screwdriver behind the seal and pry it from the

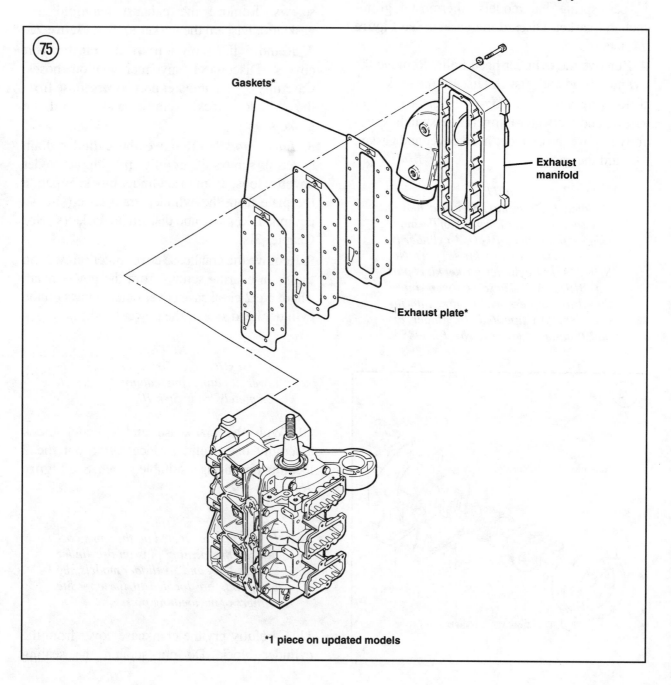

(75)

Gaskets*

Exhaust manifold

Exhaust plate*

*1 piece on updated models

bearing. Discard the seal. Remove the bearing from the crankshaft.

15. Carefully pry the retaining ring from each center main bearing race. Expand the ring just enough to remove it.

16. Remove each center bearing assembly (2 race halves and 2 roller cages). The rollers and cages are serviced as an assembly. Remove each seal ring (located just below each center main bearing area) and discard it.

NOTE
Do not remove the upper bearing unless it is going to be replaced. If replacement is necessary, thread the flywheel nut onto the crankshaft to protect the threads. Use a bearing separator plate and press the bearing off of the crankshaft. Use a suitable mandrel to press the bearing back onto the crankshaft. Support the crankshaft under the top counterweight when pressing the bearing on.

17. Reinstall the connecting rod caps and screws. Tighten the screws finger tight. Remove the piston and rod assemblies from the cylinder block.

18. Remove and discard the piston rings with the ring expander (part No. FT-8926) or equivalent. See **Figure 65**.

19A. *1984-1994 models*—If the pistons must be removed from the connecting rod, inspect the piston pin bore for snap rings or lock clips. Original 1984-1994 outboard models are not equipped with piston pin locking devices. The piston pin is retained by an interference fit between the piston pin and the piston pin bore. L-Drive models use lock clips that must be pried out with a suitable tool. If snap rings or lock clips are present on any models, remove them with the appropriate tool. Discard any lock clips or snap rings removed.

19B. *1995 models*—If the pistons are to be removed from the connecting rods, remove both snap rings from each piston with a snap ring pliers (part No. FT-1749). Discard the snap-rings.

19C. *1996-1999 models*—If the pistons are to be removed from the connecting rods, remove both lock rings from each piston by carefully prying them out with lock ring tool part No. 91-77109A-2 or equivalent. Discard the lock rings.

20A. *1984-1994 outboard models*—Place the piston in pillow block (part No. FT-2990) and insert the end of the shim bar (from FT-2990 kit) marked 295 between the spacer and needles. Press the pin from the piston with the stepped end of the driver (from FT-2990 kit). Collect the 2 spacers and 26 loose needles. Keep all rod assembly parts separate from the other rod assemblies. Repeat this step for the remaining pistons. See **Figure 66**.

20B *L-Drives and 1995 outboard models*— Place the piston in pillow block (part No. FT-2990) and press the pin from the piston with a suitable driver. Collect the 2 spacers and 26 loose needles. Keep all rod assembly parts separate from the other rod assemblies. Repeat this step for the remaining pistons. See **Figure 54**.

20C. *1996-1999 models*—Place the piston in pillow block (part No. FT-2990) and press the pin from the piston with driver (part No.

8

91-74607A-3). Collect the 2 spacers and 29 loose needles. Keep all rod assembly parts separate from the other rod assemblies. Repeat this step for the remaining pistons. See **Figure 54**.

POWER HEAD
CLEANING/INSPECTION

Cylinder Block and Crankcase

The cylinder block and crankcase cover on all models are matched and align-bored assemblies. For this reason, no attempt should be made to assemble a power head from components salvaged from other crankcase and cylinder block assemblies. If inspection indicates that either the block or cover requires replacement, replace both as an assembly.

Carefully remove all gasket and sealant residue from the cylinder block and crankcase cover mating surfaces using a suitable solvent. Clean the aluminum surfaces carefully to prevent nicks, scratches or other damage. A dull putty knife may be used, but a piece of Lucite with one edge ground to a 45° angle works well and will reduce the possibility of damage to the surfaces. When sealing the crankcase cover and cylinder block, both mating surfaces must be free of all sealant residue, dirt, oil or other contamination, or leaks will develop.

Once the gasket surfaces are thoroughly cleaned, place the mating surface of each component on a surface plate such as a large pane of glass. Apply uniform downward pressure on the component and check for warpage at several locations by trying to insert a feeler gage between the surface plate and the component mating surface. See **Figure 77**. The cylinder head on all models should be replaced if warped in excess of 0.012 in. The exhaust manifold on L-Drive models should be replaced if warped in excess of 0.003 in.

Slight warpage can often be eliminated by placing a large sheet of No. 120 emery cloth over the surface plate. Apply a slight amount of pressure and move the component in a figure-eight pattern. See **Figure 78**. Remove the component and emery cloth and recheck surface flatness on the surface plate.

If warpage exists, the high spots will be dull while low areas will remain unchanged in appearance. It may be necessary to repeat this procedure 2-3 times until the entire mating surface has been lapped. Do not remove more than 0.010 in. from the cylinder block or head. Finish the lapping procedure using No. 180 emery cloth.

1. Clean the cylinder block and crankcase cover thoroughly with solvent and brush.

2. Carefully remove all gasket and sealant from the cylinder block and crankcase cover mating surfaces.

3. Check the cylinder head and exhaust ports for excessive carbon deposits or varnish. Remove carbon using a suitable scraper or other blunt tool.

4. Check the block, cylinder head and cover for cracks, fractures, stripped threads or other damage.

5. Check the cylinder head and block gasket surfaces for nicks, grooves, cracks or excessive warpage. Any of the above defects may result in

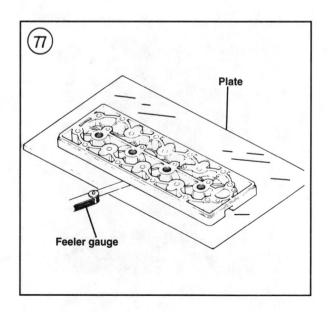

compression leakage. Replace components as required.

6. Check all oil and water passages in the block and cover for corrosion or other obstructions. Make sure any plugs are properly installed and tightened.

7. Inspect the cylinder drain plate reeds for wear or damage. Check the drain screens to make sure they are open. Replace reeds or screens as required.

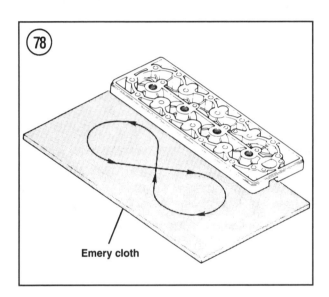

Emery cloth

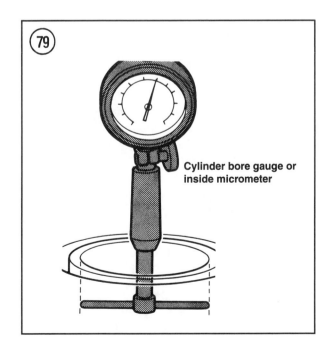

Cylinder bore gauge or inside micrometer

NOTE
Hone the cylinder walls with a medium stone even if cylinder walls appear to be in acceptable condition. Honing will remove any glazing that will interfere with proper piston ring seating (break-in).

8. Check each cylinder bore for aluminum transfer from the pistons to the cylinder walls. If light scoring is present, and the cylinder is within wear tolerances, the scoring may be removed by honing. It may be preferable to have the cylinders honed by a dealer or qualified machine shop.

9. Measure each cylinder bore at 3 points with an inside micrometer or cylinder bore gage. See **Figure 79**. Measure the cylinders at the following locations:

    a. 1/4 in. (6.3 mm) down from the top of the bore.

    b. 1/4 in. (6.3 mm) up from the exhaust port.

    c. 3/16 in. (4.8 mm) down from the lower edge of the intake port.

Repeat the measurements at 90° to the first measurements. If cylinder bore is worn, tapered in excess of 0.002 in. (0.05 mm) or measurably out of round, the cylinder bores must be bored to the next oversize by a qualified machine shop.

NOTE
The manufacturer provides pistons and rings in 0.010 in. and 0.030 in. oversizes. If the cylinders are worn, out-of-round or tapered in excess of 0.030 in., the cylinder block and crankcase cover must be replaced.

Main and Connecting Rod Bearings

Bearings may be reused if in good condition; however, it is a good idea to replace all bearings whenever the engine is disassembled. New bearings are inexpensive compared to the cost of another overhaul caused by the use of marginal bearings.

1. Remove old sealer from the outer edge of the upper or lower ball bearing with a scraper, then

clean the outer edge with Locquic Primer (part No. FT-8935).

2. Place ball bearings in a wire basket and submerge in a suitable container of fresh solvent. The bottom of the basket should not touch the bottom of the container. Agitate the basket to loosen all grease, sludge and other contamination.

3. Dry ball bearings with compressed air. Be careful not to spin the bearings.

4. Lubricate the bearings with a light coat of engine oil and inspect bearings for rust, scuffed surfaces, heat discoloration or other damage. Replace bearings as required.

5. If needle bearings are to be reused, repeat Steps 2-4, cleaning one set at a time to prevent possible mixup. Check bearings for flat spots. If one needle bearing roller is defective, replace all in the set with new bearing rollers and liners.

Piston and Connecting Rod

1. Check piston(s) for scoring, cracking, cracked or worn piston pin bores or other damage. Replace piston and pin as an assembly if any defects are noted.

2. Check piston ring grooves for distortion, loose ring locating pins or excessive wear.

NOTE
Do not use an automotive ring groove cleaning tool in Step 3 as it can damage the piston and piston ring locating pin.

3. Clean the piston ring grooves with the recessed end of a broken ring to remove any carbon deposits. Then, thoroughly clean the ring grooves with a suitable brush and solvent.

4. Immerse pistons in a carbon removal solution to remove any carbon deposits not removed in Step 3. If the solution does not remove all carbon, carefully use a fine wire brush; avoid burring or rounding of the machined edges. Clean the piston skirt with crocus cloth.

NOTE
*Refer to **Table 6** or **Table 7** for internal engine specifications. Refer to **Table 1** for connecting rod torque specifications.*

5. Measure the piston skirt and compare to specifications. If only one piston skirt specification is given, measure the skirt dimension at a right angle to the piston pin bore. If a major and minor dimension are given, the piston is cam ground and must be measured at a right angle to the piston pin bore *and* parallel to the piston pin bore as specified. The 25 hp 3-cylinder is measured at a right angle to the piston pin bore 0.050 in. (1.27 mm) from the bottom of the skirt. The 1996 40-120 hp top guided pistons are measured at a right angle to the piston pin bore 0.150 in. (3.81 mm) from the bottom of the skirt. Inspect the piston for damage to the deflector on the piston crown (cross-charged models) and wear or scuffing to the top land, ring grooves and piston skirt contact areas. Measure the piston pin bore. Replace the piston and pin if damaged, excessive wear is noted or measurements are out of specifications.

NOTE
*The connecting rod torque process for 1995 and newer 40-120 hp is the torque and turn process. Oil the rod screw threads and underside of the screw head. Install the rod cap and hand tighten the bolts. Check and adjust the alignment of the cap. Torque the rod screws to 120 in.-lb. (13.6 N•m) and then turn each rod bolt an additional 90° rotation. Refer to **Table 1** for all connecting rod screw torque specifications.*

6. Install the connecting rod cap on its respective connecting rod. Make sure the cap is orientated and aligned properly. Secure the rod in a soft jawed vise. Tighten the rod screws to the specification listed in **Table 1**. Measure the connecting rod big end and small end inside diameters. Replace the connecting rod if the measurements are out of specifications.

NOTE
The connecting rod small end bearing on 4-15 hp models can only be replaced as an assembly with the connecting rod. Also, on 9.9 and 15 hp (1984-1987A), aluminum rods are superseded to steel rods when replaced.

Crankshaft

1. Clean the crankshaft thoroughly with a suitable solvent and dry with compressed air. Lightly lubricate crankshaft with a recommended engine oil.

2. Inspect the crankshaft journals and crankpins for excessive wear, scratches, heat discoloration or other damage. Check crankshaft journal and crankpin dimensions with a micrometer and compare with specifications. Replace the crankshaft if journals or crankpins are tapered, out-of-round or excessively worn.

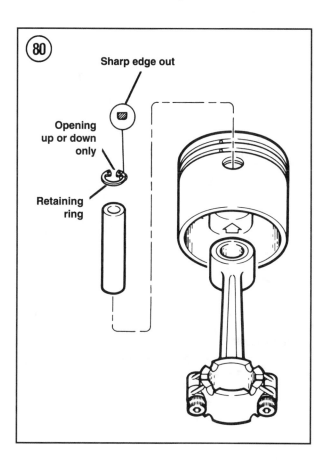

3. Inspect drive shaft splines in the crankshaft, flywheel taper, flywheel nut threads and flywheel key slot for excessive wear or damage.

4. If the upper or lower crankshaft ball bearing has not been removed, grasp inner race and attempt to work it back and forth. Replace the bearing if excessive play is noted.

5. Lubricate ball bearings with a recommended engine oil and carefully inspect bearing. Replace bearings if rusted, pitted, rough or if it does not rotate smoothly.

PISTON AND CONNECTING ROD

Assembly (4-15 hp)

If the pistons are removed from the connecting rods, they must be correctly oriented when reassembling. During the assembly operation, the piston ring groove staking pins must always face up as viewed in **Figure 80**. When the piston pin retaining ring is installed, the sharp edge of the retaining ring must face out and the retaining ring gap must face up or down (parallel to cylinder bore). Assemble the piston, connecting rod and piston pin as follows:

   a. *4 and 5 hp*—The match marks or v-slot on the connecting rod must face up (to the right). The open end of the piston pin must face up. The piston ring groove staking pins must face up.

   b. *7.5 hp*—The match marks or V-slot of the connecting rod must face up (to the right). The open end of the piston pin must face down. The piston ring groove staking pins must face up.

   c. *1984-1987A 9.9 and 15 hp*—The match marks or V-slot of the connecting rod must face down (to the left). The open end of the piston pin must face down. The piston ring groove staking pins must face up.

   d. *1988-on 9.9 and 15 hp*—The match marks or V-slot of the connecting rod (if present) must face up (to the right). The open end of

8

the piston pin must face up. The piston ring groove staking pins must face up.

1. Coat piston pin bore, piston pin and connecting rod small end bore with a recommended engine oil.

2. Place piston on pillow block (part No. FT-2990) with piston ring locating pins facing upward.

3. Warm piston pin bore with a suitable heat gun. *Do not* use open flame to heat piston.

4. Position connecting rod as described previously and install the piston pin through the piston and connecting rod with piston pin driver (part No. FT-8919). See **Figure 81**.

5. Install new piston pin retaining rings with suitable snap ring pliers. Make sure sharp edges of the rings are facing outward and that the ring openings are facing up or down. Be certain the retaining rings are properly seated in the grooves.

6. Repeat assembly procedure for the remaining piston/connecting rod on 2-cylinder models.

**Assembly
(25 hp 3-cylinder)**

If the pistons are removed from the connecting rods, they must be correctly orientated when reassembling. During the assembly operation, the piston and connecting rod scribed identification numbers must face up. Examine the piston and connecting rod and locate the scribed identification numbers before proceeding. Piston pin tool part No.91-13663A-1 or equivalent will be required for the following procedure.

Assemble the piston, connecting rod and piston pin as follows:

1. Liberally lubricate the connecting rod small end loose roller bearings with needle bearing assembly grease (**Table 8**). Insert the rollers into the connecting rod and hold them in place with the sleeve of the piston tool part No.91-13663A-1.

2. Place a thrust bearing (spacer) on each side of the connecting rod small end bore. Position both the piston and connecting rod assembly with the scribed identification numbers up and insert the rod assembly into the piston.

3. While maintaining alignment of the piston pin bore to the connecting rod bearing bore, insert the piston pin tool into the piston pin bore and push the sleeve completely from the piston.

4. Lubricate the piston pin with clean 2-cycle outboard motor oil and place the pin over the protruding portion of the piston pin tool. Tap the piston pin with a soft faced hammer into position (driving the tool back out the side it originally entered).

5. Make sure the piston pin is centered in the pin bore and install new piston pin lock rings into the grooves on both ends of the piston. Verify that the lock rings have fully seated into the grooves.

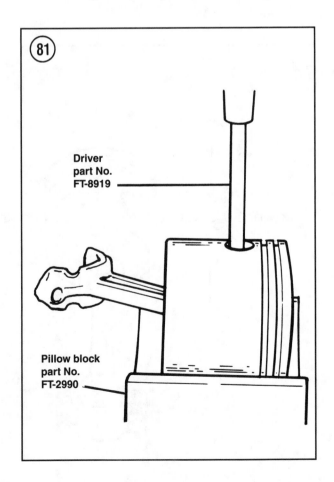

(81)

Driver
part No.
FT-8919

Pillow block
part No.
FT-2990

6. Repeat Steps 1-5 for the remaining pistons and connecting rods.

Assembly
(25 hp 2-cylinder, 35 hp, 1984-1987 50 hp, 1989b-1995 40 and 50 hp, 1995 70-120 hp Models and All L-Drive Models)

If the pistons are removed from the connecting rods, they must be correctly oriented during re-assembly. The connecting rod match marks are a bevel cut on one side of the connecting rod and

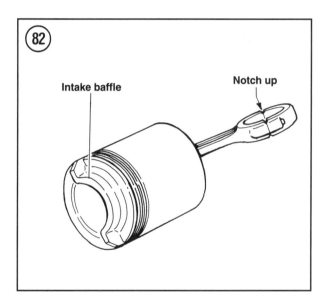

82

Intake baffle   Notch up

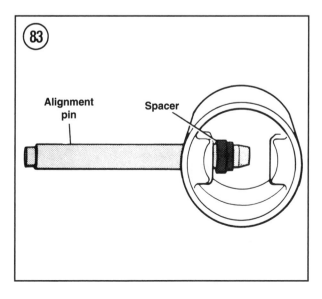

83

Alignment pin   Spacer

cap at the fracture line. Assemble the piston and connecting rod so the intake baffle side of the piston crown will face to starboard and the bevel match marks will face up. See **Figure 82**.

1. Heat the piston pin bore using a suitable heat gun. *Do not* use open flame to heat piston. Handle piston with a glove or shop cloth.

2. Fit the alignment pin from the piston tool set (part No. FT-2990) through one side of the piston and install a spacer on the pin with its small diameter facing the inside of the piston. See **Figure 83**.

3. Coat the connecting rod small end bore with needle bearing grease and install the 26 bearing rollers.

4. Install the connecting rod on the alignment pin. Make sure the piston and rod are properly oriented (**Figure 82**) and insert the other spacer with its small diameter facing the center of the piston. Push the alignment pin through the piston pin bore on the other side of the piston.

5. Position the piston assembly on the pillow block (part No. FT-2990). Carefully remove the alignment pin and insert the piston pin in its place. Fit the stepped end of the drive pin into the piston pin and drive the piston pin into the piston until it is centered.

6. Remove the drive pin and lubricate piston pin bearing with a recommended engine oil.

7A. *25hp, 35 hp and 1984-1987 50 hp*—Install new piston pin retaining rings into both piston grooves with snap ring pliers (part No. FT-1749). The sharp (lettered) side of the retaining rings must face out and the retaining ring gaps must face directly up or down (parallel with the cylinder bore). Make sure the retaining rings are fully seated in the piston grooves.

7B. *L-Drive and 1989B-1995 40 and 50 hp*—Install new piston pin lock rings into both piston grooves with special tool part No. FT-11291. Make sure the lock rings are fully seated in the piston grooves.

8. Repeat Steps 1-7 for each remaining piston and connecting rod.

8

Assembly
(1988-1989A 50 hp, 1984-1994 70-150 hp Outboard Motors)

If the pistons are removed from the connecting rods, they must be correctly oriented during re-assembly. The connecting rod match marks are a bevel cut into the rod and cap at the fracture line. The bevel match marks on the connecting rod must face upward and the intake baffle side of the piston crown must face toward starboard when assembled.

1. Insert the alignment pin from piston tool set (part No. FT-2990-1) through one side of the piston. Install one spacer on the alignment pin with the small diameter facing the inside of the piston (**Figure 84**).

2. Lubricate the connecting rod small end bore with needle bearing assembly grease and install 26 bearing rollers.

3. Install the connecting rod on the alignment pin. Make sure the piston and connecting rod are properly oriented (**Figure 82**). Insert the other spacer with the small diameter facing toward the center of the piston. Push the alignment pin through the second spacer and the other side of the piston.

4. Continue pushing the alignment pin through the piston pin bore, then install the shim bar from piston tool set (part No. FT-2990-1) with the end marked 310 between the connecting rod and the large end of the first spacer installed.

NOTE
If the end of shim bar marked 310 will not fit between the piston and spacer, insert the other end (marked 295).

5. Place the pillow block (piston tool set FT-2990-1) on a suitable press. Position the piston and rod assembly on the pillow block.

6. Place the piston pin on the stepped end of the alignment tool. Install the end of the driver tool (piston tool set FT-2990-1) into the piston pin. See **Figure 85**. Carefully, press the piston pin into the piston until exactly centered in piston.

CAUTION
Piston pin must be centered in piston. If pressed beyond center, press the pin out of the piston and repeat the installation procedure.

7. Remove the piston pin driver tool.

8. Lubricate piston pin bearings with a recommended oil. Repeat piston pin installation on remaining piston/connecting rod assemblies.

Assembly (1996-1999 40-120 hp Top-Guided Rods)

If the pistons are removed from the connecting rods, they must be correctly oriented when reas-

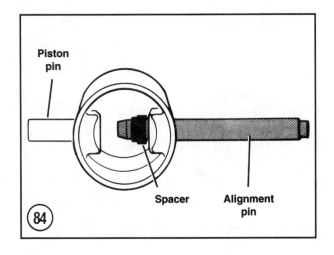

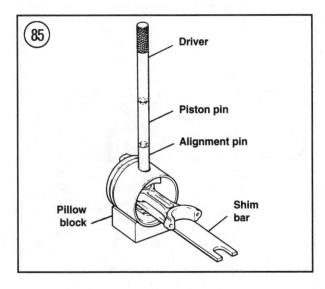

sembling. During assembly, the piston and connecting rod scribed identification numbers must face up. Examine the piston and connecting rod and locate the scribed identification numbers before proceeding. Piston pin tool part No. 91-74670A-3, lock ring removal tool part No. 91-52952A-1 and lock ring installation tool part No. 91-77109A-2 or equivalent will be required for the following procedure.

Assemble the piston, connecting rod and piston pin as follows:

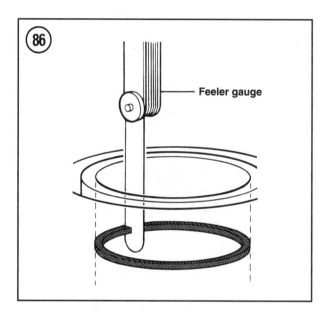

Feeler gauge

1. Liberally lubricate the connecting rod small end loose roller bearings with needle bearing assembly grease (**Table 8**). Insert rollers into the connecting rod and hold them in place with the sleeve of the piston tool part No. 91-74607A-3.

2. Place a thrust bearing (spacer) on each side of the connecting rod small end bore. Position the piston and connecting rod assembly with the scribed identification numbers up and insert the rod assembly into the piston.

3. While maintaining alignment of the piston pin bore to the connecting rod bearing bore, insert the piston pin tool into the piston pin bore and push the sleeve completely from the piston.

4. Lubricate the piston pin with clean 2-cycle outboard motor oil and place thepin over the protruding portion of the piston pin tool. Tap the piston pin with a soft faced hammer into position (driving the tool back out the side it originally entered).

5. Make sure the piston pin is centered in the pin bore and install new piston pin lock rings with tool part No. 91-77109A-2 into the grooves on both ends of the piston. Make sure the lock rings have fully seated into the grooves.

6. Repeat Steps 1-5 for the remaining pistons and connecting rods.

Piston Ring Installation (All Models)

1. Check piston ring end gap before installing on piston. Place ring in its respective cylinder just above the intake and exhaust ports. Make sure the ring is positioned squarely in the cylinder by pushing it with a piston. Measure the end gap with a feeler gauge (**Figure 86**) and compare to specifications.

2. If insufficient ring gap is present, carefully widen the gap with a suitable file.

3. If the gap is excessive with new rings, recheck the cylinder bore diameter for excessive wear.

NOTE
*Three main styles of piston rings are used. **Figure 87** (early models) shows 2*

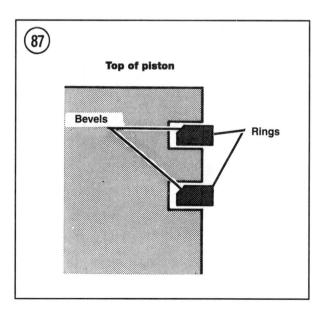

Top of piston

Bevels

Rings

8

rectangular rings. Install these rings with the bevel on the inner edge facing the top of the piston. **Figure 88** *(later models) shows a half or semi-keystone upper ring and a rectangular lower ring. Install the rectangular ring in the lower groove with the bevel on the inner edge facing the top of the piston. Install the semi-keystone ring in the upper groove with the large beveled edge facing the top of the piston.* **Figure 89** *(1996-1999 40-120 hp) shows the rings for the top guided pistons. Both rings are half or semi-keystone style. The lower ring has 2 dots on the top edge. The upper ring has 1 dot on the top edge. Install the rings with the dots facing the top of the piston.*

4. Install the lower ring on the piston with a ring expander. Spread the ring just enough to fit over the piston and place into the ring groove.

5. Repeat Step 4 to install the upper ring.

6. Make sure the ring end gaps are properly positioned around the ring groove locating pins.

Piston and Connecting Rod Installation (All Models)

1. Thoroughly lubricate the piston, rings and cylinder bore with a recommended engine oil.

> *NOTE*
> *If reusing the original pistons, be sure to install them into the cylinders from which they were removed.*

2A. *4 and 5 hp*—Place the piston assembly into the cylinder bore with the open end of the piston pin facing the *top* of the engine. See **Figure 90**.

2B. *7.5 hp*—Place the piston assembly into the cylinder bore with the open end of the piston pin facing the *bottom* of the engine.

2C. *9.9-150 hp*—Place the piston assembly into the cylinder bore with the intake baffle on the piston crown facing toward the intake ports. See **Figure 91**.

3. Insert piston into the cylinder bore. Make sure the piston ring end gaps are properly positioned around the ring locating pins.

4. Install a suitable piston ring compressor over the piston crown and rings. With the compressor resting on the cylinder head, tighten it until the rings are compressed sufficiently to enter the cylinder.

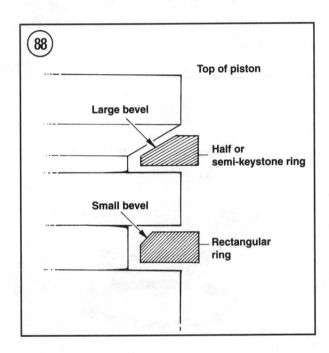

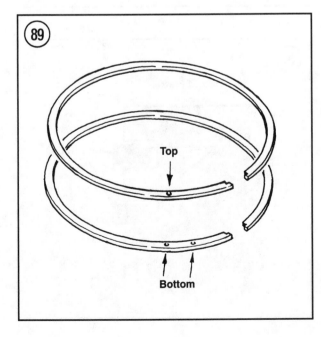

5. Hold the connecting rod end with one hand to prevent it from scraping or scratching the cylinder bore and slowly push the piston into the cylinder. See **Figure 91**.

6. Remove the ring compressor after both rings enter the cylinder. Repeat the procedure to install the remaining piston assemblies.

7. Reach through the exhaust port and lightly depress each piston ring with a pencil or small screwdriver. The ring should snap back when

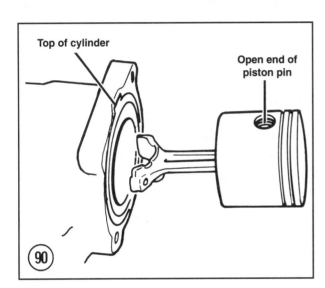

pressure is released. If not, the ring was broken during piston installation and must be replaced.

CONNECTING ROD AND CRANKSHAFT

Assembly
(4-5 hp)

Refer to **Figure 92** for this procedure.

1. Lubricate the crankshaft with a recommended engine oil. Install the crankshaft into the cylinder block making sure the retainer ring is engaged with the groove in the block.

2. Install the upper crankshaft bearing (lettered side up) with its bottom even with the inside of the crankcase wall.

3. Slide the lower seal onto the crankshaft until it bottoms. Inner sealing lip with spring must face bearing.

4. Repeat Step 3 to install the upper seal.

5. Coat connecting rod bearing cages with needle bearing assembly grease. Place one cage into the connecting rod and install the bearings.

8

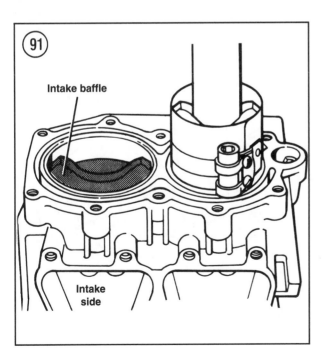

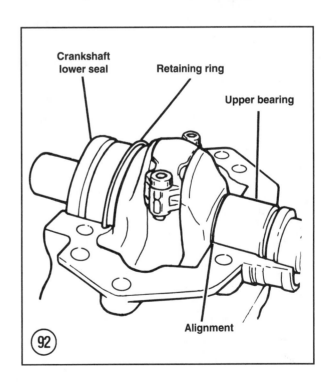

6. Position the connecting rod under the crankshaft and pull it up to the crankpin.

7. Lightly lubricate exposed area of the crankpin with needle bearing assembly grease.

8. Coat new rod cap screw threads with Loctite 271. Install rod cap and tighten the rod cap screws finger tight. Make sure the match marks on the rod and cap are aligned.

CAUTION
The procedure detailed in Step 9 is very important to proper engine operation as it affects bearing action. If not done properly, major engine damage can result. It can also be a time-consuming and frustrating process. Work slowly and with patience. If perfect alignment cannot be obtained, the connecting rod and cap assembly should be replaced.

9. Run a dental pick or pencil point along the connecting rod-to-rod cap match marks to check cap alignment. See **Figure 93**. The rod and cap must be aligned so the dental pick or pencil point will pass smoothly across the fracture line. If alignment is not correct, gently tap cap with a plastic mallet. When rod and cap are perfectly aligned, tighten rod cap screws to specifications (**Table 1**).

10. Rotate the crankshaft to check for binding at the crankpin bearing. If binding is noted, or if all crankpin bearing rollers do not rotate, remove the rod cap and check for metal chips or other contamination. Clean or replace bearing as necessary.

11. Install a new o-ring in the crankshaft lower splined bore.

**Assembly
(7.5, 9.9 and 15 hp)**

1. Press upper crankshaft ball bearing onto crankshaft, if removed. Press from lettered side of bearing. Lubricate bearing with a recommended engine oil.

2. Lubricate the lower main bearing with a recommended engine oil. Slide the bearing onto the crankshaft with the lettered side of the bearing facing outward.

3. Place the center main bearing liner into the cylinder block making sure the hole in the liner is aligned with the hole in the block.

4. Coat the main bearing liner with needle bearing assembly grease and install 13 bearing rollers into liner.

5. Carefully, place the crankshaft into the cylinder block. Make sure the lower main bearing is positioned as shown in **Figure 94**.

6. Lubricate the center crankshaft journal with needle bearing assembly grease. Install the remaining 13 center main bearing rollers, then install the remaining main bearing liner.

7A. *7.5 hp*—Lubricate each connecting rod big end bearing surface with needle bearing assembly grease (**Table 8**). Install a bearing cage and seven of the crankpin rollers into each rod.

7B. *9.9 and 15 hp (steel connecting rods)*—Lubricate each connecting rod big end bearing

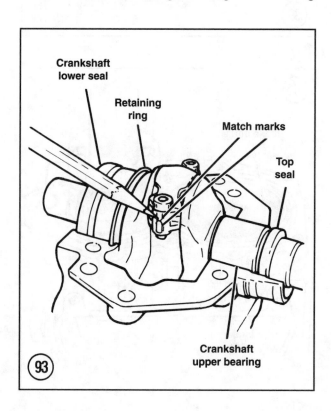

93 Crankshaft lower seal / Retaining ring / Match marks / Top seal / Crankshaft upper bearing

surface with needle bearing assembly grease (**Table 8**). Install one half (28) of the crankpin loose rollers into each rod.

7C. *9.9 and 15 hp (aluminum connecting rods)*—Install a crankpin bearing liner half into each connecting rod. Coat the liners with needle bearing assembly grease (**Table 8**) and install one half (26) of the crankpin loose rollers into each rod.

8A. *7.5 hp*—Pull the rods up to meet the crankshaft. Lubricate the crankpin journals with needle bearing assembly grease and install the remaining bearing cages and 9 needles to each crankpin journal.

8B. *9.9 and 15 hp (steel connecting rods)*—Pull the rods up to meet the crankshaft. Lubricate the crankpin journals with needle bearing assembly grease and install the remaining 28 loose rollers.

8C. *9.9 and 15 hp (aluminum connecting rods)*—Pull the rods up to meet the crankshaft. Lubricate the crankpin journals with needle bearing assembly grease and install the remaining 26 loose rollers.

9A. *7.5, 9.9 and 15 hp (steel connecting rods)*—Install the connecting rod caps. Make sure the rod and cap match marks are aligned.

9B. *9.9 and 15 hp (aluminum connecting rods)*—Install the remaining crankpin bearing liners into the rod caps. Install the rod caps, making sure the rod and cap match marks are aligned.

10. Apply Loctite 271 to new rod cap screws, then install the screws finger tight.

CAUTION
The procedure detailed in Step 11 is critical to proper engine operation. If not done properly, major engine damage can result. It can also be a time-consuming and frustrating process. Work slowly and with patience. If rod and cap cannot be perfectly aligned, the rod and cap assembly should be replaced.

11. Run a seal pick or pencil point along the ground areas (**Figure 95**) to check rod and cap alignment. The rod and cap must be aligned so that the seal pick or pencil point will pass smoothly across the fracture line. If rod and cap

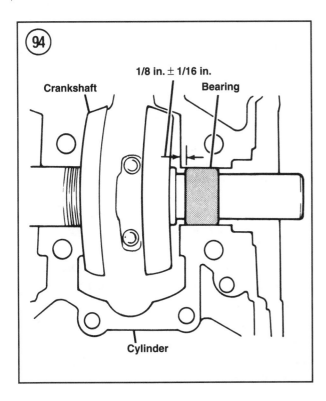

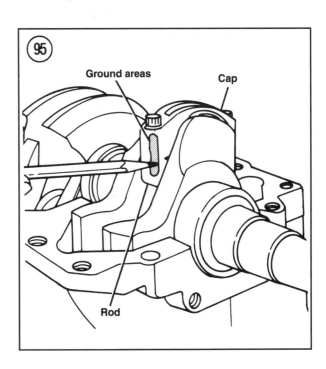

are not perfectly aligned, gently tap the rod cap using a plastic mallet to align.

12. Tighten connecting rod screws to specifications (**Table 1**). Recheck rod and cap to be certain rod and cap are aligned.

13. Rotate the crankshaft to check for binding. Make sure all crankpin rollers turn when the crankshaft is rotated. If not, remove the rod cap(s) and inspect bearings for installation damage or contamination.

14. Install a new o-ring in the crankshaft splined bore.

Assembly
(25 hp 3-cylinder)

1. If removed, press the upper main bearing back onto the crankshaft with a suitable mandrel. Support the crankshaft under the top counterweight when pressing the bearing on.

2. If removed, reinstall the 2 dowel pins (that locate the crankcase cover) into the cylinder block.

3. Lubricate the lower main bearing with clean 2-cycle outboard motor oil and slide it onto the crankshaft. Lubricate the lip of a new lower seal with clean 2-cycle outboard motor oil and slide it onto the crankshaft with the garter spring facing the crankshaft.

4. Place both center main bearing liners into the cylinder block.

5. Coat both center main bearing liners with needle bearing assembly grease (**Table 8**) and install one half (16) of each main bearings loose rollers into each liner.

CAUTION
The lubrication hole in the crankcase cover must not be blocked by the lower main bearing. Locate the hole in the crankcase cover just above the lower seal recess in the main bearing bore before proceeding.

6. Carefully lower the crankshaft into the cylinder block. Position the lower main bearing so that it will be *just above* the lubrication hole in the crankcase cover. Push the lower main seal fully into the machined recess.

7. Lubricate both center main bearing journals with needle bearing assembly grease. Install the remaining half (16) of the loose rollers to each center main journal. Install the remaining liner halves of the center main bearings. Align the dovetails in each bearing liner half to interlock securely with the liner in the cylinder block.

8. Place a bearing cage and roller half assembly in each connecting rod and pull the connecting rods up to the crankshaft. Lubricate the crankpins with clean 2-cycle outboard motor oil and install the remaining bearing cage and roller assembly halves to each crankpin.

9. Install the connecting rod caps. Make sure the rod and cap match marks are aligned.

10. Apply Loctite 271 threadlocking adhesive to new rod cap screws. Hold the cap and rod tightly together and perfectly aligned while installing the rod screws. Check that the rod and cap surfaces are still tightly together and aligned after the rod screw has entered the connecting rod threads. Tighten the rod screws hand tight.

CAUTION
The procedure in the next step is critical to proper engine operation. If not done properly, major engine damage can result. It can also be a time consuming and frustrating process. Work slowly and with patience. If the rod and cap cannot be perfectly aligned, the connecting rod assembly should be replaced.

11. Run a seal pick or pencil point along the ground areas (**Figure 95**) to check rod and cap alignment. The rod and cap must be aligned so that the seal pick or pencil point will pass smoothly across the fracture line. If the rod and cap are not perfectly aligned, gently tap the rod cap with a plastic mallet to align.

12. Torque the rod screws to 15 in.-lb. (1.7 N•m) and recheck alignment. Adjust as necessary. If the alignment is still satisfactory, apply the final torque of 95 in.-lb. (10.7 N•m) and make a final check of alignment.

13. Rotate the crankshaft to check for binding. Make sure all crankpin rollers turn when the crankshaft is rotated. If not, remove the rod cap(s) and inspect bearings for installation damage or contamination.

Assembly
(25 hp 2-cylinder and 35 hp)

1. If removed, press the lower main bearing onto the crankshaft until bearing bottoms on shoulder. Press from the lettered side of the bearing only. Lubricate bearing with a recommended engine oil. Install the crankshaft seal into the groove at the center of the crankshaft (just below center main bearing journal).

2. Place the center main bearing liner into the cylinder block making sure the hole in the liner is aligned with the dowel pin in the bearing bore.

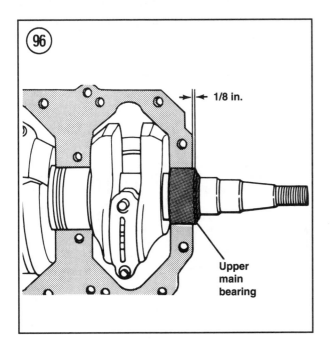

1/8 in.

Upper main bearing

3. Lubricate the bearing liner with needle bearing assembly grease. Install 14 center main bearing rollers into the liner.

4. Clean the cylinder block upper and lower main bearing bores with Locquic Primer and allow to air dry. Apply Loctite 271 to upper and lower bearing bores.

5. Lower crankshaft assembly into the cylinder block. Make sure the crankshaft is properly seated in the block and that upper main bearing is positioned as shown in **Figure 96**.

6. Carefully, rotate the crankshaft seal so the seal end gap is facing up (away from cylinders).

7. Lubricate the crankshaft center main journal with needle bearing assembly grease. Install the remaining 16 bearing rollers on the journal, then place the remaining main bearing liner on the bearing rollers.

8. Coat the connecting rod bearing bores with needle bearing assembly grease. Install the bearing cages into the rods (beveled side facing top of engine), then install 9 bearing rollers into each cage.

9. Pull the connecting rods up to meet the crankshaft. Lubricate the crankpin journals with needle bearing assembly grease. Install the remaining bearing cages onto the crankpins with the beveled side facing top of engine, then install the remaining crankpin bearing rollers into the cages.

> *NOTE*
> *Each crankpin bearing consists of 16 bearing rollers and 2 bearing roller cages.*

10. Install the connecting rod caps. Make sure the rod and cap match marks are aligned. Apply Loctite 271 to new rod cap screws and install the screws finger tight.

> *CAUTION*
> *The procedure detailed in Step 11 is critical to proper engine operation. If not done properly, major engine damage can result. It can also be a time-consuming and frustrating process. Work slowly*

8

and with patience. If rod and cap cannot be perfectly aligned, the rod and cap assembly must be replaced.

11. Run a seal pick or pencil point across the rod and cap fracture line. The pick or pencil should pass smoothly across the fracture line. If rod and cap are not perfectly aligned, tap on the rod cap with a plastic mallet to align.

12. After the proper rod and cap alignment is obtained, tighten the rod cap screws to specifications (**Table 1**).

13. Rotate the crankshaft to check for binding. Make sure all crankpin bearing rollers turn when crankshaft is rotated. If not, remove the rod cap(s) and inspect bearings for dirt, metal chips or other contamination.

14. Install a new o-ring in the crankshaft lower splined bore.

Assembly
(40 and 50 hp)

1. If removed, press the upper main bearing onto crankshaft until the bearing is bottomed on the shoulder. Lubricate the bearing with a recommended engine oil.

2. Coat the inner diameter of the center main bearing liners with needle bearing assembly grease.

NOTE
*The center main bearing assembly on 1984-1995 models uses 2 bearing cages to hold the rollers. The bearing cages final installed position must be with the beveled corners facing up. See **Figure 97**. The center main bearing assembly on 1996-1999 models uses 14 loose rollers (no cages). All center main bearing races have a retaining ring groove that must face down on final assembly.*

3A. *1984-1995 models*—Place the bearing cages into the liners and install the loose rollers.

3B. *1996-1999 models*—Install the 14 loose rollers into the bearing liners. Install the center seal ring if it was removed.

4. Install the bearing half assemblies around the center main journal with the bearing liner retaining ring groove facing down towards the labyrinth seal grooves or center seal groove. Install the retaining ring around the center main bearing assembly. Make sure the retaining ring end gap is not aligned with a bearing liner parting line.

5A. *1984-1995 models*—Lubricate the lower main bearing with clean 2-cycle outboard motor oil and slide the bearing onto the crankshaft. Lubricate the lower seal lip with clean 2-cycle outboard motor oil and slide it onto the crankshaft.

5B. *1996-1999 models*—Press a new lower seal (with the garter spring facing up during installation) into the lower main bearing using tool part No. FT9825. The garter spring must face down when the bearing is installed on the crankshaft. Lubricate the lower bearing and seal assembly with clean 2-cycle outboard motor oil and slide it onto the crankshaft.

6. Clean the upper main bearing bore in the cylinder block with Loquic primer (**Table 8**). Allow the primer to air dry, then apply a light coat of Loctite 271 threadlocking adhesive to the

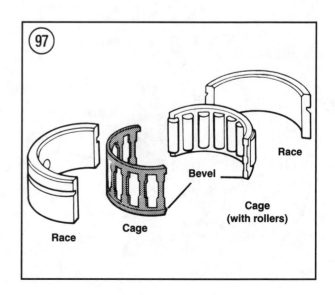

Race

Bevel

Race

Cage

Cage
(with rollers)

Race

upper main bearing bore. On 1996 models repeat Step 6 for the lower main bearing bore.

7. Install the crankshaft assembly while aligning the holes in the main bearings with the locating pins in the cylinder block. Tap the flywheel end of the crankshaft with a soft hammer to seat the crankshaft assembly.

8. *1984-1995 models*—Position the lower crankshaft seal just below the recirculation groove in the cylinder block as shown in **Figure 98**.

NOTE
The 1984-1995 models use 2 bearing cages and 16 rollers for each connecting rod. On 1996-1999 models, 2 bearing cage and roller assemblies for each connecting rod are used. If any rollers fall out of the 1996 model bearing cages, replace the bearing and cage assembly.

9A. *1984-1995 models*—Install the bearing cages into the connecting rods. Apply needle bearing assembly grease (**Table 8**) to the cages and install 9 rollers into each connecting rod cage.

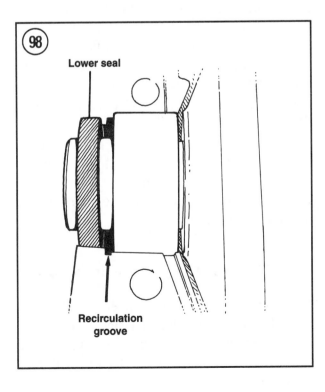

9B. *1996 models*—Install a bearing cage and roller assembly into each connecting rod. Lubricate the journals and bearing cage and roller assembly with clean 2-cycle outboard motor oil.

10. Pull the connecting rods up to meet the crankpin journals.

11A. *1984-1995 models*—Install the remaining rod bearing cages onto the crankpin journals. Apply needle bearing assembly grease to the cages, then install the final 7 rollers onto each crankpin.

11B. *1996-1999 models*—Install the remaining bearing cage and roller assembly onto each crankpin journal.

12. Install the connecting rod caps. Make sure the rod and cap match marks are aligned.

13. Apply Loctite 271 threadlocking adhesive to new rod cap screws. Hold the cap and rod tightly together and perfectly aligned while installing the rod screws. Make sure the rod and cap surfaces are still tightly together and aligned after the rod screw has entered the connecting rod threads. Tighten the rod screws hand tight.

CAUTION
The procedure in the next step is critical to proper engine operation. If not done properly, major engine damage can result. It can also be a time consuming and frustrating process. Work slowly and with patience. If the rod and cap cannot be perfectly aligned, the connecting rod assembly should be replaced.

14. Run a seal pick or pencil point along the ground areas (**Figure 95**) to check rod and cap alignment. The rod and cap must be aligned so that the seal pick or pencil point will pass smoothly across the fracture line. If the rod and cap are not perfectly aligned, gently tap the rod cap with a plastic mallet to align.

15. Torque the rod screws to specification (**Table 1**) and recheck alignment.

16. Rotate the crankshaft to check for binding. Make sure all crankpin rollers turn when the crankshaft is rotated. If not, remove the rod

cap(s) and inspect bearings for installation damage or contamination.

Assembly (60 hp)

1. If removed, press a new lower main bearing onto the crankshaft (lettered side towards the drive shaft) with a suitable mandrel. Support the crankshaft under the bottom counterweight during the pressing operation. Install the bearing retaining clip with snap ring pliers.

2. Slide the upper main bearing onto the crankshaft.

3. If removed, install a new crankshaft center seal ring into the groove next to the center main journal.

4. Coat the inner diameter of the center main bearing liners with needle bearing assembly grease (**Table 8**). Place the bearing cages into the liners and install the loose rollers.

5. Install the bearing half assemblies around the center main journal with the bearing liner retaining ring groove facing away from the center seal ring groove. Install the retaining ring around the center main bearing assembly. Make sure the retaining ring end gap is not aligned with a bearing liner parting line.

6. Clean the lower main bearing bore in the cylinder block with Loquic primer (**Table 8**). Allow the primer to air dry, then apply a light coat of Loctite 271 threadlocking adhesive to the lower main bearing bore.

7. Install the crankshaft assembly while aligning the holes in the main bearings with the locating pins in the cylinder block. Tap the drive shaft end of the crankshaft with a soft hammer to seat the crankshaft assembly.

8. Install the bearing cages into the connecting rods. Apply needle bearing assembly grease to the cages and install 9 rollers into each connecting rod cage.

9. Pull the connecting rods up to meet the crankpin journals.

10. Install the remaining rod bearing cages onto the crankpin journals. Apply needle bearing assembly grease to the cages, then install the final 7 rollers onto each crankpin.

11. Install the connecting rod caps. Make sure the rod and cap match marks are aligned.

12. Apply Loctite 271 threadlocking adhesive to new rod cap screws. Hold the cap and rod tightly together and perfectly aligned while installing the rod screws. Check that the rod and cap surfaces are still tightly together and aligned after the rod screw has entered the connecting rod threads. Tighten the rod screws hand tight.

> *CAUTION*
> *The procedure in the next step is critical to proper engine operation. If not done properly, major engine damage can result. It can also be a time consuming and frustrating process. Work slowly and with patience. If the rod and cap cannot be perfectly aligned, the connecting rod assembly should be replaced.*

13. Run a seal pick or pencil point along the ground areas (**Figure 95**) to check rod and cap alignment. The rod and cap must be aligned so that the seal pick or pencil point will pass smoothly across the fracture line. If the rod and cap are not perfectly aligned, gently tap the rod cap with a plastic mallet to align.

14. Torque the rod screws to specifications (**Table 1**) and recheck alignment.

15. Rotate the crankshaft to check for binding. Make sure all crankpin rollers turn when the crankshaft is rotated. If not, remove the rod cap(s) and inspect bearings for installation damage or contamination.

Assembly (70-150 hp [L-Drives included])

1. If removed, press a new upper main bearing onto the crankshaft (lettered side towards the flywheel) with a suitable mandrel. Support the crankshaft under the top counterweight during

the pressing operation. Lubricate the bearing with clean 2-cycle outboard motor oil.

2. Coat the inner diameter of the center main bearing liners with needle bearing assembly grease (**Table 8**).

NOTE
*The center main bearing assembly uses 2 bearing cages to hold the rollers. The bearing cages final installed position must be with the beveled corners facing up. See **Figure 97**. All center main bearing races have an alignment hole that must be between the retaining ring groove and crankshaft seal ring groove after installation.*

3. Place the center bearing cages into the center main bearing liners and install the loose rollers. If removed, install new center seal rings to the crankshaft grooves.

4. Install each bearing half assembly around the appropriate center main journal with the bearing liner alignment hole between the retaining ring groove and the center seal ring groove. Install a retaining ring around each center main bearing assembly. Make sure all retaining ring end gaps are not aligned with any bearing liner parting line. See **Figure 99**.

5. Press a new lower seal (with the garter spring facing up during installation) into the lower main

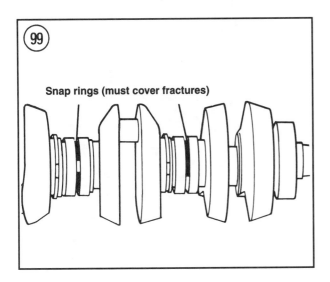

(99)

Snap rings (must cover fractures)

bearing using tool part No. FT9825. The garter spring must face down when the bearing is installed on the crankshaft. Lubricate the lower bearing and seal assembly with clean 2-cycle outboard motor oil and slide it onto the crankshaft.

6. Clean the upper main bearing bore in the cylinder block with Loquic primer (**Table 8**). Allow the primer to air dry, then apply a light coat of Loctite 271 threadlocking adhesive to the upper main bearing bore. Repeat step 6 for the lower main bearing bore.

7. Install the crankshaft assembly while aligning the holes in the main bearings with the locating pins in the cylinder block. Work carefully and take your time. Tap the flywheel end of the crankshaft with a soft hammer to seat the crankshaft assembly once all of the main bearings are properly aligned with the locating pins.

NOTE
The 1984-1995 models use 2 bearing cages and 16 rollers for each connecting rod. On 1996-1999 models, 2 bearing cage and roller assemblies for each connecting rod are used. If any rollers fall out of the 1996 model bearing cages, replace the bearing and cage assembly.

8A. *1984-1995 models*—Install the bearing cages into the connecting rods. Apply needle bearing assembly grease to the cages and install 9 rollers into each connecting rod cage.

8B. *1996-1999 models*—Install a bearing cage and roller assembly into each connecting rod. Lubricate the journals and bearing cage and roller assemblies with clean 2-cycle outboard motor oil.

9. Pull the connecting rods up to meet the crankpin journals.

10A. *1984-1995 models*—Install the remaining rod bearing cages onto the crankpin journals. Apply needle bearing assembly grease to the cages, then install the final 7 rollers onto each crankpin.

8

10B. *1996-1999 models*—Install the remaining bearing cage and roller assemblies onto each crankpin journal.

11. Install the connecting rod caps. Make sure the rod and cap match marks are aligned.

12. Apply Loctite 271 threadlocking adhesive to new rod cap screws. Hold the cap and rod tightly together and perfectly aligned while installing the rod screws. Check that the rod and cap surfaces are still tightly together and aligned after the rod screw has entered the connecting rod threads. Tighten the rod screws hand tight.

CAUTION
The procedure in the next step is critical to proper engine operation. If not done properly, major engine damage can result. It can also be a time consuming and frustrating process. Work slowly and with patience. If the rod and cap cannot be perfectly aligned, the connecting rod assembly should be replaced.

13. Run a seal pick or pencil point along the ground areas (**Figure 95**) to check rod and cap alignment. The rod and cap must be aligned so that the seal pick or pencil point will pass smoothly across the fracture line. If the rod and cap are not perfectly aligned, gently tap the rod cap with a plastic mallet to align.

14. Torque the rod screws to specifications (**Table 1**) and recheck alignment.

15. Rotate the crankshaft to check for binding. Make sure all crankpin rollers turn when the crankshaft is rotated. If not, remove the rod cap(s) and inspect bearings for installation damage or contamination.

CYLINDER BLOCK AND CRANKCASE ASSEMBLY

The cylinder block face on many early models is grooved to accommodate a rubber seal. The new seal should be fully seated in the grooves and then cut 1/2 in. (12.7 mm) longer at each end to ensure a good seal against both crankcase bearings. Apply a thin bead of sealer (part No. 92-90113—2 or equivalent) into the groove prior to installing the seal. Force the seal into the groove and allow it to set 15-20 minutes. Trim the seal ends with a sharp knife, leaving approximately 1/32 in. (0.79 mm) of the seal end to butt against the bearings. Apply additional sealant on both sides of the seal groove in the upper, center and lower main bearing areas. See **Figure 100**. Avoid excess sealant application to prevent sealant from entering the crankcase or bearings.

Sealant (part No. 92-90113—2) is also used on 150 hp models and many other engines without a mating surface groove. Some engines are equipped with a mating surface groove, but the rubber seal is not used. Sealer (part No. 92-90113—2) is also recommended to seal the crankcase on such models. The sealant should be

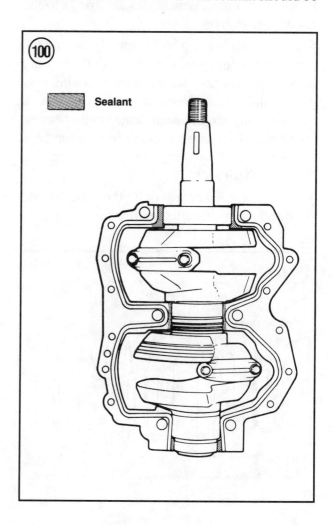

Sealant

evenly applied as shown in **Figure 101** (1-cylinder) or **Figure 102** (2-cylinder). Make sure sealant reaches lower main seal case and upper main bearing race. On engines with a seal groove, fill the groove completely with sealant to extend approximately 1/16 in. (1.6 mm) higher than the mating surface. Make sure the sealant bead is to the inside of the screw holes.

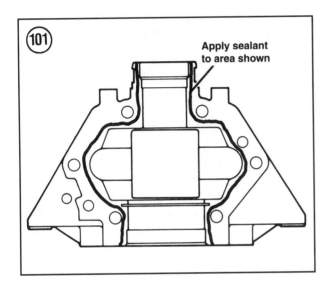

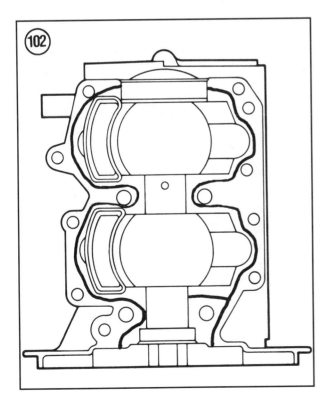

Avoid excess application to prevent sealant from entering the crankcase or bearings.

Some new model engines require Loctite Master Gasket Sealer (**Table 8**) for the crankcase halves. This sealer will be specified where required. Follow the instructions that come with the sealer kit exactly.

Assembly
(4 and 5 hp)

Refer to **Figure 40** for this procedure.

1. Apply sealant to the cylinder block and install the crankcase cover.

2. Install the 2 crankcase cover locating pins with a suitable pin punch.

3. Apply sealant to the crankcase cover screw threads. Install the screws and tighten to specifications (**Table 4**).

4. Rotate the crankshaft several turns to check for binding or unusual noise. If binding or unusual noise is noted, the power head must be disassembled and the cause determined and repaired.

5. Install the cylinder head with a new gasket. Apply sealant to the cylinder head screw threads. Install the 2 top screws with spacers and the 2 lower screws with the bracket. Tighten the cylinder head fasteners to the specifications in **Table 2**.

6. Install the power head as described in this chapter.

Assembly
(7.5, 9.9 and 15 hp)

Refer to **Figure 45** or **Figure 46** for this procedure.

1A. *7.5 hp*—Install new rubber seals with crankcase sealer (part No. 92-90113—2) or equivalent and install the crankcase cover.

1B. *9.9 and 15 hp*—Apply crankcase sealer (part No. 92-90113—2) or equivalent to the cylinder block mating surface and install the crankcase cover.

2. Install the 2 crankcase cover locating pins using a suitable punch.

3. Apply sealant to the threads of the crankcase screws. Install screws and tighten to specification (**Table 4**).

4. Rotate the crankshaft several turns to check for binding or unusual noise. If binding or unusual noise is noted, the power head must be disassembled and the cause repaired.

5. Use a scraper or other sharp tool to remove the old lower crankshaft seal stake marks from the block and crankcase cover.

6. Lubricate the lower crankcase seal lips with needle bearing assembly grease.

7. Drive the seal (garter spring side facing out) fully into the bore with seal installer (part No. FT-11202) or equivalent.

8. Use a center punch to stake the outer edge of the seal in place at 2 points 180° apart. Stake marks should be approximately 1/16 to 1/8 in. (1.59-3.18 mm) from the edge of the seal and deep enough to cover the outer edge of the seal with at least 0.005 in. (0.13 mm) of metal. See **Figure 103**.

9. Press a new upper seal (with the numbered side facing the flywheel) into the upper bearing cage with seal installer (part No. FT-3012) or equivalent. The seal should be flush to 1/32 in. (0.8mm) from the bottom of the seal bore. Lubricate the seal lip with 2-cycle outboard motor oil.

10. Place a new bearing cage gasket on the power head. Place the stator ring on top of the power head. Coat the stator ring upper surface with a 2-4-C Multi-Lube grease (**Table 8**). Install the upper bearing cage to the power head. Coat the 4 bearing cage screws with Loctite 271 thread-locking adhesive (**Table 8**). Install and tighten the screws to the specified torque (**Table 4**).

11. Install the cylinder head with a new gasket. Install the head bolts and tighten to specifications (**Table 2**) in the sequence shown in **Figure 104**

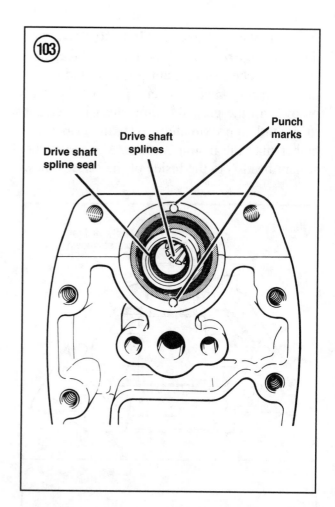

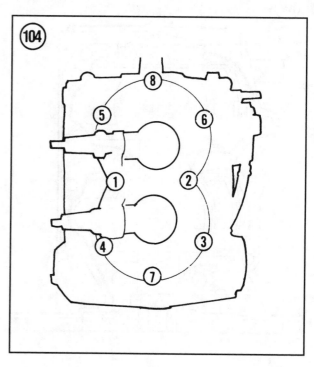

for the 9.9 and 15 hp and **Figure 105** for the 7.5 hp.

NOTE
Be sure to install trigger stator ground lead under the head of the top front screw in Step 11 on models so equipped.

12. Place the exhaust port plate between new gaskets. Fit the exhaust cover to the plate/gasket assembly, then install screws and lead wire clip (if used). Position the cover assembly on the cylinder block and tighten screws to specifications (**Table 4**). Tighten inner screws first, then outer screws.

13. Install the cylinder drain cover with a new gasket. Make sure the screens cover the cover check valves. Install hose clamp with top right hand cover screw, if used. Tighten all screws to specification (**Table 4**).

14. Install the transfer port covers (9.9 and 15 hp) with new gaskets. Tighten screws to specification (**Table 4**).

15. Install exhaust tube to the power head, if so equipped. Use Loctite 271 on the screws.

16. Install the power head as described in this chapter.

Assembly (25 hp 3-cylinder)

Refer to **Figure 47** and **Figure 48** for the following procedure.

1. Apply Loctite Master Gasket Sealer (**Table 8**) to the cylinder block mating surface. Follow the instructions in the kit exactly. Apply the sealer right up to the center main bearing liners to prevent leakage between cylinder crankcases. See **Figure 106**.

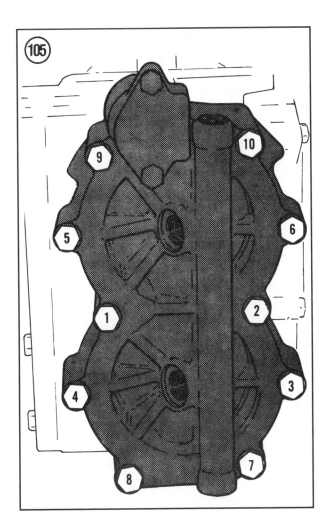

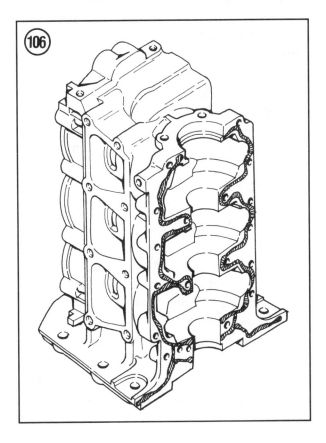

8

2. Install the crankcase cover. Carefully align the cover to the 2 locating dowels on the cylinder block. Install the 6 main bearing screws and 11 outer cover screws and hand tighten.

3. Tighten the 6 main bearing screws to the specified torque (**Table 4**). Tighten the 2 center screws first, the 2 upper screws second and the 2 lower screws last.

4. Tighten the 11 outer crankcase cover screws to the specified torque (**Table 4**). Torque from the center of the block to the outer corners in a circular pattern.

5. Rotate the crankshaft several turns to check for binding or unusual noises. If binding or unusual noise is noted, remove the crankcase cover and locate the cause.

6. Press a new seal (with the garter spring facing away from the flywheel) into the upper bearing cage with a suitable mandrel. Lubricate the seal lips with clean 2-cycle outboard motor oil.

7. Install a new upper bearing cage gasket to the power head. Install the upper bearing cage to the power head. Coat the 4 bearing cage screws with RTV sealant (**Table 8**). Install the screws and tighten to specification (**Table 4**).

8. Place the inner exhaust plate between 2 new gaskets. Assemble the outer exhaust cover to the inner plate and gasket assembly. Install the cover assembly to the power head and install the 14 screws and tighten to specification (**Table 4**). Tighten the center screws first and work outward in a circular pattern.

9. Install the transfer port covers with new gaskets. Tighten the screws to specification (**Table 4**).

10. Place a new gasket between the reed block and intake manifold. Install the intake manifold and reed block assembly to the power head with a new gasket. Install and tighten the 7 intake manifold screws to specification (**Table 4**).

11. Place a new cylinder head cover gasket on the cylinder head. Install the cylinder head cover. Install the cylinder head assembly to the cylinder head with a new gasket. Install and hand tighten the upper starboard and lower port screws with washers to hold the cylinder head assembly to the power head.

12. Install a new thermostat grommet, thermostat and thermostat spring into the cylinder head. Apply a thin layer of RTV sealant (**Table 8**) to the sealing surface of the thermostat cover. Install the thermostat cover to the cylinder head with 2 head screws without washers. Install the remaining 6 cylinder head screws with washers.

13. Torque the 10 cylinder head screws to the specification in **Table 2** following the sequence in **Figure 107**.

14. Lay the power head on its side and install the exhaust tube. Apply Loctite 271 threadlocking adhesive (**Table 8**) to the 3 screws. Install the screws, lock washers and flat washers. Tighten the screws securely.

15. Install the power head as described in this chapter.

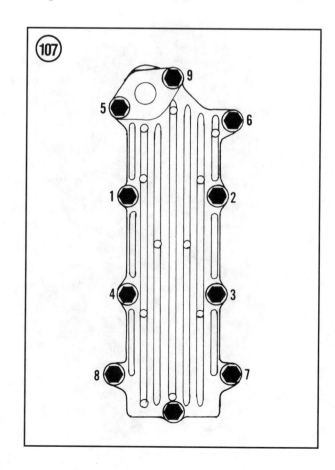

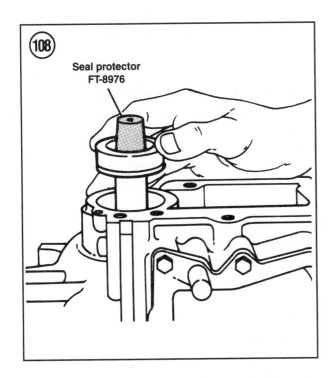

Seal protector
FT-8976

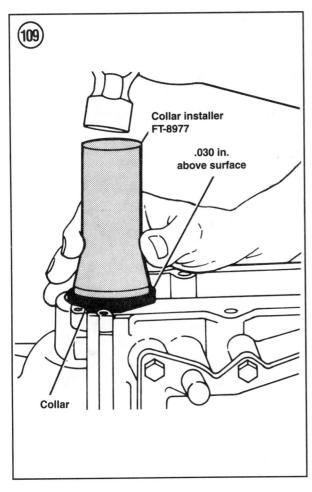

Collar installer
FT-8977

.030 in.
above surface

Collar

Assembly
(25 hp 2-cylinder and 35 hp)

Refer to **Figure 49** and **Figure 50** for this procedure.

1. Install a new crankcase seal into the cylinder block grooves.

2. Make sure the upper main bearing is positioned as shown in **Figure 96**.

3. Clean the upper and lower main bearing bores in the crankcase cover with Locquic Primer. Allow to air dry, then apply Loctite 271 to the bearing bores.

4. Apply 92-90113–2 Industrial Sealant to the mating surface of the crankcase cover.

5. Install the crankcase cover. Install the 2 crankcase cover locating pins using a suitable punch.

6. Coat the threads of the crankcase screws with sealant. Install the screws and tighten to specification (**Table 4**). Tighten the screws in a crossing pattern from the center out.

7. Rotate the crankshaft several turns to check for binding or unusual noise. If binding or unusual noise is noted, the power head must be disassembled and the cause corrected.

8. Install a new O-ring on a new lower crankcase seal collar. Lubricate the O-ring and lower seal lip with needle bearing assembly grease.

9. Place seal protector (part No. FT-8976) over end of the crankshaft. Place the lower seal and collar assembly over the seal protector (O-ring facing inward). Push the seal and collar onto the crankshaft and remove the seal protector. See **Figure 108**.

10. Make sure the O-ring is properly seated in the seal collar groove, then drive collar into crankcase with installer (part No. FT-8977) until collar is approximately 0.030 in. (0.76 mm) above surface of crankcase. See **Figure 109**.

11. Press a new seal (with the garter spring facing away from the flywheel) into the upper bearing cage with seal installer (FT-8971) or equivalent. The top of the seal should be 0.695-0.705 in.

8

(17.65-17.91 mm) from the bottom of the bearing cage chamfered ledge. Lubricate the seal lips with clean 2-cycle outboard motor oil.

12. Install a new upper bearing cage gasket to the power head. Place the stator ring onto the power head. Lubricate the bearing surfaces of the stator ring with 2-4-C Multi-Lube grease (**Table 8**).

13. Install the upper bearing cage to the power head. Coat the 4 bearing cage screws with RTV sealant (**Table 8**). Install the screws and tighten to specification (**Table 4**).

14. Install thermostat and grommet in the cylinder head. Install thermostat cover with a new gasket.

15. Install cylinder head with a new gasket. Tighten head bolts to specifications (**Table 2**) following the sequence shown in **Figure 105**.

16. Install transfer port cover with a new gasket. Tighten screws to specification (**Table 4**) in a spiral pattern starting at the center.

17. Place the exhaust port plate between new gaskets. Fit exhaust cover to the plate/gasket assembly, then install exhaust cover screws. Tighten screws to specification (**Table 4**) in a spiral pattern starting at the center.

18. Install the power head as described in this chapter.

Assembly (40-50 hp)

Refer to **Figure 55** or **Figure 56** and **Figure 57** for this procedure.

1. *1984-1993 models*—Apply sealer part No.92-90113—2 to the crankcase seal grooves. Install new crankcase seals into the cylinder block grooves.

2. Clean the crankcase cover upper and lower main bearing bores with Loquic primer (**Table 8**). Allow to air dry, then apply a light coat of Loctite 271 threadlocking adhesive to the upper and lower main bearing bores.

3. Apply crankcase sealant (part No. 92-90113—2) to the cylinder block mating surfaces. Make sure sealant is applied as shown in **Figure 100**

for 1984-1993 models or **Figure 102** for 1994-1999 models.

4. Install the crankcase cover. Install the crankcase cover locating pins using a suitable punch.

5. Apply sealant to the threads of the main bearing and crankcase cover outer screws. Install the screws. Torque the main bearing screws first and then the crankcase cover outer screws to specification (**Table 4**). Torque from the center out in a circular pattern.

6. Rotate the crankshaft several turns to check for binding or unusual noises. If binding or unusual noise is noted, remove the crankcase cover and locate the cause.

7A. *1984-1987 models*—Install a new upper seal (with the garter spring facing the power head) into the upper bearing cage with seal installer (part No. FT-3512) or equivalent. Coat the seal lips with clean 2-cycle outboard motor oil.

7B. *1988-1994 models*—Install a new upper seal into the upper bearing cage with seal installer (part No. FT-3510) or equivalent. The seal should be 0.695-0.705 in. (17.65-17.91 mm) from the bottom bearing cage chamfer. Coat the seal lips with clean 2-cycle outboard motor oil.

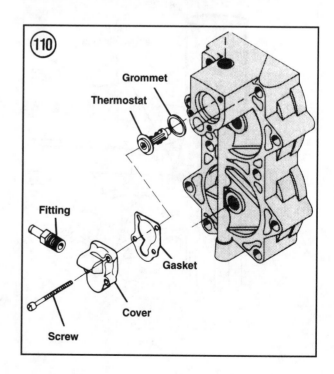

(110)

Grommet

Thermostat

Fitting

Gasket

Cover

Screw

7C. *1995-1999 models*—Install a new upper seal into the upper bearing cage with a suitable mandrel. Coat the seal lips with clean 2-cycle outboard motor oil.

8A. *1984-1987C models*—Install a new bearing cage gasket on the power head and install the bearing cage to the power head. Coat the 4 bearing cage screws with sealant (part No. 92-90113—2). Install the screws and tighten to the specified torque (**Table 4**).

8B. *1987D-1996 models*—Coat the bearing cage power head mating surface with sealant (part No. 92-90113—2) and install the bearing cage to the power head. Coat the 4 bearing cage screws with sealant (part No. 92-90113—2). Install the screws and tighten to the specified torque (**Table 4**).

9. *Early models*—Install a new thermostat grommet around the thermostat. Install the thermostat into the cylinder head with the spring side towards the cylinder head. Install a new gasket and the thermostat cover. Install the cover screws and tighten securely. See **Figure 110**.

10A. *Late models*—Apply sealant (part No. 92-90113—2) to the cylinder head cover side of the cylinder head. Install the cylinder head cover to the cylinder head. Tighten the cylinder head cover screws securely.

10B. *Late models*—Install a new thermostat grommet around the thermostat, then install the thermostat with the spring side towards the cylinder head. Place the spring over the thermostat and install the thermostat cover with a new gasket. Install the 4 thermostat cover screws and tighten securely.

10C. *Late models*—Install the water temperature switch to the cylinder head and install the snap ring with snap ring pliers (part No. FT-1749).

11. Install the cylinder head to the power head with a new gasket. Lightly lubricate the cylinder head bolt threads and underside of bolt heads with 2-cycle outboard motor oil. Install the bolts and tighten in sequence (**Figure 111**) to specification (**Table 2**).

12. *Early models*—Connect the water tube between the thermostat and cylinder block fitting and secure with clamps.

13. *Early models*—Install cylinder drain cover and plate with new gaskets. See **Figure 112**. Tighten the screws to specification (**Table 4**).

8

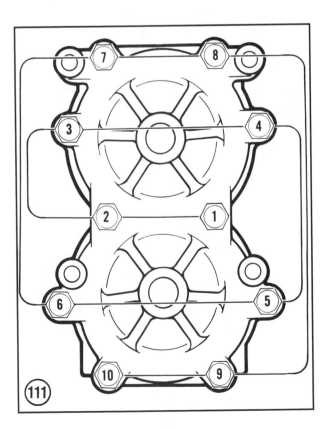

(111)

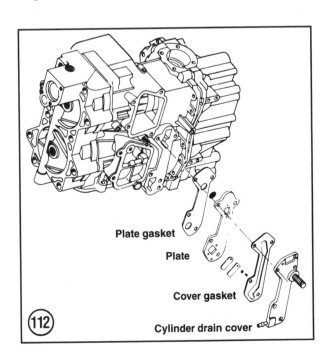

Plate gasket

Plate

Cover gasket

Cylinder drain cover

(112)

14. Install the transfer port covers with new gaskets. Tighten the screws to specification (**Table 4**).

15. Place the inner exhaust plate between 2 new gaskets. Assemble the outer exhaust cover to the inner plate and gasket assembly. Install the exhaust cover assembly to the power head. Install the screws and tighten to specification (**Table 4**). Tighten the center screws first and work outward in a circular pattern.

16. Install the intake manifold and reed block assembly with new gaskets. Tighten the screws to specification (**Table 4**).

17. Install the power head as described in this chapter.

Assembly (60 hp)

Refer to **Figure 67** and **Figure 68** for this procedure.

1. Apply sealer part No. 92-90113—2 to the crankcase seal grooves. Install new crankcase seals into the cylinder block grooves.

2. Clean the upper and lower main bearing bores with Loquic primer (**Table 8**). Allow to air dry, then apply a light coat of Loctite 271 threadlocking adhesive to the upper and lower main bearing bores.

3. Apply crankcase sealant (part No. 92-90113—2) to the cylinder block mating surfaces. Make sure sealant is applied as shown in **Figure 100**.

4. Install the crankcase cover. Install the crankcase cover locating pins using a suitable punch.

5. Apply sealant to the threads of the main bearing and crankcase cover outer screws. Install the screws. Torque the main bearing screws first, then the crankcase cover outer screws to specification (**Table 4**). Torque from the center out in a circular pattern.

6. Rotate the crankshaft several turns to check for binding or unusual noises. If binding or unusual noise is noted, remove the crankcase cover and locate the cause.

7. Install a new upper seal (with the garter spring facing the power head) into the upper bearing cage, with seal installer (part No. FT-8985) or equivalent. Coat the seal lips with clean 2-cycle outboard motor oil.

8. Coat the bearing cage power head mating surface with sealant (part No. 92-90113—2) and install the bearing cage to the power head. Coat the 6 bearing cage screws with sealant (part No. 92-90113—2). Install the screws and tighten to the specified torque (**Table 4**).

9. Press a new bearing cage small seal (with the garter spring facing away from the power head) into the lower bearing cage with seal installer (FT-3431) or equivalent. The seal must be within .030 in. (.76 mm) of bottoming in the bore.

10. Press a new bearing cage large seal (with the garter spring facing the power head) into the lower bearing cage with seal installer (FT-8985) or equivalent. The seal must be .009-.012 in. (0.23-0.30 mm) below the bearing cage surface.

11. Install a new o-ring into the lower bearing cage groove. Coat the o-ring and both bearing cage seal lips with clean 2-cycle outboard motor oil.

12. Install the lower bearing cage into the power head with the side marked *front* facing forward. Coat the 4 lower bearing cage screws with sealer. Install the screws and tighten securely.

13. Install a new thermostat grommet into the cylinder head. Install the thermostat. Install a new gasket and the thermostat cover. Install the cover screws and tighten securely.

14. Place a new gasket between the cylinder head cover and the cylinder head. Secure the cylinder head cover to the cylinder head with 2 screws. Tighten the cylinder head cover screws securely.

15. Install the water temperature switch to the cylinder head.

16. Install the cylinder head to the power head with a new gasket. Install the 8 head bolts and washers. Tighten the bolts in sequence (**Figure 111**) to specification (**Table 2**).

17. Install the water bypass cover plate with a new gasket. Install and tighten the screws securely.

18. Place the inner exhaust plate between 2 new gaskets. Assemble the outer exhaust cover to the inner plate and gasket assembly. Install the exhaust cover assembly to the power head. Install the screws and tighten to specification (**Table 4**). Tighten the center screws first and work outward in a circular pattern.

19. Install the intake manifold and reed block assembly with new gaskets. Tighten the screws to specification (**Table 4**).

20. Install the power head as described in this chapter.

Assembly (70-150 hp)

Refer to **Figure 72** or **Figure 73** for this procedure.

NOTE
Early models (85 hp, 125 hp, 90 hp 1990D and earlier, 120 hp 1990A and earlier)use a crankcase seal in a groove on each side of the cylinder block to seal the crankcase halves. See Figure 100. Later models (70 hp, 75 hp, 90 hp 1990E-on, 120 hp 1990B-on and 150 hp models) do not use a crankcase seal. See Figure 102.

1. *Early models*—Apply sealer part No. 92-90113—2 to the crankcase seal grooves. Install new crankcase seals into the cylinder block grooves.

2. Clean the crankcase cover upper and lower main bearing bores with Loquic primer (**Table 8**). Allow to air dry, then apply a light coat of Loctite 271 threadlocking adhesive to the upper and lower main bearing bores.

NOTE
The crankcase sealer must circle all of the main bearing holes. The sealer must be applied to the inside edge of the crankcase cover outer screw holes.

3. Apply crankcase sealant part No.92-90113—2 to the cylinder block mating surfaces. Make sure sealant is applied as shown in **Figure 100** for early models or **Figure 102** for late models.

4. Install the crankcase cover. Install the crankcase cover locating pins using a suitable punch.

NOTE
Two crankcase cover outer screws are installed from the opposite side.

5. Apply sealant to the threads of the main bearing and crankcase cover outer screws. Install the screws. Torque the main bearing screws first and then the crankcase cover outer screws to specification (**Table 4**). Torque from the center out in a circular pattern.

6. Rotate the crankshaft several turns to check for binding or unusual noises. If binding or unusual noise is noted, remove the crankcase cover and locate the cause.

7. Install a new upper seal (with the major seal lip facing the power head) into the upper bearing cage with seal installer (part No. FT-8903) or equivalent. Coat the seal lips with clean 2-cycle outboard motor oil.

8. Coat the bearing cage power head mating surface with sealant (part No. 92-90113—2)

9. Install seal protector (part No. FT-8927) onto the crankshaft. Slide the bearing cage over the seal protector and onto the power head.

10. Coat the bearing cage screws with sealant (part No. 92-90113—2). Install the screws and tighten to the specified torque (**Table 4**). Remove the seal protector.

11. Apply sealant (part No. 92-90113—2 to the cylinder head cover side of the cylinder head. Install the cylinder head cover to the cylinder head. Tighten the cylinder head cover screws securely.

12A. *Early models*—Install a new thermostat grommet around the thermostat, then install the thermostat into the head with the spring facing out and the bypass slot facing up. Install the thermostat cover assembly to the cylinder head with a new gasket. Install the cover screws and tighten securely.

12B. *Early models*—Install the bypass valve assembly into the power head. Install a new gasket and the cover. Install and tighten the 2 screws securely. See **Figure 72** or **Figure 73**.

13. *Late models*—Install a new thermostat seal into the cylinder head, then install the retainer, thermostat and spring. Install the thermostat cover with a new gasket. Install the 4 thermostat cover screws and tighten securely. See **Figure 74**.

14. Install the water temperature switch to the cylinder head and install the snap ring with snap ring pliers (part No. FT-1749).

CAUTION
The 1996-1999 75-120 hp models use the torque and turn method of tightening the head bolts. Follow the procedure as footnoted in Table 2.

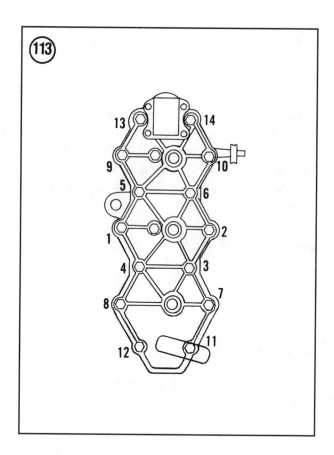

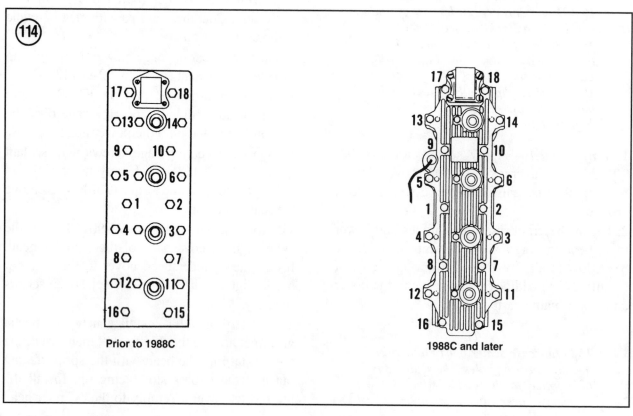

Prior to 1988C   1988C and later

15. Install the cylinder head to the power head with a new gasket. Lubricate the cylinder head bolt threads and underside of bolt heads with 2-cycle outboard motor oil. Install the bolts and tighten in sequence to specifications (**Table 2**). See **Figure 113** (3-cylinder), **Figure 114** (4-cylinder) and **Figure 115** (5-cylinder).

NOTE
Early model cylinder drain covers with reed valves use the 2 gaskets and a plate. Later models with cylinder drain cover that use check valves only use 1 gasket. See Chapter Six.

16A. *Early models*—Install the cylinder drain cover and plate with new gaskets. Tighten the screws to specification (**Table 4**).

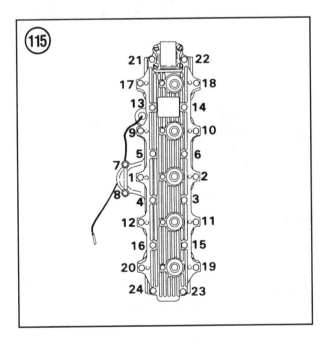

16B. *Later models*—Install the cylinder drain cover with a new gasket. Tighten the screws to specifications.

NOTE
The transfer port cover with the fuel pump mounting pad is cylinder No. 2 for 3-cylinder models and cylinder No. 3 for 4-cylinder models. Early 5-cylinder models with 2 fuel pumps use cylinders No. 3 and No. 4. Late model 5-cylinder models with 1 fuel pump use cylinder No. 4.

17. Install the transfer port covers with new gaskets. Tighten the screws to specification (**Table 4**).

18A. *Outboard models*—Place the inner exhaust plate between 2 new gaskets. Assemble the outer exhaust cover to the inner plate and gasket assembly. Install the exhaust cover assembly to the power head. Install the screws and tighten to specification (**Table 4**). Tighten the center screws first and work outward in a circular pattern.

18B. *L-Drive models*—Install the new 1 piece exhaust manifold gasket and exhaust manifold to the power head. Install the screws and tighten to specification (**Table 4**). Tighten the center screws first and work outward in a circular pattern.

19. Install the intake manifold(s) and reed block assembly(s) with new gaskets. Tighten the screws to specification (**Table 4**).

20. Install the power head as described in this chapter.

Tables 1-10 are on the following pages.

Table 1 CONNECTING ROD TORQUE SPECIFICATIONS

Outboard model (including L-Drive)	in.-lb. (N•m)
4-7.5 hp	80 (9)
9.9 and 15 hp (steel rod)	80 (9)
9.9 and 15 hp (aluminum rod)	95 (10.7)
25 hp (2 cylinder)	180-190 (20.3-21.5)
25 hp (3 cylinder)	95 (10.7)
35 hp	170 (19.2)
40 hp (1992C-1994)*	170 (19.2)
50 hp (1984-1987)	180-190 (20.3-21.5)
50 hp (1988-1994)*	170 (19.2)
40 and 50 hp (1995-1996)	Torque and turn*
60 hp	275 (31)
70 hp (1991-serial No. OE093699)*	170 (19.2)
70 hp (serial No. OE093699-on) and 75 hp	Torque and turn*
85 and 125 hp (1984-1987)	180-190 (20.3-21.5)
85 and 125 hp (1988-1989)	170 (19.2)
90 and 120 hp (up to serial No. OE093699)	170 (19.2)
90 and 120 hp (serial No. OE093700 and up)	Torque and turn*
150 hp	170 (19.2)

*Serial No. OE093700-on 40-120 hp models (1995 and newer) use a new torque procedure for the connecting rod screws. Lightly oil the threads and the underside of the head of each screw. Torque to 120 in.-lbs. (13.5 N•m). Then turn each screw an additional 90°.

Table 2 CYLINDER HEAD BOLT TORQUE SPECIFICATIONS

Outboard model	Torque specification
4-15 hp	130 in.-lbs. (14.7 N•m)
25 hp (2 cylinder) and 35 hp	190 in.-lbs. (21.5 N•m)
25 hp (3 cylinder)	250 in.-lbs. (28.2 N•m)
50 hp 1984-1989B (3/8 in. bolts)	270 in.-lbs. (30.5 N•m)
50 hp 1989C-1996 (5/16 in. bolts)	225 in.-lbs. (25.4 N•m)
40, 60, 70, 85, 125 and 150 hp	225 in.-lbs. (25.4 N•m)
75 hp	Torque and turn*
90 and 120 hp (to serial No. OE138599 including L-Drive models)	225 in.-lbs. (25.4 N•m)
90 and 120 hp (serial No. OE138600-on)	Torque and turn*

*1996 (serial No. 138600-on) 75, 90 and 120 hp models use a new torque procedure for the cylinder head bolts. Lightly oil the threads and the underside of the head of each bolt. Torque in sequence to 120 in.-lbs. (13.5 N•m). Then turn each head bolt, in sequence, an additional 90°.

Table 3 FLYWHEEL TORQUE SPECIFICATIONS

Outboard model	Torque specification
4-5 hp	17 ft.-lb. (23 N•m)
7.5 hp	40 ft.-lb. (54 N•m)
9.9-15 hp	50 ft.-lb. (67.8 N•m)
25 hp (2 cylinder)	60 ft.-lb. (81.3 N•m)
25 hp (3 cylinder)	45 ft.-lb. (61 N•m)
	(continued)

Table 3 FLYWHEEL TORQUE SPECIFICATIONS (continued)

Outboard model	Torque specification
35 hp	70 ft.-lb. (95 N•m)
40 and 50 hp (prior to 1995)	80 ft.-lb. (108.5 N•m)
40 and 50 hp (1995-1996)	125 ft.-lb. (169.5 N•m)
60 and 70 hp	90 ft.-lb. (122 N•m)
75 hp	125 ft.-lb. (169.5 N•m)
85 and 125	90 ft.-lbs. (122 N•m)
90 and 120 hp (to serial No. OE138599 including L-Drive models)	90 ft.-lbs. (122 N•m)
90 and 120 hp (serial No. OE138600-on)	125 ft.-lb. (169.5 N•m)
150 hp	130 ft.-lb. (169.5 N•m)

Table 4 SPECIAL POWER HEAD TORQUE SPECIFICATIONS

Fastener	in.-lb.	ft.-lb.	N•m
Crankcase upper bearing to crankcase			
7.5-150 hp (except 1996 40-50 hp)	70	–	7.9
40-50 hp (1996)	90	–	10.2
Crankcase cover			
4-5 hp	70	–	7.9
7.5, 9.9, 15 and 35 hp			
Outer screws	70	–	7.9
Main bearing screws	160	13.3	18.1
25 hp (2 cylinder)	standard torque		
25 hp (3 cylinder)			
Outer screws	90	–	10.2
Main bearing screws	160	13.3	18.1
40-60 hp			
Outer screws	70	–	7.9
Main bearing screws	270	22.5	30.5
70-150 hp			
Main bearing screws	270	22.5	30.5
Cylinder drain cover	70	–	7.9
Exhaust cover			
7.5 hp	70	–	7.9
9.9-15 hp	90	–	10.2
25 hp (3-cylinder)	90	–	10.2
25 hp (2-cylinder) and 35 hp	70	–	7.9
40-50 hp (1984-1999)	70	–	7.9
40-50 hp (1996-1999)	100	8.3	11.3
60, 70, 85, 125 and 150 hp (outboard)	70	–	7.9
75 hp	115	9.6	13.0
90 and 120 (1990-1994 outboard)	70	–	7.9
90 and 120 (1995-1999 outboard)	80	–	9.0
L-Drive	100	8.3	11.3
Fuel tank screws (4 and 5 hp)	90	–	10.2
Power head-to-motor leg			
4-7.5 hp	70	–	7.9
9.9-35 hp (except 25 hp 3-cylinder)	160	13.3	18.1
25 hp (3-cylinder)	350	29.2	39.5
50 hp (1984-1994)	160	13.3	18.1
40-50 hp (1995-1999)	–	55	74.6
70-85 and 125-150 hp (except 75 hp and L drive)	270	22.5	30.5

(continued)

8

Table 4 SPECIAL POWER HEAD TORQUE SPECIFICATIONS (continued)

Fastener	in.-lb.	ft.-lb.	N•m
Power head-to-motor leg (continued)			
75 hp	444	37.0	50.0
90 and 120 (1990-1994 outboard)	270	22.5	30.5
90 and 120 (1995-1999 outboard)	–	50	67.8
L-Drive	300	25	33.9
Spacer plate-to-motor leg (or power head)			
40-50 hp (1995-1999)	225	18.8	25.4
70-85 hp and 125-150 hp (outboard)	270	22.5	30.5
90 and 120 hp (1990-1994 outboard)	270	22.5	30.5
90 and 120 hp (1995-1999 outboard)	360	30	40.7
L-Drive	300	25	33.9
Stern bracket bolt (tiller models)			
4-5 hp	180	15	20.3
9.9-15 hp	125	10.4	14.1
25-35 hp	160	13.3	18.1
Steering support tube (remote models)			
35-50 hp	225	18.8	25.4
70-150 hp (outboard)	–	50	67.8
L-Drives	480	40	54.2
Steering cable jam nuts (L-Drive)	50		67.8
Stern bracket clamp screws	35		47.5
Transfer port cover screws			
9.9 and 15 hp	90	–	10.2
25-150 hp (except 1996 40-50 hp)	70	–	7.9
40-50 hp (1996-1999)	100	8.3	11.3

Table 5 STANDARD TORQUE VALUES

Screw or Nut Size	in.-lbs.	ft.-lbs.	N•m
6-32	9	–	1.0
8-32	20	–	2.3
10-24	30	–	3.4
10-32	35	–	4.0
12-24	45	–	5.1
1/4-20	70	6	7.9
1/4-28	84	7	9.5
5/16-18	160	13	18.1
5/16-24	168	14	19.0
3/8-16	270	23	30.5
3/8-24	300	25	33.9
7/16-14	–	36	48.8
7/16-20	–	40	54.2
1/2-13	–	50	67.8
1/2-20	–	60	81.3

Table 6 POWER HEAD SERVICE SPECIFICATIONS (4-60 HP)

Component	Specification—in. (mm)
Crankshaft	
Crankpin diameter	
4-7.5 hp	0.7493-0.7496 (19.03-19.04)
9.9 and 15 hp	0.7496-0.7501 (19.04-19.05)
(continued)	

Table 6 POWER HEAD SERVICE SPECIFICATIONS (4-60 HP) (continued)

Component	Specification—in. (mm)
Crankshaft	
Crankpin diameter (continued)	
25-50[3] hp 1984-1995	1.1391-1.1395 (28.93-28.94)
40 and 50 hp 1996-1999 (top-guided rod)	1.1813-1.1818 (30.01-30.02)
60 hp	1.1822-1.1827 (30.03-30.04)
Center main journal diameter	
7.5-15 hp	0.8000-0.8005 (20.32-20.33)
25 hp (2 cylinder) and 35 hp	1.3446-1.3451 (34.15-34.17)
40 and 50 hp 1984-1995	1.1388-1.1392 (28.93-28.94)
40 and 50 hp 1996-1999 (top-guided rod)	1.2160-1.2165 (30.89-30.90)
60 hp	1.3748-1.3752 (34.92-34.93)
Top main journal diameter	
4 and 5 hp	0.8125-0.8130 (20.64-20.65)
7.5-15 hp	0.9849-0.9853 (25.02-25.03)
25 hp (2 cylinder) and 35 hp	1.3774-1.3780 (34.99-35.00)
40 and 50 hp 1984-1995	1.1815-1.1821 (30.01-30.03)
40 and 50 hp 1996-1999 (top-guided rod)	1.3789-1.3793 (35.02-35.03)
60 hp	1.3744-1.3750 (34.91-34.93)
Bottom main journal diameter	
4 and 5 hp	0.7874-0.7878 (20.00-20.01)
7.5-15 hp	0.7495-0.7500 (19.04-19.05)
25 hp (2 cylinder) and 35 hp	0.9849-0.9853 (25.02-25.03)
40 and 50 hp 1984-1995	1.1245-1.1251 (28.56-28.58)
40 and 50 hp 1996-1999 (top-guided rod)	1.2500-1.2505 (31.75-31.76)
60 hp	1.3789-1.3793 (35.02-35.03)
Upper seal surface diameter	
4 and 5 hp	0.7185-0.7190 (18.25-18.26)
7.5-15 hp	0.8122-0.8135 (20.63-20.66)
25 hp (2 cylinder) and 35 hp	1.0630-1.0650 (27.00-27.05)
40 and 50 hp 1984-1995	1.1245-1.1255 (28.56-28.59)
60 hp	1.3744-1.3750 (34.91-34.93)
Lower seal surface diameter	
4-15 hp	0.7490-0.7500 (19.02-19.05)
25 hp (2 cylinder) and 35 hp	0.9345-0.9350 (23.74-23.75)
40 and 50 hp 1984-1995	1.1245-1.1251 (28.56-28.58)
60 hp	1.3740-1.3760 (34.90-34.95)
Center seal (labyrinth) surface diameter	
9.9 and 15 hp	1.0585-1.0590 (26.89-26.90)
Connecting rod	
Piston end inside diameter	
4-7.5 hp 1984-1989	0.6245-0.6250 (15.86-15.88)
5 hp 1990-1996	0.6870-0.6875 (17.45-17.46)
9.9 and 15 hp	0.6870-0.6875 (17.45-17.46)
25 hp (2 cylinder) and 35 hp 1986-1987	0.8520-0.8560 (21.64-21.74)
35 hp 1988-1991	0.8762-0.8767 (22.26-22.27)
40 and 50 hp 1984-1995	0.8762-0.8767 (22.26-22.27)
40 and 50 hp 1996-1999 (top-guided rod)	0.9568-0.9573 (24.30-24.32)
60 hp	0.9654-0.9659 (24.52-24.53)
Crankshaft end inside diameter	
4 hp and 5 hp 1988-1989	0.9399-0.9403 (23.87-23.88)
5 hp 1990-1999	0.9409-0.9413 (23.90-23.91)
7.5-15 hp	0.9399-0.9403 (23.87-23.88)
25 hp (2 cylinder) and 35 hp 1986-1987	1.4523-1.4528 (36.89-36.90)

(continued)

Table 6 POWER HEAD SERVICE SPECIFICATIONS (4-60 HP) (continued)

Component	Specification—in. (mm)
Connecting rod (continued)	
Crankshaft end inside diameter	
35 hp 1988-1991	1.4528-1.4533 (36.90-36.91)
40 and 50 hp 1984-1995	1.4528-1.4533 (36.90-36.91)
40 and 50 hp 1996-1999 (top-guided rod)	1.4986-1.4991 (38.06-38.08)
60 hp	1.5000-1.5005 (38.10-38.11)
Standard cylinder bore diameter	
4-7.5 hp 1984-1989	2.000-2.001 (50.80-50.83)
5 hp 1990-1996	2.125-2.126 (53.98-54.00)
9.9 hp 1984-1987	2.1875-2.1885 (55.56-55.59)
9.9 hp 1988-1999 and 15 hp	2.2510-2.2520 (57.18-57.20)
25 hp (3 cylinder)	2.375 (60.33)
25 hp (2 cylinder)	2.8125-2.8135 (71.44-71.46)
35 hp	3.001-3.003 (76.23-76.28)
50 hp 1984-1989A	3.1890-3.1910 (81.00-81.05)
50 hp 1989B-1992B	3.3130-3.3148 (84.15-84.20)
40 and 50 hp 1992C-1996	3.3745-3.3760 (85.71-85.75)
60 hp	3.3750-3.3762 (85.73-85.76)
Maximum cylinder out-of-round	0.0005 (0.01)
Maximum cylinder taper	0.002 (0.05)
Piston	
Skirt diameter	
4-7.5 hp 1984-1989	1.9960-1.9965 (50.70-50.71)
5 hp 1990-1996	2.122-2.123 (53.90-53.92)
9.9 hp 1984-1987	2.1845-2.1850 (55.49-55.50)
9.9 hp 1988-1996 and 15 hp	2.2470-2.2475 (57.07-57.09)
25 hp (2 cylinder)	
Major diameter (90° to pin bore)	2.8064-2.8084 (71.28-71.33)
Minor diameter (parallel to pin bore)	2.8039-2.8059 (71.22-71.27)
25 hp (3 cylinder)[1]	2.372-2.374 (60.25-60.30)
35 hp	
Major diameter (90° to pin bore)	2.9935-2.9950 (76.03-76.07)
Minor diameter (parallel to pin bore)	2.9885-2.9915 (75.91-75.98)
50 hp 1984-1987	
Major diameter (90° to pin bore)	3.184-3.185 (80.87-80.90)
Minor diameter (parallel to pin bore)	3.181-3.183 (80.80-80.85)
50 hp 1988-1989A	
Major diameter (90° to pin bore)	3.184-3.185 (80.87-80.90)
Minor diameter (parallel to pin bore)	3.179-3.181 (80.75-80.80)
50 hp 1989B-1992B	
Major diameter (90° to pin bore)	3.308-3.309 (84.02-84.05)
Minor diameter (parallel to pin bore)	3.304-3.305 (83.92-83.95)
40 and 50 hp 1992C-1995	
Major diameter (90° to pin bore)	3.3618-3.3628 (85.39-85.42)
Minor diameter (parallel to pin bore)	3.3598-3.3608 (85.34-85.36)
40 and 50 hp 1996-1999 (top-guided rod)	3.3695-3.3705 (85.59-85.61)
60 hp	
Major diameter (90° to pin bore)	3.366-3.367 (85.50-85.52)
Minor diameter (parallel to pin bore)	3.363-3.365 (85.42-85.47)
Pin bore inside diameter	
4-7.5 hp 1984-1989	0.4373-0.4376 (11.11-11.12)
9.9 and 15 hp	0.4998-0.5001 (12.69-12.70)
25 hp (2 cylinder) and 35 hp	0.6874-0.6877 (17.46-17.47)

(continued)

Table 6 POWER HEAD SERVICE SPECIFICATIONS (4-60 HP) (continued)

Component	Specification—in. (mm)
Piston (continued)	
Pin bore inside diameter	
50 hp 1984-1987	0.6874-0.6877 (17.46-17.47)
50 hp 1988-1992B	0.6876-0.6879 (17.47-17.47)
40 and 50 hp 1992C-1995	0.6878-0.6881 (17.47-17.48)
60 hp	0.7769-0.7772 (19.73-19.74)
Piston ring end gap	
4-7.5 hp 1984-1989	0.006-0.011 (0.15-0.28)
5 hp 1990-1999	0.009 (0.23)
9.9 hp 1984-1987	0.006-0.016 (0.15-0.41)
9.9 hp 1988-1999 and 15 hp	0.004-0.014 (0.10-0.36)
25 hp (2 cylinder)	0.007-0.017 (0.18-0.43)
25 hp (3 cylinder)	0.010-0.018 (0.25-0.46)
35 hp	
Top ring	0.006-0.016 (0.15-0.41)
Bottom ring	0.004-0.014 (0.10-0.36)
50 hp 1984-1989A	0.006-0.016 (0.15-0.41)
50 hp 1989B-1992B	
Top ring	0.010-0.020 (0.25-0.51)
Bottom ring	0.006-0.016 (0.15-0.41)
40 and 50 hp 1992C-1995	0.004-0.014 (0.10-0.36)
40 and 50 hp 1996-1999 (top-guided rod)	0.010-0.020 (0.25-0.51)
60 hp	
Top ring	0.004-0.014 (0.10-0.36)
Bottom ring	0.006-0.016 (0.15-0.41)
Piston pin	
Diameter	
4-7.5 hp	0.43750-0.43765 (11.11-11.12)
9.9-50[3] hp 1984-1994	0.50000-0.50015 (12.70-12.70)
40 and 50 hp 1995	0.68750-0.68765 (17.46-17.47)
40 and 50 hp 1996-1999 (top-guided rod)	0.76993-0.77003 (19.56-19.56)
60 hp	0.77675-0.77690 (19.73-19.73)
Overall length	
4-7.5 hp 1984-1989	1.730 (43.94)
5 hp 1990-1996	1.790-1.810 (45.47-45.97)
9.9-50[3] hp 1984-1994	1.800-1.810 (45.72-45.97)
40 and 50 hp 1995	2.895-2.915 (73.53-74.04)
40 and 50 hp 1996-1999	2.890-2.930 (73.41-74.42)
60 hp	3.120-3.130 (79.25-79.50)

[1]Measured .050 in. (1.27 mm) from bottom of skirt, 90° to piston pin bore.
[2]Measured .150 in. (3.81 mm) from bottom of skirt, 90° to piston pin bore.
[3]Does not include 25 hp 3-cylinder models.

Table 7 POWER HEAD SERVICE SPECIFICATIONS (70-150 HP [INCLUDING L-DRIVES])

Component	Specification - in. (mm)
Crankshaft	
Crankpin diameter	
1984-1995 models	1.1391-1.1395 (28.93-28.94)
1996-1999 models (top-guided rod)	1.1813-1.1818 (30.01-30.02)
Center main journals diameter	1.3748-1.3752 (34.92-34.93)
Top main journal diameter	1.3789-1.3793 (35.02-35.03)
(continued)	

8

**Table 7 POWER HEAD SERVICE SPECIFICATIONS
(70-150 HP [INCLUDING L-DRIVES]) (continued)**

Component	Specification - in. (mm)
Crankshaft (continued)	
Bottom main journal diameter	1.2495-1.2500 (31.74-31.75)
Upper seal surface diameter	
1984-1995 models	1.249-1.251 (31.72-31.78)
1996-1999 models (top-guided rod)	1.374-1.376 (34.90-34.95)
Lower seal surface diameter	1.2495-1.2500 (31.74-31.75)
Connecting rod	
Piston end inside diameter	
1984-1995 models	0.8762-0.8767 (22.26-22.27)
1996-1999 models (top-guided rod)	0.9568-0.9573 (24.30-24.32)
Crankshaft end inside diameter	
1984-1995 models	1.4528-1.4533 (36.90-36.91)
1996-1999 models (top-guided rod)	1.4986-1.4991 (38.06-38.08)
Standard cylinder bore diameter	
1984-1990A models	3.3130-3.3148 (84.15-84.20)
1990B-1999 models	3.3750-3.3762 (85.73-85.76)
Maximum cylinder out-of-round	0.0005 (0.01)
Maximum cylinder taper	0.002 (0.05)
Piston	
Skirt diameter	
1984-1989B models	3.3045-3.3055 (83.93-83.96)
1989C-1990A models	
Major diameter (90° to pin bore)	3.308-3.309 (84.02-84.05)
Minor diameter (parallel to pin bore)	3.304-3.305 (83.92-83.95)
1990B-1995 models	
Major diameter (90° to pin bore)	3.369-3.370 (85.57-85.60)
Minor diameter (parallel to pin bore)	3.367-3.368 (85.52-85.55)
1996-1999 models (top-guided rod)*	3.3695-3.37005 (85.59-85.60)
Pin bore inside diameter (1984-1995)	0.6878-0.6880 (17.47-17.48)
Piston ring end gap	
1984-1989B	0.006-0.016 (0.15-0.41)
1989C-1995	
Top ring	0.010-0.020 (0.25-0.51)
Bottom ring	0.006-0.016 (0.15-0.41)
1996-1999 models (top-guided rod)	0.010-0.020 (0.25-0.51)
Piston pin	
Diameter	
1984-1995 models	0.68750-0.68765 (17.46-17.47)
1996-1999 models (top-guided rod)	0.76993-0.77003 (19.56-19.56)
Overall length	
1984-1995 models	3.120-3.130 (79.25-79.50)
1996-1999 models (top-guided rod)	2.890-2.930 (73.41-74.42)

*Measured .150 in. (3.81 mm) from bottom of skirt, 90° to piston pin bore.

Table 8 RECOMMENDED LUBRICANTS, SEALANTS AND ADHESIVES

	Part No.
Lubricants	
Quicksilver Premium	
2-Cycle TC-W3 outboard oil	(normal dealer stock item)
Quicksilver Special Lubricant 101	92-13872A-1
	(continued)

Table 8 RECOMMENDED LUBRICANTS, SEALANTS AND ADHESIVES (continued)

	Part No.
Lubricants (continued)	
Quicksilver 2-4-C Multi-Lube	(normal dealer stock item in various sizes)
Quicksilver Anti-Corrosion Grease	92-78376A-6
Quicksilver Needle Bearing Grease	92-825265A-1
Quicksilver Power Trim and Steering Fluid	92-90100A12
Quicksilver Premium Blend	
Gearcase Lubricant	(normal dealer stock item)
Sealants	
Quicksilver Perfect Seal	92-34227-11
Loctite 5900 Ultra black RTV sealant	92-809826
Sealer (crankcase halves)	92-90113–2
Loctite Master Gasket Sealer	92-12564–2
Quicksilver Liquid Neoprene	92-25711–2
Loctite 567 PST pipe sealant	92-809822
Quicksilver Bellows Adhesive	92-86166–1
Adhesives	
Loquic Primer	92-809824
Loctite 271 threadlocking sealant	
(high strength)	92-809819
Loctite 242 threadlocking sealant	
(medium strength)	92-809821
Loctite RC680 high strength	
retaining compound	92-809833
Miscellaneous	
Quicksilver Power Tune Engine Cleaner	92-15104A12
Quicksilver Corrosion Guard	92-815869A12
Quicksilver Storage Seal Rust Inhibitor	92-86145A12

Table 9 POWER HEAD SPECIAL TOOLS (4-60 HP)

Description	Part No.	Models
Rod bolt socket	FT-2953	25 (2-cylinder) and 35-50 hp
Rod bolt socket	FT-8929	4-15 hp
Pin punch	FT-8919	4-15 and 60 hp
Snap ring pliers	FT-1749	4-50 hp (except 25 hp 3-cylinder)
Lock ring installation tool	FT-11291	40-50 hp (1984-1995)
Pillow block	FT-2990-1	4-50 hp
Piston ring expander	FT-8926	all
Piston ring compressor	FT-2997	4-15 hp
Piston ring compressor	FT-2996	25-60 hp
Seal installer	FT-11202	7.5 hp
Seal installer	FT-3012	7.5-15 hp
Seal installer	FT-8949	9.9 and 15 hp
Seal installer	FT-8971	25 (2-cylinder) and 35 hp
Seal installer	FT-3510	35 hp (1988-1991) and 40-50 hp
Seal installer	FT-8985	60 hp
Seal installer	FT-3431	60 hp
Seal protector	FT-8967	25 (2-cylinder) and 35 hp (84-87)
Seal protector	FT-8976	25 (2-cylinder) and 35 hp
Seal protector	FT-2908	9.9 and15 hp
Seal protector	FT-8976	25 (2-cylinder) hp

(continued)

8

Table 9 POWER HEAD SPECIAL TOOLS (4-60 HP) (continued)

Description	Part No.	Models
Seal collar installer	FT-8977	25 (2-cylinder) and 35 hp
Hose clamp pliers	FT-8900	5, 25 (2-cylinder) and 40-50 hp
Carbon removing brush	FT-2991	all
Lift hook	FT-8932	25 (2-cylinder) and 35 hp
Lift hook	FT-8933	40-60 hp (1984-1995)
Flywheel puller kit	FT-8948-1	40-60 hp (1984-1995)
Flywheel wedge	FT-2989	9.9-35 hp
Flywheel knock off tool	FT-8998	4 and 5 hp
Flywheel knock off tool	FT-2909	7.5-25 (3-cylinder) hp
Flywheel knock off tool	FT-2910	25 (2-cylinder) and 35 hp
Flywheel holding wrench	91-52344	all electric start models
1996 top-guided rod power head tools		
Piston pin tool	91-13663A-1	25 (3-cylinder) hp (1996)
Flywheel puller kit	91-73687A-2	40-50 (1996)
Crankshaft protector cap*	91-24161	40-50 (1996)
Lift eye	91-90455	40-50 (1996)
Piston ring remover	91-24697	40-50 (1996)
Piston tool (cradle and driver)	91-74607A-3	40-50 (1996)
Lock ring removal tool	91-52952A-1	40-50 (1996)
Lock ring installation tool	91-77109A-2	40-50 (1996)

*Included in 91-73687A-2 kit.

Table 10 POWER HEAD SPECIAL TOOLS (70-150 HP, INCLUDING L-DRIVES)

Description	Part No.	Models
Rod bolt socket	FT-2953	70-150 hp
Pillow block	FT-2990-1	70-150 hp
Piston ring expander	FT-8926	all
Piston ring compressor	FT-2996	all
Lock ring installation tool	FT-11291	all
Seal installer	FT-8903	70-150 hp
Seal installer	FT-8925	70-150 hp
Carbon removing brush	FT-2991	all
Lift hook	FT-8933	70-150 hp (1984-1995)
Flywheel puller kit	FT-8948-1	70-150 hp (1984-1995)
Flywheel holding wrench	91-52344	all
1996 top-guided rod power head tools		
Flywheel puller kit	91-73687A-2	75-120 (1996)
Crankshaft protector cap*	91-24161	75-120 (1996)
Lift eye	91-90455	75-120 (1996)
Piston ring remover	91-24697	75-120 (1996)
Piston tool (cradle and driver)	91-74607A-3	75-120 (1996)
Lock ring removal tool	91-52952A-1	75-120 (1996)
Lock ring installation tool	91-77109A-2	75-120 (1996)

*Included in 91-73687A-2 kit.

Chapter Nine

Gearcase

Torque is transferred from the engine crankshaft to the gearcase by a drive shaft. A pinion gear on the drive shaft meshes with the drive gears in the gearcase to change the vertical power flow (engine crankshaft and drive shaft) into a horizontal power flow (propeller shaft). The power head drive shaft rotates clockwise continuously when the engine is running, but propeller rotation is determined by the gear shifting mechanism.

On models equipped with a reverse gear, a sliding clutch engages the appropriate drive gear in the gearcase. This creates a direct coupling that transfers the power flow from the pinion gear to the propeller shaft. **Figure 1** shows the operation of the gear train.

Small outboard motors equipped with NEUTRAL but not REVERSE, use a spring-loaded clutch to shift between NEUTRAL and FORWARD gears. Gear train operation is shown in **Figure 2** (disengaged) and **Figure 3** (engaged).

The gearcase can be removed without removing the entire outboard motor or L-Drive assembly from the boat. This chapter contains removal, overhaul and installation procedures for the propeller, gearcase and water pump. **Table 1** lists

gearcase lubricant capacities and gear ratios. **Table 2** and **Table 3** list torque specifications. **Table 4** lists all gearcase service specifications. **Table 5** through **Table 8** list manufacturer recommended special tools. **Table 9** lists recommended sealants, lubricants and adhesives. All tables are at the end of the chapter.

The gearcases covered in this chapter differ somewhat in design and construction over the years covered and thus require slightly different service procedures. The chapter is arranged in a normal disassembly/assembly sequence. When only a partial repair is required, follow the procedure(s) for your gearcase to the point where the faulty parts can be replaced, then reassemble the unit.

Since this chapter covers a wide range of models from 1984-on, the gearcase assemblies shown in the accompanying illustrations are the most common. While it is possible that the components shown in the illustrations may not be identical to those being serviced, the step-by-step instructions may be used with all models covered in this manual.

Gearcases used on Force outboards and L-Drives can be divided into 12 basic designs.

Listed below are the major design features of each:

1. *4 and 5 hp*—Forward and neutral shifting only. Reverse thrust is accomplished by steering the engine backward. All bearings are bronze bushings. The exhaust exits through the anti-ventilation plate exhaust snout. Propeller uses a drive pin, plastic nut and cotter pin. There is no anode.

2. *7.5 hp*—Forward, neutral and reverse shifting. Similar to the 4-5 hp gearcase, but with a reverse gear added. The exhaust snout is a replaceable anode.

3. *9.9-15 hp (1997 and prior)*—Forward, neutral and reverse shifting. The forward and pinion gears run on roller bearings, while the reverse gear and propeller shaft run on bronze bushings. The exhaust exits a cast-in snout on the lower edge of the anti ventilation plate. The propeller uses a drive pin, plastic nut and cotter pin. There is no anode.

4. *9.9 and 15 hp (1998 only)*—Mercury gearcase with vertical shift rod travel. These models use a propeller thrust hub and elastic stop nut. Exhaust exits through the propeller

5. *25-50 hp (1984-1994)*—Scaled up 1984-1997 9.9-15 hp gearcase. Fully equipped with roller bearings. The exhaust snout is a replaceable anode.

6. *25-50 hp (1995-1999) and 70-75 hp (1995-1998)*—Mercury style gearcase with Force style vertical shift rod travel. Exhaust exits through the propeller hub. The 25 hp models use a propeller thrust hub and elastic stop nut, 40-75 hp uses a propeller thrust washer, tabbed lock washer and elastic stop nut. The trim tab is a replaceable anode. The 70 and 75 hp require shimming of internal components.

7. *60, 85-150 hp (1984-1994)*—4 major variations, all require shimming of internal components. A propeller thrust washer and elastic stop nut are used on all models, with many variations of the rear propeller retaining washer(s). Early models use a plastic coned propeller nut cover

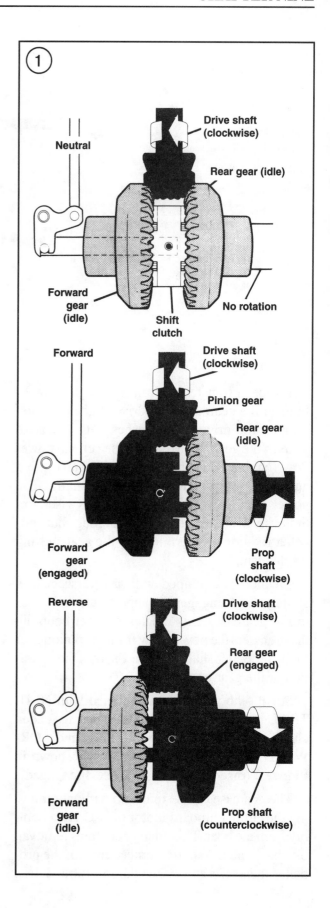

retained by a single screw. Dual-port exhaust models use a lock tab retainer under the elastic stop nut.

8. *Original (single port exhaust/one-piece drive shaft)*—Used on 60, 85 and 125 hp models (1984-1989). Exhaust exits the adjustable trim tab/exhaust snout. The drain plug is pipe thread. The anode is mounted in front of the propeller. The water intakes are on the propeller shaft centerline. A non-reusable crush ring and the water pump adapter plate secure the drive shaft

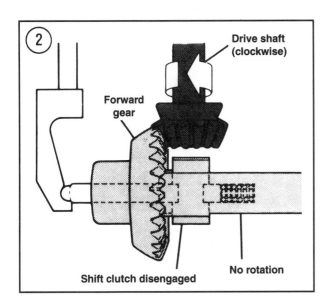

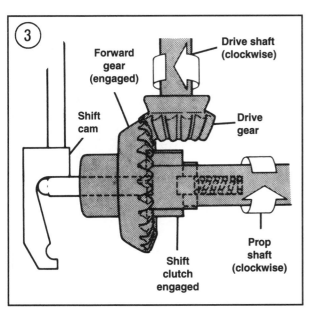

assembly to the gear housing. Shimming procedures involve the use of shim fixtures and feeler gauges.

9. *Type A (single port exhaust/two-piece drive shaft)*—Used on early 90, 120 and 150 hp outboard models. Also used on all 85 and 125 hp L-Drives and early 90 and 120 hp L-Drives. The drive shaft has a coupler that joins an upper drive shaft to the lower drive shaft just above the gearcase mounted water pump. A drive shaft lock ring is used to secure the drive shaft assembly into the gear housing. Shimming procedures require the use of code letters stamped into the gear housing and identification tags attached to new gearcase components. The water pump adapter plate and water pump assembly are redesigned.

10. *Type B (dual-port exhaust/two-piece drive shaft/internal anode)*—Used on 90, 120 and 150 hp outboard models and most late 90 and 120 hp L-Drives. Exhaust exits the adjustable trim tab/exhaust snout and the propeller hub. The anode is mounted in the upper exhaust area (requires separating gearcase from motor leg to service). The water intakes are located on the gearcase strut, above the propeller shaft centerline. A threaded lock ring secures the propeller shaft bearing carrier to the gear housing. Shimming procedures are similar to Type A design.

11. *Types C and D (dual-port exhaust/two-piece drive shaft/external anode)*—Used on most late 90, 120 and 150 hp outboard models through 1994 and the 1992 120 hp L-Drive. Service procedures are identical to the Type B design with the exception of the 2 anodes that are mounted above the anti ventilation plate, one on each side of gearcase. The Type D gearcase uses a gear set that will fit in Type B and C gearcases, however Type B and C gear sets will not fit in Type D gearcases. Type D dual-port exhaust gearcases are identified by the number 4 stamped near the water pump adapter cover or stamped above the fill plug.

9

12. *90, 120 hp (1995-1999) and 75 hp (1999) with Mercury style gearcase*—Mercury rotating cam gear shift mechanism. Exhaust exits through the propeller hub. The propeller uses a thrust washer, tabbed lock washer and elastic stop nut. The trim tab is a replaceable anode. Shimming of internal components is required.

SERVICE PRECAUTIONS

When working on a gearcase, there are several procedures to keep in mind that will make your work easier, faster and more accurate.

1. Never use elastic stop nuts more than twice. It is a good practice to replace such nuts each time they are removed. Never use an elastic stop nut that can be turned by hand (without the aid of a wrench).

2. Use special tools where noted. **Tables 5-8** list all manufacturer recommended special tools. The use of makeshift tools can damage components and may cause serious personal injury.

3. Use a vise with protective jaws to hold housings or components. If protective jaws are not available, insert blocks of wood or similar padding on each side of the component before clamping.

4. Remove and install pressed-on parts with an appropriate mandrel, support and press (arbor or hydraulic). Do not attempt to pry or hammer press-fit components on or off.

5. Refer to **Table 2** for special torque values and **Table 3** for standard torque values. Proper torque is essential to ensure long life and satisfactory service from outboard components.

6. To help reduce corrosion, especially in saltwater areas, apply Quicksilver Perfect Seal (**Table 9**) to all external surfaces of bearing carriers, housing mating surfaces and fasteners when no other sealant, adhesive or lubricant is recommended. Do not apply Perfect Seal where it can get into gears or bearings.

7. Discard all O-rings, seals and gaskets during disassembly. Apply 2-4-C Multi-Lube grease or equivalent (**Table 9**) to new O-rings and seal lips to provide initial lubrication.

8. Apply Loctite 271 threadlocking adhesive (**Table 9**) to the outer diameter of all metal-cased seals.

9. The 60 hp and larger gearcase uses precision shimmed gears. Record the location and thickness of all shims as they are removed from the gearcase. Shims are reusable as long as they are not physically damaged or corroded. Follow shimming instructions carefully. Shims control gear location and bearing preload. Incorrectly shimming a gearcase willl cause failure of the gears and/or bearings.

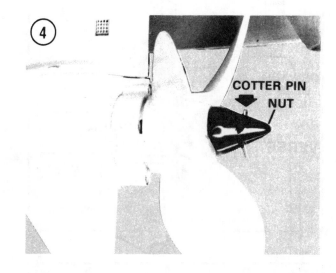

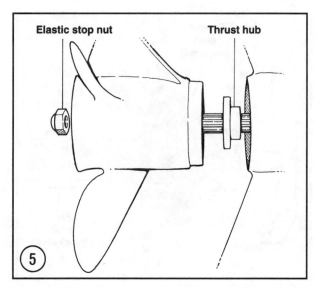

10. Work in an area with good lighting and sufficient space for component storage. Keep an ample number of clean containers available for parts storage. Cover parts and assemblies with clean shop towels or plastic bags.

CAUTION
Metric and American fasteners are used on the newer model Mercury style gearcases. Always match a replacement fas-

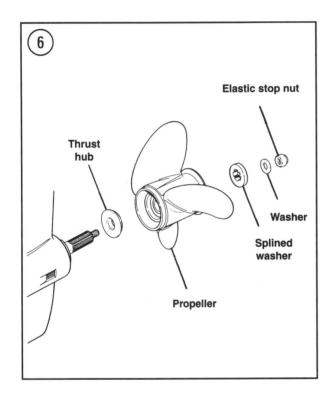

tener to the original. Do not run a tap or thread chaser into a hole (or over a bolt) without first verifying the thread size and pitch.

Refer to **Table 1** for gear ratio and lubricant capacities. Multiple gear ratios are often available within the same gearcase style to accommodate the different horsepower ratings. Do not attempt to operate an engine with the incorrect gear ratio or major power head damage will result.

PROPELLER

The outboard motors and L-Drives covered in this manual use many variations of propeller attachment.

Most smaller gearcases use a propeller drive pin that engages the propeller hub with a hole in the propeller shaft. The drive pin is secured by a cone shaped plastic nut which is secured by a cotter pin (**Figure 4**). The drive pin is designed to absorb the propeller thrust loads. The splines on the propeller shaft transfer engine torque to the propeller through the propeller's internal rubber hub.

The 25 hp 3-cylinder and 9.9 and 15 hp (1998) models use a propeller that requires a thrust hub that rides against a stepped shoulder on the propeller shaft. The small diameter end of the thrust hub must face the gearcase and the large diameter end must face the propeller. The propeller is retained by an elastic stop nut without a washer. See **Figure 5**.

Larger gearcases use propellers that push against a thrust washer that rides against a tapered step on the propeller shaft. The propeller on 60 hp and 85-150 hp single-port exhaust gearcases is retained by either a plastic flare washer, metal flat washer or elastic stop nut and tapered propeller nut cover (retained by a screw) or a spline washer, flat washer and elastic stop nut. See **Figure 6** or **Figure 7**.

The 70-75 hp and 1995-1999 40-50 hp propellers are retained by an elastic stop nut and a

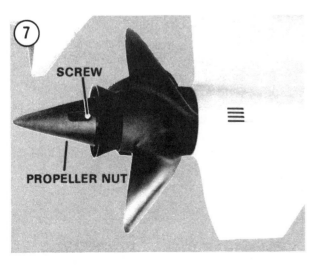

9

locking tab washer that engages 2 protrusions on the propeller hub. After the elastic stop nut is torqued, the lock tabs are bent up against the nut. See **Figure 8**.

The 85 hp and larger dual port exhaust and Mercury style gearcase propellers are retained by a spline washer (built into propeller on some models), a lock tab washer and an elastic stop nut. After the elastic stop nut is tightened, the locking tabs are driven down into the propeller hub or spline washer. See **Figure 9**.

All propellers use a rubber hub that is primarily designed to absorb gear shift shock loads. If a rubber hub fails, it will generally slip at higher throttle settings, but still allow the boater to return to port at reduced throttle. Most late model Mercury style gearcases use Mercury style propellers that incorporate a square shaped rubber or delrin (plastic) drive hub that cannot completely spin. The delrin drive hub (2, **Figure 10**) can be easily replaced should it become damaged from impact. Refer to *Delrin Drive Hub* (in this section) for instructions. Propellers with the rubber drive hub require special equipment when replacement is required. Have the hub replaced at a reputable propeller repair shop.

Removal/Installation

> *WARNING*
> *To prevent accidental starting, always disconnect and ground the spark plug wire(s) before servicing the propeller.*

Drive pin models

1. Remove and discard the cotter pin from the rear of the propeller shaft. See **Figure 4**.

2. Remove the propeller nut from the end of the propeller shaft. Remove the O-ring if so equipped.

3. Remove the drive pin from the propeller. It may be necessary to drive the pin out with a

punch and hammer if it is distorted or bent. Replace the pin if it is damaged or worn.

4. Slide the propeller from the propeller shaft.

5. Clean the propeller shaft thoroughly. Inspect the pin engagement hole for elongation, wear or cracks. Rotate the propeller shaft to check for a bent propeller shaft. Replace any damaged parts.

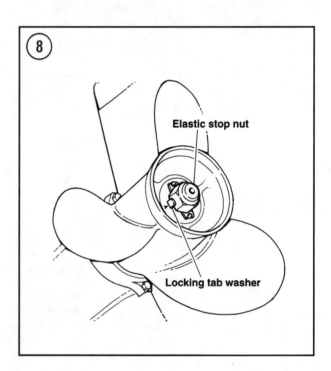

Elastic stop nut

Locking tab washer

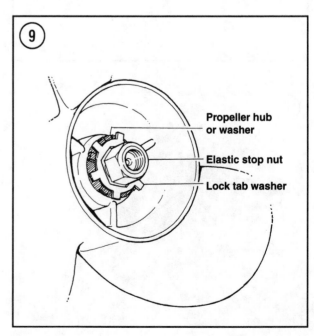

Propeller hub or washer

Elastic stop nut

Lock tab washer

6. Lubricate the propeller shaft liberally with 2-4-C Multi-Lube or Special Lubricant 101 (**Table 9**).

7. Slide the propeller onto the propeller shaft and align the drive pin bores. Insert the drive pin. Install the O-ring on models so equipped.

8. Install the propeller nut and secure it with a new stainless steel cotter pin. Bend the ends of the cotter pin to secure it in place.

Elastic stop nut models

> *CAUTION*
> *The 9.9 and 15 hp (serial No. 0E288000-on) and 25 hp 3-cylinder models use a propeller thrust hub. Install the thrust hub with its small diameter facing toward the gearcase.*

1A. *Early models*—Remove the screw securing the propeller cone to the propeller shaft. See **Figure 7**.

1B. *Lock tab models*—Pry the lock tab(s) up from the rear splined washer or down from the elastic stop nut as required using an appropriate tool.

2. Place a suitable block of wood between a propeller blade and the antiventilation plate to prevent propeller rotation. See **Figure 11**.

3. Remove the elastic stop nut with an appropriate socket. Replace the nut if it can be turned by hand.

4. Slide the propeller and all related hardware from the propeller shaft.

5. Clean the propeller shaft thoroughly. Inspect the propeller shaft for cracks, wear or damage. Rotate the propeller shaft to check for a bent propeller shaft. Inspect the propeller thrust washer and rear washers for wear or damage. Replace any damaged parts.

6. Lubricate the propeller shaft liberally with 2-4-C Multi-Lube or Special Lubricant 101 (**Table 9**).

7. Slide the propeller thrust washer onto the propeller shaft. Align the splines and seat the propeller against the thrust washer.

> *NOTE*
> *The Newer 9.9 and 15 hp (1998) and all 25 hp (3-cylinder) models do not use a rear washer or lock tab washer. The elastic stop nut is the only means of retention. Replace the nut if the locking feature is diminished.*

9

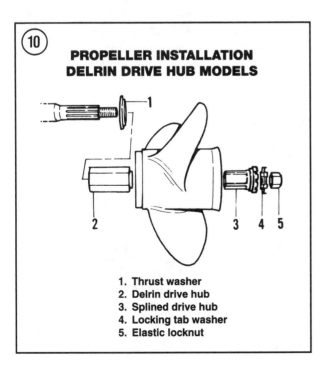

PROPELLER INSTALLATION DELRIN DRIVE HUB MODELS

1. Thrust washer
2. Delrin drive hub
3. Splined drive hub
4. Locking tab washer
5. Elastic locknut

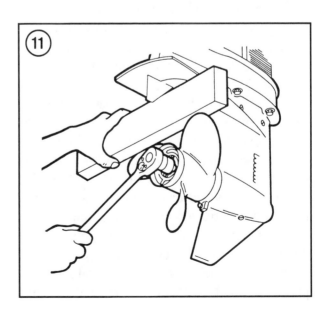

8. Install the rear washer(s), lock tab washer (if equipped) and the elastic stop nut.

9. Place a suitable block of wood between a propeller blade and the anti-ventilation plate to prevent propeller rotation and tighten the propeller nut to specification. See **Table 2**.

10A. *Early models*—Install the plastic propeller nut cover and screw. Tighten the screw securely. See **Figure 7**.

10B. *40-75 hp Lock tab models*—Bend both lock tabs securely against the appropriate flats of the elastic stop nut. See **Figure 8**. If necessary, move the propeller nut slightly to align the tabs.

10C. *85-150 hp Lock tab models*—Select 3 lock tabs that align with the notches in the propeller hub or rear splined washer. Drive the lock tabs into the notches with a hammer and punch. See **Figure 9**. If necessary move the propeller nut slightly to align the tabs.

Delrin drive hub models

Refer to (**Figure 10**) during the Removal and Installation procedure.

1. Pry the lock tab(s) up from the propeller (rear splined washer) or down from the elastic stop nut as required using an appropriate tool.

2. Place a suitable block of wood between a propeller blade and the antiventilation plate to prevent propeller rotation. See **Figure 11**.

3. Remove the propeller elastic stop nut with an appropriate socket. Replace the nut if it can be unthreaded by hand.

4. Slide the propeller and all related hardware from the propeller shaft.

5. Remove the delrin drive hub (2, **Figure 10**) from the propeller. Use a punch and drive the hub from the propeller if necessary. Inspect the hub for cracked, melted or excessively worn areas. Replace the hub if any defects are noted.

6. Clean the propeller shaft thoroughly. Inspect the propeller shaft for cracks, wear or damage. Rotate the propeller shaft to check for a bent propeller shaft. Inspect the propeller thrust

washer and rear washers for wear or damage. Replace any damaged parts.

7. Lubricate the propeller shaft liberally with 2-4-C Multi-Lube or Special Lubricant 101 (**Table 9**).

8. Place the small tapered side of the delrin drive hub into the propeller bore opening. with. Align the hub with the square bore and carefully slide the hub into the bore. When using a new delrin drive hub the 4 small tabs should face out. Use a block of wood for padding and carefully drive the hub into the bore when necessary.

9. Slide the propeller thrust washer onto the propeller shaft. Slide the propeller onto the propeller shaft until it contacts the thrust washer (1, **Figure 10**).

10. Slide the splined drive hub (3, **Figure 10**) onto the propeller shaft. Rotate the propeller until the splined drive hub aligns with its bore in the delrin drive hub and slides into the hub. Rotate the propeller until the splined drive hub aligns with the splines on the propeller shaft. The splined drive hub must slide fully into the delrin drive hub and seat against the propeller.

11. Install the locking tab washer and elastic locknut (4 and 5, **Figure 10**). Place a suitable block of wood between a propeller blade and the anti-ventilation plate (**Figure 11**) to prevent

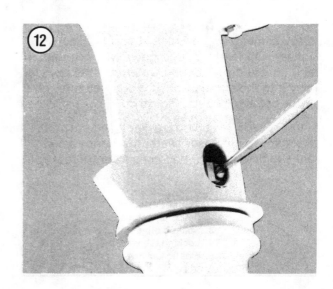

propeller rotation and tighten the propeller nut to specification. See **Table 2**.

12. Bend both lock tabs securely against the appropriate flats of the elastic stop nut. See **Figure 8**. If necessary, move the propeller nut slightly to align the tabs.

GEARCASE

Removal/Installation 4-5 hp

1. Disconnect the spark plug wire from the spark plug to prevent accidental starting.

2. Remove the propeller as described in this chapter.

3. Pry the shift coupler cover from the side of the motor leg with a screwdriver. See **Figure 12**.

4. Loosen the shift coupler screw (**Figure 12**).

5. Remove the 2 fasteners securing the gearcase to the motor leg.

6. Tilt the motor leg up and carefully separate the gearcase from the motor leg.

7. Install the gearcase into a suitable holding fixture.

8. If gearcase disassembly is required, drain gearcase lubricant as described in Chapter Four.

CAUTION
Do not grease the top of the drive shaft in Step 9. This may cause a hydraulic lock and excessively preload the drive shaft and crankshaft when the mounting screws are tightened, resulting in prema-

ture failure of the power head or gearcase.

9. To reinstall the gearcase, lightly lubricate the drive shaft splines with 2-4-C Multi-Lube Grease (**Table 9**).

10. Pull the lower shift rod upward as far as possible.

11. Apply a bead of RTV sealant along the gearcase mating surface as shown in **Figure 13**.

12. Position the gearcase under the motor leg and align the drive shaft splines with the crankshaft.

CAUTION
Do not rotate the flywheel counterclockwise in Step 13, or water pump impeller damage can result.

13. Start the gearcase into position, rotating the flywheel clockwise as required to align the drive shaft and crankshaft splines.

14. Align the water tube with the water tube seal. Align the upper shift rod with the lower shift rod coupler.

15. Seat the gearcase against the motor leg.

16. Coat the motor leg screw threads with RTV sealant. Install both screws and tighten to specification (**Table 2**).

17. Place the shift lever in NEUTRAL. Make sure the lower shift rod is all the way up, then tighten the coupler screw.

18. Position the shift coupler cover on the motor leg and tap into place with a soft mallet.

19. Install the propeller as described in this chapter.

20. Reconnect the spark plug lead and refill the gearcase (if drained) with the proper type and quantity of lubricant. See Chapter Four.

Removal/Installation 7.5 hp

1. Disconnect and ground the spark plug leads to prevent accidental starting.

2. Remove the propeller as described in this chapter.

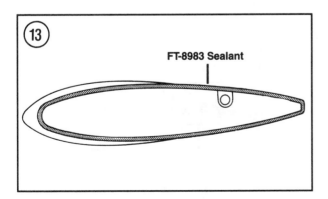

(13)

FT-8983 Sealant

3. If gearcase disassembly is required, drain the gearcase lubricant as described in Chapter Four.

4. Remove the screw joining the upper and lower shift rods together. The screw is located just above and in front of the lower shock mount covers.

5. Remove the 4 screws securing the gearcase extension to the motor leg.

6. Remove the gearcase from the motor leg. Place the gearcase in a suitable holding fixture.

7. Check the lower shift rod adjustment before reinstalling the gearcase. The centerline of the hole in the rod must be 6.12-6.20 in. (155.45-157.48 mm) above the gearcase to motor leg mating surface in NEUTRAL. Turn the lower shift rod as necessary to adjust shift rod height.

CAUTION
Do not grease the top of the drive shaft in Step 8. This may cause a hydraulic lock and excessively preload the drive shaft and crankshaft when the mounting screws are tightened, resulting in premature failure of the power head or gearcase.

8. Lightly lubricate the drive shaft splines with 2-4-C Multi-Lube grease (**Table 9**).

9. Position the gearcase under the motor leg. Align the water tube in the water pump and drive shaft with crankshaft splines.

CAUTION
Do not rotate the flywheel counterclockwise in Step 10 or water pump impeller damage can result.

10. Push the gearcase toward the motor leg, rotating the flywheel clockwise as required to align the drive shaft and crankshaft splines. Insert the lower shift rod into the upper shift rod.

11. Make sure the water tube is seated in the water pump seal, then push the gearcase against the motor leg. Install the gearcase screws and tighten to specifications (**Table 2**).

12. Align the upper and lower shift rods. Install the shift rod screw and tighten securely.

13. Install the propeller as described in this chapter.

14. Refill the gearcase (if drained) as outlined in Chapter Four. Reconnect the spark plug leads.

Removal/Installation 9.9-15 hp (1984-1997)

1. Disconnect the spark plug leads to prevent accidental starting.

2. If gearcase disassembly is required, drain the gearcase lubricant as described in Chapter Four.

3. Shift into FORWARD gear. Rotate the propeller clockwise while shifting to help engage forward gear.

4. Remove the 4 screws securing the gearcase to the motor leg.

5. Separate the gearcase from the motor leg enough to expose the shift rod screw (**Figure 14**), then remove the screw.

6. Remove the gearcase from the motor leg. Place the gearcase into a suitable holding fixture.

7. Check the lower shift rod adjustment before reinstalling the gearcase. The centerline of the hole in the rod must be 9/64 to 15/64 in. below the motor leg-to-gearcase mating surface with

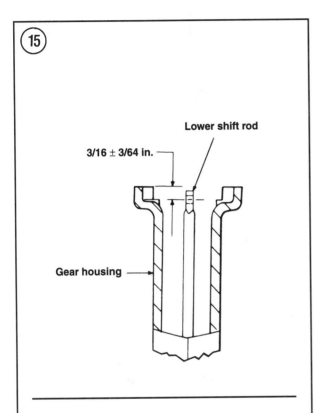

15

Lower shift rod

3/16 ± 3/64 in.

Gear housing

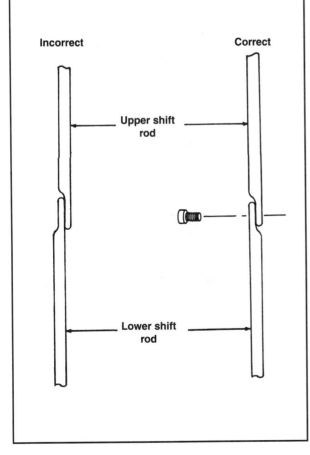

Incorrect

Correct

Upper shift rod

Lower shift rod

the gearcase in NEUTRAL. See **Figure 15**. Turn the lower shift rod as necessary to adjust shift rod height. Once the correct adjustment is obtained, position the shift rod so the flared and indented side of the hole in the rod is facing the starboard side of the gear housing.

8. To reinstall, shift the gearcase into FORWARD by pulling the lower shift rod upward. If necessary, rotate the propeller shaft clockwise to help engage forward gear.

> *CAUTION*
> *Do not grease the top of the drive shaft in Step 9. This may cause a hydraulic lock and excessively preload the drive shaft and crankshaft when the mounting screws are tightened, resulting in premature failure of the power head or gearcase.*

9. Lightly lubricate the drive shaft splines with a 2-4-C Multi-Lube grease.

10. Position the gearcase under the motor leg. Align the water tube in the water pump seal and drive shaft with crankshaft splines.

> *CAUTION*
> *Do not rotate the flywheel counterclockwise in Step 11 or water pump impeller damage can result.*

11. Push the gearcase toward the motor leg, rotating the flywheel clockwise as required to align the crankshaft and drive shaft splines. Align the upper and lower shift rods as shown in **Figure 15**.

12. Install the shift rod screw and tighten securely.

13. Make sure the water tube is seated in the water pump seal, then push gearcase against the motor leg. Install the gearcase screws and tighten to specification (**Table 2**).

14. Refill the gearcase (if drained) as outlined in Chapter Four. Reconnect the spark plug leads.

9

Removal/Installation 9.9, 15 hp (1998) and 25 hp (3-Cylinder)

1. Disconnect and ground the spark plug leads to prevent accidental starting.

2. Remove the propeller as described in this chapter.

3. If gearcase disassembly is required, drain the gearcase lubricant as described in Chapter Four.

4. Remove the rubber grommet (plug) on the port side of the motor leg to gain access to the shift rod screw. Remove the screw joining the upper and lower shift rods together (**Figure 15**).

5. On 9.9 and 15 hp models, Remove the 2 bolts on the side of the gearcase. Remove the 1 bolt above the leading edge of the mating surface for the gearcase. On 25 hp models, Remove the 4 screws securing the gearcase to the motor leg.

6. Remove the gearcase from the motor leg. Place the gearcase in a suitable holding fixture.

CAUTION
Do not grease the top of the drive shaft in Step 7. This may cause a hydraulic lock and excessively preload the drive shaft and crankshaft when the mounting screws are tightened, resulting in premature failure of the power head or gearcase.

7. To reinstall the gearcase, lightly lubricate the drive shaft splines with 2-4-C Multi-Lube grease (**Table 9**).

8. Position the gearcase under the motor leg. Align the water tube in the water pump and drive shaft with crankshaft splines.

CAUTION
Do not rotate the flywheel counterclockwise in Step 9 or water pump impeller damage can result.

9. Push the gearcase toward the motor leg, rotating the flywheel clockwise as required to align the drive shaft and crankshaft splines.

10. Make sure the water tube is seated in the water pump seal, then push the gearcase against the motor leg. Install the gearcase screws and tighten to specification (**Table 2**).

11. Align the upper and lower shift rods. Install the shift rod screw and tighten securely. Install the rubber grommet in the motor leg access hole.

12. Install the propeller as described in this chapter.

13. Refill the gearcase (if drained) as outlined in Chapter Four. Reconnect the spark plug leads.

Removal/Installation 35-50 hp (1984-1987) and 25 hp (2-Cylinder)

1. Disconnect the spark plug leads to prevent accidental starting. Disconnect the negative battery cable.

2. If gearcase disassembly is required, drain gearcase lubricant as described in Chapter Four.

3. Loosen the screws securing the gearcase to the motor leg.

4. Separate the gearcase from the motor leg sufficiently to gain access to the shift rod coupler (**Figure 16**).

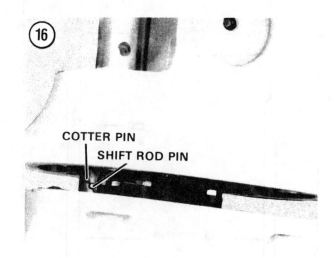

COTTER PIN
SHIFT ROD PIN

5. Remove the cotter pin and shift rod coupler pin. Separate the upper shift rod from the intermediate shift rod.

6. Remove the 4 gearcase-to-motor leg screws. Remove gearcase from the motor leg. Place the gearcase into a suitable holding fixture.

CAUTION
Do not grease the top of the drive shaft in Step 7. This may cause a hydraulic lock and excessively preload the drive shaft and crankshaft when the mounting screws are tightened, resulting in premature failure of the power head or gearcase.

7. To reinstall the gearcase, lightly lubricate the drive shaft splines with a suitable antiseize grease.

CAUTION
Do not rotate the flywheel counterclockwise in Step 8 or water pump impeller damage can result.

8. Install the gearcase on the motor leg. Rotate the flywheel clockwise to align the crankshaft and drive shaft splines.

9. Install (but do not tighten) the 4 gearcase-to-motor leg screws.

10. Connect the shift rods (**Figure 16**). Secure shift coupler pin with a new cotter pin.

11. Tighten the 4 gearcase-to-motor leg screws to specifications (**Table 2**).

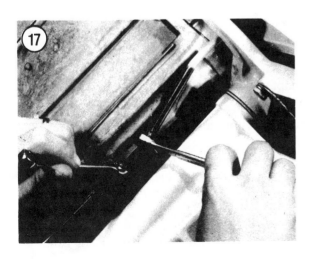

12. If drained, refill the gearcase as described in Chapter Four. Reconnect the spark plug leads.

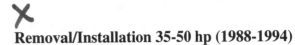

Removal/Installation 35-50 hp (1988-1994)

1. Disconnect and ground the spark plug leads to prevent accidental starting.

2. Remove the propeller as described in this chapter.

3. If gearcase disassembly is required, drain the gearcase lubricant as described in Chapter Four.

4. Shift into FORWARD gear. Rotate the propeller while shifting to assist gear engagement.

5. Loosen the jam nut above the shift coupler. See **Figure 17**.

6. Turn the shift rod coupler until the upper and lower shift rods are separated.

7. Remove the 4 screws securing the gearcase to the motor leg.

8. Remove the gearcase from the motor leg. Place the gearcase in a suitable holding fixture.

CAUTION
Do not grease the top of the drive shaft in Step 9. This may cause a hydraulic lock and excessively preload the drive shaft and crankshaft when the mounting screws are tightened, resulting in premature failure of the power head or gearcase.

9. To reinstall the gearcase, lightly lubricate the drive shaft splines with 2-4-C Multi-Lube grease (**Table 9**).

10. Shift the control box into FORWARD gear. Shift the gearcase into FORWARD gear while rotating the propeller shaft clockwise.

11. Position the gearcase under the motor leg. Align the water tube in the water pump and drive shaft with crankshaft splines.

CAUTION
Do not rotate the flywheel counterclockwise in Step 12 or water pump impeller damage can result.

9

12. Push the gearcase toward the motor leg, rotating the flywheel clockwise as required to align the drive shaft and crankshaft splines.

13. Make sure the water tube is seated in the water pump seal, then push the gearcase against the motor leg. Install the gearcase screws and tighten to specifications (**Table 2**).

14. Align the upper and lower shift rods. Reconnect the shift rods by turning the shift rod coupler (**Figure 17**).

15. Adjust the shift linkage. See *Gear Shift Linkage Adjustment* in this chapter.

16. Install the propeller as described in this chapter.

17. Refill the gearcase (if drained) as outlined in Chapter Four. Reconnect the spark plug leads.

Removal/Installation 60 hp

1. Disconnect and ground the spark plug leads to prevent accidental starting.

2. Remove the propeller as described in this chapter.

3. If gearcase disassembly is required, drain the gearcase lubricant as described in Chapter Four.

4. Remove the 2 screws from the port lower shock mount cover. Remove the port lower shock mount cover to gain access to the shift rod pin. Remove the cotter pin and shift pin joining the upper and lower shift rods together.

5. Remove the 6 screws securing the gearcase to the motor leg. The gearcase can be removed with the exhaust snout installed.

6. Remove the gearcase from the motor leg. Place the gearcase in a suitable holding fixture.

CAUTION
Do not grease the top of the drive shaft in Step 7. This may cause a hydraulic lock and excessively preload the drive shaft and crankshaft when the mounting screws are tightened, resulting in premature failure of the power head or gearcase.

7. To reinstall the gearcase, lightly lubricate the drive shaft splines with 2-4-C Multi-Lube grease (**Table 9**).

8. Position the gearcase under the motor leg. Align the water tube in the water pump and drive shaft with crankshaft splines.

CAUTION
Do not rotate the flywheel counterclockwise in Step 9 or water pump impeller damage can result.

9. Push the gearcase toward the motor leg, rotating the flywheel clockwise as required to align the drive shaft and crankshaft splines.

10. Make sure the water tube is seated in the water pump seal, then push the gearcase against the motor leg. Install the gearcase screws and tighten to specifications (**Table 2**).

11. Align the upper and lower shift rods. Install the shift rod pin and secure with a new cotter pin.

12. Install the propeller as described in this chapter.

13. Adjust the shift linkage. See *Gear Shift Linkage Adjustment* in this chapter.

14. Refill the gearcase (if drained) as outlined in Chapter Four. Reconnect the spark plug leads.

Removal/Installation
40-50 hp (1995-1999), 70 and 75 hp
and 90-120 hp (1995-1999)

1. Disconnect and ground the spark plug leads to prevent accidental starting.

2. Remove the propeller as described in this chapter.

3. If gearcase disassembly is required, drain the gearcase lubricant as described in Chapter Four.

NOTE
The 90-120 hp models do not require any shift system disengagement for gearcase removal

4A. *40-50 hp*—Shift into NEUTRAL gear.

4B. *70-120 hp*—Shift into FORWARD gear. Rotate the propeller while shifting to assist gear engagement.

5. *40-75 hp*—Loosen the jam nut above the shift coupler. See **Figure 18** for 40-50 hp and **Figure 17** for (1998 and prior) 70-75 hp.

6. *40-50 hp models and 75 hp models (prior to 1999)*—Turn the shift rod coupler until the upper and lower shift rods are separated.

7. Mark the trim tab position (with a white grease pencil or china marker) and remove the trim tab retaining screw. Remove the trim tab.

8A. *40-50 hp*—Remove the 4 screws (2 on each side) and 1 nut (in the trim tab pocket) securing the gearcase to the motor leg.

8B. *70-75 hp (prior to 1999)*—Remove the 5 screws (2 on each side and 1 in the trim tab pocket) securing the gearcase to the motor leg.

8C. *90-120 hp and 1999 75 hp*—Remove the 5 elastic stop nuts (2 on each side and 1 in the trim tab pocket) securing the gearcase to the motor leg.

9. Remove the gearcase from the motor leg. Place the gearcase in a suitable holding fixture.

CAUTION
Do not grease the top of the drive shaft in Step 10. This may cause a hydraulic lock and excessively preload the drive shaft and crankshaft when the mounting

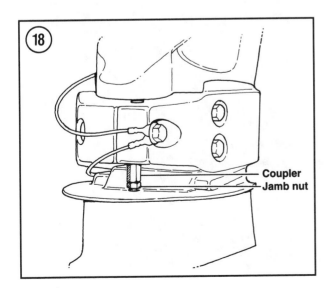

Coupler
Jamb nut

screws are tightened, resulting in premature failure of the power head or gearcase.

10. To reinstall the gearcase, lightly lubricate the drive shaft splines with 2-4-C Multi-Lube grease (**Table 9**).

11A. *40-50 hp*—Shift the control box and gearcase into NEUTRAL gear.

11B. *70-120 hp*—Shift the control box and gearcase into FORWARD gear. Rotate the propeller while shifting the gearcase to assist gear engagement. When FORWARD gear is engaged and the propeller shaft is turned clockwise, the clutch dog will ratchet.

12. Position the gearcase under the motor leg. Align the water tube in the water pump and drive shaft with crankshaft splines.

CAUTION
Do not rotate the flywheel counterclockwise in Step 13 or water pump impeller damage can result. It may be necessary to rotate the shift mechanism slightly on 90 and 120 hp models to engage the shift block splines with the gearcase shift rod splines.

13. Push the gearcase towards the motor leg, rotating the flywheel clockwise as required to align the drive shaft and crankshaft splines.

14. Make sure the water tube is seated in the water pump seal and the shift rod splines are engaged (90 and 120 hp and 75 hp models (1999), then push the gearcase against the motor leg. Install the gearcase screws or elastic stop nuts and tighten to specifications (**Table 2**).

15. *40-50 hp and 70/75 hp models (prior to 1999)*—Align the upper and lower shift rods. Reconnect the shift rods by turning the shift rod coupler (**Figure 17** or **Figure 18**).

16. Adjust the shift linkage. See *Gear Shift Linkage Adjustment* in this chapter.

17. Install the propeller as described in this chapter.

18. Refill the gearcase (if drained) as outlined in Chapter Four. Reconnect the spark plug leads.

9

Removal/Installation (1984-1994 85-150 hp [Except L-Drive])

1. Disconnect the spark plug leads to prevent accidental starting. Disconnect the negative battery cable.

2. If gearcase disassembly is required, drain the gearcase lubricant as described in Chapter Four.

3. Remove the propeller as described in this chapter.

4. Remove the cotter pin holding the shift rod pin to the upper shift rod coupler. See **Figure 19**. Remove the shift rod pin and separate the shift rods.

NOTE
A 6-point socket should be used to remove the exhaust snout screw with the thin head in Step 5.

5. Mark the position of the exhaust snout for reference during installation. Remove the 2 screws securing the exhaust snout to the gearcase and remove the snout.

6. Remove the gearcase fastener inside the exhaust snout cavity, then remove the remaining gearcase-to-motor leg screws.

7. Remove the gearcase and place into a suitable holding fixture. Make sure the drive shaft seal is removed with the drive shaft. If not, reach into the motor leg and extract the drive shaft seal.

CAUTION
Do not grease the top of the drive shaft in Step 8. This may create a hydraulic lock and excessively preload the drive shaft and crankshaft when the mounting screws are tightened, resulting in premature failure of the power head or gearcase.

8. Make sure drive shaft splines are clean. Inspect the drive shaft seal for cracking or other damage. Replace seal as required. Lightly lubricate the drive shaft splines with a 2-4-C Multi-Lube grease.

CAUTION
To prevent water pump impeller damage, do not rotate the flywheel counterclockwise in Step 9.

9. Position the gearcase under the motor leg. Align the water tube with the water pump grommet, drive shaft with the crankshaft splines and the shift rod with the shift rod coupler. Rotate the flywheel clockwise as required to align the crankshaft and drive shaft splines.

10. Install the gearcase-to-motor leg screws and tighten to specifications (**Table 2**).

11. Install the gearcase fastener inside the exhaust snout. Install the exhaust snout aligning the reference marks made during removal.

12. Connect the shift rod to the shift rod coupler. Install a new cotter pin to retain the shift rod pin.

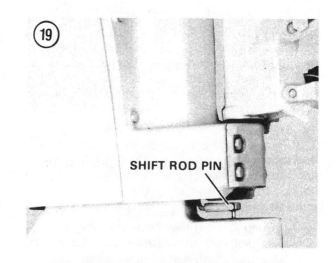

SHIFT ROD PIN

13. Adjust the shift rod. See *Gear Shift Linkage Adjustment* in this chapter.

14. Install the propeller as described in this chapter.

15. If drained, refill the gearcase with the recommended lubricant as outlined in Chapter Four.

16. Reconnect the spark plug leads.

Removal/Installation L-Drive

1. Disconnect the spark plug leads to prevent accidental starting.

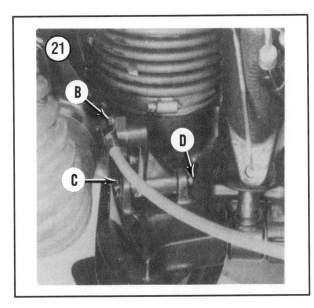

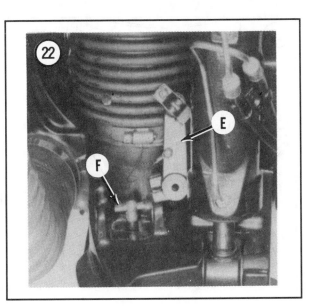

2. Lower gearcase to the fully down position.

3. If gearcase disassembly is required, drain gearcase lubricant as described in Chapter Four.

4. Remove the propeller as described in this chapter.

5. Disconnect the gear shift linkage as follows:
   a. Remove the connector (A, **Figure 20**) from the stud.
   b. Remove screw (B, **Figure 21**). Remove cotter pin (C), then push out shift lever pivot pin (D).
   c. Remove shift lever (E, **Figure 22**) and shift pin (F).

6. Place marks on the side of the exhaust snout for reference during reassemble. Remove the 2 screws securing the exhaust snout to the gearcase and remove the snout.

7. Tilt the gearcase to the fully up position.

8. Remove the screw inside the exhaust snout cavity (**Figure 23**).

9. Remove the 6 remaining screws securing the gearcase to the motor leg. Remove the gearcase and place into a suitable holding fixture.

10. Before reinstalling the gearcase, inspect the waterline seal for wear or damage and replace as required. See **Figure 24**. Be sure waterline seal is properly installed in the universal joint housing.

CAUTION
Do not grease the top of the drive shaft in Step 11. This may create a hydraulic lock

9

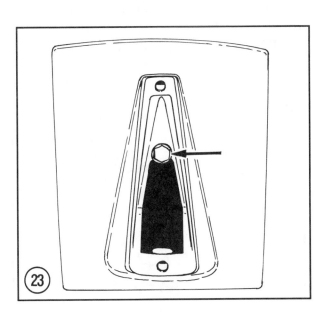

and excessively preload the drive shaft and crankshaft when the mounting screws are tightened, resulting in premature failure of the power head or gearcase.

11. Make sure the drive shaft splines are clean, then lightly lubricate splines with suitable antiseize grease.

12. Position gearcase under the universal joint housing. Align drive shaft with crankshaft, then push gearcase up against the universal joint housing. Install gearcase mounting screws. Install screw inside the exhaust snout cavity (**Figure 23**). Tighten all gearcase mounting screws to specification (**Table 2**).

13. Apply Loctite RC680 (**Table 9**) to the threads of the exhaust snout mounting screws. Install the exhaust snout, align with the marks made during disassembly, then install and securely tighten the screws.

14. Lower the gearcase to the fully down position.

15. Refer to **Figure 25** and check shift rod adjustment as follows:

    a. Install shift pin into the shift rod.

    b. Insert the shift lever pivot pin into the universal joint housing bracket.

    c. While rotating propeller shaft, pull the shift rod upward as far as it will go.

    d. The shift pin should just clear the shift lever pivot pin when the shift rod is rotated 90°. If not, turn shift rod in or out as required to obtain the desired clearance.

16. Remove the shift lever pivot pin.

17. Reassemble the shift linkage as follows:

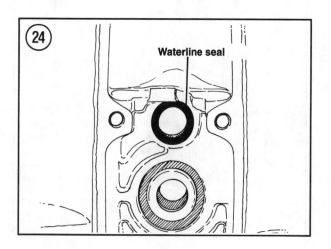

24

Waterline seal

    a. Install the shift lever (E, **Figure 22**) so it engages the flats on the shift pin (F).

    b. Install the shift lever pivot pin (D, **Figure 21**). Secure the pin with a new cotter pin (C).

    c. Secure the shift cable to the lever with screw (B, **Figure 21**).

    d. Install the shift cable connector (A, **Figure 20**) on the stud.

NOTE
*Some early models are equipped with a plastic shift cable connector (A, **Figure 20**). On models so equipped, replace the plastic connector with connector part No. 58685-2.*

18. Lubricate propeller shaft with a suitable antiseize grease. Install the propeller as described in this chapter.

19. If drained, refill the gearcase with the recommended lubricant as described in Chapter Four.

20. Reconnect the spark plug leads.

GEARCASE DISASSEMBLY/REASSEMBLY

4 and 5 hp

Refer to **Figure 26** for this procedure.

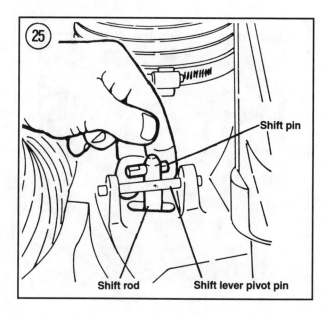

25

Shift pin

Shift rod   **Shift lever pivot pin**

GEARCASE (4 AND 5 HP)

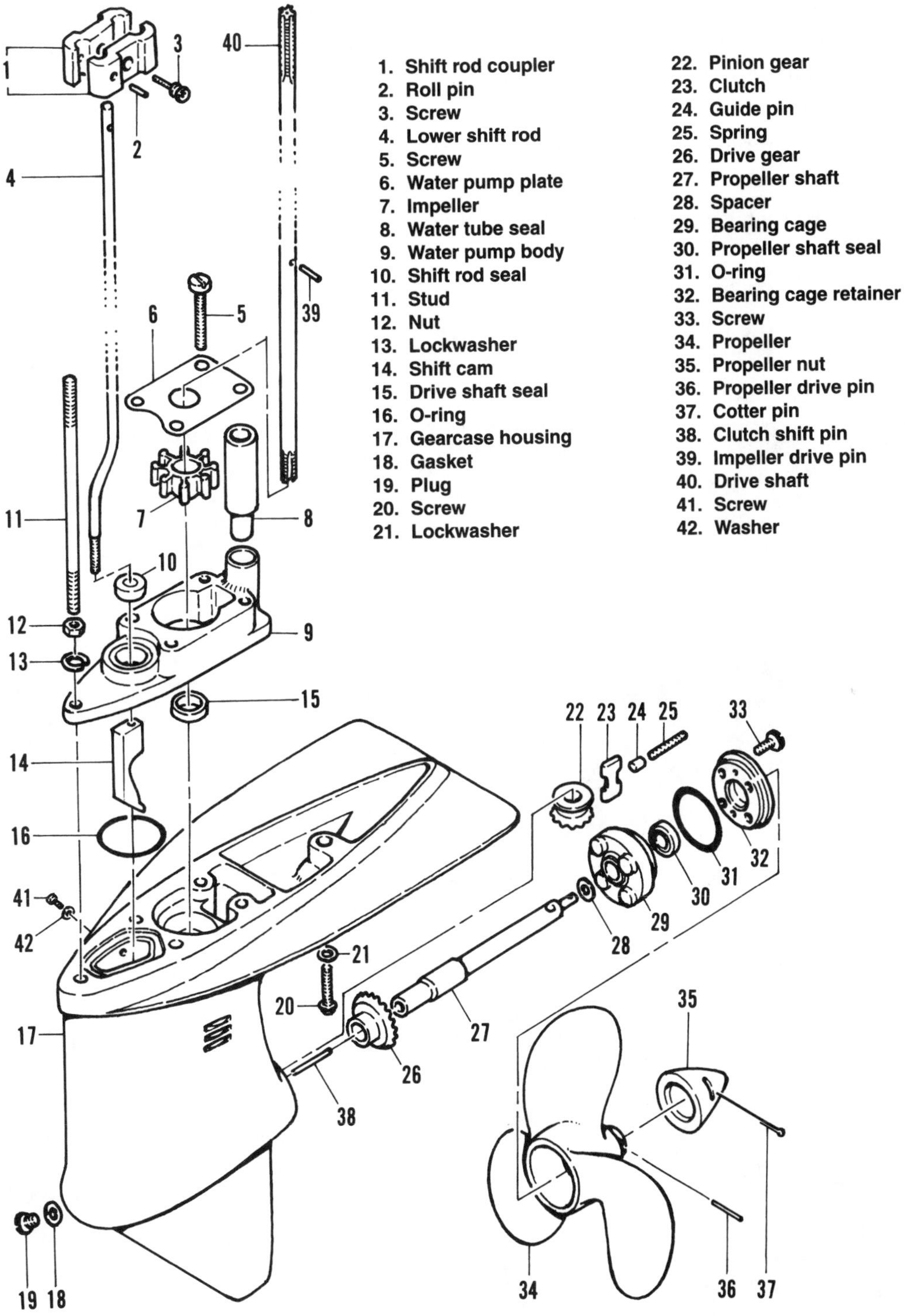

1. Shift rod coupler
2. Roll pin
3. Screw
4. Lower shift rod
5. Screw
6. Water pump plate
7. Impeller
8. Water tube seal
9. Water pump body
10. Shift rod seal
11. Stud
12. Nut
13. Lockwasher
14. Shift cam
15. Drive shaft seal
16. O-ring
17. Gearcase housing
18. Gasket
19. Plug
20. Screw
21. Lockwasher
22. Pinion gear
23. Clutch
24. Guide pin
25. Spring
26. Drive gear
27. Propeller shaft
28. Spacer
29. Bearing cage
30. Propeller shaft seal
31. O-ring
32. Bearing cage retainer
33. Screw
34. Propeller
35. Propeller nut
36. Propeller drive pin
37. Cotter pin
38. Clutch shift pin
39. Impeller drive pin
40. Drive shaft
41. Screw
42. Washer

9

1. Remove the gearcase as described in this chapter.

2. Secure the gearcase in a suitable holding fixture or a vise with protective jaws. If protective jaws are not available, position the gearcase upright with the skeg between wooden blocks in a vise.

3. Drain the gearcase lubricant as described in Chapter Four.

4. Remove the water pump as described in this chapter.

5. Remove the 4 screws holding the bearing cage retainer to the bearing cage. See **Figure 27**.

6. Install the flywheel puller (part No. FT-8948-1) as shown in **Figure 28** and remove the bearing cage retainer.

7. Remove the bearing cage O-ring.

8. Reinstall the bearing cage retainer into the gearcase housing and secure to the bearing cage with 2 screws placed 180° apart.

9. Install puller (part No. FT-8948-1) as shown in **Figure 28** and remove the bearing cage and retainer as an assembly.

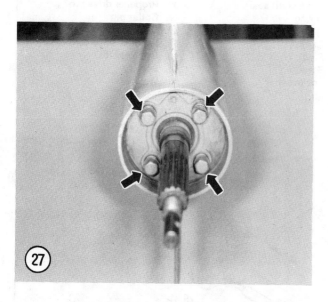

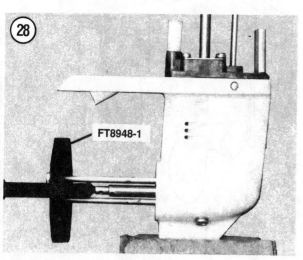

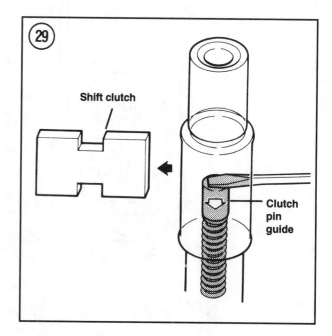

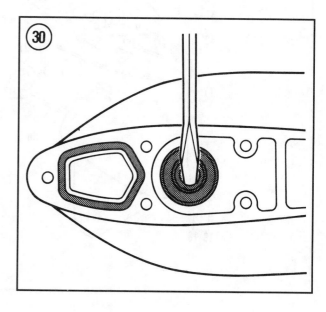

10. Withdraw the propeller shaft from the gear-case.

11. Remove the lower shift rod and shift cam.

CAUTION
Cover shaft with a shop cloth in Step 12. If spring pressure is released suddenly, the clutch guide pin may shoot out rapidly.

12. Clamp the propeller shaft (prop end down) into a vise with protective jaws. Remove the clutch shift pin. Use a small screwdriver to compress the clutch spring and remove the clutch from the shaft slot (**Figure 29**). Remove the clutch guide pin and spring.

13. Remove the drive gear and the pinion gear from the gearcase, then lift the drive shaft from the gearcase.

14. Pry the drive shaft seal from the gearcase bore with a screwdriver. See **Figure 30**.

15. Position the bearing cage face down on open vise jaws or on 2 blocks of wood. Drive the

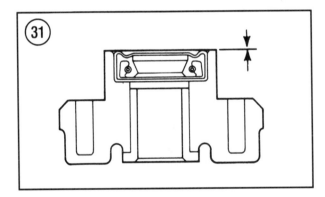

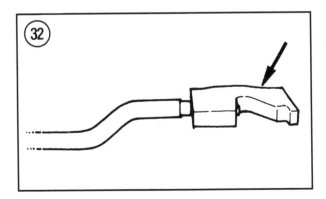

propeller shaft seal out of the bearing cage with a suitable punch.

16. Clean and inspect all components as described in this chapter. Refer to **Table 4** for all specifications. The gear housing upper drive shaft and forward gear bearings are not serviceable. Replace the gear housing if either of these bearings is excessively worn. Replace all worn or damaged parts that do not meet specifications.

17. Install a new seal into the propeller shaft bearing cage with seal installer (FT-2907) or equivalent. The spring side of the seal should face the propeller. The seal case should be flush to 0.030 in. (0.76 mm) below the bearing cage surface. See **Figure 31**.

18. Install the clutch spring in the propeller shaft cavity, then insert the clutch pin guide. Place a shop cloth over the shaft end and use a small screwdriver to compress the spring, then slide the clutch into the prop shaft slot. Install the shift pin into the propeller shaft.

19. Install a new drive shaft seal into the gearcase housing with sealer installer (FT-2907 or equivalent). Spring side of the seal should face out.

20. Position a new O-ring into the shift rod cavity groove.

21. Screw the shift cam onto the shift rod as far as possible, then back off as necessary to position the cam on the shift rod as shown in **Figure 32**. Install the shift rod and cam assembly into the gearcase.

22. Install the drive gear and pinion gear into the gearcase.

23. Install the drive shaft while holding the pinion gear in position.

24. Install the water pump as described in this chapter.

25. Install the propeller shaft into the gearcase.

26. Install the spacer and bearing cage. Push the bearing cage into the gearcase until the O-ring groove is visible. Install a new O-ring into the groove.

9

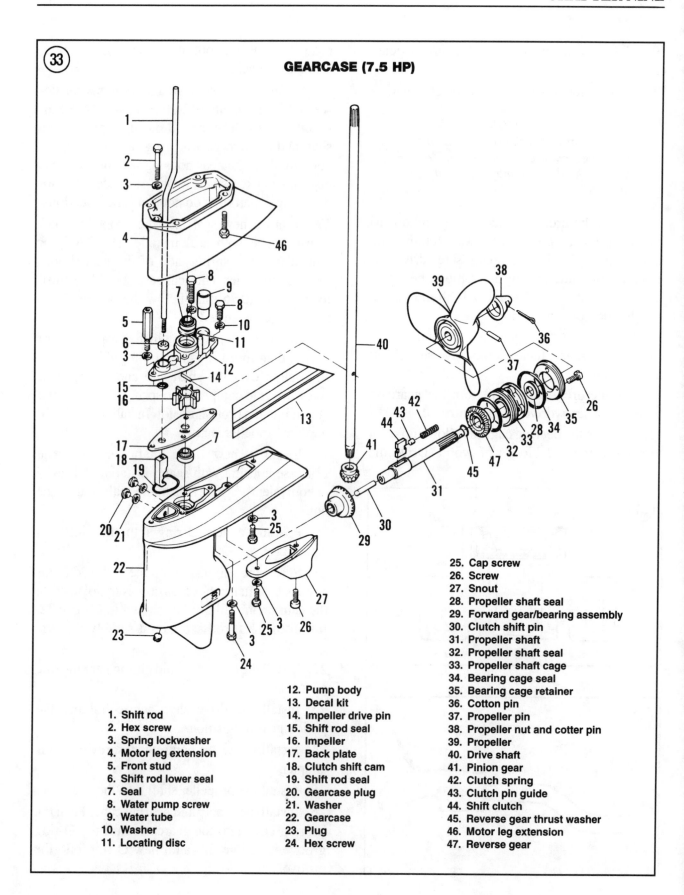

GEARCASE (7.5 HP)

1. Shift rod
2. Hex screw
3. Spring lockwasher
4. Motor leg extension
5. Front stud
6. Shift rod lower seal
7. Seal
8. Water pump screw
9. Water tube
10. Washer
11. Locating disc

12. Pump body
13. Decal kit
14. Impeller drive pin
15. Shift rod seal
16. Impeller
17. Back plate
18. Clutch shift cam
19. Shift rod seal
20. Gearcase plug
21. Washer
22. Gearcase
23. Plug
24. Hex screw

25. Cap screw
26. Screw
27. Snout
28. Propeller shaft seal
29. Forward gear/bearing assembly
30. Clutch shift pin
31. Propeller shaft
32. Propeller shaft seal
33. Propeller shaft cage
34. Bearing cage seal
35. Bearing cage retainer
36. Cotton pin
37. Propeller pin
38. Propeller nut and cotter pin
39. Propeller
40. Drive shaft
41. Pinion gear
42. Clutch spring
43. Clutch pin guide
44. Shift clutch
45. Reverse gear thrust washer
46. Motor leg extension
47. Reverse gear

27. Install the bearing cage retainer and align the screw holes. Apply RTV sealant to the retainer screw threads. Install the screws and tighten to specifications (**Table 2**).

28. Pressure test the gearcase as described in this chapter.

29. Install the gearcase assembly as described in this chapter. Refill gearcase with the recommended lubricant as described in Chapter Four.

30. Check the gearcase lubricant level after the motor has been run. Change the lubricant after the first 10 hours of operation (break-in period). See Chapter Four.

7.5 hp

Refer to **Figure 33** for this procedure.

1. Remove the propeller as described in this chapter.

2. Drain the gearcase lubricant as described in Chapter Four.

3. Remove the gearcase as described in this chapter.

4. Secure the gearcase in a suitable holding fixture or a vise with protective jaws. Two suitable blocks of wood may be used as protective jaws.

5. Remove the 2 screws securing the exhaust snout to the gearcase. Remove the snout.

6. Remove the 3 screws securing the gearcase extension to the gearcase. Remove the extension.

7. Remove the water pump as described in this chapter.

8. Remove the 4 screws holding the bearing cage retainer to the bearing cage. See **Figure 27**.

9. Install puller (FT-8948-1) as shown in **Figure 28** and pull the bearing cage retainer from the gear housing.

10. Remove the bearing cage O-ring from the gear housing bore.

11. Remove the bearing cage with puller (FT-8948-1).

12. Remove the reverse gear and thrust washer from the propeller shaft. Remove the prop shaft from the gear housing.

13. Remove the clutch shift cam. Place a shop cloth over the shift shaft cavity, hold the drive shaft in place and tilt the gearcase upside down. Catch the cam as it slides out of the shift cavity.

CAUTION
Cover the propeller shaft with a shop cloth in Step 14. If the spring pressure is suddenly released, the clutch guide pin may shoot out rapidly with great force.

14. Clamp the propeller shaft (prop end down) into a vise with protective jaws. Remove the shift clutch, clutch pin guide and spring. Use a small screwdriver to compress the clutch spring and slide the shift clutch from the shaft slot. Release the pressure on the clutch spring and remove the clutch pin guide and spring from the propeller shaft. See **Figure 29**.

15. Lift the drive shaft out of the gearcase. Remove the pinion and forward gears from the gearcase.

16. Pry the drive shaft seal from the gearcase bore with a screwdriver. See **Figure 30**. Do not damage the gearcase bore.

17. Place the propeller shaft bearing cage face down on open vise jaws or on 2 blocks of wood. Drive the propeller shaft seal out with a hammer and a suitable punch.

18. Clean and inspect all components as described in this chapter. Refer to **Table 4** for all specifications. The gear housing upper drive shaft and forward gear bearings are not serviceable. Replace the gear housing if either of these bearings is excessively worn. Replace all worn or damaged parts. Inspect the exhaust snout (anode) for deterioration. Replace the snout if it is significantly deteriorated.

19. Install a new seal into the propeller shaft bearing cage with seal installer (FT-2907) or equivalent. The spring side of the seal should

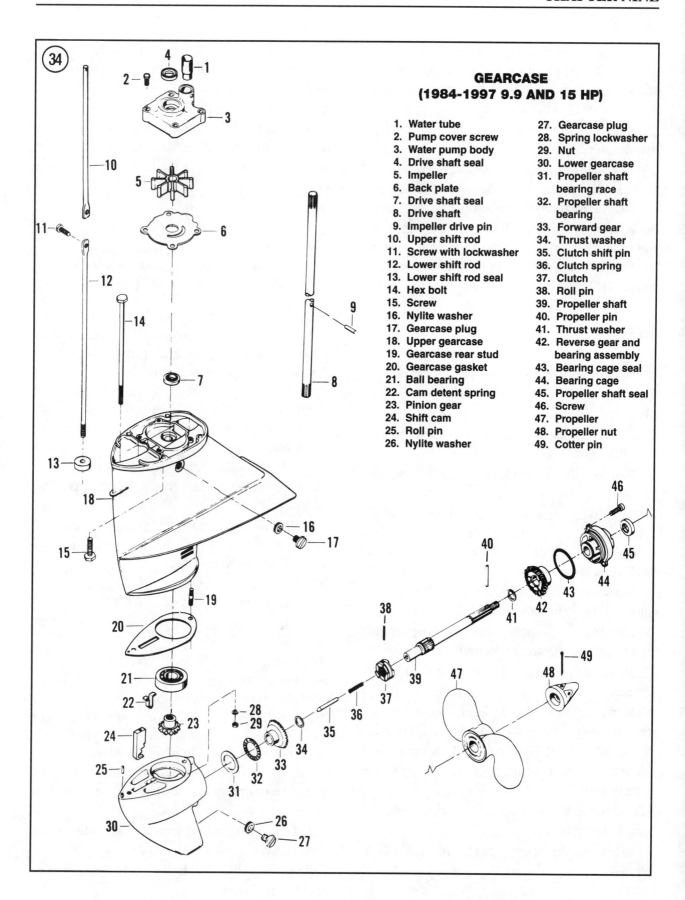

**GEARCASE
(1984-1997 9.9 AND 15 HP)**

1. Water tube
2. Pump cover screw
3. Water pump body
4. Drive shaft seal
5. Impeller
6. Back plate
7. Drive shaft seal
8. Drive shaft
9. Impeller drive pin
10. Upper shift rod
11. Screw with lockwasher
12. Lower shift rod
13. Lower shift rod seal
14. Hex bolt
15. Screw
16. Nylite washer
17. Gearcase plug
18. Upper gearcase
19. Gearcase rear stud
20. Gearcase gasket
21. Ball bearing
22. Cam detent spring
23. Pinion gear
24. Shift cam
25. Roll pin
26. Nylite washer
27. Gearcase plug
28. Spring lockwasher
29. Nut
30. Lower gearcase
31. Propeller shaft bearing race
32. Propeller shaft bearing
33. Forward gear
34. Thrust washer
35. Clutch shift pin
36. Clutch spring
37. Clutch
38. Roll pin
39. Propeller shaft
40. Propeller pin
41. Thrust washer
42. Reverse gear and bearing assembly
43. Bearing cage seal
44. Bearing cage
45. Propeller shaft seal
46. Screw
47. Propeller
48. Propeller nut
49. Cotter pin

face the propeller. The seal case should be flush to 0.030 in. (0.76 mm) below the bearing cage surface. See **Figure 31**.

20. Install the clutch spring in the propeller shaft, then insert the clutch pin guide. Place a shop cloth over the shaft end and use a small screwdriver to compress the guide and spring. Slide the shift clutch into the propeller shaft slot and carefully release the spring pressure. Install the shift guide pin into the end of the propeller shaft.

21. Install a new seal into the drive shaft bore with seal installer (FT-2907) or equivalent. The spring side of the seal should face out.

22. Position a new O-ring in the shift rod cavity groove.

23. Insert the clutch shift cam (threaded end up and ramp facing the propeller) into the shift cavity.

24. Install the water pump assembly as described in this chapter. Do not install the water pump screws at this time.

25. Insert the shift rod carefully through the shift rod seal and thread the shift rod into the clutch shift cam.

26. Lift the drive shaft approximately 5/8 in. (16 mm) and install the forward gear into the bearing at the front of the gearcase. Position the pinion gear under the drive shaft. Align the splines and seat the drive shaft and water pump to the gearcase.

27. Coat the water pump cover screws with a light coat of RTV sealant (**Table 9**). Install the screws and tighten to specification (**Table 2**).

28. Install the propeller shaft assembly into the gearcase. Move the shift rod upward to engage the clutch guide pin into the forward (deepest) notch of the clutch shift cam. Push the propeller shaft fully into the gearcase.

29. Slide the reverse gear thrust washer and then the reverse gear over the propeller shaft and into the gearcase.

NOTE
The propeller shaft bearing cage O-ring groove will be visible in Step 30 when the bearing cage is fully seated.

30. Apply 2-4-C Multi-Lube grease to the propeller shaft splines. Install the propeller shaft bearing cage over the propeller shaft and push it into the gearcase. Rotate the propeller shaft and push the shift rod down to engage reverse gear. Continue rotating the propeller to make sure the reverse gear engages the pinion gear and fits into the propeller shaft bearing cage. Seat the propeller shaft bearing cage fully into the gearcase.

31. Coat a new O-ring with 2-4-C Multi-Lube grease and install it into the groove behind the propeller shaft bearing cage.

32. Install the propeller shaft bearing cage retainer. Rotate the retainer to align the bolt holes with the propeller shaft bearing cage. Coat the propeller shaft bearing cage retainer screws with RTV sealant (**Table 9**). Install and tighten the screws to specification (**Table 2**).

33. Pressure test the gearcase as described in this chapter.

34. Fill the gearcase with the recommended lubricant as described in Chapter Four.

35. Install the gearcase extension and secure with 3 screws. Tighten the screws securely.

36. Install the exhaust snout and secure with 2 screws. Tighten the screws securely.

37. Install the gearcase and propeller as described in this chapter.

38. Check the gearcase lubricant level after the engine has been run. Change the lubricant after 10 hours of operation (break-in period). See Chapter Four.

9.9 and 15 hp (1997 and Prior)

Refer to **Figure 34** for this procedure.

1. Drain the gearcase lubricant as described in Chapter Four.

2. Remove the propeller as described in this chapter.

3. Remove the gearcase as described in this chapter.

4. Secure the gearcase in a suitable holding fixture or a vise with protective jaws. If protective jaws are not available, position the gearcase upright with the skeg between wooden blocks in a vise.

5. Remove the water pump as described in this chapter.

6. Lift the drive shaft up and out of the gearcase.

7. Remove the 2 screws securing the bearing cage assembly to the lower gearcase.

8. Install puller (part No. FT-8948-1) as shown in **Figure 28** and remove the bearing cage assembly. Remove and discard the bearing cage O-ring.

9. Remove the long hex bolt in the front of the water pump cavity.

10. Rotate the lower shift rod counterclockwise until the rod is free of the shift cam. Carefully, lift the lower shift rod out of gearcase. Avoid damaging the shift rod seal if the seal is to be reused.

11. Remove the nut and lockwasher inside the gear cavity, then separate the lower and upper gearcase housings. Remove and discard the gasket.

12. Remove the propeller shaft assembly from the lower gearcase. Remove the reverse gear, reverse gear thrust washer and clutch shift pin from the propeller shaft.

13. To remove the pinion gear, insert the drive shaft into the lower gearcase and pinion gear, then rock the drive shaft back and forth until the pinion gear is dislodged. Lift the drive shaft out of the gearcase. Reach into the gear cavity and remove the pinion gear.

14. Thread the lower shift rod into the shift cam. Lift the shift cam and detent spring out of the gearcase as an assembly.

15. Remove the forward gear with thrust bearing and race from gear cavity.

16. Slide the clutch against spring pressure (toward prop end) sufficiently to insert a 1/8 in. pin punch through the clutch slot in the propeller shaft.

17. Secure the propeller shaft in a vise with protective jaws. Drive the roll pin from the clutch with a suitable punch. See **Figure 35**. Slide the clutch off the propeller shaft.

18. Thread a 5/16 in. lag screw into the upper gearcase shift rod seal. Insert a 1/4 in. diameter rod from the other side and drive the screw and seal from the housing.

19. Pry the drive shaft seal from the upper gearcase housing.

20. Clean and inspect all parts as described in this chapter. Check the drive shaft bearing in the upper gearcase housing. If worn or damaged, replace the upper gearcase housing. Refer to **Table 4** for all specifications.

21. Inspect the bearing cage bearing. If worn or damaged, replace the bearing cage.

22. Install a new shift rod seal into the gearcase with seal installer (FT-8957) or equivalent. The raised head of the seal should face up and the seal should be flush with the bottom of the seal bore chamfer when installed correctly. Lubricate the seal lips with 2-4-C Multi-Lube grease or equivalent.

23. Install a new drive shaft seal into the gearcase with seal installer (FT-2907) or equivalent. The spring side should face the power head.

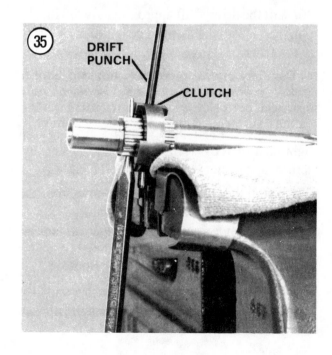

(35) DRIFT PUNCH — CLUTCH

Lubricate the seal lips with 2-4-C Multi-Lube grease (**Table 9**).

NOTE
Install metal cased propeller shaft seals with the garter spring facing the gearcase. Install rubber cased propeller shaft seals with the garter spring facing the propeller.

24. Install a new propeller shaft bearing cage seal with seal installer (FT-2907) or equivalent. Lubricate the seal lips with 2-4-C Multi-Lube grease or equivalent.

25. Install the clutch onto the propeller shaft with the chamfered edge facing the propeller end, and the hole aligned with the slot in the propeller shaft. Drive the roll pin partially into the clutch.

26. Secure the propeller shaft in a vise with protective jaws. Insert a screwdriver blade into the end of the propeller shaft and compress the clutch spring. Position the clutch over the shaft splines and carefully drive the roll pin into the shaft until flush with the clutch.

27. Install the shift pin into the propeller shaft with the flat end toward the clutch spring.

28. Install the forward gear thrust washer, forward gear, forward gear thrust bearing and race onto the propeller shaft.

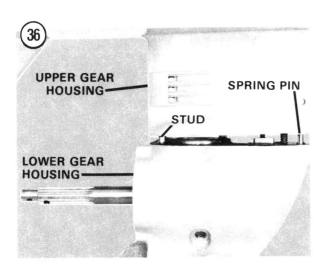

29. Insert the clutch shift cam into the lower gearcase housing. Hold top of cam about 3/16 in. (4.8 mm) out of the housing and install the propeller shaft assembly until the forward gear engages the shift pin. Install the shift cam detent spring to hold the shift cam in place.

30. Install the pinion gear and bearing assembly into the top of the lower gearcase.

31. Install the reverse gear and thrust washer onto the propeller shaft.

32. Coat both sides of a new gearcase housing gasket with RTV sealant and install the gasket into place on the lower housing.

33. Align the roll pin at the front of the lower gearcase housing with the bore in the upper housing (**Figure 36**) and mate the housing together.

34. Install the spring lockwasher and hex nut on the upper housing stud that protrudes into the lower housing gear cavity. Tighten the nut securely.

35. Coat the long hex bolt threads with RTV sealant. Install the bolt into the upper gearcase housing and tighten to 120 in.-lb. (13.6 N•m).

36. Lubricate a new bearing cage O-ring and the propeller shaft seals with a suitable antiseize grease.

37. Install the bearing cage over the propeller shaft and press into position. Install the bearing cage screws and tighten to specification (**Table 2**).

38. Install the drive shaft into the gearcase and pinion gear.

39. Lubricate the lower shift rod and shift rod seal with a suitable grease. Carefully rotate the lower shift rod through the seal and thread completely into the shift cam.

40. Install the water pump as described in this chapter.

41. Fill the gearcase with the recommended lubricant as described in Chapter Four.

42. Pressure test the gearcase as described in this chapter.

43. Install the gearcase assembly onto the motor leg as described in this chapter.

9

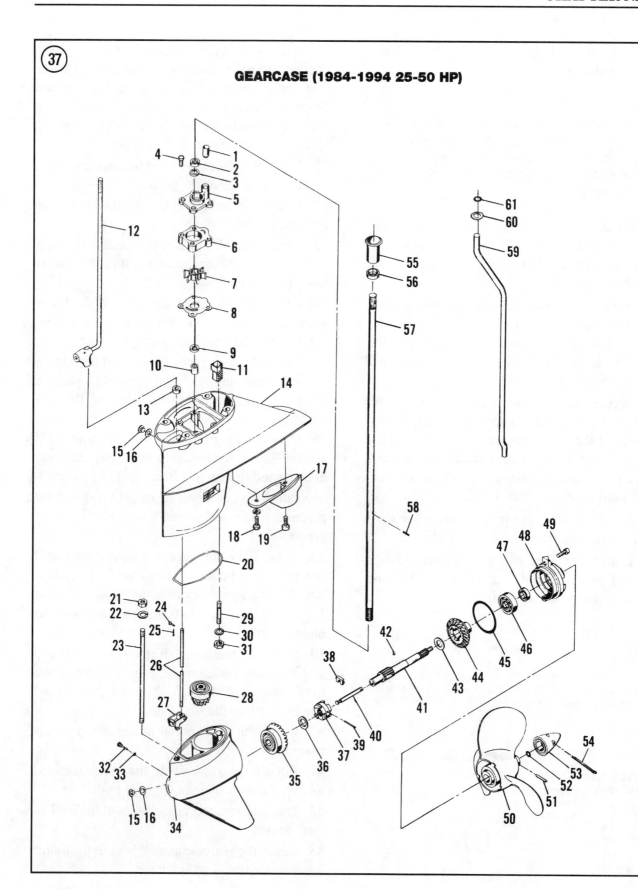

GEARCASE (1984-1994 25-50 HP)

1. Water tube seal
2. Seal
3. Water pump disc
4. Screw
5. Water pump cover
6. Water pump body
7. Impeller
8. Plate
9. Seal
10. Drive shaft upper bearing
11. Screen
12. Intermediate shift rod
13. Lower shift rod seal
14. Upper gearcase housing
15. Plug
16. Gasket
17. Exhaust snout (anode)
18. Screw
19. Screw
20. Seal
21. Nut
22. Lockwasher
23. Stud
24. Shift rod pin
25. Cotter pin
26. Lower shift rod
27. Shift arm
28. Pinion gear and bearing assembly
29. Stud
30. Lockwasher
31. Nut
32. Shift arm pivot pin
33. Seal
34. Lower gearcase housing
35. Forward gear and bearing assembly
36. Thrust washer
37. Clutch
38. Shift yoke
39. Roll pin
40. Shift arm pin
41. Propeller shaft
42. Ball
43. Thrust washer
44. Reverse gear
45. O-ring
46. Propeller shaft bearing
47. Propeller shaft seal
48. Bearing cage
49. Screw
50. Propeller
51. Propeller drive pin
52. Propeller nut seal
53. Propeller nut
54. Cotter pin
55. Drive shaft boot
56. Retainer
57. Drive shaft
58. Impeller drive pin
59. Water tube (long shaft models)
60. Washer
61. Seal

44. Check the gearcase lubricant level after the motor has been run. Change the lubricant after the first 10 hours of operation (break-in period) as described in Chapter Four.

25-50 hp (1984-1994)

Refer to **Figure 37** for this procedure.

1. Remove the propeller as described in this chapter.

2. Drain the gearcase lubricant as described in Chapter Four.

3. Remove the gearcase assembly as described in this chapter.

4. Secure the gearcase in a suitable holding fixture or a vise with protective jaws. If protective jaws are not available, position the gearcase upright with the skeg between wooden blocks in a vise.

5. Remove the cotter pin securing the shift rod pin. Push out the shift rod pin and separate the intermediate shift rod from the lower shift rod.

6. Remove the water pump as described in this chapter. Pull the drive shaft up and out of the gearcase.

7. Remove the 2 screws securing the propeller shaft bearing cage to the lower gearcase.

8. Install puller (part No. FT-8948-1) as shown in **Figure 38** and remove the bearing cage assembly.

9

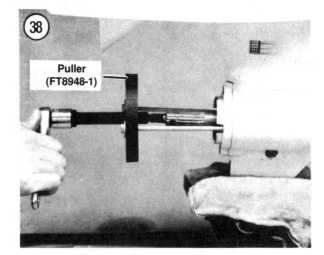

9. Remove the nut inside the lower housing gear cavity. Remove the nut on the upper housing stud (forward of lower shift rod). Separate the upper and lower gearcase housings (**Figure 39**).

10. Pull the propeller shaft assembly out of the lower gearcase.

11. To remove the pinion gear and bearing assembly, insert the drive shaft into the pinion gear splines. Dislodge the pinion gear bearing race by slightly rocking the drive shaft while pushing up on the pinion gear. Remove the pinion gear bearing race and the pinion gear and bearing assembly (**Figure 40**).

12. Remove the forward gear assembly from the gearcase.

13. Remove the forward gear thrust washer and shift yoke from the propeller shaft.

NOTE
If the original shift yoke is brass colored, it should be replaced with the new design (harder) yoke.

14. Use a suitable magnet to remove the propeller shaft ball on models so equipped.

15. Slide the reverse gear and reverse gear thrust washer from the propeller shaft.

16. Place the propeller shaft into a vise as shown in **Figure 41**. Use shop cloths to prevent damaging the propeller shaft. Carefully drive out the roll pin, then remove the clutch and shift pin from the shaft.

17. Remove the shift arm pivot pin. Remove and discard the pivot pin O-ring.

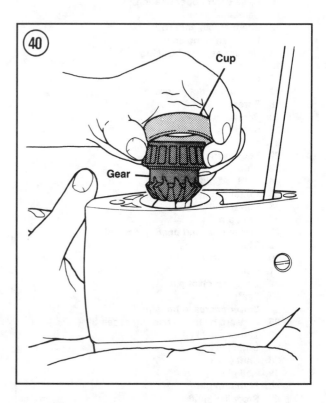

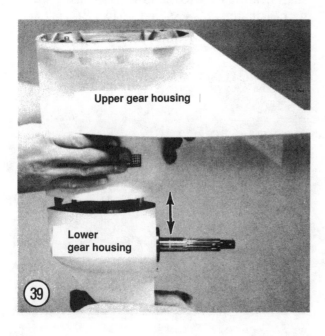

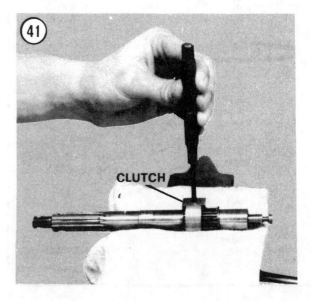

18. Lift the lower shift rod and shift arm out the top of the lower gearcase.

19. Assemble special tool (part No. FT-8964) as shown in **Figure 42** and press the drive shaft bearing and seal from the upper gearcase.

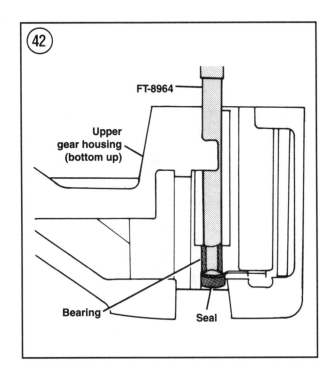

20. Remove the lower shift rod seal using a slide hammer with a hooked end as shown in **Figure 43**. An alternate method to remove the shift rod seal is to thread a 5/16 in. lag screw into the top of the seal, then drive the seal and lag screw out from the other side of the upper gearcase.

21. If the forward gear bearing requires replacement, remove the bearing cup from the lower gearcase using bearing cup remover (part No. FT-8921) and bearing guide set (part No. FT-8918), assembled as shown in **Figure 44**. Turn the nut on the tool until the bearing race is free.

22. Remove and discard the propeller shaft bearing cage O-ring.

23. Place the bearing cage on top of a vise. Use shop cloths between the vise jaws and bearing cage to prevent damaging the bearing cage. Using a brass punch, lightly tap around the bearing inner race until the bearing is removed.

24. Pry the bearing cage seal out with a screwdriver. Discard the seal.

9

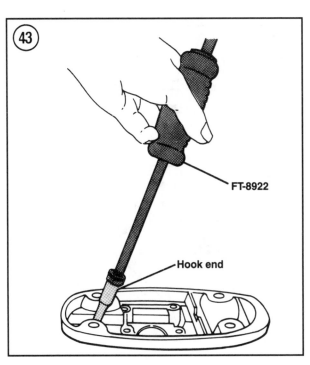

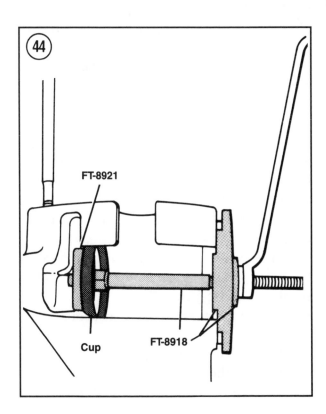

25. Clean and inspect all components as described in this chapter.

26. Press a new drive shaft bearing into the upper gearcase housing with bearing driver (part No. FT-8963), or a suitable mandrel. See **Figure 45**.

> *NOTE*
> *If the drive shaft bearing has an external groove, the groove must align with the groove in the upper gearcase housing.*

27. Install a new shift rod seal into the gearcase with seal installer (FT-8957) or equivalent. The raised head of the seal should face up and the seal should be flush with the bottom of the seal bore chamfer when installed correctly. Lubricate the seal lips with 2-4-C Multi-Lube grease or equivalent.

28. Install a new drive shaft seal into the gearcase with seal installer (FT-8972) and handle (FT-8907) or equivalent. The spring side of the seal should face the power head. Lubricate the seal lips with 2-4-C Multi-Lube grease (**Table 9**).

29. Press a new forward gear bearing cup into the lower gearcase housing using cup installer (part No. FT-8904), driver handle (part No. FT-8907) and guide plate (part No. FT-8918). Assemble the tools as shown in **Figure 46** and press the bearing cup into the housing until bottomed.

30. Install a new propeller shaft seal into the bearing cage using installer (part No. FT-3431). Seal lip should face the propeller side of the bearing cage. Lubricate the seal lip with a suitable grease.

31. Install a new bearing into the bearing cage by carefully tapping around the bearing outer race.

32. Install a new O-ring into the outer groove on the bearing cage. Lubricate the O-ring with a suitable antiseize grease.

33. Screw the lower shift rod in or out of the shift arm as necessary to position the end of the shift rod flush with the bottom of the threaded area of the shift arm. Install the shift rod and arm (fork end facing down) assembly into the lower

housing. Install the shift arm pivot pin with a new O-ring. Make sure the pivot pin properly engages the shift arm.

34. Install the propeller shaft rear thrust washer onto the propeller shaft. Position the clutch and

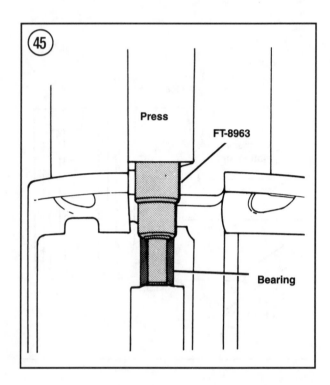

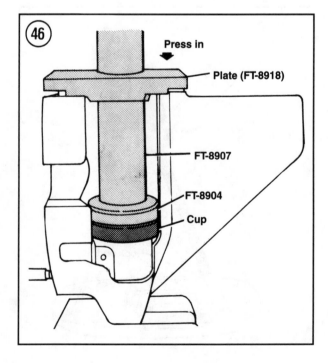

shift pin on the propeller shaft. Align the pin holes in the clutch and propeller shaft and install the roll pin. See **Figure 47**.

35. Install the reverse gear onto the propeller shaft.

36. Install the forward thrust washer onto the propeller shaft. Coat the shift pin groove with antiseize grease and install the shift yoke into the groove. Lubricate the propeller shaft ball (models so equipped) and install the ball into the shaft.

37. Install the forward gear into the lower gearcase housing.

38. Install the pinion gear, bearing and race assembly into the lower housing.

39. While pulling up on the lower shift rod, insert the propeller shaft assembly into the lower housing. The shift arm must properly engage the shift yoke. Check engagement by moving the lower shift rod up and down to check for clutch movement.

40. Install a new seal into the lower gearcase housing groove. Fit the upper and lower housings together. Install the nut and lockwasher on the stud located inside the lower housing gear cavity. Install the O-ring, lockwasher and nut on the upper stud. Tighten both nuts to specification (**Table 2**).

41. Rotate the propeller shaft to position the propeller shaft ball (models so equipped) facing upward. Install the bearing cage with the slot in the bearing inner race aligned with the propeller shaft ball. Make sure the bearing cage is seated in the housing.

42. Apply a suitable RTV sealant to the threads of the bearing cage screws. Install the screws and tighten to specification (**Table 2**).

43. Install the water pump as described in this chapter.

44. Pressure test the gearcase as described in this chapter.

45. Install the gearcase as described in this chapter.

46. Fill the gearcase with the recommended lubricant as described in Chapter Four.

47. Check the gearcase lubricant level after the motor has been run. Change the lubricant after the first 10 hours of operation (break-in period). See Chapter Four.

9.9, 15 (1998) and 25 hp (3-Cylinder)

To assist with component identification and orientation refer to the illustration for the selected model. For 9.9 and 15 hp models (1998), refer to (**Figure 48**). For 25 hp 3-cylinder models, refer to (**Figure 49**).

1. Remove the propeller as described in this chapter.

2. Drain the gearcase lubricant as described in Chapter Four.

3. Remove the gearcase as described in this chapter.

4. Secure the gearcase in a suitable holding fixture or a vise with protective jaws.

5. On 25 hp 3-cylinder models, Mark the position of the trim tab with a white grease pencil or china marker. Remove the screw securing the trim tab to the gearcase. Remove the trim tab.

6. Remove the water pump as described in this chapter.

7. On 25 hp 3-cylinder models, remove the 3 screws securing the retaining plate to the propeller shaft bearing carrier. Remove the retainer plate and large O-ring.

CAUTION
The propeller shaft bearing carrier has left-hand threads. The use of spanner

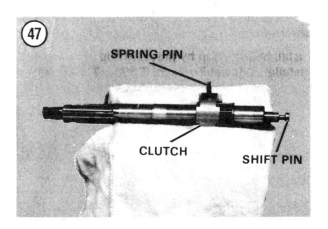

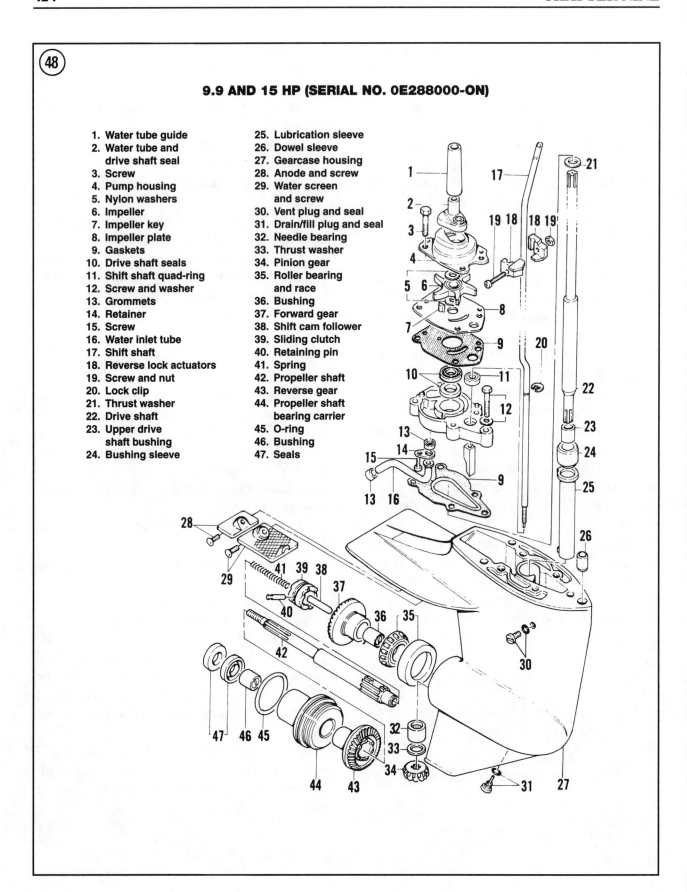

9.9 AND 15 HP (SERIAL NO. 0E288000-ON)

1. Water tube guide
2. Water tube and drive shaft seal
3. Screw
4. Pump housing
5. Nylon washers
6. Impeller
7. Impeller key
8. Impeller plate
9. Gaskets
10. Drive shaft seals
11. Shift shaft quad-ring
12. Screw and washer
13. Grommets
14. Retainer
15. Screw
16. Water inlet tube
17. Shift shaft
18. Reverse lock actuators
19. Screw and nut
20. Lock clip
21. Thrust washer
22. Drive shaft
23. Upper drive shaft bushing
24. Bushing sleeve
25. Lubrication sleeve
26. Dowel sleeve
27. Gearcase housing
28. Anode and screw
29. Water screen and screw
30. Vent plug and seal
31. Drain/fill plug and seal
32. Needle bearing
33. Thrust washer
34. Pinion gear
35. Roller bearing and race
36. Bushing
37. Forward gear
38. Shift cam follower
39. Sliding clutch
40. Retaining pin
41. Spring
42. Propeller shaft
43. Reverse gear
44. Propeller shaft bearing carrier
45. O-ring
46. Bushing
47. Seals

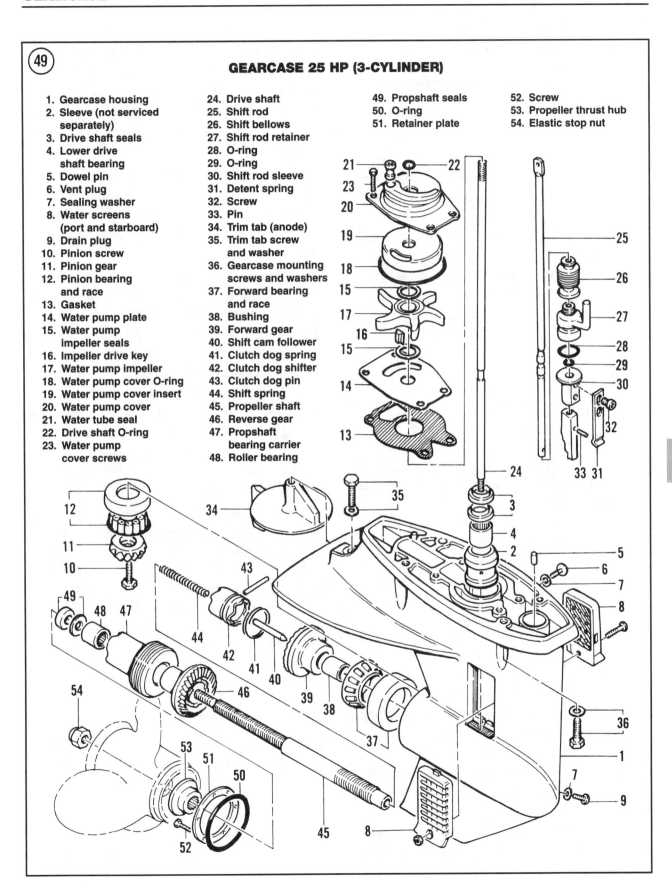

(49) **GEARCASE 25 HP (3-CYLINDER)**

1. Gearcase housing
2. Sleeve (not serviced separately)
3. Drive shaft seals
4. Lower drive shaft bearing
5. Dowel pin
6. Vent plug
7. Sealing washer
8. Water screens (port and starboard)
9. Drain plug
10. Pinion screw
11. Pinion gear
12. Pinion bearing and race
13. Gasket
14. Water pump plate
15. Water pump impeller seals
16. Impeller drive key
17. Water pump impeller
18. Water pump cover O-ring
19. Water pump cover insert
20. Water pump cover
21. Water tube seal
22. Drive shaft O-ring
23. Water pump cover screws
24. Drive shaft
25. Shift rod
26. Shift bellows
27. Shift rod retainer
28. O-ring
29. O-ring
30. Shift rod sleeve
31. Detent spring
32. Screw
33. Pin
34. Trim tab (anode)
35. Trim tab screw and washer
36. Gearcase mounting screws and washers
37. Forward bearing and race
38. Bushing
39. Forward gear
40. Shift cam follower
41. Clutch dog spring
42. Clutch dog shifter
43. Clutch dog pin
44. Shift spring
45. Propeller shaft
46. Reverse gear
47. Propshaft bearing carrier
48. Roller bearing
49. Propshaft seals
50. O-ring
51. Retainer plate
52. Screw
53. Propeller thrust hub
54. Elastic stop nut

9

wrench part No. 91-13664 (for 9.9 and 15 hp models) and part No. 91-83843—1 (for 25 hp models) is recommended for removing the carrier. An alternative procedure for 25 hp models is listed in the following steps.

8. On 25 hp models, remove the thrust hub cap from the propeller thrust hub. Install the thrust hub cap over the propeller shaft and engage the thrust hub cap ears to the recesses on the bearing carrier.

9. On 25 hp models, install the propeller and tighten the nut to hold the propeller firmly against the thrust hub cap and bearing carrier.

10A. On 25 hp models, turn the propeller *clockwise* to remove the bearing carrier. A socket wrench may be used on the propeller nut, if necessary. Unscrew the carrier and remove the propeller nut, propeller and thrust cap from the propeller shaft.

10B. On all 9.9 and 15 hp models and when necessary on 25 hp models, use spanner wrench part No. 91-13664 for 9.9 and 15 hp models or part No. 91-83843—1 for 25 hp models to remove the carrier. Engage the tool into the slots within the bearing carrier. Turn the tool clockwise (as viewed from the propeller shaft) to unthread the carrier from the gearcase.

11. Pull the propeller shaft and propeller shaft bearing carrier out as an assembly. Slide the cam follower from the forward end of the propeller shaft.

12. Remove the reverse gear and propeller shaft bearing carrier from the propeller shaft.

13A. Secure the propeller shaft bearing carrier in a soft-jawed vise. On 9.9 and 15 hp models, use a punch to carefully drive the seals from the bearing carrier. Work carefully to avoid damaging the seal contact areas of the carrier.

13B. On 25 hp models, use drift (part No. FT-8919) or equivalent to drive the seals from the bearing carrier.

14A. Inspect the propeller shaft in the area that contacts the bushing or bearing in the bearing carrier. Remove and replace the bushing or

bearing along with the propeller shaft when pitted, rough or discolored surfaces are noted.

14B. On 9.9 and 15 hp models, use driver part No. 91-824787 or an appropriately sized section of tubing to carefully drive the bushing from the bearing carrier.

14C. On 25 hp models, carefully drive the bearing from the bearing carrier using a suitable punch or appropriately sized section of tubing. Work carefully to avoid damaging the bearing bore surfaces in the bearing carrier.

15A. Inspect the clutch for worn or damaged surfaces. Remove and replace the clutch when defects are noted. On 9.9 and 15 hp models, Locate the side of the cross pin that is grooved on the end. Use a small punch and drive on the *ungrooved* side of the pin to remove it from the clutch. Discard the pin upon removal.

15B. On 25 hp models, remove the clutch dog spring with a small screwdriver or awl. Insert the tool under one end of the spring and rotate the propeller shaft to unwind the spring. Discard the spring upon removal.

16. On 25 hp models, insert the shift cam follower into the propeller shaft with the beveled end facing out. Place the cam follower against a solid surface and push on the propeller shaft to unload the spring pressure on the clutch dog cross pin. Remove the pin with a suitable punch. Carefully release the pressure on the cam follower and spring.

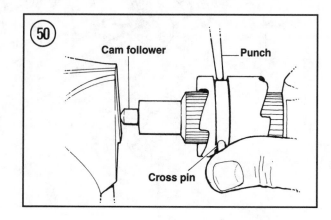

17. On 9.9 and 15 hp models, carefully pry the water pump base loose from the gearcase. Remove the e-clip from the shift shaft then rotate the shift shaft (LH) to release it from the shift cam. Slide the shift shaft from the water pump base.

18. On all models, remove the cam follower, spring and clutch dog (**Figure 50**) from the propeller shaft.

19A. Remove the drive shaft, pinion gear, forward gear and related components from the gearcase. On 9.9 and 15 hp models, place a shop towel inside the gearcase to provide support for the pinion gear. Carefully pull the drive shaft from the gearcase. Remove the pinion gear, thrust washer and forward gear assembly from the gearcase.

19B. On 25 hp models, clamp the drive shaft in a soft-jawed vise. Remove the screws securing the pinion nut to the drive shaft. Lift the drive shaft out of the gearcase. Remove the pinion and forward gears from the gearcase.

20A. On 9.9 and 15 hp models, note the seal lip direction then carefully pry the seals from the water pump base.

20B. On 25 hp models, remove the drive shaft seals from the gearcase with puller (part No. 91-27780) or equivalent. See **Figure 51**.

21. On 25 hp models, remove the shift shaft assembly from the gearcase. Remove and discard the outer O-ring from the shift shaft retainer. Inspect the retainer, boot, inner O-ring,

detent springs and shift cam. Replace any worn or damaged parts. Do not remove the inner O-ring unless replacement is necessary. The shift retainer is plastic and should be inspected carefully for cracks.

22. Clean and inspect all components as described in this chapter. Refer to **Table 4** for all specifications. The gear housing lower drive shaft roller bearing cup, forward gear roller bearing and cup, upper drive shaft caged roller bearing and forward gear bushing should not be removed unless they are to be replaced. Replace all worn or damaged parts that do not meet specifications. Inspect the trim tab (anode) for deterioration. Replace the trim tab if it is significantly deteriorated.

23. If the lower drive shaft roller bearing must be replaced, remove the bearing cup from the gearcase by driving it down into the propeller shaft bore with bearing puller kit (part No. 91-31229A7) or equivalent.

24A. On 9.9 and 15 hp models, Remove the upper drive shaft bushing and sleeve with a suitable slide hammer. Work carefully to avoid damaging the bearing bore.

24B. If the upper drive shaft caged roller bearing is to be replaced on 25 hp models, drive it down into the propeller shaft bore with a suitable mandrel.

25A. If the lower drive shaft bearing must be replaced on 9.9 and 15 hp models, carefully pull the lubrication sleeve from the gearcase. See **Figure 48**. Use bearing removal tool (part No. 91-824788a 1) or an appropriately sized socket to carefully drive the bearing into the gearcase opening.

25B. If the lower drive shaft bearing must be replaced on 25 hp models, use an appropriately sized socket or section of tubing to drive the bearing into the gearcase opening. Work carefully to avoid damaging the gearcase housing.

26. If the forward gear roller bearing must be replaced, remove the cup from the gearcase with slide hammer (part No. 91-34569A-1) or equivalent. Remove the roller bearing from the forward

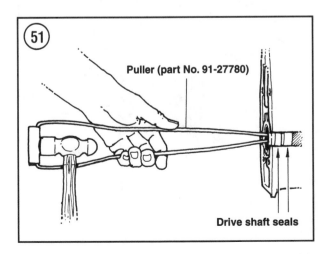

(51)

Puller (part No. 91-27780)

Drive shaft seals

9

gear with bearing separator plate (part No. 91-37241) or equivalent and a suitable mandrel.

27. If the bushing in the forward gear bore must be replaced, remove the bushing by securing the gear in a soft-jawed vise. Drive the bushing out with a suitable punch and hammer. Do not damage the forward gear roller bearing (if installed) during this operation.

28. Install the forward bearing cup that came with the replacement forward gear bearing (when replacement is required. Lubricate all surfaces of the bearing cup with gearcase lubricant prior to installation. On 9.9 and 15 hp models, use mandrel (part No. 91-13658) and the bearing carrier removal tool to carefully drive the bearing cup into the gearcase. Ensure that the cup is fully seated into the housing.

29. On 25 hp models, lubricate the outside of the new bearing cup with gear oil and set the cup into the gearcase bearing bore. Place a suitable mandrel from bearing installer kit (part No. 91-31229A7) over the cup. Place the propeller shaft into the mandrel hole. Install the propeller shaft bearing carrier 4 or 5 full turns into the gearcase (to hold the propeller shaft centered). Thread a scrap propeller nut onto the propeller shaft. Use a mallet and drive the propeller shaft against the mandrel until the bearing cup is fully seated in the gearcase bearing bore. Remove the propeller nut, propeller shaft, bearing carrier and mandrel. Coat the bearing race with gear oil.

30. Set the forward gear on a press with the gear teeth facing down. Lubricate the new roller bearing inner diameter with gear oil. Set the bearing onto the gear with the wide end of the bearing facing toward the gear. Press the bearing fully onto the gear with a suitable mandrel. Do not press on the roller cage. Leave the gear in the press for Step 31.

31. Lubricate the outside diameter of a new forward gear bushing with gear oil. Set the bushing on the forward gear and press it into the forward gear with a suitable mandrel.

32A. On 9.9 and 15 hp models, carefully slide the lubrication sleeve into the drive shaft bore until fully seated. Use drive shaft bushing installation tool (part No. 91-824790-1) to pull the bushing and sleeve into the drive shaft bore. If using other means to install the bushing, ensure that the bushing and sleeve are installed to the same depth as the original components.

32B. On 25 hp models, lubricate the outside diameter of a new driveshaft upper bearing with gear oil. Set the bearing into the drive shaft bore with its numbered side facing the power head. Drive the bearing into the gearcase with a suitable mandrel. Drive the bearing just far enough to uncover the oil hole (**Figure 52**).

33A. On 9.9 and 15 hp models, place the lower bearing into the housing with the numbered side facing the gearcase opening or down. Use drive shaft bearing installation tool (part No. 91-824790a 1) to carefully pull the bearing into the drive shaft bore. When using other means to install the bearing, ensure the bearing is installed to the proper depth within the bore.

33B. On 25 hp models, install a new drive shaft lower bearing cup into the gearcase with bearing installer kit (part No. 91-31229A7) or equivalent. Oil the outside of the cup and install it with

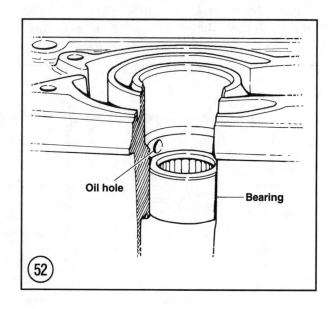

Oil hole — Bearing

(52)

the small diameter facing the top of the gearcase. Seat the cup fully in the bearing bore.

34. The drive shaft seal are installed into the gearcase or water pump base. Prior to installation, Coat the outside diameter of 2 new drive shaft seals with Loctite 271 threadlocking adhesive (**Table 9**).

35A. On 9.9 and 15 hp models, place the first seal into the water pump base with the seal lip facing Down. Use mandrel (part No. 91-13665) or an appropriately sized socket then carefully drive the seal into the seal bore. Ensure the seal is fully seated. Install the second seal into the opening with the seal lip facing UP. Ensure the seal is seated against the first seal. Lubricate the seal lips with 2-4-C Multi-Lube grease or equivalent.

35B. On 25 hp models, install the first seal with its lip facing down. Press the seal with a suitable mandrel until it is just below flush with the drive shaft bore. Install the second seal with its lip facing up. Press both seals to a depth of 3/16 in. (4.76 mm) from the top of the drive shaft bore. Lubricate the seal lips with 2-4-C Multi-Lube grease or equivalent.

36. Rotate the gearcase so that the propeller shaft bore is pointing upward. Install the forward

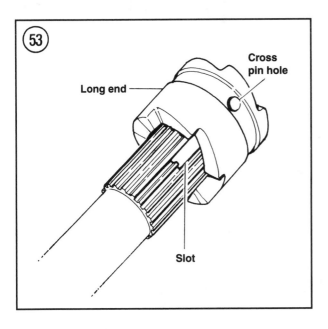

53

Long end

Cross pin hole

Slot

gear and bearing assembly into the forward bearing cup.

37. Place the lower drive shaft roller bearing into the lower cup. Place the pinion gear in position on top of the bearing.

38A. On 9.9 and 15 hp models, position the grooved side of the lower thrust washer against the top side of the pinion gear. Place the pinion gear and thrust washer into the gearcase. Ensure the pinion gear teeth engage the forward gear teeth. Rotate the drive shaft and slide it into its bore. The drive shaft will drop into position when the lower splined section aligns with the splines in the pinion gear. Place the upper thrust washer over upper end of the drive shaft and slide it into position against the upper drive shaft bushing.

38B. On 25 hp models, carefully insert the drive shaft through the drive shaft seals and into the gear housing. Hold the pinion gear and lower bearing in position and engage the drive shaft splines to the pinion gear splines.

39. Apply Loctite 271 threadlocking adhesive (**Table 9**) to the pinion screw. Install the pinion screw and hand tighten. Clamp the drive shaft in a soft-jawed vise and tighten the pinion screw to the specified torque (**Table 2**).

40. On 25 hp models, reassemble the shift rod assembly with new O-rings and a new boot. Grease the O-rings with 2-4-C Multi-Lube grease or equivalent. Install the shift rod into the gearcase with the notched ramp of the shift cam facing the propeller. Seat the retainer firmly into the shift cavity.

41. Assemble the propeller shaft. Align the cross pin holes of the clutch dog with the slot in the propeller shaft. Position the long end of the clutch dog (**Figure 53**) toward the propeller and slide it onto the propeller shaft. Lubricate the shift spring with gear oil and install it into the propeller shaft. Install the cam follower with the beveled end out. Press the cam follower against a solid object to compress the spring. Insert a small punch through the clutch dog holes *between* the spring and the cam follower.

9

Remove the cam follower. Insert the clutch dog cross-pin (opposite side of the punch) into the clutch dog (ungrooved side on 9.9 and 15 hp models) and slide the pin into the clutch dog as you pull the punch out. See **Figure 50**. When finished, the cross-pin must be in front of the spring.

42A. On 9.9 and 15 hp models, drive on the grooved side of the cross pin using a suitable punch until the end of the cross pin is flush with the clutch surface.

42B. On 25 hp models, secure the pin to the clutch dog with a new retainer spring. Do not open the spring any more than necessary to install it.

43. Grease the cam follower with 2-4-C Multi-Lube grease or equivalent and install it into the propeller shaft with the beveled end out.

44. On 9.9 and 15 hp models, install a new water pump base gasket (9, **Figure 48**) onto the gearcase. Slide the shift shaft through its opening in the water pump base. Install the e-clip onto its groove on the shift shaft. Thread the shift cam onto the lower end of the shift shaft until fully seated. Unthread the cam just enough to allow the tapered side to face the reverse gear when the assembly is installed into the gearcase. Ensure the water inlet tube (16, **Figure 48**) is properly seated into the sealing grommets (13, **Figure 48**) as you slide the water pump base and shift shaft into position. Lubricate it with grease then slide a new shift shaft quad ring (11, **Figure 48**) over the shift shaft and position it onto the water pump base. Install the front bolt and washer into the water pump base and tighten it securely.

45. Turn the gearcase so that the propeller shaft bore is horizontal. Move the shift rod to the forward position (upper detent) and install the propeller shaft into the center of the forward gear. Slide the reverse gear over the propeller shaft into mesh with the pinion gear.

46. If the propeller shaft bearing carrier bearing was removed, lubricate a new bearing or bushing with gear oil and place it into the carrier with

lettered end facing the propeller. Use a suitable mandrel and press the bearing flush with the end of the bearing bore as shown in **Figure 54**.

47. Coat 2 new propeller shaft seals with Loctite 271 threadlocking adhesive (**Table 9**). Install the small diameter seal with the spring facing the gearcase. Press the seal in with a suitable mandrel until the seal bottoms in its bore. Install the large diameter seal with the spring facing the propeller. Press the seal in with a suitable mandrel until the seal bottoms in its bore. Coat the seal lips with 2-4-C Multi-Lube grease or equivalent. See **Figure 54**.

48. On 9.9 and 15 hp models, install a new O-ring (45, **Figure 48**) into the bearing carrier. Ensure the O-ring is fully seated into the groove of the bearing carrier. Coat the O-ring with 2-4-C Multi-Lube grease or its equivalent.

49. Coat the threads of the propeller shaft bearing carrier with Special Lubricant 101

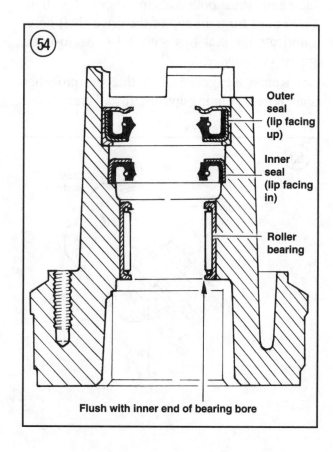

Outer seal (lip facing up)

Inner seal (lip facing in)

Roller bearing

Flush with inner end of bearing bore

(**Table 9**) and thread the carrier *counterclockwise* into the gearcase as far as possible by hand.

CAUTION
The propeller shaft bearing carrier has left-hand threads. The use of spanner wrench (part No. 91-13664) for 9.9 or 15 hp models and (part No. 91-83843—1) for 25 hp models is recommended for installing the carrier. An alternative procedure is listed in the following steps.

50. On 25 hp models only, Install the propeller thrust hub cap over the propeller shaft and engage the thrust hub cap ears to the recesses on the bearing carrier. Install the propeller and tighten the nut to hold the propeller firmly against the cap and bearing carrier. Turn the propeller *counterclockwise* to tighten the bearing carrier securely to the gearcase. Tighten the propeller nut as necessary to hold the propeller against the bearing carrier. Unscrew the carrier and remove the propeller nut, propeller and thrust cap from the propeller shaft.

51. Use spanner wrench (part No. 91-13664) for 9.9 or 15 hp models and (part No. 91-83843—1) for 25 hp models to tighten the carrier securely.

52. On 25 hp models, coat a new propeller shaft carrier O-ring with 2-4-C Multi-Lube grease or equivalent and position it behind the bearing carrier in the gearcase bore. Install the retainer plate over the O-ring and align the holes with bearing carrier. Coat the 3 retainer screws with Perfect Seal (**Table 9**). Install and tighten the screws to specification (**Table 2**).

53. On 25 hp models, install the propeller thrust hub cap to the thrust hub. Tap the cap onto the hub with a small ball peen hammer.

54. Coat the splines of the thrust hub with Perfect Seal and install the thrust hub onto the propeller shaft as shown in **Figure 5**.

55. Pressure test the gearcase as described in this chapter.

56. Install the water pump as outlined in this chapter.

57. Fill the gearcase with the recommended lubricant as described in Chapter Four.

58. Install the gearcase and propeller as described in this chapter.

59. Check the gearcase lubricant level after running the engine. Change the lubricant after 10 hours of operation (break-in period). See Chapter Four.

40 and 50 hp (1995-1999)

Refer to **Figure 55** for this procedure.

1. Remove the propeller as described in this chapter.

2. Drain the gearcase lubricant as described in Chapter Four.

3. Remove the gearcase as described in this chapter.

4. Secure the gearcase in a suitable holding fixture or a vise with protective jaws.

5. Remove the water pump as described in this chapter.

6. Inspect the exhaust deflector. Remove and replace the deflector if it is damaged.

7. Remove the 2 screws and washers securing the propeller shaft bearing carrier to the gearcase. Remove the propeller shaft bearing carrier with puller (part No. 91-27780) or equivalent.

8. Pull the propeller shaft assembly from the gearcase. If the shift cam follower falls out of the propeller shaft, retrieve it from the gearcase.

9. Remove the pinion nut. Use drive shaft socket (part No. 91-825196) and an appropriate wrench or socket. Lift the drive shaft assembly from gearcase.

10. Remove the pinion gear, pinion roller bearing and forward gear from the propeller shaft bore.

11. Remove the shift shaft assembly from the gearcase.

12. Remove the drive shaft seal carrier from the drive shaft assembly. Remove and discard the O-ring from the seal carrier. Place the large beveled end of the seal carrier down (on a suitable

9

GEARCASE 40-50 HP (1995-1999)

1. Gearcase housing
2. Exhaust deflector and seal
3. Vent plug
4. Sealing washer
5. Magnetic drain plug
6. Pinion nut
7. Pinion gear
8. Pinion bearing and race
9. Gasket
10. Water pump plate
11. Gasket
12. Water pump impeller seals
13. Impeller drive key
14. Water pump impeller
15. Water pump cover
16. Water pump cover screws
17. Water tube seal
18. Drive shaft seals
19. Drive shaft seal carrier
20. O-ring
21. Ball bearing
22. Drive shaft
23. Nut
24. Tie-strap
25. Shift bellows
26. Shift rod retainer

27. O-ring
28. O-ring
29. Washer
30. Washer
31. Shift rod
32. Pin
33. Shift cam
34. Pin
35. Trim tab (anode)
36. Trim tab screw and washer
37. Water screen
38. Rubber plug
39. Water tube
40. Gasket
41. Dowel pins
42. Gearcase mounting screws and washers
43. Forward bearing and race
44. Roller bearing
45. Forward gear
46. Shift cam follower
47. Shift spring
48. Clutch dog pin
49. Clutch dog shifter
50. Clutch dog spring
51. Propeller shaft
52. Reverse gear

53. Ball bearing
54. O-ring
55. Propshaft bearing carrier
56. Roller bearing

57. Screw and washer
58. Propshaft seals
59. Propeller thrust washer
60. Lock tab washer
61. Elastic stop nut

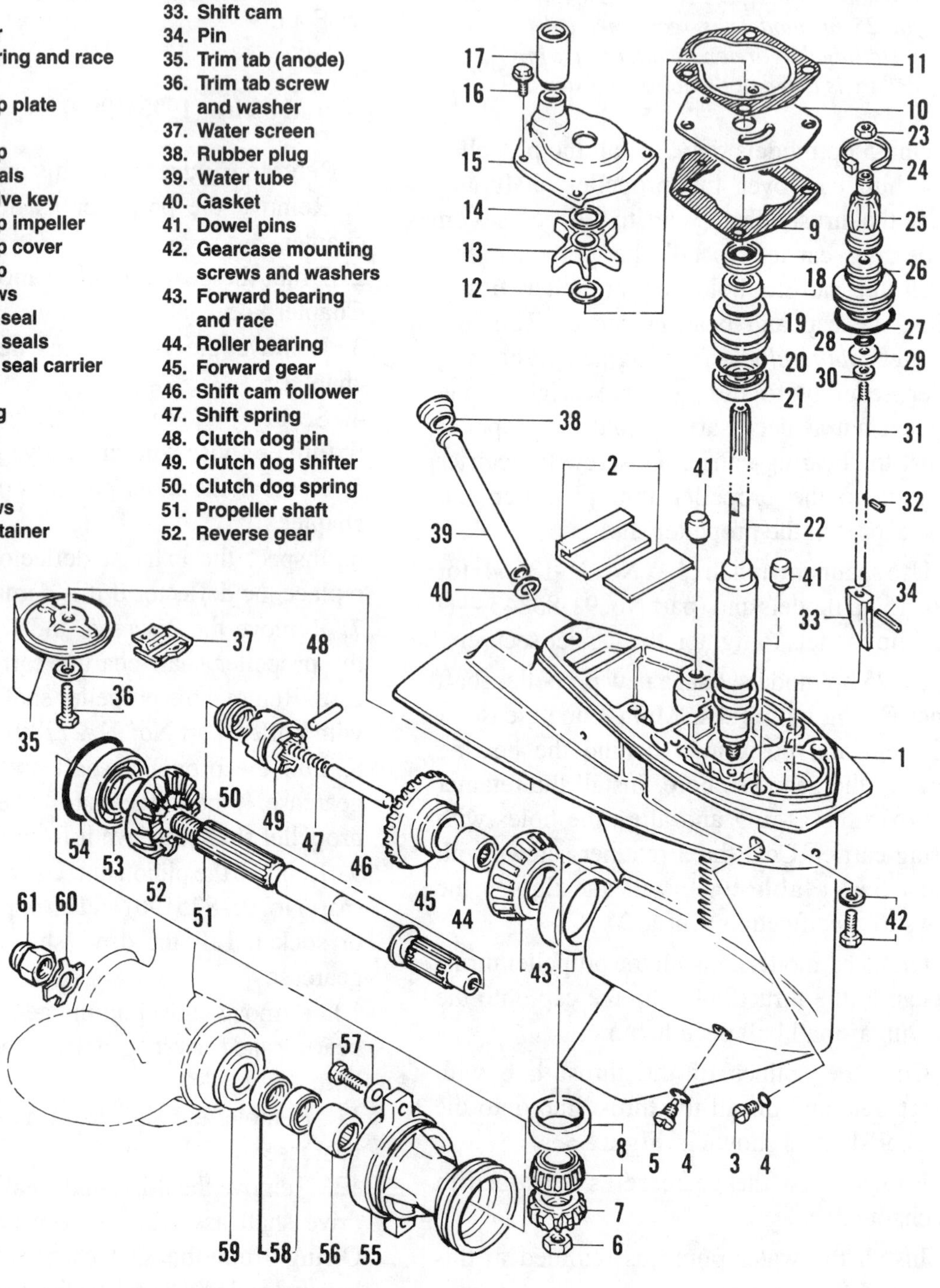

open support) and press both seals from the carrier with a suitable mandrel. Discard the seals.

13. Secure the propeller shaft bearing carrier in a soft-jawed vise. Remove the reverse gear and bearing assembly with puller (part No. 91-27780) or equivalent.

NOTE
If the propeller shaft bearing is removed, the propeller shaft seals will also be removed in the process. If the seals must be replaced, but not the bearing, remove the seals with a suitable puller.

14. Place the propeller shaft bearing carrier (seal end down) on a suitable open support. Press the bearing and seals out of the carrier with driver (part No. 91-37312) and rod (part No. 91-37323) or equivalent. Discard the seals and bearing.

15. Remove and discard the clutch dog spring with a small screwdriver or awl. Insert the tool under one end of the spring and rotate the propeller shaft to unwind the spring.

16. Insert the shift cam follower into the propeller shaft with the beveled end facing out. Place the cam follower against a solid surface and push on the propeller shaft to unload the

spring pressure on the clutch dog cross pin. Remove the pin with a suitable punch. Carefully release the pressure on the cam follower and spring. Remove the cam follower, spring and clutch dog from the propeller shaft. See **Figure 50**.

17. Remove the shift shaft assembly from the gearcase. Remove and discard the inner and outer O-rings from the shift shaft retainer. Remove and discard the shift boot. Inspect the shift cam for wear. Replace any worn or damaged parts. The shift retainer is plastic and should be inspected carefully for cracks.

18. Clean and inspect all components as described in this chapter. Refer to **Table 4** for all specifications. The drive shaft lower bearing cup, forward gear outer roller bearing and cup, forward gear inner bearing, reverse gear ball bearing and the upper drive shaft ball bearing should not be removed unless they must be replaced. Replace all worn or damaged parts that do not meet specifications. Inspect the trim tab (anode) for deterioration. Replace the trim tab if it is significantly deteriorated.

19. If the reverse gear bearing must be replaced, remove the bearing from the gear by pressing it off of the gear. Support the bearing in a press with bearing separator plate (part No. 91-37241) or equivalent. Press the gear from the bearing with driver (part No. 91-37312) or equivalent.

20. If the drive shaft lower roller bearing must be replaced, remove the bearing cup from the gearcase by driving it down into the propeller shaft bore with bearing puller (part No. 91-825200A1) and driver (part No. 91-13779) or equivalent. Insert the puller (A, **Figure 56**) from the propeller shaft bore. Insert the driver (B, **Figure 56**) through the drive shaft bore. Place a shop cloth under the bearing puller. Use a suitable mallet and drive the bearing cup out into the propeller shaft bore.

21. If the upper drive shaft ball bearing must be replaced, place the drive shaft, with the pinion end down, into a vise with the jaws opened just wide enough to support the ball bearing. Strike

9

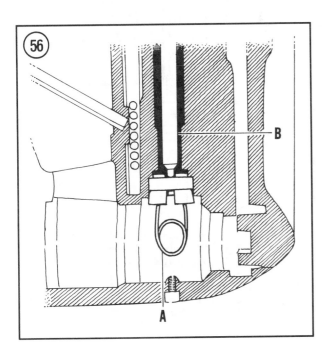

the power head end of the drive shaft with a lead or rawhide hammer and drive the drive shaft from the bearing. Be prepared to catch the drive shaft as it comes free.

22. If the forward gear roller bearing must be replaced, remove the cup from the gearcase with puller (part No. 91-27780) or equivalent. Remove the roller bearing from the forward gear with bearing separator plate (part No. 91-37241) or equivalent and a suitable mandrel.

23. If the forward gear inner roller bearing must be replaced, remove the bearing by pressing it out of the gear with a suitable mandrel. Do not damage the forward gear roller bearing (if installed) during this operation.

24. If the forward gear bearing cup was removed, lubricate the outside of the new bearing cup with gear oil and set the cup into the gearcase bearing bore. Place mandrel (part No. 91-36571) or equivalent over the cup. Place the propeller shaft into the mandrel hole. Install the propeller shaft bearing carrier into the gearcase (to hold the propeller shaft centered). Thread a scrap propeller nut onto the propeller shaft. Use a mallet and drive the propeller shaft against the mandrel until the bearing cup is fully seated in the gearcase bearing bore. Remove the propeller nut, propeller shaft, bearing carrier and mandrel. Coat the bearing race with gear oil.

25. Set the forward gear on a press with the gear teeth facing down. Lubricate the new roller bearing inner diameter with gear oil. Set the bearing onto the gear with the wide end of the bearing facing the gear. Press the bearing fully onto the gear with a suitable mandrel. Do not press on the roller cage. Leave the gear in the press for Step 26.

26. Lubricate the outside diameter of a new forward gear internal bearing with gear oil and press it into the forward gear (numbered side up) with driver (part No. 91-826872) or equivalent.

27. If the drive shaft ball bearing was removed, lubricate the inside diameter of a new bearing with gear oil. Slide the bearing over the drive shaft. Place the drive shaft and bearing in a press and support the ball bearing inner race with separator plate (part No. 91-37241) or equivalent. Thread an old pinion nut 3/4 of the way onto the drive shaft. Press the bearing onto the drive shaft until it is seated.

28. If the lower drive shaft bearing was removed, install a new cup into the gearcase as shown in **Figure 57**. Oil the outside of the cup and install it with the small diameter facing the top of the gearcase. Tighten the nut to seat the cup fully in the bearing bore.

29. Set the drive shaft bearing carrier in a press with the large beveled edge facing up. Coat the outside diameter of 2 new drive shaft seals with Loctite 271 threadlocking adhesive (**Table 9**). Install the metal cased seal with its lip facing down. Press the seal from the large stepped side

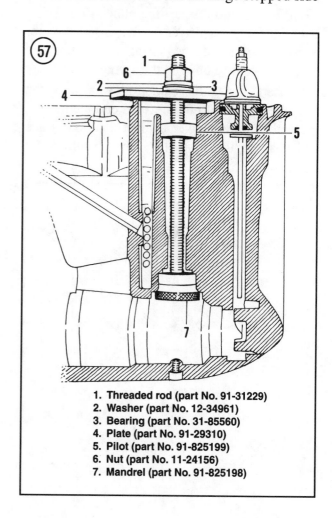

1. **Threaded rod (part No. 91-31229)**
2. **Washer (part No. 12-34961)**
3. **Bearing (part No. 31-85560)**
4. **Plate (part No. 91-29310)**
5. **Pilot (part No. 91-825199)**
6. **Nut (part No. 11-24156)**
7. **Mandrel (part No. 91-825198)**

of mandrel (part No. 91-825197) or equivalent until the tool bottoms on the carrier. Install the rubber cased seal with the lip facing up. Press the seal from the small stepped side of mandrel (part No. 91-825197) or equivalent until the tool bottoms on the carrier. Lubricate the seal lips with 2-4-C Multi-Lube grease or equivalent.

30. Lubricate a new drive shaft carrier O-ring with 2-4-C Multi-Lube grease or equivalent and install it in the carrier groove.

31. Rotate the gearcase so the propeller shaft bore is pointing upward. Lubricate the forward gear bearing with gear oil and place the gear and bearing assembly into the gearcase forward bearing cup.

32. Place the lower drive shaft roller bearing into the lower cup. Place the pinion gear in position on top of the bearing.

33. Spray the threads of the drive shaft with Loquic primer (**Table 9**). Insert the drive shaft into the gear housing. Hold the pinion gear and lower bearing in position and engage the drive shaft splines to the pinion gear splines.

34. Apply Loctite 271 threadlocking adhesive (**Table 9**) to the pinion nut. Install the pinion nut with the rounded corners *against* the pinion gear and hand tighten. Use drive shaft socket (part No. 91-825196) and a suitable socket or wrench to tighten the pinion nut to specifications (**Table 2**).

35. If the shift shaft was disassembled, reassemble the shift rod assembly with new O-rings and a new boot. Grease the O-rings with 2-4-CMulti-Lube grease or equivalent. Install the shift rod to the gearcase with the ramp of the shift cam facing the propeller. Seat the retainer firmly into the shift cavity.

36. Assemble the propeller shaft. Align the cross pin holes of the clutch dog with the slot in the propeller shaft. Position the long end of the clutch dog (**Figure 53**) towards the propeller and slide it onto the propeller shaft. Lubricate the shift spring with gear oil and install it into the propeller shaft. Install the cam follower with the beveled end out. Press the cam follower against

a solid object to compress the spring. Insert a small punch through the clutch dog holes *between* the spring and the cam follower. Remove the cam follower. Insert the clutch dog cross-pin into the clutch dog (opposite of the punch) and slide the pin into the clutch dog and the punch out. See **Figure 50**. When finished, the cross-pin must be in front of the spring.

37. Secure the pin to the clutch dog with a new retainer spring. Do not open the spring any more than necessary to install it. Grease the cam follower with 2-4-C Multi-Lube grease or equivalent and install it into the propeller shaft with the beveled end out.

38. Turn the gearcase so that the propeller shaft bore is horizontal. Move the shift rod upward to the forward position and install the propeller shaft into the center of the forward gear.

39. If the propeller shaft bearing carrier roller bearing was removed, lubricate a new bearing with gear oil and place it into the carrier with lettered end facing the propeller. Use mandrel (part No. 91-817011) or equivalent and press the bearing until the tool seats against the carrier.

40. Coat 2 new propeller shaft seals with Loctite 271 threadlocking adhesive (**Table 9**). Install the small diameter seal with its spring facing the gearcase. Press the seal in with the large stepped end of mandrel (part No. 91-817007) or equivalent until the tool bottoms against the carrier. Install the large diameter seal with its spring facing the propeller. Press the seal in with the small stepped end of mandrel (part No. 91-817007) or equivalent until the tool bottoms against the carrier. Coat the seal lips with 2-4-C Multi-Lube grease or equivalent.

41. If the reverse gear bearing was removed, install a new bearing with its numbered side away from the gear. Lubricate the inner diameter of the bearing with gear oil. Press the bearing onto the gear with a suitable mandrel. Press on the inner race only.

42. Lubricate the outside diameter of the reverse gear bearing. Press the reverse gear and bearing

9

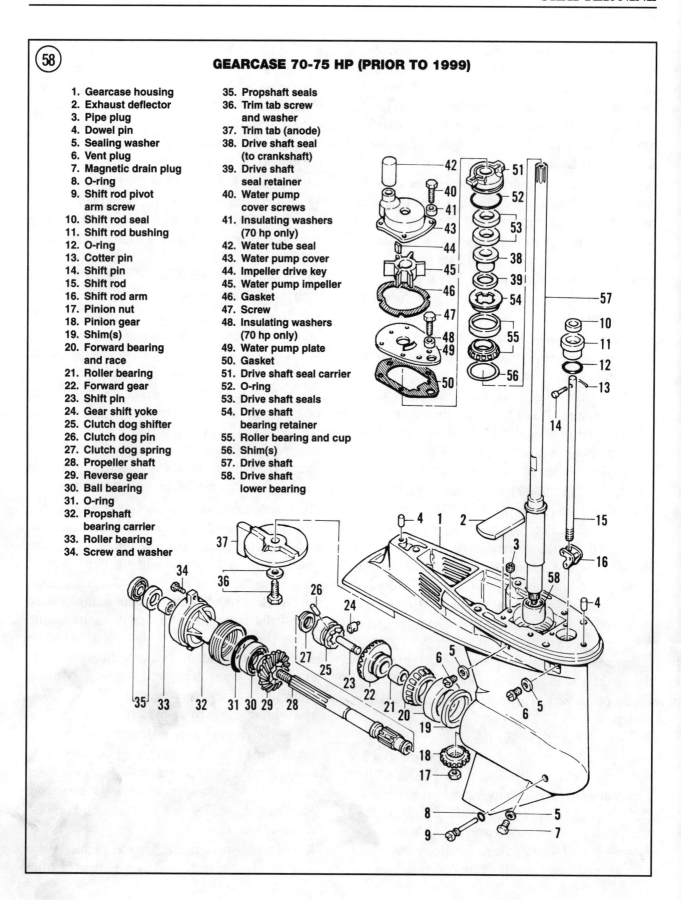

58

GEARCASE 70-75 HP (PRIOR TO 1999)

1. Gearcase housing
2. Exhaust deflector
3. Pipe plug
4. Dowel pin
5. Sealing washer
6. Vent plug
7. Magnetic drain plug
8. O-ring
9. Shift rod pivot arm screw
10. Shift rod seal
11. Shift rod bushing
12. O-ring
13. Cotter pin
14. Shift pin
15. Shift rod
16. Shift rod arm
17. Pinion nut
18. Pinion gear
19. Shim(s)
20. Forward bearing and race
21. Roller bearing
22. Forward gear
23. Shift pin
24. Gear shift yoke
25. Clutch dog shifter
26. Clutch dog pin
27. Clutch dog spring
28. Propeller shaft
29. Reverse gear
30. Ball bearing
31. O-ring
32. Propshaft bearing carrier
33. Roller bearing
34. Screw and washer
35. Propshaft seals
36. Trim tab screw and washer
37. Trim tab (anode)
38. Drive shaft seal (to crankshaft)
39. Drive shaft seal retainer
40. Water pump cover screws
41. Insulating washers (70 hp only)
42. Water tube seal
43. Water pump cover
44. Impeller drive key
45. Water pump impeller
46. Gasket
47. Screw
48. Insulating washers (70 hp only)
49. Water pump plate
50. Gasket
51. Drive shaft seal carrier
52. O-ring
53. Drive shaft seals
54. Drive shaft bearing retainer
55. Roller bearing and cup
56. Shim(s)
57. Drive shaft
58. Drive shaft lower bearing

assembly into the propeller shaft bearing carrier with a suitable mandrel.

43. Coat a new propeller shaft carrier O-ring with 2-4-C Multi-Lube grease or equivalent and position it in the bearing carrier groove. Install the propeller shaft bearing carrier and reverse gear assembly into the gearcase.

44. Coat the threads of the 2 retaining screws with perfect seal (**Table 9**). Install new lock tab washers onto the screws and install the screw assemblies to the gearcase. Tighten the screws to specifications (**Table 2**). Bend a lock tab over each screw.

45. Slide the drive shaft seal carrier (large beveled edge up) over the drive shaft and seat it into the gearcase bore.

46. Install water pump as outlined in this chapter.

47. Pressure test the gearcase as described in this chapter.

48. Fill the gearcase with the recommended lubricant (**Table 9**) as described in Chapter Four.

49. Install the gearcase and propeller as described in this chapter.

50. Check the gearcase lubricant level after running the engine. Change the lubricant after 10 hours of operation (break-in period). See Chapter Four.

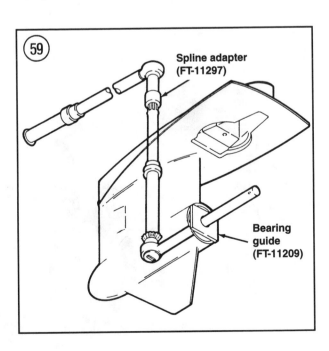

Spline adapter (FT-11297)

Bearing guide (FT-11209)

70 and 75 hp (Prior to 1999)

Refer to **Figure 58** for this procedure.

1. Remove propeller as described in this chapter.

2. Drain the gearcase lubricant (Chapter Four).

3. Remove the gearcase assembly as described in this chapter.

4. Secure the gearcase in a suitable holding fixture or a vise with protective jaws. If protective jaws are not available, position the gearcase upright with the skeg between wooden blocks.

5. Remove water pump as described in this chapter.

6. Remove the 2 screws securing the bearing carrier to the gearcase housing. Use a suitable jaw-type puller to extract the bearing carrier from the gearcase housing. When the bearing carrier is free of the housing, pull the propeller shaft from housing along with the bearing carrier and the propeller shaft components as an assembly.

7. Remove the shift yoke from the propeller shaft. Shift yoke may remain inside the gearcase housing when the propeller shaft is removed. If so, reach into the gear cavity and remove the yoke.

8. Slide the bearing carrier and the reverse gear and bearing assembly off the propeller shaft.

9. Remove and discard the bearing carrier O-ring.

10. Remove the propeller shaft seals the from bearing carrier.

11. Inspect the propeller shaft needle bearing inside the bearing carrier. If the bearing is rusted, pitted, excessively worn or damaged, remove the bearing from the carrier using a suitable driver.

12. Using a suitable punch, drive the clutch roll pin from the clutch. Remove the shift pin and slide the clutch off the propeller shaft.

13. Install drive shaft spline adapter (part No. FT-11297) onto the drive shaft splines. Hold the pinion gear nut using a 11/16 in. 6-point socket and flex handle. Support the flex handle using bearing guide (part No. FT-11209), or pad the flex handle with shop towels to prevent damage to gearcase housing. Place an appropriate size wrench or socket on the drive shaft spline adapter and turn the drive shaft to remove the pinion nut and washer. See **Figure 59**.

9

14. Remove the drive shaft upper bearing retainer using retainer wrench (part No. FT-11293).

15. Lift the drive shaft, along with the upper bearing and race out the top of the housing.

16. Remove any shims present under the upper drive shaft bearing.

> *NOTE*
> *One or more shims (or none) may be present under the upper drive shaft bearing. Note the number, thickness and location of shims for reference during assembly.*

17. Reach into the housing gear cavity and remove the pinion nut, washer and pinion gear.

18. Remove the forward gear and bearing assembly from the gear cavity.

19. Turn the lower shift rod counterclockwise until disengaged from the shift arm, then lift the shift rod and shift rod bushing out of the housing.

20. Remove the shift arm pivot pin from the lower starboard side of the gearcase housing. Reach into the housing gear cavity and remove the shift arm.

21. If forward gear bearing requires replacement, remove the forward gear bearing race as follows:

   a. Assemble the bearing race remover (part No. FT-11207-1) and bearing guide set (part No. FT-11209) as shown in **Figure 60**.

   b. Turn the bearing tool nut until the bearing race is free. Remove the special tools and discard the bearing race.

22. Remove any shims behind the forward gear bearing race.

> *NOTE*
> *One or more (or none) shims may be present behind the forward gear bearing race. Note the number, thickness and location of the shim(s) for reference during reassemble.*

23. Remove the forward gear tapered roller bearing using a suitable bearing plate and arbor press.

24. If the forward gear needle bearing requires replacement, carefully drive the bearing from the inner diameter of the gear using a punch.

25. If the upper drive shaft bearing requires replacement, press the bearing off the drive shaft using a suitable bearing plate and mandrel.

26. If the drive shaft lower bearing requires replacement, drive the bearing downward into the gear cavity using the special tool arrangement shown in **Figure 61**.

27. Remove and discard the shift rod bushing O-ring. Pry the shift rod seal from the bushing using a screwdriver or similar tool.

28. Clean and inspect all gearcase components as described in this chapter.

> *NOTE*
> *The forward gear position must be adjusted if a new gearcase housing or new forward gear is used. The pinion gear depth must be reshimmed if a new gearcase housing or drive shaft is used. See* **Gearcase Shimming** *in this chapter prior to proceeding with reassemble.*

29. Coat the outer diameter of a new shift rod seal with a suitable sealant. Press the seal into the shift rod bushing with the seal lip facing up.

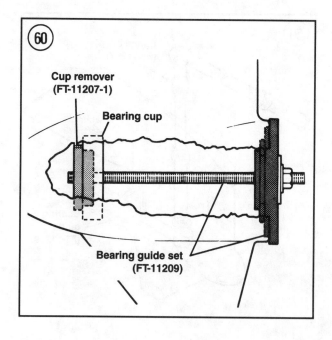

60

Cup remover
(FT-11207-1)

Bearing cup

Bearing guide set
(FT-11209)

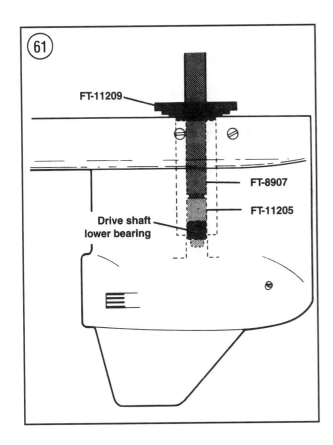

(61)

FT-11209

FT-8907

FT-11205

Drive shaft
lower bearing

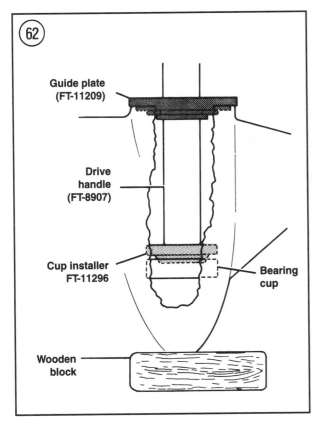

(62)

Guide plate
(FT-11209)

Drive
handle
(FT-8907)

Cup installer
FT-11296

Bearing
cup

Wooden
block

Install a new O-ring on the shift rod bushing. Lubricate the O-ring with a suitable grease.

30. Install a new seal on the shift arm pivot pin. Install the shift arm into the gearcase housing with the forked end facing down. Install the shift arm pivot pin making sure the pin properly engages the shift arm.

31. Install the lower shift rod into the gearcase. Screw the shift rod into the shift arm until bottomed out, then back off four complete turns. Place the lower shift rod bushing over the shift rod and push the bushing into the gearcase.

32. To install the forward gear bearing race, position the gearcase as shown in **Figure 62**. Install the original forward gear shim(s) into the gearcase. Install a new bearing race with installer (part No. FT-11296), driver handle (part No. FT-8907) and bearing guide plate (part No. FT-11209). Drive bearing race into gearcase housing until fully seated.

33. Lubricate a new drive shaft lower bearing with needle bearing assembly grease. Drive the bearing into the gearcase housing using bearing installation tool (Mercury Marine part No. 91-817058A1). Drive bearing from the numbered side, into the housing until the tool bottoms on the top of the gearcase housing. If the bearing installation tool is not available, position the top of the bearing 7.05-7.07 in. (179.1-179.6 mm) from the top surface of the gearcase housing (**Figure 63**) using a suitable driver.

34. Lubricate a new propeller shaft needle bearing with needle bearing assembly grease. Using a suitable installation tool, press the bearing (from numbered side) into the bearing carrier until the bearing is 0.82 in. (20.8) from the face of the carrier as shown in **Figure 64**.

35. Apply Loctite 271 to the outer diameter of the small propeller shaft seal. Place the seal into the bearing carrier with the seal lip facing down. Press the seal into the bearing carrier until top of seal is 0.44 in. (11.2 mm) from face of carrier as shown in **Figure 64**.

9

36. Apply Loctite 271 onto the outer diameter of the large propeller shaft seal. Place the seal into the bearing carrier with the lip facing up, until the seal is 0.04 in. (1.02 mm) from the face of the carrier measured as shown in **Figure 64**. Lubricate the seal lips and the cavity between the seals with needle bearing assembly grease.

37. If removed, press a new bearing onto the reverse gear.

38. Press the reverse gear and bearing assembly into the bearing carrier.

39. Install a new O-ring onto the bearing carrier. Lubricate the O-ring with Quicksilver Special Lube 101.

40. Lightly lubricate the outside diameter of a new forward gear needle bearing. Press the needle bearing into the forward gear until bottomed in the gear. Be sure to press from the lettered side of the bearing. Lubricate the bearing rollers with needle bearing assembly grease.

41. Press a new tapered roller bearing onto the forward gear until fully seated. Lubricate the bearing with needle bearing assembly grease.

42. Install the forward gear assembly into the gearcase.

43. If removed, press a new upper drive shaft bearing onto the drive shaft until fully seated. Lubricate the bearing with a recommended gearcase lubricant.

44. Install the pinion gear depth shims into the upper drive shaft bearing bore.

45. Install the drive shaft with the upper bearing and race into the gearcase.

NOTE
If the pinion depth requires reshimming, install the original pinion gear nut in Step 46 and omit the Loctite application. During final reassemble, always use a new nut and apply Loctite.

46. Install the pinion gear onto the drive shaft. Apply Loctite 271 onto the threads of a *new*

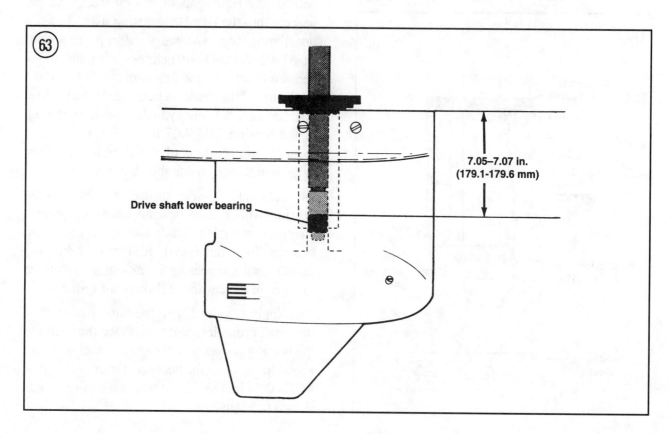

63

Drive shaft lower bearing

7.05–7.07 in.
(179.1-179.6 mm)

pinion gear nut and install the washer and nut onto the drive shaft. Make sure the recessed side of the nut is facing the pinion gear. Tighten the nut finger tight.

47. Install the upper drive shaft bearing retainer with the OFF mark facing upward (smooth side toward bearing race). Using retainer wrench (part No. T-11293), tighten the retainer to specification (**Table 2**).

48. Using the tool arrangement shown in **Figure 59**, tighten the pinion gear nut to specification (**Table 2**).

49. Align the hole in the clutch with the slot in the propeller shaft, then install the clutch on the shaft. Insert the shift pin into the forward end of the propeller shaft. Align the hole in the shift pin with hole in the clutch, then install a new roll pin.

50. Place the shift yoke on the shift pin with the opening facing down. Use grease to hold the yoke in place.

51. Pull upward on the lower shift rod so the forked end of the shift arm is facing aft.

52. Position the gearcase housing so the gear cavity is facing upward. Install the propeller shaft into the gearcase. Make sure the shift yoke properly engages the shift arm. Raise and lower the lower shift rod while watching for clutch movement to check shift yoke engagement.

53. Slide the bearing carrier assembly over the propeller shaft and into the gearcase. Install the bearing carrier screws and tighten to specification (**Table 2**).

54. Install the water pump as described in this chapter.

55. Check the propeller shaft end play and gear backlash as described in this chapter.

56. Pressure test the gearcase as described in this chapter.

57. Install the gearcase as described in this chapter.

58. Fill the gearcase with a recommended lubricant (Chapter Four).

59. Check the gearcase lubricant level after operating the motor. Change the lubricant after the first 10 hours of operation (break-in period). See Chapter Four.

90 and 120 hp (1995-1996) and 1999 75 hp

Refer to **Figure 65** for this procedure.

1. Remove the propeller as described in this chapter.

2. Drain the gearcase lubricant as described in Chapter Four.

3. Remove the gearcase as described in this chapter.

9

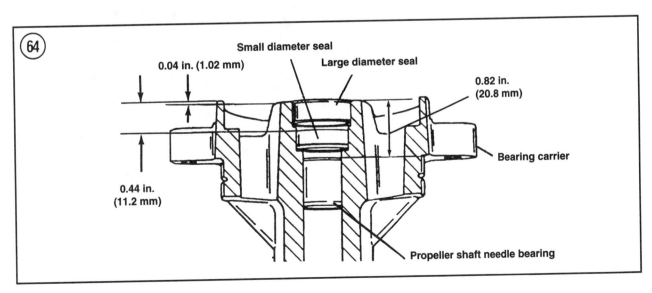

64

Small diameter seal

0.04 in. (1.02 mm)

Large diameter seal

0.82 in. (20.8 mm)

Bearing carrier

0.44 in. (11.2 mm)

Propeller shaft needle bearing

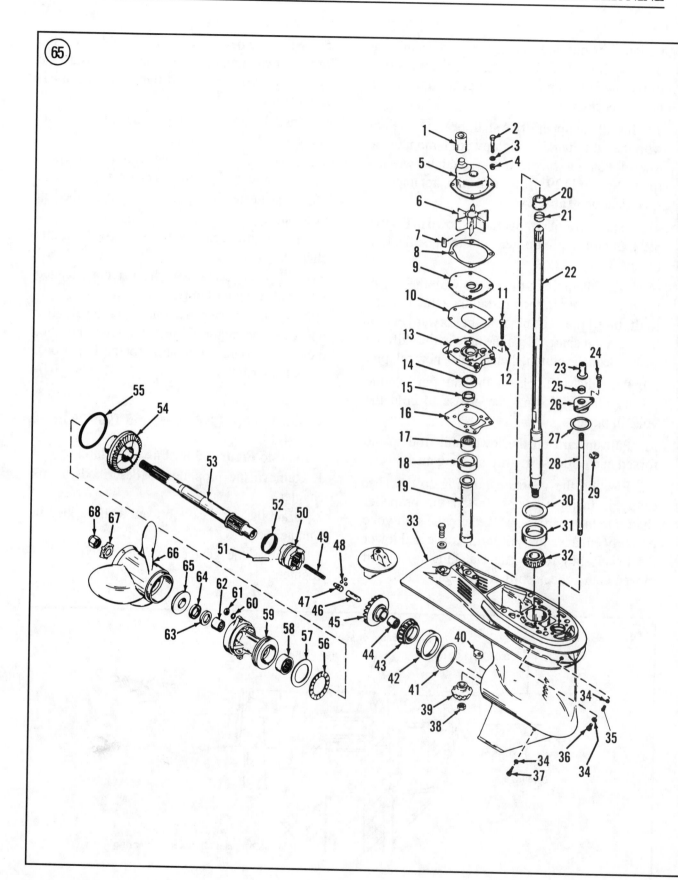

GEARCASE 90 AND 120 HP MODELS (1995-1999), 1999 75 HP MODELS

1. Water tube seal
2. Screw
3. Washer
4. Insulator
5. Water pump cover
6. Impeller
7. Impeller drive key
8. Gasket
9. Face plate
10. Gasket
11. Screw
12. Washer
13. Water pump base
14. Seal
15. Seal
16. Gasket
17. Roller bearing
18. Carrier
19. Sleeve
20. Wear sleeve
21. Seal ring
22. Drive shaft
23. Shift shaft coupler
24. Screw
25. Seal
26. Shift shaft retainer
27. O-ring
28. Shift shaft
29. Retaining ring
30. Shim pack
31. Bearing race
32. Tapered roller bearing
33. Gear housing
34. Gasket
35. Plug
36. Plug
37. Plug
38. Pinion gear nut
39. Pinion gear
40. Shift cam
41. Shim pack
42. Bearing race
43. Tapered roller bearings
44. Roller bearing
45. Forward gear
46. Shift cam follower
47. Guide
48. Balls
49. Spring
50. Sliding clutch
51. Cross pin
52. Cross pin retainer
53. Propeller shaft
54. Reverse gear
55. O-ring
56. Thrust bearing
57. Thrust washer
58. Roller bearing
59. Bearing carrier
60. Washer
61. Nut
62. Roller bearing
63. Seal
64. Seal
65. Thrust hub
66. Propeller
67. Tab washer
68. Propeller nut

4. Secure the gearcase in a suitable holding fixture or a vise with protective jaws.

5. Remove the water pump and water pump adapter base as described in this chapter.

6. Remove the 2 elastic stop nuts and washers securing the propeller shaft bearing carrier to the gearcase. Remove the propeller shaft bearing carrier with puller (part No. 91-46086A-1) or equivalent. Slide the propeller thrust washer onto the propeller shaft and position it to keep the jaws of the puller secured out against the propeller shaft bearing carrier.

7. Remove the reverse gear, thrust bearing and thrust washer from the propeller shaft bearing carrier. Remove and discard the O-ring.

8. Pull the propeller shaft assembly from the gearcase. Remove and discard the clutch dog spring with a small screwdriver or awl. Insert the tool under one end of the spring and rotate the propeller shaft to unwind the spring.

9. Place the shift cam follower against a solid surface and push on the propeller shaft to unload the spring pressure on the clutch dog cross pin (**Figure 50**). Remove the pin with a suitable punch. Carefully release the pressure on the cam follower and spring. Remove the cam follower, 3 metal balls, guide block, spring and clutch dog from the propeller shaft.

10. Remove the pinion nut. Use drive shaft socket (part No. 91-56775) and appropriate

9

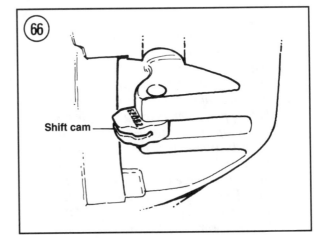

Shift cam

wrenches or sockets. Lift the drive shaft assembly from gearcase.

11. Remove the pinion gear, pinion roller bearing and forward gear from the propeller shaft bore.

12. Remove the 2 screws securing the shift shaft retainer to the gearcase. Carefully pry the shift shaft retainer from the gearcase. Remove the shift shaft assembly from the gearcase.

13. Remove the shift cam from the front of the gearcase bore. See **Figure 66**.

14. Remove the o-ring and seal from the shift shaft retainer. Discard the seal and o-ring.

NOTE
If the propeller shaft bearing must be replaced, the propeller shaft seals will also be removed in the process. If the seals are to be replaced, but not the bearing, remove the seals with a suitable puller.

15. Place the propeller shaft bearing carrier (seal end down) on a suitable open support. Press the bearing and seals out of the carrier with mandrel (part No. 91-26569) and rod (part No. 91-37323) or equivalent. Discard the seals and bearing.

16. Clean and inspect all components as described in this chapter. Refer to **Table 4** for all specifications. Replace any other worn or damaged parts that do not meet specifications. Inspect the trim tab (anode) for deterioration. Replace the trim tab if it is significantly deteriorated.

CAUTION
*Do not remove the following components unless replacement is needed. The forward gear outer roller bearing, forward gear inner roller bearing, drive shaft upper roller bearing and sleeve, both propeller shaft bearing carrier roller bearings, the drive shaft wear sleeve and the gear case oil sleeve (19, **Figure 65**). These components are typically damaged in the removal process. Gear positioning shims are located under the forward gear bearing cup and the*

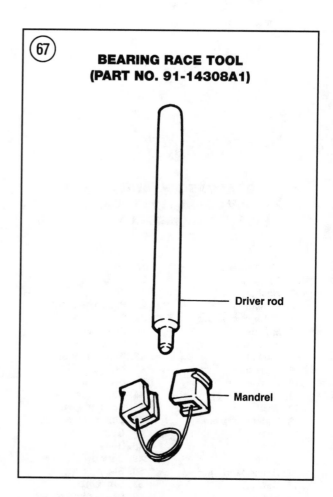

BEARING RACE TOOL
(PART NO. 91-14308A1)

Driver rod

Mandrel

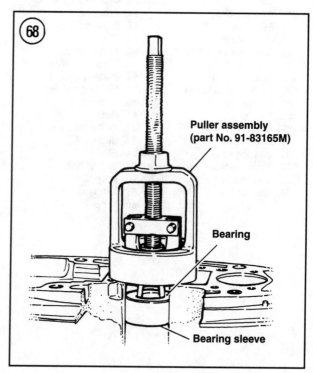

Puller assembly
(part No. 91-83165M)

Bearing

Bearing sleeve

lower drive shaft bearing cup. Record the thickness and location of all shims removed from the gear housing. Shims are normally reused unless they are damaged.

17. If the propeller shaft bearing carrier bearings must be replaced, clamp the carrier in a vise. Remove the inner bearing with slide hammer (part No. 91-34569A-1) or equivalent. Discard the bearing. The rear roller bearing is removed as described in Step 15.

18. If the lower drive shaft roller bearing must be replaced, remove the bearing cup from the gearcase by driving it down into the propeller shaft bore with bearing puller (part No. 91-14308A-1) or equivalent. Insert the puller jaws (mandrels) from the propeller shaft bore. Insert

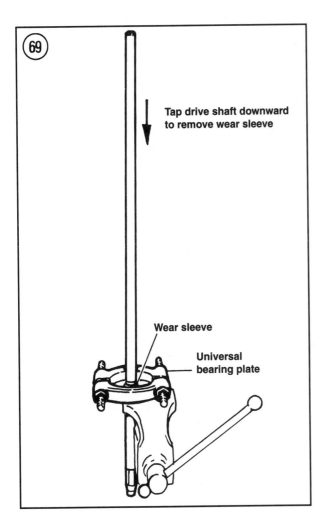

69

Tap drive shaft downward
to remove wear sleeve

Wear sleeve

Universal
bearing plate

the driver handle through the drive shaft bore. Place a shop cloth under the puller jaws. Use a suitable mallet and drive the bearing cup out into the propeller shaft bore. Retrieve the shims for later reference. See **Figure 67**.

19. If the upper drive shaft bearing and sleeve are to be replaced, remove the bearing with a 2-jaw puller (part No. 91-83165M) or equivalent. Expand the jaws tightly behind the bearing and tighten the puller nut to remove the bearing. Repeat the process for the sleeve. See **Figure 68**.

20. If the drive shaft wear sleeve and seal must be replaced, place the drive shaft into bearing separator plate (part No. 91-37241) with the pinion end down. Support the drive shaft and separator in a vise with the jaws opened just wide enough to allow the drive shaft to fit. Adjust the separator plate to catch the edge of the wear sleeve. Strike the power head end of the drive shaft with a lead or rawhide hammer and drive the shaft from the wear sleeve. Be prepared to catch the drive shaft as it comes free. Remove the rubber seal from the drive shaft. Discard the seal and wear ring. See **Figure 69**.

21. If the forward gear roller bearing must be replaced, remove the cup from the gearcase with a slide hammer (part No. 91-34569A-1) or equivalent (**Figure 70**). Retrieve the shims from in front of the bearing cup for later reference. Remove the roller bearing from the forward gear with bearing separator plate (part No. 91-37241) or equivalent and a suitable mandrel.

22. If the forward gear inner roller bearing must be replaced, support the gear in a soft-jawed vise. Drive the bearing from the gear with a suitable punch. Do not damage the forward gear roller bearing (if attached) during this operation.

23. If the forward gear bearing cup was removed, install the original shims into the bearing bore. If the original shims were lost, start with 0.010 in. (0.254 mm) shim(s). Lubricate the outside of the new bearing cup with gear oil and set the cup into the gearcase bearing bore. Place mandrel (part No. 91-31106) or equivalent over

9

the cup. Place the propeller shaft into the mandrel hole. Install the propeller shaft bearing carrier into the gearcase (to hold the propeller shaft centered). Thread a scrap propeller nut onto the propeller shaft. Use a mallet and drive the propeller shaft against the mandrel until the bearing cup is fully seated in the gearcase bearing bore. Remove the propeller nut, propeller shaft, bearing carrier and mandrel. Coat the bearing race with gear oil.

24. Set the forward gear on a press with the gear teeth facing down. Lubricate the new roller bearing inner diameter with gear oil. Set the bearing onto the gear with the wide end of the bearing towards the gear. Press the bearing fully onto the gear with mandrel (part No. 91-37350) or equivalent. Do not press on the roller cage. Leave the gear in the press for Step 25.

25. Lubricate the outside diameter of a new forward gear internal bearing with gear oil and press it into the forward gear (numbered side up) with a suitable mandrel until it bottoms.

26. If the drive shaft wear sleeve and seal were removed, install a new rubber seal to the drive shaft groove. Coat the outside diameter of the rubber seal with Loctite 271 threadlocking adhesive (**Table 9**). Place a new wear sleeve into the holder from sleeve installation kit (part No. 91-14310A-1) Slide the drive shaft into the sleeve and holder. Place the driver (from sleeve installation kit) over the pinion end of the drive shaft. Place the drive shaft and tool assembly in a press. Press the driver against the holder until they contact each other.

27. If the lower drive shaft bearing was removed, install a new cup into the gearcase as shown in **Figure 71**. Oil the outside of the cup and place the original shims on top of the cup. If the original shims are lost, install 0.025 in. (0.635 mm) shim(s). Install the cup with the small diameter facing the top of the gearcase. Tighten the nut to seat the cup fully in the bearing bore.

28. If the drive shaft oil sleeve was removed, lubricate a new sleeve with gear oil. Position the tab at the top of the sleeve to the rear of the gearcase and press the sleeve into the gearcase with hand pressure.

29. If drive shaft bearing and sleeve were removed, lubricate the inner diameter of a new sleeve with 2-4-C Multi-Lube grease or equivalent.

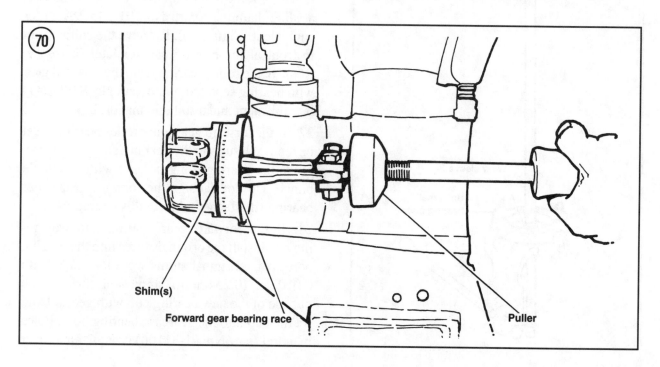

Shim(s)

Forward gear bearing race

Puller

Place the sleeve in a press (tapered side down) and set the bearing on top of the sleeve (numbered side up). Press the bearing into the sleeve with mandrel (part No. 91-14309A-1) or equivalent.

NOTE
The drive shaft oil sleeve must be installed before proceeding with the next step.

30. Install the bearing and sleeve (tapered side down) into the gearcase as shown in **Figure 72**. Tighten the nut to fully seat the bearing and sleeve in the gearcase.

31. Coat the outside diameter of a new shift shaft seal with Loctite 271 threadlocking adhesive.

Press the seal into the shift shaft retainer until it is flush with the retainer upper surface. Grease a new O-ring with 2-4-C Multi-Lube grease or equivalent and install it into the retainer groove. If removed, install the E-ring onto the shift shaft. Lubricate the shift shaft with 2-4-C Multi-Lube grease or equivalent and carefully insert the shift shaft into the shift shaft retainer and seal.

32. Place the shift cam into the gear housing with its numbered side up as shown in **Figure 66**. Install the shift shaft assembly into the gearcase and engage the shift shaft splines to the shift cam internal splines.

33. Apply Loctite 271 threadlocking adhesive to the threads of the 2 shift shaft retainer screws. Install and tighten the screws to specification (**Table 2**).

9

1. Nut (part No. 11-24156)
2. Mandrel (from kit
   part No. 91-31229)
3. Threaded rod
   (part No. 91-31229)
4. Mandrel (from kit
   part No. 91-14309A-1)
5. Bearing cup
6. Shim(s)

⑦¹

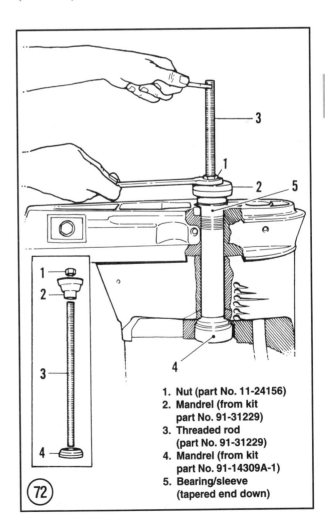

1. Nut (part No. 11-24156)
2. Mandrel (from kit
   part No. 91-31229)
3. Threaded rod
   (part No. 91-31229)
4. Mandrel (from kit
   part No. 91-14309A-1)
5. Bearing/sleeve
   (tapered end down)

⑦²

34. Rotate the gearcase so that the propeller shaft bore is pointing upward. Lubricate the forward gear bearing with gear oil and place the gear and bearing assembly into the gearcase forward bearing cup.

35. Place the lower drive shaft roller bearing into the lower cup. Place the pinion gear in position on top of the bearing.

36. Spray the threads of the drive shaft with Loquic primer (**Table 9**). Insert the drive shaft into the gear housing. Hold the pinion gear and lower bearing in position and engage the drive shaft splines with the pinion gear splines.

NOTE
*Apply Loctite to a **new** pinion nut **after** the pinion gear depth and gear lash have been verified. Install the old pinion nut without sealant to check the gear depth and backlash.*

37. Apply Loctite 271 threadlocking adhesive (**Table 9**) to a new pinion nut. Install the pinion nut and hand tighten. Use drive shaft socket (part No. 91-56775) and a suitable socket or wrench to tighten the pinion nut to specification (**Table 2**).

38. Proceed to *Gearcase Shimming* and verify/set the pinion gear depth and forward gear backlash. Continue at the next step when shimming has been properly verified.

39. Assemble the propeller shaft. Align the cross pin holes of the clutch dog with the slot in the propeller shaft . Position the grooved end of the clutch dog towards the propeller and slide it onto the propeller shaft. Lubricate the shift spring with gear oil and install it into the propeller shaft, followed by the guide block, 3 metal balls and the cam follower as shown in **Figure 73**. Press the cam follower against a solid object to compress the spring. Insert a small punch through the clutch dog holes *and* through the guide block. Remove the cam follower. Insert the clutch dog cross-pin into the clutch dog (opposite of the punch) and slide the pin into the clutch dog as the punch is pulled out. See **Figure**

50, typical. When finished, the cross-pin must be through the guide block.

40. Secure the pin to the clutch dog with a new retainer spring. Do not open the spring any more than necessary to install it. Grease the cam follower with 2-4-C Multi-Lube grease or equivalent and install it into the propeller shaft with the beveled end out.

41. If the propeller shaft bearing carrier roller bearings were removed, lubricate a new inner (forward) bearing with gear oil and place it into the carrier with the lettered end facing out. Use bearing installer (part No. 91-13945) or equivalent and press the bearing into the carrier until the tool seats. Lubricate a new outer (rear) bearing with gear oil and place it into the carrier with lettered end facing out. Set the carrier on tool part No. 91-13945 to protect the carrier. Use mandrel (part No. 91-37263) or equivalent and press the bearing into the carrier until the bearing bottoms. Leave the carrier sitting on tool part No. 91-13945 for Step 42.

42. Coat 2 new propeller shaft seals with Loctite 271 threadlocking adhesive (**Table 9**). Install the small diameter seal with the lip facing the gearcase. Press the seal in with the large stepped end of mandrel (part No. 91-31108) or equivalent until the tool bottoms against the carrier. Install the large diameter

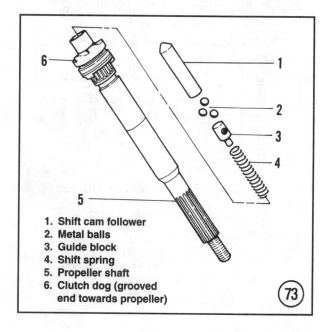

1. **Shift cam follower**
2. **Metal balls**
3. **Guide block**
4. **Shift spring**
5. **Propeller shaft**
6. **Clutch dog (grooved end towards propeller)**

73

seal with the lip facing the propeller. Press the seal in with the small stepped end of mandrel (part No. 91-31108) or equivalent until the tool bottoms against the carrier. Coat the seal lips with 2-4-C Multi-Lube grease or equivalent.

43. Lubricate the propeller shaft bearing carrier thrust washer with needle bearing assembly grease (**Table 9**). Install the thrust washer onto the propeller shaft carrier. Lubricate the thrust bearing with needle bearing assembly grease and place it on top of the thrust washer. Install the reverse gear in to the propeller shaft bearing carrier being careful not to disturb the position of the thrust washer and bearing.

44. Carefully slide the propeller shaft into the propeller shaft bearing carrier assembly.

45. Obtain a piece of 1-1/4 or 1-1/2 in. diameter PVC pipe 6 in. long. Install the PVC pipe over the propeller shaft, then install the propeller locking tab washer and propeller nut. Hand tighten the nut to hold the propeller shaft securely into the bearing carrier. See **Figure 74**.

46. Coat a new propeller shaft carrier O-ring with 2-4-C Multi-Lube grease or equivalent and position it in the bearing carrier groove. Install the propeller shaft bearing carrier and reverse gear assembly into the gearcase with the casting mark *TOP* facing up.

47. Coat the studs with Loctite 271 threadlocking adhesive and install the washers and new elastic stop nuts. Tighten the nuts to specifications (**Table 2**). Remove the propeller nut, lock tab washer and PVC pipe.

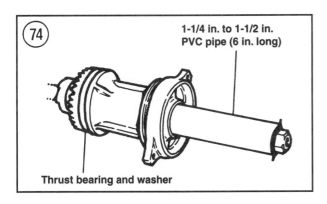

(74)

1-1/4 in. to 1-1/2 in.
PVC pipe (6 in. long)

Thrust bearing and washer

48. Install the water pump and water pump adapter base as outlined in this chapter.

49. Pressure test the gearcase as described in this chapter.

50. Fill the gearcase with the recommended lubricant (**Table 9**) as described in Chapter Four.

51. Install the gearcase and propeller as described in this chapter.

52. Check the gearcase lubricant level after running the engine. Change the lubricant after 10 hours of operation (break-in period). See Chapter Four.

60 hp and 85-150 hp (1984-1994)

Identification

Three basic gearcase designs are used on 85-150 hp models. The three designs are:

    a. 1-piece drive shaft/single-port exhaust (1984-1989 60, 85 and 125 hp).

    b. 2-piece drive shaft/single-port exhaust (90-150 hp).

    c. 2-piece drive shaft/dual-port exhaust (90-150 hp). Furthermore, variations within the basic designs are used. Consequently, positive identification of the various gearcase assemblies is necessary to perform certain service procedures and when ordering replacement parts.

The gearcase assemblies can be identified as follows:

1. One-piece drive shaft/single-port exhaust (1984-1989 60, 85 and 125 hp):

    a. The cooling water intake is aligned with the propeller shaft centerline.

    b. The lubricant drain plug is a 1/16 in. pipe plug.

    c. The anode is located inside the gearcase forward of the propeller.

    d. A 3 or 4 is stamped in the gearcase, between the fill and vent plugs. A 3 indicates an 85 hp model with a 2:1 gear ratio. A 4 indicates a 125 hp model with a 1.73:1 gear ratio.

2. Type A 2-piece drive shaft/single-port exhaust (90-150 hp):

9

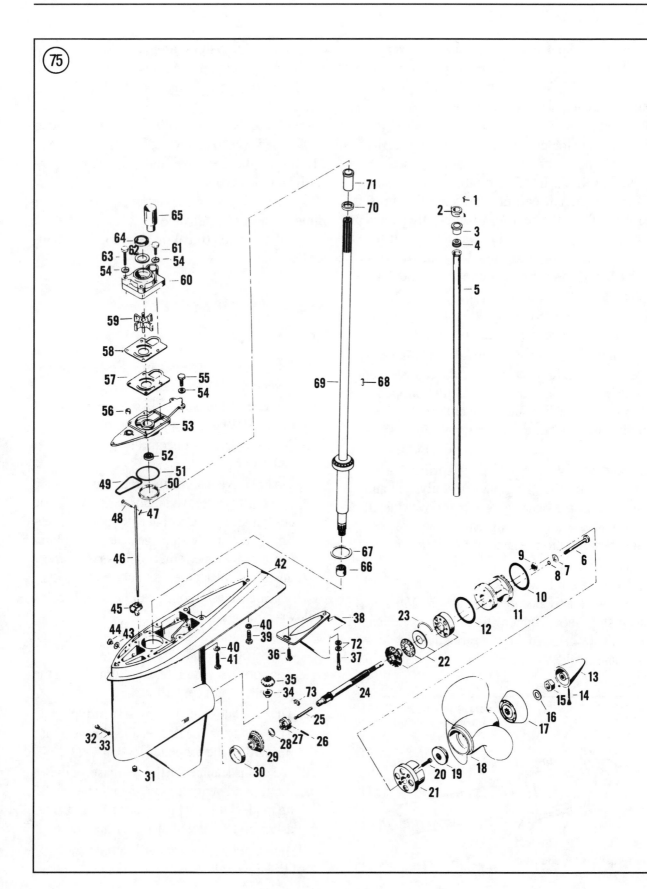

GEARCASE, 1 PIECE
DRIVE SHAFT/SINGLE PORT EXHAUST
(60 HP AND 85-125 HP 1984-1989)

1. Cap screw
2. Water tube bracket
3. Upper water tube seal
4. Water tube grommet
5. Water tube
6. Cap screw
7. Washer
8. Bearing spool bolt O-ring
9. Propeller shaft seal
10. Bearing spool O-ring
11. Bearing spool
12. Bearing spool seal
13. Propeller nut
14. Propeller nut pin
15. Stop nut
16. Plain washer
17. Flare washer
18. Propeller
19. Propeller spacer
20. Screw
21. Zinc anode
22. Reverse gear and bearing assembly
23. Retaining ring
24. Propeller shaft
25. Shift pin
26. Roll pin
27. Clutch
28. Forward gear thrust washer
29. Forward gear and bearing assembly
30. Bearing cup
31. Gearcase plug
32. Shift arm pivot pin
33. Seal
34. Pinion nut
35. Pinion gear
36. Snout retainer
37. Hex socket cap screw
38. Exhaust snout
39. Cap screw
40. Spring lockwasher
41. Cap screw
42. Gearcase
43. Plug washer
44. Gearcase plug
45. Shift coupler
46. Lower shift rod
47. Cotter pin
48. Lower shift rod pin
49. O-ring
50. Crush ring
51. O-ring
52. Drive shaft seal
53. Gearcase cover
54. Spring lockwasher
55. Cap screw
56. Shift rod seal
57. Water pump gasket
58. Back plate
59. Impeller
60. Water pump body
61. Cap screw
62. Locating disc
63. Cap screw
64. Water pump seal
65. Lower water tube seal
66. Lower drive shaft bearing
67. Shim
68. Impeller drive key
69. Drive shaft
70. Crankshaft spline seal retainer
71. Drive shaft spline seal
72. Washer
73. Shift yoke

a. Uses a 2-piece drive shaft assembly.

b. The water intake is aligned with the propeller shaft centerline.

c. The drain and vent plugs are screws with washers (gaskets).

d. Uses a 1.93:1 gear ratio on all models.

3. Type B 2-piece drive shaft/dual-port exhaust (90-150 hp):

a. The water intake is located in the gearcase strut area, above the propeller shaft centerline.

b. The anode is located inside the gearcase, in the exhaust area.

c. Uses a 2-piece drive shaft.

d. Uses a 1.93:1 gear ratio.

4. Type C 2-piece drive shaft/dual-port exhaust (90-150 hp):

a. The water intake located in the gearcase strut area, above the propeller shaft centerline.

b. Uses a 2-piece drive shaft assembly.

c. Has 2 anodes, one on each side of the gearcase, above the anti-ventilation plate.

d. Uses a 1.93:1 standard gear ratio or an optional high-altitude 2.2:1 gear ratio (90 and 120 hp only).

5. Type D 2-piece drive shaft/dual port exhaust (90-150 hp):

a. The water intake is located in the gearcase strut area, above the propeller shaft centerline.

b. Uses a 2-piece drive shaft assembly.

c. Has 2 anodes, one on each side of the gearcase, above the anti-ventilation plate.

d. Uses a 1.93:1 standard gear ratio or an optional high-altitude 2.2:1 gear ratio (90 and 120 hp only).

e. A 4 is stamped in the gearcase. On early models the 4 is stamped above the fill plug. On later models, the 4 is stamped in the gearcase-to-motor leg mating surface, adjacent to the housing cover.

Disassembly/assembly

Refer to **Figure 75** (single-port exhaust) or **Figure 76** (dual-port exhaust) for this procedure.

9

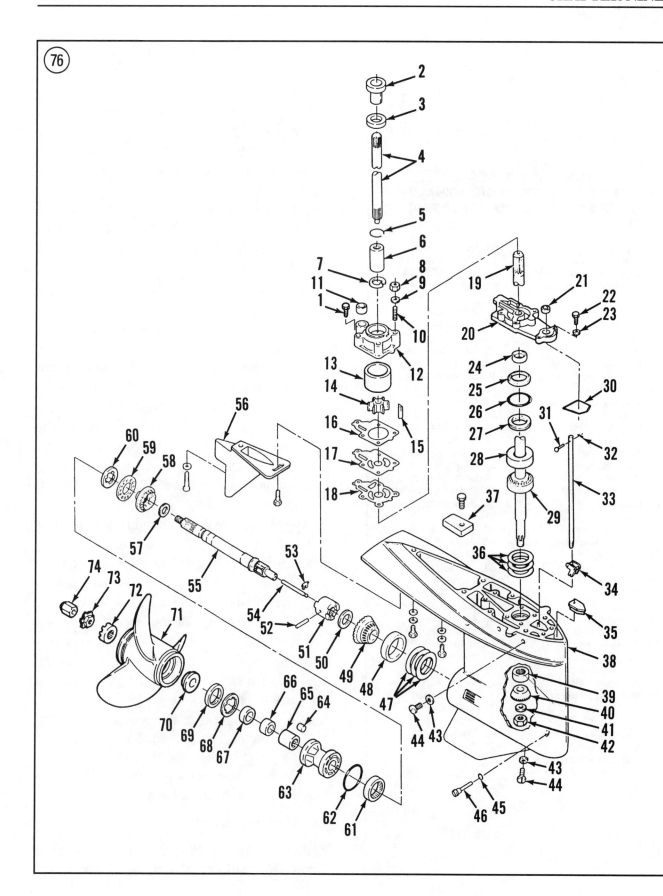

GEARCASE, 2-PIECE DRIVE SHAFT/DUAL-PORT EXHAUST
(1990-1994 90-150 HP [TYPICAL TYPE C])

1. Screw
2. Spline seal (except L-Drive)
3. Seal (except L-Drive)
4. Upper drive shaft (except L-Drive)
5. Retaining ring (except L-Drive)
6. Coupling (except L-Drive)
7. Seal
8. Nut
9. Washer
10. Stud
11. Water tube seal
12. Water pump housing
13. Water pump liner
14. Impeller
15. Impeller drive key
16. Gasket
17. Plate
18. Gasket
19. Lower drive shaft
20. Gearcase cover
21. Shift rod seal
22. Screw
23. Washer
24. Seal
25. Seal
26. Seal
27. Retainer
28. Bearing race
29. Bearing
30. Seal
31. Pin
32. Cotter pin
33. Lower shift rod
34. Shift arm
35. Pitot plug
36. Shim(s)
37. Anode
38. Gear housing
39. Drive shaft lower bearing
40. Pinion gear
41. Washer
42. Nut
43. Gasket
44. Plug
45. O-ring
46. Shift arm pivot pin
47. Shim(s)
48. Bearing race
49. Forward gear and bearing assembly
50. Spacer (some models)
51. Clutch
52. Pin
53. Shift yoke
54. Shift pin
55. Propeller shaft
56. Exhaust snout
57. Spacer
58. Reverse gear
59. Thrust bearing
60. Thrust washer
61. Bearing
62. O-ring
63. Bearing spool
64. Key
65. Bearing
66. Seal
67. Seal
68. Tab washer
69. Retainer
70. Thrust hub
71. Propeller
72. Spline washer
73. Tab washer
74. Stop nut

9

1. Drain gearcase lubricant as described in Chapter Four.

2. Remove gearcase as described in this chapter.

3. Secure the gearcase in a suitable holding fixture or vise with protective jaws. If protective jaws are not available, position the gearcase upright with the skeg between wooden blocks.

4. Remove the spline seal and the seal retainer from the upper end of the drive shaft.

5. Remove the water pump as described in this chapter.

6. Remove the screws and lockwashers holding the gearcase cover to the gearcase. To dislodge the cover, pull up while rocking the cover side-to-side. If necessary, carefully pry the cover upward at the center. *Do not* pry on the ends of the cover.

7A. *One-piece drive shaft*—Remove the crush ring from the gearcase bore.

7B. *Two-piece drive shaft*—Remove drive shaft bearing retainer using retainer wrench (part No. FT-11293).

8. Invert the gearcase cover and remove the O-ring seals (A, **Figure 77**). Pry the drive shaft seal from the cover bore (B, **Figure 77**).

9. The shift rod seal in the gearcase cover may be a bellows or a conventional seal. To remove a bellows type seal, invert the cover and push off the bellows with a suitable punch through the holes provided on the underside of the cover. To remove a conventional seal, thread a 5/16 in. lag screw into the top of the seal. Invert the cover and drive the screw and the seal out of the cover using a 1/4 in. diameter punch or rod.

10. Dual exhaust—Rotate the lower shift rod counterclockwise until unscrewed from the shift arm coupler. Remove the shift rod.

11. Single exhaust:

    a. Remove the 2 screws securing the anode to the propeller shaft bearing spool and remove the anode. See **Figure 78**.

    b. Remove the 4 screws and O-rings holding the propeller shaft bearing spool to the bearing cage. Discard the O-rings.

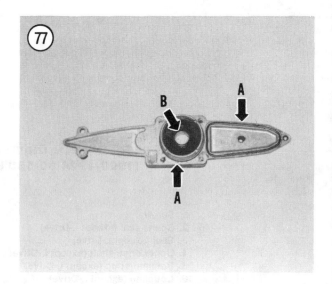

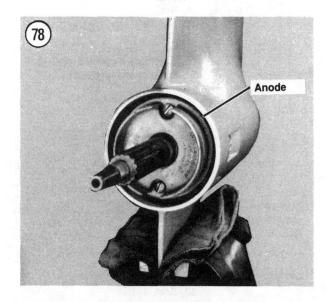

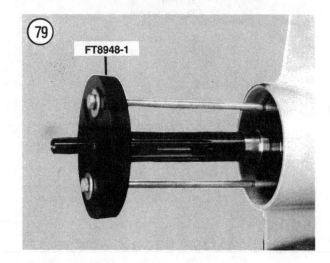

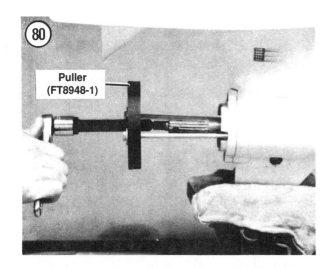

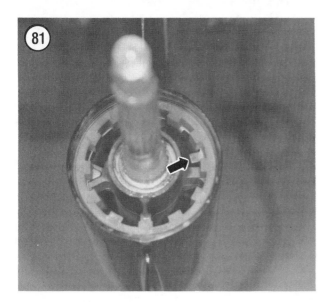

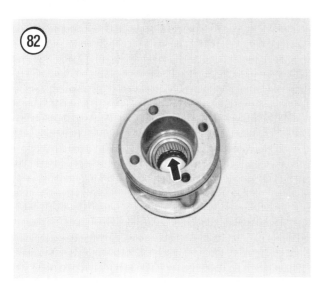

12A. *5/8 in. propeller shaft (except dual exhaust):*

a. Thread the puller plate from puller set (part No. FT-8948-1) completely onto the propeller shaft. Install 2 bolts (1/4 × 7 in.) as shown in **Figure 79**.

b. Shift gearcase into forward or reverse gear by pushing down or pulling up on the lower shift rod.

c. Install drive shaft spline socket part No. FT-11208 (60 hp), part No. FT-7848 (85-125 hp 1 piece drive shaft) or part No. FT-16536 (2 piece drive shaft) onto the drive shaft splines and rotate drive shaft. The puller will unthread from the propeller shaft as shaft rotates, drawing the bearing spool from the gearcase. Remove and discard the bearing spool O-rings.

12B. *3/4 in. propeller shaft (except dual exhaust):*

a. Install puller (part No. FT-8948-1) using long 1/4 in. bolts as shown in **Figure 80**. Make sure the bolts are set at equal lengths.

b. Turn the puller center screw until the bearing spool is free of the gearcase. Remove puller and spool from the gearcase. Remove and discard the bearing spool O-rings.

12C. *Dual exhaust*—Remove the bearing spool as follows:

a. Bend the locking tab away from the bearing spool locking ring. See **Figure 81**.

b. Place locking ring wrench (part No. FT-11275) over the propeller shaft and engage with the locking ring. Turn the locking ring wrench counterclockwise to remove the locking ring.

c. Remove the bearing spool from the gearcase using a suitable puller with hooked jaws. Be sure to retrieve the dowel pin located at the top of the spool. Remove and discard the bearing spool O-ring.

13. Using a suitable punch, drive the propeller shaft seal from the bearing spool. See **Figure 82**. Inspect the propeller shaft needle bearing inside

the spool. If the bearing is rusted, pitted, excessively worn or damaged, replace the bearing spool assembly.

14. All models except dual exhaust:

    a. To remove the reverse gear bearing carrier retaining rings, push downward on the beveled end of each ring as shown in **Figure 83**.

    b. Reinstall the bearing spool (without O-rings) into the gearcase. Secure the spool to the reverse gear bearing carrier with 2 bearing spool bolts.

    c. Using puller set (part No. FT-8948-1), repeat Step 12A or 12B to pull the bearing spool and the reverse gear bearing carrier from the gearcase as an assembly.

15. Remove the propeller shaft assembly along with the reverse gear from the gearcase. Be sure the shift yoke is removed with the propeller shaft. If not, reach into the gearcase and retrieve the yoke.

16. Slide the reverse gear along with the bearing and race off the propeller shaft.

17. Place the propeller shaft into a vise. Cushion the shaft assembly with shop cloths to prevent damage to the shaft. Drive the clutch roll pin out with a suitable punch. Remove the shift pin and slide the clutch off the propeller shaft.

18. Install drive shaft spline socket part No. FT-11208 (60 hp), part No. FT-7848 (85-125 hp 1 piece drive shaft) or part No. FT-16536 (2 piece drive shaft) onto the drive shaft splines.

19. Hold the pinion gear nut with a 3/4 in. (1 piece drive shaft) or 7/8 in. (2 piece drive shaft) 6 point socket and breaker bar. Pad the handle of the breaker bar with a shop cloth to prevent damage to the gearcase housing.

20. Place an appropriate size wrench or socket on the spline adapter. Loosen the pinion gear nut by turning the drive shaft while holding the pinion nut from turning. Remove the pinion nut.

21. To separate the drive shaft from the pinion gear, clamp the drive shaft into a vise with protective jaws or between wooden blocks, clamping as close to the housing as possible.

22. Using a plastic or soft-faced mallet *only*, tap around the drive shaft bore until the drive shaft separates from the pinion gear. Slide the drive shaft and bearing from the housing. Remove the pinion gear from the gear cavity.

> *NOTE*
> *One or more (or none) shims may be present under the upper drive shaft bearing. Note the number, thickness and location of the shim(s) for reference during reassemble.*

23. Remove any shims located in the drive shaft bearing bore.

24. Reach into the gear cavity and remove the forward gear and bearing assembly along with the forward gear thrust washer.

> *NOTE*
> *The forward gear, bearing and race can be replaced as a set only.*

25. Remove the shift arm pivot pin and O-ring from the gearcase. Discard the O-ring.

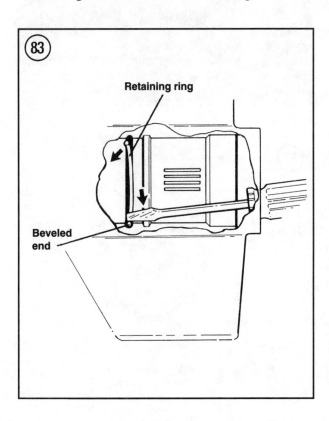

Retaining ring

Beveled end

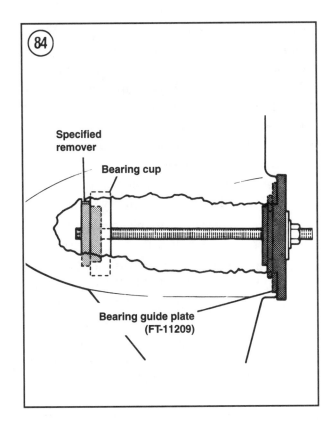

Specified remover

Bearing cup

Bearing guide plate
(FT-11209)

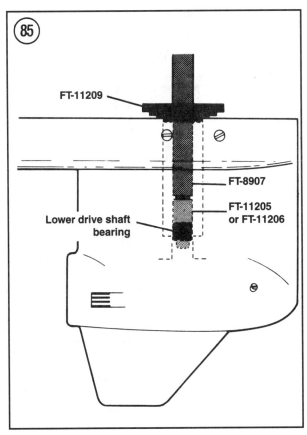

FT-11209

FT-8907

FT-11205
or FT-11206

Lower drive shaft
bearing

26A. *1 piece drive shaft models*—Lift the lower shift rod and shift arm out the top of the housing.

26B. *2 piece drive shaft/single port exhaust models*—Unscrew the lower shift rod from the shift arm. Lift the shift rod out the top of the housing and reach into the gear cavity and extract the shift arm.

26C. *Dual port exhaust models*—Reach into the gear case and extract the shift arm.

> *NOTE*
> *Do not remove the forward gear bearing race (Step 27) from the gearcase unless the forward gear or bearing requires replacement.*

27. Remove the forward gear bearing race with race remover part No. FT-11206 (60 hp), part No. FT-11207 (85-125 hp 1 piece drive shaft) or part No. FT-16813 (2-piece drive shaft) and bearing guide plate part No. FT-11209 as shown in **Figure 84**. Turn the bearing tool nut until the forward gear bearing race is free of the gearcase.

> *NOTE*
> *One or more (or none) shims may be present behind the forward gear bearing race. Note the number, thickness and location of the shim(s) for reference during reassemble.*

28. Remove any shims located behind the forward gear bearing race.

> *NOTE*
> *Do not remove the lower drive shaft bearing (Step 29A or Step 29B) unless bearing replacement is required.*

29A. *1 piece drive shaft*—Remove the lower drive shaft bearing with remover part No. FT-11205 (85-125 hp) or part No. FT-11206 (60 hp). Insert the drive handle (part No. FT-8907) through the guide plate (part No. FT-11209) and install the specified remover. Install the tool to the gearcase as shown in **Figure 85** and drive the bearing downward into the gear cavity.

9

29B. *2 piece drive shaft*—The bearing rollers must be installed in the drive shaft bearing race for removal. Apply a suitable grease on the bearing to hold the rollers in place. Insert bearing driver (part No. FT-16433) into the drive shaft bore and lower bearing, then drive the bearing downward into the gear cavity to remove.

30. Clean and inspect all gearcase components as described in this chapter.

NOTE
*The forward gear position must be adjusted if a new gearcase housing is used or a new forward gear is installed. The drive shaft (pinion depth) must be adjusted if a new gearcase housing is used or a new pinion gear or drive shaft is installed. The propeller shaft end play must be adjusted if a new gearcase housing is used or a new reverse gear, forward gear or propeller shaft is installed. Refer to **Gearcase Shimming** in this chapter.*

31A. *Except dual exhaust*—Install a new propeller shaft seal into the propeller shaft bearing spool. Lubricate the seal lip with gearcase lubricant or a suitable grease.

31B. *Dual exhaust*—Position new propeller shaft seals so the inner seal lip faces forward and the outer seal lip faces rearward. Press both seals into the bearing spool until the outer seal is flush with the rear surface of the spool.

32. Install the shift arm coupler with the forked end facing down. Install the shift arm pivot pin with a new O-ring and tighten securely.

33A. *1 piece drive shaft*—Insert the lower shift rod and shift arm assembly into the housing and secure the shift arm with the shift arm pivot pin and a new O-ring.

33B. 2 piece drive shaft—Apply Loctite 271 on the threads of the lower shift rod. Insert the shift rod into the gearcase and screw it into the shift arm until fully bottomed, then back out 4 complete turns.

34. Position the gearcase housing as shown in **Figure 86**. Install any shims required behind the

forward gear bearing race. Refer to *Gearcase Shimming* in this chapter. Using bearing race installer part No. FT-11203 (60 hp), part No. FT-11204 (85-125 hp 1 piece drive shaft) or part No. FT-16814 (2-piece drive shaft), handle part No. FT-8907 and guide plate part No. FT-11209, drive the race into the housing until fully seated.

35A. *One-piece drive shaft:*

a. Lubricate a new drive shaft lower bearing with needle bearing assembly grease.

b. Place the bearing into the gearcase with the lettered side facing up.

c. Using bearing installer part No. FT-11206 (60 hp) or part No. FT-11205 (85-125 hp), driver handle (part No. FT-8907) and bearing guide plate (part No. FT-11209), drive the bearing into the gearcase until the top edge is flush with the top of the bearing bore. Refer to **Figure 85**.

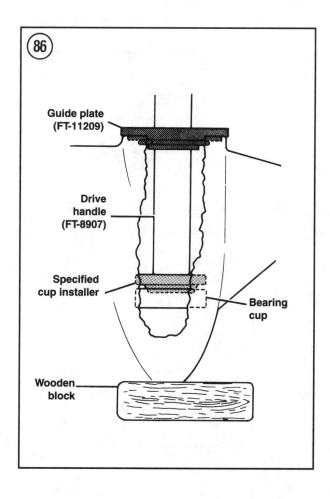

(86)

Guide plate (FT-11209)

Drive handle (FT-8907)

Specified cup installer

Bearing cup

Wooden block

35B. *Two-piece drive shaft:*

  a. Install 18 bearing rollers into the drive shaft lower bearing outer race. Hold the rollers in place using a suitable grease.

  b. Assemble the bearing installer (part No. FT-16496B), top plate (part No. FT-16496A) and rod and washers from bearing tool set (part No. FT-16496) as shown in **Figure 87**. Lettered side of the bearing must face upward.

  c. While holding the bearing tool lower nut, tighten the upper nut until the top of the bearing contacts the shoulder of the bearing bore.

36. Lubricate the forward gear bearing with gearcase lubricant. Install the gear into the gearcase. If necessary, select the correct thickness forward gear thrust washer as described in this chapter. Install the thrust washer using grease to hold the washer to the forward gear.

37. Install the required shims into the drive shaft upper bearing bore. Refer to *Gearcase Shimming* in this chapter.

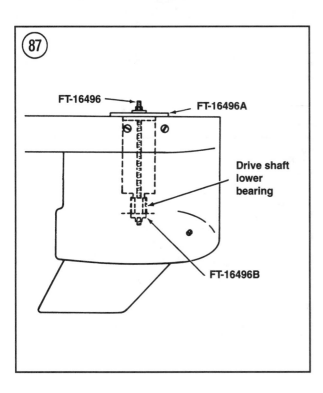

87

FT-16496

FT-16496A

Drive shaft
lower
bearing

FT-16496B

38. If the drive shaft upper bearing was removed, press a new bearing onto the drive shaft until fully seated.

39. Install the drive shaft with the bearing and race into the gearcase housing.

40. Install the pinion gear on the drive shaft.

41. Apply Loctite 271 to the threads of a new pinion gear nut. Install the pinion gear washer and nut. Make sure the recessed side of the nut is facing the pinion gear.

42A. *1 piece drive shaft*—Tighten the pinion nut to specification (**Table 2**) by turning the drive shaft using spline adapter part No. FT-11208 (60 hp) or part No. FT-8949 (85-125 hp). Hold the pinion nut with a 3/4 in. 6-point socket and breaker bar.

42B. *2 piece drive shaft*—Finger tighten the pinion nut, then install the drive shaft upper bearing retainer. Make sure the "OFF" mark on the retainer is facing upward. Tighten the retainer to specification (**Table 2**) using retainer wrench (part No. FT-11293). Now tighten the pinion gear nut to specification (**Table 2**) by turning the drive shaft using spline adapter (part No. FT-16536). Hold the pinion nut with a 7/8 in. 6-point socket and flex handle.

43. Insert the shift pin into the propeller shaft aligning the hole in the pin with the slot in the propeller shaft.

44. Install the clutch on the propeller shaft aligning the hole in the clutch with the hole in the shift pin.

45. Install the clutch roll pin.

46. Install the shift yoke onto the shift pin with the open side facing down. Apply a suitable grease to the yoke to hold it in place.

47. Position the gearcase so the gear cavity is facing up. Insert the propeller shaft assembly into the gearcase while holding up on the lower shift rod. Make sure the shift arm properly engages the shift yoke by moving the shift rod and watching for clutch movement.

9

48. Assemble the reverse gear bearing, spacer and bearing cage. Lubricate the bearing and spacer with a suitable grease.

49. Install the reverse gear assembly into the gearcase. Rotate the bearing cage so the bolt holes are squared in the gearcase opening.

50A. *Except dual exhaust:*

a. Install the propeller shaft bearing cage retaining rings, making sure the rings are properly seated in their grooves.

b. Install new O-rings onto the propeller shaft bearing spool. Lubricate the O-rings and propeller shaft seals and bearing with gearcase lubricant.

c. Install the bearing spool into the gearcase, aligning the spool bolt holes with the bearing cage bolt holes.

d. Place new O-rings on the bearing spool bolts, install the bolts and tighten to specification (**Table 2**).

e. Install the zinc anode over the propeller shaft. Apply Loctite 271 onto the anode screws and tighten to specification (**Table 2**).

50B. *Dual exhaust:*

a. Install a new O-ring onto the bearing spool. Lubricate the O-ring, propeller shaft seals and bearing with gearcase lubricant.

b. Install the spool into the gearcase with the locating pin groove facing up (aligned with groove in gearcase). Install the locating pin.

c. Install the locking tab washer into the gearcase. Apply a suitable antiseize grease to the threads of the spool retaining ring and install the ring into the gearcase with the mark OFF facing outward. Tighten the retaining ring to specification (**Table 2**).

d. Select one of the locking tab washer tabs that is centered between one notch in the retaining ring. Bend the tab outward to secure the ring. Bend the remaining 3 tabs inward toward the bearing spool.

51. *Single port exhaust/1 piece drive shaft*—Install a new crush ring over the drive shaft into the bearing bore.

52. *Single port exhaust/2 piece drive shaft*—Screw the intermediate shift rod into the lower shift rod until fully seated, then back out 4 complete turns.

53. Install the shift rod seal or bellows into the gearcase housing cover.

54. Install new drive shaft seal (B, **Figure 77**) into the gearcase cover. Install the seals with the seal lips facing away from each other. Install new gearcase cover O-rings (A, **Figure 77**).

55A. *Single exhaust*—Apply a continuous bead of a suitable RTV sealant onto the sealing surface of the water inlet passage only. See **Figure 88**.

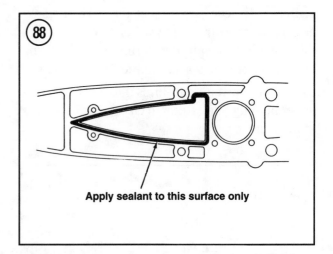

Apply sealant to this surface only

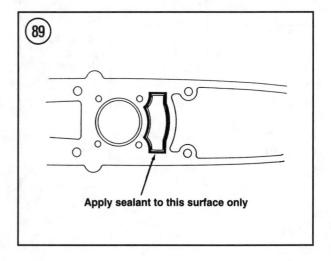

Apply sealant to this surface only

55B. *Dual exhaust*—Apply a continuous bead of a suitable RTV sealant onto the water inlet sealing surface only. See **Figure 89**.

55C. *All models*—Apply a suitable RTV sealant onto the threads of the gearcase cover screws. Install the cover and tighten the screws to specification (**Table 2**).

56. Install the water pump as described in this chapter.

57. Coat the drive shaft splines with antiseize grease and install a new spline seal and retainer.

58. Pressure test the gearcase as described in this chapter.

59. Install the gearcase as described in this chapter.

60. Fill the gearcase with a recommended lubricant. See Chapter Four.

61. Check the gearcase lubricant level after operating the motor. Change the lubricant after 10 hours of operation (break-in period). See Chapter Four.

GEARCASE CLEANING AND INSPECTION

1. Clean all components in fresh solvent and dry with compressed air.

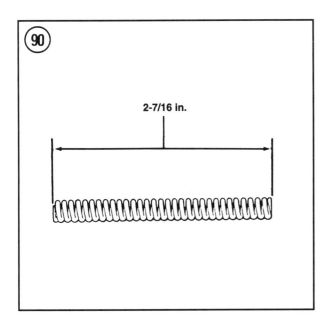

2. Clean all nut and screw threads thoroughly if RTV sealant or Loctite has been used. Soak nuts and screws in solvent and use a fine wire brush to remove any residue.

3. Remove and discard all O-rings, gaskets and seals. Clean all gasket and sealant residue from the mating surfaces.

4. Check the drive shaft splines for wear or damage. If the gearcase has struck a submerged object, the drive shaft and propeller shaft may be damaged. Replace the drive shaft as required and check the crankshaft splines for similar wear or damage.

5. Check the propeller shaft splines and threads for wear, rust or corrosion damage. Replace the shaft as required.

6. Support the drive shaft with V-blocks placed under the bearing surfaces at each end of the shaft. Slowly rotate the shaft while checking for excessive wobble or runout. Replace the shaft if bent. See **Table 4**.

7. Repeat Step 6 with the propeller shaft. Also check the shaft for excessive wear at seal contact areas.

8. Check the propeller shaft bearing cage or spool and needle bearing for excessive wear or damage. Replace the cage or spool if the bearing requires replacement.

9. Check the bearing cage or spool contact points on the propeller shaft. Replace the shaft and bearings if pitting, scoring, heat discoloration or embedded metallic particles are noted.

10. Check the water pump as described in this chapter.

11. Check all shift components for wear or damage:

    a. Inspect the clutch and drive gears for excessive wear on engagement surfaces. Replace the clutch and drive gears if pitted, chipped, broken or excessively worn.

    b. On models so equipped, measure the clutch spring free length (**Figure 90**). Replace the spring if the free length is not 2-7/16 in. (6.19 cm).

c. Check the clutch for cracks at shear points (**Figure 91**) and rounded areas that contact the forward and reverse gear engagement dogs. Replace as required.

d. Check the shift pin and cam for wear. See **Figure 92**. Excessive wear on the shift cam can allow the gearcase to drop out of gear. Replace as required.

12. Clean all bearings with solvent and dry with compressed air. Lubricate the bearings to prevent rusting. Check all bearings for rust, corrosion, flat spots or excessive wear and replace as required.

13. Check the forward, reverse and pinion gears for excessive wear or damage. If gear teeth are pitted, chipped, broken or excessively worn, replace the gears as a set. Check the pinion gear splines for excessive wear and replace the gear as required.

14. Check the propeller for nicks, cracks or damaged blades. Minor nicks can be removed with a file, taking care to retain the shape of the propeller. Replace (or have repaired) the propeller if bent, cracked or badly chipped blades are noted.

GEARCASE SHIMMING

The pinion gear depth, drive gear backlash and propeller shaft end play must be correctly adjusted to ensure the proper gear engagement. If the clearance is not within specification, excessive gear and bearing wear will occur, resulting in premature gearcase failure.

70-75 hp, 90 and 120 hp (1995-1999)

Pinion gear depth

1. Install the forward gear and drive shaft assemblies into the gearcase housing as described in this chapter.

2. Using a clean shop towel, thoroughly clean the gear cavity, especially the area around the bearing carrier shoulder.

3. Position the gearcase with the drive shaft facing up.

> *NOTE*
> *Drive shaft bearing preload tool part No. 91-14311A2 is necessary to properly check and adjust pinion gear depth and gear backlash. See **Figure 93**.*

4. Install the bearing preload tool (part No. 91-14311A2 onto the drive shaft in the order shown in **Figure 93**.

a. Make sure the thrust bearing and washer are clean and lightly oiled.

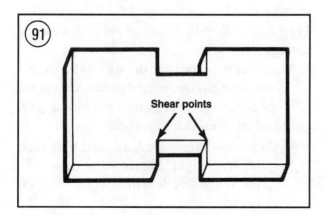

Shear points

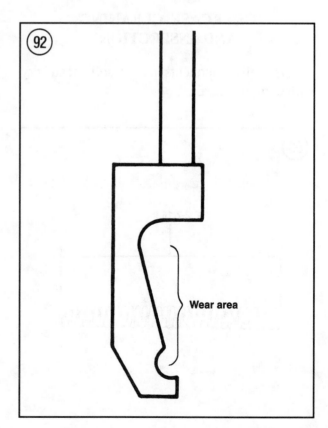

Wear area

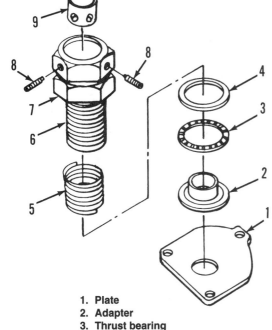

DRIVE SHAFT BEARING PRELOAD TOOL (PART NO. 91-14311A2)

1. Plate
2. Adapter
3. Thrust bearing
4. Thrust washer
5. Spring
6. Bolt
7. Nut
8. Set screws
9. Sleeve

(93)

(94)

b. Screw the nut (7, **Figure 93**) completely on to the bolt (6), then securely tighten the set screws (8), making sure the holes in the sleeve (9) are aligned with the set screws.

c. Measure the distance (D, **Figure 94**) between the top of the nut and the bottom of the bolt head. Then screw the nut downward increasing the distance (D, **Figure 94**) by 1 in. (25.4 mm).

d. Rotate the drive shaft 10-12 turns to seat the drive shaft bearing(s).

5. *70-75 hp (1998 and prior)*—Insert the pinion locating tool (part No. 91-817008A2) into the gearcase. Make sure the tool engages the forward gear, with the access hole facing up, exposing the pinion gear.

6A. *75 hp (1999 only) and 90-120 hp*—Assemble the pinion shim tool (part No. 91-12349A2) as shown in **Figure 95**. Face the numbered side of the gauge block out so the numbers can be seen as the tool is being used. Tighten the split

9

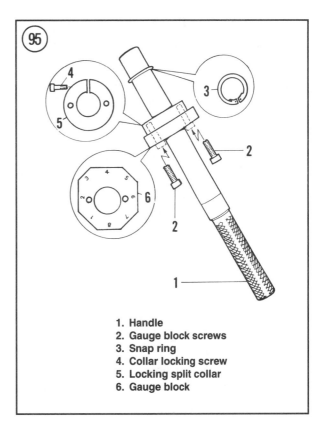

(95)

1. Handle
2. Gauge block screws
3. Snap ring
4. Collar locking screw
5. Locking split collar
6. Gauge block

collar retaining screw to the point where the collar can still be slid back and forth on the handle with moderate hand pressure.

6B. *75 hp (1999 only) and 90-120 hp*—Insert the tool into the gearcase. Make sure the tool engages the forward gear. Slide the gauge block back and forth as necessary to position the gauge block directly under the pinion gear teeth as shown in **Figure 96**.

6C. *75 hp (1999 only) and 90-120 hp*—Carefully remove the tool and tighten the collar retaining screw without changing the gauge block position.

6D. *75 hp (1999 only) and 90-120 hp*—Reinsert the tool into the gearcase with Flat No. 8 (75 hp and 90 hp) or Flat No. 2 (120 hp) facing the pinion gear. Install the No. 3 alignment disc from the shim tool over the handle and into the propeller shaft bore. Position the access hole upward, exposing the pinion gear. See **Figure 97**.

7. Insert a 0.025 in. (0.63 mm) flat feeler gauge between the gauging block and the bottom of the pinion gear. See **Figure 98**. The clearance between the gear and gauging block should be 0.025 in. (0.63 mm).

8. If the clearance is not correct, add shim(s) under the drive shaft upper bearing race to increase pinion gear clearance, or subtract shim(s) to decrease clearance.

9. If the clearance in Step 6 is correct, leave the drive shaft bearing preload tool installed, but remove the pinion gear locating tool and continue at *Forward gear backlash* in this chapter.

Forward gear backlash

Do not attempt to adjust forward gear backlash until the pinion gear depth is correctly established.

1. Make sure the drive shaft preload tool is correctly installed as described under *Pinion gear depth* in this chapter.

2. Install the propeller shaft and fully assembled bearing carrier into the gearcase. Then, install bearing carrier puller jaws (part No. 91-46086A1) and puller bolt (part No. 91-85716) as shown in **Figure 99**. Tighten the puller bolt to 45 in.-lb. to preload the propeller shaft bearings. Rotate the propeller shaft 10-12 revolutions to seat the bearings, then retighten the puller bolt to 45 in.-lb. (5.1 N·m).

3. Fasten a suitable threaded rod (**Figure 100**) to the gear housing using flat washers and nuts. Install a dial indicator to the threaded rod (**Figure 100**).

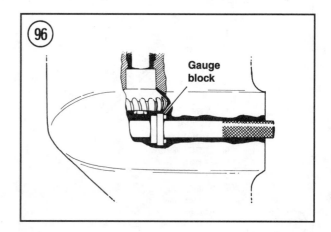

Gauge block

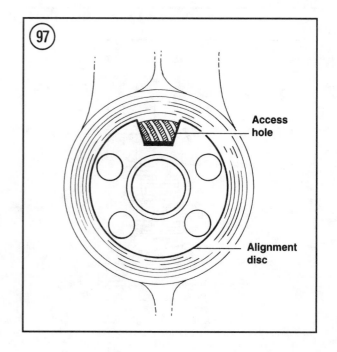

Access hole

Alignment disc

4. Install the backlash tool (**Table 8**) onto the drive shaft and tighten it securely. Adjust the dial indicator as necessary to align with the specified mark (**Table 4**) on the backlash indicator tool.

5. Zero the dial indicator needle. Lightly turn the drive shaft back and forth (propeller shaft should not move) while noting the dial indicator. The amount of travel in the drive shaft without moving the propeller shaft is forward gear backlash. The backlash should be within specification (**Table 4**).

6. If forward gear backlash is not as specified, remove the forward gear bearing race as described in this chapter. Subtract shim(s) behind the race to increase backlash or add shim(s) behind the race to decrease backlash.

7. After establishing the correct pinion gear depth and forward gear backlash, remove the drive shaft bearing and propeller shaft preload tools. Then, remove the bearing carrier and propeller shaft. Apply Loctite 271 to the threads of a *new* pinion gear nut and install it as described in the appropriate section of this chapter. Complete gearcase assembly as described in this chapter.

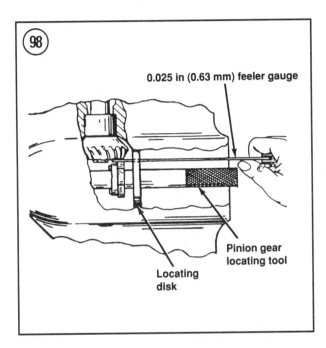

0.025 in (0.63 mm) feeler gauge

Pinion gear locating tool

Locating disk

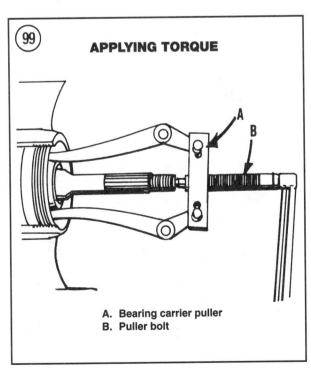

APPLYING TORQUE

A. Bearing carrier puller
B. Puller bolt

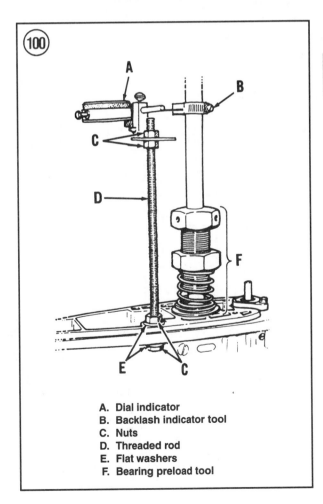

A. Dial indicator
B. Backlash indicator tool
C. Nuts
D. Threaded rod
E. Flat washers
F. Bearing preload tool

9

Stamped-in gearcase housing code	DRIVE SHAFT/FORWARD GEAR CODE (101)																		
	3	4	5	6	7	8	9	10	11	12	13	14	15	16	17	18	19	20	21	22
0	.003	.004	.005	.006	.007	.008	.009	.010	.011	.012	.013	.014	.015	.016	.017	.018	.019	.020	.021	.022
1	.004	.005	.006	.007	.008	.009	.010	.011	.012	.013	.014	.015	.016	.017	.018	.019	.020	.021	.022	.023
2	.005	.006	.007	.008	.009	.010	.011	.012	.013	.014	.015	.016	.017	.018	.019	.020	.021	.022	.023	.024
3	.006	.007	.008	.009	.010	.011	.012	.013	.014	.015	.016	.017	.018	.019	.020	.021	.022	.023	.024	.025
4	.007	.008	.009	.010	.011	.012	.013	.014	.015	.016	.017	.018	.019	.020	.021	.022	.023	.024	.025	.026
5	.008	.009	.010	.011	.012	.013	.014	.015	.016	.017	.018	.019	.020	.021	.022	.023	.024	.025	.026	.027
6	.009	.010	.011	.012	.013	.014	.015	.016	.017	.018	.019	.020	.021	.022	.023	.024	.025	.026	.027	.028
7	.010	.011	.012	.013	.014	.015	.016	.017	.018	.019	.020	.021	.022	.023	.024	.025	.026	.027	.028	.029
8	.011	.012	.013	.014	.015	.016	.017	.018	.019	.020	.021	.022	.023	.024	.025	.026	.027	.028	.029	.030
9	.012	.013	.014	.015	.016	.017	.018	.019	.020	.021	.022	.023	.024	.025	.026	.027	.028	.029	.030	.031
	23	24	25	26	27	28	29	30	31	32	33	34	35	36	37	38	39	40	41	42
0	.023	.024	.025	.026	.027	.028	.029	.030	.031	.032	.033	.034	.035	.036	.037	.038	.039	.040	.041	.042
1	.024	.025	.026	.027	.028	.029	.030	.031	.032	.033	.034	.035	.036	.037	.038	.039	.040	.041	.042	.043
2	.025	.026	.027	.028	.029	.030	.031	.032	.033	.034	.035	.036	.037	.038	.039	.040	.041	.042	.043	.044
3	.026	.027	.028	.029	.030	.031	.032	.033	.034	.035	.036	.037	.038	.039	.040	.041	.042	.043	.044	.045
4	.027	.028	.029	.030	.031	.032	.033	.034	.035	.036	.037	.038	.039	.040	.041	.042	.043	.044	.045	.046
5	.028	.029	.030	.031	.032	.033	.034	.035	.036	.037	.038	.039	.040	.041	.042	.043	.044	.045	.046	.047
6	.029	.030	.031	.032	.033	.034	.035	.036	.037	.038	.039	.040	.041	.042	.043	.044	.045	.046	.047	.048
7	.030	.031	.032	.033	.034	.035	.036	.037	.038	.039	.040	.041	.042	.043	.044	.045	.046	.047	.048	.049
8	.031	.032	.033	.034	.035	.036	.037	.038	.039	.040	.041	.042	.043	.044	.045	.046	.047	.048	.049	.050
9	.032	.033	.034	.035	.036	.037	.038	.039	.040	.041	.042	.043	.044	.045	.046	.047	.048	.049	.050	.051

Stamped-in gearcase housing code	DRIVE SHAFT/FORWARD GEAR CODE																		
	3	4	5	6	7	8	9	10	11	12	13	14	15	16	17	18	19	20	21	22
A	.002	.003	.004	.005	.006	.007	.008	.009	.010	.011	.012	.013	.014	.015	.016	.017	.018	.019	.020	.021
B	.001	.002	.003	.004	.005	.006	.007	.008	.009	.010	.011	.012	.013	.014	.015	.016	.017	.018	.019	.020
C	.000	.001	.002	.003	.004	.005	.006	.007	.008	.009	.010	.011	.012	.013	.014	.015	.016	.017	.018	.019
D		.000	.001	.002	.003	.004	.005	.006	.007	.008	.009	.010	.011	.012	.013	.014	.015	.016	.017	.018
E			.000	.001	.002	.003	.004	.005	.006	.007	.008	.009	.010	.011	.012	.013	.014	.015	.016	.017
F				.000	.001	.002	.003	.004	.005	.006	.007	.008	.009	.010	.011	.012	.013	.014	.015	.016
G					.000	.001	.002	.003	.004	.005	.006	.007	.008	.009	.010	.011	.012	.013	.014	.015
H						.000	.001	.002	.003	.004	.005	.006	.007	.008	.009	.010	.011	.012	.013	.014
I							.000	.001	.002	.003	.004	.005	.006	.007	.008	.009	.010	.011	.012	.013
J								.000	.001	.002	.003	.004	.005	.006	.007	.008	.009	.010	.011	.012
K									.000	.001	.002	.003	.004	.005	.006	.007	.008	.009	.010	.011
	23	24	25	26	27	28	29	30	31	32	33	34	35	36	37	38	39	40	41	42
A	.022	.023	.024	.025	.026	.027	.028	.029	.030	.031	.032	.033	.034	.035	.036	.037	.038	.039	.040	.041
B	.021	.022	.023	.024	.025	.026	.027	.028	.029	.030	.031	.032	.033	.034	.035	.036	.037	.038	.039	.040
C	.020	.021	.022	.023	.024	.025	.026	.027	.028	.029	.030	.031	.032	.033	.034	.035	.036	.037	.038	.039
D	.019	.020	.021	.022	.023	.024	.025	.026	.027	.028	.029	.030	.031	.032	.033	.034	.035	.036	.037	.038
E	.018	.019	.020	.021	.022	.023	.024	.025	.026	.027	.028	.029	.030	.031	.032	.033	.034	.035	.036	.037
F	.017	.018	.019	.020	.021	.022	.023	.024	.025	.026	.027	.028	.029	.030	.031	.032	.033	.034	.035	.036
G	.016	.017	.018	.019	.020	.021	.022	.023	.024	.025	.026	.027	.028	.029	.030	.031	.032	.033	.034	.035
H	.015	.016	.017	.018	.019	.020	.021	.022	.023	.024	.025	.026	.027	.028	.029	.030	.031	.032	.033	.034
I	.014	.015	.016	.017	.018	.019	.020	.021	.022	.023	.024	.025	.026	.027	.028	.029	.030	.031	.032	.033
J	.013	.014	.015	.016	.017	.018	.019	.020	.021	.022	.023	.024	.025	.026	.027	.028	.029	.030	.031	.032
K	.012	.013	.014	.015	.016	.017	.018	.019	.020	.021	.022	.023	.024	.025	.026	.027	.028	.029	.030	.031

Forward Gear Shim Selection
(1990-1994 90-150 hp 2 Piece Drive Shaft)

The forward gear position must be adjusted if a new forward gear or gearcase housing is used. Refer to the shim selection chart in **Figure 101** during this procedure.

Installing new forward gear into original housing

1. Note the forward gear code stamped in the top of the housing. See **Figure 102**.

2. The new forward gear is provided with a tag which contains the forward gear shim code. Note the code number.

3. Refer to the shim selection chart (**Figure 101**) and locate where the stamped-in gear housing code intersects with the drive shaft/forward gear

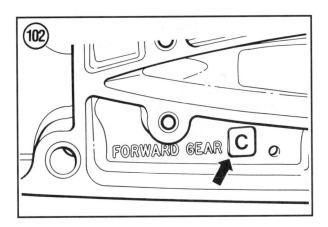

code. This is the required thickness of shim(s) to be installed behind the forward gear bearing race. Be certain all original shims are removed from the gearcase.

Installing original forward gear into a new gearcase housing

1. Note the forward gear code stamped in the top of the *original* gearcase housing (**Figure 102**).

2. Using a micrometer, measure the thickness of the *original* shim(s) removed from behind the forward gear bearing race.

3. To determine the forward gear code, refer to the shim selection chart (**Figure 101**). Locate the stamped-in gear housing code on the chart, then find the thickness of the original forward gear shims (measured in Step 2) on the chart. The forward gear code is the number directly above the intersection of these 2 points (drive shaft/forward gear numbers). For example, if the forward gear code stamped in the gearcase housing is 2 and the thickness of the original forward gear shims is 0.007 in., the forward gear code is 5.

4. Note the forward gear code stamped in the top of the *new* gearcase housing.

5. Using the code of the *original* forward gear found in Step 3, determine the required forward gear thickness on the shim selection chart.

Pinion Gear Depth Shim Selection
(1990-1994 90-150 hp 2 Piece Drive Shaft)

The pinion gear depth must be adjusted if a new drive shaft (includes pinion gear) is installed or if a new gearcase housing is used. Refer to the shim selection chart in **Figure 101**.

Installing new drive shaft into original gearcase housing

1. Note the drive shaft code stamped in the top of the housing. See **Figure 103**.

9

2. The new drive shaft/pinion gear assembly is provided with a tag which contains the drive shaft code. Note the code number or letter.

3. Refer to the shim selection chart (**Figure 101**) and locate where the stamped-in gear housing code intersects with the drive shaft/forward gear code on the chart. This is the required thickness of shim(s) to be installed under the drive shaft upper bearing. Be certain all original shims are removed from the bearing bore.

Installing original drive shaft assembly into a new gearcase housing

1. Note the drive shaft code stamped in the top of the *original* gearcase housing.

2. Using a micrometer, measure the thickness of the *original* shim(s) removed from under the upper drive shaft bearing.

3. To determine the drive shaft code, refer to the appropriate shim selection chart (**Figure 101**). Locate the stamped-in gear housing code on the chart, then find the thickness of the *original* drive shaft shims (measured in Step 2) on the chart. The drive shaft code is the number directly above the intersection of these 2 points (drive shaft/forward gear numbers). For example, if the drive

shaft code stamped in the gearcase housing is 3 and the thickness of the original drive shaft shims is 0.010 in., the drive shaft code is 7.

4. Note the drive shaft code stamped in the top of the *new* gearcase housing.

5. Using the code of the *original* drive shaft found in Step 3, determine the required drive shaft shim thickness on the shim selection chart.

Propeller Shaft End Play and Gear Backlash (1990-1994 90-150 hp 2 Piece Drive Shaft)

Refer to *Gearcase Disassembly/Reassemble* in this chapter.

> *NOTE*
> *Propeller shaft end play adjustment is only necessary when a forward gear thrust washer (spacer) is used. To determine if a spacer is required, measure the distance (A, Figure 104). If the measurement (A, Figure 104) is within 2.637-2.643 in. (67-67.1 mm), a thrust washer is installed between the propeller shaft and forward gear. If the distance (A, Figure 104) is within 2.697-2.703 in. (68.5-68.7 mm), no thrust washer is used*

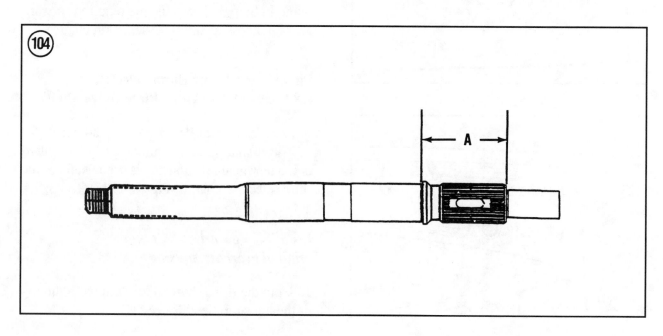

and propeller shaft end play is not adjustable.

1. Remove the forward gear thrust washer and install a thrust washer 0.050 in. thick in its place. Make sure the thrust washer is centered on the forward gear. See **Figure 105**.

2. Remove the shift yoke from the propeller shaft assembly.

3A. *Except dual exhaust:*

   a. Position the gearcase so the gear cavity is facing up. Install the propeller shaft assembly (including clutch, reverse gear and re-

verse gear bearing cage) into the gearcase. Be sure the propeller shaft is fully seated.

   b. Install the bearing cage retaining rings.

   c. Remove the O-rings from the propeller shaft bearing spool. Install the bearing spool into the gearcase. Tighten the bearing spool mounting bolts to 160 in.-lb. (18 N·m).

3B. *Dual exhaust:*

   a. Position the gearcase so the gear cavity is facing up. Install the propeller shaft assembly (including clutch, reverse gear and reverse gear bearing). Make sure the propeller shaft assembly is fully seated.

   b. Install the propeller shaft bearing spool without the O-ring. Install the bearing spool retaining ring and tighten to 130 ft.-lbs.

4A. *Except dual exhaust:*

   a. Install dial indicator post (part No. FT-8997-E) into one anode mounting screw hole in the bearing spool.

   b. Attach a dial indicator to the post with the indicator plunger resting on the end of the propeller shaft.

   c. Push down on the propeller shaft and zero the dial indicator.

   d. Pull up on the propeller shaft and note the indicator reading. Repeat this step several times to ensure consistent readings.

4B. *Dual exhaust:*

   a. Affix a dial indicator to the propeller shaft using a suitable hose clamp. Position the indicator so the plunger is resting on the lip of the gearcase housing.

   b. Push down on the propeller shaft and zero the dial indicator.

   c. Pull up on the propeller shaft and note the indicator reading. Repeat this step several times to ensure consistent readings.

5. Propeller shaft end play should be 0.005-0.020 in. (0.13-0.51 mm). Change thickness of the forward gear thrust washer as required to obtain the specified end play.

9

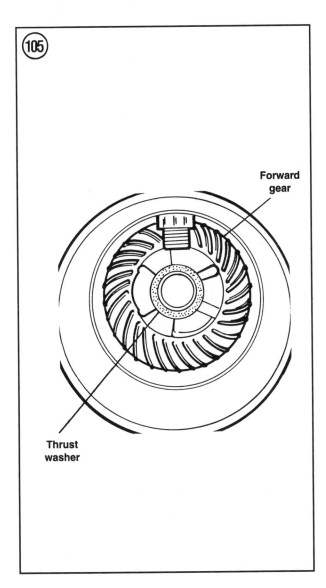

(105)

Forward gear

Thrust washer

6A. *Dual exhaust*—To check gear backlash, install locking pliers or similar tool onto one spoke of the propeller shaft bearing spool as shown in **Figure 106**.

6B. *Except dual exhaust*—To check gear backlash, thread dial indicator post (part No. FT-8997-E) or a suitable bolt into one anode screw hole in the bearing spool.

7. Mount a dial indicator onto the propeller shaft using a suitable hose clamp (**Figure 106**). Position the dial indicator so the plunger is resting on the locking pliers (dual exhaust) or the dial indicator post (except dual exhaust).

8. Turn the drive shaft either direction until the propeller shaft just begins to move. Next, turn the drive shaft in the opposite direction until all gear slack is removed and the propeller shaft just begins to move.

9. Zero the dial indicator. While holding up on the drive shaft, rotate the propeller shaft back and forth, just taking up the slack in the gears while noting indicator reading. Gear backlash should be 0.009-0.018 in. (0.23-0.46 mm). If not as specified, recheck the gearcase component reassemble, and pinion depth and forward gear shimming procedures.

Pinion Gear Depth and Gear Backlash (1984-1989 60, 85-125 hp 1 Piece Drive Shaft)

1. Insert the master shim from shimming tool set (part No. FT-8997) into the drive shaft upper bearing bore.

2. Install the drive shaft assembly into the gearcase. Install the pinion gear on the drive shaft and secure with an old pinion nut.

3. Install the drive shaft spline adapter over the drive shaft splines. Attach a torque wrench and suitable socket to the adapter. Hold the pinion nut with a suitable socket and flex handle. Pad the flex handle to prevent damage to the gearcase housing. Tighten the pinion nut to 85 ft.-lbs. (115 N•m).

4. Insert the shimming plug part No. FT-8997-B (60 hp) or part No. FT-8997-A (85-125 hp) into the forward gear. Rotate the plug until the flat area is facing the pinion gear. Install the plug cradle between the plug and gearcase bottom. See **Figure 107**.

5. Pull up on the drive shaft to provide the maximum clearance between the pinion gear and the shimming plug.

> *NOTE*
> *Do not insert the feeler gauge blade farther than 1/4 in. (6.35 mm) in Step 6.*

6. Insert a flat feeler gauge between the bottom of the pinion gear and the larger outer diameter of the shimming plug.

7. Holding the feeler gauge in place, depress the drive shaft sharply and remove the feeler gauge. There should be a slight drag when the feeler gauge is removed. If the feeler gauge does not slide out easily and the drive shaft drops down when the feeler gauge is removed, repeat Step 6 with a thinner gauge. If a slight drag is not noted when the feeler gauge is removed, repeat Step 6 with a thicker gauge.

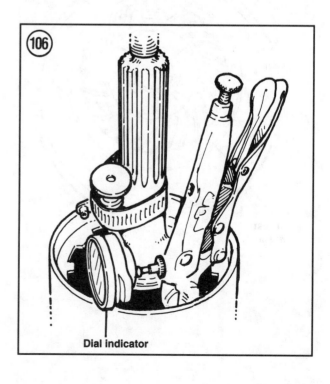

(106)

Dial indicator

NOTE
The desired clearance between the pinion gear and the shimming plug is 0.064-0.066 in. (1.63-1.68 mm) on 85 and 90 hp models and 0.004-0.006 in. (0.10-0.15 mm) on 60, 120 and 125 hp models.

8. Subtract the desired clearance from the clearance measured in Step 7.

9. Subtract the remainder obtained in Step 8 from 0.050 in. (1.27 mm) (master shim thickness). This Figure is the required shim thickness. For example, if 0.085 in. (2.16 mm) was measured with the feeler gauge in Step 7, subtracting 0.065 in. (1.65 mm) (desired clearance on 85 and 90 hp) leaves a reduction factor of 0.020 in. (0.51 mm). Next, subtract the 0.020 in. (0.51 mm) reduction factor from 0.050 in. (1.27 mm) (master shim thickness), leaving 0.030 in. (0.76 mm) as the shim thickness required to properly shim the drive shaft.

10. Remove the shim plug and cradle.

11. Remove the drive shaft. Refer to *Gearcase Disassembly/Reassemble*. Remove the master shim and install the required shim pack (Step 9).

12. Reinstall the drive shaft and pinion gear using the *old* pinion nut. Tighten the nut to 85 ft.-lb. (115 N•m).

13. Repeat Steps 1-7 to recheck pinion gear clearance. Clearance must be 0.064-0.066 in. (1.63-1.68 mm) on 85 and 90 hp models and 0.004-0.006 in. (0.10-0.15 mm) on 60, 120 and 125 hp models. If not, repeat shimming procedure. If the clearance is as specified, remove the old pinion gear nut. Apply Loctite 271 to the threads of a *new* nut. Install the nut and tighten to 85 ft.-lb. (115 N•m).

14. Install a 0.054 in. (1.37 mm) forward gear thrust washer into the forward gear. Hold the thrust washer in place with grease, making sure it is centered on the gear.

15. Assemble the clutch and shift pin on the propeller shaft. Install the clutch roll pin.

16. Lightly lubricate the bearing cage spacer and assemble the bearing cage, spacer bearing and reverse gear as shown in **Figure 108**. Install the reverse gear assembly on the propeller shaft.

CAUTION
Make sure the bearing cage spacer does not move out of place in Step 17. If it

9

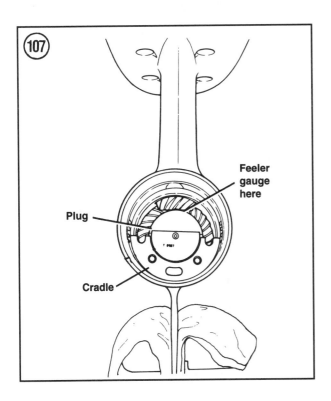

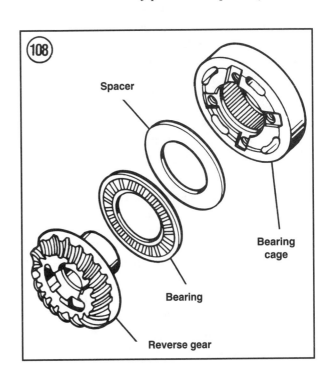

*does, remove the propeller shaft assem-
bly and reposition the spacer to prevent
serious gearcase damage.*

17. Install the propeller shaft assembly into the gearcase housing. When properly seated, the gearcase retaining ring grooves will be visible. Install and seat the 2 retaining rings.

18. Install the propeller shaft bearing spool (without O-rings) into the gearcase housing. Tighten the bearing spool bolts to 160 in.-lb. (18 N.m).

19. Install a dial indicator so the plunger will contact the machined surface on the end of the propeller shaft.

20. Depress and rotate the propeller shaft to remove all forward gear bearing clearance.

21. Zero the dial indicator. Pull up on the propeller shaft while noting the indicator reading. Repeat this step several times to ensure consistent readings. The propeller shaft end play should be 0.009-0.011 in (0.23-0.28 mm). If not, proceed to Step 22.

22. To calculate the required thrust washer thickness, subtract 0.010 in. (0.25 mm) (desired end play) from the dial indicator reading obtained in Step 21. Then, add the remainder to 0.054 in. (1.37 mm) (thickness of the thrust washer installed in Step 14). This Figure is the required forward gear thrust washer thickness.

23. Remove the dial indicator, propeller shaft bearing spool, retaining rings and propeller shaft assembly from the gearcase.

24. Remove the 0.054 in. (1.37 mm) thrust washer and replace with the washer determined in Step 22.

25. Complete reassemble as described in this chapter.

GEARCASE PRESSURE TESTING

When a gearcase assembly is overhauled, it should be pressure tested after reassemble to ensure that no leakage is present. If the gearcase fails the pressure test, it must be disassembled

and the source of the leakage located and corrected. Failure to correct any leakage can result in major gearcase damage.

1. Remove the vent plug from the gearcase housing.

2. Thread pressure tester adapter (part No. FT-8950) into the vent hole. Tighten the adapter securely.

3. Pressurize the gearcase to 10 psi (69 kPa). Push, pull and rotate the drive shaft, propeller shaft and actuate the shift rod while observing the pressure gauge for 5 minutes. If the pressure does not remain steady, submerge the gearcase in water and pressurize to 10 psi (69 kPa). Check for air bubbles to locate the source of the leak.

4. If the source of the leak cannot be located, disassemble the gearcase and inspect and/or replace seals and gaskets.

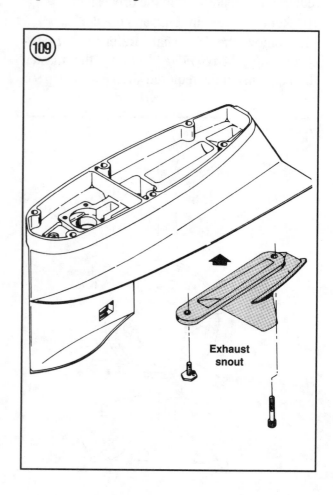

Exhaust snout

ZINC ANODE

Some outboards are fitted with a sacrificial zinc anode to help protect the gearcase from galvanic corrosion. The 7.5 hp and 25-50 hp Force gearcases (1984-1994) cast the anode as a replaceable exhaust snout (**Figure 109**). The newer Mercury style gearcases cast the anode as a replaceable trim tab. The anode on all other models is mounted in front of the propeller (**Figure 78**) or in the exhaust cavity (37, **Figure 76**).

The anode should not be painted, as this destroys its protective value. Check the anode periodically for erosion. If badly eroded, the anode should be replaced. Make sure that defective wiring or ground circuits on the boat or on a boat moored nearby is not causing excessive corrosion (stray current corrosion).

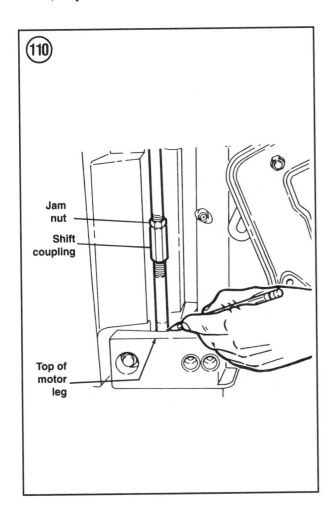

110

Jam nut

Shift coupling

Top of motor leg

GEAR SHIFT LINKAGE ADJUSTMENT

These procedures cover adjustments that synchronize the engine shift linkage to the gearcase shift mechanism. Remote control cable adjustments are covered in Chapter Twelve. The smaller engines (4-15 hp and 25 hp 3-cylinder) do not have gear shift adjustments. 1984-1992 models have starter interlock switches mounted on the engine. The linkage must be adjusted to provide interlock switch activation when the gearcase is in NEUTRAL. Neutral is defined as the mid-point of gearcase shift travel between maximum engagement in forward gear and maximum engagement in reverse gear. Always spin the propeller when shifting to ensure full clutch engagement.

The 1993-1999 models have the starter interlock switch located in the remote control box. The gear shift linkage on these models is adjusted to ensure full clutch engagement can be made in each gear before the linkage runs out of travel. The 1999 75 hp and 1995-1999 90 and 120 hp models use a splined shift rod. If the splines are not indexed properly when the gearcase is installed, it will be impossible to properly engage both gears. Remove the gearcase and re-index the shift rod as instructed in *Gearcase Removal/Installation* in this chapter.

25-50 hp and 70 hp Models with Interlock Switch (1984-1992)

NOTE
It may be necessary to remove the lower leg covers on 1984-1987 models in order to gain access to the shift coupling shown in Figure 110, typical.

1. Disconnect the remote control shift cable from the engine.
2. Manually move the power head gear shift lever to forward gear while spinning the propeller to ensure full clutch engagement.

9

3. Place a mark on an accessible part of the shift rod, referenced from a motor leg component. See **Figure 111**, typical.

4. Manually move the power head gear shift lever to reverse gear while spinning the propeller to ensure full clutch engagement.

5. Make another mark on the shift rod from the same reference point as Step 3.

6. Make a final mark on the shift rod at the midpoint (center) of the 2 previous marks. This mark represents true mechanical neutral for the gearcase.

7. Manually move the power head gear shift lever to align the center mark with the reference point on the motor leg.

8. With the shift rod in this position, the interlock switch plunger should be depressed. See **Figure 111**, typical. If not, loosen the jam nut and turn the shift rod coupler to adjust. Retighten the jam nut.

9. Verify proper adjustment by repeating Steps 2-8.

10. Reconnect the remote control shift cable.

60 hp with Interlock Switch

1. Remove the starboard support plate. See Chapter Eight, *Power Head Removal*.

2. Remove and discard the cotter pin from the gear shift pin. Remove the gear shift pin.

3. Manually shift the gearcase into FORWARD by pushing down on the shift rod while spinning the propeller to fully engage the shift clutch.

4. Loosen the lock nut under the shift rod coupler. Adjust the coupler until the shift pin hole is 1.38 in. (35 mm) above the steering arm. Retighten the lock nut. See **Figure 112**.

5. Reinstall the gear shift pin and secure with a new cotter pin.

6. Shift the control box into NEUTRAL. Adjust the remote control shift cable to align the gear shift arm with the starter (neutral) interlock switch. See **Figure 113**.

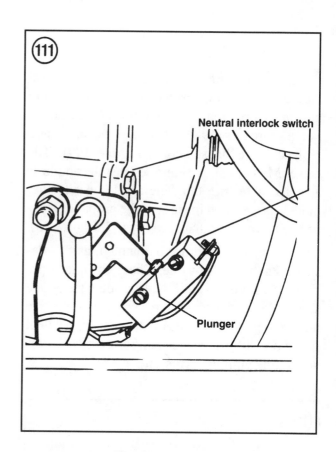

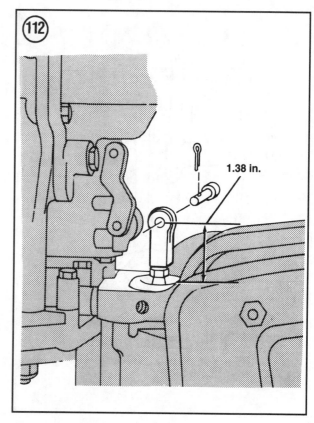

7. Disconnect the shift arm link. Shift the remote control box into FORWARD. Manually move the gearcase shift linkage to FORWARD while spinning the propeller to ensure full clutch engagement. Loosen the lock nut on the shift arm link and adjust the shift link connector until it aligns with the shift arm pin. Refer to **Figure 114**.

8. Reinstall the shift link and washer. Secure the link and washer with a new cotter pin.

40-50 hp (1993-1999) and 70-75 hp (1998 and Prior) Models without Interlock Switch

1. Disconnect the remote control shift cable from the engine.

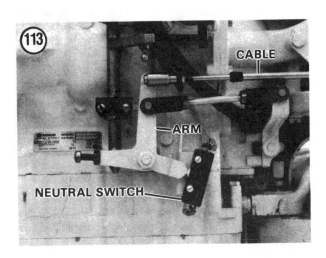

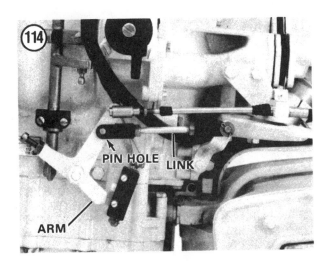

2. Manually move the power head gear shift lever to FORWARD gear while spinning the propeller to ensure full clutch engagement.

3. Place a mark on an accessible part of the shift rod, referenced from a motor leg component. See **Figure 111**, typical.

4. Manually move the power head gear shift lever to REVERSE gear while spinning the propeller to ensure full clutch engagement.

5. Make another mark on the shift rod from the same motor leg reference point as Step 3.

6. Make a final mark on the shift rod at the midpoint (center) of the 2 previous marks. This mark represents true mechanical neutral for the gearcase.

7. Manually move the power head gear shift lever to align the center mark with the reference point on the motor leg. Note the position of the power head gear shift lever in neutral.

8. Manually shift into each gear while rotating the propeller. Note the travel required to engage each gear as referenced from the neutral position in Step 7.

9. Gear shift lever travel at the power head should be equal in each gear. If the shift lever moves further to engage one gear than the other, adjust the shift rod coupler to provide equal shift travel into each gear. Retighten the jam nut when finished.

10. Reconnect the remote control shift cable.

85-150 hp (1984-1994)

1. Disconnect the remote control shift cable from the engine.

2. Manually move the power head gear shift lever to forward gear while spinning the propeller to ensure full clutch engagement.

3. Place a mark on the shift rod as shown in **Figure 115**.

9

4. Manually move the power head gear shift lever to reverse gear while spinning the propeller to ensure full clutch engagement.

5. Make another mark on the shift rod as shown in **Figure 116**.

6. Make a final mark on the shift rod at the midpoint (center) of the 2 previous marks. This mark represents true mechanical neutral for the gearcase. See **Figure 117**.

7. Manually move the power head gear shift lever to align the center mark with the reference point on the motor leg. The neutral interlock lever arm connected to the upper shift rod should align with the lower tower shaft as shown in **Figure 118**.

8. If the interlock lever arm and tower shaft do not align properly, adjust the 2 elastic stop nuts on the upper shift rod to position the interlock arm as shown in **Figure 118**. The stop nuts sandwich the interlock lever arm. Adjustment requires moving both nuts up or down the shift rod as necessary.

9. *Interlock switch models*—With the gear shift mechanism in the neutral position and the interlock lever and tower shaft aligned, the interlock switch plunger (1, **Figure 119**) should be depressed. If not, loosen the adjustment screws (2, **Figure 119**) and align the cam with

the interlock switch. Tighten the adjustment screws securely.

10. Reconnect the remote control shift cable to the engine.

WATER PUMP

The outboard motors and L-Drives covered in this manual use a water pump located on the top of the gearcase housing. The pump body impeller on small models is secured to the drive shaft by a pin that fits into the drive shaft and a similar cutout in the impeller hub. On larger models, a drive shaft key engages a flat on the drive shaft and a cutout in the impeller hub. As the drive

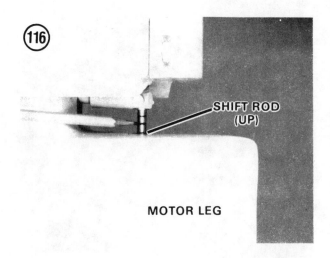

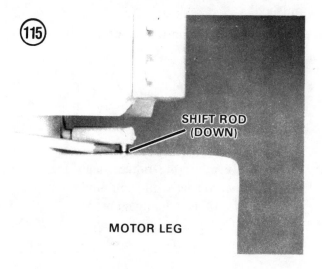

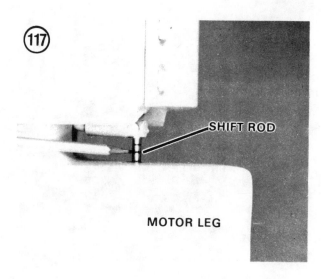

shaft rotates, the impeller rotates along with it. Water between the impeller blades and pump housing is pumped into the power head through the water tube.

The offset center of the pump housing causes the impeller vanes to flex during rotation. At low speeds, the pump functions as a displacement type; at high speeds, water resistance forces the vanes to flex inward and the pump functions as a centrifugal type. See **Figure 120**.

All seals and gaskets should be replaced anytime the pump is removed. Since proper water pump operation is critical to engine operation, it is also recommended to replace the pump impeller at the same time.

Never turn a used impeller over and reuse it. The impeller rotates in a clockwise direction with the drive shaft and the vanes gradually take a set in one direction. Turning the impeller over will cause the vanes to move in the opposite direction of the set and result in premature impeller failure and possible power head damage.

Removal and Disassembly (4 and 5 hp)

Refer to **Figure 121** for this procedure.

1. Secure the gearcase in a holding fixture or a vise with protective jaws. If protective jaws are not available, place the gearcase upright in the vise with the skeg between wooden blocks.

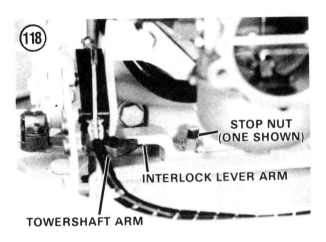

STOP NUT
(ONE SHOWN)

INTERLOCK LEVER ARM

TOWERSHAFT ARM

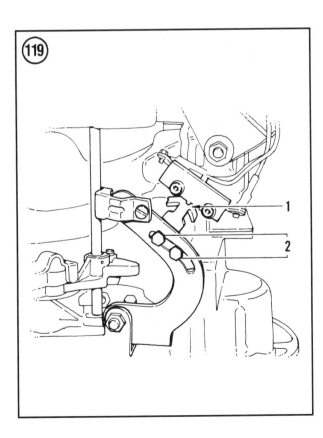

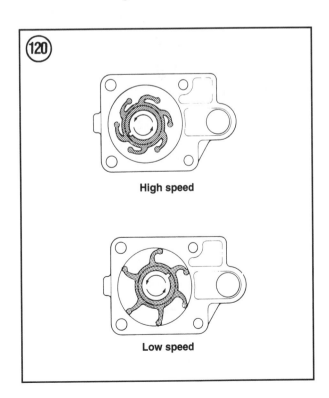

High speed

Low speed

2. Remove the screws securing the pump plate to the pump body. Remove the pump plate.

3. Make sure the drive shaft is clean and free of corrosion. Clean with sandpaper if necessary.

4. Slide the impeller up and off the drive shaft.

NOTE
Do not raise the drive shaft too far in Step 5 or pinion gear will disengage from the shaft requiring gearcase disassembly to repair.

5. Raise the drive shaft just enough to remove the impeller drive pin using needlenose pliers.

6. Remove the roll pin securing the shift rod coupling to the lower shift rod.

7. Remove the extension stud holding the pump body to the gearcase.

8. Carefully pry the pump body free and slide up and off of the drive shaft.

9. Remove and discard the gearcase O-ring under the pump body.

10. Thread a self-tapping screw into the top of the shift rod seal. Then, invert the pump body and drive the seal and self-tapping screw from the pump body using a suitable punch.

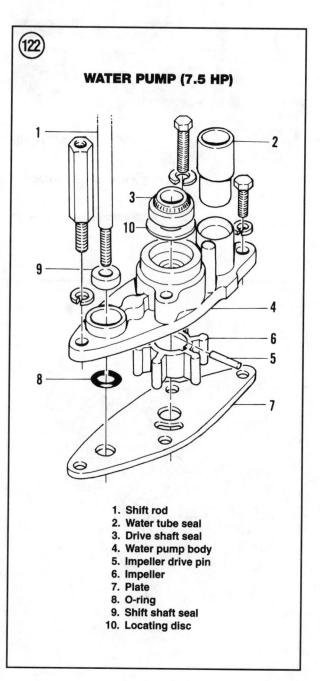

(122)

WATER PUMP (7.5 HP)

1. Shift rod
2. Water tube seal
3. Drive shaft seal
4. Water pump body
5. Impeller drive pin
6. Impeller
7. Plate
8. O-ring
9. Shift shaft seal
10. Locating disc

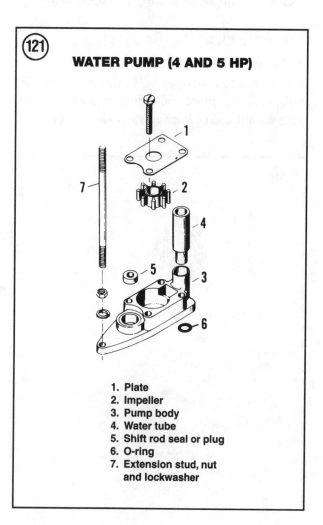

(121)

WATER PUMP (4 AND 5 HP)

1. Plate
2. Impeller
3. Pump body
4. Water tube
5. Shift rod seal or plug
6. O-ring
7. Extension stud, nut and lockwasher

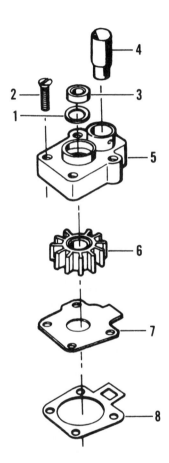

(123)

**WATER PUMP
9.9-15 HP, 25-50 HP
(1984-1994)**

1. Locating disc
2. Screw
3. Drive shaft seal
4. Water tube
5. Pump body
6. Impeller
7. Back plate
8. Gasket

Removal and Disassembly (7.5 hp)

Refer to **Figure 122** for this procedure.

1. Secure the gearcase in a suitable holding fixture or a vise with protective jaws. If protective jaws are not available, clamp the gearcase in a vise with the skeg between 2 wooden blocks.

2. Unscrew the shift rod and remove it from the gearcase.

3. Remove the front stud and 3 screws securing the water pump body to the gearcase. Lift the water pump body from the gearcase. Do not lift the drive shaft while removing the pump body.

3. Slide the impeller off of the drive shaft. Do not lift the drive shaft while removing the impeller.

4. Remove the impeller drive pin and slide the water pump plate up and off of the drive shaft.

5. Remove and discard the O-ring from the gearcase shift cavity groove.

6. Remove the O-ring from the water pump body. Pry the drive shaft seal from the water pump body. Do not damage or misplace the locating disc. Discard the seal and O-ring.

7. Thread a 1/4 in. screw into the shift rod seal from the top. Invert the pump body and drive the screw and seal out of the water pump body with a small punch. Discard the seal.

**Removal and Disassembly 9.9-15 hp
(1997 and Prior) and 25-50 hp (1984-1994)**

Refer to **Figure 123**, typical for this procedure.

1. Secure the gearcase in a suitable holding fixture or a vise with protective jaws. If protective jaws are not available, place the gearcase upright in a vise with the skeg between wooden blocks.

2. Remove the water tube from the pump body.

NOTE
Hold down on the drive shaft while lifting the pump body and impeller off the

9

drive shaft. If the drive shaft is badly corroded, it may be necessary to remove the drive shaft along with the pump components.

3. Remove the screws securing the pump body to the gearcase. Slide the pump body up and off the drive shaft.

4. Remove the impeller drive key from the drive shaft.

5. Carefully pry the back plate and gasket from the gearcase. Remove the plate and discard the gasket.

6. Remove the impeller from the pump body.

7. Using a screwdriver or similar tool, carefully pry the drive shaft seal and the water pump centering disc from the pump body.

Removal and Disassembly
9.9 and 15 hp (1998)

Refer to **Figure 124** for this procedure.

1. Secure the gearcase in a suitable holding fixture or a vise with protective jaws. If protective jaws are not available, clamp the gearcase in a vise with the skeg between 2 wooden blocks.

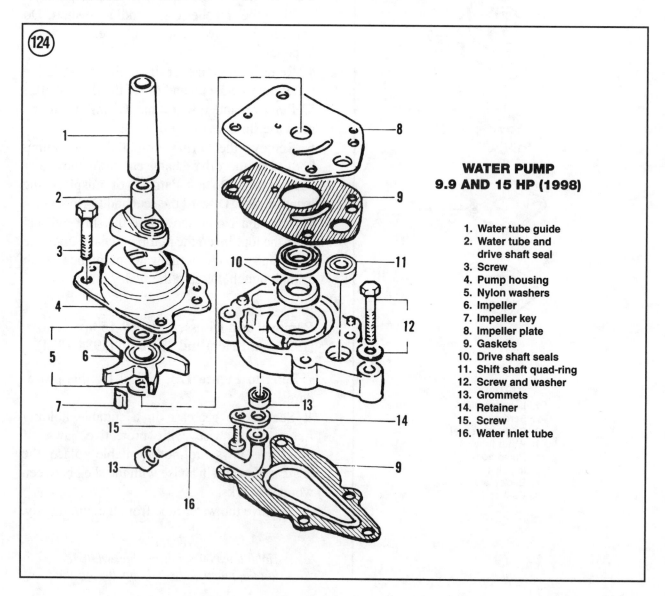

(124)

WATER PUMP
9.9 AND 15 HP (1998)

1. Water tube guide
2. Water tube and drive shaft seal
3. Screw
4. Pump housing
5. Nylon washers
6. Impeller
7. Impeller key
8. Impeller plate
9. Gaskets
10. Drive shaft seals
11. Shift shaft quad-ring
12. Screw and washer
13. Grommets
14. Retainer
15. Screw
16. Water inlet tube

2. Carefully pull the tube guide and water tube/drive shaft seal (1 and 2, **Figure 124**) from the pump housing (4, **Figure 124**). Pull the water tube/drive shaft seal over the drive shaft.

3. Remove the 4 water pump body screws (3, **Figure 124**) and carefully pry the pump housing from the pump base.

4. Remove the washer from the top of the impeller. Slide the impeller up and off the drive

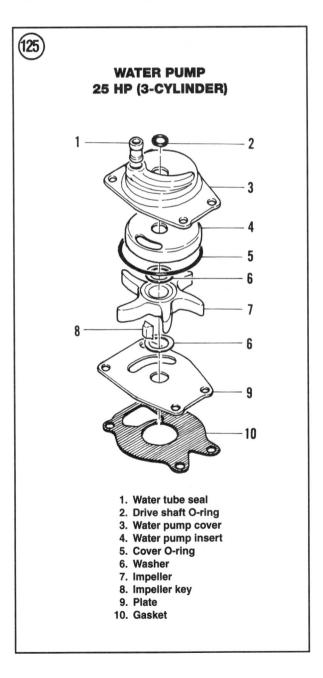

**WATER PUMP
25 HP (3-CYLINDER)**

1. Water tube seal
2. Drive shaft O-ring
3. Water pump cover
4. Water pump insert
5. Cover O-ring
6. Washer
7. Impeller
8. Impeller key
9. Plate
10. Gasket

shaft. Remove the impeller drive key and bottom impeller washer. Pry the plate (8, **Figure 124**) from the water pump base. Discard the gasket.

5. Remove the bolt and washer (12, **Figure 124**) from the water pump base. Carefully pry the water pump base loose from the gearcase. Pull the water inlet tube (16, **Figure 124**) from the grommet (13, **Figure 124**) as you pull the water pump base over the drive shaft. Remove and discard the gasket (9, **Figure 124**).

6. Remove the screw and retainer (14 and 15, **Figure 124**) then pull the water inlet tube from the water pump base. Refer to Gearcase Disassembly/Reassemble (in this chapter) for procedures when replacement of the drive shaft seals or shift shaft quad-ring seal is required.

Removal and Disassembly 25 hp (3-cylinder) and 40-50 hp (1995-1999)

1. Refer to **Figure 125** (25 hp) or **Figure 126** (40-50 hp) for this procedure.

2. Remove the water pump body screws. Slide the pump body up and off of the drive shaft. Remove the pump body liner (25 hp) from the pump body. Remove and discard the O-ring or gasket.

3. Remove the washer from the top of the impeller. Slide the impeller up and off the drive shaft. Remove the impeller drive key and bottom impeller washer.

4. Pry the plate from the gearcase. Discard the gasket.

Removal and Disassembly 70-75 hp (1998 and Prior)

Refer to **Figure 127** for this procedure.

1. Secure the gearcase in a suitable holding fixture or a vise with protective jaws. If protective jaws are not available, place the gearcase upright in a vise with the skeg between wooden blocks.

9

2. Remove the 6 screws securing the water pump cover.

NOTE
*The isolators (4, **Figure 127**) and (10) are not the same. Be sure to keep them separate for reference during reassembly.*

3. Lift the pump cover up and off the drive shaft.

4. Lift the impeller up and off the drive shaft.

5. Remove the impeller drive key.

6. Remove the plate and gasket. Discard the gasket.

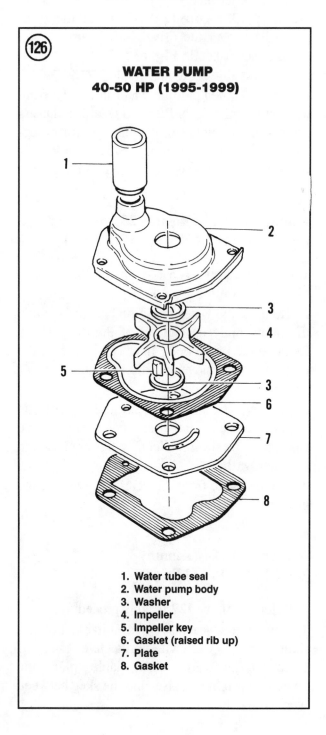

(126)

**WATER PUMP
40-50 HP (1995-1999)**

1. Water tube seal
2. Water pump body
3. Washer
4. Impeller
5. Impeller key
6. Gasket (raised rib up)
7. Plate
8. Gasket

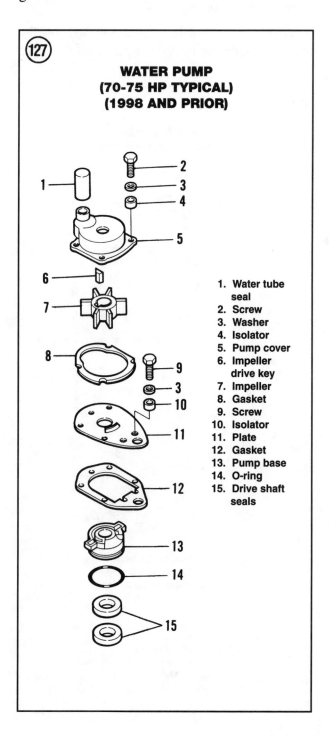

(127)

**WATER PUMP
(70-75 HP TYPICAL)
(1998 AND PRIOR)**

1. Water tube seal
2. Screw
3. Washer
4. Isolator
5. Pump cover
6. Impeller drive key
7. Impeller
8. Gasket
9. Screw
10. Isolator
11. Plate
12. Gasket
13. Pump base
14. O-ring
15. Drive shaft seals

7. Carefully pry pump base from the gearcase. Lift the base up and off the drive shaft.

8. Remove the pump base O-ring. Carefully pry the drive shaft seals from the pump base.

Removal and Disassembly 75 hp (1999) and 90-120 hp (1995-1999)

Refer to **Figure 128** for this procedure.

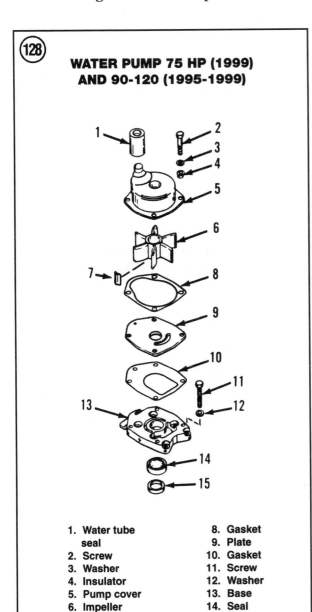

128

WATER PUMP 75 HP (1999) AND 90-120 (1995-1999)

1. Water tube seal	8. Gasket
2. Screw	9. Plate
3. Washer	10. Gasket
4. Insulator	11. Screw
5. Pump cover	12. Washer
6. Impeller	13. Base
7. Drive key	14. Seal
	15. Seal

1. Secure the gearcase in a suitable holding fixture or a vise with protective jaws. If protective jaws are not available, clamp the gearcase in a vise with the skeg between 2 wooden blocks.

2. Remove the water pump body screws. Slide the pump body up and off of the drive shaft. Remove and discard the gasket.

3. Slide the impeller up and off the drive shaft. Remove the impeller drive key.

4. Pry the plate from the water pump base. Remove and discard the gasket.

5. Remove the screws holding the water pump base to the gearcase.

6. Carefully pry the base from the gearcase. Remove and discard the gasket.

7. Remove and discard the seals in the water pump base.

Removal and Disassembly 60 hp and 85-150 hp (1984-1994)

Refer to **Figure 129** for early models and **Figure 76** for late models.

1. Secure the gearcase in a suitable holding fixture or a vise with protective jaws. If protective jaws are not available, place the gearcase upright in a vise with the skeg between wooden blocks.

2. Remove the water tube from the pump body.

3. Remove the screws or nuts and lockwashers securing the pump body to the gearcase cover. Carefully pry the pump body loose and lift it up and off the drive shaft.

4. Remove the impeller drive key from the drive shaft.

5. Carefully pry the water pump plate and gasket from the gearcase cover. Discard the gasket.

NOTE
It is not necessary to remove the gearcase cover for normal water pump service.

9

6. Remove the impeller from the water pump body. Push the impeller insert from the pump body on models so equipped.

7. Carefully pry the drive shaft seal and locating disc from the pump body.

Cleaning and Inspection

When removing seals from the pump body or base, note and record the direction in which the lip of each seal is facing for reference during reassemble.

1. Check the pump body for cracks, distortion or melting. Replace as required.

2. Clean the pump body and back plate in solvent and dry with compressed air or shop towels.

3. Carefully remove all gasket residue from the mating surfaces.

4. If the original impeller is reused, check the bonding to the impeller hub. Check the side seal surfaces and vanes for cracks, tears, excessive wear or a glazed and melted appearance. If any of these defects are noted, *replace* the impeller.

Assembly and Installation (4 and 5 hp)

1. Install a new shift rod seal into the pump body. The metal side should face up, with the top of the seal flush to 0.010 in. (0.25 mm) below the seal bore chamfer. See **Figure 130**.

2. Install a new O-ring seal into the gearcase groove.

3. Install the pump body over the shift rod and drive shaft and seat it onto the gearcase.

4. Coat the extension stud threads with RTV sealant. Install the stud but do not tighten the nut at this time.

NOTE
Do not raise the drive shaft too far in Step 5 or pinion gear will disengage from the shaft requiring gearcase disassembly to repair.

5. Carefully lift the drive shaft just enough to install the impeller drive pin using needlenose pliers. Slide the impeller over the drive shaft and into position on the gearcase.

6. Install the water pump plate on the pump body and tighten the screws securely. Tighten the extension stud nut securely.

7. Install the shift rod coupler to the lower shift rod with the roll pin.

Assembly and Installation (7.5 hp)

1. Install a new O-ring in the gearcase shift cavity groove. Slide the water pump plate over the drive shaft and into position on the gearcase.

CAUTION
The manufacturer recommends installation of a new water pump impeller anytime the pump is disassembled. If the

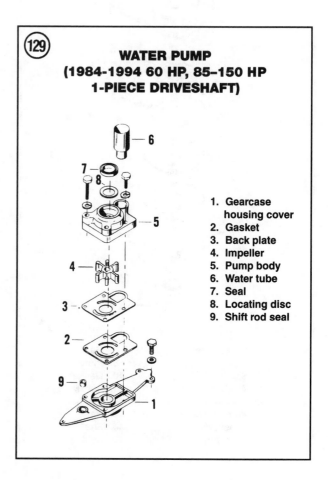

WATER PUMP
(1984-1994 60 HP, 85–150 HP
1-PIECE DRIVESHAFT)

1. Gearcase housing cover
2. Gasket
3. Back plate
4. Impeller
5. Pump body
6. Water tube
7. Seal
8. Locating disc
9. Shift rod seal

original impeller must be reused, install it in the same rotational direction as removed or water pump failure will result.

2. Insert the impeller drive pin into the drive shaft. Slide a new impeller over the drive shaft and engage it to the impeller drive pin.

3. Install a new shift rod seal into the pump body. Press the seal (with the metal capped end up) into the pump body with installer (part No. FT8957) or equivalent. The seal should be flush to 0.010 in. (0.25 mm) below the seal bore. See **Figure 130**.

4. Install a new drive shaft seal into the pump body. Press the seal (with the spring end up) into

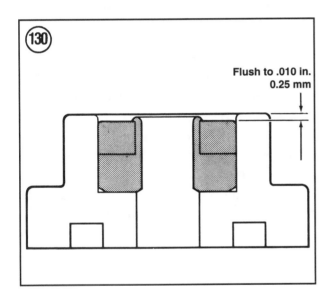

the pump body with installer (part No. FT2915) or equivalent.

5. Install a new O-ring into the pump body groove. Use 2-4-C Multi-Lube grease or equivalent to hold the O-ring in the groove during installation.

6. Slide the pump body over the drive shaft and into position over the impeller. Turn the drive shaft clockwise and press the body down to feed the impeller into the body. Seat the pump body against the plate.

7. Coat the threads of the water pump fasteners with RTV sealant (**Table 9**). Install and tighten the screws and stud to specification (**Table 2**).

8. Lubricate the shift rod with 2-4-C Multi-Lube grease or equivalent. Carefully thread the shift rod through the shift rod seal and into the shift cam. Set shift rod height before reinstalling the gearcase.

Assembly and Installation 9.9-15 hp (1997 and prior) and 25-50 hp (1984-1994)

1. Insert the centering disc into the pump body.

2. Install the drive shaft seal into the pump body with the lip side facing up. Use installer (part No. FT-2907 [9.9-15 hp] or part No. FT-8972 [25-50]) or equivalent tool and press the seal into the body until bottomed. Lubricate the seal lip with a suitable grease.

3. Install the pump back plate and gasket (if used).

4. Install the impeller drive pin into the drive shaft.

CAUTION
If the original impeller is reused, install it in the same rotational direction as removed to prevent premature water pump failure. The drive pin groove must be visible and the bend in the impeller blades positioned as shown in Figure 131.

5. Lightly lubricate the inner diameter of the water pump body. Install the impeller into the body by rotating in a counterclockwise direction. Be sure the drive pin slot is facing away from the pump body.

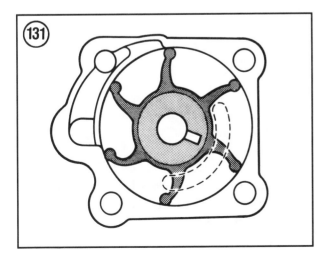

6. Place the pump body and impeller over the drive shaft. Align the impeller slot with the drive pin and seat the pump body on the gearcase.

7. Insert the pump body screws and tighten securely.

8. Install the water tube into the pump body.

Assembly and Installation 9.9 and 15 hp (1998)

1. Refer to Gearcase Disassembly and Assembly to install the water pump base to the gearcase.

2. Ensure the quad-ring (11, **Figure 124**) is properly positioned in the water pump base. Place a new gasket onto the water pump base. Slide the water pump plate over the drive shaft and position it on the gasket.

3. Install a washer (5, **Figure 124**) over the drive shaft and position it against the plate. Grease the impeller key with 2-4-C Multi-Lube grease or equivalent and position it on the drive shaft. Slide the impeller onto the drive shaft and engage the key. Install the top washer over the drive shaft and into position on top of the impeller.

4. Slide the pump body over the drive shaft and into position over the impeller. Turn the drive shaft clockwise and press the body down to feed the impeller into the body. Seat the pump body against the plate.

5. Coat threads of water pump fasteners with Loctite 271 threadlocking adhesive (**Table 9**). Install and tighten screws to specification (**Table 2**).

6. Place the water tube and drive shaft seal (2, **Figure 124**) into position on the pump housing. Install the water tube guide (1, **Figure 124**) onto the water tube and drive shaft seal.

Assembly and Installation (25 hp [3-cylinder] and 40-50 hp [1995-1999])

1. Place a new gasket onto the gearcase. Slide the water pump plate over the drive shaft and into position on the gasket.

2A. *25 hp*—Install the pump liner into the pump body. Glue a new O-ring into the pump body groove with a suitable contact adhesive (**Table 9**).

2B. *40-50 hp*—Install a new gasket (with the raised rib up) on top of the water pump plate.

CAUTION
The manufacturer recommends installation of a new water pump impeller anytime the pump is disassembled. If the original impeller must be reused, install it in the same rotational direction as removed or water pump failure will result.

3. Install a washer over the drive shaft and position it against the plate. Grease the impeller key with 2-4-C Multi-Lube grease or equivalent and position it on the drive shaft. Slide the impeller onto the drive shaft and engage the key. Install the top washer over the drive shaft and into position on top of the impeller.

4. Slide the pump body over the drive shaft and into position over the impeller. Turn the drive shaft clockwise and press the body down to feed the impeller into the body. Seat the pump body against the plate.

5. Coat the threads of the water pump fasteners with Loctite 271 threadlocking adhesive (**Table 9**). Install and tighten the screws to specification (**Table 2**).

6A. *25 hp*—Install the water tube seal and drive shaft O-ring.

6B. *40-50 hp*—If the water tube guide and seal is removed it must be reattached or replaced. Secure the water tube with Loctite 405 adhesive (obtained locally).

Assembly and Installation 70-75 hp (1998 and Prior)

1. Apply Loctite 271 to the outer diameter of the drive shaft seals. Press seals into the pump base using seal driver (part No. 91-817006) with the seal lips facing down (toward gearcase). Lubricate the seal lips with a suitable grease.

2. Install a new O-ring on the pump base. Install the base into the gearcase housing. Make sure the base is fully seated.

3. Install a new pump plate gasket and install the plate.

CAUTION
The manufacturer recommends install-ing a new water pump impeller any time the pump is disassembled. If the original impeller must be reused, install it in the same rotational direction as removed or water pump failure will result.

4. Install a new pump cover gasket. Place the impeller drive key into the drive shaft slot and slide the impeller over the drive shaft. Make sure the impeller properly engages the drive key.

5. Install the pump cover over the impeller while rotating the drive shaft in a clockwise direction. Install pump cover screws and tighten to 60 in.-lb.

6. Install the water tube seal into the pump cover.

Assembly and Installation
75 hp (1999) and 90-120 hp (1995-1999)

1. Coat the outer cases of 2 new water pump base oil seals with Loctite 271 threadlocking adhesive. Set the water pump base (stepped side facing up) into a press. Install the teflon coated seal (flat brown/black color) with the spring facing the power head onto the longer stepped side of seal installer (part No. 91-13949) or equivalent. Press the seal into the water pump base until the tool bottoms. Install the non-teflon coated seal (glossy black color) with spring facing the gearcase onto the short stepped side of the seal installer (part No. 91-13949) or equivalent. Press the seal into the water pump base until the tool bottoms. Coat the seal lips with 2-4-C Multi-Lube grease or equivalent.

2. Place a new gasket onto the gearcase. Slide the water pump base over the drive shaft and into position on the gasket. Make sure the water pump

base is piloted into the gearcase bore and has not pinched the gasket in the gearcase bore.

3. Coat the water pump base screws with Loctite 271 threadlocking adhesive (**Table 9**). Install the screws and washers. Tighten the screws to specification (**Table 2**).

4. Install a new gasket on top of the water pump base. Slide the water pump plate over the drive shaft and into position on the gasket.

CAUTION
The manufacturer recommends installa-tion of a new water pump impeller anytime the pump is disassembled. If the original impeller must be reused, install it in the same rotational direction as removed or water pump failure will result.

5. Install a new gasket on top of the water pump plate. Grease the impeller key with 2-4-C Multi-Lube grease or equivalent and position it on the drive shaft. Slide the impeller onto the drive shaft and engage the key.

6. Slide the pump body over the drive shaft and into position over the impeller. Turn the drive shaft clockwise and press the body down to feed the impeller into the body. Seat the pump body against the plate.

7. Coat the threads of the water pump fasteners with Loctite 271 threadlocking adhesive (**Table 9**). Install and tighten the screws to specification (**Table 2**).

8. Install the water tube guide and seal. Lubri-cate the seal with 2-4-C Multi-Lube grease or equivalent.

Assembly and Installation
(60 hp and 85-150 hp [1984-1994])

One-piece drive shaft models

1. Insert the centering disc into the pump body seal bore.

2. Install a new drive shaft seal (with the lip facing up) into the pump body bore with seal installer (part No. FT-3012) or equivalent. Coat

the seal lips with 2-4-C Multi-Lube grease or equivalent.

CAUTION
The manufacturer recommends installation of a new water pump impeller anytime the pump is disassembled. If the original impeller must be reused, install it in the same rotational direction as removed or water pump failure will result.

3. Lightly coat a new impeller with 2-4-C Multi-Lube grease or equivalent and install the impeller into the pump body with a counterclockwise rotation.

4. Install a gasket on the water pump adapter base. Slide the water pump plate over the drive shaft and into position on the gasket.

5. Install the impeller key into the drive shaft slot. Install the water tube guide into the pump body.

6. Slide the pump body and impeller assembly over the drive shaft and into position over the impeller key. Align the impeller slot with impeller key. Seat the pump body against the plate.

7. Coat the threads of the water pump screws with RTV sealant (**Table 9**). Install the screws and lock washers. Tighten the screws to specification (**Table 2**).

Two-piece drive shaft models

1. Insert the water tube seal into the pump body.

2. Install a gasket on the water pump adapter base. Slide the water pump plate over the drive shaft and into position on the gasket. Install a gasket on the water pump plate.

CAUTION
The manufacturer recommends installation of a new water pump impeller anytime the pump is disassembled. If the original impeller must be reused, install it in the same rotational direction as removed or water pump failure will result.

3. Lightly coat a new impeller with 2-4-C Multi-Lube grease or equivalent and install the impeller into the pump liner with a counterclockwise rotation.

4. Install the impeller key into the drive shaft slot.

5. Slide the pump liner and impeller assembly over the drive shaft and into position over the impeller key. Align the impeller slot with impeller key. Seat the pump liner assembly against the plate.

6. Rotate the liner assembly until the tab on the upper surface of the liner is positioned pointing directly at the shift rod.

7. Install the pump housing over the drive shaft and liner, making sure the tab on the liner engages the recessed slot in the pump housing. Seat the housing against the plate.

8. Install the washers and new elastic stop nuts. Tighten the nuts to specification (**Table 2**).

9. Install the rubber seal over the drive shaft and seat it against the pump housing.

Table 1 GEAR RATIO AND APPROXIMATE LUBRICANT CAPACITY

Outboard model	Gear ratio (tooth count)	Lubricant capacity
4 and 5 hp	2:1 (13:26)	4 oz. (118 ml)
7.5 hp	2:1 (13:26)	5 oz. (148 ml)
9.9 and 15 hp	1.57:1 (14:22)	5 oz. (148 ml)
25 hp (2 cylinder)	2:1 (13:26)	12 oz. (355 ml)
25 hp (3 cylinder)	2.25:1 (12:27)	7.6 oz. (225 ml)
(continued)		

Table 1 GEAR RATIO AND APPROXIMATE LUBRICANT CAPACITY (continued)

Outboard model	Gear ratio (tooth count)	Lubricant capacity
35 hp	2:1 (13:26)	12 oz. (355 ml)
40-50 hp (through 1994)	1.62:1 (13:21)	12 oz. (355 ml)
40-50 hp (1995-on)	2:1 (13:26)	14.9 oz. (441 ml)
60 hp	not available	26 oz. (769 ml)
70 and 75 hp (prior to 1999)	1.64:1 (14:23)	12 oz. (355 ml)
85 hp (through 1989)	2:1 (15:30)	26 oz. (769 ml)
125 hp (through 1989)	1.73:1 (15:26)	26 oz. (769 ml)
90 and 120 hp (1990-1994)	1.93:1 (14:27)	35 oz. (1035 ml)
90 hp (1995-on) and		
75 hp (1999 only)	2.3:1 (13:30)	22.5 oz. (665 ml)
120 hp (1995-on)	2.07:1 (14:29)	22.5 oz. (665 ml)
150 hp (through 1991I)	1.93:1 (14:27)	26 oz. (769 ml)
150 hp (1991J-on)	1.93:1 (14:27)	35 oz. (1035 ml)
L-Drive models	1.93:1 (14:27)	26 oz. (769 ml)

Table 2 GEARCASE TORQUE VALUES

Fastener	in.-lb.	ft.-lb.	N•m
Drain plugs			
4 and 5 hp			
Upper	30	–	3.4
Lower	45	–	5.1
7.5 hp	90-115	–	10.2-13.0
25 hp (3-cylinder)	40	–	4.5
40 and 50 hp (1995-1996)	60	–	6.8
90 and 120 hp (1995-1996)			
Large plug	60	–	6.8
Small plug	20	–	2.3
Drive shaft retainer			
70 and 75 hp (prior to 1999)	–	75	101.7
85-125 hp (2 piece drive shaft)	–	90	122.0
Gear housing to motor leg			
(universal joint housing [L-Drive])			
4 and 5 hp	110	–	12.4
9.9 and 15 hp	130	–	14.7
25 (2-cylinder), 40 hp (1992-1994)			
and 50 hp (1984-1994)	270	23	31.2
25 hp (3-cylinder)	270	23	31.2
40 and 50 hp (1995-1996)	–	40	54.2
70 and 75 hp (prior to 1999)	–	40	54.2
85-125 hp (5/16 in. hardware)	160	–	18.1
Gear housing to motor leg (universal			
joint housing [L-Drive]) (continued)			
85-125 hp (3/8 in. hardware)	270	23	31.2
90 and 120 hp (1995-1996)	–	40	54.2
Gear shift arm retaining pin	30	–	3.4
Pinion screw			
25 hp (3-cylinder)	150	–	16.9

(continued)

9

Table 2 GEARCASE TORQUE VALUES (continued)

Fastener	in.-lb.	ft.-lb.	N•m
Pinion nut			
40 and 50 hp (1995-1996)	–	50	67.8
60 hp	–	85	115.2
70 and 75 hp (prior to 1999)	–	50	67.8
85-150 hp (1984-1994)	–	85	115.2
90 and 120 hp (1995-1996)			
and 75 hp (1999)	–	70	94.9
Propeller nut			
25 hp (3-cylinder)	120	–	13.6
70 and 75 hp (prior to 1999)	–	55	74.6
90 and 120 hp (1995-1996)			
and 75 hp (1999)	–	55	74.6
Propshaft bearing carrier			
(bearing spool)			
9.9 and 15 hp	70	–	7.9
25 hp (3-cylinder)	204	17	23.0
40 and 50 hp (1995-1996)	200	17	22.6
60 hp	160	–	18.1
70 and 75 hp (prior to 1999)	150	–	16.9
90 and 120 hp (1995-1996)			
and 75 hp (1999)	300	25	33.9
85-125 hp (single port exhaust)	160	–	18.1
90-150 hp (dual port exhaust)	–	130	176.3
Upper gearcase to lower gearcase			
9.9 and 15 hp	125	–	14.1
25 (2-cylinder), 40 hp (1992-1994)			
and 50 hp (1984-1994)	270	22.5	30.5
Shift rod cover			
90 and 120 hp (1995-1996)			
and 75 hp (1999)	60	–	6.8
Trim tab (anode)			
40 and 50 hp (1995-1996)	190	15.8	21.4
70 and 75 hp (prior to 1999)	270	22.5	30.5
90 and 120 hp (1995-1996)			
and 75 hp (1999)	270	22.5	30.5
Water pump cover			
25 hp (3-cylinder)	60	–	6.8
40 and 50 hp (1995-1996)	60	–	6.8
60 hp	70	–	7.9
70 and 75 hp (prior to 1999)	60	–	6.8
90 and 120 hp (1995-1996)			
and 75 hp (1999)	60	–	6.8
85 and 125 hp (1-piece drive shaft)	70	–	7.9
85-150 hp (Single port exhaust,			
2-piece drive shaft)			
Long studs	70	–	7.9
Short stud	40	–	4.5
90-150 hp (Dual port exhaust,			
2 piece drive shaft)			
Long studs	50	–	5.6
Short stud	15	–	1.7
Water pump adapter plate			
60-150 hp (1984-1994)	70	–	7.9
90 and 120 hp (1995-1996)			
and 75 hp (1999)	60	–	6.8

Table 3 STANDARD TORQUE VALUES

Screw or nut size	in.-lb.	ft.-lb.	N•m
6-32	9	–	1.0
8-32	20	–	2.3
10-24	30	–	3.4
10-32	35	–	4.0
12-24	45	–	5.1
1/4-20	70	6	7.9
1/4-28	84	7	9.5
5/16-18	160	13	18.1
5/16-24	168	14	19.0
3/8-16	270	23	30.5
3/8-24	300	25	33.9
7/16-14	–	36	48.8
7/16-20	–	40	54.2
1/2-13	–	50	67.8
1/2-20	–	60	81.3

Table 4 GEARCASE SERVICE SPECIFICATIONS

Component	Specification—in. (mm)
Shift pin length	
9.9 and 15 hp	1.706-1.712 (43.33-43.48)
Clutch spring uncompressed length	
4 -15 hp	2-7/16 in. (61.91)
Forward gear bearing (in gear housing)	
4 and 5 hp	0.8766-0.8789 (22.27-22.32)
7.5 hp	0.8787-0.8794 (22.32-22.34)
Forward gear internal bearing	
4, 5 and 7.5 hp (inside diameter)	0.5000-0.5007 (12.70-12.72)
9.9 and 15 hp (inside diameter)	0.5630-0.5635 (14.30-14.31)
Reverse gear internal bearing	
9.9 and 15 hp (inside diameter)	0.5630-0.5635 (14.30-14.31)
Propeller shaft bearing housing	
4 and 5 hp	
Propeller shaft bearing (inside diameter)	0.4990-0.4997 (12.67-12.69)
Internal thrust face to rear of flange	0.645-0.652 (16.38-16.56)
7.5 hp	
Reverse gear support bearing (inside diameter)	0.8787-0.8794 (22.32-22.34)
Propeller shaft bearing (inside diameter)	0.500-0.501 (12.70-12.73)
9.9 and 15 hp	
Propeller shaft bearing (inside diameter)	0.5630-0.5637 (14.30-14.32)
Propeller shaft straightness (run-out)	0.006 in. (0.152 mm) maximum
Shift rod height (in neutral unless otherwise specified)	
7.5 hp	
(gear housing to center of hole)	6.12-6.20 (155.45-157.48)
9.9 and 15 hp	
(gear housing to center of hole)	0.1406-0.2344 (3.57-5.95)
60 hp	1.38 (35.05)

(continued)

9

Table 4 GEARCASE SERVICE SPECIFICATIONS (continued)

Component	Specification—in. (mm)
Pinion gear height	
60 hp	0.004-0.006 (0.10-0.15)
70 and 75 hp (prior to 1999)	0.025 (0.64)
85 and 90 hp (1 piece drive shaft)	0.064-0.066 (1.63-1.68)
90 hp (1995-1996) gauge block flat No. 8 and 75 hp (1999)	0.025 (0.64)
120 hp (1995-1996) gauge block flat No. 1	0.025 (0.64)
120 and 125 hp (1 piece drive shaft)	0.004-0.006 (0.10-0.15)
Forward gear backlash	
70 and 75 hp (measured at mark No. 3) (prior to 1999)	0.013-0.019 (0.33-0.48)
90 hp (1995-1996) (measured at mark No. 4) and 75 hp (1999)	0.012-0.019 (0.30-0.48)
120 hp (1995-1999) (measured at mark No. 1)	0.015-0.022 (0.38-0.56)
60, 85-150 hp (1984-1994)	0.009-0.018 (0.23-0.46)
Propshaft end play	
60 hp	0.009-0.011 (0.23-0.28)
85-150 hp (1984-1994)	0.005-0.020 (0.13-0.51)

Table 5 GEARCASE SPECIAL TOOLS
(4-15 HP [1984-1996] AND 25-60 HP [1984-1994])

Description	Part No.	Models
Puller kit	FT-8948-1	All
Pressure tester	FT-8950	All
Seal installer	FT-2907	5, 9.9 and 15 hp
Seal installer	FT-2915	7.5 hp
Seal installer	FT-8957	5-15 hp
Drift	FT-8919	9.9-60 hp
Seal installer	FT-3431	25-50 hp
Bearing installer	FT-8904	25-50 hp
Bearing remover	FT-8921	25-50 hp
Seal installer	FT-8957	25-50 hp
Seal installer	FT-8963	25-50 hp
Seal remover	FT-8964	25-50 hp
Seal installer	FT-8972	25-50 hp
Driver handle	FT-8907	25-60 hp
Bearing guide set	FT-8918	25-60 hp
Seal installer	FT-3012	60 hp
Dial indicator adaptor	FT-8901	60 hp
Dial indicator	FT-8902	60 hp
Bearing installer	FT-8985	60 hp
Shim tool kit	FTA-8997	60 hp
Bearing cup installer	FT-11203	60 hp
Bearing remover/installer	FT-11206	60 hp
Bearing cup remover	FT-11207	60 hp
Bearing guide plate	FT-11209	60 hp
Drive shaft spline socket	FT-11297	60 hp

Table 6 GEARCASE SPECIAL TOOLS
(85-150 HP [1984-1994], INCLUDING L-DRIVES)

Description	Part No.	Models
Dial indicator adaptor	FT-8901	All
Dial indicator	FT-8902	All
Driver handle	FT-8907	All
Drift	FT-8919	All
Seal installer	FT-8925	All
Puller kit	FT-8948-1	All
Pressure tester	FT-8950	All
Seal installer	FT-8985	All
Dial indicator post	FT-8997-E	All
Master shim	FT-8997-F	All
Bearing guide plate	FT-11209	All
Seal installer	FT-8957	Standard shift rod seal models
Seal installer	FT-16535	Shift rod bellows models
Seal installer	FT-3012	1 piece drive shaft models
Drive shaft spline socket	FT-7848	1 piece drive shaft models
Pinion gear shim set	FTA-8997	1 piece drive shaft models
Bearing cup installer	FT-11204	1 piece drive shaft models
Bearing remover/installer	FT-11205	1 piece drive shaft models
Bearing cup remover	FT-11207	1 piece drive shaft models
Drive shaft puller	FT-11292	2 piece drive shaft models
Drive shaft retainer wrench	FT-11293	2 piece drive shaft models
Bearing remover	FT-16433	2 piece drive shaft models
Bearing service kit	FT-16496	2 piece drive shaft models
Drive shaft spline socket	FT-16536	2 piece drive shaft models
Bearing cup remover	FT-16813	2 piece drive shaft models
Bearing cup installer	FT-16814	2 piece drive shaft models
Propshaft retainer wrench	FT-11275	Dual port exhaust models

9

Table 7 GEARCASE SPECIAL TOOLS
(25 HP [3-CYLINDER], 40 AND 50 HP [1995-1999])

Description	Part No.	Models
Pressure tester	FT-8950	All
Bearing puller	91-27780	All
Bearing service kit	91-31229A7	All
Nut[1]	11-24156	All
Washer (2)[1]	12-34961	All
Plate[1]	91-29310	All
Threaded rod[1]	91-31229	All
Slide hammer	91-34569A-1	All
Bearing separator plate	91-37241	All
Bearing carrier tool	91-93843–1	25 hp
Bearing	31-85560	40 and 50 hp
Driver[2]	91-13779	40 and 50 hp
Mandrel	91-36571	40 and 50 hp
Driver	91-37312	40 and 50 hp
Driver rod	91-37323	40 and 50 hp
Driver	91-817007	40 and 50 hp
Driver	91-817011	40 and 50 hp
Drive shaft spline socket	91-825196	40 and 50 hp

(continued)

Table 7 GEARCASE SPECIAL TOOLS
(25 HP [3-CYLINDER], 40 AND 50 HP [1995-1999]) (continued)

Description	Part No.	Models
Driver	91-825197	40 and 50 hp
Mandrel	91-825198	40 and 50 hp
Pilot	91-825199	40 and 50 hp
Spring hook assembly	91-825200A1	40 and 50 hp
Driver	91-826872	40 and 50 hp

[1] Included in the 91-31229A7 bearing service kit.
[2] Part of the 91-14308A1 bearing race tool, used on the 90 and 120 hp (1995-1996)

Table 8 GEARCASE SPECIAL TOOLS
(70-75 HP, 90 and 120 HP [1995-1999])

Description	Part No.	Models
Drift	FT8919	All
Pressure tester	FT8950	All
Bearing preload tool	91-14311A-2	All
Slide hammer	91-34569A-1	All
Bearing separator plate	91-37241	All
Driver rod	91-37323	All
Puller jaws	91-46086A-1	All
Dial indicator	91-58222A-1	All
Dial indicator adaptor kit	91-83155	All
Puller bolt	91-85716	All
Bearing cup remover	FT11207	70-75 hp
Bearing guide set	FT11209	70-75 hp
Retainer wrench	FT11293	70-75 hp
Bearing cup installer	FT11296	70-75 hp
Drive shaft spline socket	FT11297	70-75 hp
Mandrel	91-24273	70-75 hp
Bearing puller assembly	91-27780	70-75 hp
Mandrel	91-37312	70-75 hp
Bearing installer	91-817005	70-75 hp
Seal installer	91-817006	70 and 75 hp (prior to 1999)
Seal installer	91-817007	70 and 75 hp (prior to 1999)
Pinion gear shim tool	91-817008A-2	70 and 75 hp (prior to 1999)
Bearing installer	91-817011	70 and 75 hp (prior to 1999)
Drive handle	91-824892	70 and 75 hp (prior to 1999)
Backlash indicator	91-19660–1	70 and 75 hp (prior to 1999) and 120 hp
Backlash indicator	91-78473	75 hp (1999) and 90 hp
Nut*	11-24156	75 hp (1999), 90 hp and 120 hp
Pinion gear shim tool	91-12349A-2	75 hp (1999), 90 hp and 120 hp
Bearing installer	91-13945	75 hp (1999), 90 hp and 120 hp
Seal installer	91-13949	75 hp (1999), 90 hp and 120 hp
Bearing race tool	91-14308A-1	75 hp (1999), 90 hp and 120 hp
Bearing installer	91-14309A-1	75 hp (1999), 90 hp and 120 hp
Wear sleeve installer	91-14310A-1	75 hp (1999), 90 hp and 120 hp
Mandrel*	91-15755	75 hp (1999), 90 hp and 120 hp
Mandrel	91-31106	75 hp (1999), 90 hp and 120 hp
Seal installer	91-31108	75 hp (1999), 90 hp and 120 hp
Threaded rod*	91-31229	75 hp (1999), 90 hp and 120 hp

(continued)

Table 8 GEARCASE SPECIAL TOOLS
(70-75 HP, 90 and 120 HP [1995-1999]) (continued)

Description	Part No.	Models
Mandrel*	91-36569	75 hp (1999), 90 hp and 120 hp
Mandrel	91-37350	75 hp (1999), 90 hp and 120 hp
Drive shaft holding tool	91-56775	75 hp (1999), 90 hp and 120 hp
Bearing puller assembly	91-83165M	75 hp (1999), 90 hp and 120 hp

* From bearing removal and installation kit part No. 91-31229A7

Table 9 RECOMMENDED LUBRICANTS, SEALANTS AND ADHESIVES

	Part No.
Lubricants	
Quicksilver Premium 2-Cycle TC-W3 outboard oil	(normal dealer stock item)
Quicksilver Special Lubricant 101	92-13872A-1
Quicksilver 2-4-C Multi-Lube	(normal dealer stock item in various sizes)
Quicksilver Anti-Corrosion Grease	92-78376A-6
Quicksilver Needle Bearing Grease	92-825265A-1
Quicksilver Power Trim and Steering Fluid	92-90100A12
Quicksilver Premium Blend Gearcase Lubricant	(normal dealer stock item)
Sealants	
Quicksilver Perfect Seal	92-34227-11
Loctite 5900 Ultra black RTV sealant	92-809826
Sealer (crankcase halves)	92-90113–2
Loctite Master Gasket Sealer	92-12564–2
Quicksilver Liquid Neoprene	92-25711–2
Loctite 567 PST pipe sealant	92-809822
Quicksilver Bellows Adhesive	92-86166–1
Adhesives	
Loquic Primer	92-809824
Loctite 271 threadlocking sealant	
(high strength)	92-809819
Adhesives (continued)	
Loctite 242 threadlocking sealant	
(medium strength)	92-809821
Loctite RC680 high strength	
retaining compound	92-809833
Miscellaneous	
Quicksilver Power Tune Engine Cleaner	92-15104A12
Quicksilver Corrosion Guard	92-815869A12
Quicksilver Storage Seal Rust Inhibitor	92-86145A12

9

Chapter Ten

L-Drive Lower Assembly and Exhaust System

The L-Drive system is basically an outboard power head mounted inside the boat and turned 90°. The lower unit assembly protrudes through a lip on the transom and swivels to provide steering. It also hinges through a set of universal joints to provide trim/tilt functions.

This chapter provides service procedures for the L-Drive system lower assembly and exhaust system. Refer to **Table 1** for torque specifications and **Table 2** for lubricants, sealants and adhesives. All Tables are at the end of the chapter.

> *NOTE*
> *Water hose kit, part No. 819069T is available to improve water hose attachment security on early model L-Drives. The kit consists of 2 new fittings, hose clamps and a new water hose. Follow the instructions supplied with the kit.*

LOWER ASSEMBLY REMOVAL/INSTALLATION

The lower assembly consists of the transom plate, mounting base, steering yoke and univer-sal joint housing. Refer to **Figure 1** for this procedure.

1. Disconnect the spark plugs leads and the negative battery cable.

2. Remove the power head. See Chapter Eight.

3. Remove the gearcase assembly. See Chapter Nine.

4. Loosen the clamps and disconnect the exhaust bellows from the universal joint housing (**Figure 2**).

5. Label the power trim/tilt hydraulic lines for reference during reinstallation. Disconnect the lines from the transom plate and plug the lines to prevent leakage or contamination. See **Figure 3**.

6. Connect a suitable lifting chain at the points shown (**Figure 4**). Attach a suitable engine hoist to the chain and remove slack from the lifting chain.

7. Remove the 4 transom clamps (**Figure 4**). Carefully, lower the assembly down and out of the boat transom.

8. Remove and discard the transom plate O-ring. Thoroughly clean all adhesive residue from the transom plate O-ring groove.

9. To reinstall the L-Drive lower assembly, apply a suitable contact adhesive to the transom plate

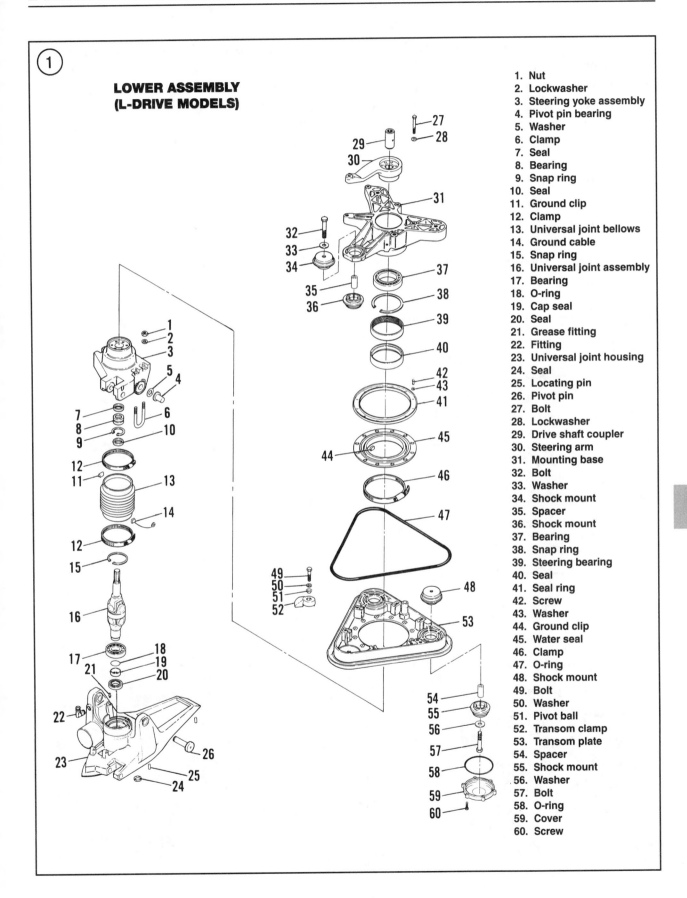

**LOWER ASSEMBLY
(L-DRIVE MODELS)**

1. Nut
2. Lockwasher
3. Steering yoke assembly
4. Pivot pin bearing
5. Washer
6. Clamp
7. Seal
8. Bearing
9. Snap ring
10. Seal
11. Ground clip
12. Clamp
13. Universal joint bellows
14. Ground cable
15. Snap ring
16. Universal joint assembly
17. Bearing
18. O-ring
19. Cap seal
20. Seal
21. Grease fitting
22. Fitting
23. Universal joint housing
24. Seal
25. Locating pin
26. Pivot pin
27. Bolt
28. Lockwasher
29. Drive shaft coupler
30. Steering arm
31. Mounting base
32. Bolt
33. Washer
34. Shock mount
35. Spacer
36. Shock mount
37. Bearing
38. Snap ring
39. Steering bearing
40. Seal
41. Seal ring
42. Screw
43. Washer
44. Ground clip
45. Water seal
46. Clamp
47. O-ring
48. Shock mount
49. Bolt
50. Washer
51. Pivot ball
52. Transom clamp
53. Transom plate
54. Spacer
55. Shock mount
56. Washer
57. Bolt
58. O-ring
59. Cover
60. Screw

10

at the locations shown in **Figure 5**. Install a *new* transom plate O-ring. Make sure the O-ring is held firmly in place by the contact adhesive.

10. Connect a lifting chain at the points shown in **Figure 4**. Using a hoist, lift the assembly into place in the boat transom.

11. Apply Loctite 271 to the threads of the transom clamp bolts. Install the bolts and tighten to specification (**Table 1**).

12. Disconnect the hoist and remove the lifting chain.

13. Reconnect the power trim/tilt hydraulic lines (**Figure 3**).

14. Using alcohol, thoroughly clean the inside diameter of the exhaust bellows and the bellows mounting surface of the universal joint housing. Install the exhaust bellows to the universal joint housing. Tighten the bellows clamps (**Figure 2**) to specification (**Table 1**).

15. Install the gearcase assembly. See Chapter Nine.

16. Install the power head. See Chapter Eight.

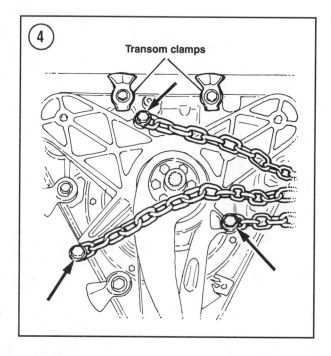

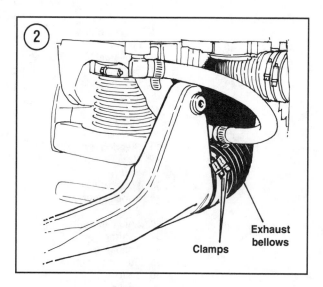

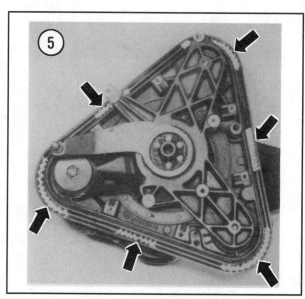

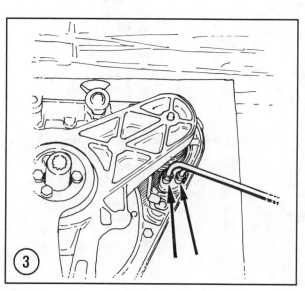

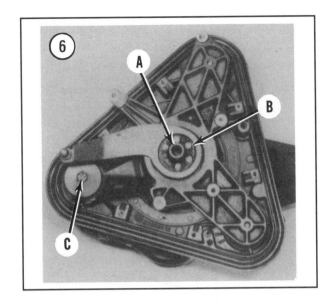

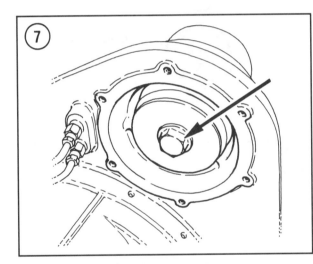

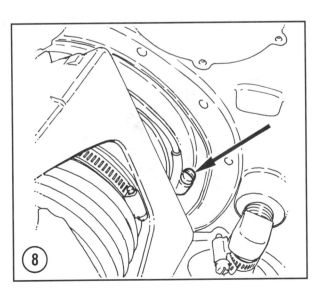

Servicing Shock Mounts and Mounting Base

It is not necessary to remove the lower assembly from the boat to inspect or replace the transom plate and mounting base shock mounts; however, it will be necessary to support the assembly with blocks during shock mount service.

Refer to **Figure 1** for this procedure.

1. Remove the power head. See Chapter Eight.

2. Remove the drive shaft coupler (A, **Figure 6**).

3. Remove the 5 bolts (B, **Figure 6**) and washers securing the steering arm to the steering yoke. Remove the steering arm.

4. Remove the shock mount bolt (C, **Figure 6**) and washer from the mount base.

5. Remove the screws securing the 2 transom plate shock mount covers. Remove the covers (59, **Figure 1**) and discard the cover O-rings (58).

6. Remove the 2 transom plate shock mount bolts and washers. See **Figure 7**.

7. Loosen the transom plate water seal clamp (**Figure 8**).

8. Attach a lifting chain to the mounting base (A, **Figure 9**) and lift off the transom plate (B). If

10

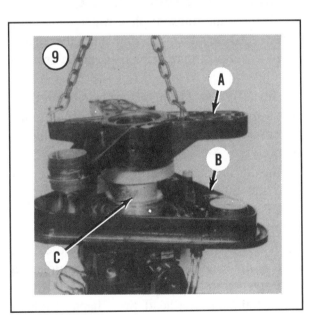

necessary, tap lightly around the steering yoke (C, **Figure 9**) to dislodge the mounting base.

9. Inspect the shock mounts for excessive wear, cracking or other damage.

10. If replacement is necessary, pry the upper and lower shock mounts from the transom plate or mounting base. Remove the spacer. See **Figure 10**.

11. Thoroughly clean all sealant from each side of the transom plate or mounting base.

12. Apply RTV sealant onto the mating surfaces of each shock mount. Install the lower shock mount and spacer, then install the upper shock mount. See **Figure 10**.

13. Prior to installing the mounting base, replace the transom plate water seal as described in this chapter.

14. If necessary, service the mounting base bearings and seal as described in this chapter.

15. To reassemble, make sure the grounding clip is in place as shown in **Figure 11**.

16. Lubricate the transom plate water seal and the sealing surface of the mounting base with a soap and water solution. Position mounting base as shown (**Figure 11**) and lower into place.

17. Apply Loctite 271 onto the threads of the shock mount bolts. Install the bolts and washers and tighten to specification (**Table 1**).

18. Tighten the transom plate water seal clamp (**Figure 8**) securely, making sure the clamp screw is *not* positioned directly over the grounding clip.

19. Install a new O-ring on each transom plate shock mount cover. Apply Loctite 242 onto the cover screws. Install the cover screws and tighten securely.

20. Install the steering arm. Apply Loctite 271 onto the threads of the steering arm screws. Install the screws and washers and tighten to specification (**Table 1**).

21. Apply 2-4-C multilube grease onto the drive shaft coupler splines and install the coupler on the universal joint shaft.

22. Install the power head. See Chapter Eight.

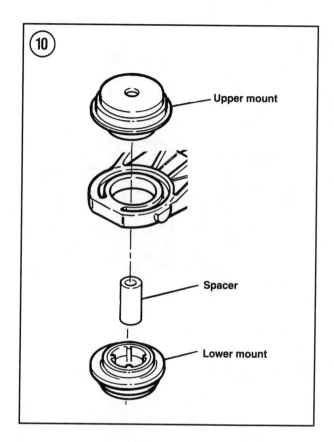

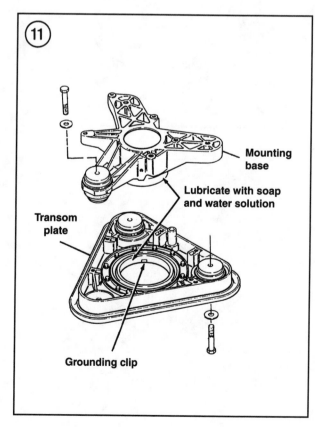

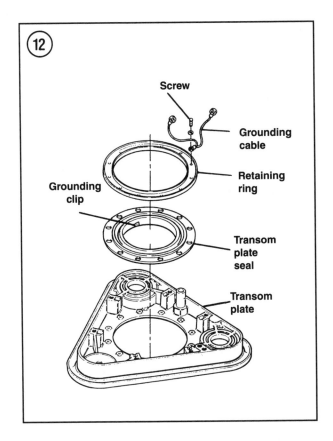

⑫

Screw

Grounding cable

Retaining ring

Grounding clip

Transom plate seal

Transom plate

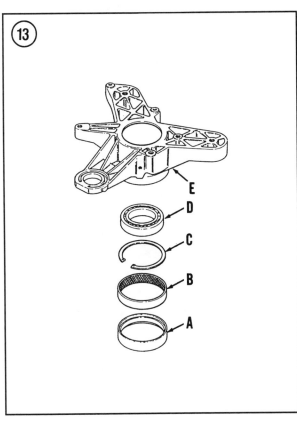

⑬

E
D
C
B
A

Replacing Transom Plate Water Seal

Refer to **Figure 1** for this procedure.

1. Remove the lower assembly mounting base as described in *Servicing Shock Mounts and Mounting Base*.

2. Remove the screws securing the water seal retaining ring to the transom plate. Remove the retaining ring and transom plate seal. See **Figure 12**.

3. Installation is the reverse of removal plus the following:

   a. Install a *new* grounding clip at the location shown in **Figure 12**.

   b. Install a *new* grounding cable at the location shown in **Figure 12**.

   c. Apply Loctite 242 onto the threads of the seal retaining ring screws. Install the screws and washers and tighten securely.

   d. Reinstall the mounting base as described in this chapter.

Servicing the Mounting Base

Refer to **Figure 1** for this procedure.

1. Remove the mounting base as described in *Servicing Shock Mounts and Mounting Base*.

2. Remove seal (A, **Figure 13**) and steering bearing (B) from the mounting base (E).

3. Remove snap ring (C, **Figure 13**).

4. Remove bearing (D, **Figure 13**) from the mounting base (E).

5. Inspect the bearings for excessive wear or other damage and replace as required.

6. Thoroughly clean the bearing bore of the mounting base.

7. To reassemble the mounting base, apply Loctite RC680 onto the mounting base inner diameter.

8. Lubricate the bearing (D, **Figure 13**) with 2-4-C multilube grease. Press the bearing into the mounting base until seated. Press on the bearing outer race only.

10

9. Install the snap ring into the mounting base. Make certain the flat surface of the snap ring is facing the bearing (D, **Figure 13**).

10. Apply Loctite RC680 onto the steering bearing bore in the mounting base.

11. Using a suitable piston ring compressor, compress the steering bearing. Position the steering bearing with the gap facing rearward and press into the mounting base until seated. Lubricate the steering bearing with 2-4-C multilube grease.

12. Install a new seal (A, **Figure 13**) into the mounting base with the seal lip facing away from the steering bearing.

13. Install the mounting base as described in this chapter.

Steering Yoke Removal/Installation

Refer to **Figure 1** for this procedure.

1. Remove gearcase assembly. See Chapter Nine.

2. Remove the power head. See Chapter Eight.

3. Remove the L-Drive lower assembly as described in this chapter.

4. Remove the mounting base as described in *Servicing the Shock Mounts and Mounting Base*.

5. Label the trim/tilt hydraulic lines (**Figure 14**) for reference during reassembly. Disconnect and plug the lines to prevent leakage or contamination.

6. Disconnect the water inlet hose from the transom plate and universal joint housing.

7. Remove the transom plate from the steering yoke.

8. Disconnect the grounding cable from the tilt cylinder, steering yoke and universal joint housing (**Figure 15**).

9. Remove the tilt cylinder. See Chapter Twelve.

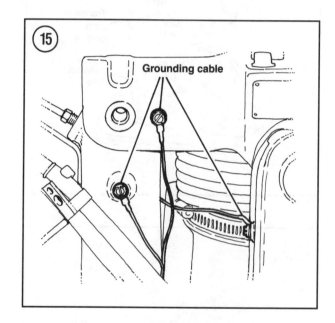

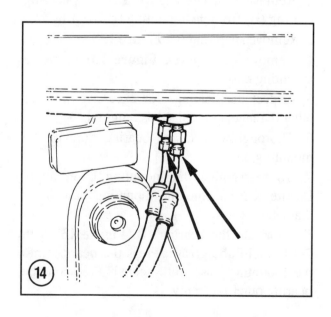

10. Loosen the steering yoke nuts (A, **Figure 16**).

11. Loosen the universal joint bellows clamp (A, **Figure 17**).

12. Remove snap rings and washers (B, **Figure 17**).

13. To remove the pivot pins, thread a nut onto an appropriate size bolt as shown in **Figure 18**. Place a flat washer on the bolt, then insert the bolt and nut through a suitable socket or piece of pipe as shown. Thread the bolt into the pivot pin, then turn the nut clockwise while holding the

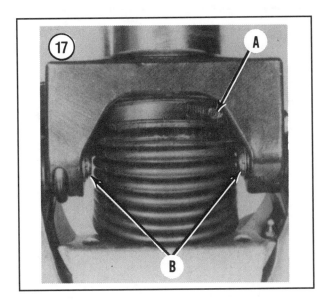

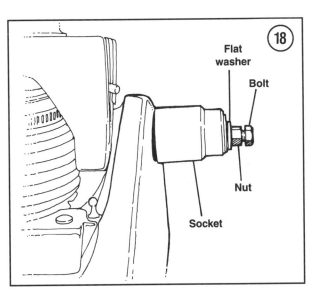

bolt to extract the pivot pin from the steering yoke and universal joint housing.

14. Repeat Step 13 to remove the remaining pivot pin. Lift the steering yoke off the universal joint housing.

15. To reinstall, place the steering yoke into position on the universal joint housing. Tap the pivot pins into position using a rubber mallet.

16. Install the washers and *new* snap rings (B, **Figure 17**) on the inner end of the pivot pins. Make sure the sharp edge of the snap rings face inward (toward bellows).

17. Slide the bellows onto the steering yoke and tighten the clamp (A, **Figure 17**). Make sure the clamp screw is not directly over the bellows grounding clip.

18. Tighten the steering yoke clamp nuts (A, **Figure 16**) evenly to specification (**Table 1**).

19. Install the tilt cylinder. See Chapter Twelve.

20. Connect a *new* grounding cable as shown in **Figure 15**.

21. Install the transom plate on the steering yoke.

22. Connect the water inlet hose to the transom plate.

23. Connect the trim/tilt hydraulic lines to the bottom fittings of the transom plate.

24. Reinstall the lower assembly as described in this chapter.

25. Install the power head. See Chapter Eight.

26. Install the gearcase. See Chapter Nine.

Steering Yoke Disassembly and Reassembly

Refer to **Figure 19** for this procedure.

1. Pry out the steering yoke lower seal (A).

2. Remove the snap ring (B).

3. Remove the bearing (C).

4. Remove the upper seal (D).

5. Inspect the bearings and steering yoke for excessive wear or other damage. Replace as required.

6. To reassemble, press a new upper seal (D, **Figure 19**) into the steering yoke with the seal lip facing the bottom of the yoke. Pack the seal with bearing assembly compound (**Table 2**).

7. Press the bearing (C, **Figure 19**) into the steering yoke until seated against the seal. Pack the bearing with bearing assembly compound (**Table 2**).

8. Install the snap ring (B, **Figure 19**) using snap ring pliers. Make sure the flat surface of the snap ring faces away from the bearing (C, **Figure 19**).

9. Place a new lower seal (A, **Figure 19**) into the steering yoke with the seal lip facing the bottom of the yoke. Press seal into the yoke until seated against the snap ring. Pack the seal with bearing assembly compound (**Table 2**).

Universal Joint Assembly and Universal Joint Housing Removal/Installation

1. Remove the steering yoke as described in this chapter.

2. Using snap ring pliers (part No. FT-11282) or equivalent, remove the universal joint assembly snap ring (**Figure 20**).

3. Pull the universal joint assembly up and out of the universal joint housing.

4. Remove and discard the water tube seal from the gearcase side of the universal joint housing (**Figure 21**).

5. Remove and discard the universal joint housing seal (**Figure 22**).

6. Remove the pivot pin bearings from the pivot pin holes in the universal joint housing to complete disassembly.

7. Thoroughly clean all components in solvent and dry with compressed air.

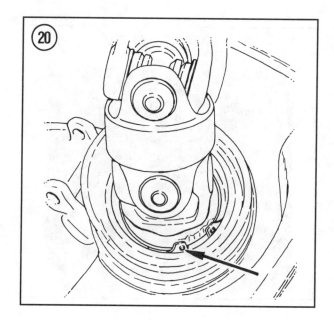

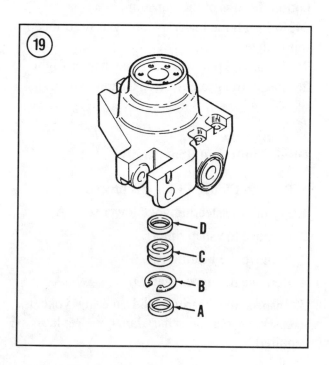

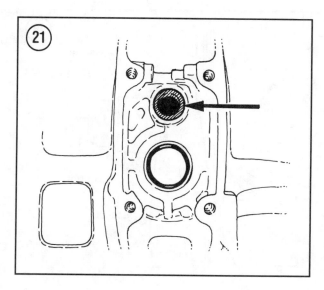

8. Inspect the universal joint housing for excessive wear, cracks or other damage. Replace the housing as required.

9. Inspect the universal joint assembly for binding, excessive wear or other damage. Inspect the universal joint bearing for binding, excessive wear, rust or other damage. Replace as required. Inspect the universal joint bellows for dryness,

cracks, tears or other damage and replace the bellows as necessary.

> *NOTE*
> *The universal joint assembly has conventional grease zerks on some models, while other models will require a needle adapter (part No. FT-11274) to lubricate the universal joints. Use 2-4-C multilube grease.*

10. Lubricate the universal joints using a grease gun or grease gun with needle point adapter.

11. If removed, thoroughly clean all oil or grease from the seal cap (**Figure 23**) and the seal cap area of the universal joint assembly. Apply Loctite RC680 to the inside diameter of the seal cap and press onto the universal joint.

12. Press the universal joint bearing (**Figure 23**) onto the joint assembly until seated.

13. Install a *new* O-ring onto the seal cap.

14. Reassembly and reinstallation is the reverse of disassembly, plus the following.

15. Install a *new* universal joint seal (**Figure 22**) with the seal lip facing down.

16. Install a *new* water tube seal (**Figure 21**).

17. Pack the universal joint housing with 2-4-C grease. Press the universal joint assembly into place in the housing, then install a *new* snap ring (**Figure 20**) using snap ring pliers (part No. FT-11282) or equivalent.

18. Make sure the grounding clips are installed on the universal joint bellows. Tighten the bellows clamps to specification (**Table 1**).

19. Install the steering yoke as described in this chapter.

EXHAUST SYSTEM

Disassembly/Reassembly

Refer to **Figure 24** for an exploded view of the exhaust system used on the 1989 A L-Drive models. The exhaust system used on later models is similar.

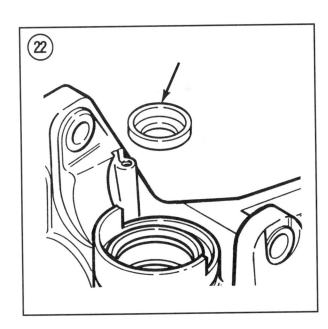

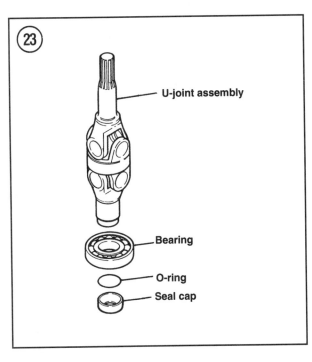

10

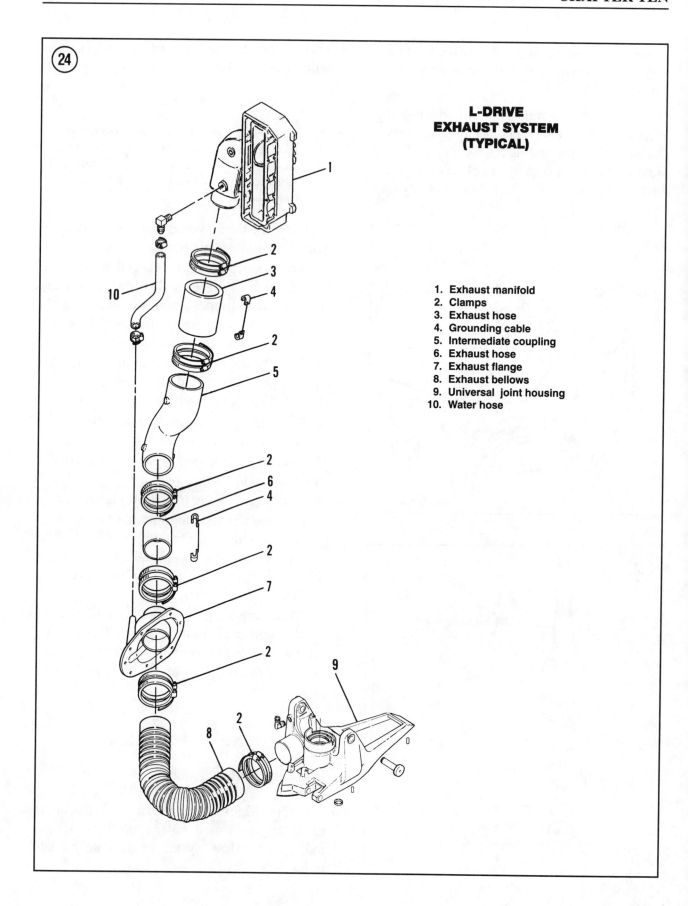

(24)

**L-DRIVE
EXHAUST SYSTEM
(TYPICAL)**

1. Exhaust manifold
2. Clamps
3. Exhaust hose
4. Grounding cable
5. Intermediate coupling
6. Exhaust hose
7. Exhaust flange
8. Exhaust bellows
9. Universal joint housing
10. Water hose

The power head requires removal to service exhaust components that are located inside the hull of the boat, including the exhaust flange.

1. Remove the power head. See Chapter Eight.

2. Loosen the clamps and remove the exhaust hose (3, **Figure 24**) from the intermediate coupling.

3. Loosen the clamps and remove the intermediate coupling (5, **Figure 24**).

4. Loosen the clamps and remove exhaust hose (6) from the exhaust flange.

5. To remove the exhaust flange, loosen the clamp and remove the water hose from the flange. Remove the flange mounting screws and remove the flange.

6. Inspect all hoses for excessive wear, dryness or other damage. Replace hoses as necessary.

Inspect the exhaust flange, intermediate coupler, clamps and grounding cables for rust, corrosion or damage and replace as necessary.

7. To reassemble the exhaust system, apply a suitable marine sealant to the exhaust flange-to-hull mating surface. Make sure the sealant surrounds each screw hole. Install the flange to the hull and tighten the screws securely.

8. Clean the mating surfaces of the exhaust bellows, exhaust flange and universal joint housing with alcohol.

9. Reassemble the exhaust system by reversing the disassembly procedure while noting the following:

    a. Tighten the exhaust hose and bellows clamps to specification (**Table 1**).

CAUTION
*After tightening the clamps (C, **Figure 25**), be certain the clamps do not rub on the water inlet hose during turns. Position the clamp screws so they do not contact the water hose.*

    b. Be sure the grounding cables are properly positioned. The grounding clips should not be located directly under the clamp screws.

NOTE
If a problem with the exhaust bellows slipping off the exhaust flange is noted, clean the flange and bellows mating surfaces thoroughly with alcohol, then install the bellows and tighten the clamps to 150 in.-lb. (17 N•m). Next, drill a small hole between the bellows clamps and install a self-tapping stainless steel screw to secure the bellows.

10

Tables 1 and 2 are on the following page.

Table 1 L-DRIVE SYSTEM TIGHTENING TORQUES*

Fastener	in.-lb.	ft.-lb.
Exhaust bellows clamps	150	—
Exhaust hose clamps	150	—
Shock mount bolts	—	55
Steering arm screws	—	25
Water hose clamps	55	—
Steering yoke clamp nuts	—	25
Transom clamp screws	—	25
Standard screws		
6-32	9	—
8-32	20	—
10-24	30	—
10-32	35	—
12-24	45	—
1/4-20	70	—
5/15-18	160	—
3/8-16	270	—

*Use standard torque value if the specific fastener is not listed.

Table 2 RECOMMENDED LUBRICANTS, SEALANTS AND ADHESIVES

	Part Number
Lubricants	
Quicksilver Premium 2-Cycle TC-W3 outboard oil	(normal dealer stock item)
Quicksilver Special Lubricant 101	92-13872A-1
Quicksilver 2-4-C Multi-Lube	(normal dealer stock item in various sizes)
Quicksilver Anti-Corrosion Grease	92-78376A-6
Quicksilver Needle Bearing Grease	92-825265A-1
Quicksilver Power Trim and Steering Fluid	92-90100A12
Quicksilver Premium Blend Gearcase Lubricant	(normal dealer stock item)
Sealants	
Quicksilver Perfect Seal	92-34227-11
Loctite 5900 Ultra black RTV sealant	92-809826
Sealer (crankcase halves)	92-90113–2
Loctite Master Gasket Sealer	92-12564–2
Quicksilver Liquid Neoprene	92-25711–2
Loctite 567 PST pipe sealant	92-809822
Quicksilver Bellows Adhesive	92-86166–1
Adhesives	
Loquic Primer	92-809824
Loctite 271 threadlocking sealant (high strength)	92-809819
Loctite 242 threadlocking sealant (medium strength)	92-809821
Loctite RC680 high strength retaining compound	92-809833
Miscellaneous	
Quicksilver Power Tune Engine Cleaner	92-15104A12
Quicksilver Corrosion Guard	92-815869A12
Quicksilver Storage Seal Rust Inhibitor	92-86145A12

Chapter Eleven

Manual Rewind Starters

All 4-15 hp models and 25 hp 3-cylinder models are equipped with rope-operated rewind starter. On models with an integral fuel tank, the starter assembly is mounted on the power head and attached to the fuel tank. Models without an integral fuel tank may have the starter bracket-mounted to the front of the power head or mounted in a housing above the flywheel.

Pulling the rope handle causes the starter spindle or spool shaft to rotate against spring tension, moving the drive pawl(s) or pinion gear to engage the flywheel to turn the engine. When the rope handle is released, the spring inside the assembly reverses direction of the spindle or spool shaft and rewinds the rope around the pulley or spool.

A starter interlock feature is used on all models without an integral fuel tank. The interlock prevents operation of the rewind starter unless the shift lever is in the NEUTRAL position.

Rewind starters are relatively trouble free, with a broken or frayed rope the most common failure. This chapter covers rewind starter and rope/rewind spring service.

ENGINE COVER STARTER

4 hp and Early 5 hp

This starter is used on all models equipped with an integral fuel tank. See **Figure 1** (starter removed).

Removal/Installation

1. Disconnect the spark plug lead to prevent accidental starting.
2. Pry the retainer from the starter rope handle. Remove the rope from the retainer and pull the rope through the engine cover hole. Tie a suitable knot in the rope to prevent it from winding into the starter.
3. Remove the fuel tank cap. Remove the upper engine cover. Reinstall the fuel tank fill cap.

4. Remove the 4 nuts and lockwashers holding the starter assembly to the fuel tank (**Figure 2**). Lift the starter off the fuel tank.

5. Installation is the reverse of removal. Pull the starter rope to engage the friction shoes with the starter cup prior to tightening the mounting nuts.

Starter Rope and Rewind Spring Replacement

WARNING
Disassembling this starter mechanism without holding the rewind spring securely in place can result in the spring unwinding violently, resulting in serious personal injury. Wear safety glasses and gloves during this procedure.

1. Invert the starter housing on a flat surface.

2. Remove the screw and washer securing the friction shoe assembly (**Figure 3**).

3. Remove the 2 shoe plates, the brake cover and 2 springs, the conical brake spring, washer and bearing.

4. Untie the knot in the rope and allow the rope pulley to unwind slowly.

5A. If the spring is good but the rope requires replacement, carefully lift one edge of the rope pulley, insert a thin screwdriver blade under it and disengage the spring loop from the pulley slot. Remove the pulley and rope.

5B. If the rewind spring requires replacement, place the starter assembly on the floor (right side up) and gently tap on the top of the housing. The spring will drop out of the housing and unwind inside the housing. Remove and discard the spring.

6. Check the pulley bore bearing, brake spring and friction shoes for excessive wear. Replace as

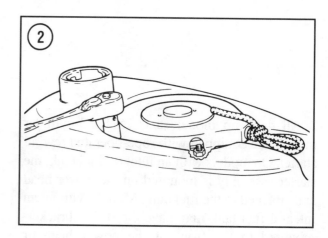

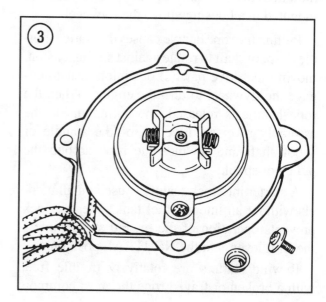

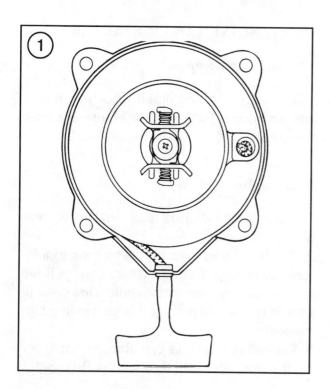

necessary. If the shoe edges are not sharp, dress them with a file.

7. Tie a knot in one end of the new starter rope. Insert the rope through the pulley hole, then fold the rope end over and pull into the pulley recess to lock the rope in place. Wind the rope counterclockwise (**Figure 4**).

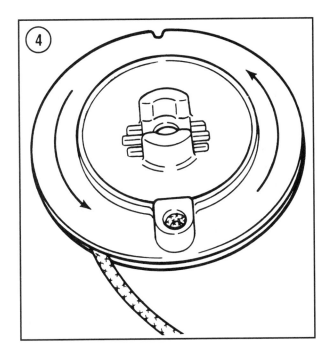

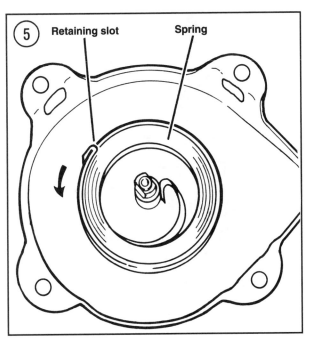

8. If a new rewind spring is being installed, place it in the housing. Align the outer loop with the housing retaining slot (**Figure 5**) and remove the spring retainer carefully to prevent it from ejecting from the housing.

9. Lubricate the pulley shaft bore with a suitable water-resistant grease. Carefully insert the pulley into the housing, engaging the looped end of the rewind spring with the pulley slot.

10. Insert the loose end of the rope into the slot located on the outer edge of the pulley. Turn the pulley counterclockwise 3 full turns to preload the spring.

11. While holding the pulley to maintain spring tension, insert the rope end through the housing rope guide hole and tie a large slip knot to secure the rope in place.

12. Pull the rope out as far as possible and hold in that position, then attempt to rotate the pulley counterclockwise. If it will not turn at least an addition 1/8 to 3/8 of turn, the spring is bottomed out. In this case, carefully disassemble the starter and repeat the reassembly procedure.

13. Insert the pulley bearing into the bore, then place the washer and brake spring on the pulley shaft. Install the shoe plates, springs and lever on the pulley as shown in **Figure 6**. Install the screw and washer and tighten securely.

14. Install the starter as described in this chapter.

11

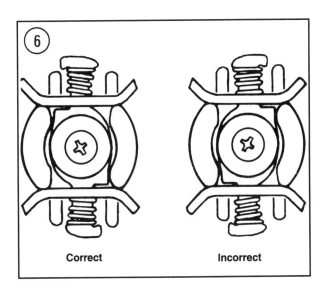

Correct   Incorrect

SPOOL STARTER

7.5, 9.9 and 15 hp (1984-1986)

This starter is bracket-mounted to the power head. The starter rope is wound around a spring-loaded spool. A pinion gear at the top of the spool (**Figure 7**) engages the flywheel when the rope is pulled. A neutral interlock bracket and link connected to the pinion gear prevents the engine from being started while in gear. **Figure 8** and **Figure 9** identify the starter components.

Starter Pinion Gear and Rewind Spring Removal/Installation

1. Remove the engine cover.

2. Remove the flywheel. See Chapter Eight.

3. Hold a punch against the pinion gear pin and remove the starter spring arbor screw.

4. Push the pinion gear pin 1/2 way out of the gear.

5. Install the rewind key (**Table 1**) in place of the screw removed in Step 3.

6. Hold the rewind key to prevent the starter spring from unwinding abruptly, then remove the pinion gear pin. Use the rewind key to allow the rewind spring to unwind slowly, then remove the key and starter spring arbor from the spool shaft. Remove the key from the arbor.

7. Remove the pinion gear and slide the pinion spring off the gear.

8. Remove the rewind spring, spring retainer and spring end from the spool.

9. Lightly lubricate the inner and outer diameter of the rewind spring and the inner diameter and groove of the pinion gear with a suitable water-resistant grease.

10. Insert the arbor shaft into the rewind spring. The shaft groove should engage the spring end.

11. Install the arbor and spring assembly into the spool shaft. Align the spring end notch with the pin in the lower starter bracket.

12. Install the pinion spring into the pinion gear groove.

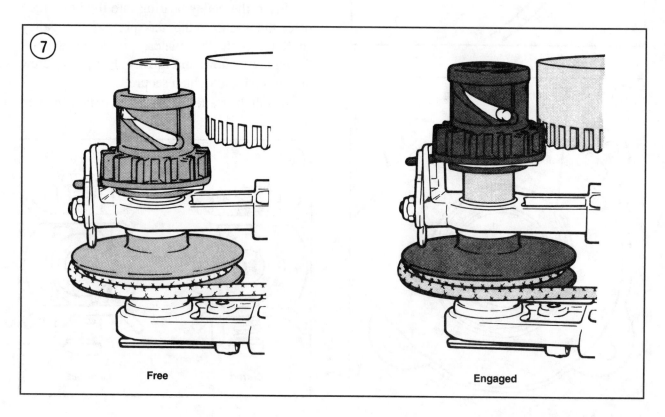

⑦

Free

Engaged

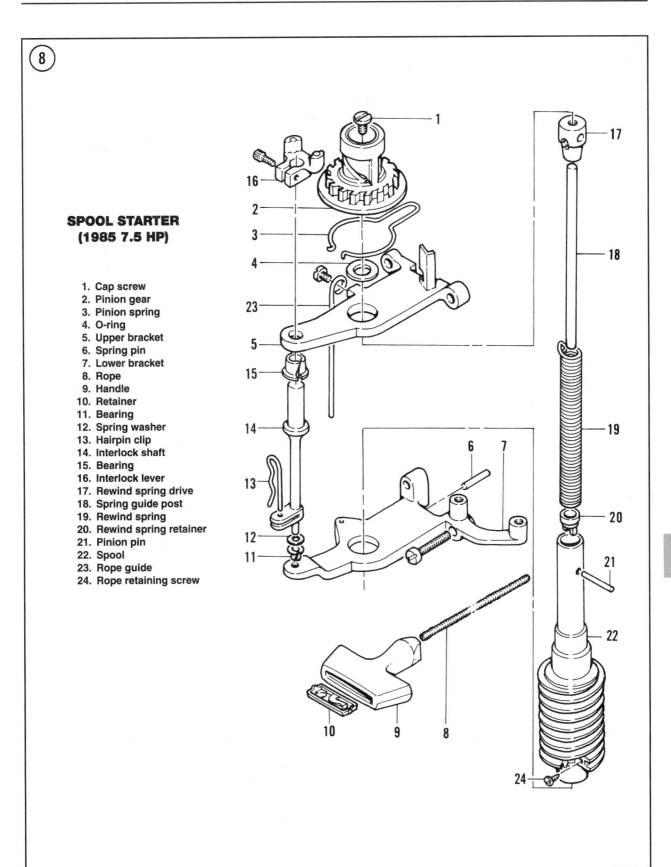

**SPOOL STARTER
(1985 7.5 HP)**

1. Cap screw
2. Pinion gear
3. Pinion spring
4. O-ring
5. Upper bracket
6. Spring pin
7. Lower bracket
8. Rope
9. Handle
10. Retainer
11. Bearing
12. Spring washer
13. Hairpin clip
14. Interlock shaft
15. Bearing
16. Interlock lever
17. Rewind spring drive
18. Spring guide post
19. Rewind spring
20. Rewind spring retainer
21. Pinion pin
22. Spool
23. Rope guide
24. Rope retaining screw

11

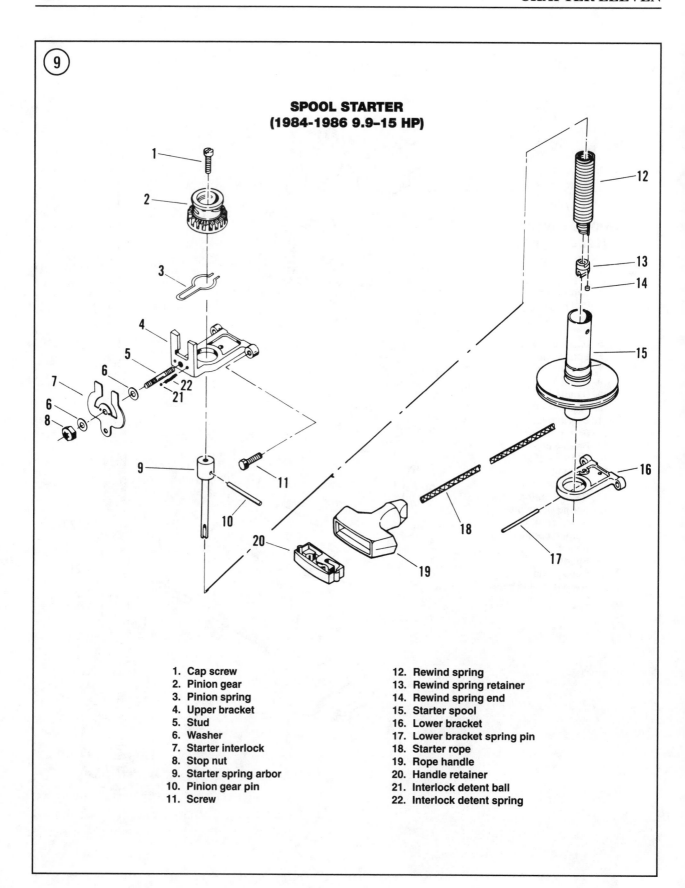

**SPOOL STARTER
(1984-1986 9.9–15 HP)**

1. Cap screw
2. Pinion gear
3. Pinion spring
4. Upper bracket
5. Stud
6. Washer
7. Starter interlock
8. Stop nut
9. Starter spring arbor
10. Pinion gear pin
11. Screw
12. Rewind spring
13. Rewind spring retainer
14. Rewind spring end
15. Starter spool
16. Lower bracket
17. Lower bracket spring pin
18. Starter rope
19. Rope handle
20. Handle retainer
21. Interlock detent ball
22. Interlock detent spring

13. Place the pinion gear on the spool shaft with the spring loop protruding through the starter bracket slot.

14. Install the rewind key (**Table 1**) into the tapped hole of the rewind spring arbor.

15. Align the pin slot in the gear with the pin holes in the spool shaft and spring arbor. Insert the pinion gear pin through the gear slot and partially into the spool shaft and arbor pin holes. Hold the end of the pinion pin and tighten the rewind key on the end of the arbor.

16. Remove the pin and turn the rope spool to remove all slack. Turn the rewind key counterclockwise until the spring tension just begins to be felt. At this point, continue rewinding to the specification in **Table 1**.

17. Align the gear slot and pin holes. Insert the pin partially as in Step 15. Hold the end of the pin and remove the rewind key. Install the pin completely. Be sure the pin is centered in the gear.

18. Install the cap screw to retain the pin.

19. Install the flywheel. See Chapter Eight.

20. Install the engine cover.

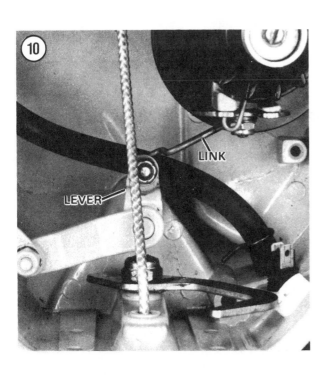

Starter Spool and Rope Removal/Installation

1. Remove the engine cover.

2. Pry the rope handle retainer free and remove the rope from the retainer.

3. Remove the pinion gear and rewind spring as described in this chapter.

4. *9.9 and 15 hp*—Remove the stop nut, washer and 2 O-rings holding the interlock connecting link to the gear shift shaft lever. See **Figure 10**

5. *7.5 hp*—Remove the cotter clip from the interlock linkage and separate the link. Remove the interlock lever retaining screw. Remove the interlock lever. See 16, **Figure 8**.

6. Remove the upper bracket screws. Remove the upper bracket and interlock assembly.

7. *9.9 and 15 hp*—Hold the upper bracket upright and remove the stop nut. Remove the interlock, 2 washers, interlock link, 2 detent balls and 2 springs from the bracket. See **Figure 9**.

8. Remove the starter spool from the power head.

9. Unwind and remove the rope from the spool.

10. Install the end of a new rope through the spool hole and pull it through until about 3/16 in. of the rope end is exposed in the spool. Install and tighten the screw.

11. Wind the rope counterclockwise (as viewed from the top of the spool) around the spool grooves.

12. Lightly lubricate the spool bore with a suitable grease. Install the spool into the lower bracket.

13. Route the rope around the rope pulley on the manifold and through the support plate grommet.

14. Install the rope into the handle retainer. Install the retainer into the handle.

15. *7.5 hp*—Assemble the interlock shaft, spring washer and both bearings. Lubricate the bearings and shaft friction points with a suitable grease. Install the interlock shaft assembly to the lower bracket.

11

16. Position the upper bracket on the spool shaft. Install the upper bracket and spool shaft assembly to the engine and tighten the screws securely.

17. *9.9 and 15 hp*—Reassemble and install the interlock assembly onto the upper bracket. Connect the interlock link onto the shift lever (**Figure 10**).

18. *7.5 hp*—Install the interlock lever on top of the interlock shaft with the ears pointing up and towards the pinion gear. Shift the engine into NEUTRAL.

19. *7.5 hp*—Push and hold the interlock shaft down to compress the spring washer in the lower bracket. Pull up and hold the starter spool shaft to remove all end play.

20. *7.5 hp*—Adjust the interlock lever so that there is a .020 in. (0.51 mm) clearance between the lower edge of the ears on the interlock lever and the top of the pinion gear flange. Align the curved edge between the ears of the interlock lever to align with the outside diameter of the pinion gear flange.

21. *7.5 hp*—Tighten the interlock lever locking screw securely.

22. Check the operation of the interlock system. Shift the engine into both FORWARD and

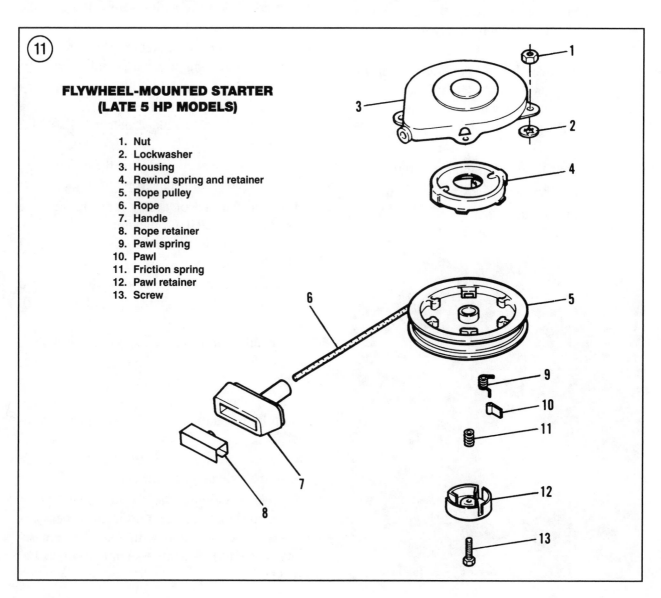

FLYWHEEL-MOUNTED STARTER (LATE 5 HP MODELS)

1. Nut
2. Lockwasher
3. Housing
4. Rewind spring and retainer
5. Rope pulley
6. Rope
7. Handle
8. Rope retainer
9. Pawl spring
10. Pawl
11. Friction spring
12. Pawl retainer
13. Screw

REVERSE. Pull the starter rope in both locations. The pinion gear should not engage the flywheel when the gear shift is in FORWARD or REVERSE. Shift into NEUTRAL. Pull the starter rope. The interlock system must allow the pinion to engage the flywheel when the gear shift is in NEUTRAL.

23. *9.9 and 15 hp*—To adjust the interlock system, disconnect the gear shift lever and shift rod. Rotate the shift rod connector on the rod as required. Reconnect the rod to the lever and retest Step 22.

24. *7.5 hp*—To adjust the interlock system, loosen the interlock lever locking screw and shift the engine into NEUTRAL. Readjust Steps 19-21 as required and recheck Step 22.

FLYWHEEL-MOUNTED STARTER

Rope and Rewind Spring Replacement (Late 5 hp Models)

Refer to **Figure 11** for this procedure.
1. Remove the engine cover.
2. Disconnect the spark plug lead to prevent accidental starting.
3. Remove the nuts securing the starter assembly to the power head. Lift the starter off the power head.
4. Invert the starter, remove the screw securing the pawl retainer. Remove the pawl retainer.
5. Remove the starter pawls, pawl springs and friction spring from the rope pulley.
6. While holding the rope pulley securely, remove the rope handle, then allow the pulley to unwind slowly, relieving rewind spring tension.

WARNING
Remove the rope pulley and rewind spring carefully to prevent the spring from unwinding violently and causing personal injury. Wear safety glasses and gloves during starter disassembly.

7. Remove the rope and pulley from the housing.

NOTE
If only the rope is to be replaced, do not remove the rewind spring and retainer assembly as described in Step 8.

8. Lift the rewind spring and retainer out of the housing. *Do not* attempt to remove the rewind spring from its retainer. Replacement rewind spring comes assembled in a new retainer.
9. Thoroughly clean the starter pawls and inspect for excessive wear. The engagement edge of the pawls must be sharp. Replace the pawls as necessary.
10. Inspect the springs and replace if worn or bent.
11. Inspect the starter pulley and replace if excessively worn, cracked or broken.
12. New rope should be 53 in. long. Insert the rope through the hole in the rope pulley and secure with a suitable knot. Wind the rope onto the pulley in a counterclockwise direction as viewed from the bottom of the pulley.
13. Thoroughly lubricate the rewind spring with a suitable water-resistant grease. Install the rewind spring assembly on the rope pulley. Make sure the spring properly engages the slots in the rope pulley.
14. Lubricate the inside diameter of the rope pulley bore with water-resistant grease. Install the pulley assembly into the starter housing.
15. Install the friction spring, pawl springs and pawls into the rope pulley.
16. Install the pawl retainer onto the pulley. Apply Loctite 222 onto the threads of the pawl retainer screw. Install the screw and tighten securely.
17. While holding the handle end of the rope, rotate the rope pulley 2 full turns in a counterclockwise direction. Hold the pulley in this position and insert the rope through the rope guide in the housing, then install the rope handle.
18. Check the rewind spring tension by fully extending the rope. The rope pulley should be able to rotate an additional 1/8 to 3/8 turn counterclockwise with the rope fully pulled out.

11

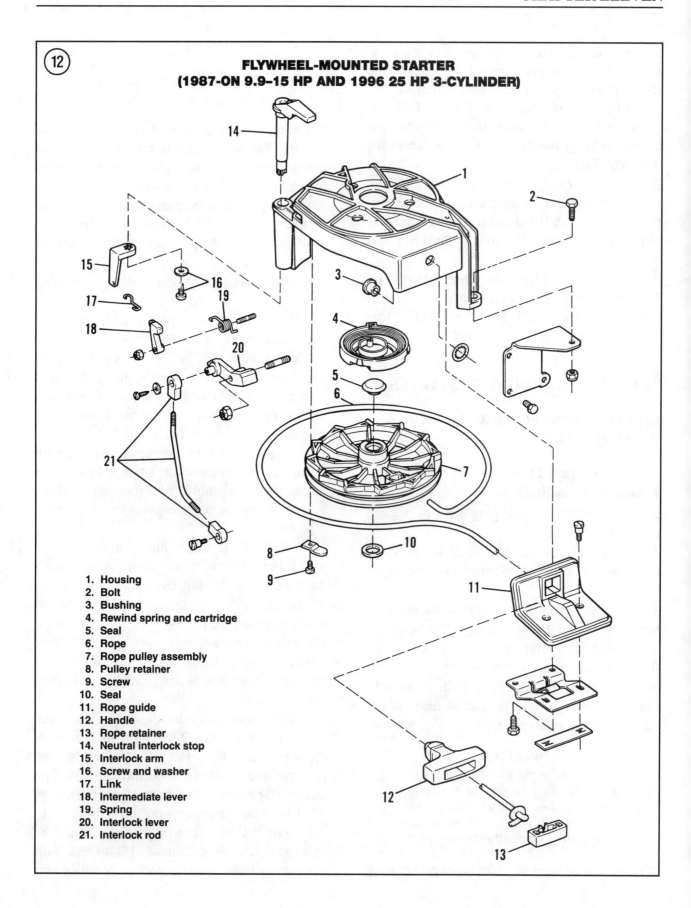

⑫ **FLYWHEEL-MOUNTED STARTER**
(1987-ON 9.9–15 HP AND 1996 25 HP 3-CYLINDER)

1. Housing
2. Bolt
3. Bushing
4. Rewind spring and cartridge
5. Seal
6. Rope
7. Rope pulley assembly
8. Pulley retainer
9. Screw
10. Seal
11. Rope guide
12. Handle
13. Rope retainer
14. Neutral interlock stop
15. Interlock arm
16. Screw and washer
17. Link
18. Intermediate lever
19. Spring
20. Interlock lever
21. Interlock rod

If not, remove some of the tension from the rewind spring to prevent spring breakage.

19. Install the starter assembly on the power head.

Starter Rope and Rewind Spring Replacement (1987-on 9.9-15 hp and 1996 25 hp 3-cylinder)

Refer to **Figure 12** for this procedure.

1. Remove the engine cover.

2. Disconnect the spark plug leads to prevent accidental starting.

3. Remove the 3 screws and 1 nut holding the starting housing to the power head. Do not loose the spacers located in each mounting hole.

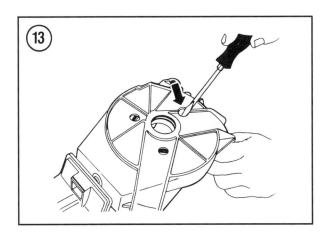

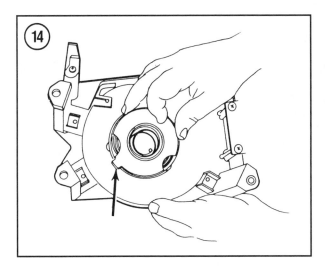

4. Lift the starter assembly off the power head then tilt it forward to disconnect the neutral interlock link from the intermediate lever.

5. Pry the rope retainer from the rope handle. While firmly holding the pulley, remove the rope retainer and handle, then allow the pulley to unwind slowly, relieving the rewind spring tension.

> *WARNING*
> *Remove the rope pulley and rewind spring carefully to prevent the spring from unwinding violently and causing personal injury. Wear safety glasses and gloves during starter disassembly.*

6. Invert the starter assembly and remove the 3 pulley retainers. Lift the rope pulley with the rope from the housing.

> *NOTE*
> *If the rewind spring does not require replacement, do not remove it during Step 7.*

7. Remove the rewind spring and cartridge assembly by pushing out with a screwdriver through the hole provided in the housing (**Figure 13**). *Do not* remove the rewind spring from the cartridge. The replacement spring comes assembled in a new cartridge.

8. Thoroughly clean and inspect all components for excessive wear or other damage.

9. Insert a new rope through the hole in the pulley and secure with a knot.

10. Wind the rope onto the pulley in a counterclockwise direction as viewed from the power head side of the pulley.

11. Install the rewind spring and cartridge into the starter housing. Make sure the tab (**Figure 14**) properly engages the slot in the housing.

12. Place the loose end of the rope into the notch located in the outer periphery of the rope pulley to prevent the rope from unwinding.

13. Install the pulley and rope into the housing, making sure the notch in the inner hub of the

11

pulley engages the hook in the inner coil of the rewind spring.

14. Rotate the pulley counterclockwise until the notch and rope are facing the rope guide. A screwdriver can be inserted through the interlock slot in the housing to hold the pulley in place (**Figure 15**).

15. Install the 3 pulley retainers. Tighten the retainer screws securely.

16. Insert the rope through the rope guide and attach to the handle.

17. Apply a light coat of water-resistant grease onto the shaft of the flywheel bolt (A, **Figure 16**).

18. Position the starter assembly as shown in **Figure 16** and connect the interlock link to the intermediate lever.

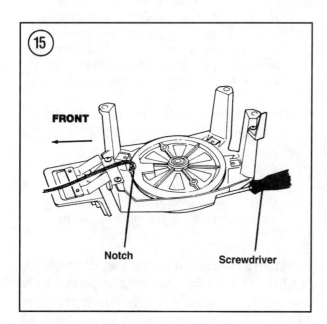

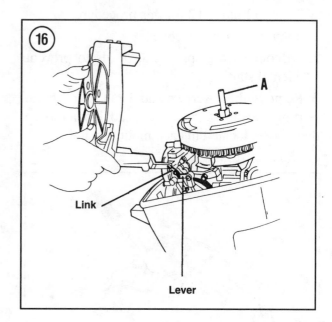

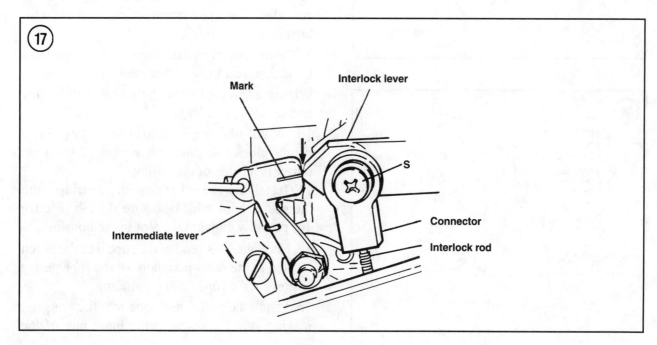

19. Install the starter assembly onto the power head. Tighten the 3 screws and 1 nut securely.

Adjusting Neutral RPM Limiter
(1987-on 9.9-15 hp
and 1996-1998 25 hp 3-cylinder)

1. Remove the engine cover.

2. Disconnect the spark plug leads to prevent accidental starting.

3. Place the shift lever into the NEUTRAL position.

4. Check that the mark on the interlock lever is aligned as shown in **Figure 17**.

5. If not, remove screw (S, **Figure 17**) and disconnect the interlock rod. Adjust the rod connector up or down on the rod as necessary to align the mark as shown.

6. Install the screw (S) and tighten securely.

Table 1 SPOOL STARTER SPECIFICATIONS

Rewind key part No.	
7.5 hp	FT-3139-1
9.9 and 15 hp	FT-2985
Starter spring preload	
7.5 hp	3-1/2 to 4 turns counter-clockwise
9.9 and 15 hp	7-1/2 to 8 turns counter-clockwise
Interlock clearance*	
7.5 hp	.020 in. (0.51 mm)

*Measured between the bottom of the interlock lever and the top of the pinion gear flange.

11

Chapter Twelve

Power Trim and Tilt and Remote Control Systems

POWER TRIM AND TILT

On models without power trim and tilt, the raising and lowering of the motor is a mechanical process. The reverse lock must be released and the motor lifted manually. To change the running position of the gearcase thrust line to the boat (trim angle), the trim pin must be moved to another one of the 4 or 5 different positions available in the stern brackets. Different operating conditions and changes to the boat load will require frequent changes to the trim pin position to maximize boat performance and efficiency.

Power trim and tilt was developed to provide an easy and convenient way to infinitely change the trim angle while under way and allow hands free tilting of the motor for trailer loading or beaching. The term *integral* refers to components being located in between the stern brackets, while the term *external* refers to components being located outside of the stern brackets.

The typical system will consist of:

1. A reversible electric motor controlled from the control box or dash.

2. A hydraulic pump and fluid reservoir assembly.

3. A single hydraulic trim and tilt cylinder or separate trim and tilt cylinders.

4. Hydraulic hoses and fittings.

5. Electrical wiring, a fuse or circuit breaker and 2 relays or 2 solenoids.

6. A separate shock absorbing cylinder on some models.

A power trim/tilt system is standard equipment on large outboards and L-Drives and optional equipment on midsize models. Power trim is not available for 4-25 hp models.

Power trim/tilt systems can be divided into the following basic designs.

1. *85-150 hp (1984-1994)*—Force style system. External pump, integral trim cylinder and separate integral tilt cylinder. Incorporates a separate integral shock absorber. There are 2 versions of the pump and motor. See **Figure 1**.

2. *35 hp (1988A-1991) and 50 hp (1984-1991)*—Force style system. External pump, integral trim cylinder and separate integral tilt cylinder. There is no separate shock absorber. See **Figure 2**.

3. *40-50 hp (1992-1994) and 70-75 hp*—External pump and single integral ram. 2 pump and motor versions. See **Figure 3**.

4. *40-50 hp (1995-1999)*—Mercury style 1 piece integral system. Equipped with a manual release valve. See **Figure 4**.

5. *90-120 hp (1995-1999)*—Mercury style 1 piece integral system. Equipped with a manual

release valve. There are 2 versions of the pump and motor. See **Figure 5**.

6. *L-Drive models*—Pump and reservoir mounted in the boat and 1 external ram. See **Figure 6**.

Two basic types of electric motors are used. If the electric motor has 2 wires, it is a permanent magnet motor. There are no field windings and electricity flows only through the rotating armature. Strong permanent magnets are glued to the main housing. Permanent magnet motors should never be struck with a hammer as this will crack the magnets and destroy the motor. The 2 motor wires are blue and green. When the blue wire is connected to positive and the green wire is grounded, the motor runs in the *up* direction. When the green wire is connected to positive and the blue wire is grounded, the motor runs in the *down* direction. 2 relays take care of switching the polarity of the green and blue wires to change the motor direction.

If the electric motor has 3 wires, it is a field wound motor. Electricity flows through the rotating armature and the main housing field windings. The 3 wires are blue, green and black. The black wire is permanently hooked to ground. When the blue wire is hooked to positive the motor runs in the *up* direction. When the green wire is hooked to positive the motor runs in the *down* direction. The black provides the ground in both directions. The green and blue wires must never be hooked to positive at the same time. 2 solenoids provide for the switching of the blue and green wires to positive.

This chapter includes maintenance, troubleshooting procedures and component replacement procedures. **Table 1** lists recommended tools and test equipment. **Table 2** lists recommended sealants, lubricants and adhesives. **Table 3** lists special torque and dimensional specifications. **Table 4** lists general torque specifications. All tables are at the end of the chapter.

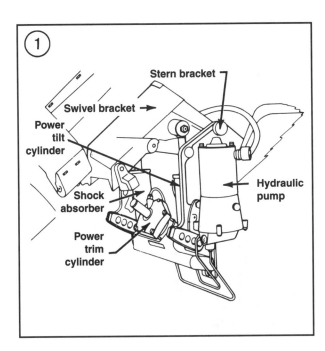

① Stern bracket
Swivel bracket →
Power tilt cylinder
Shock absorber
Power trim cylinder
Hydraulic pump

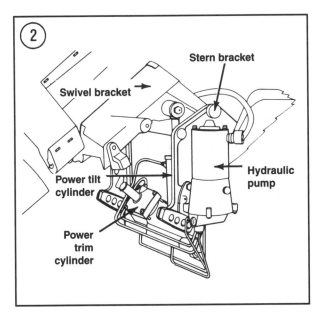

② Stern bracket
Swivel bracket →
Power tilt cylinder
Power trim cylinder
Hydraulic pump

12

③

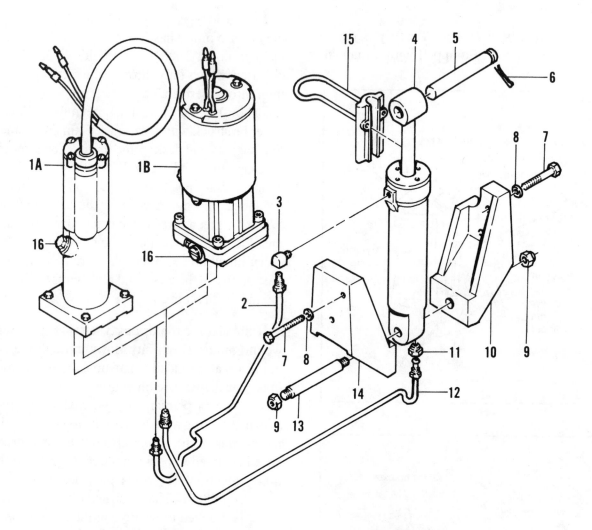

TRIM AND TILT SYSTEM
40-50 HP (1992-1994) AND 70-75 HP (1998 AND PRIOR)

1A. Trim motor, reservoir
   and pump assembly (early models)
1B. Trim motor, reservoir
   and pump assembly (late models)
 2. Hydraulic line (down)
 3. Elbow
 4. Trim and tilt cylinder assembly
 5. Pin (upper)
 6. Cotter pin
 7. Mounting screw

 8. Washer
 9. Elastic stop nut
10. Port mounting bracket
11. Fitting
12. Hydraulic line (up)
13. Pin (lower)
14. Starboard mounting bracket
15. Trailer lock kit (optional)
16. Reservoir fill plug

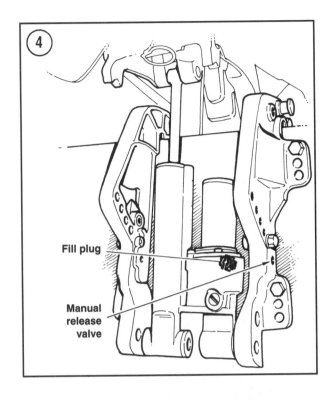

Fill plug

Manual
release
valve

Operation (Typical)

Moving the trim switch to LIFT closes the pump motor circuit. The motor drives the oil pump, forcing oil into the base of the trim and tilt cylinders. The larger trim cylinder diameter produces more force and the trim cylinder extends first. Once it has fully extended, the tilt cylinder starts to extend. When it reaches maximum extension, the drive motor stalls. If the trim switch is not released at this time, a thermal relay opens to shut off power to the motor. **Figure 7** shows a typical operational sequence.

Moving the trim switch to DOWN also closes the pump motor circuit. The reversible motor runs in the opposite direction, driving the oil pump to force oil to the rod end of the trim and tilt cylinders. The weight of the gearcase causes the tilt cylinder to retract first. As the gearcase lowers, it contacts the trim cylinder rod and both cylinders continue retracting until they are fully collapsed. **Figure 8** shows a typical operational sequence.

The power tilt will temporarily maintain the gearcase at any angle within its range to allow shallow water operation at slow speed, launching, beaching or trailering.

To prevent damage from striking an underwater object, spring-loaded check valves in the tilt cylinder and hydraulic pump allow the gearcase to pivot upward quickly and return slowly.

Manual Release Valve Operation

Mercury style 1 piece integral system used on 1995-1999 40-50 hp, 75 hp (1999) and 90-120 hp (1995-1999) models incorporate a manual release valve. The valve is accessed through a hole in the starboard stern bracket. See **Figure 4**, 40-50 hp or A, **Figure 5**, 75 hp (1999) and 90-120 hp (1995-1999). The manual release valve allows the motor to be raised or lowered to

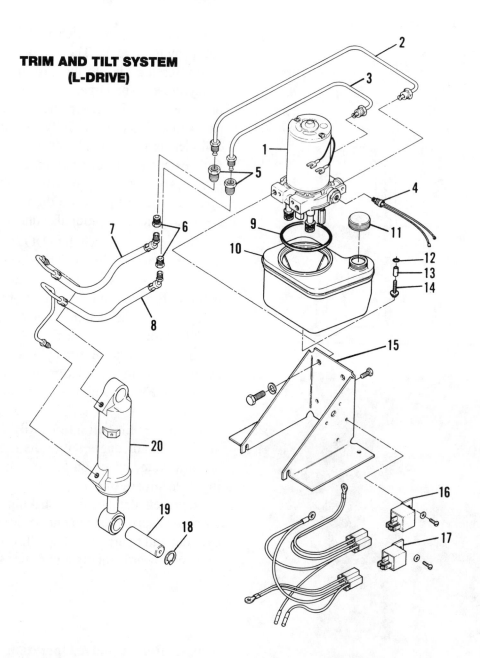

**TRIM AND TILT SYSTEM
(L-DRIVE)**

1. Motor, pump and valve body assembly
2. UP hydraulic line
3. DOWN hydraulic line
4. Pressure switch (some models)
5. Fittings
6. Fittings
7. UP hydraulic hose
8. DOWN hydraulic hose
9. O-ring
10. Reservoir
11. Fill cap
12. O-ring
13. Spacer
14. Screw
15. Bracket
16. UP relay
17. DOWN relay
18. Snap ring
19. Pin
20. Cylinder

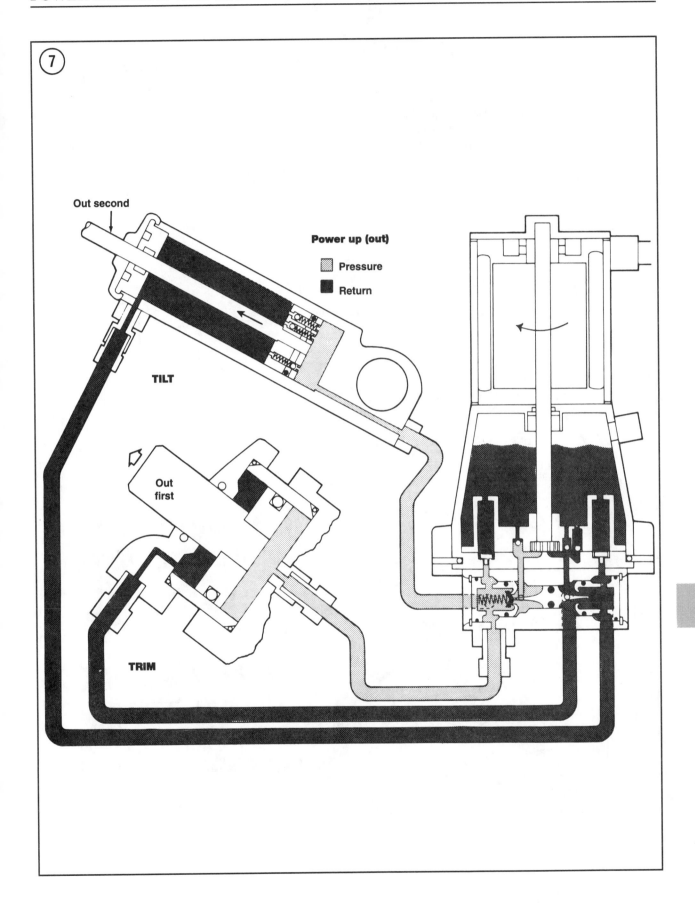

any position if the electric motor has failed for any reason.

WARNING
Do not operate the engine with the manual release valve in the open position.

Reverse lock protection will be disabled. There would be nothing to prevent the engine from tilting out of the water when backing up in reverse gear and when decelerating in forward gear. This will cause a loss of directional control. Retighten the manual release valve se-

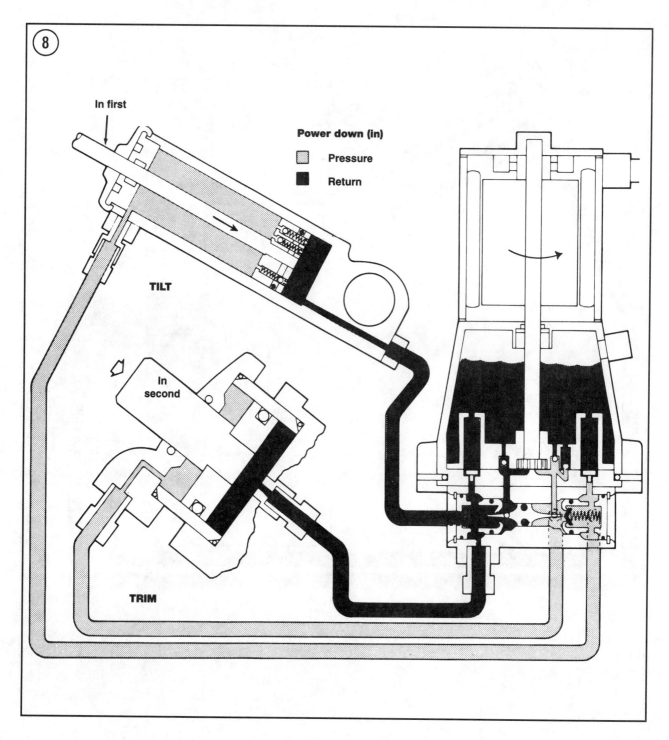

curely once the motor has been positioned as desired.

1A. *40-50 hp*—To raise or lower the motor manually, open the manual release valve no more than 3 full turns. Do not open the valve further than recommended

1B. *75 hp (1999) and 90-120 hp (1995-1999)*— To raise or lower the motor manually, open the manual release valve 3-4 full turns. Do not open valve further than recommended.

2. Position the engine at the tilt or trim position desired.

3. Retighten the manual release valve securely.

Maintenance

Periodically check the wiring system for corrosion and loose or damaged connections. Tighten any loose connections, replace damaged components and clean corroded terminals as necessary. Coat the terminals and connections with anti-corrosion grease or liquid neoprene (**Table 2**). Check the reservoir fluid level as outlined in the following procedures.

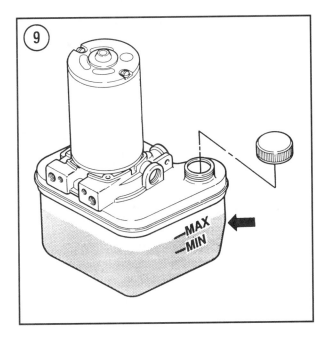

Reservoir fluid check (L-Drive)

1. Trim the drive to the full *down* position. Fluid level should be between the *MIN* and *MAX* marks on the pump reservoir. See **Figure 9**. If necessary, remove reservoir cap and add SAE 10W-40 engine oil as necessary to bring the level up to the *MAX* mark. See **Figure 9**.

2. Cycle the trim/tilt system fully up and down to bleed any air that might be in the system.

3. Recheck the fluid level as described in Step 1.

Reservoir fluid check (1-piece integral pumps)

1. Trim the outboard to the full *UP* position. Clean the area around the fill plug. Carefully remove the fill plug while holding a shop cloth over the plug to block any oil spray.

2. The fluid level should be even with the bottom of the fill plug hole. If necessary add Quicksilver Power Trim Fluid (**Table 2**) or Dexron II transmission fluid to bring the level up to the bottom of the oil level hole. See **Figure 4** or B, **Figure 5**.

3. Install the fill plug. Cycle the outboard fully down and up several times to bleed any air that might be in the system.

4. Recheck the fluid level as described in Steps 1 and 2.

Reservoir fluid check (Outboards with external pumps)

1. Trim the outboard to the full *DOWN* position. Clean the area around the fill plug. Carefully remove the fill plug while holding a shop cloth over the plug to block any oil spray.

2. The fluid level should be even with the bottom of the fill plug hole. If necessary add SAE 10W-40 engine oil to bring the level up to the

12

bottom of the oil level hole. See **Figure 10** or **Figure 11**, typical.

3. Install the fill plug. Cycle the outboard fully up and down several times to bleed any air that might be in the system.

4. Recheck the fluid level as described in Steps 1 and 2.

Hydraulic Troubleshooting

Whenever a problem develops in the trim/tilt system, the initial step is to determine whether the problem is located in the electrical system or in the hydraulic system. If the electric motor runs normally, the problem is hydraulic in nature. If the electric motor does not run or runs slowly, go to *Electric system testing* in this chapter. It is possible for an internal hydraulic component problem to cause the pump to turn slowly or lock up completely, but not likely.

> *NOTE*
> *Always replace all O-rings, seals and gaskets that are removed. Clean the outside of the component before disassembly. Always use a lint-free cloth when handling trim/tilt components. Dirt or lint can cause blocked passages, sticking valves and prevent O-rings from sealing.*

On 40-50 and 75 hp (1999) and 90-120 hp (1995-1999) models with 1 piece integral Mercury style trim/tilt units, the unit is removed and installed as an assembly. There are no specific troubleshooting procedures to isolate the trim cylinder from the pump and manifold. Parts are available to service most of the cylinder and pump/valve body components. Begin troubleshooting at *Mercury 1-piece trim/tilt system troubleshooting*.

On 85-150 hp (1984-1994) models with the Force system, the trim cylinder and tilt cylinders are serviceable. The shock absorber is replaced as an assembly. The valve body is not serviceable

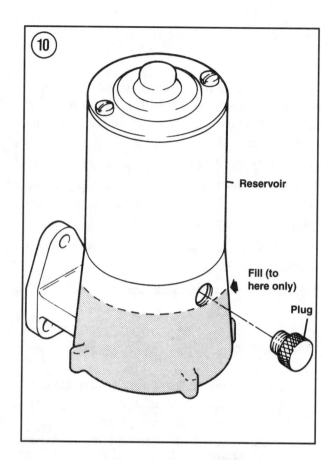

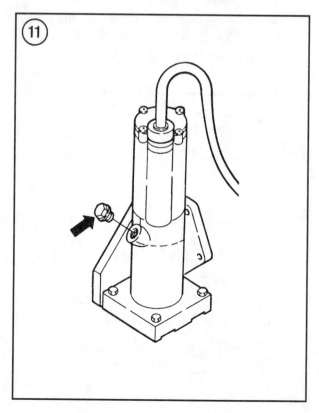

and is replaced as an assembly. Begin troubleshooting at *Tilt cylinder leak-down testing*.

On 35 hp (1988A-1991) and 50 hp (1984-1991) models with the Force system, the trim cylinder and tilt cylinders are serviceable. The valve body is not serviceable and is replaced as an assembly. Begin troubleshooting at *Tilt cylinder leak-down testing*.

On 40-50 hp (1992-1994) and 70-75 hp models, the trim/tilt cylinder is not serviceable and is replaced as an assembly. The pump and valve body are serviced as separate assemblies, but most internal pump and valve body components are not available. Begin troubleshooting at *Tilt cylinder leak-down testing*. See **Figure 12** for 40-70 hp and early 75 hp models pump assembly

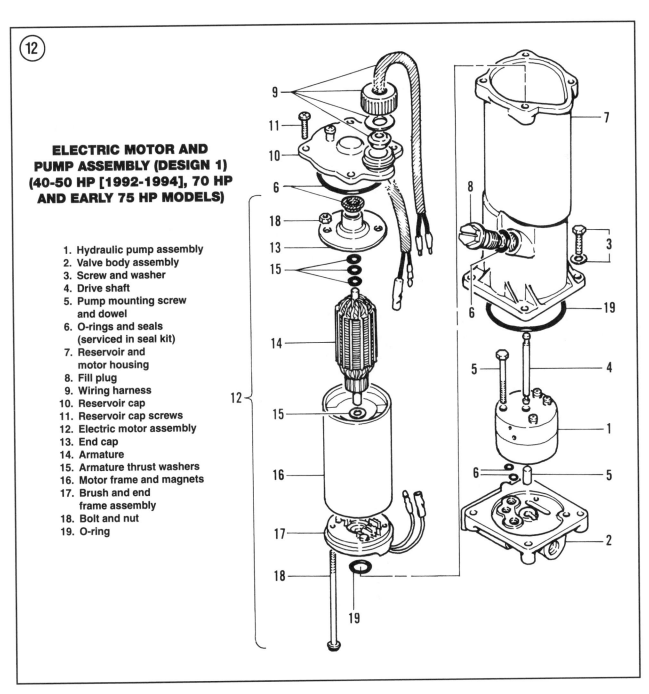

ELECTRIC MOTOR AND PUMP ASSEMBLY (DESIGN 1) (40-50 HP [1992-1994], 70 HP AND EARLY 75 HP MODELS)

1. Hydraulic pump assembly
2. Valve body assembly
3. Screw and washer
4. Drive shaft
5. Pump mounting screw and dowel
6. O-rings and seals (serviced in seal kit)
7. Reservoir and motor housing
8. Fill plug
9. Wiring harness
10. Reservoir cap
11. Reservoir cap screws
12. Electric motor assembly
13. End cap
14. Armature
15. Armature thrust washers
16. Motor frame and magnets
17. Brush and end frame assembly
18. Bolt and nut
19. O-ring

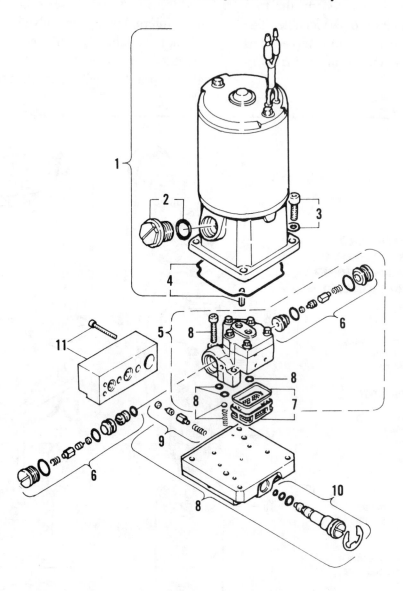

**ELECTRIC MOTOR AND PUMP ASSEMBLY
75 HP MODELS (PRIOR TO 1999)**

1. Electric motor assembly
2. Fill plug and O-ring
3. Screw and washer
4. Drive shaft and motor seal
5. Pump assembly
6. Piston operating spool valve assembly
7. Filter and seal
8. Manifold assembly
9. Trim limit valve assembly
10. Manual release valve assembly
11. Manifold adapter and screws

break-down. See **Figure 13** for late 75 hp models (to 1998) pump assembly break-down.

On L-Drive models, the pump and reservoir is not serviceable and is replaced as an assembly. The trim/tilt cylinder is not serviceable and is replaced as an assembly. Begin troubleshooting at *Tilt cylinder leak-down testing*.

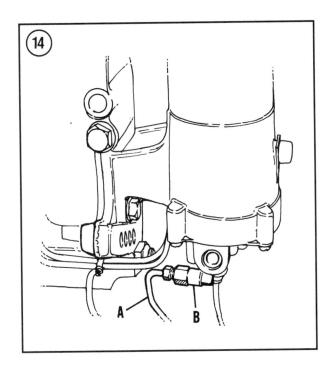

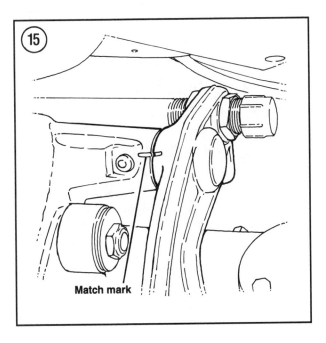

Tilt cylinder leak-down testing

The following test is a simple, yet effective test to determine if the cause of leak-down is the tilt cylinder (or trim/tilt cylinder). To prevent testing errors and unnecessary parts replacement, perform the test in the order described. This test is for all models except those equipped with the 1 piece Mercury style integral trim units.

It will be necessary to obtain (locally) the following to perform this test.

 a. 3/16 in. inverted flare (female) connector with one end plugged.
 b. 3/16 in. inverted flare (male) plug.

1. Tilt the gearcase to the fully UP position. Support the gearcase with a suitable block, then relieve the pressure in the hydraulic system by tilting DOWN slightly.

> *CAUTION*
> *When disconnecting any hydraulic line or fitting, pressure may still be present in the system. Cover all fittings and connections with a shop cloth during removal to block any oil spray.*

2A. *Force systems*—Remove the line from the pump assembly that connects to the bottom of the tilt cylinder. Plug the line (A, **Figure 14**) with the 3/16 in. female plug (B).

2B. *Single cylinder outboards*—Remove the line from the pump assembly that connects to the bottom of the trim/tilt cylinder. Plug the line with the 3/16 in. female plug.

2C. *L-Drive models*—Remove the line from the pump assembly that is marked *UP*. Plug the line with the 3/16 in. female plug.

3. Remove the block supporting the gearcase.

> *NOTE*
> *At this point the gearcase is being supported by the tilt cylinder on Force style units or the Trim/tilt cylinder assembly on all others.*

4. Place a pencil mark across the swivel and stern brackets (outboard models, **Figure 15**) or across

12

the steering yoke and universal joint housing (L-Drive models, **Figure 16**).

5. Observe the pencil marks for indication of leak-down (downward movement of the gearcase). It may take several hours to show noticeable movement.

6A. *Force systems*—If leak-down is noted in Step 5, repair or replace the tilt cylinder. If leak-down is not noted in Step 5, continue to *Valve body leak-down testing*.

6B. *Single cylinder outboards*—If leak-down is noted in Step 5, replace the trim/tilt cylinder. If leak-down is not noted in Step 5, but does occur with the trim/tilt cylinder line connected to the pump assembly, replace the valve body in the pump assembly.

6C. *L-Drive models*—If leak-down is noted in Step 5, replace the trim/tilt cylinder. If leak-down is not noted in Step 5, but does occur with the trim/tilt cylinder line connected to the pump assembly, replace the pump assembly.

Valve body leak-down testing (Force system)

1. Lower the outboard motor to the fully trimmed in position.

2. Remove the lower trim cylinder line from the valve body and plug the line with the 3/16 in. female plug (A, **Figure 17**).

3. Plug the lower trim cylinder port in the valve body (B, **Figure 17**).

4. Tilt the motor to the fully up position.

5. Place pencil marks across the swivel and stern brackets (**Figure 15**).

6. Observe the pencil marks for indication of leak-down (downward movement of the gearcase). It may take several hours to show noticeable movement.

7. If leak-down occurs in Step 6, replace the valve body (if available). If the valve body is not available, replace the pump assembly.

8. If leak-down does not occur in Step 6 and the tilt cylinder tested acceptably, repair or replace the trim cylinder.

Mercury 1-piece trim/tilt system troubleshooting

The Mercury 1 piece system troubleshooting is divided into 2 failure modes: The unit has no reverse lock (kicks up in reverse or trails out on deceleration) or the unit leaks down (will not hold a trim position in forward gear). Refer to **Figure 18** for 40-50 hp models and **Figure 19** for 90-120 hp design 1 models and **Figure 20** for 75 hp (1999) and 90-120 hp design 2 models.

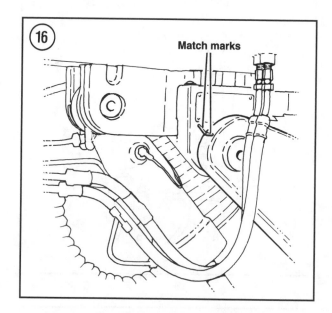

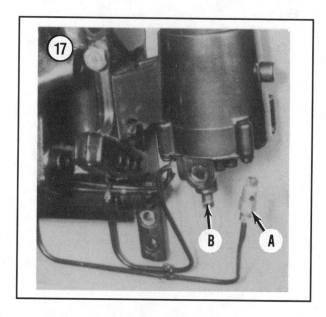

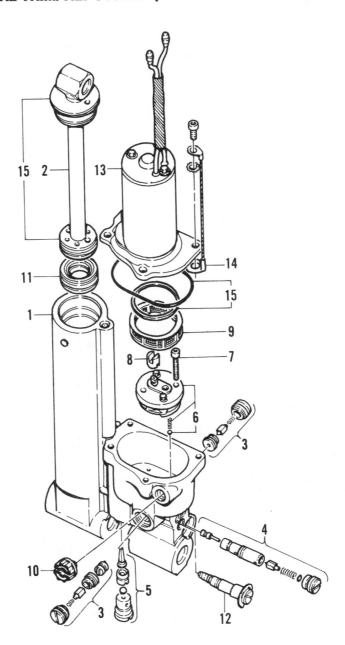

18

INTEGRAL TRIM/TILT SYSTEM (1995-1999 40-50 HP MODELS)

12

1. Cylinder and main body
2. Cylinder rod, end cap and piston
3. Piston operating spool valve assembly
4. Tilt relief valve assembly
5. Suction valve and seat assembly
6. Pump assembly with
   spring and check ball
7. Pump mounting bolt

8. Drive shaft coupler
9. Filter
10. Fill plug
11. Memory piston
12. Manual release valve assembly
13. Electric motor assembly
14. Ground cable
15. O-rings and seals (Seal kit)

⑲

**DESIGN 1 INTEGRAL TRIM/TILT SYSTEM
(1995-1999 90-120 HP MODELS)**

1. Cylinder rod assembly
2. End cap
3. Cylinder O-rings and seals
4. Memory piston
5. Cylinder assembly
6. Check valve assembly
7. Cylinder to manifold screws
8. Rocker arm and bolt
9. Reservoir to pump screws
10. Drive shaft
11. Pump and valve body assembly
12. Reservoir
13. Fill plug and O-ring
14. Manual release valve and E-clip
15. Pump O-rings and seals
16. Armature and thrust washers
17. Motor frame with field windings
18. Brush plate assembly
19. End cap and harness
    (serviced with frame)
20. Brushes and springs
21. Anchor pin (lower)
22. Anchor pin (upper)
23. Trilobe lock pin

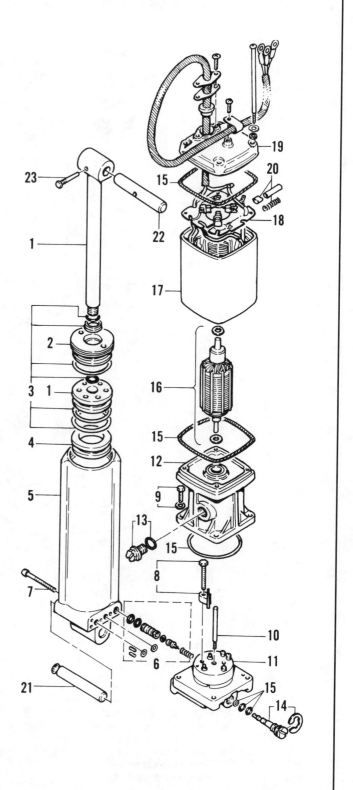

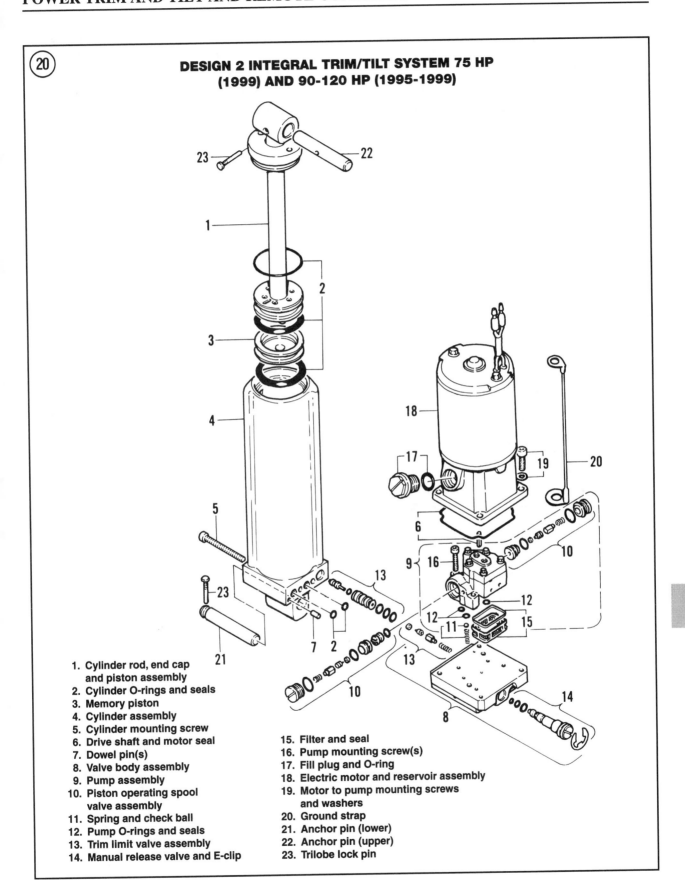

⑳

**DESIGN 2 INTEGRAL TRIM/TILT SYSTEM 75 HP
(1999) AND 90-120 HP (1995-1999)**

1. Cylinder rod, end cap
   and piston assembly
2. Cylinder O-rings and seals
3. Memory piston
4. Cylinder assembly
5. Cylinder mounting screw
6. Drive shaft and motor seal
7. Dowel pin(s)
8. Valve body assembly
9. Pump assembly
10. Piston operating spool
    valve assembly
11. Spring and check ball
12. Pump O-rings and seals
13. Trim limit valve assembly
14. Manual release valve and E-clip

15. Filter and seal
16. Pump mounting screw(s)
17. Fill plug and O-ring
18. Electric motor and reservoir assembly
19. Motor to pump mounting screws
    and washers
20. Ground strap
21. Anchor pin (lower)
22. Anchor pin (upper)
23. Trilobe lock pin

12

1. Unit leaks down:
   a. Remove, clean and inspect the manual release valve and O-ring(s). Replace the manual release valve if it or the O-ring(s) are damaged. Install the manual release valve and tighten the valve securely to prevent leaks. Retest the system for leak-down. Continue to the next step if leak-down is still noted.
   b. Remove, clean and inspect the tilt relief valve. Replace the tilt relief valve if it or any of the O-rings are damaged. Reassemble the unit and retest for leak-down. Continue to the next step if leak-down is still noted.
   c. Remove, clean and inspect the piston operating spool valve assembly (if equipped). Replace the piston operating spool valve if any of the components are damaged. Reassemble the unit and retest for leak-down. Continue to the next step if leak-down is still noted.
   d. Remove, clean and inspect the memory piston and the shock piston. If the O-rings are undamaged and the cylinder wall is not scored, replace the memory piston and shock piston. On 40-50 hp models, if the cylinder wall is scored or damaged the trim/tilt unit will have to be replaced as a complete assembly. On 75 hp (1999) and 90-120 hp, if the cylinder wall is scored or damaged, replace the cylinder assembly. On all models, reassemble the unit with new seals and O-rings. Retest the system for leak-down. Continue to the next step if leak-down is still noted.
   e. If leak-down is still noted, replace the trim system as a complete assembly on 40-50 hp models. On 75 hp (1999) and 90-120 hp, replace the pump and valve body assembly.
2. Unit has no reverse lock:
   a. Remove, clean and inspect the manual release valve and O-ring(s). Replace the manual release valve if it or the O-ring(s) are damaged. Install the manual release valve and tighten the valve securely to prevent leaks. Retest the system for reverse lock function. Continue to the next step if reverse lock still does not function correctly.
   b. Remove, clean and inspect the piston rod assembly for debris or damage to the shock rod valves. Replace the piston rod assembly if any damage is noted. Reassemble the unit with new O-rings and seals and retest for reverse lock function. Continue to the next step if reverse lock still does not function correctly.
   c. Remove, clean and inspect the piston operating spool valve assembly (except design 1, 75 hp [1999] and 90-120 hp). Replace the piston operating spool valve if any of the valve components are damaged. Reassemble the unit with new O-rings and retest for reverse lock function. On 40-50 hp models, continue to the next step if reverse lock still does not function correctly. On 90-120 hp models, replace the pump and manifold assembly if the reverse lock still does not function correctly.
   d. *40-50 hp*—Remove, clean and inspect the suction seat assembly. Replace the suction seat assembly if any damage is noted. Reassemble the unit with new O-rings and retest the system for reverse lock function. If reverse lock still does not function properly, replace the trim/tilt unit as a complete assembly.

Electrical System Testing

Electrical system testing is divided into 3 distinct procedures depending on the unit being tested. Refer to the appropriate section heading when troubleshooting a trim/tilt electrical system problem.
1. Testing very early models without solenoids or relays.
2. Testing models with trim relays (2-wire electric motors).
3. Testing models with trim solenoids (3-wire electric motors).

Green colored wires are primarily used for the up circuits. Blue colored wires are primarily used for the down circuits. Newer models will not have a circuit breaker for the trim motor. The switching circuits for the trim/tilt system are normally protected by the main 20 amp fuse or circuit breaker. Electrical testing is performed most accurately with a multimeter (**Table 1**). A 12 volt test lamp and a self-powered continuity meter may be used if a multimeter is unavailable. Before beginning any troubleshooting with a test lamp, connect the test lamp directly to the battery and observe the brightness of the bulb. You must reference the rest of your readings against this test. Whenever the bulb does not glow as brightly as when it was hooked directly to the battery, a problem is indicated. If using a multimeter, take a battery voltage reading to reference all of your readings against. When the voltmeter reads 1 or more volts less than battery voltage, a definite problem is indicated. When checking continuity with a ohmmeter, a zero reading is good. The higher the ohmmeter reads above zero, the worse the condition of that circuit.

Models without solenoids or relays

> *NOTE*
> *If the motor runs, but tilts the engine slowly, check the trim/tilt fluid level as described in this chapter before proceeding.*

1. Test the battery. The battery should be fully charged and the battery terminals cleaned and tightened. Substitute a known good battery if necessary.
2. Remove the trim switch from the dash and check for continuity with a self-powered test light or an ohmmeter. Continuity should be present between the center terminal and blue wire terminal with the switch held in the trim UP position. Continuity should be present between the center terminal and green wire terminal with the switch held in the trim DOWN position.

Replace the switch if it shows no continuity or high resistance.
3. Disconnect the trim/tilt motor and check the continuity of the green and blue wires from the trim motor connector to the dash mounted switch terminals. If either wire shows no continuity or high resistance, repair or replace the wire(s) as necessary.
4. Locate the black ground wire from the trim/tilt motor and follow it to ground on the engine or at the battery. Check the black wire for continuity and loose connections. Clean and tighten connections or replace defective wiring as necessary.
5. Remove the electric motor from the pump assembly. Reconnect the blue, green and black wires to the wiring harness. Activate the trim switch in both directions. If the motor runs normally now, the trim/tilt pump assembly is binding internally. Repair or replace the trim/tilt pump assembly. If the motor still does not run or runs very slowly, rebuild or replace the electric motor.

Models with relays (2-wire motors)

Refer to **Figure 21** (outboards) or **Figure 22** (L-Drives) for this procedure.

The 2-wire motor is reversed by switching the polarity of the trim motor blue and green wires. There are 2 relays, one for each trim motor wire. Both relays hold their trim motor wire (blue or green) to ground when they are not activated. When the UP relay is activated it takes the blue trim motor lead off of ground and connects it to positive. The DOWN relay is inactive and holds the green wire to ground. Current can then flow from the positive terminal to the UP relay to the trim motor and back to ground through the down relay causing the motor to run in the UP direction. When the Down relay is activated it takes the green trim motor wire off of ground and connects it to positive. The UP relay is inactive and holds the blue wire to ground. Current can then flow from the positive terminal to the

12

DOWN relay to the trim motor and back to ground through the up relay causing the motor to run in the DOWN direction. If the motor will run in one direction, but not the other, the problem cannot be the trim motor. Some L-Drive models have a simple oil pressure switch in the *manifold* that operates a light on the dash to let the boat operator know that the drive is down. Testing of this switch is covered later in this chapter.

1. Connect the test lamp lead to the *positive* terminal of the battery and touch the test lamp probe to metal anywhere on the engine block. The test lamp should light. If the lamp does not light or is dim, the battery ground cable connections are loose or corroded, or there is an

open circuit in the battery ground cable. Check connections on both ends of the ground cable.

2. Connect test lamp lead to a good engine ground.

3. Connect the test lamp probe to the starter solenoid input terminal (Test point A). The test lamp should light. If the lamp does not light or is very dim, the battery cable connections are loose or corroded, or there is an open in the cable between the battery and the solenoid. Clean and tighten connections or replace the battery cable as required.

4. Connect the test lamp probe to the input side of the circuit breaker (Test point B, if so equipped). The test lamp should light. If not,

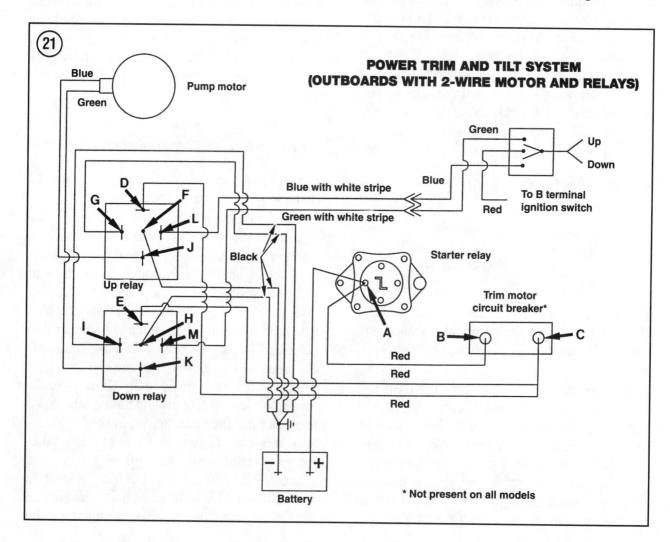

repair or replace the wire between the starter solenoid and the circuit breaker.

5. Connect the test lamp probe to the output side of the circuit breaker (Test point C, if so equipped). The test lamp should light. If not, reset or replace the circuit breaker.

6. Disconnect the trim/tilt relays from their connector bodies.

7. Connect the test lamp probe to the input side of each relay (Test point D, up relay and Test point E, down relay). The test lamp should light at each point. If not, repair or replace the wire from the circuit breaker (or starter solenoid) to each relay.

8. Connect the test lamp lead to the *positive* terminal of the battery and touch the test lamp

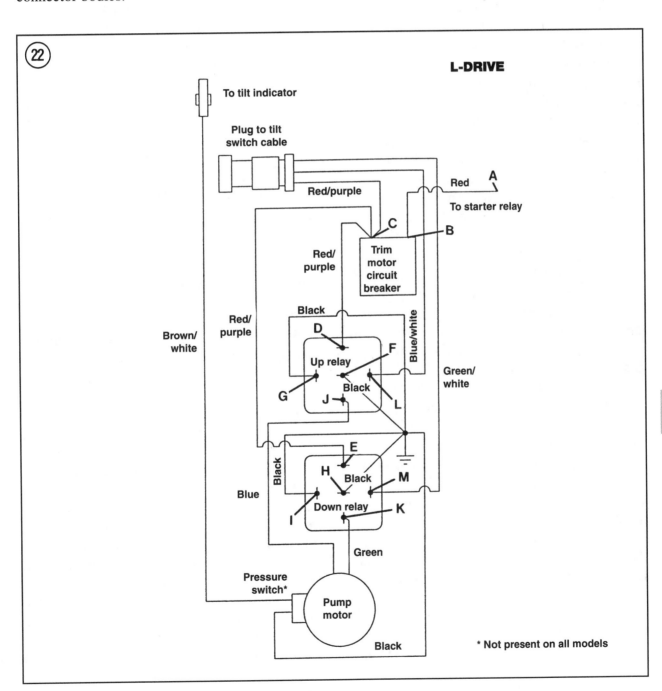

probe to each of the following relay connector test points: F, G, H and I. The test lamp should light at each point. If not, repair or replace each wire (from the relay connector body to ground) that failed.

9. *Outboards*—Connect the test lamp lead to a clean engine ground. Connect the test lamp probe to terminal B on the key switch. If the lamp does not light, repair or replace the wire, main engine harness connector and the fuse or circuit breaker between the starter solenoid positive terminal and the key switch terminal B.

10. Connect the test lamp probe to the center terminal (red or red/purple wire) of the trim/tilt switch. The test lamp should light. If it does not light, repair or replace the wire from the ignition switch terminal B to the trim/tilt switch center terminal on outboards. On L-Drives, repair or replace the wire from the trim motor circuit breaker (C, **Figure 22**) to the trim/tilt switch center terminal.

11. Connect the test lamp probe to test point L in the up relay connector body. Hold the trim switch in the UP position and observe the test lamp. The test lamp should light. If not, connect the test lamp probe to the blue/white wire at the trim switch. Hold the trim switch in the UP position and observe the test lamp. The test lamp should light. If not, replace the trim/tilt switch. If the test lamp lights at the trim switch, but not at test point L, repair or replace the blue/white wire from the trim/tilt switch to the up relay connector.

12. Connect the test lamp probe to test point M in the down relay connector body. Hold the trim switch in the DOWN position and observe the test lamp. The test lamp should light. If not, connect the test lamp to the green/white wire at the trim switch. Hold the trim switch in the DOWN position and observe the test lamp. The test lamp should light. If not, replace the trim/tilt switch. If the test lamp lights at the trim switch, but not at test point M, repair or replace the green/white wire from the trim/tilt switch to the relay connector.

13. Reconnect the trim/tilt relays to the wiring harness connectors. Connect the test lamp probe to test point J in the up relay connector body. Hold the trim switch in the UP position and observe the test lamp. The test lamp should light. If not, replace the up trim relay.

14. Connect the test lamp probe to test point K in the down relay connector body. Hold the trim switch in the DOWN position and observe the test lamp. The test lamp should light. If not, replace the down trim relay.

15. Connect the test lamp lead to the (bf ital)positive(bf ital) terminal of the battery and touch the test lamp probe to each of the following test points from the back side of the connector (with relays installed): H and F. The test lamp should light at each test point. If not, replace the defective relay(s).

16. If all previous tests are satisfactory and the electric motor still does not operate correctly, repair or replace the electric motor.

Models with solenoids (3-wire motors)

Refer to **Figure 23** for this procedure.

The 3-wire motor is reversed by switching the power on to only one of the blue or green wires at a time. The black wire is direct wired to ground. There are 2 solenoids, one for each trim motor positive wire. Both solenoids hold the (blue or green) wire open from battery power when they are not activated. When the UP solenoid is activated it connects the blue trim motor lead to positive. The black wire is already hooked to ground. Current can then flow from the positive terminal through the UP solenoid to the trim motor and back to ground through the black wire causing the motor to run in the UP direction. When the Down solenoid is activated it connects the green trim motor wire to positive. The black wire is already hooked to ground. Current can then flow from the positive terminal through the DOWN relay to the trim motor and back to ground through the black wire causing the motor to run in the DOWN direction. If the motor will run in one direction, but not the other, the problem can be in the trim motor.

1. Connect the test lamp lead to the (bf ital)positive(bf ital) terminal of the battery and touch the test lamp probe to metal anywhere on the engine block. The test lamp should light. If the lamp does not light or is dim, the battery ground cable connections are loose or corroded, or there is an open circuit in the battery ground cable. Check connections on both ends of the ground cable.

2. Connect test lamp lead to a good engine ground.

3. Connect the test lamp probe to the starter solenoid input terminal (test point A). The test lamp should light. If the lamp does not light or is very dim, the battery cable connections are loose or corroded, or there is an open in the cable between the battery and the solenoid. Clean and tighten connections or replace the battery cable as required.

4. Connect the test lamp probe to the large positive input stud of each solenoid (test point C, up solenoid and test point B, down solenoid). The test lamp should light at each point. If not, repair or replace the wire from the starter solenoid to each solenoid.

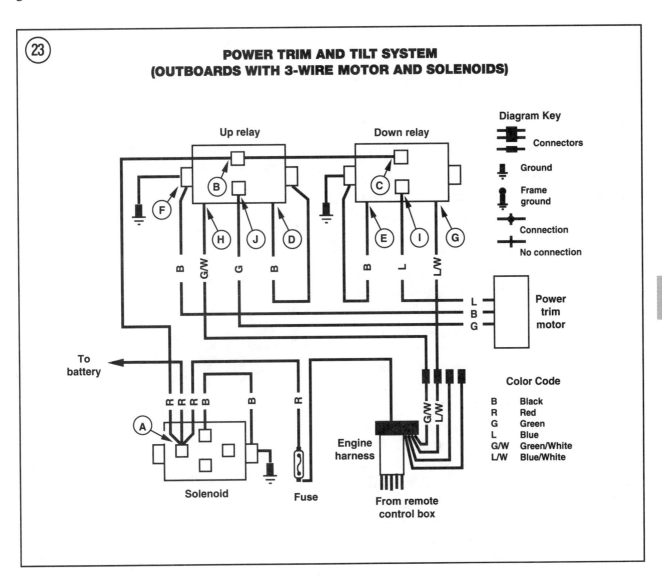

POWER TRIM AND TILT SYSTEM
(OUTBOARDS WITH 3-WIRE MOTOR AND SOLENOIDS)

5. Connect the test lamp lead to the *positive* terminal of the battery and touch the test lamp probe to the small black wire stud (test point D, down solenoid and test point E, up solenoid) on each solenoid. The test lamp should light at each test point. If not, repair or replace the black wire(s) from the solenoids to ground.

6. Connect the test lamp probe to the large black wire coming from the trim/tilt motor. The wire will be hooked to one of the solenoid mounting bolts (test point F). The test lamp should light. If not, remove and clean the wire terminal and bolt. Reinstall the bolt and terminal and retest.

7. Connect the test lamp lead to a clean engine ground. Connect the test lamp probe to terminal B on the key switch. If the lamp does not light, repair or replace the wire, main engine harness connector and the fuse between the starter solenoid positive terminal and the key switch terminal B.

8. Connect the test lamp probe to the center terminal (red or red/purple wire) of the trim/tilt switch. The test lamp should light. If not, repair or replace the wire from the ignition switch terminal B to the trim/tilt switch center terminal.

9. Connect the test lamp probe to the up solenoid blue/white stud (test point G). Hold the trim switch in the UP position and observe the test lamp. The test lamp should light. If not, connect the test lamp probe to the blue/white wire at the trim switch. Hold the trim switch in the UP position and observe the test lamp. The test lamp should light. If not, replace the trim/tilt switch. If the test lamp lights at the trim switch, but not at test point G, repair or replace the blue/white wire from the trim/tilt switch to the up solenoid.

10. Connect the test lamp probe to the down solenoid green/white stud (test point H). Hold the trim switch in the DOWN position and observe the test lamp. The test lamp should light. If not, connect the test lamp to the green/white wire at the trim switch. Hold the trim switch in the DOWN position and observe the test lamp. The test lamp should light. If not, replace the

trim/tilt switch. If the test lamp lights at the trim switch, but not at test point M, repair or replace the green/white wire from the trim/tilt switch to the down solenoid.

11. Connect the test lamp probe to the up solenoid large blue stud (test point I). Hold the trim switch in the UP position and observe the test lamp. The test lamp should light. If not, replace the up solenoid.

12. Connect the test lamp probe to the down solenoid large green stud (test point J). Hold the trim switch in the DOWN position and observe the test lamp. The test lamp should light. If not, replace the down solenoid.

13. If all previous tests are satisfactory and the electric motor still does not operate correctly, repair or replace the electric motor.

Pump Removal/Installation (Outboards with External Pump)

Make sure the outboard motor is in the fully down position.

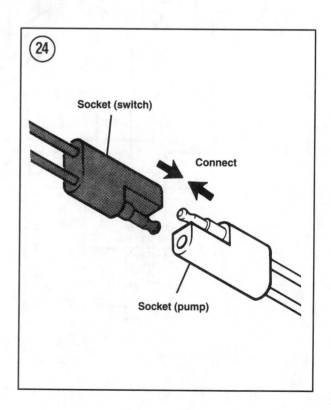

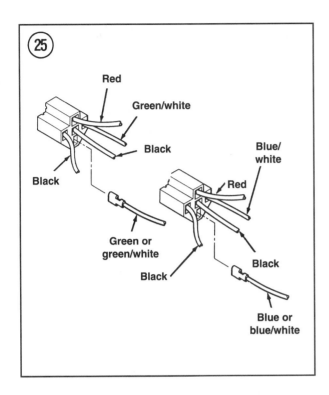

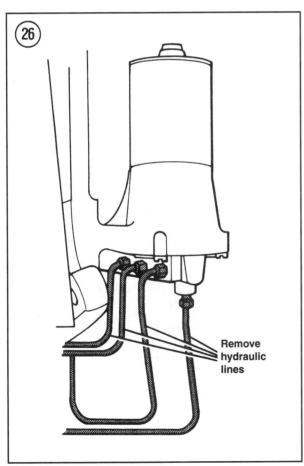

1. Disconnect the negative battery cable.

2A. *1984-1987:*

   a. Disconnect the black pump assembly ground wire at the negative battery cable.

   b. Disconnect the red trim/tilt switch wire at the positive battery cable.

   c. Disconnect the trim/tilt switch from the pump assembly at the connector (**Figure 24**).

2B. *1988-on:*

   a. Disconnect the harness connectors from the trim/tilt relays.

   b. Remove the green wire from the DOWN relay connector and the blue wire from the UP relay connector. See **Figure 25**. Use a small screwdriver to push down the tab on the relay side of the connectors, then pull the wires from the connectors.

WARNING
The oil in the hydraulic system may be under pressure. Use caution when removing the lines in Step 3.

3. Disconnect all hydraulic lines from the pump assembly. See **Figure 26**, typical. Place shop towels under the pump to absorb spilled oil.

4. Remove the fasteners mounting the pump assembly to the stern bracket. Remove the pump assembly.

5. Installation is the reverse of removal. Fill the pump reservoir with a recommended oil and bleed the hydraulic system as described in this chapter.

Pump Removal/Installation (L-Drive)

Make sure the gearcase is in the fully down position.

1. Disconnect the negative battery cable.

12

2. Disconnect the harness connectors from the trim/tilt relays. See **Figure 27**.

3. Remove the green/white wire from the DOWN relay connector and the blue/white wire from the UP relay connector. See **Figure 25**. Use a small screwdriver to push down the tab on the relay side of the connectors, then pull the wires from the connectors.

4. Place a suitable container under the pump assembly to catch spilled oil.

5. Disconnect the hydraulic lines from the pump assembly. See **Figure 28**. Plug the lines to prevent leakage.

6. Remove the 2 fasteners securing the pump assembly to the mounting bracket. Remove the pump assembly.

7. Remove the reservoir fill cap and drain the reservoir into a suitable container.

8. Remove the screw at the bottom center of the reservoir. Remove the screw, spacer and O-ring and separate the reservoir from the pump assembly. Remove and discard the O-ring between the pump and reservoir.

9. Installation is the reverse of removal. Replace the reservoir-to-pump O-ring and the reservoir screw O-ring. Apply Loctite 271 onto the threads of the pump assembly mounting screws.

10. Fill and bleed the hydraulic system as described in this chapter.

Trim and Tilt Cylinder Housing Assembly Removal/Installation (Force Style Systems)

1. Disconnect the negative battery cable.

2. Raise the outboard until the upper shaft clears the stern brackets. See **Figure 29** (pump shown removed).

3. Suspend a rope around the gearcase and attach it to a hoist or other solid object to support the gearcase.

4. Hold the lower shaft stop nut on one side with a suitable wrench and loosen the stop nut on the other side of the shaft. Remove both stop nuts.

5. Repeat Step 3 to remove the upper shaft stop nuts and washers.

6. Place a jack under the cylinder housing assembly or have an assistant help support it while you tap the upper and lower shafts out.

7. Remove the cylinder housing assembly from the stern brackets.

NOTE
The tilt cylinder and shock absorber (if equipped) can be removed from the

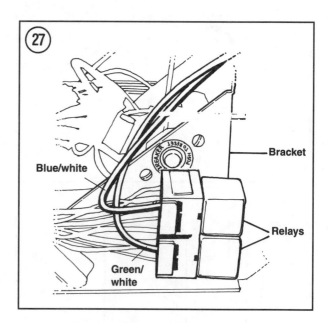

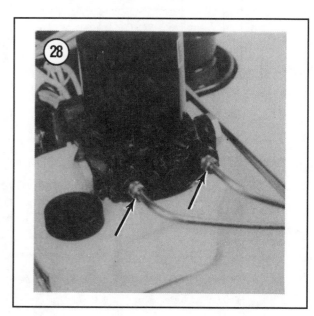

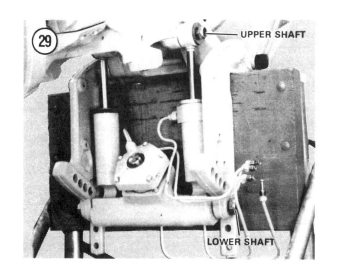

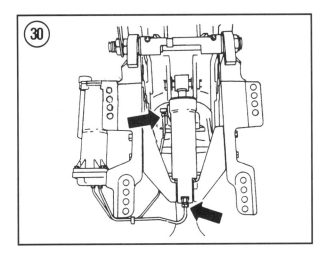

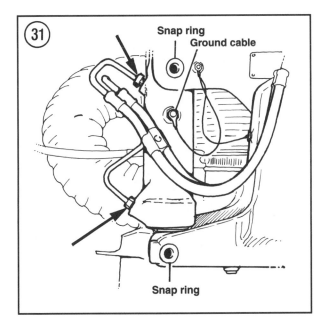

housing assembly. The trim cylinder is an integral part of the housing base.

8. Disconnect the hydraulic lines at the tilt cylinder. Remove the tilt cylinder and shock absorber from the cylinder housing assembly.

9. Installation is the reverse of removal. Be sure the stop nuts are tightened securely.

Tilt/Trim Cylinder Removal/Installation (1992-1994 40-50 hp and 70-75 hp [Prior to 1999] [1-Ram System])

1. Remove the outboard motor from the boat. Suspend the outboard from a suitable hoist.

2. Disconnect hydraulic lines from the tilt/trim cylinder. See **Figure 30**.

3. Remove the nuts securing the cylinder lower mounting shaft. Remove the mouting shaft.

4. Remove the cotter pin securing the cylinder upper mounting shaft. Remove the shaft and cylinder.

5. To reinstall, place the tilt/trim cylinder into position in the boss on the swivel bracket, then install the upper mounting shaft. Secure the shaft to the swivel bracket using a new cotter pin.

6. Install the lower mounting shaft and nuts.

7. Fill and bleed the hydraulic system as described in this chapter.

Tilt/Trim Cylinder Removal/Installation (L-Drive)

1. Disconnect the negative battery cable.

2. Remove the 2 hydraulic lines from the cylinder. See **Figure 31**. Plug the lines to prevent leakage.

3. Remove the ground cable from the cylinder (**Figure 31**).

4. Remove the snap rings securing the cylinder mounting pins using suitable snap ring pliers. See **Figure 31**.

5. To remove the cylinder pins, proceed as follows:

12

a. Obtain a bolt that will thread into the cylinder mounting pins.

b. Thread an appropriate size nut on the bolt and place a flat washer on the bolt.

c. Insert the bolt, nut and washer into a suitable piece of pipe as shown in **Figure 32**. Make sure the inside diameter of the pipe is large enough for the pin to pass through.

d. Screw the bolt into the pin, then while holding the bolt, turn the nut clockwise until the pin is extracted.

6. Repeat Step 5 on the remaining pin.

7. To reinstall the trim/tilt cylinder, lubricate the mounting pins with a suitable antiseize compound.

8. Install the cylinder into position and tap the pins into the bores. Make sure the flat side of the pins are facing outward.

9. Using snap ring pliers, install the mounting pin snap rings. Make sure the flat side of the snap rings is facing outward.

10. Attach the ground cable to the cylinder and connect the hydraulic lines.

11. Fill the pump reservoir, if necessary, then bleed the hydraulic system by operating the trim/tilt system through several up and down cycles.

Testing Pressure Switch (L-Drive)

The pressure switch is not used on all models. Refer to **Figure 33** for this procedure.

1. Disconnect the brown pressure switch wire (A, **Figure 33**).

2. Remove the bolt and nut (C) and remove the black pressure switch ground wire.

3. Lower the motor leg to the full DOWN position.

4. Connect a suitable ohmmeter or self-powered test lamp between the pressure switch brown and black wires.

5. Continuity should be present between the wires with the motor leg in the down position. If

no continuity is noted, replace the pressure switch.

6. Tilt the motor leg to the fully UP position.

7. No continuity should be present between the brown and black pressure switch wires with the motor leg tilted fully up. If continuity is noted, replace the switch.

8. If the switch requires replacement, unscrew the switch from the pump assembly using an appropriate size wrench. Install a new switch into the pump and tighten securely. Reconnect

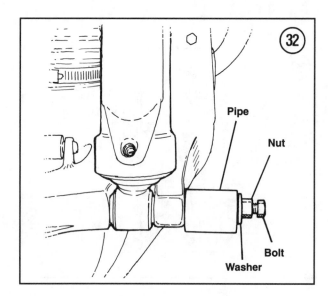

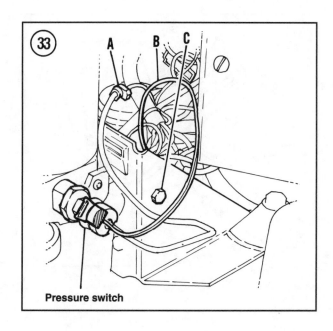

the brown wire to the wiring harness and the black wire to the bolt and nut in the bracket.

Sender Switch Adjustment
(Except L-Drive)

Refer to **Figure 34** for this procedure.

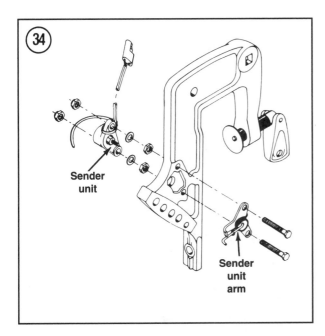

1. Remove the sender unit from the stern bracket.

2. Raise and support the engine at the No. 4 lock bar position.

3. Adjust the sender potentiometer until the dash gage indicates the No. 4 position.

4. Reinstall the sender unit on the stern bracket.

5. Check the sender unit arm for free operation.

CAUTION
Metric and American fasteners are used on the newer model Mercury style trim/tilt units. Always match a replacement fastener to the original. Do not run a tap or thread chaser into a hole (or over a bolt) without first verifying the thread size and pitch.

System Removal/Installation
(Mercury 1-Piece Integral System, 40-50 hp Models)

1. Tilt the outboard to the full tilt position and engage the tilt lock. If it is necessary to use the manual release valve, do not open the manual release valve more than 3 full turns.

2. Disconnect the negative battery cable.

3. Disconnect the power trim blue and green motor wires from the main engine harness bullet connectors.

4. Loosen any wire clamps or tie-straps and pull the trim motor wires through the lower support plate. Remove the trim harness wire clamp on the starboard stern bracket. Pull the trim motor wire harness through and free from the starboard stern bracket

5. Use a diagonal pliers and pry the upper retaining pin (trilobe pin) from the swivel bracket. See **Figure 35**. Drive the upper pivot pin from the swivel bracket with a suitable punch and hammer.

6. Remove the anode from the lower stern brackets to free the motor ground cable.

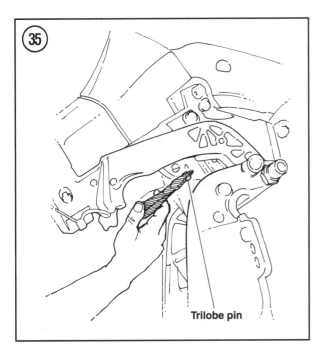

12

7. Remove the nuts and washers from the lower pivot pin. Remove the pivot pin from the stern brackets.

8. Lift the trim/tilt unit upward and out of the stern brackets. Remove the pivot pin bushing from each stern bracket and the 2 bushings from the trim/tilt unit.

9. To install the trim/tilt unit, lift the outboard motor to the full tilt position and engage the reverse lock.

10. Lubricate the pivot pin bushings with 2-4-C multilube grease or equivalent and install a bushing into each stern bracket bore and 2 bushings into the trim/tilt unit.

11. Insert the trim/tilt unit between the stern brackets, bottom first. Lubricate the pivot pin shaft with 2-4-C multilube grease or equivalent. Align the pivot pin bores and install the lower pivot pin. Install the washers and elastic stop nuts. Tighten the nuts to specification (**Table 3**).

12. Install the anode to the stern brackets. Place the trim motor ground lead between the anode and the starboard stern bracket. Tighten the anode screws securely.

13. Route the trim motor harness through the starboard stern bracket and into the lower support plate. Install the harness clamps to the starboard stern brackets as shown in **Figure 36**. The trim motor harness must loop around the steering cable as shown.

14. Lubricate the upper pivot pin with 2-4-C multilube grease or equivalent. Align the upper pivot pin bore with the trim ram bore. Drive the upper pivot pin in until it is flush with the swivel bracket.

15. Drive the trilobe pin into the swivel bracket pin bore until it is seated.

16. Connect the trim motor wires to the engine harness bullet connectors. Secure the harness as it was removed with clamps or ty-straps.

17. Reconnect the negative battery cable.

18. Check the reservoir fluid level as described in this chapter.

System Removal/Installation (Mercury 1-Piece Integral System, 75 hp [1999] and 90-120 hp Models)

1. Tilt the outboard to the full tilt position and engage the tilt lock. If it is necessary to use the manual release valve, do not open the manual release valve more than 3 full turns.

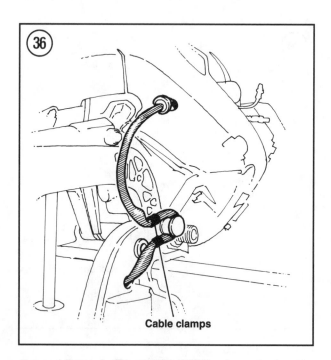

Cable clamps

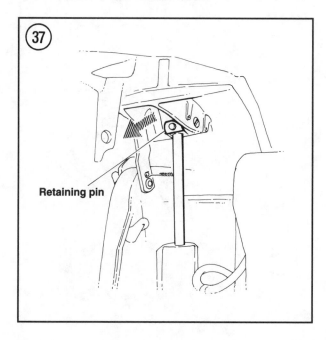

Retaining pin

2. Disconnect the negative battery cable.

3. Disconnect the power trim motor blue and green motor wires from the up and down solenoids. Disconnect the power trim motor black lead from the solenoid mounting screw.

4. Loosen any wire clamps or ty-straps and pull the trim motor wires through the lower support plate. Remove the trim harness wire clamp on the starboard stern bracket. Pull the trim motor wire harness through and free from the starboard stern bracket.

NOTE
If the upper pivot pin retaining pin cannot be removed in the following step, it may be necessary to drive the upper

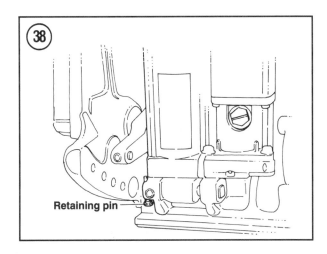

Retaining pin

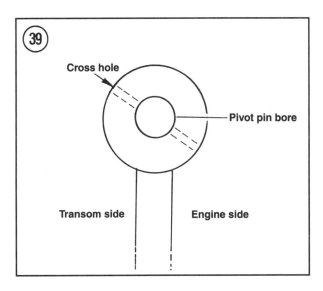

Cross hole

Pivot pin bore

Transom side   Engine side

pivot pin out, shearing the retaining pin. After the pivot pin has been driven out, remove the remaining pieces of the retaining pin.

5. Use a diagonal pliers and pry the upper retaining pin (cross pin) from the swivel bracket. See **Figure 37**. Drive the upper pivot pin from the swivel bracket with a suitable punch and hammer.

6. Use a suitable punch and drive out the lower retaining pin (cross pin) as shown in **Figure 38**. Drive the lower pivot pin from the stern brackets.

7. Rotate the top of the trim/tilt unit to the rear and lift the unit up and out of the stern brackets.

8. To install the trim/tilt unit, lift the outboard motor to the full tilt position and engage the reverse lock.

9. Lubricate the upper and lower pivot pins with 2-4-C multilube grease or equivalent.

10. Insert the trim/tilt unit between the stern brackets, bottom first. Align the pivot pin bores and install the lower pivot pin. Drive the lower pivot pin in until it is flush with the port stern bracket. Install the lower retaining pin (cross pin) and drive it in until it is flush.

11. Route the trim motor harness through the starboard stern bracket and into the lower support plate. Install the harness clamp to the starboard stern bracket.

12. Align the upper pivot pin bore with the trim ram bore. The trim ram bore must be facing as shown in **Figure 39**. Drive the upper pivot pin in until it is flush with the swivel bracket.

13. Drive the upper retaining pin (cross pin) into the trim ram pin bore until it is seated.

14. Connect the trim motor wires to the trim solenoids and mounting screw. Secure the harness as it was removed with clamps or ty-straps.

15. Reconnect the negative battery cable.

16. Check the reservoir fluid level as described in this chapter.

12

Maximum Trim In Limit Adjustment (Mercury 1-Piece Integral System)

On the 40-50 hp models there are 2 stop bolts, 1 on each stern bracket (**Figure 40**) that control how much negative (down) trim the unit can achieve. The 75 hp (1999) and 90-120 hp models use bolt kit part No.10-96930A1 that uses a single long bolt that passes through both stern brackets. On some boats, excessive negative trim can cause instability at high speeds. The simplest solution is to educate the operator not to trim the unit down too far at high speeds. However, this adjustment should be considered when education of the operator is not feasible (rental fleets or boats that will have many different operators). In these cases, the bolt(s) should be moved out-

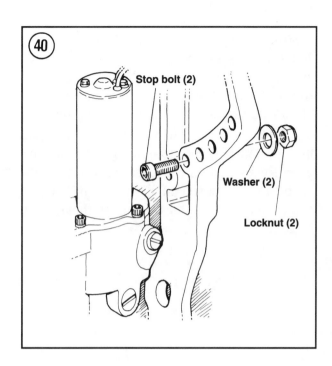

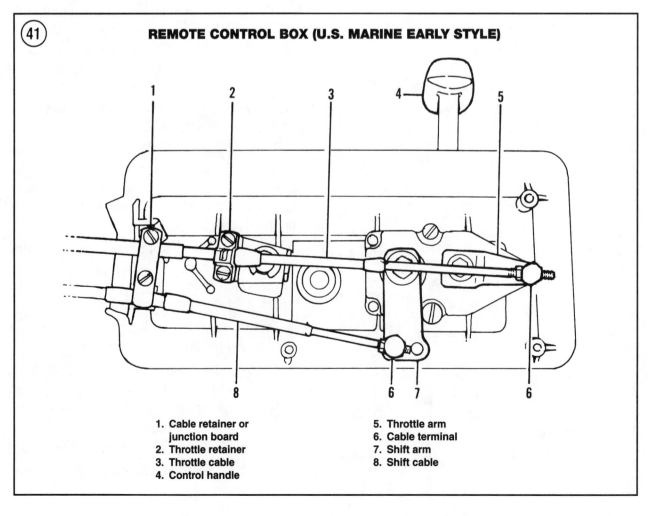

REMOTE CONTROL BOX (U.S. MARINE EARLY STYLE)

1. Cable retainer or junction board
2. Throttle retainer
3. Throttle cable
4. Control handle
5. Throttle arm
6. Cable terminal
7. Shift arm
8. Shift cable

ward (equally) to limit the negative trim. Test run the boat after each adjustment. The moving of the bolt(s) outward will cause the boat to take longer to achieve planing speed because of less available negative trim. Therefore, do not move the bolt(s) further outward than necessary to eliminate any high speed instability.

REMOTE CONTROLS

On 1984-1992 outboard models, the U.S. Marine remote control box is primarily used. Refer to **Figure 41** for early models and **Figure 42** for late models. These control boxes and model year engines used SAE style remote control cables,

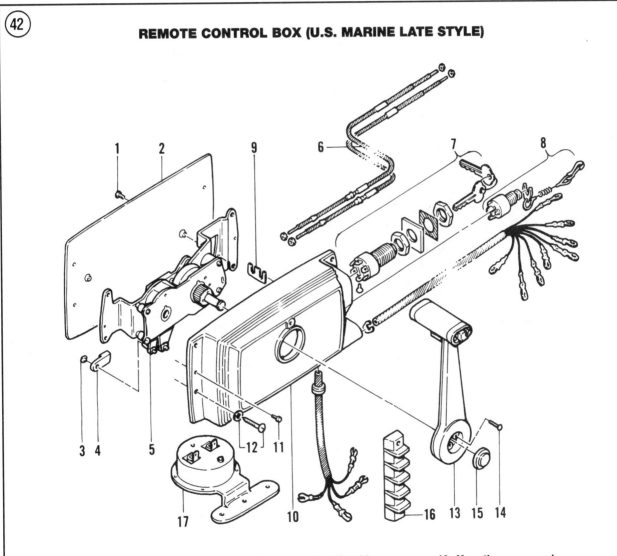

REMOTE CONTROL BOX (U.S. MARINE LATE STYLE)

1. Rear cover screw
2. Rear cover
3. E-clip or cotter pin
   (cable retainer)
4. Cable connector end
5. Control mechanism
   (not serviced separately)
6. Throttle and shift cables
   (with jam nuts)
7. Ignition switch assembly
8. Emergency stop lanyard
   switch assembly
9. Cable retainer
10. Front cover
11. Front cover screws
12. Mounting screw and
    washer
13. Control handle
14. Screw
15. Cover
16. Accessory terminal block
    (under dash)
17. Overheat horn (under dash)

12

commonly called *universal* cables. Adapters must be threaded onto both ends of the cable at the engine and the control box. Incorrectly installing the adapters at the control box causes the common problem of not being able to correctly adjust the control cables at the engine. The adapters for the engine end are adjustable, quick-connect links. The throttle cable adapter is spring-loaded and much longer than the shift cable adapter. 1984-1992 Force outboards use terminal strip connectors for the main engine harness. Early model control systems typically have the key switch mounted in the dash, but later model control systems will have the key switch and associated harness in the remote control box. An accessory terminal block will be mounted under the dash to connect the control box or dash mounted ignition switch and accessories to the main engine harness. The neutral interlock switch is factory mounted on the engine.

On 1993-1999 models, the Mercury Commander style control boxes are primarily used. These control boxes and model year engines use standard Mercury control cables. Mercury control cables do not require any adapters. All adjustments are made at the engine end adjustable anchor block. On 1993 and newer Force outboards also use the Mercury style single plug-in main engine harness. The neutral interlock switch must be mounted in the remote control box. Many Mercury remote control boxes also feature the main wiring harness, key switch, trim switch and emergency stop lanyard switch in the control box. Refer to **Figure 43**, **Figure 44** and **Figure 45** for typical wiring diagrams. Refer to **Figure 46** for a typical Mercury Commander 3000 control box internal component diagram.

U.S. Marine Remote Control Box (Typical early model)

Removal/Installation

1. Disconnect the negative battery cable.

2. Remove the 3 screws securing the remote control unit. Remove the unit.

3. From the back of the unit, remove the cotter pin holding the throttle cable terminal.

4. Remove the 2 screws holding the throttle cable clamp to the swivel. Disconnect the cable.

5. Remove the clutch cable terminal cotter pin.

6. Remove the 2 screws holding the junction board to the remote control unit housing. See **Figure 47**.

7. Disconnect the shift cable.

8. Installation is the reverse of removal.

Disassembly

Refer to **Figure 48** for this procedure.

1. Remove the hex bolt and lockwasher holding the throttle arm to the control unit housing.

2. Remove the hex bolt and lockwasher holding the clutch arm to the control unit housing.

3. Remove the 2 screws holding the retaining plate to the housing.

> *WARNING*
> *The detent ball and spring are under tension. Cover the throttle gear assembly with shop towels to prevent them from flying out unexpectedly and possibly causing personal injury.*

4. Cover the throttle gear assembly with shop towels and remove the setscrew holding the remote control handle to the throttle gear shaft.

> *WARNING*
> *The detent ball and spring are under tension. Cover the throttle gear assembly with shop towels to prevent them from flying out unexpectedly and possibly causing personal injury.*

5. Remove the 2 bearings, bowed washer, throttle gear, detent ball and spring from the housing.

6. Pull the clutch bearing, gear and shaft from the housing, then remove the detent ball and spring.

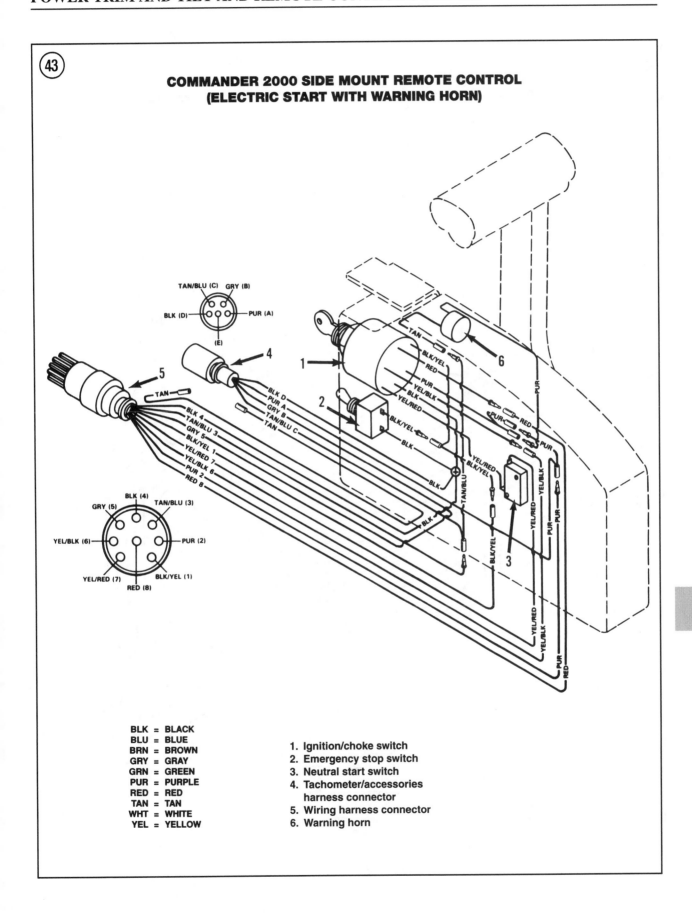

COMMANDER 2000 SIDE MOUNT REMOTE CONTROL
(ELECTRIC START WITH WARNING HORN)

BLK = BLACK
BLU = BLUE
BRN = BROWN
GRY = GRAY
GRN = GREEN
PUR = PURPLE
RED = RED
TAN = TAN
WHT = WHITE
YEL = YELLOW

1. Ignition/choke switch
2. Emergency stop switch
3. Neutral start switch
4. Tachometer/accessories harness connector
5. Wiring harness connector
6. Warning horn

12

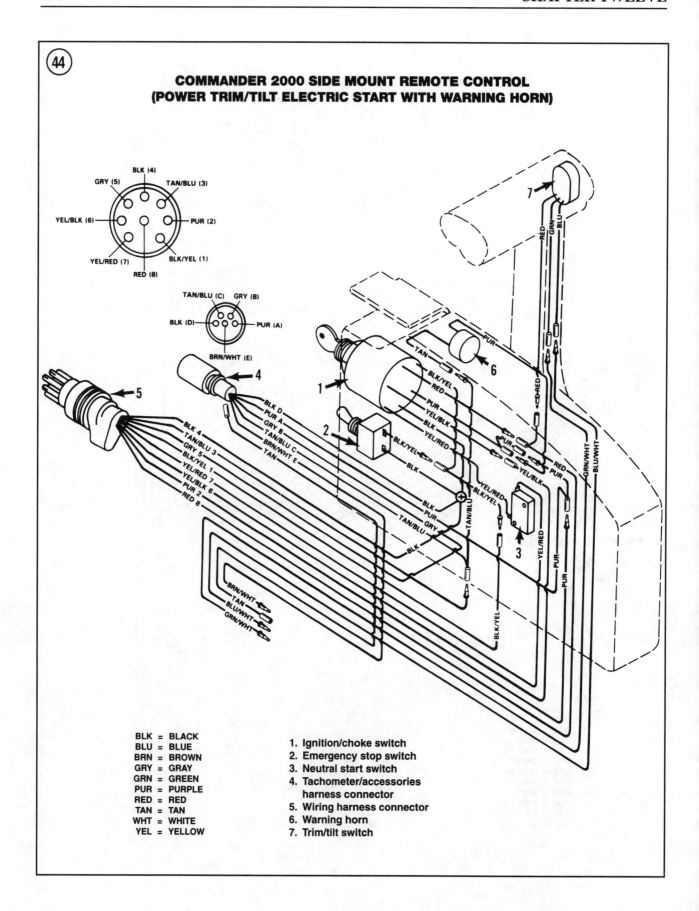

COMMANDER 2000 SIDE MOUNT REMOTE CONTROL (POWER TRIM/TILT ELECTRIC START WITH WARNING HORN)

BLK (4)
GRY (5)
TAN/BLU (3)
YEL/BLK (6)
PUR (2)
YEL/RED (7)
BLK/YEL (1)
RED (8)

TAN/BLU (C)
GRY (B)
BLK (D)
PUR (A)
BRN/WHT (E)

BLK = BLACK
BLU = BLUE
BRN = BROWN
GRY = GRAY
GRN = GREEN
PUR = PURPLE
RED = RED
TAN = TAN
WHT = WHITE
YEL = YELLOW

1. Ignition/choke switch
2. Emergency stop switch
3. Neutral start switch
4. Tachometer/accessories harness connector
5. Wiring harness connector
6. Warning horn
7. Trim/tilt switch

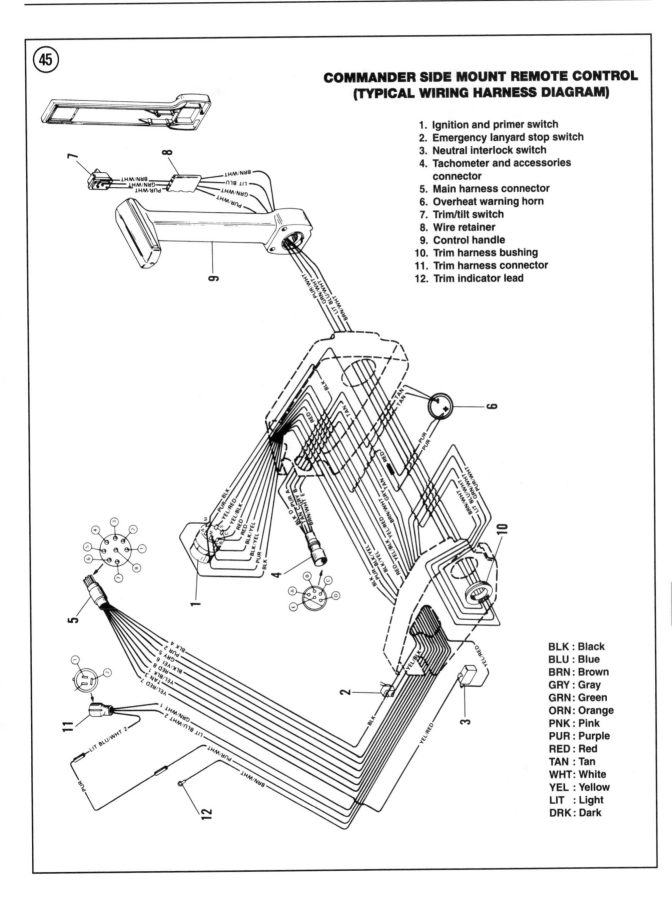

**COMMANDER SIDE MOUNT REMOTE CONTROL
(TYPICAL WIRING HARNESS DIAGRAM)**

1. Ignition and primer switch
2. Emergency lanyard stop switch
3. Neutral interlock switch
4. Tachometer and accessories connector
5. Main harness connector
6. Overheat warning horn
7. Trim/tilt switch
8. Wire retainer
9. Control handle
10. Trim harness bushing
11. Trim harness connector
12. Trim indicator lead

BLK : Black
BLU : Blue
BRN : Brown
GRY : Gray
GRN : Green
ORN : Orange
PNK : Pink
PUR : Purple
RED : Red
TAN : Tan
WHT : White
YEL : Yellow
LIT : Light
DRK : Dark

12

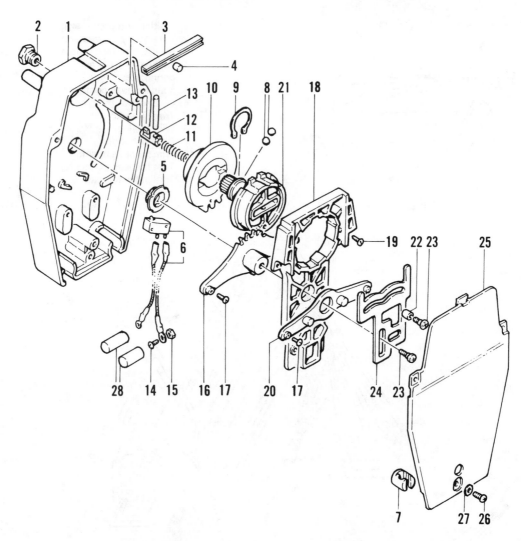

**COMMANDER 3000 SIDE MOUNT CONTROL BOX
(TYPICAL INTERNAL COMPONENT DIAGRAM)**

1. Main housing
2. Handle lock bolt
3. Detent spring
4. Detent roller
5. Bushing
6. Neutral interlock switch and leads
7. Cable anchor
8. Steel ball
9. C-clip
10. Shift gear
11. Spring, shift lock-out
12. Shift lock-out shaft
13. Pin
14. Screw (wire connector)
15. Nut (wire connector)
16. Shift arm
17. Screw
18. Support housing
19. Screw
20. Throttle arm
21. Main handle shaft
22. Throttle plate roller
23. Shoulder screw
24. Throttle plate
25. Rear cover
26. Cover screw
27. Washer
28. Insulator

7. If the handle requires removal, remove the collar, felt washer and indicator tape. Carefully pry the cap from the top of the handle.

8. Remove the snap ring holding the swivel to the housing.

Cleaning and Inspection

1. Clean all metal parts in solvent and dry with compressed air.

2. Check the clutch and throttle gears and shaft for excessive wear or damage.

3. Check the detent springs for wear or damage.

4. Check the throttle and clutch arms for excessive wear or damage.

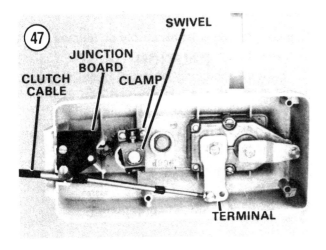

5. Discard the felt washer.

6. Check all plastic parts and housing for chips, cracks or breaks.

Reassembly

1. Fit the cap on the handle, then place the collar with indicator and a new felt washer on the handle.

2. Insert the handle assembly into the housing.

3. Drop one bearing into the housing throttle gear shaft bore.

4. Install the throttle gear, bowed washer and the second bearing into the housing. See **Figure 49**.

5. Install and tighten the handle setscrew to hold the handle to the gear assembly.

6. Install the clutch shaft, gear and bearing into the housing. See **Figure 50**.

7. Install the clutch detent ball and spring (smaller one) into the slot (**Figure 50**).

8. Install the throttle detent ball and spring in the slot.

9. Install the remaining plate over the throttle and clutch gear assembly. See **Figure 51**.

10. Install the swivel and secure with the snap ring.

11. Install the clutch and throttle arms (**Figure 52**).

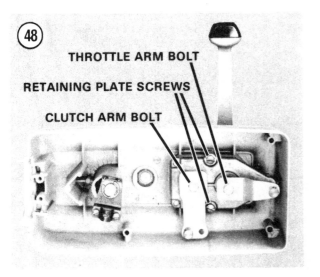

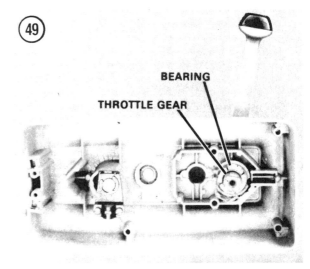

Control cable removal/installation (U.S. Marine control boxes)

Early model control box

Refer to **Figure 41** for this procedure.

1. Disconnect the negative battery cable. Disconnect and ground the spark plug leads.

2. Remove the 3 screws securing the control box to the boat.

3. Remove the 2 screws from the throttle cable clamp on the swivel anchor.

4. Remove the 2 screws from the shift cable retainer (or junction board).

5. Remove the cotter pins from both cable terminals at the control arms.

6. Remove both cables from the control box. Remove the terminals from the cables if the cables are being replaced.

7. Install the shift cable. Thread the terminal onto the cable and set the terminal to the 3/16 in. (4.8 mm) dimension as shown in **Figure 53**. Tighten the jam nut securely against the cable terminal. Grease the cable boots and sleeve with 2-4-C multilube grease or equivalent.

8. Secure the shift cable terminal to the shift control arm rear hole with a new cotter pin.

9. Install the throttle cable. Thread the terminal onto the cable and set the terminal to the 3/16 in.

dimension as shown in **Figure 54**. Tighten the jam nut securely against the cable terminal. Grease the cable boots and sleeve with 2-4-C multilube grease or equivalent.

10. Secure the throttle cable terminal to the throttle arm with a new cotter pin.

11. Secure the throttle cable clamp to the swivel with 2 screws. Tighten the screws securely.

12. Secure the shift cable retainer (or junction board) with 2 screws. Tighten the screws securely.

13. Reinstall the control box to the boat with 3 screws. Tighten the screws securely.

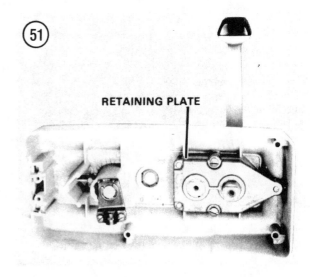

(51)

RETAINING PLATE

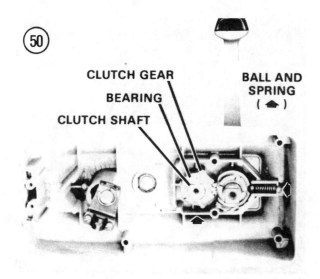

(50)

CLUTCH GEAR

BEARING

CLUTCH SHAFT

BALL AND SPRING
(◆)

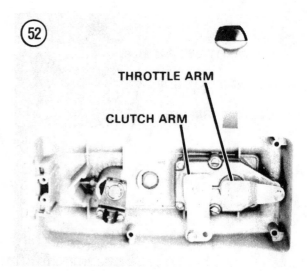

(52)

THROTTLE ARM

CLUTCH ARM

14. Reconnect the spark plug leads and the negative battery cable.

Late model control box

Refer to **Figure 42** for this procedure.

1. Disconnect the negative battery cable. Disconnect and ground the spark plug leads.

2. Remove the 4 screws (typical) holding the control box to the boat.

3. Remove the 2 screws from the rear cover of the control box. Remove the rear cover.

4. Disconnect both cables from the control arms by removing either an E-clip or a cotter pin from each cable connector end.

5. Slide the cable retainer and cables out of the control box. Remove the retainer from the cables.

6. Remove the cable connector ends from the control cables if the cables are being replaced.

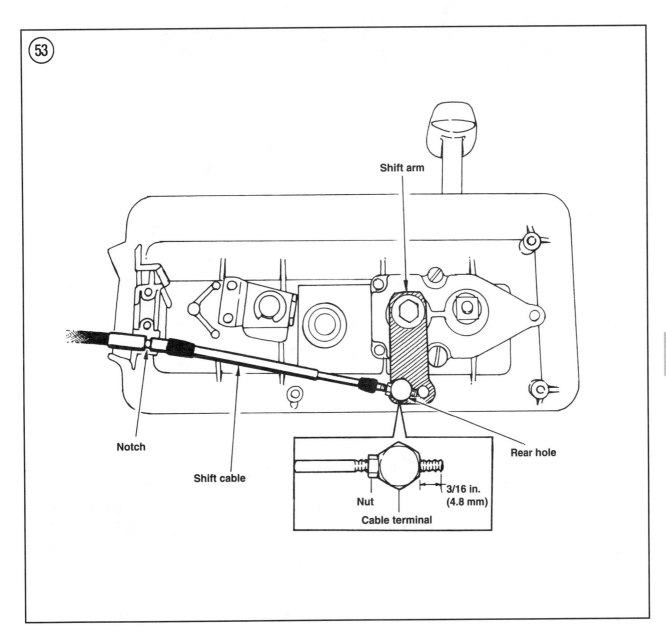

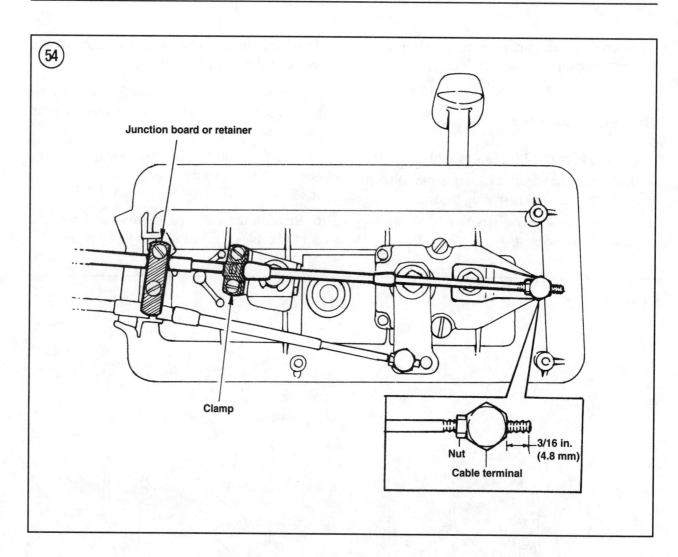

Junction board or retainer

Clamp

Nut

Cable terminal

3/16 in.
(4.8 mm)

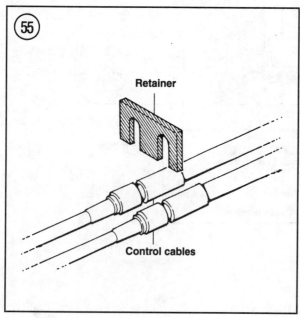

Retainer

Control cables

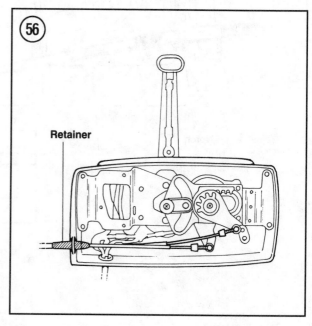

Retainer

7. Install both control cables into the retainer as shown in **Figure 55**. The shift cable will be the cable furthest into the control box. Grease the cable boots and sleeves with 2-4-C multilube grease or equivalent.

8. Slide the cables and retainer into the control box. Be careful not to pinch any wires on models with built in wiring harnesses. See **Figure 56**.

9. Initially install the connector ends onto both cables as shown in **Figure 57**. Adjust the connector to obtain the specified dimension (**Table 3**). Tighten the jam nuts securely.

10. Secure the throttle cable connector to the throttle arm with an E-clip or new cotter pin.

11. Secure the shift cable connector to the shift arm hole with an E-clip or new cotter pin.

12. Install the rear cover and secure with 2 screws. Tighten the screws securely.

13. Reinstall the control box to the boat with 4 screws (typical). Tighten the screws securely.

14. Reconnect the spark plug leads and the negative battery cable.

Control cable removal/installation (engine)

1. Disconnect the negative battery cable. Disconnect and ground the spark plug leads.

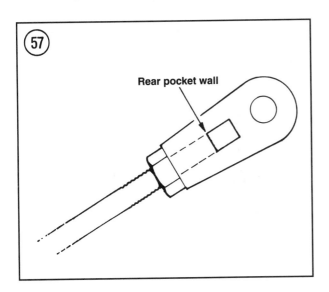

Rear pocket wall

2. Remove the shift cable anchor screw from the clamp.

3. Pull back on the outer sleeve of the shift connector and remove the connector from the stud.

4. Remove the throttle cable anchor screw from the clamp.

5. Pull back on the outer sleeve of the throttle connector and remove the connector from the stud.

6. Pull both control cables out through the lower support plate grommet.

7. Remove both control cable connector ends if the cables are to be replaced.

8. To install the cables, route both cables through the lower support plate grommet and position each cable near the respective cable anchor.

9. Install the cable connector to each cable. The throttle cable connector is longer than the shift connector and is spring loaded.

10. Install the throttle cable into the fixed clamp and align the detent in the swinging clamp with the groove in the throttle cable. Close the swinging clamp. Install and tighten the clamp screw securely.

11. Shift the remote control into the NEUTRAL position. Hold the throttle linkage on the engine against the idle stop screw. Pull the throttle connector towards the stud and adjust the throttle connector until the throttle connector will just touch the stud with the slack pulled out of the cable. See **Figure 58**.

12. Tighten the jam nut securely against the throttle connector.

13. Stretch the connector over the stud, pull back on the outer sleeve and install the connector over the stud.

14. Shift the remote control into the FORWARD gear, full throttle position. Rotate the propeller to ensure full gear engagement. Return the remote control to the idle position. The throttle

12

connector should stretch approximately 1/4 in. (6.3 mm) when properly adjusted. See **Figure 59**.

15. Install the shift connector into the fixed clamp and align the detent in the swinging clamp with the groove in the shift cable. Close the swinging clamp. Install and tighten the clamp screw securely.

16. Shift the control box into the NEUTRAL position. Manually shift the engine shift linkage until the interlock switch is activated by the interlock cam. The propeller should spin freely in either direction. If the propeller engages either gear when the interlock switch is aligned with the cam, refer to *Gear Shift Linkage Adjustment* in Chapter Nine.

17. Pull gently out on the shift cable to remove slack and adjust the connector until it is centered over the shift linkage stud. Tighten the jam nut securely against the shift connector.

18. Pull back on the connector outer sleeve and install it over the shift stud.

19. Reconnect the spark plug leads and the negative battery cable.

Mercury Remote Control Box (1993-1999 models)

When servicing Mercury control boxes, lubricate all internal friction points with 2-4-C multi-lube grease or equivalent (**Table 2**). Apply Loctite 242 threadlocking adhesive (**Table 2**) to all internal threaded fasteners. Refer to **Table 3** for all torque specifications.

Control cable removal/installation (engine)

NOTE
On 1993-1994 40-50 hp models, the shift cable must be installed and adjusted first. On 70-150 hp models the throttle cable must be installed and adjusted first. See Figure 60 for typical anchor stud style control cable attachment. The

1995-1999 (except the 70-75 hp) models use a cable latch and retainer cup assembly to anchor the barrel of the shift and throttle cables, no tools are required to remove or install the cable latch. See Figure 61, (90-120 hp throttle cable) and Figure 62, (90-120 hp shift cable). The control cables on the 1995-1999 40-50 hp must be adjusted separately (one at a time), but installed to the retainer cup assembly at the same time.

1. Disconnect the negative battery cable. Disconnect and ground the spark plug leads.

2. Remove both anchoring stud elastic stop nuts or open the retaining cup latch or latches.

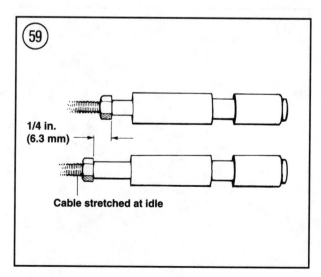

1/4 in. (6.3 mm)

Cable stretched at idle

3. Remove the elastic stop nut from each actuator stud. Remove the nylon washers, if so equipped.

4. Remove both cables from the motor. Retrieve the 2 plastic grommets (each cable) on anchoring stud models.

5. Pull both control cables out through the lower support plate grommet(s).

6. To install the cables, route both cables through the lower support plate grommet(s) and position each cable near the respective cable anchoring stud or retainer cup(s).

NOTE
On 1993-1994 40-50 hp models, the shift cable must be installed and adjusted first. On 70-150 hp models the throttle cable must be installed and adjusted first. On 1995-1999 40-50 hp models temporarily install and adjust each cable separately, then install both cables into the retainer cup at the same time.

7. Install the throttle cable onto the actuator stud. Install the nylon washer on models so equipped.

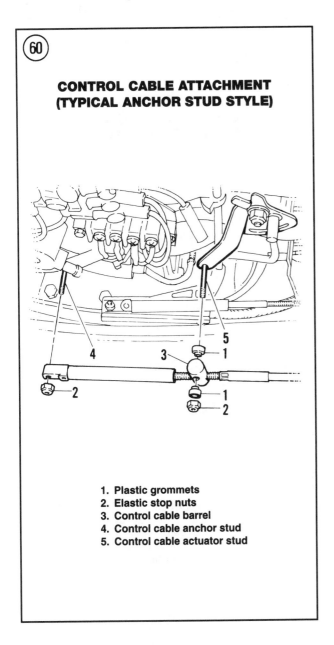

60

**CONTROL CABLE ATTACHMENT
(TYPICAL ANCHOR STUD STYLE)**

1. Plastic grommets
2. Elastic stop nuts
3. Control cable barrel
4. Control cable anchor stud
5. Control cable actuator stud

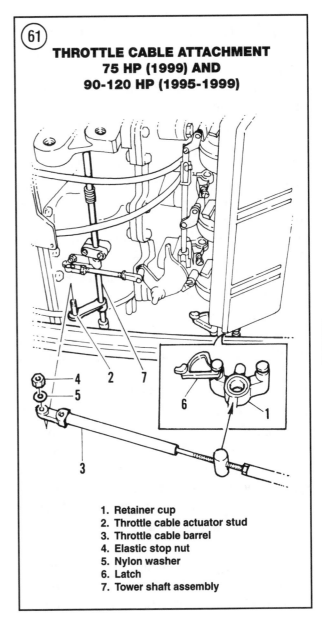

61

**THROTTLE CABLE ATTACHMENT
75 HP (1999) AND
90-120 HP (1995-1999)**

1. Retainer cup
2. Throttle cable actuator stud
3. Throttle cable barrel
4. Elastic stop nut
5. Nylon washer
6. Latch
7. Tower shaft assembly

12

Install the elastic stop nut and tighten it securely. On models with nylon washers, loosen the nut 1/4 turn to prevent cable binding.

8. Shift the remote control into the NEUTRAL position. Hold the throttle linkage on the engine against the idle stop screw. Measure the distance between the anchoring stud or retainer cup and the actuator stud (center to center). Adjust the throttle cable barrel to provide a dimension that is 1/8 in. (3.18 mm) longer. This will add the correct preload to ensure that the throttle returns to the idle stop without binding the control system.

9. Install the throttle cable barrel over the anchoring stud (sandwiched by the plastic grommets) or into the retainer cup. Install the elastic stop nut and tighten it securely or close the retainer cup latch.

10. Shift the remote control into the FORWARD gear, full throttle position. Rotate the propeller to ensure full gear engagement. Return the remote control to the idle position. Manually push the throttle linkage towards the idle stop screw. If any movement is noted, adjust the cable barrel to increase the dimension set in Step 8. Reinstall the cable and repeat this step. The throttle cable must positively return the throttle linkage to the idle stop screw.

11. Install the shift cable onto the actuator stud. Install the nylon washer on models so equipped. Install the elastic stop nut and tighten it securely. On models with nylon washers, loosen the nut 1/4 turn to prevent cable binding.

12. Shift the remote control into the NEUTRAL position. Manually move the engine shift linkage to the NEUTRAL position (the exact center of total shift linkage travel). The propeller should spin freely in both directions. Adjust the shift cable barrel to fit over the anchoring stud or into the retainer cup with a slight pre-load towards reverse gear.

13. Install the shift cable barrel over the anchoring stud (sandwiched by the plastic grommets) or into the retainer cup. Install the

elastic stop nut and tighten it securely or close the retainer cup latch.

14. Shift the remote control into FORWARD gear. Rotate the propeller and verify gear engagement in forward. Return the remote control to NEUTRAL and verify the propeller spins freely in each direction. Shift the control box into REVERSE gear. Rotate the propeller and verify gear engagement in reverse. Adjust the shift cable barrel as necessary if gear engagements are not satisfactory.

15. Reconnect the spark plug leads and the negative battery cable.

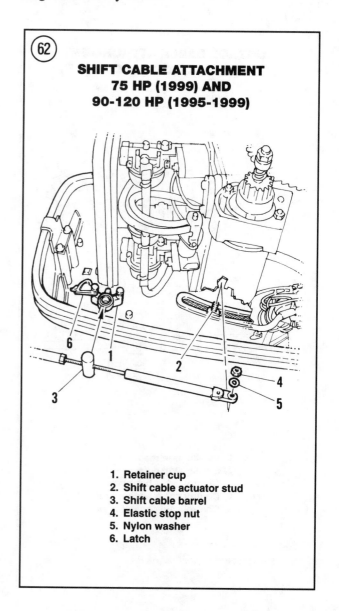

62

**SHIFT CABLE ATTACHMENT
75 HP (1999) AND
90-120 HP (1995-1999)**

1. Retainer cup
2. Shift cable actuator stud
3. Shift cable barrel
4. Elastic stop nut
5. Nylon washer
6. Latch

Table 1 TRIM/TILT TEST EQUIPMENT AND TOOLS

Description	Part No.	Models
Multimeter	91-99750	All
Spanner wrench	FT-11240	Force style units
Snap ring pliers	FT-1749	Force style units
Spanner wrench	91-74951	Mercury 1-piece integral units
Internal snap ring pliers	Craftsman 4735	Mercury 1-piece integral units
Heat lamp	91-63209	Mercury 1-piece integral units

Table 2 RECOMMENDED LUBRICANTS, SEALANTS AND ADHESIVES

	Part Number
Lubricants	
Quicksilver Premium	
2-Cycle TC-W3 outboard oil	(normal dealer stock item)
Quicksilver Special Lubricant 101	92-13872A-1
Quicksilver 2-4-C Multi-Lube	(normal dealer stock item in various sizes)
Quicksilver Anti-Corrosion Grease	92-78376A-6
Quicksilver Needle Bearing Grease	92-825265A-1
Quicksilver Power Trim and Steering Fluid	92-90100A12
Quicksilver Premium Blend Gearcase Lubricant	(normal dealer stock item)
Sealants	
Quicksilver Perfect Seal	92-34227-11
Loctite 5900 Ultra black RTV sealant	92-809826
Sealer (crankcase halves)	92-90113–2
Loctite Master Gasket Sealer	92-12564–2
Quicksilver Liquid Neoprene	92-25711–2
Loctite 567 PST pipe sealant	92-809822
Quicksilver Bellows Adhesive	92-86166–1
Adhesives	
Loquic Primer	92-809824
Loctite 271 threadlocking sealant	
(high strength)	92-809819
Loctite 242 threadlocking sealant	
(medium strength)	92-809821
Loctite RC680 high strength	
retaining compound	92-809833
Miscellaneous	
Quicksilver Power Tune Engine Cleaner	92-15104A12
Quicksilver Corrosion Guard	92-815869A12
Quicksilver Storage Seal Rust Inhibitor	92-86145A12

Table 3 SPECIAL POWER TRIM/TILT SYSTEM TORQUE SPECIFICATIONS

Fastener	in.-lb.	ft.-lb.	N•m
90-120 hp Mercury			
1-piece integral trim/tilt system			
Manifold to cylinder screws	100	–	11.3
Reservoir to pump body	70	–	7.9
Motor to reservoir (design 1)	13	–	1.5

(continued)

12

Table 3 SPECIAL POWER TRIM/TILT SYSTEM TORQUE SPECIFICATIONS (continued)

Fastener	in.-lb.	ft.-lb.	N•m
40-50 hp Mercury			
1-piece integral trim/tilt system			
Motor to main body	80	–	9.0
Cylinder end cap	–	45	61
Suction valve	120	–	13.6
Piston operating spool valve(s)	120	–	13.6
Lower pivot pin	–	18	24.4
Mercury Commander 3000			
style remote control box			
Control handle lock bolt	150	–	16.9
Control arm screw (8-32)	25	–	2.8
Support assembly screw (10/32)	35	–	4.0
Shoulder screw	35	–	4.0
Cover screw	10	–	1.1

Table 4 STANDARD TORQUE VALUES

Screw or Nut Size	in.-lbs.	ft.-lbs.	N•m
6-32	9	–	1.0
8-32	20	–	2.3
10-24	30	–	3.4
10-32	35	–	4.0
12-24	45	–	5.1
1/4-20	70	6	7.9
1/4-28	84	7	9.5
5/16-18	160	13	18.1
5/16-24	168	14	19.0
3/8-16	270	23	30.5
3/8-24	300	25	33.9
7/16-14	–	36	48.8
7/16-20	–	40	54.2
1/2-13	–	50	67.8
1/2-20	–	60	81.3

Table 5 REMOTE CONTROL CONNECTOR SPECIFICATIONS

Connector	Specification
U.S. Marine late model control box (1987B-1992)	
Shift cable	
35 hp (1987B-1991)	Flush to rear pocket wall.
50 hp (1987B-1992)	Threaded fully onto cable.
85-125 hp (1987B-1989)	Threaded fully onto cable.
70-150 hp (1990A-1992)	Threaded onto cable 8 full turns.
Throttle cable	
35 hp (1987B-1991)	Flush to rear pocket wall.
50 hp (1987B-1992)	Recess cable 2 turns from rear pocket wall.
70-150 hp (1987B-1992)	Thread cable 2 turns past rear pocket wall.

Index

A

Alternator,
    charging system 46-50, 249-253
Anticorrosion maintenance 128

B

Battery 243-249
    and starter motor check,
        electric start models 138
    breaker point ignition 263-265
    system 56-58
Breaker point
    ignition system service 135-138
    magneto ignition 260-263
Breakerless ignition,
    module, BIM 282-284
    system 89-91

C

Capacitor discharge module,
    CDM, ignition 92-100
    40-120 hp models 285-290
Carburetor 179
    cleaning and inspection 213-214
    disassembly, reassembly
        and adjustment 187-213
    removal/installation 179-187
Charging system, alternator 46-50

E

Electrical
    alternator charging
        system 249-253
    battery 243-249
    starting system 253
Engine
    cover starter 509-511
    flushing 128-129
    operation 2

Choke solenoid 222-223
    or fuel primer valve circuits 43-46
Compression check 129-130
Connecting rod
    and piston 355-361
    and crankshaft 361-370
Core plugs and lead shot 214-215
Corrosion
    anticorrosion maintenance 128
    galvanic 11-13
        protection from 13-14
Crankcase assembly
    and cylinder block 370-381
Crankshaft
    and connecting rod 361-370
Cylinder
    block and
        crankcase assembly 370-381
    head bolt torque 130-131

F

synchronization
    and adjustment 139
    and linkage adjustments . . . .
        See synchronization
    and timing 145-146
    wiring diagrams 572-611
Exhaust system 505-507

F

Fasteners 2-8
    and torque specifications,
        power head 296-300
Flywheel-mounted starter 517-521
Force model
    numbering system 295-296
Fuel system 101-102
    carburetor 179
        cleaning and inspection . . . 213-214
        disassembly, reassembly
            and adjustment 187-213
        removal/installation 179-187
    choke solenoid 222-223
    core plugs and lead shot 214-215
    hose and primer bulb 224-226
    integral tank 223
    portable tank 223-224
    primer valve 223
        circuits or choke solenoid . . . 43-46
    pump 168-178
    recirculation system 226-239
    reed valve assembly 215-222
    service 134-135

G

Gasket sealant. 10-11
Gear shift linkage adjustment. . . 473-476
Gearcase 399-408
  and water pump check 134
  cleaning and inspection 461-462
  disassembly/reassembly
    9.9 and 15 hp, 1998,
      and 25 hp, 3-cylinder . . . 423-431
    25-50 hp, 1984-1994 419-423
    4 and 5 hp. 408-413
    40 and 50 hp,
      1995-1999 431-437
    60 hp and 85-150 hp,
      1984-1994 449-461
    7.5 hp 413-415
    70 and 75 hp,
      prior to 1999 437-441
    9.9 and 15 hp,
      1997 and prior 415-419
    90 and 120 hp, 1995-1996,
      and 1999 75 hp. 441-449
  gear shift
    linkage adjustment 473-476
  pressure testing. 472
  propeller 395-399
  service precautions 394-395
  shimming 462-472
  water pump. 476-488
  zinc anode. 473
General information
  engine operation 2
  fasteners 2-8
  gasket sealant 10-11
  lubricants 8-10
  propellers 14-20
  torque specifications. 2

I

Ignition system 50-52, 260
  battery breaker point. 56-58
  battery breaker point. 263-265
  breaker point service 135-138
  breaker point magneto 260-263
  breakerless ignition
    module, BIM 89-91, 282-284
  capacitor discharge
    module, CDM. 92-100
    40-120 hp models. 285-290
  magneto 52-56
  Prestolite magneto capacitor
    discharge 58-81, 265-277
  Sem-walbro 284-285
    capacitor discharge. 91-92
  starter motor system 253-260
  switch 100-101
  Thunderbolt capacitor
    discharge. 81-88, 277-282

Integral fuel tank. 223

L

L-Drive, lower assembly
  removal/installation 496-505
Lubrication 115-124
  lubricants. 8-10

M

Magneto ignition system 52-56
Maintenance
  anticorrosion 128
  complete submersion 127-128
  engine flushing 128-129
  storage. 124-127
  tune-up 129
Manual rewind starters
  engine cover 509-511
  flywheel-mounted. 517-521
  spool 512-517
Mechanic's techniques 31-32

O

Operating requirements 33-34

P

Performance test, on boat 139-140
Piston and connecting rod 355-361
Portable fuel tank 223-224
Power head 102-105
  cleaning/inspection 352-355
  connecting rod and
    crankshaft 361-370
  cylinder block and
    crankcase assembly 370-381
  disassembly. 320-322
    25 hp, 2-cylinder, and 35 hp. . . 331
    25 hp, 3-cylinder. 328-331
    40 and 50 hp 331-340
    60 hp 340-345
    7.5, 9.9 and 15 hp 322-328
    70-150 hp,
      including L-Drive 345-352
  fasteners and
    torque specifications. 296-300
  Force model
    numbering system. 295-296
  piston
    and connecting rod 355-361
  removal/installation 300-320
Power trim and tilt 522-523
  cylinder removal/installation
    housing assembly,
      Force style systems. 546-547

1992-1994 40-50 hp and
    70-75 hp, 1998 and prior,
    1-ram system. 547
  L-Drive 547-548
  electrical system testing 538-544
  hydraulic troubleshooting . . . 530-538
  maintenance 529-530
  manual release
    valve operation 525-529
  maximum trim in limit adjustment,
    Mercury 1-piece
    integral system 552-553
  operation, typical. 525
  pump removal/installation
    L-Drive 545-546
    outboards with
      external pump 544-545
  sender switch adjustment,
    except L-Drive 549
  system removal/installation,
    Mercury 1-piece integral system,
    40-50 hp models 549-550
    Mercury 1-piece integral system,
    75 hp, 1999 only, and
    90-120 hp models 550-551
  testing pressure switch,
    L-Drive 548-549
Prestolite magneto capacitor
  discharge ignition 58-81, 265-277
Primer valve 223
Propeller 14-20, 395-397

R

Reed valve assembly. 215-222
Remote controls 553-566

S

Sem-walbro
  capacitor discharge ignition . . . 91-92
  ignition system 284-285
Spark plugs 131-134
Special tips 30-31
Spool starter 512-517
Starting system 34-43
  electric. 253
  motor
    check, electric start models
      and battery. 138
    system 253-260
Storage 124-127
Synchronization
  and adjustment 139
  and linkage adjustments
    25 hp 2-cylinder and
      35 hp models. 148-150
    25 hp 3-cylinder models . . 150-151
    4, 5, 7.5, 9.9. 146-148

40, 50 and 60 hp models . . 151-158
70-150 hp models,
    including L-Drive. 159-163
and timing. 145-146
Submersion, complete 127-128

T

Test equipment 26-28
Thunderbolt capacitor
    discharge ignition 81-88, 277-282
Tools, basic hand 21-26
Torque specifications 2
Troubleshooting
    alternator charging system 46-50
    choke solenoid or
        fuel primer valve circuits 43-46
    fuel primer valve circuits
        or choke solenoid 43-46
    fuel system 101-102
    ignition system 50-52
        battery breaker point. 56-58

breakerless ignition
    module, BIM 89-91
capacitor discharge
    module, CDM 92-100
magneto 52-56
Prestolite magneto
    capacitor discharge 58-81
Sem-walbro
    capacitor discharge 91-92
switch 100-101
Thunderbolt capacitor
    discharge. 81-88
operating requirements 33-34
power head 102-105
starting system 34-43
Tune-up. 129
battery and starter motor check,
    electric start models 138
breaker point ignition
    system service. 135-138
compression check 129-130
cylinder head bolt torque 130-131

engine synchronization
    and adjustment 139
fuel system, service. 134-135
gearcase and
    water pump check. 134
performance test, on boat . . . 139-140
spark plugs 131-134
wiring harness check. 138-139

W

Water pump 476-487
    check and gearcase 134
Wiring harness check 138-139
Wiring diagrams 572-611

Z

Zinc anode. 473

13

5 HP (BIM 1 IGNITION)

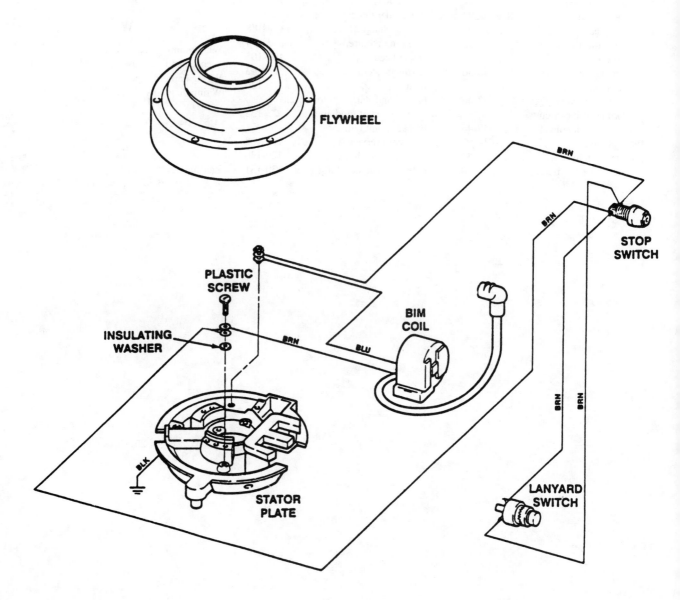

FLYWHEEL

PLASTIC
SCREW

INSULATING
WASHER

BRN

BIM
COIL

BLU

BLK

STATOR
PLATE

BRN

STOP
SWITCH

BRN

BRN   BRN

LANYARD
SWITCH

5 HP (BIM 2 IGNITION)

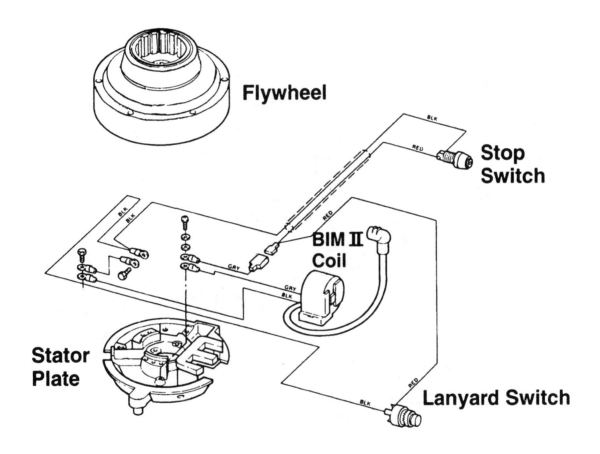

Flywheel

Stop Switch

BIM II Coil

Stator Plate

Lanyard Switch

5 HP (SEM IGNITION)

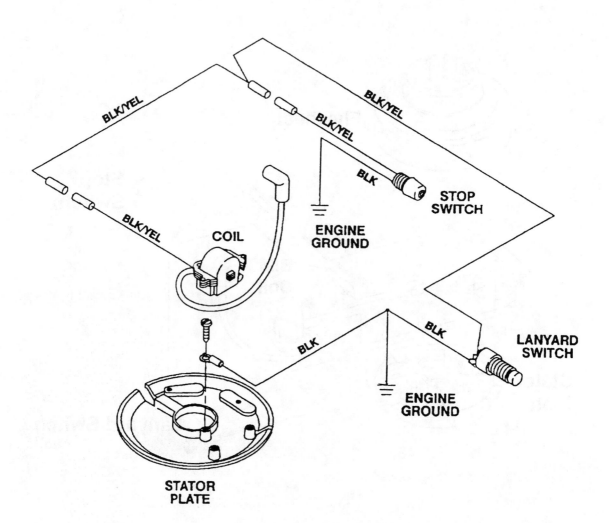

7.5 HP ELECTRICAL SYSTEM

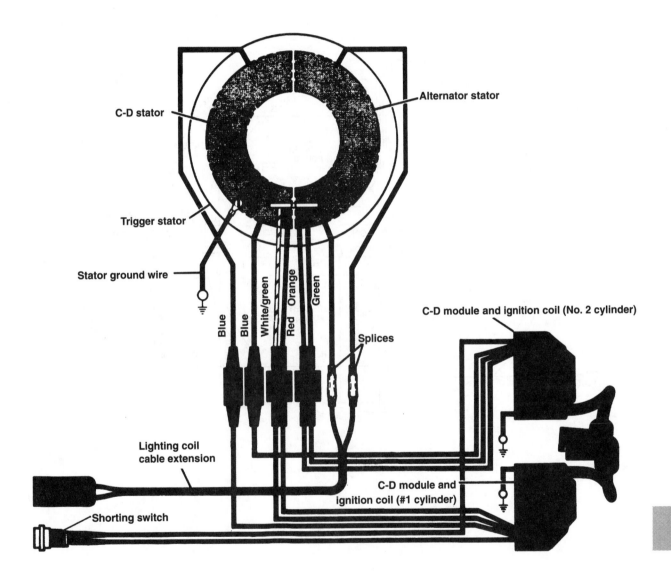

C-D stator

Alternator stator

Trigger stator

Stator ground wire

Blue

Blue

White/green

Red

Orange

Green

Splices

C-D module and ignition coil (No. 2 cylinder)

Lighting coil
cable extension

C-D module and
ignition coil (#1 cylinder)

Shorting switch

14

9.9 AND 15 HP BREAKER-POINT IGNITION

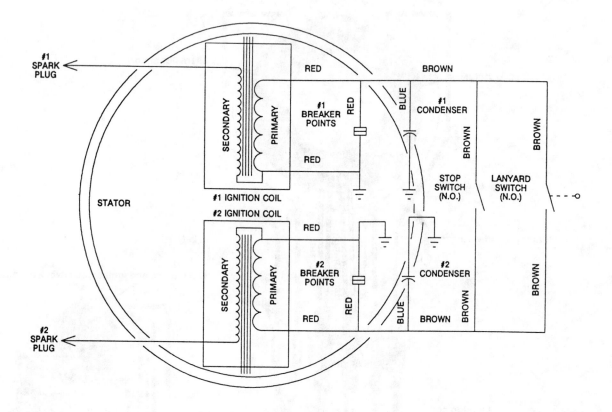

9.9 AND 15 HP BIM 1 IGNITION

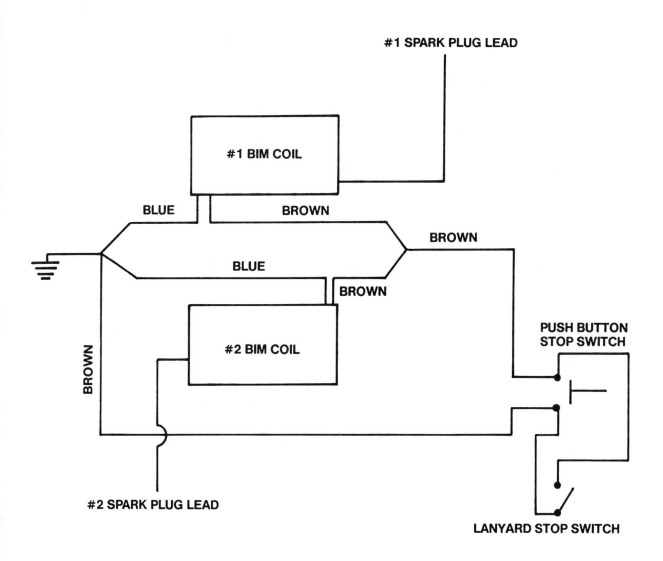

14

9.9 AND 15 HP BIM 2 IGNITION

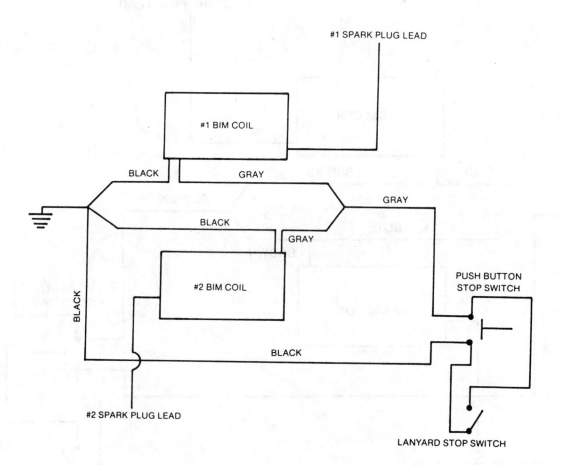

9.9 AND 15 HP SEM IGNITION

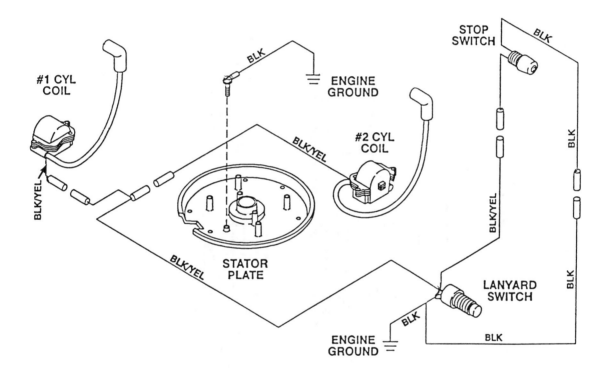

14

IGNITION SYSTEM DIAGRAM
(25 HP 3-CYLINDER 1996-SEM IGNITION)

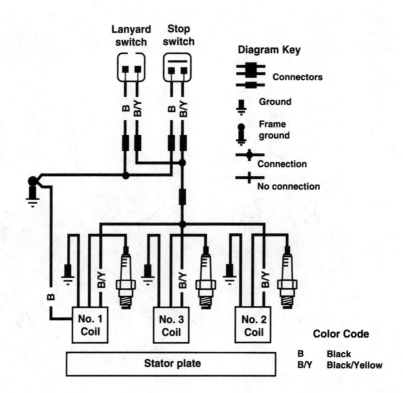

1984-1986 35 HP AND 1989 25 HP CD IGNITION
(ELECTRIC START)

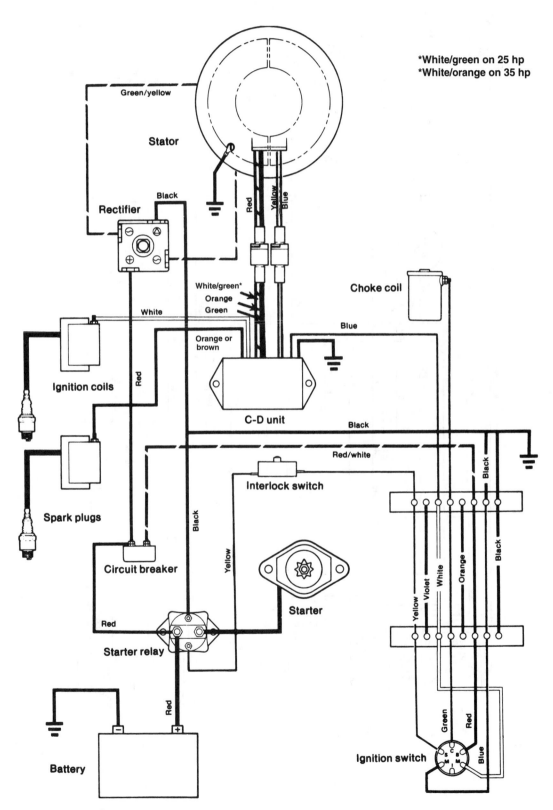

1987-ON 35 HP CD IGNITION

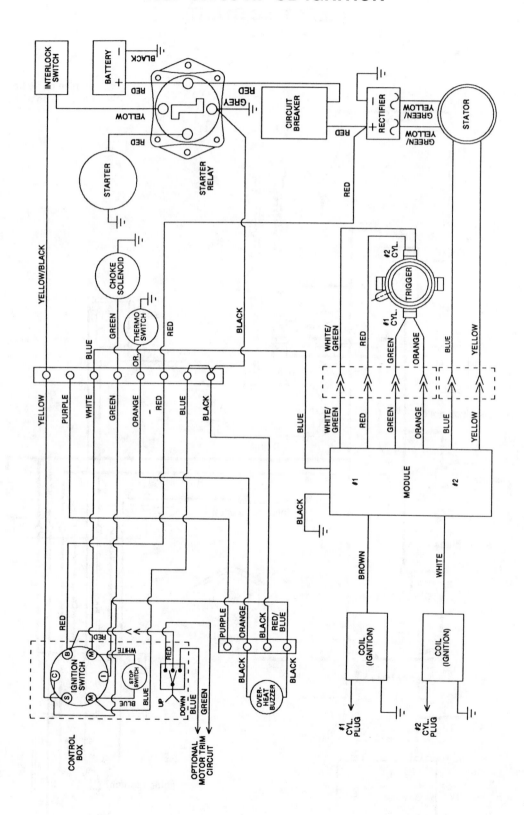

1984-1987B 50 HP BATTERY BREAKER POINT IGNITION WITH ALTERNATOR

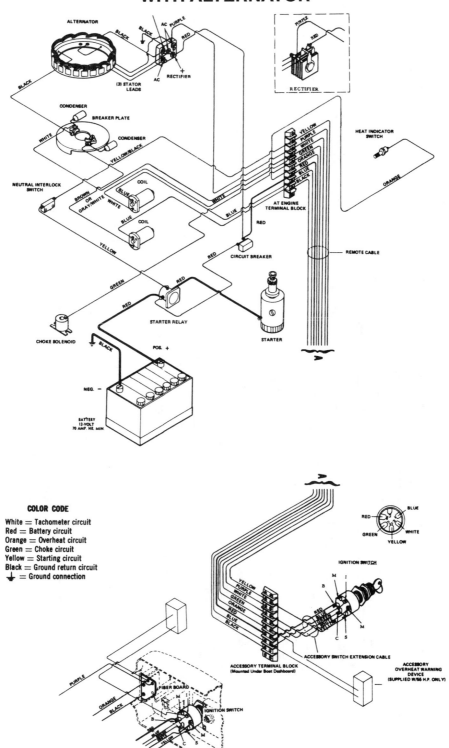

COLOR CODE

White = Tachometer circuit
Red = Battery circuit
Orange = Overheat circuit
Green = Choke circuit
Yellow = Starting circuit
Black = Ground return circuit
⏚ = Ground connection

14

1987C-1988C 50 HP CD IGNITION

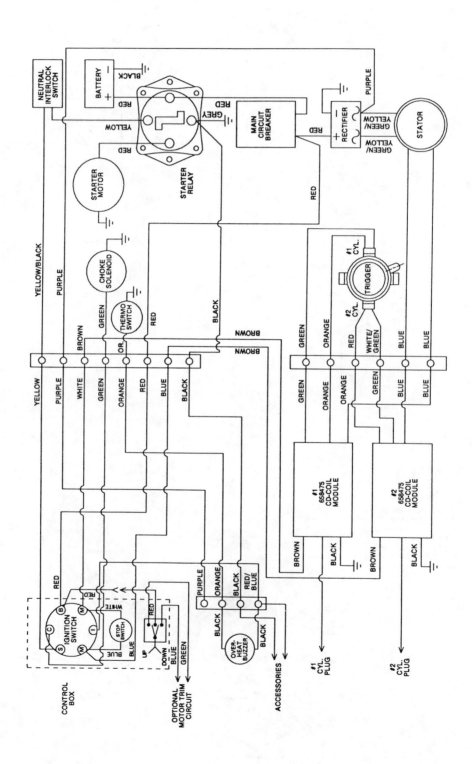

1988D-1992B 50 HP CD IGNITION

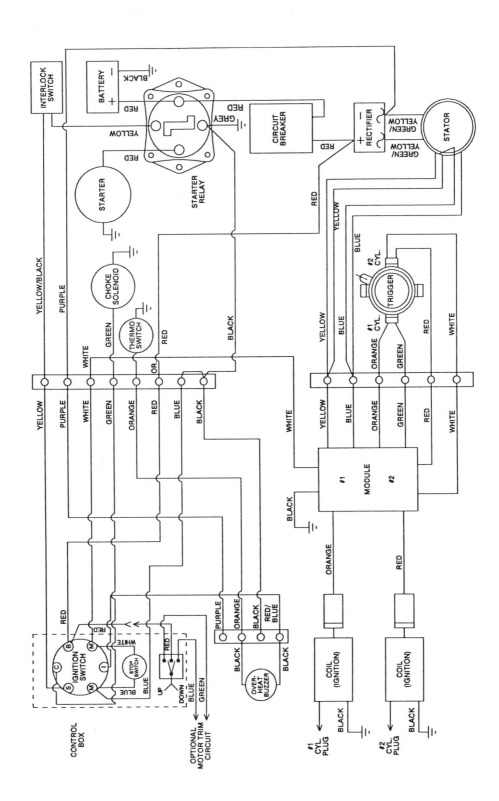

14

1992C-1995 40 AND 50 HP
THUNDERBOLT CDI IGNITION CIRCUIT

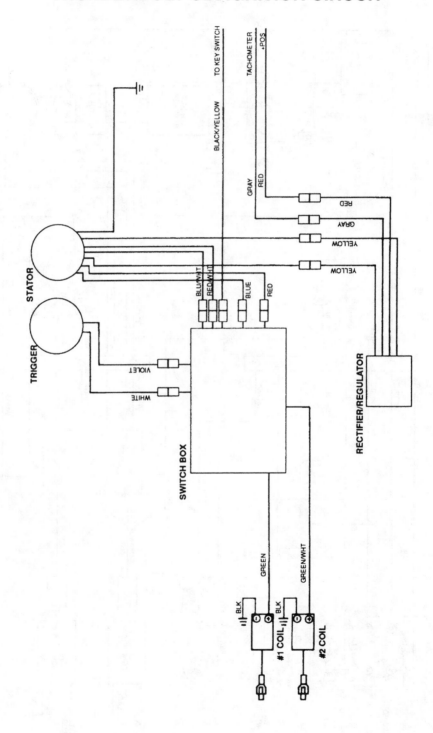

1992-ON 40 AND 50 HP (STARTING/CHARGING CIRCUIT)

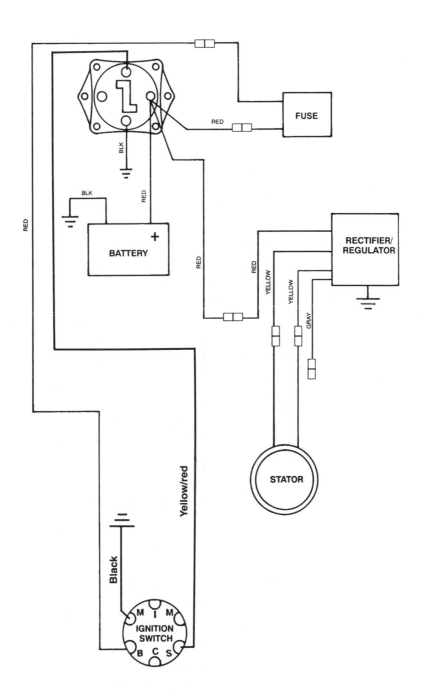

14

1996 40-50 HP MODELS (CDM IGNITION)

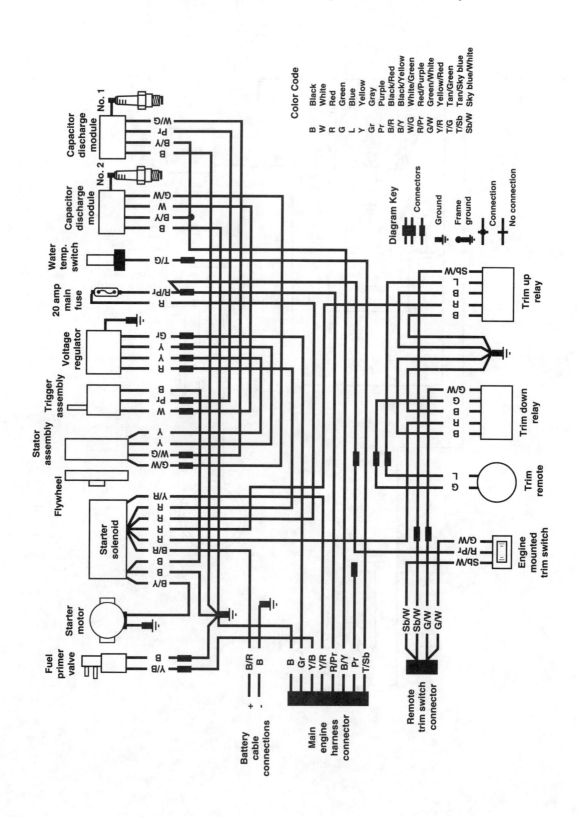

1985 60 HP MODELS (PRESTOLITE CD IGNITION)

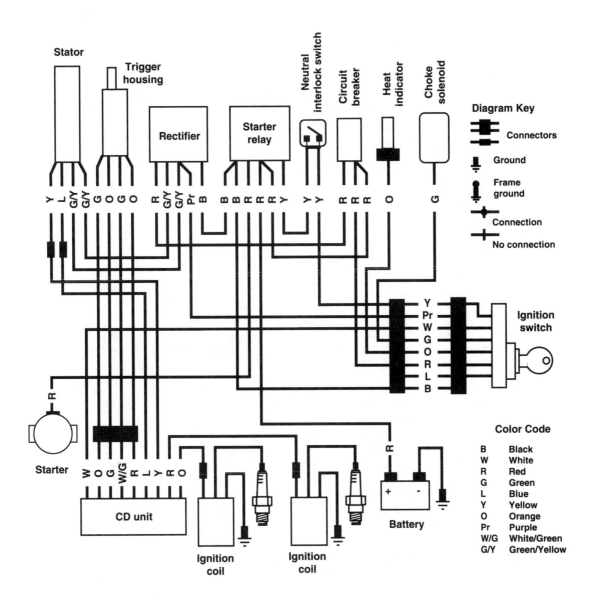

70 HP

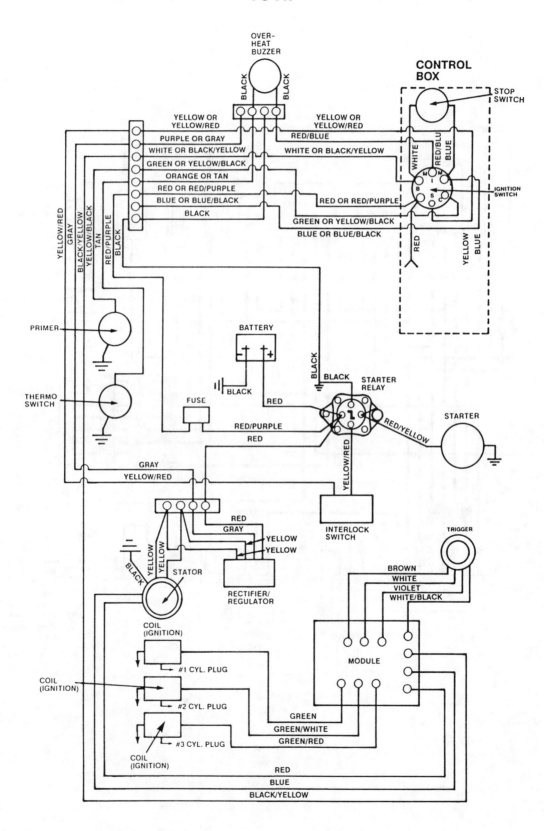

1996 75 HP MODELS (CDM IGNITION)

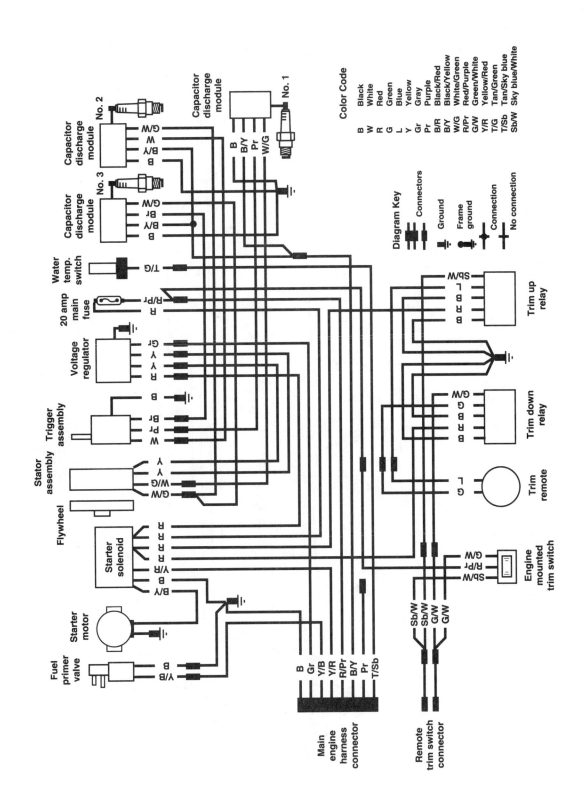

1984-1986 85 HP MODELS

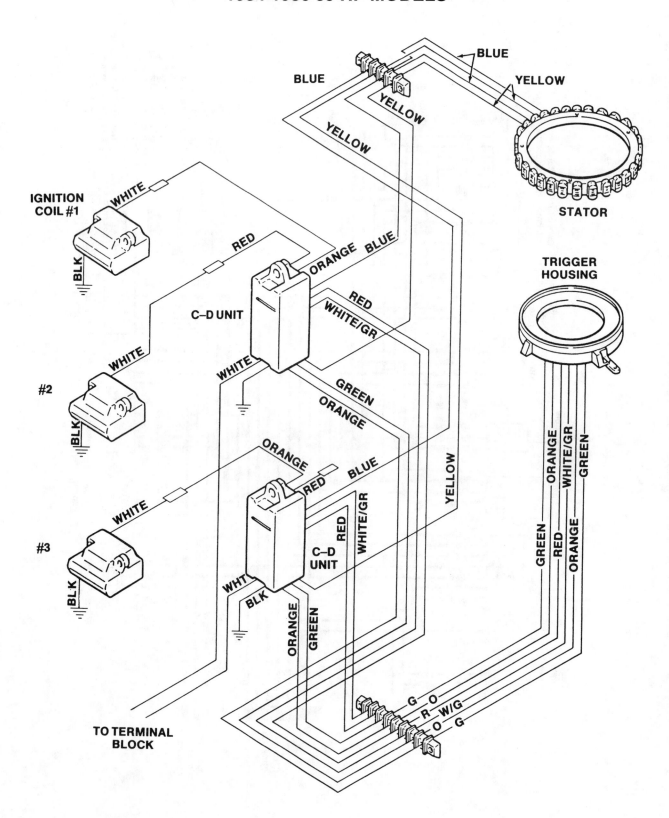

1987-1989 85 HP MODELS (PRESTOLITE IGNITION)

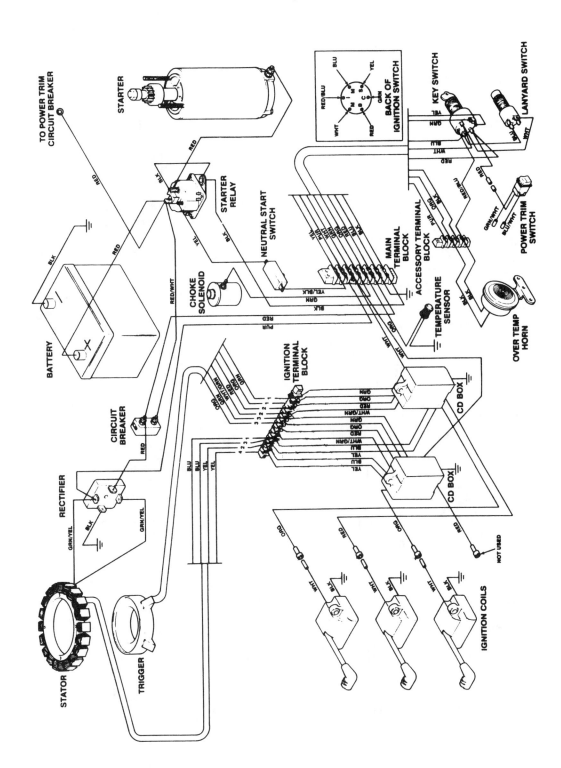

90 HP (PRESTOLITE IGNITION)

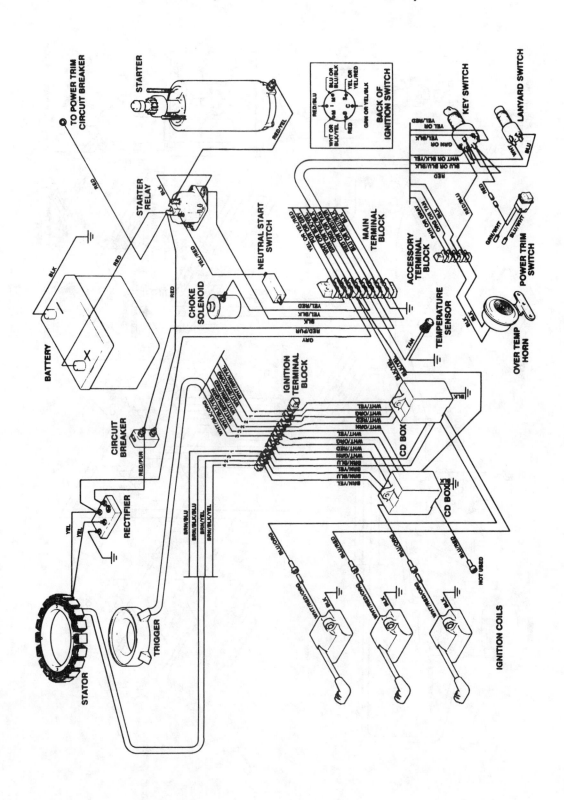

90 HP (THUNDERBOLT IGNITION)

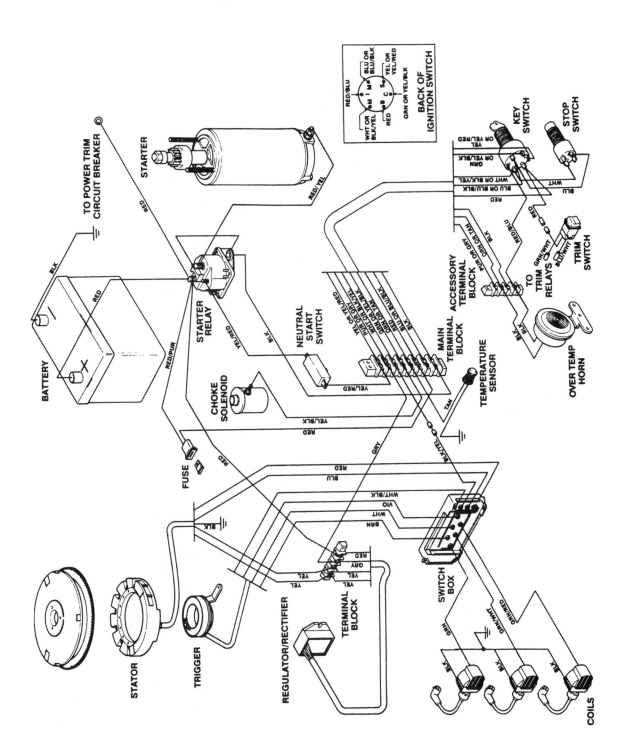

14

90 HP L-DRIVE (THUNDERBOLT IGNITION)

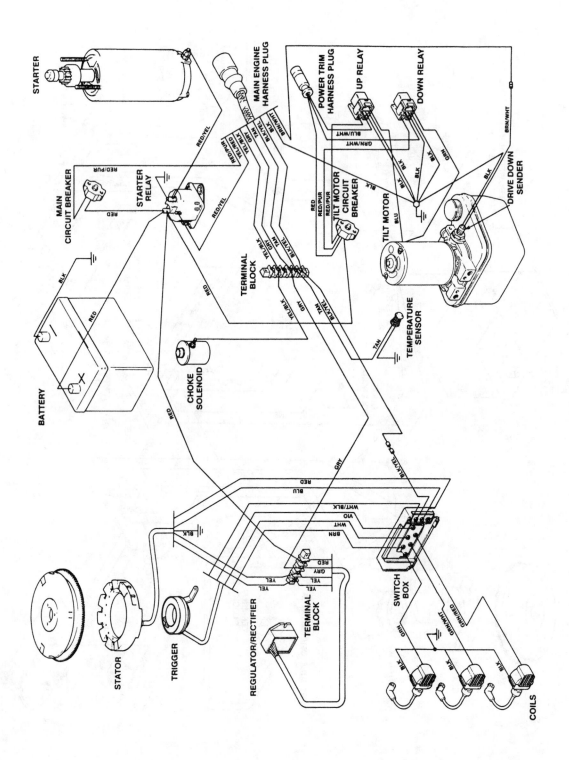

1996 90 HP MODELS (CDM IGNITION)

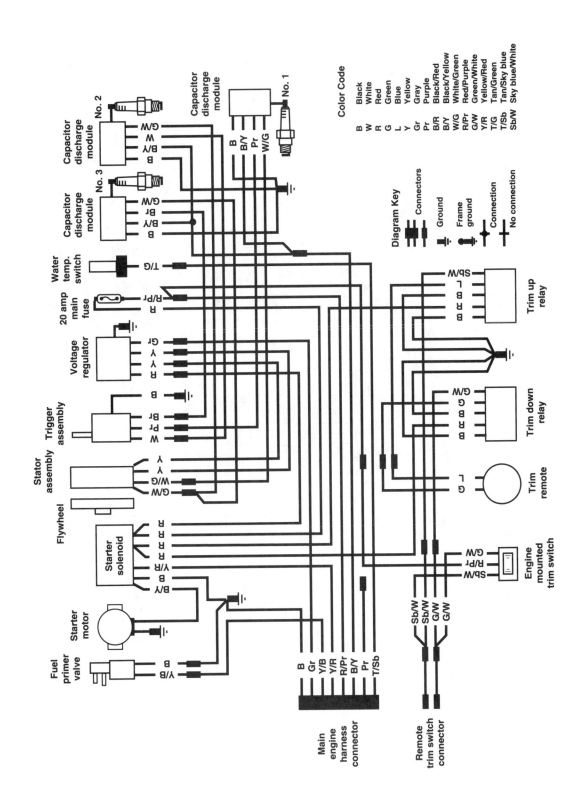

120 HP (PRESTOLITE IGNITION)

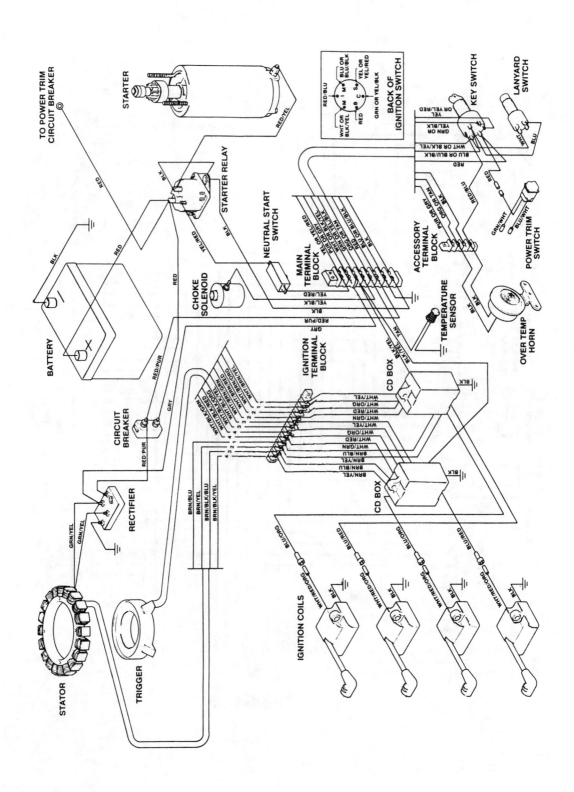

120 HP (THUNDERBOLT IGNITION)

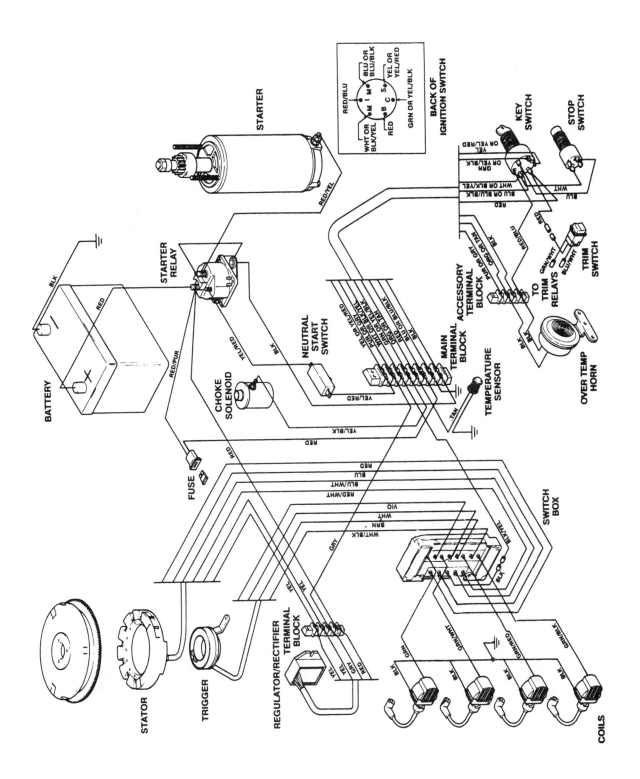

120 HP L-DRIVE (THUNDERBOLT IGNITION)

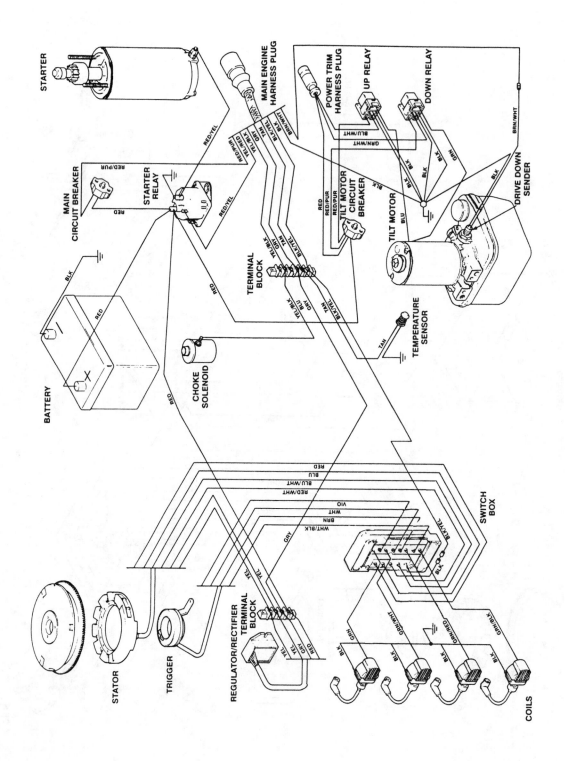

1996 120 HP (CDM IGNITION)

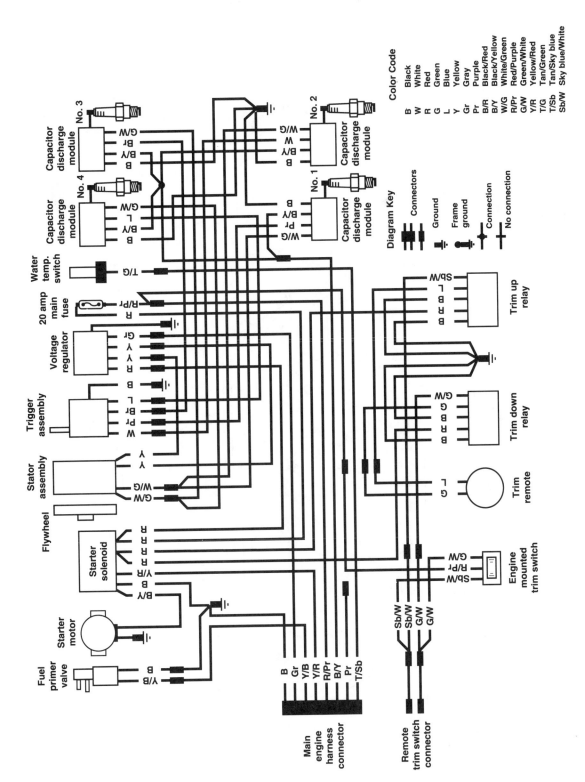

1984-1986 125 HP MODELS

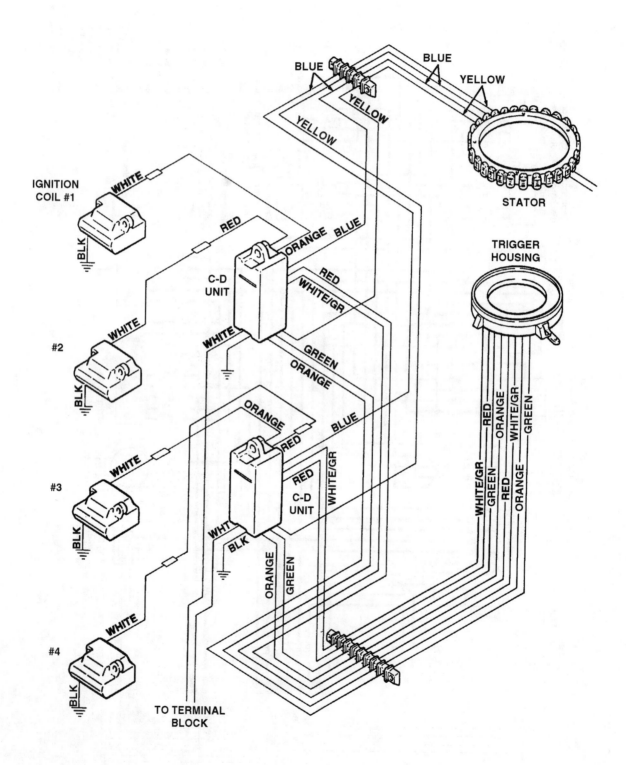

1987-1989 125 HP MODELS (PRESTOLITE IGNITION)

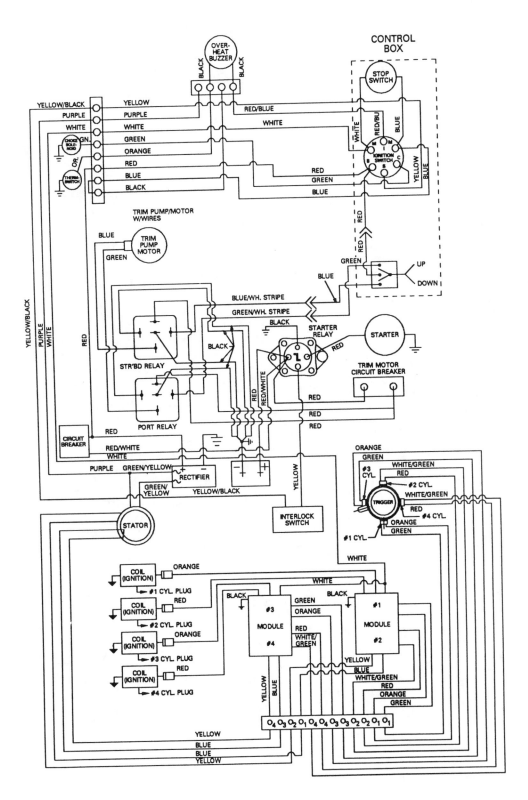

150 HP (THUNDERBOLT IGNITION)

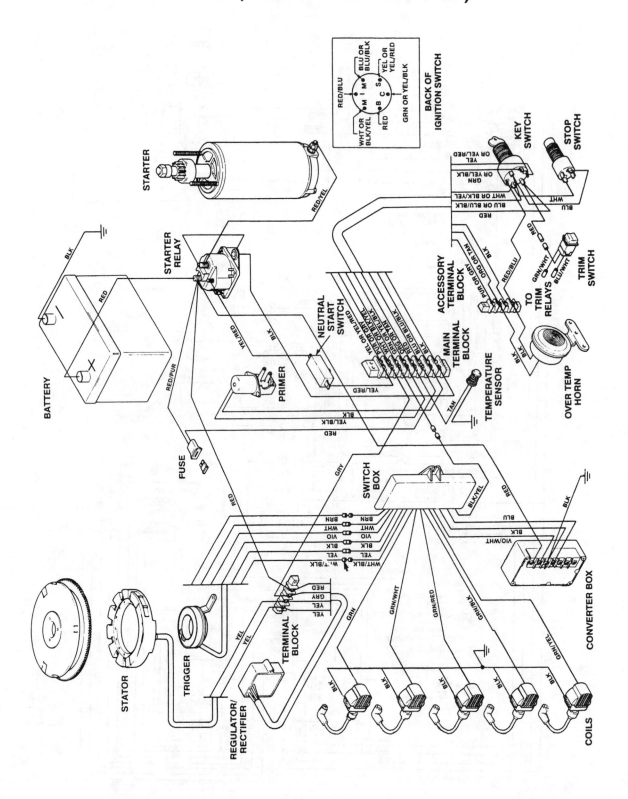

5-CYLINDER MODELS (PRESTOLITE IGNITION)

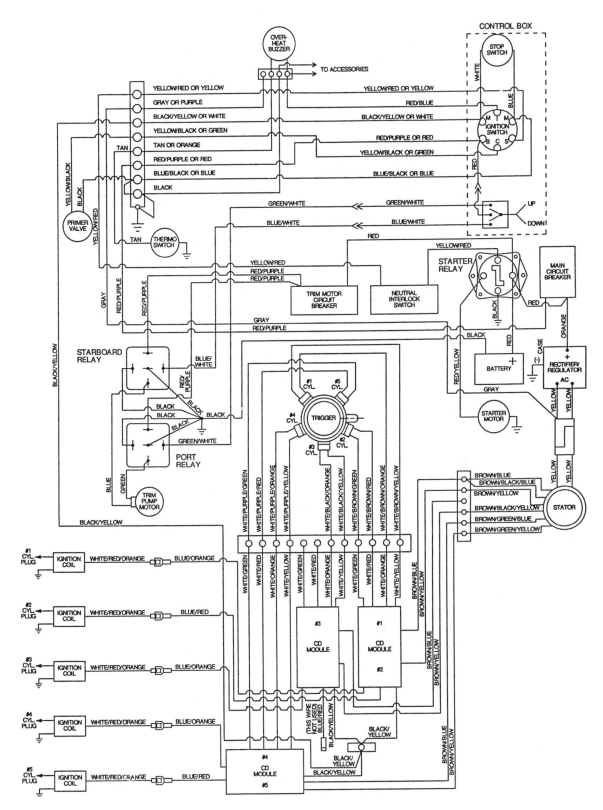

3-CYLINDER L-DRIVE (PRESTOLITE IGNITION)

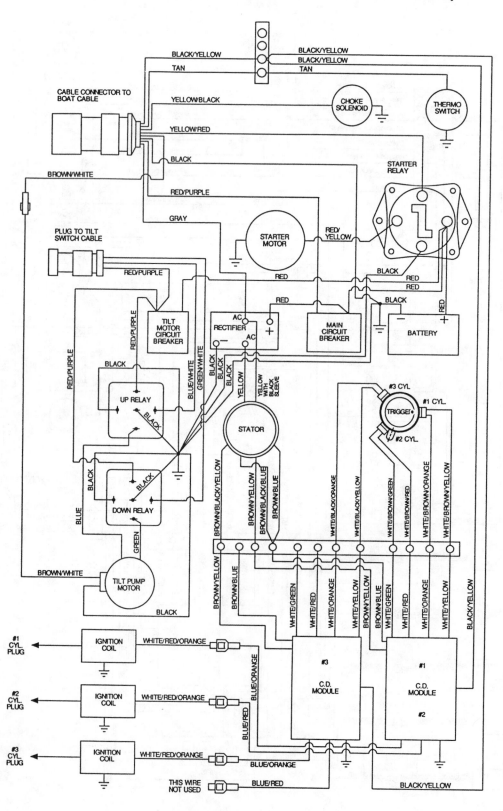

4-CYLINDER L-DRIVE (PRESTOLITE IGNITION)

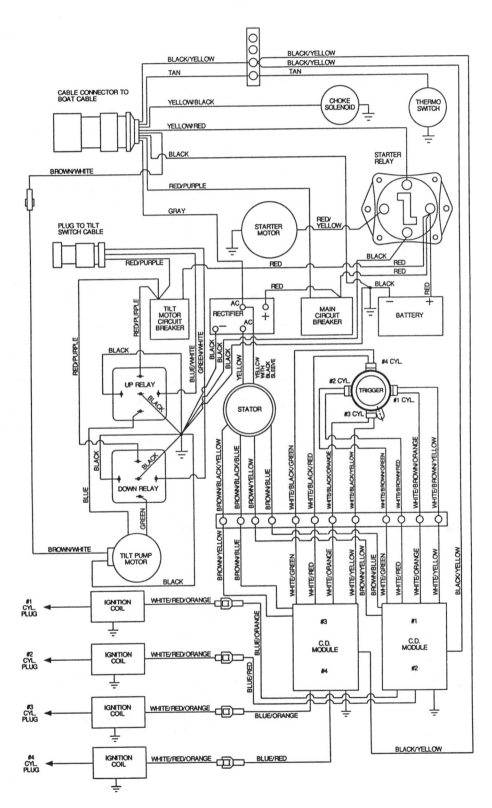

L-DRIVE BOAT AND INSTRUMENT PANEL

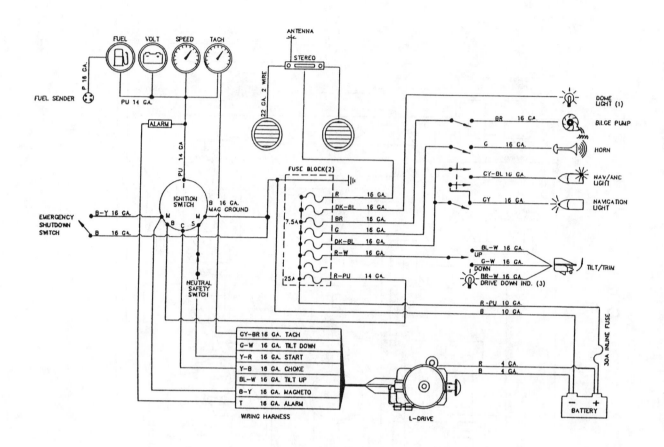

CAPRI 1870, 2070 AND 2072

COLOR CODE
B - BLACK
BR- BROWN
BL - BLUE
G - GREEN
GY- GRAY
P - PINK
PU- PURPLE
R - RED
T - TAN
W - WHITE
Y - YELLOW
LT - LIGHT
DK- DARK

SYMBOLS
SWITCH

FUSE (2)

CONNECTION

NO CONNECTION

GROUND

DPST SWITCH

NOTES
(1) 2072 ONLY.
(2) 10 AMP UNLESS OTHERWISE NOTED.
(3) LOCATED AT DASH.

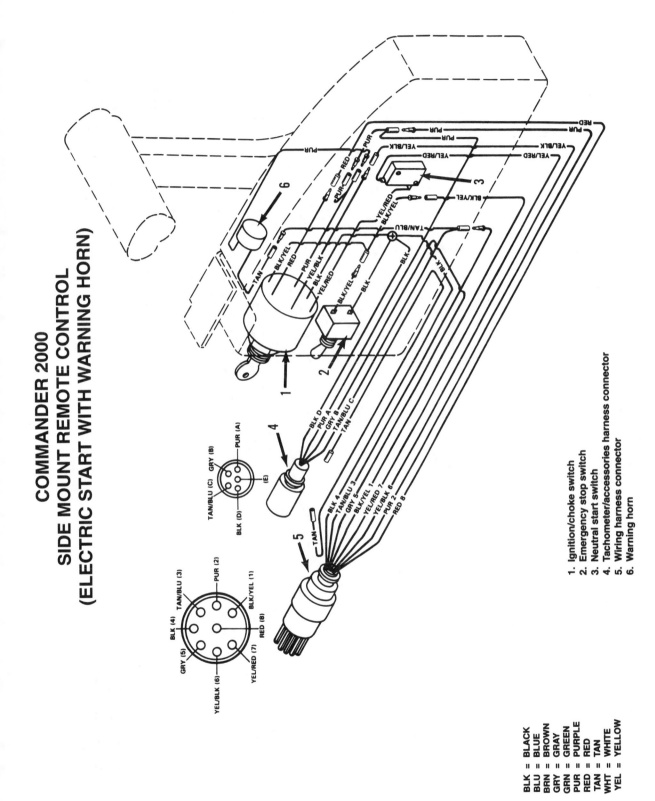

COMMANDER 2000
SIDE MOUNT REMOTE CONTROL
(ELECTRIC START WITH WARNING HORN)

1. Ignition/choke switch
2. Emergency stop switch
3. Neutral start switch
4. Tachometer/accessories harness connector
5. Wiring harness connector
6. Warning horn

BLK = BLACK
BLU = BLUE
BRN = BROWN
GRY = GRAY
GRN = GREEN
PUR = PURPLE
RED = RED
TAN = TAN
WHT = WHITE
YEL = YELLOW

14

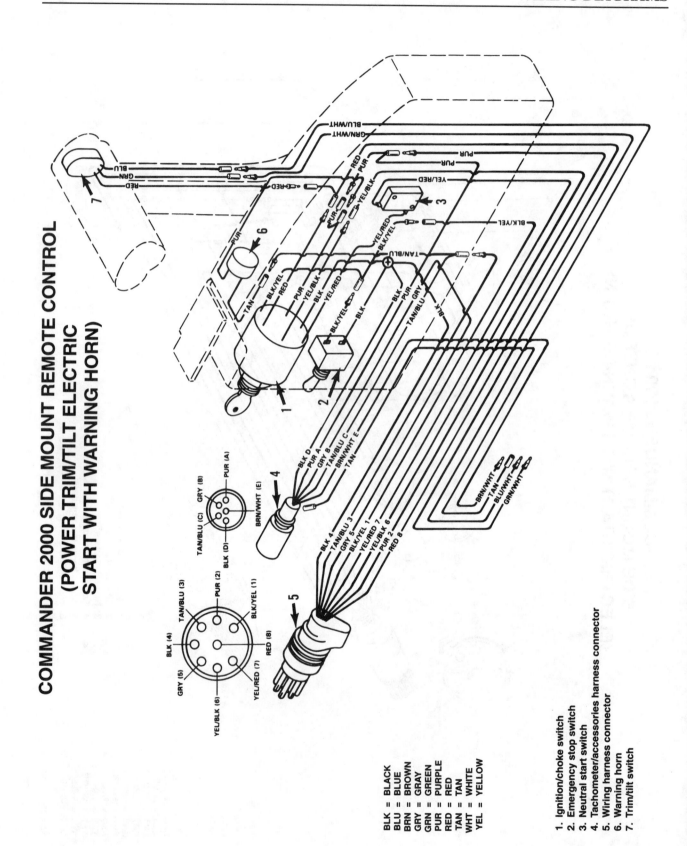

**COMMANDER 2000 SIDE MOUNT REMOTE CONTROL
(POWER TRIM/TILT ELECTRIC
START WITH WARNING HORN)**

BLK = BLACK
BLU = BLUE
BRN = BROWN
GRY = GRAY
GRN = GREEN
PUR = PURPLE
RED = RED
TAN = TAN
WHT = WHITE
YEL = YELLOW

1. Ignition/choke switch
2. Emergency stop switch
3. Neutral start switch
4. Tachometer/accessories harness connector
5. Wiring harness connector
6. Warning horn
7. Trim/tilt switch

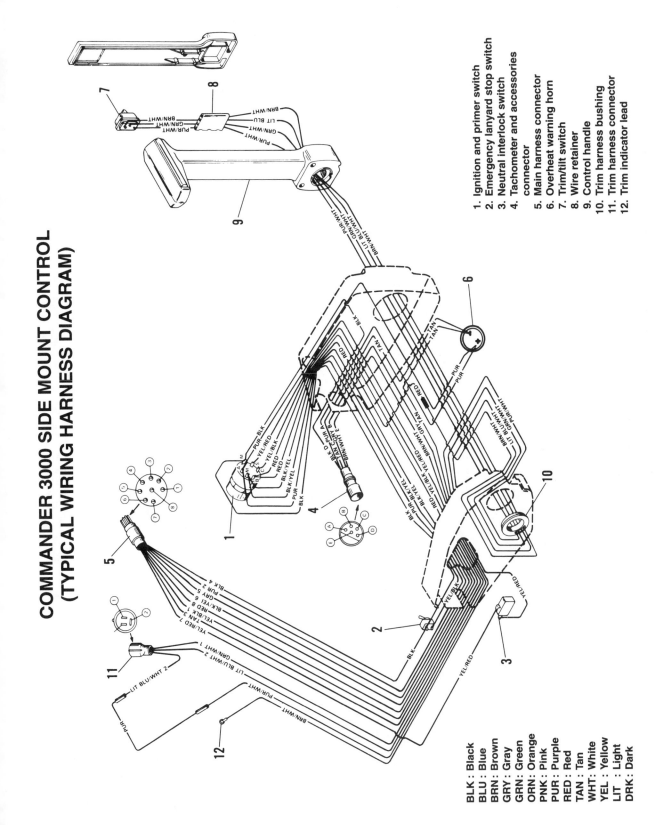

COMMANDER 3000 SIDE MOUNT CONTROL
(TYPICAL WIRING HARNESS DIAGRAM)

1. Ignition and primer switch
2. Emergency lanyard stop switch
3. Neutral interlock switch
4. Tachometer and accessories connector
5. Main harness connector
6. Overheat warning horn
7. Trim/tilt switch
8. Wire retainer
9. Control handle
10. Trim harness bushing
11. Trim harness connector
12. Trim indicator lead

BLK : Black
BLU : Blue
BRN : Brown
GRY : Gray
GRN : Green
ORN : Orange
PNK : Pink
PUR : Purple
RED : Red
TAN : Tan
WHT : White
YEL : Yellow
LIT : Light
DRK : Dark

14

NOTES

NOTES

NOTES

NOTES

MAINTENANCE LOG

Date	Maintenance performed	Engine hours